A New Star-Rating System & Other Exciting News from Frommer's!

In our continuing effort to publish the savviest, most up-to-date, and most appealing travel guides available, we've added some great new features.

Frommer's guides now include a new **star-rating system.** Every hotel, restaurant, and attraction is rated from 0 to 3 stars to help you set priorities and organize your time.

We've also added **seven brand-new features** that point you to the great deals, in-the-know advice, and unique experiences that separate travelers from tourists. Throughout the guide, look for:

Finds	Special finds—those places only insiders know about
Fun Fact	Fun facts—details that make travelers more informed and their trips more fun
Kids	Best bets for kids—advice for the whole family
Moments	Special moments—those experiences that memories are made of
Overrated	Places or experiences not worth your time or money
Tips	Insider tips—some great ways to save time and money
Value	Great values—where to get the best deals

Here's what the critics say about Frommer's:

Peru

1st Edition

by Neil E. Schlecht

Wiley Publishing, Inc.

About the Author

Neil E. Schlecht first trekked to Machu Picchu in 1983 as a college student spending his junior year abroad in Quito, Ecuador. The author and co-author of a dozen travel guides (including *Spain For Dummies*, *Frommer's South America*, *Frommer's Texas*, and *Frommer's Cuba*), as well as articles on art and culture and art catalog essays, and a photographer, he has lived for extensive periods in Brazil and Spain. He now resides in northwestern Connecticut.

Published by:

Wiley Publishing, Inc.

909 Third Ave.
New York, NY 10022

ISBN 0-7645-6512-5
ISSN 1537-8136

Editor: Myka Carroll
Production Editor: Suzanna R. Thompson
Photo Editor: Richard Fox
Cartographer: Roberta Stockwell
Production by Wiley Indianapolis Composition Services

Front cover photo: Peruvian child with Andean flute
Back cover photo: Machu Picchu

For information on our other products and services or to obtain technical support, please contact our Customer Care Department within the U.S. at (800) 762-2974, outside the U.S. at (317) 572-3993 or fax (317) 572-4002.

Wiley also publishes its books in a variety of electronic formats. Some content that appears in print may not be available in electronic formats.

Manufactured in the United States of America

5 4 3 2 1

Contents

List of Maps

An Invitation to the Reader

In researching this book, we discovered many wonderful places—hotels, restaurants, shops, and more. We're sure you'll find others. Please tell us about them so that we can share the information with your fellow travelers in upcoming editions. If you were disappointed with a recommendation, we'd love to know that, too. Please write to:

Frommer's Peru, 1st Edition
Wiley Publishing, Inc. • 909 Third Ave. • New York, NY 10022

An Additional Note

Please be advised that travel information is subject to change at any time—and this is especially true of prices. We therefore suggest that you write or call ahead for confirmation when making your travel plans. The authors, editors, and publisher cannot be held responsible for the experiences of readers while traveling. Your safety is important to us, however, so we encourage you to stay alert and be aware of your surroundings. Keep a close eye on cameras, purses, and wallets, all favorite targets of thieves and pickpockets.

New! Frommer's Star Ratings & Icons

Every hotel, restaurant, and attraction listing in this guide has been ranked for quality, value, service, amenities, and special features using a star-rating scale. In country, state, and regional guides, we also rate towns and regions to help you narrow down your choices and budget your time accordingly. Hotels and restaurants in the Very Expensive and Expensive categories are rated on a scale of one (highly recommended) to three stars (exceptional). Those in the Moderate and Inexpensive categories rate from zero (recommended) to two stars (very highly recommended). Attractions, towns, and regions are rated according to the following scale: zero stars (recommended), one star (highly recommended), two stars (very highly recommended), and three stars (must-see).

In addition to the rating system, we also use seven icons to highlight insider information, useful tips, special bargains, hidden gems, memorable experiences, kid-friendly venues, places to avoid, and other useful information:

(Finds   (Fun Fact   (Kids   (Moments   (Overrated   (Tips   (Value

The following abbreviations are used for credit cards:

AE American Express	DISC Discover	V Visa
DC Diners Club	MC MasterCard	

FROMMERS.COM

Now that you have the guidebook to a great trip, visit our website at **www.frommers.com** for travel information on nearly 2,500 destinations. With features updated regularly, we give you instant access to the most current trip-planning information available. At Frommers.com, you'll also find the best prices on airfares, accommodations, and car rentals—and you can even book travel online through our travel booking partners. At Frommers.com, you'll also find the following:

- Online updates to our most popular guidebooks
- Vacation sweepstakes and contest giveaways
- Newsletter highlighting the hottest travel trends
- Online travel message boards with featured travel discussions

The Best of Peru

Peru is legendary among world travelers looking for new experiences. A stunningly endowed country, Peru offers much more than most short trips can hope to take in: charming Andean highlands towns with colonial architecture; remote jungle lodges in the Amazon basin; soaring snowcapped mountains and volcanoes; a 3,220km (2,000-mile) Pacific coastline; and, of course, the legacies of the Incas and other sophisticated pre-Columbian civilizations. The following lists are some of my favorite places and activities, from hotels and restaurants to outdoor experiences and festivals. But the fun of traveling to a fascinating country like Peru is compiling your own list.

1 The Most Unforgettable Travel Experiences

- **Flying over the Nasca Lines:** One of South America's great enigmas are the ancient, baffling lines etched into the desert sands along Peru's southern coast. There are giant trapezoids and triangles, the identifiable shapes of animal and plant figures, and more than 10,000 lines that can only really be seen from the air. Variously thought to be signs from the gods, agricultural and astronomical calendars, or even extraterrestrial airports, the Nasca Lines were constructed between 300 B.C. and A.D. 700. Small-craft overflights dip and glide, and passengers strain their necks against the window to see mysterious figures such as "the Astronaut." See "Nasca," in chapter 5.

- **Gazing upon Machu Picchu:** However you get to it—whether you hike the fabled Inca Trail, hop aboard one of the prettiest train rides in South America, or zip in by helicopter—Machu Picchu more than lives up to its reputation as one of the most spectacular sites on earth. The ruins of the legendary "lost city of the Incas" sit majestically among the massive Andes, swathed in clouds. The ceremonial and agricultural center, never discovered or looted by the Spaniards, dates to the mid-1400s but seems even more ancient. Exploring the site is a thrilling experience, especially at sunrise, when dramatic rays of light creep over the mountaintops. See "Machu Picchu & the Inca Trail," in chapter 7.

- **Hiking the Inca Trail:** The legendary trail to Machu Picchu, the Camino del Inca, is one of the world's most rewarding eco-adventures. The 4-day trek leads across astonishing Andes mountain passes and through some of the greatest natural and manmade attractions in Peru, including dozens of Inca ruins, dense cloud forest, and breathtaking mountain scenery. At the end of the arduous trail lie the glorious ruins of Machu Picchu, shrouded in mist at your feet. See "Machu Picchu & the Inca Trail," in chapter 7.

The Best of Peru

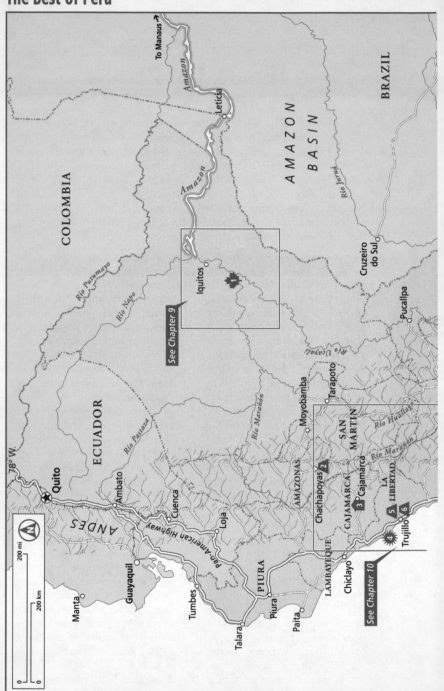

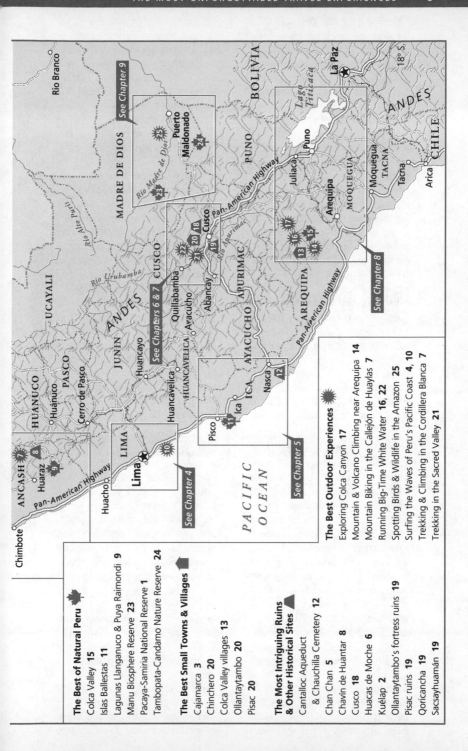

The Best of Natural Peru

Colca Valley **15**
Islas Ballestas **11**
Lagunas Llanganuco & Puya Raimondi **9**
Manu Biosphere Reserve **23**
Pacaya-Samiria National Reserve **1**
Tambopata-Candamo Nature Reserve **24**

The Best Small Towns & Villages

Cajamarca **3**
Chinchero **20**
Colca Valley villages **13**
Ollantaytambo **20**
Pisac **20**

The Most Intriguing Ruins
& Other Historical Sites

Cantalloc Aqueduct
  & Chauchilla Cemetery **12**
Chan Chan **5**
Chavín de Huantar **8**
Cusco **18**
Huacas de Moche **6**
Kuélap **2**
Ollantaytambo's fortress ruins **19**
Pisac ruins **19**
Qoricancha **19**
Sacsayhuamán **19**

The Best Outdoor Experiences

Exploring Colca Canyon **17**
Mountain & Volcano Climbing near Arequipa **14**
Mountain Biking in the Callejón de Huaylas **7**
Running Big-Time White Water **16, 22**
Spotting Birds & Wildlife in the Amazon **25**
Surfing the Waves of Peru's Pacific Coast **4, 10**
Trekking & Climbing in the Cordillera Blanca **7**
Trekking in the Sacred Valley **21**

- **Floating on Lake Titicaca:** Lake Titicaca, the world's highest navigable body of water, straddles the border between Peru and Bolivia. To locals, it is a mysterious and sacred place. An hour's boat ride from Puno takes you to the Uros floating islands, where communities dwell upon soft patches of reeds. Visitors have a rare opportunity to experience the ancient cultures of two inhabited natural islands, Amantaní and Taquile, by staying with a local family. The views of the ocean-like lake, at more than 3,600m (12,000 ft.) above sea level, and the star-littered night sky are worth the trip. See "Puno & Lake Titicaca," in chapter 8.
- **Watching the Condors Soar at Colca Canyon:** The world's second-deepest canyon (but twice as deep as the Grand Canyon), Colca is the best place in South America to see giant Andean condors, majestic birds with wingspans of up to 3.5m (11½ ft.). From a stunning lookout point nearly 1,200m (4,000 ft.) above the canyon river, you can watch as the condors appear, slowly circle, and gradually gain altitude with each pass, until they soar silently above your head and head off down the river. A truly spine-tingling spectacle, the flight of the big birds may make you feel quite small and insignificant—and certainly less graceful. See "Colca Valley," in chapter 8.
- **Plunging Deep into the Jungle:** However you do it, and in whichever part of the Amazon-basin rain forest you do it, Peru's massive tracts of jungle are not to be missed. The northern jungle is most accessible from Iquitos, and the southern Amazon, which features two phenomenal national reserves, Manu and Tambopata, is approachable from Cusco and Puerto Maldonado. You can take a river cruise, stay at a rustic jungle lodge, or lose yourself with a private guide, making camp and catching dinner along the way. See chapter 9.

2 The Most Intriguing Ruins & Other Historical Sights

- **Cantalloc Aqueduct & Chauchilla Cemetery:** An incredible necropolis dating to around A.D. 1000 and a sophisticated irrigation system in the area around Nasca are two of the south's most interesting archaeological sites. Of the thousands of graves at Chauchilla, 12 underground tombs have been exposed. What they hold is fascinating: the bleached bones of children and adults with Rasta-like dreadlocks, and some of the garments and goodies they were buried with. Close to town, nearly 3 dozen aqueducts represent a spectacular engineering feat of the Incas and their predecessors. The canals have air vents forming spirals descending to the water current and are still in use today by local farmers. See "Nasca," in chapter 5.
- **Cusco:** Vibrant Cusco is a living museum of Peruvian history, with Spanish colonial churches and mansions sitting atop perfectly constructed Inca walls of exquisitely carved granite blocks that fit together without mortar. Streets still have evocative, Quechua-language names that date back to Inca times, such as Saqracalle ("Where the demons dwell") and Pumaphaqcha ("Puma's tail"). See chapter 6.
- **Qoricancha:** Qoricancha—the Inca Temple of the Sun—is an exceptional example of the Incas' masterful masonry. Dedicated to

sun worship, the greatest temple in the Inca empire was a gleaming palace of gold before the Spaniards raided it. During the summer solstice, the sun still magically illuminates a niche where the Inca chieftain held court. A sensuously curved wall of stone is one of the greatest remaining examples of Inca stonework. See "What to See & Do," in chapter 6.

- **Sacsayhuamán:** On a hill overlooking Cusco, the monumental stonework at Sacsayhuamán forms massive zigzagged defensive walls of three tiers. Built by the Inca emperor Pachacútec in the mid–15th century, some blocks weigh as much as 300 tons, and they fit together seamlessly without mortar. The main pageant of the splendid Inti Raymi festival, one of the greatest expressions of Inca and Quechua culture, is celebrated every June 24 at Sacsayhuamán. See "What to See & Do," in chapter 6.

- **The Pisac Ruins:** At the beginning of the Sacred Valley, just 45 minutes from Cusco, are some of the most spectacular Inca ruins in Peru. Equal parts city, religious temple, and military complex— and perhaps a royal estate of the Inca emperor—the ruins enjoy stunning views of the valley. A hike up the hillside to the ruins, beginning at Pisac's main square, is one of the most rewarding climbs you're likely to take. See "Pisac," in chapter 7.

- **Ollantaytambo's Fortress Ruins:** The Incas never finished this temple for worship and astronomical observation, but it is still extraordinary. On a rocky outcrop perched above the valley, dozens of rows of incredibly steep stone terraces are carved into the hillside; high above are elegant examples of classic Inca masonry in pink granite. See "Ollantaytambo," in chapter 7.

- **Huacas de Moche:** On the outskirts of Trujillo, this complex of mysterious Moche adobe pyramids, the Temple of the Sun and Temple of the Moon, dates to A.D. 500. The Temple of the Sun (Huaca del Sol), today sadly eroded, is still mammoth—it was once probably the largest manmade structure in the Americas. The smaller Temple of the Moon (Huaca de la Luna) has been excavated; revealed inside are cool polychromatic friezes of a scary figure, the decapitator god. See "Trujillo," in chapter 10.

- **Chan Chan:** A sprawling city of adobe in the Moche Valley, just beyond Trujillo, Chan Chan was the capital of the formidable Chimú empire. Begun around A.D. 1300, it is the largest adobe complex of pre-Columbian America. Among the nine royal palaces, the partially restored Tschudi Palace has unusual friezes and is evocative enough to spur thoughts of the unequalled size and sophistication of this compound of the Chimú kingdom, which reached its apogee in the 15th century before succumbing to the Incas. Chan Chan includes three other sites, all quite spread out, including a modern museum. See "Trujillo," in chapter 10.

- **The Ruins of Kuélap:** The remote site of Kuélap, hidden by thick cloud forest and more than 800 years old, is one of the manmade wonders of Peru waiting to be discovered. The ruins are still tough and time-consuming to get to, but the fortress complex of 400 round buildings, surrounded by a massive defensive wall, rewards the efforts of adventurous amateur archaeologists. See "The Ruins of Kuélap," in chapter 10.

- **Chavín de Huántar:** About 110km (70 miles) from Huaraz and the Cordillera Blanca are the 3,000-year-old ruins of Chavín de Huántar, a fortress-temple with excellent stonework constructed by the Chavín culture from about 1200 to 300 B.C. These are the best-preserved ruins of one of Peru's most sophisticated and influential ancient civilizations. In a subterranean tunnel is the Lanzón, a handsome stone carving and cult object shaped like a dagger. See "Huaraz & the Cordillera Blanca," in chapter 10.

3 The Best Museums

- **Museo Arqueológico Rafael Larco Herrera,** Lima: The world's largest private collection of pre-Columbian art focuses on the Moche dynasty (A.D. 200–700) and its extraordinary ceramics. Packed shelves in this 18th-century colonial building hold an incredible 45,000 pieces. And it wouldn't be a proper presentation of the Moche culture without a Sala Erótica, dedicated to the culture's shockingly explicit ceramic sexual depictions. See p. 132.

- **Museo de la Nación,** Lima: The National Museum traces the art and history of the earliest inhabitants to the Inca empire, the last before colonization by the Spaniards. It's sprawling, but very well designed, with scale models of major archaeological sites and great carved totems and textiles. See p. 133.

- **Museo de Oro del Perú,** Lima: The private Gold Museum is a glittering treasure trove of ceremonial objects, weaponry, textiles, jewelry, and above all, gold, from the Incas and pre-Inca civilizations. It's not well-documented, but it is almost overwhelming in its reach. See p. 133.

- **Convento y Museo de San Francisco,** Lima: The capital's best colonial-era church, the Convent of St. Francis is a striking 17th-century baroque complex with gorgeous glazed ceramic tiles and carved ceilings. The museum holds excellent examples of religious art and a splendid library, but deep beneath the church are some creepy catacombs, dug in the 16th century to house the remains of tens of thousands of priests and parishioners. See p. 128.

- **Casa-Museo María Reiche,** Nasca: One of Peru's best small museums, named for the German woman who dedicated herself to the study of the Nasca Lines, displays a good collection of Paracas textiles, Nasca ceramics, mummies, and colonial art. Outside of Lima, it's one of the best spots for a primer on southern Peru's rich history and archaeology. See p. 162.

- **Museo Antonini,** Nasca: A private archaeology museum with a mission, this Italian initiative presents finds of the sophisticated Nasca culture and details the process of archaeological excavations. In the museum's backyard is the Bisambra aqueduct, an ancient Nasca stone irrigation canal. The museum is in possession of the world's greatest collection of painted textiles, from the huge adobe city of Cahuachi nearby, but as of yet has no place to display them. See p. 163.

- **Museo Inka,** Cusco: This fine collection of exhibits and artifacts from pre-Inca civilizations and Inca culture poses an excellent introduction to the Incas. The handsome colonial-era mansion that houses the museum, built on top of an Inca palace, is one of Cusco's most important. Women weave Andean textiles in the courtyard. See p. 195.

- **Monasterio de Santa Catalina,** Arequipa: The Convent of Santa Catalina, founded in 1579, is hands-down the greatest religious monument in Peru. More than a convent, it's an extraordinary and evocative small village, with Spanish-style cobblestone streets, passageways, plazas, and cloisters, where more than 200 sequestered nuns once lived (only a handful remain). Spending a sunny afternoon here is like being transported to another world: a small village in Andalucía, Spain. See p. 275.

- **Museo Santuarios Andinos,** Arequipa: Down the street from the Convent of Santa Catalina at the Museum of Andean Sanctuaries is a singular exhibit, one of the most important recent archaeological finds in Peru: Juanita, the Ice Maiden of Ampato. A 13- or 14-year-old girl sacrificed in the 1500s by Inca priests on a volcano at more than 6,000m (20,000 ft.), "Juanita" was discovered in almost perfect condition in 1995. Her frozen remains, kept inside a high-tech chamber, have been studied by scientific teams from the U.S. and Peru to elicit clues from her DNA. See p. 277.

- **Museo Arqueológico Brüning,** Lambayeque: Housing one of Peru's most important archaeological discoveries, the glittering royal tomb of the Lord of Sipán, this terrifically designed museum is a must-see. The Moche royal figure, buried 1,700 years ago and his tomb unearthed in all its undisturbed glory of ceremonial treasures, is astounding. Also on the premises is a wide-ranging collection of 1,500 items from the Lambayeque, Moche, Chavín, Vicus, and Inca civilizations, including a memorable gold room. See p. 353.

- **Conjunto Monumental de Belén,** Cajamarca: A historic architectural complex of carved volcanic stone, Belén comprises an extraordinary colonial church and two former hospitals housing medical and archaeological exhibits, including textiles and ceramics dating back to 1500 B.C. and interesting ethnographic displays. See p. 364.

4 The Best of Natural Peru

- **Islas Ballestas:** The Ballestas Islands, considered the "Peruvian Galápagos," are home to an amazing roster of protected species, including huge colonies of sea lions, endangered turtles and Humboldt penguins, red boobies, pelicans, turkey vultures, and red-footed cormorants. The islands are so covered with migratory and resident sea birds that they are known for their production of *guano*, or bird droppings. The Ballestas are part of the Paracas National Reserve, which is two-thirds ocean. See "Pisco & the Reserva Nacional de Paracas," in chapter 5.

- **Colca Valley:** The Colca Canyon is an awe-inspiring site and the best place in South America to witness giant condors, but the entire area, which Mario Vargas Llosa called the "Valley of Wonders," is extraordinarily scenic. From snowcapped volcanoes to patchwork valleys of green, narrow gorges, and beautiful desert landscapes, Colca has it all. On the way to Colca Canyon, you pass the Salinas and Aguada Blanca Nature Reserve, where you can glimpse vicuñas, llamas, and alpacas from the road. See "Colca Valley," in chapter 8.

• **Tambopata-Candamo Nature Reserve:** A huge reserve of rain forest in the *departmento* (province) of Madre de Dios, Tambopata has outstanding biodiversity: more species of birds (nearly 600) and butterflies (1,200) than any place of similar size on earth, as well as a dozen different types of forest and gorgeous oxbow lakes and at least 13 endangered animal species. The famous Tambopata macaw clay lick, where thousands of brilliantly colored macaws and parrots gather daily for feedings, ranks as one of the wildlife highlights of Peru. See "The Southern Amazon Jungle," in chapter 9.

• **Manu Biosphere Reserve:** Remote Manu—about as close as you're likely to come to virgin rain forest anywhere—is the second-largest protected area in Peru. Its incredibly varied habitats include Andes highlands, cloud forests, and lowland tropical rain forests. One hectare (2.5 acres) of forest in Manu may have 10 times the number of species of trees found in a hectare of temperate forest in Europe or North America, and Manu has the highest bird, mammal, and plant diversity of any park on the planet. The reserve is one of the world's finest for birding (greater even than all of Costa Rica), and other wildlife include giant river otters, cocks-of-the-rock, and perhaps 15,000

animal species, as well as native Amerindian tribes that remain untouched by the modern world. See "The Southern Amazon Jungle," in chapter 9.

• **Pacaya-Samiria National Reserve:** The reserve, nearly 322km (200 miles) south of Iquitos, is the largest protected area in Peru and one of the best conserved in the world. Its dense, pristine rain forest and wetlands comprise 1.5% of Peru's total surface area and contain some of the Amazon's greatest wildlife, including pink dolphins, macaws, black caimans, spider monkeys, and giant river turtles. Found in the reserve (at last count) are 539 species of birds, 101 species of mammals, 256 kinds of fish, and 22 species of orchids. See "Into the Wild: Farther Afield from Iquitos," in chapter 9.

• **Lagunas Llanganuco & Puya Raimondi:** Near Huaraz, the snowcapped peaks of the Cordillera Blanca are the biggest natural draw for trekkers, but the area is replete with all kinds of natural wonders. The Llanganuco lakes are two turquoise, glacier-fed alpine lakes, which reflect the snowy summits of several 6,000m (20,000-ft.) mountains. In the valley of Pachacoto, 56km (35 miles) from Huaraz, are the famous Puya Raimondi plants: trippy bromeliad plants, which soar up to 12m (36 ft.), flower just once in 100 years and immediately die. The colorful flowers, against the backdrop of the Cordillera Blanca mountains, makes for one of the prettiest pictures in Peru. See "Huaraz & the Cordillera Blanca," in chapter 10.

5 The Best Small Towns & Villages

• **Pisac:** The first of the Sacred Valley settlements outside Cusco,

Pisac has a greatly colorful and lively artisans' market and some of the most splendid Inca ruins this side of Machu Picchu. A massive fortress complex clings to a cliff high above town, affording sensational views of the valley. See "Pisac," in chapter 7.

- **Chinchero:** Just beyond Cusco, but not technically part of the Sacred Valley, Chinchero is best known for its bustling Sunday artisans' market, one of the best in Peru. But the graceful, traditional Andean town, higher even than Cusco, has mesmerizing views of snowy mountain ranges, a lovely colonial church, and its own Inca ruins. In the pretty main square, you can still see the huge stones and 10 trapezoidal niches of an Inca wall, originally part of a royal palace. See "Urubamba & Yucay," in chapter 7.

- **Ollantaytambo:** One of the principal villages of the Sacred Valley of the Incas, Ollanta (as the locals call it) is a spectacularly beautiful place along the Urubamba River; the gorge is lined by agricultural terraces, and snowcapped peaks rise in the distance. The ruins of a formidable temple-fortress overlook the old town, a perfect grid of streets built by the Incas, the only such layout remaining in Peru. See "Ollantaytambo," in chapter 7.

- **Colca Valley Villages:** Chivay, on the edge of Colca Canyon, is the valley's main town, but it isn't much more than a laid-back market town with fantastic hot springs on its outskirts. Dotting the Colca Valley and its extraordinary agricultural terracing are 14 charming colonial villages dating to the 16th century, each marked by its attractively decorated church. Yanque, Coporaque, Maca, and Lari are among the cutest towns. Natives in the valley are descendants of the pre-Inca ethnic communities Collaguas and Cabanas, and they maintain the vibrant style of traditional dress, highlighted by fantastically embroidered and sequined hats. See "A Typical Guided Tour of Colca Valley," in chapter 8.

- **Cajamarca:** A gem of a small town, a mini-Cusco in the northern highlands, delightful Cajamarca surprisingly doesn't get much tourist traffic. Beautifully framed by the Andes and sumptuous green countryside, with a historic core of colonial buildings where an important Inca city once stood, Cajamarca is elegant and easygoing. It's also very well-positioned for day trips into the country and to fascinating archaeological sites; indeed, several of Peru's nicest and most relaxing country hotels are located here. See "Cajamarca," in chapter 10.

6 The Best Outdoor Experiences

- **Trekking in the Sacred Valley:** The most famous trek outside Cusco is, of course, the Inca Trail to Machu Picchu. But if you're not up to 4 strenuous days with a group along a highly structured trail, there are plenty of additional hiking options in the Sacred Valley. Other trails are much less crowded and share some of the same extraordinary scenery. Ollantaytambo and Yucay are the best bases for walks in the pretty countryside of the Urubamba Valley. See chapter 7.

- **Running Big-Time White Water:** Just beyond Cusco in the Urubamba Valley are some excellent river runs, ranging from mild to world-class. Novices can do 1-day trips to get a taste of this thrilling sport, while more experienced rafters can take multi-day trips and even hard-core rafting journeys along the Tambopata River in the Amazon jungle. The area around Arequipa and the Colca Canyon in southern Peru is even better for rafting. The easiest and most convenient runs from Arequipa are on the Río Chili. More advanced rafting, ranging up to Class VI, beckons on the Río Majes, Río Colca, and Río Cotahuasi. See "Extreme Sacred Valley: Outdoor Adventure Sports," in chapter 7, and "Colca Valley," in chapter 8.

- **Exploring Colca Canyon:** Perhaps second only to the Callejón de Huaylas Valley in northern Peru for quality independent hiking is Colca Canyon. One of the most celebrated is the descent into the canyon itself, from the Cruz del Cóndor lookout. There are others that are even longer and more demanding, but more accessible hikes are also possible; walking from one village to another in the valley should satisfy most peoples' urges to get outdoors. Excursions on horseback throughout the valley and into the canyon are also possible. Hard-core sports enthusiasts might take on remote Cotahuasi Canyon, deeper and more rugged even than Colca. See "Colca Valley," in chapter 8.

- **Mountain & Volcano Climbing near Arequipa:** For mountaineers (and fit, adventurous travelers), the volcanoes just beyond Arequipa are perfect for some of Peru's best ascents. Several don't demand technical skills. Towering El Misti, which forms part of the Arequipa skyline, is an extremely popular climb, and the city's other major volcano, Chachani, also presents an accessible ascent. Peaks in the Colca Valley are great for serious climbers, such as the

Ampato Volcano and Coropuna, which at more than 6,425m (21,200 ft.) is perhaps the most stunning mountain in the Cotahuasi Valley and is for specialists only. See "Colca Valley," in chapter 8.

- **Spotting Birds & Wildlife in the Peruvian Amazon:** Peru's Amazon rain forest is some of the most biologically diverse on the planet. The southeastern jungle and its two principal protected areas, the Tambopata-Candamo Nature Reserve and the Manu Biosphere Reserve, are terrific for viewing wildlife and more than 1,000 species of birds. One of the great birding spectacles is the sight of thousands of macaws and parrots feeding at a clay lick. Keep your eyes peeled for more elusive wildlife, such as caimans, river otters, and even jaguars and tapirs. See "The Southern Amazon Jungle," in chapter 9.

- **Surfing the Waves of Peru's Pacific Coast:** Brazil may have more popular recognition as a surfing destination, but wave connoisseurs dig Peru, with 2,000km (1,200 miles) of Pacific coastline and a great variety of left and right reef breaks, point breaks, and big-time waves. Beaches are mostly uncrowded, but the water's cold, and most surfers wear wet suits year-round. More than 2 dozen beaches attract *surfistas*. Northern Peru, best from October to March, is the top choice of many; surfers hang out in the easygoing fishing village of Huanchaco, but the biggest and best waves in Peru are found at Puerto Chicama (also called Puerto Malabrigo), about 80km (50 miles) up the coast from Trujillo. The best beaches in southern Peru, where surfing is best from April to December (and at its peak in May), are Punta

Hermosa, Punta Rocas, Cerro Azul, and Pico Alto. See "Side Trips from Lima," in chapter 4, and "Trujillo," in chapter 10.

- **Trekking & Climbing in the Cordillera Blanca:** The Cordillera Blanca, the highest tropical mountain chain in the world, is almost wholly contained in the protected Huascarán National Park. For walkers and mountaineers, the scenery of snowcapped peaks, glaciers, lakes, and rivers is unrivaled in Peru. Fifty summits soar between 4,800 and 6,662m (16,000–22,205 ft.) high, so naturally, expert mountaineers are drawn to the Cordillera, but trekking and climbing opportunities abound for less-experienced outdoors types. The classic trek is the 4- to 5-day Santa Cruz–Llanganuco route, one of the most beautiful in South America. See "Huaraz & the Cordillera Blanca," in chapter 10.

- **Mountain Biking in the Callejón de Huaylas:** Mountain biking is just really developing some legs in Peru. The top spot is the valley near the Cordillera Blanca, the pristine mountain range in central Peru. Hundreds of mountain and valley horse trails lace lush fields and push past picturesque Andean villages and alpine lakes. Hardcore peddlers can test their lung capacity climbing to 5,000m (16,400-ft.) mountain passes. For cycling camaraderie, check out the Semana del Andinismo in Huaraz, which features a mountain-bike competition. See "Huaraz & the Cordillera Blanca," in chapter 10.

7 The Best Architecture

- **Colonial Lima:** The old center of Lima Centro preserves a wealth of fine colonial-era buildings that have survived fires, earthquakes, and decades of inattention. Churches include San Pedro (the best-preserved example of early colonial religious architecture in the city), La Merced, and San Agustín. Equally interesting are the historic quarter's few remaining *casas coloniales,* such as Casa Riva-Agüero, Casa Aliaga, and Casa de Osambela Oquendo. Others, including the famous Palacio Torre Tagle, are no longer open to the public. See "What to See & Do," in chapter 4.

- **Cusco's Inca Masonry:** Everywhere in Cusco's old center are stunning Inca walls, made of giant granite blocks so amazingly carved that they fit together, without mortar, like jigsaw puzzle pieces. The colonial architecture has, for the most part, not stood up nearly as well as the Incas' bold structures, which are virtually earthquake-proof. The best examples are Hatunrumiyoc, an alleyway lined with polygonal stones and featuring a 12-angled stone. Another pedestrian-only alleyway, Inca Roca, has a series of stones said to form the shape of a puma. See "The Magic of Inca Stones: A Walking Tour," in chapter 6.

- **Moray:** A peculiar Inca site with a mystical reputation, Moray isn't the Inca version of the Nasca Lines, though it sure looks like it could be. A series of inscrutable ringed terraces sculpted in the earth, the deep-set bowls formed an experimental agricultural center to test new crops and conditions. The different levels produce microclimates, with remarkable differences in temperature from top to bottom. See "Urubamba & Yucay," in chapter 7.

- **Ollantaytambo's Old Town:** Though Ollanta is best known for its Inca ruins perched on an outcrop, equally spectacular is the grid of perfectly constructed *canchas,* or city blocks, that reveal the Incas as masterful urban planners as well as stonemasons. The 15th-century canchas, amazingly preserved, each had a single entrance opening onto a main courtyard. Rippling alongside the lovely stone streets run canals that carry water down from the mountains. See "Ollantaytambo," in chapter 7.
- **Machu Picchu's Temple of the Sun:** Even as ruins, Machu Picchu rises to the stature of great architecture. Its brilliant elements of design and stonemasonry are to be found around every corner, but perhaps the greatest example of architectural prowess is the Temple of the Sun. A finely tapered tower, it has the finest stonework in Machu Picchu. A perfectly positioned window allows the sun's rays to come streaming through at dawn on the South American winter solstice in June, illuminating the stone at the center of the temple. A cave below the temple, carved out of the rock, has a beautifully sculpted altar and series of niches that create mesmerizing morning shadows. See "Machu Picchu & the Inca Trail," in chapter 7.
- **Colonial Arequipa:** The colonial core of Arequipa, Peru's second city, is the most graceful and harmonious in the country. Most of its elegant mansions and churches are carved from *sillar,* or white volcanic stone. The Plaza de Armas is one of the prettiest main squares in Peru, even though the cathedral was recently damaged by a major earthquake. Other colonial churches of note are La Compañía, San Francisco, San

Agustín, and the Monasterio de la Recoleta. Arequipa also has some of Peru's finest colonial seigniorial homes, which feature beautiful courtyards, elaborately carved stone facades, and period furnishings. Don't miss Casa del Moral, Casa Ricketts, and Casa Arróspide. See "Arequipa," in chapter 8.
- **Iquitos's Unique Structures:** A humid Amazon river city, Iquitos might not be a place you'd expect to find distinguished architecture, but the rubber barons who made fortunes in the 19th century lined the Malecón Tarapacá riverfront with handsome mansions covered in colorful Portuguese glazed tiles, or *azulejos.* The best are Casa Hernández, Casa Cohen, Casa Morey, and the Logia Unión Amazónica. Also check out the Casa de Fierro, designed by Gustave Eiffel and entirely constructed of iron in Paris and shipped to Peru, or the wild wooden houses on stilts in the often-flooded shantytown district of Belén. See "Iquitos & the Northern Amazon," in chapter 9.
- **Trujillo's Casas Antiguas:** The colorful pastel facades and unique iron window grilles of Trujillo's colonial- and republican-era houses represent one of Peru's finest architectural ensembles. Several have splendid interior courtyards and *mudéjar*-style (Moorish-Christian) details. Fine homes grace the lovely Plaza de Armas and the streets that radiate out from it. Among those outfitted with historic furnishings and open to the public are Palacio Iturregui, Casa Urquiaga (where Simón Bolívar once lived), Casa de la Emancipación, Casa Ganoza Chopitea, and Casa Orbegoso. See "Trujillo," in chapter 10.

- **Cumbe Mayo's Aqueduct:** This weird and wonderful spot near Cajamarca draws visitors for its strange rock formations, which mimic a stone forest, but a structure engineered by man, a pre-Inca aqueduct constructed around 1000 B.C., is pure genius. The extraordinary, 8km (5-mile) canal is carved from volcanic stone in perfect lines to collect and redirect water on its way to the Pacific Ocean. Right angles slow the flow of water and ease the effects of erosion. The aqueduct is likely the oldest man-made structure in South America. See "Cajamarca," in chapter 10.

8 The Best Festivals & Celebrations

- **Fiesta de la Cruz** (across Peru): The Festival of the Cross isn't as solemnly Catholic as it might sound. Best in Lima, Cusco, and Ica, the festival does features cross processions (though the decorated crosses are vibrant), but it also displays a surfeit of folk music and dance, the highlight being the daring "scissors dancers," who once performed on top of churches.
- **El Señor de los Milagros** (Lima): The Artist Once Again Known as Prince would love this highly religious procession, with tens of thousands of participants all clad in bright purple. The Lord of Miracles, the largest procession in South America, lasts a full 24 hours. It venerates a miraculous painting of Jesus Christ, which was created by an Angolan slave and survived the devastating 1746 earthquake, even though almost everything around it was felled.
- **Inti Raymi** (Cusco): The Festival of the Sun, one of the greatest pageants in South America, celebrates the winter solstice and honors the Inca sun god with a bounty of colorful Andean parades, music, and dance. It takes over Cusco and transforms the Sacsayhuamán ruins overlooking the city into a majestic stage.

- **Virgen del Carmen** (Paucartambo): The tiny, remote Andean colonial village of Paucartambo is about 4 hours from Cusco, but it hosts one of Peru's wildest festivals. Its 3 days of dance, revelry, drinking, and outlandish, scary costumes pack in thousands who camp all over town (there's almost nowhere to stay) and then wind up at the cemetery.
- **Virgen de la Candelaria** (Puno): Puno, perhaps the epicenter of Peruvian folklore, imbues its festivals with a unique vibrancy. Candlemas, (or Virgen de la Candelaria), which is spread over 2 weeks, is one of the greatest folk religious festivals in South America, with an explosion of music, dance, and some of the most fantastic costumes and masks seen anywhere.
- **Puno Week** (Puno): Puno, the fiesta capital of Peru, rises to the occasion for a full week every November to mark its Amerindian roots. A huge procession from Lake Titicaca into town remembers the legend of the first Inca emperor, who emerged from the world's highest navigable lake to establish the Inca Empire. The procession deviates into dance, music, and oblivion.

9 The Best Hotels

- **Miraflores Park Plaza,** Lima (© 01/242-3000): Perhaps the top business traveler's hotel in Lima, this oasis of refinement and luxury is small enough to cater to your every whim. The Park Plaza is the epitome of style, with handsome, spacious rooms, huge bathrooms, and an elegant restaurant and bar. There's a small pool and a gym/sauna on the top floor, overlooking the malecón, parks, and the coastline. See p. 115.

- **Hotel Antigua Miraflores,** Lima (© 01/241-6116): This charming midsize hotel is in a century-old mansion, full of Peruvian touches. The house is tastefully decorated with colonial Peruvian art, but with a laid-back atmosphere. Built around a leafy courtyard, it's a peaceful respite within the hubbub of Miraflores and the rest of Lima. See p. 115.

- **Country Club Lima Hotel,** Lima (© 01/611-9000): A recently revived hacienda-style hotel from the 1920s, this grand estate is luxurious and has plenty of character, but it remains a relaxed place that's good for families. Given its high standards, it's not a bad deal, either. A good retreat from the stress of modern Lima, the country club aspect isn't neglected: Golf and tennis are both available. See p. 118.

- **Hotel Libertador,** Cusco (© 084/231-961): This dignified five-star hotel in Cusco, with excellent service, is just a couple of blocks from the Plaza de Armas and right across the street from the Inca Temple of the Sun. Elegant and traditional, the Libertador inhabits a colonial house where Francisco Pizarro once lived. Full of art and antiques, the rooms are refined with colonial touches. See p. 173.

- **Hotel Monasterio,** Cusco (© 084/241-777): Extraordinarily carved out of a 16th-century monastery, itself built over the foundations of an Inca palace, this Orient-Express hotel is the most dignified and historic place to stay in Peru. With its own gilded chapel and 18th-century Cusco School art collection, it's an attraction in its own right. Rooms are gracefully decorated with colonial touches, particularly the rooms off the serene first courtyard. See p. 174.

- **Sonesta Posada del Inca Sacred Valley,** Yucay (© 084/201-107, or 01/222-4777 for reservations): One of the coolest hotels in the Sacred Valley, this former 17th-century monastery and hacienda looks like a colonial village—it even has a small chapel. Spread over nice grounds and gardens, with great views of the valley and hill terraces, the hotel has rooms with loads of character, a good restaurant, and a neat museum of ancient ceramics and textiles. See p. 220.

- **Hotel Pakaritampu,** Ollantaytambo (© 084/204-020): More of an inn than a hotel, this new place is rustic and intimate, with a great fireplace bar and lovely gardens, but also it's big enough for some privacy. It's eminently tasteful but still fits in very well with its low-key surroundings. See p. 226.

- **Machu Picchu Pueblo Hotel,** Aguas Calientes (© 084/211-032, or 084/245-314 for reservations): It's not next to the ruins, but this rustic hotel is a compound of bungalows ensconced in lush tropical gardens and cloud forest, and it's the nicest place in Aguas Calientes. With lots of nature trails and guided activities, it's also great for naturalists. And after a day at Machu Picchu, the spring-fed pool is a great alternative to the thermal baths in town. Junior suites, with fireplaces and small terraces, are good deals. See p. 248.

- **Sonesta Posada del Inca Lake Titicaca,** Puno (© 054/363-672): Gracing the shores of Lake Titicaca, this hotel is warmly designed, with a roaring fireplace and lots of Peruvian art. Rooms are spacious and comfortable, and many have great views of the lake. For families, there's a tiny version of a Lake Titicaca floating community. See p. 264.
- **Hotel Libertador Arequipa,** Arequipa (© 054/215-110): Housed in a nice 1940s-era colonial-style building a bit removed from the colonial center of Arequipa, this upscale hotel has a relaxed, almost homey feel. It has authentic colonial touches and plenty of space to stretch out, as well as a large outdoor pool and lush gardens. A good family hotel, it has a game area for children. See p. 280.
- **Hotel El Dorado Plaza,** Iquitos (© 094/222-555): Although not overly fancy or oozing with character, the El Dorado Plaza is by far the best place to stay in Iquitos. It was the first-ever luxury hotel in town, and it boasts a perfect location on the Plaza de Armas and good service. Rooms are large, and the great pool is a fine place to relax after a jungle excursion. A very good value if you get a deal, too. See p. 327.
- **Hotel Posada del Puruay,** Cajamarca (© 044/828-318, or 01/336-7869 for reservations): In the gorgeous highland countryside just outside Cajamarca, this country hotel is a restored 1830 farmhouse. The great grounds, with gardens, horses, and amenities such as a barbecue pit, are sure-fire selling points, but the inn also has huge rooms, friendly personal service, a very good restaurant, and an extensive video library as well. See p. 369.

10 The Best Small Hotels & Hostales

- **Hotel España,** Lima (© 01/427-9196): A funky budget hotel in the old center, across from the Convento de San Francisco, this is the perfect place to hang out with other backpackers traipsing around Peru. In a character-filled colonial building replete with curious decor and a maze of rooms, it's simple but cheap and cheery, with a great rooftop terrace. See p. 114.
- **Mochileros,** Lima (© 01/477-4506): A cool backpackers' inn in Barranco, Lima's most bohemian district, this former theater offers bundles of flair for the money. The brightly colored communal rooms and genial atmosphere are great, and rooms are more than adequate for a comfortable stay. A fun Irish-style pub operates in the front of the building. See p. 121.
- **The Niños Hotel,** Cusco (© 084/231-424): Even if this great little inn had no redeeming social and moral value, it would still be one of the best informal places to stay in Peru. The fact that it operates as part of a foundation that dedicates its profits to helping and housing Cusco's street children is a welcome bonus. The small, Dutch-owned hotel, located in a restored and nicely if simply decorated colonial house, is charming, immaculate, and a great value. The trick is getting a reservation—try many months in advance of your arrival. See p. 179.
- **Casa de Campo Hostal,** Cusco (© 084/243-069): Way up in the hills of the San Blas district, this exuberantly friendly place enjoys some of the best views in all of Cusco. The chalet-style rooms are

chilly but comfortable and a good value. The hike up the hill and the unending stairs leading to the hotel are tough, so it's nice that you can relax on the fantastic terraces or in the fireplace lounge. See p. 181.

- **Hostal Pisaq,** Pisac (© and fax **084/203-062**): On the main square of Pisac, which is overrun on market days, this friendly little inn has neat features for a budget hostel: hand-painted murals, a sauna, an attractive courtyard, and a little cafe serving great pizza from a wood-burning oven and home-cooked meals. See p. 216.

- **El Albergue,** Ollantaytambo (© and fax **084/204-014**): An American-owned hostel right next to the railroad tracks—but much quieter than that would indicate—this comfortable little place has just a few rooms and shared bathrooms, but beds are excellent, and the vibe, with relaxing gardens and Labrador retrievers running around, is great. There's also a cool wood-fired sauna. See p. 226.

- **La Casa de Melgar Hostal,** Arequipa (© and fax **054/222-459**): In a pretty colonial house made of sillar stone, this small inn exudes style and charm. With thick walls, multiple interior courtyards, and gardens, it's much nicer than most inexpensive hotels. Ground floor rooms with vaulted brick ceilings look like they're straight out of a movie shoot. See p. 281.

- **La Casa de Mi Abuela Hostal,** Arequipa (© **054/241-206**): Though this extremely friendly and well-run small hotel continues to grow, it retains much its original B&B character. A self-contained resort, it now features a restaurant, a *peña* music bar, a pool, a game room, great gardens, and an excellent travel agency. Some rooms pale in comparison with the facilities, but you can't beat the services and security. See p. 281.

- **Parador de Colca,** Yanque (© **054/288-440**): There is a burgeoning number of rustic, country-style inns along the edge of Colca Canyon, any one of which is easily recommended, but this is a travelers' favorite. In a local nature reserve near Yanque, this Swedish-owned ecolodge has great views of Colca. Rooms have loft spaces, and there are private patios with fire pits, as well as lots of hiking and horseback-riding opportunities. See p. 295.

- **Hacienda San Vicente,** Cajamarca (© and fax **044/822-644**): A small and funky inn in a former hacienda, this unique place probably isn't for everyone. Its oddball rooms are like caves carved into the hillside (rock walls even form a headboard or two). Everything is just a tad "off," but delightfully so. With skylights for moon views and a Gaudí-esque chapel on the premises, this place isn't afraid to be itself. See p. 369.

11 The Best Local Dining Experiences

- **Barbecuing Peruvian-Style:** The Peruvian version of a BBQ get-together is called a *pachamanca;* it's basically cooking meat and veggies over coals or hot stones in a hole in the ground. On weekends in the countryside, mostly in the mountains, you'll see families gathered around smoky subterranean grills, cooking up pork or beef and potatoes and vegetables. (You can also get pachamanca-style dishes in some traditional restaurants.)

- **Chugging *Chicha:*** An ancient Andean tradition is the brewing of chicha, beer made from fermented maize. You can find it at a few traditional restaurants, but for an authentic Andean experience, the best place to get it is at a simple bar or home that flies the chicha flag—a long pole with a red flag or, often, balloon—which is the local way of advertising that there's home-brewed chicha available inside. Served warm, in monstrous tumblers for a few pennies, it's not to many foreigners' liking, but it's one of the best ways to go native. *Chicha morada,* a refreshment made from blue corn, is something altogether different—it's sweet, nonalcoholic, and it actually tastes good (especially with *ceviche*).

- **Going Native with Jungle Cuisine:** Peru's vast Amazon is full of exotic critters and plants, so it's logical that it would produce its own unique cuisine. Some of what restaurateurs deal in is endangered animals, though, so I don't advise satisfying your curiosity to try sea-turtle soup or caiman, even if the locals do it. Local jungle dishes you don't have to feel bad about trying include *patarashca,* a steamed river fish wrapped in banana leaves; *juanes,* a kind of rice tamale; *timbuche,* a thick soup made with local fish; *paiche,* an Amazon-size local fish; and *chonta,* a hearts of palm salad. See chapter 9.

- **Relaxing at a *Quinta*:** There are elegant restaurants in Lima, Cusco, Arequipa, and Iquitos, but there's nothing quite like an informal *quinta*—an open-air restaurant specializing in Andean home-cooking. It's an Andean tradition perhaps best explored in the crisp air of Cusco, which has a trio of quintas that are especially popular with locals on weekends.

Look for informal garden or courtyard settings, large portions of Peruvian cooking, and reasonable prices. Most quintas are open only for lunch, so plan on it as your main meal of the day. You'll not only eat well but it's also a great way to spend a sunny afternoon. See "Cusco's *Quintas,*" in chapter 6.

- **Savoring a Pisco Sour:** Peru's national drink is the pisco sour, a delicious concoction made from the white grape brandy called *pisco.* Made frothy when mixed with egg whites, lemon juice, sugar, and bitters, it's cold and complex, the closest thing to a Peruvian margarita. Try one with ceviche or a robust Andean meal—or just knock 'em back late at night at a gringo-filled bar.

- **Self-Medicating with *Mate de Coca*:** Coca-leaf tea, a perfectly legal local drink that's been a tradition in the Andes for centuries, is a great way to deal with the high altitude of the mountains, which can make your head spin and your body reel. As soon as you hit Cusco or Puno, head straight for the mate de coca—most hotels have it at the ready for their guests. And if that doesn't work, strap on the oxygen tank (many hotels supply that for their guests, too).

- **Sucking on Ceviche:** Though cooking varies greatly across Peru, there are few things more satisfying than a classic Peruvian ceviche: raw fish and shellfish marinated in lime or lemon juice and hot chili peppers, served with raw onion, sweet potato, and toasted corn. It's wonderfully refreshing and spicy. The best place to try one? A seaside *cevichería,* specializing in umpteen varieties of deliciously fresh ceviche.

- **Touring Ica's** *Bodegas:* Peru, one of the great winemaking countries of the world? Probably not, but the southern desert coast does have a thriving wine industry. The most famous product is pisco, but the many traditional bodegas (wineries) throughout the Ica countryside also make regular table wines. A few bodegas give tours and tastings. Ica hosts a hopping Wine Festival in March, a good time to tour the region if you're into wine and general merriment. Harvest time, late February through April, is the other time to visit, when you can see people crushing grapes the old-fashioned way—with their feet. See "Ica," in chapter 5.

12 The Best Restaurants

- **L'Eau Vive,** Lima (© 01/427-5612): Run by a French order of nuns who perform "Ave Maria" nightly after dinner, this French-Peruvian restaurant donates its proceeds to charity and cooks up good-value meals in the process. The menu's tasty, and the daily set lunch is a bargain. Did I mention that the proceeds go to the poor of Peru? See p. 122.
- **Astrid y Gastón,** Lima (© 01/444-1496): One of the coolest restaurants in the country is this stylish modern place serving a creative brand of creole-Mediterranean fare. Behind a nondescript facade in the Miraflores district, a husband/wife team cooks and runs the colorful colonial dining room and cozy bar, favored by Limeño regulars. See p. 123.
- **Las Brujas de Cachiche,** Lima (© 01/447-1883): Celebrating 2,000 years of local culture and pre-Columbian Peruvian cuisine with ancient recipes and ingredients, this sophisticated place is a favorite of local businesspeople and diplomats. It serves classic Peruvian dishes, such as *ají de gallina* (chili cream chicken), with innovative twists. For a treat, check out the daily lunch buffet and frequent gastronomic festivals. See p. 123.
- **Manos Morenas,** Lima (© 01/467-0421): The best place for dinner and a show in Lima, this sleek Barranco restaurant serves good *criollo* (creole) cooking and features peña and Afro-Peruvian music and dance nightly. It's housed in an elegant early-1900s house, very appealingly converted. The show's not inexpensive, but it's usually a great evening out. See p. 127.
- **Inka Grill,** Cusco (© 084/262-992): A popular place on the Plaza de Armas, Inka Grill serves Andean cooking with a fresh twist in relaxed surroundings—perfect for Cusco. Try something spicy and new, or an international standby, such as pizza, pasta, and risotto. See p. 184.
- **La Retama,** Cusco (© 084/226-372): One of Cusco's most traditional longtime favorites, with good second-floor views of the Plaza de Armas, La Retama has nightly folklore shows and good traditional cooking. The restaurant is very popular with the gringo set. See p. 185.
- **Greens,** Cusco (© 084/243-820): A small and stylish restaurant in the cool San Blas district, Greens has a creative menu and funky decor, including low, comfy sofas and hipster tunes. The excellent, surprising menus of international and Peruvian dishes are reasonably priced. See p. 186.
- **La Casa de la Abuela,** Urubamba (© 084/622-975): Probably the

best restaurant in the Sacred Valley is this crowd-pleasing, family-run place. Warm and friendly, it's the kind of place you want to keep going back to for the homemade pizza, pasta, and Peruvian meals. Keep an eye peeled for Carnaval fiestas and frequent criollo-themed nights, which feature peña music. See p. 221.

- **Indio Feliz,** Aguas Calientes (© 084/211-090): The town at the bottom of Machu Picchu is a little scrappy, so this Peruvian-French restaurant really stands out. In an attractive and very popular two-level dining room, it offers a great-value three-course menu. If by chance you just completed the 4-day Inca Trail trek, treat yourself to a meal here. See p. 250.

- **Sol de Mayo,** Arequipa (© 054/254-148): This is the best place in town for traditional Arequipeño cooking, which has quite a reputation in Peru. The setting, around a courtyard garden where strolling musicians play, is delightful. It's a perfect place to sink your teeth into local Peruvian specialties and a great place to splurge. See p. 284.

- **Zig Zag,** Arequipa (© 054/206-020): This cute, chic, and inviting restaurant has a unique specialty: stone-grilled ostrich. Healthier than other meats, ostrich is really good, as is another popular dish served here, alpaca (which is also healthier than red meat). In a two-level space with sillar walls and vaulted ceilings, the grilled meat is not the only thing that makes this a memorable dining experience. See p. 285.

- **Montecarlo,** Iquitos (© 094/232-246): The northern Amazon city of Iquitos has a handful of good restaurants serving Peruvian and jungle specialties, but this new upscale place—glitzy on the outside but relaxed and elegant on the inside—is the best. Fish dishes are excellent, as is the service. If you want, you can gamble downstairs at the casino. See p. 329.

- **Club Colonial,** Huanchaco (© 044/461-015): An unexpectedly chic and stylish restaurant in the low-key beach resort of Huanchaco, this Belgian-French place has the kind of ambience you'd look to find in Barranco in Lima, not the north coast. The candlelit dining room is like a cool expatriate's house, and the menu is a tantalizing mix of Peruvian and Franco-Belgian items. Whether you order meat or fresh fish, or even a Belgian standard, you're in for a treat. See p. 349.

- **Pueblo Viejo,** Chiclayo (© 074/228-863): Chiclayo may not be the dining capital of Peru, but its best restaurant is very good. An attractive two-story eatery that serves traditional but creative Chiclayano cooking and *comida criolla* (creole cooking), Pueblo Viejo really stands out in the north of Peru. See p. 360.

- **El Querubino,** Cajamarca (© 044/830-900): A new, brightly decorated restaurant just off the Plaza de Armas, El Querubino is refined and stylish, but relaxed enough to be popular with locals. Dinner often features live but low-key music, and at lunch, there's a nice daily list of value specials. See p. 371.

13 The Best Markets & Shopping

- **Miraflores,** Lima: The Peruvian capital has the biggest number of shops and selection of goods from across the country, as might be expected. The Miraflores district has dozens of shops stocked to the rafters with handicrafts from around Peru. For one-stop shopping, there are mini-malls of many stalls selling ceramics, textiles, and other souvenirs. The best silver jewelry and antiques shops are also in Miraflores. See "Shopping," in chapter 4.

- **Barrio de San Blas,** Cusco: The picturesque and bohemian neighborhood of San Blas, which rises into the hills above Cusco, is bursting with the studios and workshops of artists and artisans, as well as art galleries and ceramics shops. You can pop into several studios and see artists at work. See "Shopping," in chapter 6.

- **Pisac's Market:** Thousands of tourists descend each Sunday morning on Pisac's liveliest handicrafts market, which takes over the central plaza and spills across adjoining streets. Many sellers, decked out in the dress typical of their villages, come from remote populations high in the mountains. Pisac is one of the best spots for colorful Andean textiles, including rugs, alpaca sweaters, and ponchos. See "Pisac," in chapter 7.

- **Pablo Seminario,** Urubamba: Urubamba leaves the Sunday tourist handicrafts markets to other towns in the Sacred Valley, but it's home to one of the coolest ceramics shops in Peru. Pablo Seminario, originally from the north of the country, now operates out of a lovely place that is equal parts home, workshop, storefront, and zoo. His work features funky pre-Columbian motifs. See "Urubamba & Yucay," in chapter 7.

- **Chinchero's Handicrafts Market:** It's not as popular as Pisac's market, but in many ways,

Chinchero's is more authentic, and the setting is just as spectacular. The big one is on Sunday, when the tourist buses come through, but less-hectic Tuesday and Thursday are probably better for making a deal. The quality of handicrafts is usually quite excellent. Take your camera; the sellers still wear traditional garments. See "Urubamba & Yucay," in chapter 7.

- **Isla Taquile,** Lake Titicaca: The Taquile islanders are famous for their dress and exquisite textiles. Travelers can pick up some of the finest woven and embroidered waistbands and wool stocking caps in Peru, including some that are normally reserved for community authorities. Because they're so finely made, Taquile textiles are more expensive than the mass-produced handicrafts you'll find elsewhere in Peru. Islanders operate a co-op on the main plaza, and sell from stalls during festivals. See "Puno & Lake Titicaca," in chapter 8.

- **Arequipa:** Alpaca sweaters, ponchos, and hats are classic Peruvian souvenirs, and you can score them across the Andes and in Lima, but Arequipa is the top spot for really excellent, export-quality goods. You'll find great designs in baby alpaca, vicuña, and wool. Visit any of the shops near the Plaza de Armas, including the alpaca boutiques that now inhabit the old cloisters of the La Compañía church. Another good spot, for slightly less swank goods, is the general handicrafts market (*mercado de artesanía*), whose stalls are in what used to be the old town jail. See "Arequipa," in chapter 8.

- **Barrio Belén,** Iquitos: Handicrafts, particularly textiles and other items from the Shipibo tribe in the Amazon, are available at the large artisans' market out by the airport, but shopping of a very different sort is pursued at the popular market in the waterfront Barrio de Belén. The wildly colorful market, which spreads over several long blocks and is a riot of activity, sells everything under the Amazon sun; let your senses be the judge. Look for unusual Amazon fish and fruits, and exotic jungle meats, such as monkey and caiman. When it becomes too much, take a breather at the fresh juice stands. See "Iquitos & the Northern Amazon," in chapter 9.

14 The Best Reasons for Bragging Rights

- **Surfing Big Sand:** The southern desert of Peru is a strange, unrelenting landscape, but it has the highest sand dunes in South America. An X-sport fast gaining in popularity is surfing the dunes on sand boards and *areneros* (dune buggies). The biggest are near Nasca, but probably the prettiest spot is the dunes that ring the Huacachina Lagoon outside of Ica. See "Ica," in chapter 5.

- **Gazing at the Stars at Sacsayhuamán:** The Sacsayhuamán ruins are amazing enough by day; imagine those immense, elegantly laid stones at night, high above Cusco. Night visits to the ruins are permitted. If your visit coincides with a full moon in that gargantuan sky, you'll be talking about it back home for months. At night, it won't be hard to perceive the Incas' worship of the natural world, in which the moon was a deity. A similar experience would be hiking along the Inca Trail and spending that last night before pushing on to Machu Picchu under a full moon. See "What to See & Do," in chapter 6.

- **Lighting It Up at Tres Cruces:** Beyond the remote Andean village of Paucartambo, known for its Virgen de Carmen festival, is Tres Cruces, perched on a mountain ridge on the edge of the Amazon basin. Famous for its almost hallucinogenic, multihued sunrise, the spot was held sacred by the Incas, and it's not hard to see why. During the winter months (May–July), the special effects are beyond belief. To enhance your bragging rights, note that Tres Cruces is a royal pain to reach. See "Side Trips from Cusco," in chapter 6.

- **Taking a Copter to Machu Picchu:** OK, it doesn't resound with the same adventure cred as walking 4 days over tortuous mountain passes, but exclaiming that you cruised into Machu Picchu by helicopter surely has a certain panache. The views may not be as great as you'd hope, but you're still soaring over the amazing Andes, and you'll arrive at Machu Picchu in no time. See "Machu Picchu & the Inca Trail," in chapter 7.

- **Scaling Huayna Picchu in Record Time:** Huayna Picchu hovers above Machu Picchu in the classic postcard shot of the ruins. People of all ages and decent physical condition can climb to the summit; to properly boast, you've got to race the steep stone path in close to record time (about 22 min. at last report). Even if you don't beat the record, you can savor the stunning, indescribable view as you wait for your heart rate to return to normal. See "Machu Picchu & the Inca Trail," in chapter 7.

- **Making It Over the Top of "Dead Woman's Pass":** Hiking the Inca Trail to Machu Picchu is one of the greatest eco-adventures on the planet. Enough said. See

"Machu Picchu & the Inca Trail," in chapter 7.

- **Running a Class VI in Colca Canyon:** Extremely technical white-water rafting in the Colca (as well as Cotahuasi) Canyon is the stuff that bragging was made for. Imagine telling your friends that you hurtled down the river at the bottom of a canyon more than twice as deep as the Grand Canyon! For hard-core runners only; trips are expensive and lengthy. See "Colca Valley," in chapter 8.

- **Rumbling by Truck to Puerto Maldonado:** If you like tests of sheer perseverance, travel by truck from Cusco to Puerto Maldonado, the gateway to the Tambopata Reserve in the southern Amazon. It'll take between 3 and 10 days on a road that's 95% unpaved, but what's time (and a sore body) to a good story? See "The Southern Amazon Jungle," in chapter 9.

- **Trippin' Amazon-Style:** If spotting wildlife and trekking through primary rain forest isn't stimulating enough, you can do your best to imitate the ancient ways of Amazon tribes and shamans by taking part in an *ayahuasca*

ceremony. The natural hallucinogenic potion, made of herbs, roots, and other plants, is supposed to mess with your mind. But for locals, it's a deeply respected ritual. See "Iquitos & the Northern Amazon," in chapter 9.

- **Fishing for Piranha:** If you visit a jungle lodge, you may have the opportunity to head out on the Amazon or its tributaries in a dugout canoe to fish for piranha. Most are surprisingly small, but their famous teeth are very much present. For a special dinner, have the lodge cook fry 'em up for you that night. See "Iquitos & the Northern Amazon," in chapter 9.

- **Bagging 6,000m Peaks in the Cordillera Blanca:** For expert climbers, the Cordillera Blanca is a mountaineering mecca. From May to September, fit climbers can score several 6,000m (20,000-ft.) summits in the Parque Nacional Huascarán in just a couple weeks. Huascarán, at 6,768m (22,300 ft.), is the big one, the highest mountain in the Peruvian Andes and the tallest tropical mountain in the world. See "Huaraz & the Cordillera Blanca," in chapter 10.

15 The Best of Peru Online

- **www.andeantravelweb.com:** The Andean Travel Web, a private website run by gringos in Peru, is a miniguide to the country, with information on all the major destinations and activities, transportation, the latest in Inca Trail regulations, local tour operators, and helpful things such as ecotourism links.

- **www.gorp.com:** The travel wholesaler GORP features an entire page of personal essays on the great outdoors and adventure

sports in Peru, including pieces on running the Amazon, birding, and a top 20 of adventure activities.

- **www.peru.org.pe:** The most comprehensive official Peru site, recently revamped, is the website of PromPerú. It has detailed sections on Peruvian history, festivals, trip-planning, and outdoor "adrenaline rushes," all with extensive pull-down menus, as well as a stock of photo and video images and audio files.

- **www.saexplorers.org**: The site of the rightly famous South American Explorers (based in Ithaca, N.Y., with clubhouses in Lima, Cusco, and Quito, Ecuador) has vital information such as travel advisories, insurance providers, and links to websites on specific Peruvian destinations. You can order the club's "Information Packet" of fact sheets and member tips.

- **www.traficoperu.com**: This is an online travel agent with details on practical matters—domestic airlines, bus transportation, and hotels—plus a few cheap domestic packages.

2

Planning Your Trip to Peru

Peru—a land of pre-Columbian ruins and lost cities, Andes mountains and Amazon jungle—has a reputation for exoticism, but it is a destination about which many first-time travelers know very little. This chapter details everything you need to know to make planning your trip to Peru less daunting, from the lay of the land and how to get there to money and health concerns. It also covers other critical information for planning your trip, such as tour operators and travel packages, and tips on Peruvian accommodations, dining, and shopping.

1 The Regions in Brief

Peru, which lies just below the equator, is the third largest country in South America, covering an area of nearly 1,300,000km² (500,000 sq. miles). It is larger than France and Spain combined. Peru shares borders with Ecuador and Colombia to the north, Brazil and Bolivia to the east, and Chile to the south.

Peruvians like to say that their country consists of three distinct geological components: coast, *sierra* (highlands), and *selva* (jungle). Though the capital, Lima, lies on the coast, the bold Andes mountain range and Amazon rain forest, which makes up nearly two-thirds of Peru, dominate the country. Its considerable size, natural barriers, and a lack of efficient transportation alternatives make Peru a somewhat difficult and time-consuming place to get around.

LIMA & THE SOUTHERN COAST The Pacific coastal region is a narrow strip that runs from one end of the country to the other (a distance of some 2,200km/1,400 miles) and is almost entirely desert. Lima lies about halfway down the coast. To the south, in one of the driest areas on earth, are Pisco, Ica, and Nasca, the cradle of several of Peru's most important

ancient civilizations, as well as the famously mysterious Nasca Lines and the Ballestas Islands, promoted locally as "Peru's Galápagos" for their diverse indigenous fauna.

CUSCO & THE SACRED VALLEY The dramatic Andes mountains in south-central Peru contain the country's most famous sights, including the former Inca capital of Cusco and scenic highland villages that run the length of the beautiful Sacred Valley. The valley is dotted with singularly impressive Inca ruins, of which Machu Picchu (and the Inca Trail leading to it) is undoubtedly the star. Cusco sits at an elevation of some 3,300m (11,000 ft.). Indigenous culture is particularly strong in the region.

SOUTHERN PERU Massive Lake Titicaca, shared with Bolivia, is the largest lake in South America and the world's highest navigable body of water (at 3,800m/12,540 ft.). Indigenous peoples inhabit ancient villages on islands (some of them man-made) in the middle of this huge body of water. Puno, at the edge of Lake Titicaca, is a rough-and-tumble town that hosts some of Peru's liveliest festivals. The

Peru's UNESCO World Heritage Sites

- Cusco city (designated in 1983)
- Machu Picchu Historic Sanctuary (1983)
- Archaeological Site of Chavín (1985)
- Huascarán National Park (1985)
- Manu National Park (1987)
- Chan Chan Archaeological Zone (1988)
- Río Abiseo National Park (1990)
- Historic Center of Lima (1991)
- Nasca Lines (1994)
- Historic Center of Arequipa (2000)

elegant colonial city of Arequipa is one of Peru's most gorgeously situated, at the base of three snowcapped volcanoes, and nearby is Colca Canyon, twice as deep as the Grand Canyon and site of perhaps the best place in all South America to view the regal condor.

THE AMAZON BASIN Though about 60% of Peru is Amazon rain forest, only about 5% of the country's human inhabitants reside there. One of the world's most dazzling arrays of wildlife—over 1,700 species of birds (more than the population found in the continental U.S.) and 2,000 species of fish—make it their home. For the visitor, there are two primary jungle destinations. The northern jungle, of which Iquitos is the principal gateway (but accessible only by plane or boat), is the most explored and has the most facilities. Much less trafficked, and more controlled, is the Madre de Dios department in the south, which contains Manu Biosphere Reserve, Puerto Maldonado, and Tambopata-Candamo Nature Reserve. These can be reached by land or air from Cusco.

NORTHERN PERU Peru's north is much less visited than the south, even though it possesses some of the country's most outstanding archaeological sights. Trujillo, Chiclayo, and Cajamarca (a lovely small city in the highlands), are the main colonial towns of interest. Near Trujillo and Chiclayo are Chan Chan, Túcume, and Sipán, extraordinary adobe cities, pyramids, and royal tombs and treasures that predate the Incas.

The mountain ranges in the center of Peru, north of Lima, are among the highest in Peru. Within Huascarán National Park, the Cordillera Blanca stretches 200km (124 miles) and contains a dozen peaks over 5,000m (16,500 ft.); the highest is Huascarán, at 6,768m (22,334 ft.). The region is a favorite of trekkers and outdoor-adventure travelers who come to Peru with white-water rafting, ice climbing, and other sports in mind. The main jumping-off point for these activities is the town of Huaraz. In valleys east of the capital is the important archaeological site Chavín de Huántar, one of Peru's most ancient.

2 Visitor Information

BEFORE YOU GO

Peru doesn't maintain national tourism offices abroad, so your best official source of information before you go is

www.peru.org.pe, the website of PromPerú (Commission for the Promotion of Peru). Peruvian embassies and consulates usually offer some brochures and other information on traveling to Peru, but it's probably best not to expect too much.

Other helpful websites include **www.peruemb.org**, the Peruvian embassy in Washington, D.C.; **www.traficoperu.com/english**, the site for Tráfico on Line Perú, a travel agency with information about flights, hotels, and special deals; **www.perurail.com**, the official PeruRail website with route and service information; and **www.saexplorers.org**, the South American Explorers website, which is especially good for trekking and adventure travel information.

IN PERU

Visitor information is not handled by a single, centralized government agency across Peru. PromPerú, the main national organization responsible for tourism promotion and information, works alongside the Ministry of Industry, Tourism & International Business Negotiation (MITINCI) and several private entities. The result is

---

 Red Alert Checklist

- Have you taken care of all special requirements for your destination, such as yellow fever vaccinations and antimalarial drugs if you're visiting the jungle?
- Did you secure your place on any organized tours that require reservations (such as the Inca Trail)?
- Did you make sure your favorite attraction is open? Some attractions may be closed for special events or inaccessible because of weather conditions. Scheduled tours, festivals, and special events may also be cancelled. Confirm fixed-departure dates for tours and expeditions.
- If you purchased traveler's checks, have you recorded the check numbers and stored the documentation separately from the checks?
- Did you pack your camera and an extra set of camera batteries, and did you purchase enough film? (Good slide film is especially hard to come by in Peru.) If you packed film in your checked baggage, did you invest in protective pouches to shield film from airport X-rays?
- Do you have a safe, accessible place to store money, such as a money belt?
- Did you bring ID cards that could entitle you to discounts? Did you make copies of your passport?
- Did you bring emergency drug prescriptions and extra glasses and/or contact lenses?
- Do you have your credit card personal identification numbers (4-digit PINs are required for use in Peru)?
- If you have an E-ticket, do you have your printed E-ticket, your ID, and the credit card you used to purchase the ticket?
- Did you leave a copy of your itinerary and passport with someone at home?
- Did you check to see if any travel advisories have been issued by the U.S. State Department (http://travel.state.gov) regarding your destination?
- Do you have the address and phone number of your country's embassy with you?

that tourism information is confusingly dispersed among sometimes poorly equipped, small municipal offices and is often limited to regional or, worse, only local information. Occasionally, private travel agencies are more adept at dispensing information, though their goal is, of course, to hawk their services.

PromPerú maintains a large bureaucratic office in Lima at Edificio Mitinci, 14th floor, Calle Uno Oeste 50, Urbanización Córpac, San Isidro (℃ **01/224-9355**); however, it is not convenient for tourists seeking basic information about the country. PromPerú also operates a 24-hour information booth (℃ **01/574-8000**) in the international terminal of Lima's Jorge Chávez International Airport.

The **Tourist Protection Bureau,** which handles complaints and questions about consumer rights, operates a 24-hour traveler's assistance line at ℃ **0800/42-579,** or 01/224-7888 in

Lima. The Tourist Protection Bureau office is at Calle La Prosa 138, San Borja, Lima (℃ **01/224-8600**). For local branch locations and telephone numbers of the Tourist Protection Bureau, see "Fast Facts" in individual destination chapters.

The **South American Explorers,** with clubhouses in Lima and Cusco, is an excellent source of information, particularly on trekking and mountaineering in Peru. They stock a good selection of guides, maps, and dossiers on travel and trails, which is available to members. Yearly membership is $40, and for many travelers, particularly independent and outdoor types, it is an excellent investment. You can contact them in the United States at ℃ **800/274-0568** or 607/277-0488; otherwise, visit their Lima office at Piura 135, Miraflores (℃ **01/445-3306**), or the Cusco office at Choquechaca 188, no. 4 (℃ **084/245-484**). You can also check out their website at www.samexplo.org.

3 Entry Requirements & Customs

ENTRY REQUIREMENTS

Citizens of the United States, Canada, Great Britain, South Africa, New Zealand, and Australia do not require visas to enter Peru as tourists—only valid passports. Citizens of any of these countries conducting business or enrolled in formal educational programs in Peru do require visas; contact the embassy or consulate in your home country for more information.

Tourist (or landing) cards, distributed on arriving international flights or at border crossings, are good for stays of up to 90 days. Keep a copy of the tourist card for presentation upon departure from Peru. (If you lose it, you'll have to pay a $4 fine.) A maximum of three extensions of 30 days each, for a total of 180 days, is allowed.

No immunizations are required for entry, although if you plan to travel to

jungle regions, I advise you to read "Insurance, Health & Safety," later in this chapter.

IN THE U.S. The Embassy of Peru is located at 1700 Massachusetts Ave. NW, Washington, DC 20036 (℃ **202/833-9860;** www.peruemb.org). There are Peruvian consulates in New York, Los Angeles, Miami, Boston, Chicago, Denver, Houston, and San Francisco. For their contact information, visit the Peruvian Ministry of Foreign Relations website at www.rree.gob.pe.

IN CANADA The Embassy of Peru is located at 130 Albert St., Ste. 1901, Ottawa, Ontario K1P 5G4 (℃ **613/238-1777**). There are Peruvian consulates in Montreal (℃ **514/844-5123**), Toronto (℃ **416/963-9696**), and Vancouver (℃ **604/662-8880**).

IN THE U.K. The Embassy of Peru is located at 52 Sloane St., London

SW1X 9SP (ℭ 020/7235-1917; www.peru-embassy.uk).

IN AUSTRALIA The Embassy of Peru is located at 40 Brisbane Ave., Ste. 8, ground floor, Barton ACT 2600 (ℭ 02/6273-8752; www.embaperu. org.au). The Peruvian consulate has an office in Sydney at 30 Clarence St., level 3, NSW 2000 (ℭ 02/9262-6464).

IN NEW ZEALAND The Embassy of Peru is located at Cigna House, 40 Mercer St., level 8, Wellington (ℭ 04/499-8087).

PASSPORT INFORMATION

Safeguard your passport in an inconspicuous, inaccessible place such as a money belt and keep a copy of the critical pages with your passport number in a separate place. If you lose your passport, visit the nearest consulate of your native country as soon as possible for a replacement. Passport applications are downloadable from some of the websites listed below.

IN THE U.S. If you're applying for a first-time passport, you need to do it in person at one of 13 passport offices throughout the United States; a federal, state, or probate court; or a major post office. (Call the number below to find post offices that accept applications.) You must present a certified birth certificate as proof of citizenship, and it's wise to bring along your driver's license, state or military ID, and social security card as well. You also need two identical passport-size photos (2 in. × 2 in.), taken at any corner photo shop (not one of the strip photos from a photo-vending machine).

For people over 15, a passport is valid for 10 years and costs $60 ($45 plus a $15 handling fee); for those 15 and under, it's valid for 5 years and costs $40. If you're over 15 and have a valid passport that was issued within the past 12 years, you can renew it by mail and bypass the $15 handling fee. Allow plenty of time before your trip

to apply; processing normally takes 3 weeks but can take longer during busy periods (especially spring). To find your regional passport office, either check the U.S. State Department website (http://travel.state.gov) or call the National Passport Information Center (ℭ 900/225-5674); the fee is 35¢ per minute for automated information and $1.05 per minute for operator-assisted calls.

American Passport Express (ℭ 800/841-6778; www.american passport.com) will process your passport for you in a week for $50, plus the cost of the passport itself ($75 for a renewal; $95 for a first-time or lost passport). If you need the passport in 3 to 4 days, the cost is $100, and for $150 you can receive your passport in 24 hours.

IN CANADA Canadian passports are valid for 5 years and cost C$60. Children under 16 may be included on a parent's passport but need their own to travel unaccompanied by the parent. Applications, which must be accompanied by two identical passport-size photographs and proof of Canadian citizenship, are available at passport offices throughout Canada, at post offices, or from the central Passport Office, Department of Foreign Affairs and International Trade, Ottawa, Ontario K1A 0G3 (ℭ 800/567-6868; www.dfait-maeci. gc.ca/passport). Processing takes 5 to 10 days if you apply in person, or about 3 weeks by mail.

IN THE U.K. To pick up an application for a standard 10-year passport (5-year passport for children under 16), visit the nearest passport office, major post office, or travel agency. You can also contact the United Kingdom Passport Service at ℭ 0870/571-0410 or visit its website at www.ukpa. gov.uk. Passports are £30 for adults and £16 for children under 16, with an additional £15 fee if you apply in person at a passport office. Processing takes about 2 weeks.

IN IRELAND   You can apply for a 10-year passport, costing 57€, at the main **Passport Office,** Setanta Centre, Molesworth St., Dublin 2 (© 01/ 671-1633; www.gov.ie/iveagh/services/ passports/passportforms.htm). You can also apply at 1A South Mall, Cork (© 021/272-525), or over the counter at most main post offices. Travelers under 18 and over 65 must apply for a 3-year passport, which costs 12€.

IN AUSTRALIA   You can pick up an application from your local post office or any **Australian State Passport Office,** but you must schedule an interview at a passport office to present your application materials. Call the passport office information service at © 131-232 or visit the government website at www.passports.gov.au for complete details. Passports for adults are A$136; for children under 18, A$68.

IN NEW ZEALAND   You can pick up a passport application at any New Zealand Passports Office or download it from their website. Contact the **Passports Office** at © 0800/225-050 in New Zealand or 04/474-8100, or log on to www.passports.govt.nz. Passports for adults are NZ$80; for children under 16, NZ$40.

CUSTOMS
WHAT YOU CAN BRING INTO PERU

You are allowed to bring 3 liters of alcohol and 400 cigarettes (20 packs) or 50 cigars into Peru duty free. New items for personal use, including camera equipment and adventure-sports gear such as mountain bikes and kayaks, are allowed. Travelers may bring in up to $300 in varied gifts, as long as no individual item exceeds $100. To avoid the possibility of having to fill out forms or pay a bond, it's best not to draw attention to expensive, new-looking items that

officials might believe you are intent on reselling. (It helps to take them out of their original boxes.)

WHAT YOU CAN TAKE HOME

Exports of protected plant and endangered animal species—live or dead— are strictly prohibited by Peruvian law and should not be purchased. This includes headpieces and necklaces made with macaw feathers, and even common "rain sticks," unless authorized by the Natural Resources Institute (INRENA). Vendors in jungle cities and airports sell live animals and birds, as well as handicrafts made from insects, feathers, or other natural products. Travelers have been detained and arrested by the Ecology Police for carrying such items.

It is also illegal to take pre-Columbian archaeological items, antiques, and artifacts, including ceramics and textiles, and colonial-era art out of Peru. Reproductions of many such items are available, but even their export may cause difficulties at Customs or with overly cautious international courier services if you attempt to send them home. To be safe, look for the word REPRODUC-CION or an artist's name stamped on reproduction ceramics, and keep business cards and receipts from shops where you have purchased them. Particularly fine items may require documentation from Peru's National Institute of Culture (INC) verifying that the object is a reproduction and may be exported. You may be able to obtain a certificate of authorization from the National Institute of Culture (INC) kiosk at Lima's Jorge Chávez International Airport or the INC office at the National Museum Building, 6th floor, 2465 Av. Javier Prado Este, San Borja (© 01/476-9900).

FOR U.S. CITIZENS   Returning U.S. citizens who have been away for at least 48 hours are allowed to bring back, once every 30 days, $400 worth of merchandise duty-free. You'll be charged a flat rate of 4% duty on the next $1,000 worth of purchases. Be sure to have your receipts handy. On mailed gifts, the duty-free limit is $100. You cannot bring fresh foodstuffs into the United States; tinned foods, however, are allowed. For more information, contact the **U.S. Customs Service,** 1300 Pennsylvania Ave. NW, Washington, DC 20229 (© 877/287-8867) and request the free pamphlet *Know Before You Go.* It's also available online at www.customs.gov.

FOR CANADIAN CITIZENS If you've been out of the country for more than 48 hours, you may bring back C$200 worth of goods, and if you've been gone for 7 consecutive days or more, not counting your departure, the limit is C$750. The limit for alcohol is up to 1.5 liters of wine or 1.14 liters of liquor, or 24 12-ounce cans or bottles of beer; and up to 200 cigarettes, 50 cigars, or 200 grams of tobacco. You may not ship tobacco or alcohol, and you must be of legal age for your province to bring these items through Customs. For the helpful booklet *I Declare,* call the **Canada Customs and Review Agency** at © 800/461-9999 in Canada or 204/983-3500, or visit its website at www.ccra-adrc.gc.ca.

FOR U.K. CITIZENS U.K. citizens returning from a non-EU country have an allowance of 200 cigarettes; 50 cigars; 250 grams of smoking tobacco; 2 liters of still table wine; 1 liter of spirits or strong liqueurs (over 22% volume); 2 liters of fortified wine, sparkling wine or other liqueurs; 60cc (ml) perfume; 250cc (ml) of toilet water; and £145 worth of all other goods, including gifts and souvenirs. People under 17 cannot have the tobacco or alcohol allowance. For more information, call the **HM Customs & Excise** at © 0845/010-9000, or log on to www.hmce.gov.uk.

FOR AUSTRALIAN CITIZENS The duty-free allowance in Australia is A$400 or, for those under 18, A$200. Citizens can bring in 250 cigarettes or 250 grams of loose tobacco, and 1,125 milliliters of alcohol. If you're returning with valuables you already own, such as foreign-made cameras, you should file Form B263. A helpful brochure available from Australian consulates or Customs offices is *Know Before You Go.* For more information, call the **Australian Customs Service** at © 1300/363-263, or log on to www.customs.gov.au.

FOR NEW ZEALAND CITIZENS The duty-free allowance for New Zealand is NZ$700. Citizens over 17 can bring in 200 cigarettes, 50 cigars, or 250 grams of tobacco (or a mixture of all three if their combined weight doesn't exceed 250g); plus 4.5 liters of wine and beer; or 1.125 liters of liquor. New Zealand currency does not carry import or export restrictions. Fill out a certificate of export, listing the valuables you are taking out of the country; that way, you can bring them back without paying duty. Most questions are answered in *New Zealand Customs Guide for Travellers, Notice no. 4,* a free pamphlet available at New Zealand consulates and Customs offices. For more information, contact **New Zealand Customs,** The Customhouse, 17–21 Whitmore St., Box 2218, Wellington (© 04/473-6099 or 0800/428-786; www.customs.govt.nz).

4 Money

Peru is inexpensive by North American and European standards, though it's slightly more expensive than its Andean neighbors Ecuador and Bolivia. Peruvians tend to haggle over prices and accept that others haggle also, except in major stores and restaurants. In the bigger cities, prices for virtually everything are higher, especially in Lima; in addition, prices can rise in the high season, such as the Independence Day holidays (late July), Easter week (Mar or Apr), or Christmas, due to heavy demand, especially for hotel rooms and bus and plane tickets.

CURRENCY

Peru's official currency is the **nuevo sol** (S/), divided into 100 *centavos*. Coins are issued in denominations of 5, 10, 20, and 50 centavos, and banknotes in denominations of 10, 20, 50, 100, and 200 soles. At press time, the rate of exchange was approximately S/3.50 to $1 (rates are pretty consistent across the country). The U.S. dollar is the second currency; many hotels post their rates in dollars, and plenty of shops, taxi drivers, restaurants, and hotels across Peru accept U.S. dollars for payment. It is often difficult to pay with large banknotes (in either soles or dollars). Try to carry denominations of 50 and lower in both.

It's a good idea to exchange some money—at least enough to cover airport incidentals and transportation to your hotel—before you leave home, so you can avoid the less-favorable rates you'll get at airport currency-exchange desks. Check with the local American Express or Thomas Cook office or your bank. American Express cardholders can order foreign currency over the phone at ℂ **800/807-6233.**

EXCHANGING MONEY

Peru is still very much a cash society. In villages and small towns, it may be impossible to cash traveler's checks or use credit cards. Make sure that you have cash (in both soles and U.S. dollars) on hand. If you pay in dollars, you will likely receive change in soles, so be aware of the correct exchange rate. U.S. dollars are by far the easiest

foreign currency to exchange. Currencies other than U.S. dollars receive very poor exchange rates.

Banks are no longer the place of choice in Peru for exchanging money: Lines are too long, the task is too time-consuming, and rates are often lower than at *casas de cambio* (exchange houses) or by using credit- or debit-card ATMs or money-changers, who are legal in Peru. If you can't avoid banks, all cities and towns have branches of major international and local banks; see "Fast Facts" in individual destination chapters for locations. Money-changers, often wearing colored smocks with "$" insignias, can be found on the street. They offer current rates of exchange, but you are advised to count your money carefully (you can simplify this by exchanging easily calculable amounts, such as $10 or $100) and make sure you have not received any counterfeit bills.

Counterfeit banknotes and even coins are common, and merchants and consumers across Peru vigorously check the authenticity of money before accepting payment or change. (The simplest way: Hold the banknote up to the light to see the watermark.) Many people also refuse to accept banknotes that are not in good condition (including those with small tears, that have been written on, and even that are simply well worn), and visitors are wise to do the same when receiving change to avoid problems with other payments. Do not accept bills with tears (no matter how small) or taped bills.

Making change in Peru is often a problem. You should carry small bills and even then be prepared to wait for change. At one bar in Iquitos, I tried to pay with a S/20 note (less than $6) and the waiter said, "Hold on, I'm going to get change"—and he hopped on a bicycle and took off, not reappearing with correct change for nearly a half hour.

The Peruvian Sol

For American Readers   At this writing, $1 equals approximately S/3.50. This was the rate of exchange used to calculate the dollar equivalents given throughout this edition.

For Canadian Readers   At this writing, C$1 equals approximately S/2.20. This was the rate of exchange used to calculate the Canadian dollar values in the table below.

For British Readers   At this writing, £1 equals approximately S/4.95. This was the rate of exchange used to calculate the pound values in the table below.

Nuevo sol	US$	CAN$	UK£
S/10	$3	C$5	£2
S/20	$6	C$9	£4
S/30	$9	C$14	£6
S/40	$11	C$18	£8
S/50	$14	C$23	£10
S/100	$29	C$45	£20
S/200	$57	C$91	£40
S/300	$86	C$136	£61
S/400	$114	C$182	£81
S/500	$143	C$227	£101
S/1,000	$286	C$455	£202

ATMS

Automatic teller machines are the best way of getting cash in Peru; they're found in most towns and cities, though not on every street corner. ATMs allow customers to withdraw money in either Peruvian soles or U.S. dollars. Screen instructions are in English as well as Spanish. Some bank ATMs dispense money only to those who hold accounts there. Most ATMs in Peru accept only one type of credit/debit card and international money network, either **Cirrus** (© **800/424-7787;** www.mastercard.com) or **PLUS** (© **800/843-7587;** www.visa.com). Visa and MasterCard ATM cards are the most widely accepted; Visa/PLUS is the most common. It's advisable to carry both Visa and MasterCard debit and credit cards in case one doesn't work (or in case, heaven forbid, a machine eats your card). Your personal identification number (PIN) must contain 4 digits.

Be sure to find out your daily withdrawal limit before you depart. You can also get cash advances on your credit card at an ATM. Keep in mind that credit-card companies try to protect themselves from theft by limiting the funds you can withdraw away from home. It's therefore best to call your credit-card company before you leave and let them know where you're going and how much you plan to spend. You'll get the best exchange rate if you withdraw money from an ATM, but keep in mind that many banks impose a fee every time a card is used at an ATM in a different city or bank. On top of this, the bank from which you withdraw cash may charge its own fee.

TRAVELER'S CHECKS

Once the predominant method of payment for travelers, traveler's checks in Peru are exchanged at fewer places and at a considerably lower rate than cash. With the proliferation of ATMs, traveler's checks are less necessary as an alternative to carrying large amounts of cash. If you use traveler's checks, American Express is the brand most easily exchanged. In Peru, the exchange rate for traveler's checks is perhaps 2% lower than for cash. Replacing traveler's checks outside of Lima can be very problematic, if not impossible. Keep a record of check numbers and the original bill of sale in a safe place.

These days, traveler's checks seem less necessary because most cities have 24-hour ATMs that allow you to withdraw small amounts of cash as needed. However, you're likely to be charged an ATM withdrawal fee if the bank is not your own, so if you're withdrawing money every day, you might be better off with traveler's checks—provided that you don't mind showing identification every time you want to cash one.

You can get traveler's checks at almost any bank. **American Express** offers denominations of $20, $50, $100, $500, and (for cardholders only) $1,000. You'll pay a service charge ranging from 1% to 4%. You can also get American Express traveler's checks over the phone by calling © **800/221-7282;** Amex gold and platinum cardholders who use this number are exempt from the 1% fee. AAA members can obtain checks without a fee at most AAA offices.

Visa offers traveler's checks at Citibank locations, as well as at several other banks. The service charge ranges between 1.5% and 2%; checks come in denominations of $20, $50, $100, $500, and $1,000. Call © **800/ 732-1322** for information. **Master-Card** also offers traveler's checks. Call © **800/223-9920** for a location near you.

CREDIT CARDS

Credit cards are invaluable when traveling. They are a safe way to carry money and provide a convenient record of all your expenses. You can also withdraw cash advances from your credit cards at any bank (though you'll start paying hefty interest on the advance the moment you receive the cash). At most banks, you don't even need to go to a teller; you can get a cash advance at the ATM if you know your PIN. If you've forgotten yours, or didn't even know you had one, call the number on the back of your credit card and ask the bank to send it to you. It usually takes 5 to 7 business days, though some banks will provide the number over the phone if you tell them your mother's maiden name or pass some other security clearance. Keep in mind, though, that your credit-card company will likely charge a commission (1% or 2%) on every foreign purchase you make.

Many establishments in Peru accept the major international credit cards, including Visa, MasterCard, Diners Club, and American Express. Visa is the most widely accepted card in Peru. However, many shops and restaurants charge the consumer an additional 10% for paying with a credit card. Ask about this practice when asking whether an establishment accepts credit cards. When using a credit card, be careful to check the amount you are being charged. In rural areas and small towns, cash is essential for payment. At the very least, you should carry a supply of U.S. dollars in these areas.

The general information telephone numbers for major credit cards in Peru are **American Express,** © 01/424-6410; **MasterCard,** © 01/422-1290; **Diners Club,** © 01/221-2050; and **Visa,** © 01/442-6410.

What Things Cost in Cusco

A short taxi ride	$2–$3	£1.40–£2.10
Double room in a budget hotel	$20	£14
Double room in a moderate hotel	$40–$80	£28–£56
Double room in an expensive hotel	$80–$150	£56–£105
A coffee or soft drink	50¢	35p
A bottle of mineral water	$1	70p
A beer	$2	£1.40
Lunch	$2–$10	£1.40–£7
Dinner	$5–$20	£3.50–£14
A movie ticket	$3	£2.10

WHAT TO DO IF YOUR WALLET GETS STOLEN

Be sure to block charges against your account the minute you discover a card has been lost or stolen. Then be sure to file a police report.

Almost every credit-card company has an emergency number to call if your card is stolen. They may be able to wire you a cash advance off your credit card immediately, and in many places, they can deliver an emergency credit card in a day or two. The toll-free emergency numbers for major credit cards in Peru are **American Express,** ✆ 01/330-4484; **Master-Card,** ✆ 01/444-1891; **Diners Club,** ✆ 01/221-2050; and **Visa,** ✆ 01/44-2112.

Odds are that, if your wallet is gone, the police won't be able to recover it for you. However, it's still worth informing the authorities. Your credit-card company or insurer may require a police report number or record of the theft.

If you choose to carry traveler's checks, be sure to keep a record of their serial numbers separate from your checks. You'll get a refund faster if you know the numbers.

If you need emergency cash over the weekend when all banks and American Express offices are closed, you can have money wired to you from **Western Union** (✆ **0800/ 12-080** or 0800/20-007 in Peru; www.westernunion.com). You must present valid ID to pick up the cash at the Western Union office. However, in most countries, you can pick up a money transfer even if you don't have valid identification, as long as you can answer a test question provided by the sender. Be sure to let the sender know in advance that you don't have ID. If you need to use a test question instead of ID, the sender must take cash to his or her local Western Union office, rather than transferring the money over the phone or online.

5 When to Go

PEAK SEASON

Peak travel season for foreigners is in great part determined by weather. Peru experiences two very distinct seasons, wet and dry—terms that are much more relevant than "summer" and "winter." Peru's high season for travel coincides with the driest months: May through September, with by far the greatest number of visitors in July and August. May and September are particularly fine months to visit much of the country. Airlines and hotels also consider the period mid-December to mid-January as peak season.

From June to September (winter in the Southern Hemisphere) in the highlands, days are clear and often spectacularly sunny, with chilly or downright cold nights, especially at high elevations. For trekking in the mountains, including the Inca Trail, these are by far the best months. This is also the best time of the year to visit the Amazon basin: Mosquitoes are fewer, and many fauna stay close to the rivers (though some people prefer to travel in the jungle during the wet season, when higher water levels allow more river penetration). Note that Peruvians travel in huge numbers around July 28, the national holiday, and finding accommodations in popular destinations around this time can be difficult.

CLIMATE

Generally speaking, May through October is the dry season; November through April is the rainy season, and the wettest months are January through April. In mountain areas, roads and trek paths may become impassable. Peru's climate, though, is markedly different among its three vastly different regions. The coast is predominantly arid and mild, the Andean region is temperate to cold, and the eastern lowlands are tropically warm and humid.

On the desert **coast,** summer (Dec–Apr) is hot and dry, with temperatures reaching 25° to 35°C (77°–95°F) or more along the north coast. In winter (May–Oct), temperatures are much milder, though with high humidity. Much of the coast, including Lima, is shrouded in a gray mist called *garúa.* Only extreme northern beaches are warm enough for swimming.

In the **highlands** from May to October, rain is scarce. Daytime temperatures reach a warm 20° to 25°C (68°–77°F), and nights are often quite cold (near freezing), especially in June and July. Rainfall is very abundant from December to March, when temperatures are slightly milder—18° to 20°C (64°–68°F) dropping only to 15°C (59°F) at night. The wettest months are January and February. Most mornings are dry, but clouds move in during the afternoon and produce heavy downpours.

Though the Amazon **jungle** is consistently humid and tropical, with significant rainfall year-round, it, too, experiences two clearly different seasons. During the dry season (May–Oct), temperatures reach 30° to 35°C (86°–100°F) during the day. From November to April, there are frequent rain showers (which last only a few hours at a time), causing the rivers to swell, and temperatures are similarly steamy.

Lima's Average Temperatures & Precipitation

	Jan	Feb	Mar	Apr	May	June	July	Aug	Sept	Oct	Nov	Dec
Av. High/Low (°C)	25/19	26/20	26/19	24/18	21/16	19/15	17/14	17/13	17/13	19/14	20/16	23/17
Av. High/Low (°F)	77/66	79/68	79/66	75/65	70/61	66/59	63/57	63/56	63/56	66/57	68/61	73/63
Wet Days	1	0	0	0	1	1	1	2	1	0	0	0

Cusco's Average Temperatures & Precipitation

	Jan	Feb	Mar	Apr	May	June	July	Aug	Sept	Oct	Nov	Dec
Av. High/Low (°C)	19/7	19/7	19/7	20/5	20/3	19/1	19/1	20/1	20/4	21/6	20/6	20/6
Av. High/Low (°F)	66/44	66/44	67/44	68/41	68/37	67/34	67/34	68/34	68/39	70/42	69/43	68/43
Wet Days	12	11	10	6	4	3	4	3	2	2	1	5

PUBLIC HOLIDAYS

National public holidays in Peru include New Year's Day (Jan 1); Three King's Day (Jan 6); Maundy Thursday and Good Friday (Easter week, Mar or Apr); Labor Day (May 1); Fiestas Patrias (July 28–29); Battle of Angamos (Oct 7); All Saints' Day (Nov 1); Feast of the Immaculate Conception (Dec 8); and Christmas (Dec 24–25).

For additional information about regional festivals, see individual destination chapters.

PERU CALENDAR OF EVENTS

January

Entrega de Varas, Cusco. Community elders (*yayas*) designate the highest authorities of their villages in this pre-Columbian festival, which is celebrated with *chicha* (fermented maize beer) and *llonque* (sugar-cane alcohol); the mayor accepts the scepter symbolizing his power. This custom has been glossed over with Occidental formalities. January 1.

Fiesta de la Santa Tierra, Lake Titicaca. The main festival on Isla Amantaní sees the population split in two—half at the Temple of Pachamama and the other half at the Temple of Pachatata, symbolizing the islanders' ancient, dualistic belief system. Third Thursday in January.

Marinera Dance Festival, Trujillo. One of the stateliest dances in Peru, the flirtatious marinera involves a couple, each partner with a handkerchief in his or her right hand. The man wears a wide-brimmed hat and poncho, the woman a lace Moche dress. For 10 days, the festival, which draws couples from all over the country, is held in the Gran Chimú soccer stadium. There are also float processions throughout the city and dancing in the Plaza de Armas. January 20 to 30.

February

Virgen de la Candelaria (Candlemas), Puno. Puno lives up to its billing as Folk Capital of the Americas with this festival, which gathers more than 200 groups of musician and dance troupes. On the festival's main day, February 2, the Virgen is led through the city in a colorful procession of priests and pagans carefully maintaining the hierarchy. Especially thrilling is the dance of the demons, or *la diablada.* Dancers in wild costumes and masks blow panpipes and make offerings to the earth goddess Pachamama. February 1 to 14.

Carnaval. Lively pre-Lenten festivities. (Look out for water balloons and worse.) Cajamarca is reputed to have the best and wildest parties; Puno and Cusco are also good. The weekend before Ash Wednesday.

March

Festival Internacional de la Vendimia (Wine Festival), Ica. A celebration of the grape harvest and the region's wine and pisco brandy, with fairs, beauty contests, floats, and musical festivals, including Afro-Peruvian dance. Second week of March.

Las Cruces de Porcón, Porcón. Near Cajamarca, a dawn procession of massive, decorated wooden crosses through the valley of Porcón recreates the entry of Christ into Jerusalem. The main day of the festival, Palm Sunday, presents four separate ceremonies. Ultimately, the crosses are decorated with mirrors (symbolizing the souls of the dead), and locals hang metal bells to announce the arrival of the crosses to the community. Mid-March to first week of April.

Semana Santa. Handsome and spectacularly reverent processions mark Easter Week. The finest are in

Cusco and Ayacucho. Late March/early April.

Lord of the Earthquakes, Cusco. Representing a 17th-century painting of Christ on the cross that is said to have saved the city from a devastating earthquake, the image of the Lord of Earthquakes (El Señor de los Temblores) is carried through the streets of Cusco in a reverential procession, much like the Incas once paraded the mummies of their chieftains and high priests. Easter Monday, late March/early April.

April

Peruvian Paso Horse Festival, Pachacámac. The Peruvian Paso horse, one of the world's most beautiful breeds, is celebrated with the most important annual national competition at the Mamacona stables near Pachacámac, 30km (20 miles) south of Lima. April 15 to 20.

May

Fiesta de la Cruz. The Festival of the Cross features folk music and dance, including "scissors dancers," and processions in which communities decorate crosses and prepare them for the procession to neighboring churches. The *danzantes de tijeras* (scissors dancers) recreate old times, when they would perform on top of church bell towers. Today, the objective is still to outdo one another with daring feats. Celebrations are especially lively in Lima, Cusco, and Ica. May 2 and 3.

Qoyllur Rit'i, Quispicanchis, near Cusco. A massive indigenous pilgrimage marks this ritual, which is tied to the fertility of the land and the worship of Apus, the spirits of the mountains. It forms part of the greatest festival of native Indian nations in the hemisphere: Qoyllur Rit'i. The main ceremony is held at the foot of Mount Ausangate, with 10,000 pilgrims climbing to the snowline along with dancers in full costume representing mythical characters. Others head to the summit, in search of the Snow Star, and take huge blocks of ice back down on their backs—holy water for irrigation purposes. First week in May.

Fiesta de Mayo, Huaraz. Also known as El Señor de la Soledad, the festival is celebrated with traditional dances, ski races, and a lantern procession. May 2 to 10.

June

Corpus Christi, Cusco. A procession of saints and virgins arrives at the Catedral to "greet" the body of Christ. Members of nearby churches also take their patron saints in a procession. An overnight vigil is followed by a new procession around the Plaza de Armas, with images of five virgins clad in embroidered tunics and the images of four saints: Sebastian, Blas, Joseph, and the Apostle Santiago (St. James). Early June.

Semana del Andinismo, Huaraz and Callejón de Huaylas. For the outdoors fanatics, this celebration of outdoor adventure includes opportunities to partake of trekking, skiing, mountain biking, rafting, rock climbing, hang gliding—and plenty of parties to accompany them. Mid- to late June.

Inti Raymi, Cusco. The Inca Festival of the Sun—the mother of all pre-Columbian festivals—celebrates the winter solstice and honors the sun god with traditional pageantry, parades, and dances. One of the most vibrant and exciting of all Andean festivals, it draws thousands of visitors that fill Cusco's hotels. The principal event takes place at the Sacsayhuamán ruins and includes the sacrifice of a pair of llamas. General celebrations last several days. June 24.

San Juan, Cusco and Iquitos. The feast day of St. John the Baptist, a symbol of fertility and sensuality, is the most important date on the festival calendar in the entire Peruvian jungle. John the Baptist has taken on a major symbolic significance because of the importance of water as a vital element in the entire Amazon region. Events include fiestas with lots of music and regional cuisine. In Iquitos, don't miss the aphrodisiac potions with suggestive names. June 24 in Cusco, June 25 in Iquitos.

San Pedro/San Pablo, near fishing villages in Lima and Chiclayo. The patron saints of fishermen and farmers, Saint Peter and Saint Paul, are honored; figures of the saints are carried with incense, prayers, and hymns down to the sea and taken by launch around the bay to bless the waters. June 29.

Virgen del Carmen, Paucartambo. In a remote highland village 4 hours from Cusco, thousands come to honor the Virgen del Carmen, or Mamacha Carmen, patron saint of the mestizo population, with 4 days of splendidly festive music and dance, as well as some of the wildest costumes in Peru. Dancers even perform daring moves on rooftops. The festival ends in the cemetery in a show of respect for the souls of the dead. Pisac also celebrates the Virgen del Carmen festival, almost as colorfully. June 15 to 18.

July

Fiesta de Santiago, Isla Taquile. A festive and very traditional pageant of color, with exuberant dances and women in layered, multicolored skirts. July 25 and August 1 and 2.

Fiestas Patrias. A series of parties with patriotic fervor mark Peru's independence from Spain in 1821. Official parades and functions are augmented by cockfighting, bullfighting, and Peruvian Paso horse exhibitions in other towns. The best celebrations are in Cusco, Puno, Isla Taquile, and Lima. July 28 and 29.

August

Santa Rosa de Lima, Lima. Major devotional processions honor the patron saint of Lima. August 30.

September

International Spring Festival, Trujillo. Trujillo celebrates the festival of spring with marinera dance, decorated streets and houses, floats, and schoolchildren dancing in the streets—led, of course, by the pageant beauty queen. Last week in September.

October

El Señor de los Milagros, Lima. The Lord of Miracles is the largest procession in South America, and it dates from colonial times. Lasting nearly 24 hours and involving tens of thousands of purple-clad participants, it celebrates a Christ image (painted by an Angolan slave) that survived the 1746 earthquake and has since become the most venerated image in the capital. October 18.

November

Todos Santos and **Día de los Muertos.** Peruvians salute the dead by visiting cemeteries with flowers and food. Families hold candlelight vigils in the cemetery until dawn. The holiday is most vibrantly celebrated in the highlands. November 1 and 2.

Puno Week, Puno. A major procession from the shores of the lake to the town stadium celebrates Manco Cápac, who, according to legend, rose from the waters of Lake Titicaca to establish the Inca Empire. Dances and music take over Puno, with events often taking a turn for the inebriated. First week of November.

December
    Santuranticuy Fair, Cusco. One of
    the largest arts-and-crafts fairs in
    Peru—literally, "saints for sale"—is
    held in the Plaza de Armas. Artisans
    lay out blankets around the square,

as in traditional Andean markets,
and sell figurines and Nativity
scenes as well as ceramics, carvings,
pottery, and *retablos* (gradines).
Vendors sell hot rum punch called
ponche. December 24.

6 Insurance, Health & Safety

TRAVEL INSURANCE AT A GLANCE

Check your existing insurance policies
before you buy travel insurance to
cover trip cancellation, lost luggage, or
medical expenses, or car-rental insurance. You're likely to already have partial or complete coverage. But if you
still need some, ask your travel agent
about a comprehensive package. The
cost of travel insurance varies widely,
depending on the cost and length of
your trip, your age and overall health,
and the type of trip you're taking.
Insurance for extreme sports or adventure travel, for example, will cost more
than coverage for a cruise.

Some insurers provide packages for
specialty vacations, such as skiing or
backpacking. Rescue or evacuation
insurance for mountaineers and ice
climbers is a good idea, as rescue operations in the Andes are time-sensitive
and extremely costly. "Dangerous"
activities may be excluded from basic
policies. Trip-cancellation insurance in
a country such as Peru, with a rather
volatile political and economic history
over the past decade—not to mention
a history of earthquakes—also may be
a wise decision.

For information, contact one of the
following popular insurers:

- **Access America** (© 800/284-8300; www.accessamerica.com)
- **Travel Guard International** (© 800/826-1300; www.travelguard.com)
- **Travel Insured International** (© 800/243-3174; www.travelinsured.com)

- **Travelex Insurance Services** (© 800/228-9792; www.travelexinsurance.com)

TRIP-CANCELLATION INSURANCE (TCI)

There are three major types of trip-
cancellation insurance—one, in the
event that you prepay a cruise or tour
that gets cancelled, and you can't get
your money back; a second when you
or someone in your family gets sick or
dies, and you can't travel (but beware
that you may not be covered for a pre-
existing condition); and a third, when
bad weather makes travel impossible.
Some insurers provide coverage for
events such as jury duty; natural disas-
ters close to home, such as floods or
fire; even the loss of a job. Although a
few insurers have provisions for cancel-
lations due to terrorist activities, keep
in mind that in the aftermath of the
September 11, 2001, terrorist attacks,
a number of airlines, cruise lines, and
tour operators are no longer covered by
insurers. *The bottom line:* Always check
the fine print before signing on; more
and more policies have built-in exclu-
sions and restrictions that may leave
you out in the cold if something does
go awry. Don't buy trip-cancellation
insurance from the tour operator that
may be responsible for the cancellation; buy it only from a reputable
travel-insurance agency. And don't
overbuy. You won't be reimbursed for
more than the cost of your trip.

MEDICAL INSURANCE

Most health-insurance policies cover
you if you get sick away from home—
but check, particularly if you're insured

Tips Medical Insurance Warning

Under U.S. law, insurance companies are not required to cover any medical expenses incurred in countries on the U.S. State Department's Travel Advisory List, even if their policies indicate that they will cover out-of-country medical expenses. Some supplemental carriers (such as the ones listed in this chapter) will sell travelers coverage for these areas. You can view the Travel Advisory List on the State Department's website at **http://travel.state.gov**. Peru (or specific regions in the country) has appeared on this list in the recent past.

by an HMO. With the exception of certain HMOs and Medicare/Medicaid, your medical insurance should cover medical treatment—even hospital care—overseas. However, most overseas hospitals make you pay your bills upfront and send you a refund after you've returned home and filed the necessary paperwork. Members of **Blue Cross/Blue Shield** can now use their cards at select hospitals in most major cities worldwide (© **800/810-BLUE** or www.bluecares.com for a list of hospitals).

Some credit cards (American Express and certain gold and platinum Visa and MasterCards, for example) offer automatic flight insurance against death or dismemberment in case of an airplane crash if you charged the cost of your ticket.

If you require additional insurance, try one of the following companies:

- **MEDEX International,** 9515 Deereco Rd., Timonium, MD 21093-5375 (© **888/MEDEX-00** or 410/453-6300; www.medexassist.com).
- **Travel Assistance International,** 9200 Keystone Crossing, Ste. 300, Indianapolis, IN 46240 (© **800/821-2828;** www.travelassistance.com; for general information on services, call the company's Worldwide Assistance Services, Inc., at © 800/777-8710).
- **The Divers Alert Network** (DAN) (© **800/446-2671** or

919/684-8181; www.diversalert network.org).

The cost of travel medical insurance varies widely. Check your existing policies before you buy additional coverage. Also, check to see if your medical insurance covers you for emergency medical evacuation: If you have to buy a one-way same-day ticket home and forfeit your nonrefundable round-trip ticket, you may be out of big bucks.

LOST-LUGGAGE INSURANCE

On international flights (including U.S. portions of international trips), checked baggage is covered for approximately $9.07 per pound, up to approximately $635 per checked bag per ticketed passenger. If you plan to check items more valuable than the standard liability, you may purchase "excess valuation" coverage from the airline, up to $5,000. Be sure to take any valuables or irreplaceable items with you in your carry-on luggage. If you file a lost luggage claim, be prepared to answer detailed questions about the contents of your baggage, and be sure to file a claim immediately, as most airlines enforce a 21-day deadline. Before you leave home, compile an inventory of all packed items and a rough estimate of the total value to ensure you're properly compensated if your luggage is lost. You will only be reimbursed for what you lost, no more. Once you've filed a complaint, persist in securing your reimbursement; there are no laws governing the length of time it takes for a carrier to reimburse you. If you arrive at a destination without your bags, ask the airline to forward them to your hotel or to your next destination; they will usually comply. If your bag is delayed or lost, the airline may reimburse you for reasonable expenses, such as a toothbrush or a set of clothes, but the airline is under no legal obligation to do so.

Lost luggage may also be covered by your homeowner's or renter's policy. Many platinum and gold credit cards cover you as well. If you choose to purchase additional lost-luggage insurance, be sure not to buy more than you need. Buy in advance from the insurer or a trusted agent. (Prices will be much higher at the airport.)

CAR-RENTAL INSURANCE (LOSS/DAMAGE WAIVER OR COLLISION DAMAGE WAIVER)

If you hold a private auto-insurance policy, you probably are not covered abroad for loss or damage to the car, or for liability in case a passenger is injured. The credit card you use to rent the car also may provide some coverage; check with your auto-insurance policy and credit-card company to see if you would be covered in Peru.

Car-rental insurance probably does not cover liability if you cause the accident. Check your own auto-insurance policy, the rental-company policy, and your credit-card coverage for the extent of coverage: Is your destination covered? Are other drivers covered? How much liability is covered if a passenger is injured? (If you rely on your credit card for coverage, you may want to bring a second credit card with you, as damages may be charged to your card and you may find yourself stranded with no money.)

THE HEALTHY TRAVELER
HEALTH CONCERNS

As a tropical South American country, Peru presents certain health risks and concerns, but major concerns are limited to those traveling outside urban areas and to the Amazon jungle. The most common ailments for visitors to Peru are common traveler's diarrhea and altitude sickness, or **acute mountain sickness (AMS)**, called *soroche* locally.

ALTITUDE SICKNESS Cusco sits at an elevation of about 3,300m (11,000 ft.), and Lake Titicaca sits at about 3,900m (13,000 ft.). At these altitudes, shortness of breath and heart pounding are normal, given the paucity of oxygen. Some people may experience headaches, loss of appetite, extreme fatigue, and nausea. Most symptoms develop the first day at high altitude, though, occasionally, travelers have delayed reactions. The best advice is to rest on your first day in the highlands. Drink plenty of liquids, including the local remedy *mate de coca*, or coca-leaf tea. (It's perfectly legal.) Avoid alcohol and heavy food intake. Give yourself at least a day or two to acclimatize before launching into strenuous activities. Many hotels in Cusco offer oxygen for those severely affected with headaches and

---

Tips **Quick ID**

Tie a colorful ribbon or piece of yarn around your luggage handle, or slap a distinctive sticker on the side of your bag. This makes it less likely that someone will mistakenly appropriate it. And if your luggage gets lost, it will be easier to find.

shortness of breath. If symptoms persist or become more severe, seek medical attention. People with heart or lung problems and persons with the sickle cell trait may develop serious health complications at high altitudes, or even die from medical conditions exacerbated by high altitude.

IMMUNIZATIONS Though no vaccinations are officially required of travelers to Peru, you are wise to take certain precautions, especially if you are planning to travel to jungle regions. A yellow-fever vaccine is strongly recommended for trips to the Amazon—in July 2001, the Ministry of Health reported an outbreak of eight cases of and two deaths from yellow fever in the department of Loreto, in the districts of Puinahua, San Pablo, and Iquitos. In the airport at Puerto Maldonado, in the southern jungle, public nurses are usually on hand to administer yellow-fever shots to travelers without documentation of proper vaccination. Carry your records with you to avoid getting pricked right after you hop off the plane. The Centers for Disease Control and Prevention also recommend taking antimalarial drugs at least 1 week prior to arrival in the jungle, during your stay there, and for at least 4 weeks afterwards. Consult your doctor about antimalarial treatments. The CDC says that there is a risk of malaria in all departments except Arequipa, Moquegua, Puno, and Tacna, though Lima or the highland tourist areas (Cusco, Machu Picchu, and Lake Titicaca) are not at risk.

The CDC also recommends vaccines for Hepatitis A and B and typhoid, as well as booster doses for tetanus, diphtheria, and measles, though you may wish to weigh your potential exposure before getting all these shots. For additional information on travel to tropical South America, including World Health Organization news of disease outbreaks in particular areas, see the Centers for Disease Control and Prevention website at **www.cdc.gov**.

SUN EXPOSURE Limit your exposure to the sun, especially during the first few days of your trip and at high altitudes, from 11am to 2pm. Even though it can be chilly or cold in the Andes, the sun is a killer (the higher the altitude and thinner the air, the more dangerous the sun's harmful rays). Along Peru's desert coast, the sun is also extremely potent and likely to burn visitors who don't take adequate precautions. Wear a hat and use a sunscreen with a high protection factor (SPF 30 or higher) and apply it liberally. Remember that children require more protection than do adults. Heat exhaustion and heat stroke are serious maladies and are not difficult to get if you don't take proper precautions in Peru.

WATER & FOOD Visitors should drink only bottled water, which is widely available. Do not drink tap water, even in major hotels, and try to avoid drinks with ice. If you're trekking in the mountains or visiting remote rural areas where bottled water is not available, boil water to purify it or use water-purification tablets. Carry bottled water with you at all times (and especially on long bus or train rides); the heat of the desert and high altitudes of the Andes will dehydrate you very quickly.

You're safer eating fruits you can peel or salads and fruits washed with purified water, as well as foods that have been thoroughly cooked. Shellfish should be avoided by most; while *ceviche* is one of Peru's classic dishes, travelers should at least know that the fish and shellfish in it are not cooked, but marinated. That said, many, if not most, travelers eat it with few or no problems. (Your best bet is to eat ceviche only at clean, upscale places.)

Vegetarian restaurants can be found in most cities (look for branches of the chain Govinda in the largest cities). If no vegetarian restaurant is available, most others will be able to accommodate you with salads, fruits, and vegetables such as *papas* (potatoes) and *palta* (avocado), though *palta rellena* is usually stuffed with chicken or tuna.

MEDICAL ATTENTION   It's wise to get all vaccinations and obtain malarial pills prior to arriving in Peru, but if you decide at the last minute to go to the jungle and need to get a vaccine in the country, you may go to the following **Oficinas de Vacunación** in Lima: Calle Independencia 121, Breña (next to the Hospital del Niño); Jorge Chávez International Airport, 2nd floor; and the International Vaccination Center, Dos de Mayo National Hospital, Avenida Grau, block 13.

Prescriptions can be filled at *farmacias* and *boticas;* it's best to know the generic name of your drug. For most health matters that are not serious, a pharmacist will be able to help and prescribe something. In the case of more serious health issues, contact your hotel, the tourist information office, or in the most extreme case, your consulate or embassy for a doctor referral. Hospitals with English-speaking doctors are listed in individual destination chapters.

WHAT TO DO IF YOU GET SICK AWAY FROM HOME

If you worry about getting sick away from home, consider purchasing **medical travel insurance** and carry your ID card in your purse or wallet. In most cases, your existing health plan will provide the coverage you need. See "Medical Insurance," above, for more information.

If you suffer from a chronic illness, consult your doctor before your departure. For conditions such as epilepsy, diabetes, or heart problems,

wear a **Medic Alert Identification Tag** (© 800/825-3785; www.medicalert.org), which will immediately alert doctors to your condition and give them access to your records through Medic Alert's 24-hour hot line.

Pack **prescription medications** in your carry-on luggage, and carry prescription medications in their original containers. Also bring along copies of your prescriptions in case you lose your pills or run out. Carry the generic name of prescription medicines, in case a local pharmacist is unfamiliar with the brand name. And don't forget to bring sunglasses and an extra pair of contact lenses or prescription glasses.

Contact the **International Association for Medical Assistance to Travelers (IAMAT)** (© 716/754-4883 or 416/652-0137; www.iamat.org) for tips on travel and health concerns and lists of local, English-speaking doctors. The **Centers for Disease Control and Prevention** (© 800/311-3435; www.cdc.gov) provides up-to-date information on necessary vaccines and health hazards by region or country. Its booklet, *Health Information for International Travel,* is $25 by mail; on the Internet, it's free.

THE SAFE TRAVELER

Peru has not earned a great reputation for safety among travelers, although the situation is fast improving, especially since the violent crime wave and terrorist threats of the late 1980s and early '90s subsided. Personal safety is an issue to be taken very seriously in most large Peruvian cities, especially Lima, Cusco, and Arequipa. Simple theft and pickpocketing remain fairly common; assaults and robbery are more rare. Most thieves look for moments when travelers, laden with bags and struggling with maps, are distracted.

Although most visitors travel freely throughout Peru without incident, warnings must be heeded. In downtown Lima and the city's residential and hotel areas, the risk of street crime remains high. Carjackings, assaults, and armed robberies are not unheard of in Lima. Occasional armed attacks at automatic teller machines occur. However, in most heavily touristed places in Peru, a heightened police presence is noticeable. Use ATMs during the daytime, with other people present.

Street crime is prevalent in Cusco, Arequipa, and Puno, and pickpockets are known to patrol public markets. In Cusco, "strangle" muggings (in which victims are choked unconscious, and then relieved of all belongings) were reported in recent years, particularly on the streets leading off the Plaza de Armas, in the San Blas neighborhood, and near the train station. This form of violent assault seems to have subsided, but you should still not walk alone late at night on deserted streets.

In major cities, taxis hailed on the street can lead to assaults—I highly recommend using telephone-dispatched radio taxis, especially at night. Ask your hotel or restaurant to call a cab, or call one yourself from the list of recommended taxi companies in the individual city chapters.

Travelers should exercise extreme caution on public city transportation, where pickpockets are rife, and on long-distance buses and trains (especially at night), where thieves employ any number of strategies to relieve passengers of their bags. You need to be supremely vigilant, even to the extreme of locking your backpack and suitcases to luggage racks. Be extremely careful in all train and bus stations.

In general, do not wear expensive jewelry; keep expensive camera equipment out of view as much as possible; and use a money belt inside your pants or shirt to safeguard cash, credit cards, and passport. Wear your daypack on your chest rather than your back when walking in crowded areas. The time to be most careful is when you have most of your belongings on your person—for example, when going from airport or train or bus station to your hotel. At airports, it's best to spend a little more for official airport taxis; if in doubt, request the driver's official ID. Don't venture beyond airport grounds for a street taxi. Have your hotel call a taxi for your trip to the airport or bus station.

Report any criminal activity to the nearest police station or tourism police office; contact information is listed in the "Fast Facts" section in individual destination chapters.

In addition to safety and health concerns, travelers planning a trip to Peru should keep a close watch on current events. The U.S. State Department reported a resurfacing of the long-dormant Maoist terrorist network Sendero Luminoso in parts of the central highlands in late 2001, and in March 2002, a radical offshoot of the Sendero Luminoso was blamed for

Tips A Second Opinion

Peru and other Andean countries, including Ecuador and Bolivia, have earned a reputation for theft among some travelers, especially independent hikers. Although I've tried to be frank without being alarmist about the reality of crime in Peru, you may wish to read another opinion. Sacred Earth, a grass-roots organization of ethnobotanists and eco-travelers, features an essay about robbery and safety in the Andes on its website at www.sacredearth.com/travel_info/resources/thieves.html.

Tips **Discrimination in Peru**

In Peru's larger cities, including Lima and Arequipa, Afro-Peruvians and Amerindian populations occupy the bottom rung of the economic ladder, and they are frequently blamed by the white population for much of the cities' crime. That perception may be consciously or subconsciously directed at travelers of color, who may experience some discrimination, most often expressed in less-than-welcoming receptions at hotels or restaurants.

Women and gay travelers should refer to "Travelers with Special Needs," below, for additional information about harassment.

---

a car bomb attack near the U.S. Embassy in Lima. Peru elected a new president in 2001 after a decade of political unrest; Peru's political situation remains a bit tenuous, though at present it should not deter anyone from traveling to the country. Before you depart, check for travel advisories from the **U.S. State Department**
(http://travel.state.gov), the **Canadian Department of Foreign Affairs** (http://voyage.dfait-maeci.gc.ca), the **U.K. Foreign & Commonwealth Office** (www.fco.gov.uk/travel), and the **Australian Department of Foreign Affairs** (www.dfat.gov.au/consular/advice).

7 Tips for Travelers with Special Needs

TRAVELERS WITH DISABILITIES

Most disabilities shouldn't stop anyone from traveling. There are more options and resources out there than ever before. However, Peru is considerably less equipped for disabled-friendly travel than are most parts of North America and Europe. Comparatively few hotels are outfitted for disabled travelers, and only a smattering of restaurants, museums, and means of public transportation make special accommodations for disabled patrons. There are few ramps, very few wheelchair-accessible bathrooms, and almost no telephones for the hearing-impaired. Representatives of Peru's National Tourism Ministry were present at a recent Society for Accessible Travel and Hospitality conference; Peru was the only country in South America that attended, indicating its willingness to make its travel offerings more attractive to disabled travelers.

One Peruvian hotel chain, **Posadas del Inca** (www.sonesta.com), stands out in a country where few places are equipped for disabled travel. With properties in Lima, Cusco, Yucay, and Puno, it maintains rooms in every hotel that are accessible for disabled travelers. See individual destination chapters for full reviews.

AGENCIES & OPERATORS
- **Flying Wheels Travel** (© 800/535-6790; www.flyingwheels travel.com) offers escorted tours and cruises that emphasize sports and private tours in minivans with lifts. At press time, the only standard South American tour is in Argentina, but custom itineraries are available anywhere in the world.
- **Accessible Journeys** (© 800/TINGLES or 610/521-0339; www.disabilitytravel.com) caters specifically to slow walkers and wheelchair travelers and their

Tips For Disabled Travelers

Though Peru has relatively few facilities equipped for disabled travelers, things are slowly changing. Request a copy of "Tourism for the People with Disabilities: The First Evaluation of Accessibility to Peru's Tourist Infrastructure" (2001) from the Peruvian embassy in your home country before your visit to Peru. The 99-page report features evaluations of hotels, restaurants, museums, attractions, airports, and other services in Lima, Cusco, Aguas Calientes, Iquitos, and Trujillo. An executive summary of the report is available for downloading at **www.peru.org.pe**.

families and friends. The organization offers a 10-day "Peru Explorer" trip to Lima, Paracas, Cusco, the Sacred Valley, and Machu Picchu.

ORGANIZATIONS
- **The Moss Rehab Hospital** (© 215/456-9603; www.moss resourcenet.org) provides friendly, helpful phone assistance through its Travel Information Service.
- **The Society for Accessible Travel and Hospitality** (© 212/447-7284; fax 212-725-8253; www.sath.org) offers a wealth of travel resources for all types of disabilities and informed recommendations on destinations, access guides, travel agents, tour operators, vehicle rentals, and companion services. Annual membership costs $45 for adults; $30 for seniors and students.
- **The American Foundation for the Blind** (© 800/232-5463; www.afb.org) provides information on traveling with Seeing Eye dogs.

PUBLICATIONS
- **Mobility International USA** (© 541/343-1284; www.miusa. org) publishes _A World of Options,_ a 658-page book of resources, covering everything from biking trips to scuba outfitters, and a biannual newsletter, _Over the Rainbow._ Annual membership is $35.

- **Twin Peaks Press** (© 360/694-2462) publishes travel-related books for travelers with special needs.
- _Open World for Disability and Mature Travel_ magazine, published by the Society for Accessible Travel and Hospitality (see above), is full of good resources and information. A year's subscription is $13 ($21 outside the U.S.).

WEBSITES
- **Access-Able Travel Source** (www.access-able.com) offers detailed destination articles on accessible travel in Peru and a wealth of specific information about Aguas Calientes, Chiclayo, Cusco, Huanchaco, Iquitos, Lima, the Chicama and Moche valleys, Pisac, Trujillo, and Yucay. Within individual reviews, you'll find information on ramps, door sizes, room sizes, bathrooms, and wheelchair availability.
- **Inkanatura Travel** (www. inkanatura.com) is particularly well equipped to deal with travelers with disabilities. Beyond the site's specifics on Peru, it is an excellent resource with all kinds of general information and answers to frequently asked questions about traveling with disabilities.

GAY & LESBIAN TRAVELERS
Though the Inca nation flag looks remarkably similar to the gay rainbow

flag, Peru, a predominantly Catholic and socially conservative country, could not be considered among the world's most progressive in terms of societal freedoms for gays and lesbians. It is still a male-dominated, macho society where homosexuality is considered deviant. Across Peru, there is still considerable prejudice exhibited toward gays and lesbians who are out, or men—be they straight or gay—who are thought to be effeminate. *Maricón* (fag) is a commonly used derogatory term.

In the larger cities, especially Lima and Cusco, there are a number of establishments—bars, discos, inns, and restaurants—that are either gay-friendly or predominantly gay. Outside those areas, and in the small towns and villages of rural Peru, openly gay behavior is unlikely to be tolerated by the general population. Gay life is not out in the open across Peru. Many gays and lesbians may wish to err on the side of discretion.

AGENCIES & OPERATORS

- **The International Gay & Lesbian Travel Association** (© 800/448-8550 or 954/776-2626; www.iglta.org) links travelers up with gay-friendly hoteliers, tour operators, and airline and cruise-line representatives. It offers monthly newsletters, marketing mailings, and a membership directory. Membership is $150 yearly, plus a $100 administration fee for new members.
- **Above and Beyond Tours** (© 800/397-2681; www.abovebeyond tours.com) offers gay and lesbian tours worldwide and is the exclusive gay and lesbian tour operator for United Airlines.
- **Now, Voyager** (© 800/255-6951; www.nowvoyager.com) is a San Francisco–based gay-owned and -operated travel service. You can search for Peru tours, cruises, and packages on its website.

PUBLICATIONS

- ***Out and About*** (© 800/929-2268 or 415/644-8044; www.out andabout.com) offers guidebooks and a newsletter 10 times a year, all packed with solid information on the global gay and lesbian scene.
- ***Spartacus International Gay Guide*** and ***Odysseus*** are good, annual English-language guidebooks focused on gay men, with some information for lesbians. You can get them from most gay and lesbian bookstores, or order them from **Giovanni's Room** (© 215/923-2960; www.giovannisroom. com).
- ***Gay Travel A to Z: The World of Gay & Lesbian Travel Options at Your Fingertips,*** by Marianne Ferrari (Ferrari Publications), is a very good gay and lesbian guidebook series.

WEBSITES

- **Gay Peru** (www.gayperu.com) has a section on gay travel (including gay-oriented package tours), news items, and nightclubs and hotels.
- **Purple Roofs** (www.purpleroofs. com) has a decent listing of gay and lesbian lodgings, restaurants, and nightclubs throughout Peru.
- **Gay Lima** (http://gaylimape. tripod.com) covers Lima and other parts of Peru, with information on nightclubs and gay-friendly establishments and activities. There's a version of the website in English.
- **deCajon.com** (www.decajon. com), which lists events, restaurants, and bars, has a special category of gay establishments. If you can read Spanish, **deambiente. com** (www.deambiente.com) also has a detailed listings and articles about gay life in Peru.
- The **GlobalGayz** website (www. travelandtranscendence.com) includes a very interesting article

on gay life in Peru. Among other things, it details the Fujimori government's dismissal of homosexual diplomats and other public servants.

SENIOR TRAVEL

Peru as a nation greatly respects the contributions and wisdom of society's elders, but that consideration doesn't necessarily translate into automatic deferential treatment of senior tourists. Discounts for seniors are virtually unheard of in Peru. Still, you should mention the fact that you're a senior citizen when you first make your travel reservations; all major airlines offer discounts for seniors, and you may find hotels (particularly international chains) that do so as well.

Members of **AARP,** 601 E. St. NW, Washington, DC 20049 (© **800/ 424-3410** or 202/434-2277; www. aarp.org), get discounts on hotels, airfares, and car rentals. AARP offers members a wide range of benefits, including *Modern Maturity* magazine and a monthly newsletter. Anyone over 50 can join.

AGENCIES & OPERATORS

- **SAGA Holidays** (© **800/343- 0273;** www.sagaholidays.com) offers inclusive tours and cruises for those 50 and up. SAGA also offers a number of single-traveler tours and vacations with an educational bent. The "South American Odysseys" trip goes to Lima, Cusco, the Sacred Valley, and Machu Picchu at the tail end of a 19-day tour of other highlights on the continent, with an optional Peruvian Amazon extension.
- **Elderhostel** (© **877/426-8056;** www.elderhostel.org) arranges study programs for people 55 and up (and a spouse or companion of any age) in more than 80 countries, including Peru. Most courses last 2 to 4 weeks, and many include airfare, accommodations

in university dormitories or modest inns, meals, and tuition.
- **Interhostel** (© **800/733-9753;** www.learn.unh.edu/interhostel), organized by the University of New Hampshire, also offers educational travel for people 50 and up (with companions over 40). On these escorted tours, the days are packed with seminars, lectures, and field trips, with sightseeing led by academic experts.

PUBLICATIONS

- *101 Tips for the Mature Traveler,* available from Grand Circle Travel (© **800/221-2610** or 617/ 350-7500; fax 617/346-6700)
- *The 50+ Traveler's Guidebook* (St. Martin's Press)
- *Unbelievably Good Deals and Great Adventures That You Absolutely Can't Get Unless You're Over 50* (Contemporary Publishing Co.)

FAMILY TRAVEL

The family vacation is a rite of passage for many households, one that in a split second can devolve into a *National Lampoon* farce. But as any veteran family vacationer will assure you, a family trip can be among the most pleasurable and rewarding experiences of your life.

Peruvians are extremely family-oriented, and children arouse friendly interest in locals. Although there aren't many established conventions, accommodations, or discounts for families traveling with children, Peru can be an excellent country in which to travel, as long as families remain flexible and are able to surmount difficulties in transportation, food, and accommodations.

Few hotels automatically offer discounts for children or allow children to stay free with their parents. Negotiation with hotels is required. On buses, children have to pay full fare if they occupy a seat (which is why you'll see most kids sitting on their parent's or sibling's lap). Many museums and other attractions offer discounts for children under 6. Children's meals are rarely found at restaurants in Peru, but sometimes it's possible to specially order smaller portions. Peruvian food may be very foreign to many children—how many kids, or adults, for that matter, will be keen on tasting roasted guinea pig?—but familiar foods, such as fried chicken, pizza, and spaghetti, are easy to find in almost all Peruvian towns. Throughout this guide, look for the icons designating kid-friendly attractions, hotels, and restaurants, as well as boxed items on kid-friendly hotels and restaurants.

Note: Parents need to exercise special care with regard to sun exposure for children in Peru, whether on the coast or in the Andes, where the sun is particularly strong. Sunscreen and sun hats are essential gear.

AGENCIES & OPERATORS

• **Familyhostel** (© 800/733-9753; www.learn.unh.edu/familyhostel) takes the whole family on moderately priced domestic and international learning vacations. All trip details are handled by the program staff, and lectures, field trips, and sightseeing are guided by a team of academics. For kids 8 to 15 accompanied by parents and/or grandparents.

PUBLICATION

• *How to Take Great Trips with Your Kids* (The Harvard Common Press) is full of good general advice that can apply to travel anywhere.

WEBSITES

• **Travel for Kids** (www.travel forkids.com) contains "Fun Things for You and Your Kids To Do in Peru," which includes a discussion of foods and a breakdown of kid-friendly sights around the country. It also has tips on travel

essentials and a Medical Resource Directory for travel abroad.

• **Family Travel Network** (www. familytravelnetwork.com) offers travel tips and reviews of family-friendly destinations, vacation deals, and thoughtful features such as "What to Do When Your Kids Are Afraid to Travel" and "Kid-Style Camping."

• **Travel with Your Children** (www.travelwithyourkids.com) is a comprehensive site offering sound advice for traveling with children.

STUDENT TRAVEL

You'd be wise to arm yourself with an **international student ID card,** which offers substantial savings on rail passes, plane tickets, and entrance fees. It also provides you with basic health and life insurance and a 24-hour help line. The card is available for $22 from the **Council on International Educational Exchange,** or CIEE (www. ciee.org). The CIEE's travel branch, **Council Travel** (© 800/226-8624; www.counciltravel.com), is the biggest student travel agency in the world. If you're no longer a student but are still under 26, you can get a **GO 25 card** from the same agency, which entitles you to insurance and some discounts (but not on museum admission). **STA Travel** (© 800/781-4040; www.sta travel.com) is another travel agency catering especially to young travelers, although their bargain-basement prices are available to people of all ages. In Canada, **Travel CUTS** (© 800/667-2887 or 416/614-2887; www.travel cuts.com), offers similar services.

WOMEN TRAVELERS

Peru continues to be a very macho, male-dominated society, and while women are a growing part of the professional workforce and a relatively recent feminist movement is evident in urban areas, women do not yet occupy the (still unequal) position they do in many Western societies. Still, women should not encounter any insurmountable difficulties traveling in Peru.

However, women should not be surprised to encounter perhaps unwelcome attention from men, especially if traveling alone. Many Peruvian men consider *gringas*—essentially, any foreign women—to be more sexually open than Peruvian women and, thus, foreigners are frequently the targets of their advances. Blonde women are frequently singled out. *Piropos,* come-ons that are usually meant as innocuous compliments rather than as crude assessments of a woman's physical attractiveness or sexuality, are common in Latin America. However, comments can occasionally be crude and demeaning, and groping is not unheard of in public places (such as on crowded buses). Sexual assaults are rare, but the threat felt by some women, especially if they do not comprehend the Spanish slang employed in come-ons, is understandable.

Many men, as well as Peruvian women, may be curious as to why a woman isn't married or traveling with a boyfriend. A woman traveling alone may elicit comments of sympathy or even pity. Wearing a ring on your wedding finger and deflecting comments and advances with a story about your husband working in Lima and meeting you in 2 days (or something to that effect) may be a useful tactic. In general, the problem is much more pronounced in large cities than in small towns and the countryside. Amerindian populations are conservative and even shy in dealing with foreigners, including women.

Women should be able to travel safely in Peru as long as they take some sensible precautions. Women on the receiving end of catcalls and aggressive come-ons should do what Peruvian women do: Ignore them. If that doesn't succeed, contact the tourist police (offices are listed in the "Fast Facts" section of individual destination chapters). While some Peruvian men may be innocently interested in meeting a foreign woman, it is not a good idea to accept an invitation to go anywhere alone with a man. Women traveling in a group with other females or, especially, with a man, are less likely to attract unwanted attention from men. While I would hesitate to tell a woman friend she should not travel alone in Peru, traveling with even one other woman might, at least psychologically, feel like a safer situation for many women. If you are traveling alone, never walk alone at night anywhere—always call for a registered taxi. It's also a good idea to have a whistle handy; a piercing sound blast will deter almost any aggressor.

For general common-sense advice and tips on safe travel, pick up a copy of *Safety and Security for Women Who Travel,* by Sheila Swan Laufer and Peter Laufer (Travelers' Tales, Inc.). Another helpful resource is **Journeywoman** (www.journey woman.com), a lively travel website just for women.

AGENCIES & OPERATORS

- **Women Welcome Women World Wide (5W)** (© 203/259-7832; www.womenwelcomewomen.org. uk) works to foster international friendships by enabling women of different countries to visit one another. (Men can come along on the trips; they just can't join the club.) It's a big, active organization, with more than 3,000 members from all walks of life in some 70 countries.

- **The Women's Travel Club** (© 800/480-4448; www.womens travelclub.com) was designed by a woman in search of female travel companions because her husband preferred work to travel. Now, the group organizes 25 to 30 tours a year, with an emphasis on foreign culture, scenery, and safety.

SINGLE TRAVELERS

Many people prefer to travel alone. Unfortunately, the solo traveler is often forced to pay a punishing "single supplement" charged by many resorts, cruise companies, and tour agencies for the privilege of sleeping alone.

OPERATORS & ROOMMATE FINDERS

- **Travel Companion Exchange (TCE)** (© 631/454-0880; www. travelcompanions.com) is one of the nation's oldest roommate finders for single travelers. Register with it and find a travel mate who will split the cost of the room with you and be around as little, or as often, as you like during the day.
- **Travel Buddies Singles Travel Club** (© 800/998-9099; www. travelbuddiesworldwide.com) runs small, intimate, single-friendly group trips and will match you with a roommate free of charge and save you the cost of single supplements.
- **TravelChums** (© 212/799-6464; www.travelchums.com) is an Internet-only travel-companion matching service hosted by respected New York–based Shaw Guides travel service.
- **The Single Gourmet Club** (© 212/980-8788; fax 212/980-3138; www.singlegourmetny.com), is the charter club of an international social, dining, and travel club for singles of all ages, with offices in 21 cities in the United States and Canada. Membership costs $75 for the first year; $40 to renew.

PUBLICATIONS

- *Traveling Solo: Advice and Ideas for More Than 250 Great Vacations,* by Eleanor Berman (Globe Pequot), gives advice on traveling alone, whether on your own or in a group tour.
- *Outdoor Singles Network* (P.O. Box 781, Haines, AK 99827; http://kcd.com/ci/osn) is a quarterly newsletter for outdoor-loving singles, ages 19 to 90. The network will help you find a travel companion, pen pal, or soul mate. Subscriptions are $55, and your personal ad is printed free in the next issue. Current issues are $15.

8 Getting There

BY BUS

You can travel overland to Peru through Ecuador, Bolivia or Chile. Though the journey isn't short, Lima can be reached from major neighboring cities. If traveling from Quito or Guayaquil, you'll pass through the major northern coastal cities on the way to Lima. From Bolivia, there is frequent service from La Paz and Copacabana to Puno and then on to Cusco. From Chile, most buses travel from Arica to Tacna, making connections to either Arequipa or Lima.

BY PLANE

All overseas flights from North America and Europe arrive at Lima's **Jorge** Chávez International Airport (© 01/575-1434). International flights to Iquitos in the northern Amazon region may be resumed at some point in the near future, perhaps from Miami, but it is only a possibility at this point.

In Peru, it is very important to reconfirm airline tickets in advance. For local flights, reconfirm 48 hours in advance; for international flights, reconfirm 72 hours before traveling. The airport tax on domestic flights is S/12 ($3.50), $25 on international flights. The tax must be paid—in cash only—before boarding.

FROM NORTH AMERICA From the United States, there are direct flights to Lima from Miami, the main hub for Latin America, as well as New York, Newark, Houston, Dallas, and Atlanta. The major carriers are **American** (through Dallas or Miami, with infrequent nonstops from New York; ✆ 800/433-7300; www.aa.com), **Delta** (Atlanta; ✆ 800/241-4141; www.delta.com), **Continental** (Houston and Newark; ✆ 800/231-0856; www.continental.com), **United** (Atlanta; ✆ 800/538-2929; www.ual.com), **Aero Continente** (Miami; ✆ **877/359-7378;** www.aerocontinente.com.pe), **LanPeru** (New York and Miami; ✆ 800/735-5590; www.lanperu.com), and **LanChile** (Los Angeles; ✆ 800/735-5526; www.lanchile.com).

Continental has probably the most comprehensive service to Lima, with daily nonstops from Newark and Houston. Usually the lowest fares from the United States are with **Aero Continente** and **LanPeru. American** also occasionally features very good deals on airfares to Lima from the United States.

From Canada, American, Continental, Delta, and United all fly to Peru, making stops at their hubs in the United States first. **Air Canada** (✆ 888/247-2262; www.aircanada.com) makes connections with other carriers at U.S. stops, usually Miami. **LanPeru** (✆ 416/862-0807) and **LanChile** (✆ 416/862-0807) use other carriers to the United States, making stops in New York, Miami, or Los Angeles on the way to Lima. (For example, you can purchase a LanPeru or LanChile ticket from Canada to Peru, with a layover in the U.S., but you will fly a partner airline to the U.S. and then change to a LanPeru or LanChile airliner for travel on to Peru.)

FROM THE U.K. There are no direct flights to Lima from London or any other part of the United Kingdom or Ireland; getting to Peru involves a layover in either another part of Europe or the United States. **American** (✆ 020/8572-5555 in London, or 0845/778-9789), **Continental** (✆ 0800/776-464), **Delta** (✆ 003/110-271-2051), and **United** (✆ 0845/844-4777) fly through their U.S. hubs on the way to Lima. European carriers make stops in continental Europe: **Iberia** (through Madrid; ✆ 0845/601-2854; www.iberia.com); **KLM** (Amsterdam; ✆ 08705/074-074; www.klm.com); and **Lufthansa** (✆ 0845/773-7747; www.lufthansa.com).

FROM AUSTRALIA & NEW ZEALAND From Australia and New Zealand, you can either fly to Buenos Aires on **Aerolíneas Argentinas** (✆ 800/22-22-15; www.aerolineas.com.au) and then connect to Lima, or go through Los Angeles (or Buenos Aires), with **Qantas** (✆ 0800/808-767; www.qantas.com) or **Air New Zealand** (✆ 0800/737-000; www.airnz.co.nz). **LanPeru** (✆ 02/9321-9333 in Australia and 09/912-7435 in New Zealand) and **LanChile** (✆ 1300/361-400 in Australia and 09/309-8673 in New Zealand) also make stops in Los Angeles on the way to Lima.

FLYING FOR LESS: TIPS FOR GETTING THE BEST AIRFARE

Passengers within the same airplane cabin are rarely paying the same fare. Business travelers who need to purchase tickets at the last minute, change their itinerary at a moment's notice, or get home for the weekend pay the premium rate. Passengers who can book their ticket long in advance, who can stay over Saturday night, or who are willing to travel on a Tuesday, Wednesday, or Thursday after 7pm, will pay a fraction of the full fare. On

Air Travel Security Measures

In the wake of the terrorist attacks on September 11, 2001, the airline industry implemented sweeping security measures in airports. Although regulations vary from airline to airline, you can expedite the checking-in process by taking the following steps:

- **Arrive early.** Arrive at the airport 2 hours or more before your scheduled flight.
- **Try not to drive your car to the airport.** Parking and curbside access to the terminal may be limited. Call ahead and check.
- **Don't count on curbside check-in.** Some airlines and airports have stopped curbside check-in altogether, whereas others offer it on a limited basis. For up-to-date information on specific regulations and implementations, check with the individual airline.
- **Be sure to carry plenty of documentation.** A government-issued photo ID (federal, state, or local) is now required. You may need to show this at various checkpoints. With an E-ticket, you may also be required to show your printed confirmation of purchase and the credit card with which you bought your ticket. This varies from airline to airline, so call ahead to make sure you have the proper documentation. And be sure that your ID is up-to-date: An expired driver's license, for example, may keep you from boarding the plane altogether.
- **Know what you can carry on—and what you can't.** Passengers are now limited to one carry-on bag, plus one personal bag (such as a purse or a briefcase). The FAA has also issued a list of restricted carry-on items; visit its website at www.faa.gov for an updated list of what you can and can't carry onto an aircraft.
- **Prepare to be searched.** Expect spot-checks. Electronic items, such as a laptop or cellphone, should be readied for additional screening; make sure your batteries are charged so you can turn them on and off if requested to do so during inspection. Limit the metal items you wear on your person.
- **It's no joke.** When a check-in agent asks if someone other than you packed your bag, don't decide that this is the time to be funny. The agents will not hesitate to call an alarm.
- **No ticket, no gate access.** Only ticketed passengers are allowed beyond the screener checkpoints, except for those people with specific medical or parental needs.

many flights, even the shortest hops, the full fare is close to $1,000 or more, while a 7- or 14-day advance-purchase ticket may cost less than half that amount. Here are a few other easy ways to save.

- Airlines periodically lower prices on their most popular routes.

Check the travel section of your Sunday newspaper for advertised discounts or call the airlines directly and ask if any **promotional rates** or special fares are available. If your schedule is flexible, say so, and ask whether you can secure a cheaper fare by staying an extra day, by flying midweek, or by flying at less-trafficked hours. If you already hold a ticket when a sale breaks, it may even pay to exchange your ticket, which usually incurs a $100 to $150 charge.

Note: The lowest-priced fares are often nonrefundable, require advance purchase of 1 to 3 weeks and a certain length of stay, and carry penalties for changing dates of travel.

• **Consolidators,** also known as bucket shops, are a good place to find low fares. Consolidators buy seats in bulk from the airlines and then sell them back to the public at prices usually below even the airlines' discounted rates. Their small ads usually run in Sunday newspaper travel sections. Before you pay, request a confirmation number from the consolidator and then call the airline to confirm your seat. Be aware that bucket-shop tickets are usually nonrefundable or rigged with stiff cancellation penalties, often as high as 50% to 75% of the ticket price. Protect yourself by paying with a credit card rather than cash. Keep in mind that if there's an airline sale going on, or if it's high season, you can often get the same or better rates by contacting the airlines directly, so do some comparison shopping before you buy. Also check out the name of the airline; you may not want to fly on some obscure airline, even if you're saving $10. And check whether you're flying on a charter or a scheduled airline; the latter is more expensive but more reliable. **Council Travel** (© 800/226-8624; www.counciltravel.com) and **STA Travel** (© 800/781-4040; www.statravel.com) cater especially to young travelers, but their bargain-basement prices are

available to people of all ages. **The TravelHub** (© 888/AIR-FARE; www.travelhub.com) represents nearly 1,000 travel agencies, many of whom offer consolidator and discount fares. Other reliable consolidators include **1-800-FLY-CHEAP** (www.1800flycheap. com); **TFI Tours International** (© 800-745-8000 or 212/736-1140; www.lowestprice.com), which serves as a clearinghouse for unused seats; or "rebators" such as **Travel Avenue** (© 800/333-3335; www.travelavenue.com) and the **Smart Traveller** (© 800/448-3338 in the U.S. or 305/448-3338), which rebate part of their commissions to you.

• Search **the Internet** for cheap fares. Great last-minute deals are available through free weekly e-mail services provided directly by the airlines. See "Planning Your Trip Online," later in this chapter, for more information.

• Look into **courier flights.** These companies hire couriers to hand-deliver packages or mail, and use your luggage allowance for themselves; in return, you get a deeply discounted ticket. Flights often become available at the last minute, so check in often. **Halbart Express** has offices in New York (© 718/656-8189), Los Angeles (© 310/417-9790), and Miami (© 305/593-0260). **Jupiter Air** (www.jupiterair.com) has offices in New York (© 718/656-6050), Los Angeles (© 310/670-5123), and San Francisco (© 650/697-1773).

• Join a travel club such as **Moment's Notice** (© 718/234-6295; www.momentsnotice.com) or **Sears Discount Travel Club** (© 800/433-9383, or 800/255-1487; www.travelersadvantage. com), which supply unsold tickets

---

⌐ *Tips* **Cancelled Plans**

If your flight is cancelled, don't book a new fare at the ticket counter. Find the nearest phone and call the airline directly to reschedule. You'll be relaxing while other passengers are still standing in line.

---

at discounted prices. You pay an annual membership fee to get the club's hot-line number. Of course, you're limited to what's available, so you have to be flexible.

• Join **frequent-flier clubs.** It's best to accrue miles on one program so that you can rack up free flights and achieve elite status faster. But it makes sense to open as many accounts as possible, no matter how seldom you fly a particular airline. It's free, and you'll get the best choice of seats, faster response to phone inquiries, and prompter service if your luggage is stolen, your flight is canceled or delayed, or if you want to change your seat.

HOW TO HAVE AN (ALMOST) FIRST-CLASS EXPERIENCE IN COACH

Anyone who has traveled in coach or economy class in recent years can attest to the frustrating reality of cramped seating. But with a little savvy and advance planning, you can make an otherwise unpleasant coach experience downright comfy.

Here are some tips for finding the right seat:

• For more legroom, check in early and ask for an aisle seat in an emergency-exit row or bulkhead.
• To have two seats for yourself, try for an aisle seat in a center section toward the back of coach.
• To sleep, avoid the last row or the row in front of the emergency exit, as these seats are the least likely to recline. You also may want to reserve a window seat so

that you can rest your head and avoid being bumped in the aisle.
• If you're traveling with a companion, book an aisle and a window seat. Middle seats are usually booked last, so chances are good that you'll end up with three seats to yourselves. And in the case that a third passenger is assigned the middle seat, they'll probably be more than happy to trade for a window or an aisle.
• Unless you love noise, avoid seats in the very back or near toilets and pantries.

Here are some tips for making yourself comfortable during your flight:

• Wear comfortable, low-heeled shoes and dress in loose-fitting layers that you can remove as cabin temperature fluctuates. Don't underdress: Airline cabins can be notoriously chilly and blankets may be unavailable. Wear breathable natural fabrics instead of synthetics.
• Hydrate before, during, and after your flight to combat the lack of humidity in airplane cabins—which can be as dry as the Sahara. Bring a bottle of water onboard.
• Pre-order a special meal. The airlines' vegetarian and kosher meals are usually fresher than standard plane fare. Or brown-bag your own meal.
• Get up and walk around whenever you can or perform stretching exercises in your seat to keep your blood flowing.
• Bring a toothbrush and moisturizer to stay fresh.

- If you're flying with kids, don't forget a deck of cards, toys, extra bottles, pacifiers, diapers, and chewing gum to help the kids relieve ear pressure buildup during ascent and descent. Let each child pack his or her own backpack with favorite toys.
- If you're flying with a cold or chronic sinus problems, use a decongestant 10 minutes before ascent and descent, to minimize pressure buildup in the inner ear.
- Try to acclimate yourself to the local time as quickly as possible. Stay up as long as you can the first day, then try to wake up at a normal hour the next morning.

COPING WITH JET LAG

Jetlag is a pitfall of traveling across time zones. If you're flying north to south—say, from Canada to Peru—and you feel sluggish when you touch down, your symptoms are the byproduct of dehydration and the general stress of air travel. When you travel east to west or vice versa, however, the bodily functions that operate cyclically—your hormone levels, blood pressure, body temperature, digestive enzymes, kidney, heart, and brain activity—fall into a sort of time warp. This is because they are, in part, someplace else, inclined to do the things they normally would have been doing back home. Traveling east, say, from Sydney to Lima, is more difficult on your internal clock than traveling west, say from London to Lima. Traveling east, you lose time, whereas traveling west, you gain time, and thus gain sleep, which will help your body recover more quickly.

Here are some tips for combating jet lag:

- Drink lots of water before, during, and after your flight.
- Reset your watch according to your destination time before you board the plane.

- Avoid drinking alcohol before and during your flight.
- Exercise, sleep well, and eat especially healthy foods during the few days before your trip.
- Eat more lightly than you normally would, both before and during your flight.
- When you reach your destination, don't sleep longer than you normally would to try to "catch up."
- Push yourself to stay as active as you can when you reach your destination, until the normal bedtime there. Likewise, wake at the same hour that locals do. The more you expose your body to daily rhythms in your destination, the faster your body will adjust.
- Some doctors recommend melatonin 2 hours before bedtime. A natural, sleep-inducing hormone, it's thought that melatonin will trick your body into thinking night has fallen earlier and help you adjust to a new time zone.
- Remember that eating carbohydrates (such as pasta or wholegrain bread) before bedtime will allow you to sleep better. High protein foods—such as meats, fish, eggs, and dairy products—eaten before bedtime will give you energy.

If you have trouble sleeping on planes, consider taking a flight that departs in the morning and arrives in the evening, as opposed to a flight that departs in the late afternoon or evening and arrives the following morning. If you arrive in the evening, you'll be able to settle into your hotel at a reasonable hour, get a good's night sleep, and wake up refreshed the next morning. The problem with this strategy is that you waste a full day on the plane and you will likely still suffer the effects of jet lag for a few days at least.

Flying with Film & Video

Never pack unprotected, undeveloped film in checked bags, which may be scanned. The film you carry with you can be damaged by scanners, too. X-ray damage is cumulative; the slower the film, and the more times you put it through a scanner, the more likely the damage. Film under 800 ASA is usually safe for up to five scans. If you're taking your film through additional scans, request a hand inspection. In international airports, though, you're dependent on the kindness of airport officials. On international flights, store your film in transparent baggies so that you can remove it easily before you go through scanners. Keep in mind that airports are not the only places where your camera may be scanned: Highly trafficked attractions are X-raying visitors' bags with increasing frequency.

Most photo-supply stores sell protective pouches designed to block damaging X-rays. The pouches fit both film and loaded cameras. They should protect your film in checked baggage, but they also may raise alarms and result in a hand inspection.

An organization called **Film Safety for Traveling on Planes (FSTOP)** (© **888/301-2665;** www.f-stop.org), can provide additional tips for traveling with film and camera equipment.

Carry-on scanners will not damage videotape in a video camera, but the magnetic fields emitted by the walk-through security gateways and handheld inspection wands will. Always place your loaded camcorder on the screening conveyor belt or have it hand-inspected. Be sure your batteries are charged, as you will probably be required to turn the device on to ensure that it's what it appears to be.

9 Package Deals, Escorted Tours & Special-Interest Vacations

Before you start your search for the lowest airfare, you may want to consider booking your flight as part of a travel package such as an escorted tour or a package tour. What you lose in adventure, you'll gain in time and money saved when you book accommodations, and maybe even food and entertainment, along with your flight. But not all package deals are light on adventure: Some tours specifically target special interests, such as bird-watching, jungle hikes, or mountain treks.

group rate. Packages usually include airfare, a choice of hotels, and car rentals, and packagers often offer several options at different prices. In many cases, a package that includes airfare, hotel, and transportation to and from the airport will cost you less than just the hotel alone would have, had you booked it yourself. That's because packages are sold in bulk to tour operators—who resell them to the public at a cost that drastically undercuts standard rates.

PACKAGE TOURS FOR INDEPENDENT TRAVELERS

Package tours are not the same thing as escorted tours. With a package tour, you travel independently but pay a

THE PROS & CONS OF PACKAGE TOURS

Packages can save you money by offering group prices, but they allow for independent travel. The disadvantages are that you're usually required to make a large payment upfront; you may end up on a charter flight; and you have to deal with your own luggage and with transfers between your hotel and the airport, if transfers are not included in the package price. Packages often don't allow for complete flexibility or a wide range of choices. For instance, you may prefer a quiet inn but have to settle for a popular chain hotel instead. Your choice of travel days may be limited as well.

QUESTIONS TO ASK IF YOU BOOK A PACKAGE TOUR

• What are the **accommodation choices** available and are there price differences? Once you find out, look them up in this Frommer's guide. Most countries rate their hotels, so ask about the rating of the hotel in question. Or get this information from the government tourist office or its website.

• What **type of room** will you be staying in? Don't take whatever is thrown your way. Request a non-smoking room, a quiet room, a room with a view, or whatever you fancy.

• Look for **hidden expenses.** Ask whether airport departure fees and taxes are included in the total cost.

RECOMMENDED PACKAGE TOUR OPERATORS

One good source of package deals is the airlines themselves. Most major airlines offer air/land packages, including **American Airlines Vacations** (© 800/321-2121; http://www.aavacations. com), **Delta Vacations** (© 800/221-6666; www.deltavacations.com), **US Airways Vacations** (© 800/455-0123 or 800/422-3861; www.usairways vacations.com), **Continental Airlines Vacations** (© 800/301-3800; www. coolvacations.com), and **United Vacations** (© 888/854-3899; www.united vacations.com).

Online Vacation Mall (© 800/839-9851; www.onlinevacationmall. com) allows you to search for and book packages offered by a number of tour operators and airlines. The **United States Tour Operators Association**'s website (www.ustoa.com) has a search engine that allows you to look for operators that offer packages to a specific destination. Travel packages are also listed in the travel section of your local Sunday newspaper. **Liberty Travel** (© 888/271-1584; www.libertytravel.com), one of the biggest packagers in the Northeast, often runs full-page ads in Sunday papers. Check out the current specials on the **Frommer's** website (www. frommers.com), and check the ads in the national travel magazines such as *Arthur Frommer's Budget Travel Magazine, Travel & Leisure, National Geographic Traveler,* and *Condé Nast Traveler.*

Miami is the place for package deals to Peru. **Analie Tours** (© 800/811-6027; www.analietours.com) offers a 6-day/5-night $790 deal to Lima and Cusco, including round-trip airfare, city tours, a day trip to Machu Picchu, daily breakfast, and all transfers within Peru. You can fly out of a number of other U.S. gateways for an additional $240, and Lake Titicaca and Amazon extensions are possible. **Marnella Tours** (© 866/993-0033 or 305/716-9995; www.marnellatours. com) offers a similar 6-night package, including airfare and day tours in Cusco, for $977, as well as Iquitos, Arequipa, and Nasca extensions. **Tara Tours** (© 800/327-0080; www. taratours.com) is also worth a look; it usually offers several air/land packages to Peru, as well as tours such as the "Inka Journey" (Cusco, Machu Picchu, Lima, and the Amazon) and tours to the ruins at Kuélap, Sipán, and Machu Picchu.

Fly Latin America, based in Costa Rica (© **888/246-1431**; www.flylatin america.net/peru) has good airfares to Peru from North America and all over, as well as air/hotel and tour packages. **Intervac Tours** (© **800/401-5897** or 305/670-8990; latinamerica@intervac tours.com) also offers good-value air/ land packages to Peru, such as a recent offer for 5 nights (2 in Lima, 3 in Cusco) with round-trip airfare from Miami from $799. Another good source is **BET Tours** (© **800/438- 4448** or 305/385-8400), which recently offered a similar package to Lima and Cusco for just under $700.

ESCORTED TOURS

Escorted tours are structured group tours, with a group leader. The price usually includes everything from air- fare to hotels, meals, tours, admission costs, and local transportation.

THE PROS & CONS OF ESCORTED TOURS

If you book an escorted tour, most everything is paid for upfront, so you deal with fewer money issues. They allow you to enjoy the maximum number of sites in the shortest time, with the least amount of hassle, as all the details are arranged by others. Escorted tours give you the security of traveling in a group and are conven- ient for people with limited mobility. Many escorted tours are theme tours, putting together people who share the same interest (such as cooking or sailing).

On the downside, if you book an escorted tour, you often have to pay a lot of money upfront, and your lodging and dining choices are predetermined. Escorted tours can be jam-packed with activities, leaving little room for indi- vidual sightseeing, whims, or adven- ture. They also often focus only on the heavily touristed sites, so you miss out on the lesser-known gems. Plus, you may not always be happy rubbing suit- cases with strangers.

QUESTIONS TO ASK IF YOU BOOK AN ESCORTED TOUR

- What is the **cancellation policy?** Do they require a deposit? Can they cancel the trip if they don't get enough people? Do you get a refund if they cancel? If *you* can- cel? How late can you cancel if you are unable to go? When do you pay in full? *Note:* If you choose an escorted tour, think strongly about purchasing trip- cancellation insurance from an independent agency, especially if the tour operator asks you to pay upfront. See "Travel Insurance at a Glance," earlier in this chapter.

- How busy is the **schedule?** How much sightseeing is planned each day? Is ample time allowed for relaxing or wandering solo?

- What is the **size** of the group? Generally, the smaller the group, the more flexible the itinerary, and the less time you'll spend waiting for people to get on and off the bus. Tour operators may be evasive about this, because they may not know the exact size of the group until everyone has made reserva- tions; but they should be able to give you a rough estimate. Some tours have a minimum group size and may cancel the tour if they don't book enough people.

- What is included in the **price?** You may have to pay for transportation to and from the airport. A box lunch may be included in an excur- sion, but drinks may cost extra. Beer may be included, but wine may not. Can you opt out of cer- tain activities, or does the bus leave once a day, with no exceptions? Are all your meals planned in advance? Can you choose your entree at din- ner? Are tips included?

- What are the **names of the hotels** where you'll be staying? Once you've gotten the names, look them up in this Frommer's guide. Foreign countries rate their hotels, so ask about the rating of the hotel in question. This information is usually available for free from government tourist offices and their websites.
- What **type of room** will you be staying in? Don't take whatever is thrown your way. Request a non-smoking room, a quiet room, a room with a view, or whatever your fancy.
- What are the **demographics** of the group with whom you'll be traveling? What is the age range? What is the gender breakdown? Is this mostly a trip for couples?
- If you plan to be traveling alone, what is the **single supplement?** Will they find you a roommate at your request?

RECOMMENDED ESCORTED TOUR OPERATORS
North America– and Europe-Based Companies

- **Abercrombie & Kent** (© 800/ 323-7308; www.abercrombiekent. com) recently introduced South America into its extensive lineup of luxury trips, which are well managed and pampered, with stays in many of the finest hotels available (in Peru, grand places such as Swiss-ôtel, Hotel Monasterio, and the Machu Picchu Sanctuary Lodge). The tours aren't cheap, but if you want to go in style, A&K is the way to go. Group size is generally limited to 16 people. Several Peru itineraries are available; check the website for occasional discounts on selected tours and dates.
- **Adventure Life Journeys** (© 800/ 344-6118 or 406/541-2677; www. adventure-life.com), based in Missoula, Montana, has a roster of interesting Peru trips to suit most travelers. Trips are a good mix of hotels and home stays.
- **Adventures Abroad** (© 800/ 665-3998; www.adventures-abroad.com), based in Washington state, has a massive database of trips. The tour operator prides itself on small group travel, from 4 to 21 participants. Peruvian offerings are highlights tours, ranging from 7 to 21 days, but longer trips include good features such as hiking the Inca Trail. Several trips combine either Ecuador or Bolivia with Peruvian attractions.
- **Exito Latin American Travel** (© 800/655-4053; www.exito-travel.com/land.html) has several Peru packages, including the Inca Trail to Machu Picchu and jungle lodge tours. It's also a very good source for finding the best airfares to Peru and elsewhere in Latin America, as well as language programs.
- **GAP Adventures** (© 800/692-5495 in the U.S., or 800/465-5600 in Canada; www.gap adventures.com) focuses on adventure-oriented "independent travel with the security of a group" in Central and South America and Cuba. Trips range from a 21-day "Absolute Peru" trip to a 13-day "Essence of Peru" trip (Cusco, Machu Picchu, Sacred Valley, jungle lodge, and Lake Titicaca). Some trips are more comfortable; others are a bit more raw. Most trips have a maximum size of 12 travelers.
- **Latin America Escapes, Inc.** (© 800/510-5999; www.latin americanescapes.com) offers fully escorted adventure trips, cultural tours, and natural history programs in Peru, as well as customized trips with your own private guide and driver and fully hosted independent tours with all major details (transportation,

hotels, and tours) included. Check the website for current specials.

- **Ladatco Tours,** (© 800/327-6162; www.ladatco.com) has specialized in tours to Central and South America for 3 decades. Its Explorer Tours are locally hosted and include hotel, sightseeing with an English-speaking guide, and all land, cruise, and air transportation. Tours are grouped by theme such as "Mystic" and "Inca." There are also "Pampered Adventure" programs and custom-designed tours—in all, more than 2 dozen trips to Peru throughout high season. Tours are a bit pricey but well designed, and prices include airfare from Miami.

- **Nature Expeditions International** (© 800/869-0639 or 954/693-8852; www.naturexp.com) has a good reputation for package tours. It offers a good 10-day highlights trip to Lima, Cusco, the Sacred Valley, and Arequipa, and a 7-day trip to Lima, Cusco, and Machu Picchu.

- **Overseas Adventure Travel** (© 800/493-6824; www.oattravel.com) is an English outfit with economical small-group (10–16 people) tours, such as its 10-day "Real Affordable Peru" trip. Another tour combines Machu Picchu and the Galápagos Islands.

- **Peru Discover** (© and fax 305/716-9216; www.perudiscover.com) has an extensive roster of tours, flights, and packages, including plenty of plan-your-own trips to Peru. Good economical package deals include one to Lima, Cusco, and Machu Picchu with a short jungle lodge stay in Tambopata.

- **Peru for Less** (© 800/523-1272; www.peruforless.com) lives up to its plain-spoken name, guaranteeing "the lowest prices outside

Peru." It has at least a half dozen Peru tour packages, such as "Archaeological Peru," which visits Lima, Paracas, Nasca, Arequipa, Cusco, and Machu Picchu. Tours include guides, hotels, all visits and transfers, plus daily breakfast. There are plenty of extra day options, such as the Salt Mines and Moray, and backpackers "super specials."

- **Peru Horizons Travel & Tours** (© 800/333-9361; www.perutravel.com) offers economical vacation packages to most parts of Peru, including Machu Picchu, Cusco, Lima, the Nasca Lines, the Amazon, the Inca Trail, Trujillo, Lake Titicaca, Puno, Arequipa, Ica, and Urubamba.

- **Southwind Adventures** (© 800/377-9463; www.southwindadventures.com) plans fascinating, distinctive, and high-end trips with a cultural emphasis in South America. Among them are 16 Peruvian trips, from mountain biking to specialty tours such as the Kuélap ruins, and cool offerings such as "Inca Visions," a photography workshop tour. Custom trips include a 21-day Grand Andean Traverse trekking expedition, with possibilities for birdwatching, rafting, and family adventure.

- **Sunny Land Tours** (© 800/783-7839 or 201/487-2150; www.sunnylandtours.com) has a number of Peru programs available, such as its 13-day "Best of Peru" tour, 8 days in the Amazon, or a 4-day "Cusco Discovery" tour.

- **Trafalgar Tours** (© 800/854-0103; www.trafalgartours.com), the massive mass-market tour operator, has jumped on the South America bandwagon and now offers a 10-day "Best Of Peru" with fully escorted visits (and set hotels with no choices) to

Lima, Cusco, Machu Picchu, Puno, and Lake Titicaca. The only way to piggyback a Galápagos tour, for example, would be to do back-to-back trips. Trips to Peru are during (Northern Hemisphere) winter, spring, and fall only.

Peru-Based Companies

- **Class Adventure Travel** (© 01/ 444-2220; www.cat-travel.com) is a young but very professional, Dutch-owned and -operated firm with offices in Lima and Cusco. It offers adventure (rafting and trekking) and jungle tours; long trips (a 17-day "Ancient Cultures of Peru" trip) and short trips (a 7-day Cusco and Puno trip); and design-your-own tours. If you arrive in Peru and then decide to book a tour, CAT is one of the best general agencies to contact.
- **Fiesta Tours International** (© 01/225-1336; www.fiesta toursperu.com) has 22 different trips within Peru, such as its 6-day "Discover Peru" tour. It also deals in airfares from Miami or Los Angeles.
- **Kon-Tiki Tours** has offices in Miami Beach (© 877/566-8454 or 305-673-0092) and Lima (© 01/445-4929) and offers rainforest expeditions, spiritual sojourns, trekking and adventure-sports tours, and targeted cultural programs.
- **Peru Gateway** (© 01/444-3031; www.peru-explorer.com) also has an extensive roster of Peru tours and selection of hotels.

SPECIAL-INTEREST TOURS

Though Helena, Alabama, might not be the first place you'd necessarily go to plan an Amazon cruise, the city's **International Expeditions** (© 800/ 633-4734 or 205/428-1700; www.internationalexpeditions.com) features a number of Amazon cruises and jungle-lodge tours (including the most luxurious river cruises, run by Junglex), as well as an interesting 9-day Machu Picchu Ecological Workshop, which has hands-on classes and culture visits.

Magical Journeys (© 888/737-8070; www.travelperu.com) has a singular focus on "authentic sacred tours." All its trips take aim at the spiritual elements and mystery that were a significant part of many Andean pre-Columbian civilizations, including the Incas. Choose from a 2-week Machu Picchu and Cusco tour, a 10-day "Yoga in the Andes" trip, or "Artist Spiritual" journeys. All groups stay at the Willka T'ika guest lodge in the Sacred Valley. The agency is careful to market its trips to "open-minded people with an adventurous spirit."

Myths and Mountains (© 800/ 670-MYTH or 775/832-5454; www.mythsandmountains.com) offers some of the more unique tours you'll find. It specializes in what it terms learning journeys, folk medicine and traditional healing tours, and culture and crafts trips. For example, the 13-day "Weavings and Crafts of the Andes" tour includes meetings with textile experts and craftsmen and visits with rural families. Another trip of interest is the 9-day "Inca Rituals and Power Places," an exploration of ancient Inca myths and ceremonies. There are also more standard wildlife and environment tours to the Andes and the Amazon.

10 Planning Your Trip Online

Researching and booking your trip online can save time and money. Then again, it may not. It is simply not true that you always get the best deal online. Most booking engines do not include schedules and prices for budget airlines, and, from time to time, you'll get a better last-minute

Frommers.com: The Complete Travel Resource

For an excellent travel-planning resource, we highly recommend **Frommers.com** (www.frommers.com). We're a little biased, of course, but we think you'll find the travel tips, reviews, monthly vacation give-aways, and online-booking capabilities thoroughly indispensable. Among the special features are our popular **Message Boards,** where Frommer's readers post queries and share advice (sometimes even our authors show up to answer questions); **Frommers.com Newsletter,** for the latest travel bargains and inside travel secrets; and **Frommer's Destinations Section,** where you'll get expert travel tips, hotel and dining recommendations, and advice on the sights to see for more than 2,500 destinations around the globe. When your research is done, the **Online Reservation System** (www.frommers.com/booktravelnow) takes you to Frommer's favorite sites for booking your vacation at affordable prices.

price by calling the airline directly, so it's best to call the airline to see if you can do better before booking online.

On the plus side, Internet users today can tap into the same travel-planning databases that were once accessible only to travel agents—and do it at the same speed. Sites such as **Frommers.com, Travelocity.com, Expedia.com,** and **Orbitz.com** allow consumers to comparison shop for air-fares, access special bargains, book flights, and reserve hotel rooms and rental cars.

But don't fire your travel agent just yet. Although online booking sites offer tips and hard data to help you bargain shop, they cannot endow you with the hard-earned experience that makes a seasoned, reliable travel agent an invaluable resource, even in the Internet age. And for consumers with a complex itinerary, a trusty travel agent is still the best way to arrange the most direct flights to and from the best airports.

Still, there's no denying the Internet's emergence as a powerful tool in researching and plotting travel time. The benefits of researching your trip online can be well worth the effort.

Last-minute specials, such as weekend deals or Internet-only fares, are offered by airlines to fill empty seats. Most of these are announced on Tuesday or Wednesday and must be purchased online. They are only valid for travel that weekend, but some can be booked weeks or months in advance. Sign up for weekly e-mail alerts at airline websites or check megasites that compile comprehensive lists of last-minute specials, such as **Smarter Living** (www.smarterliving.com) or **WebFlyer** (www.webflyer.com).

Some sites, such as Expedia.com, will send you **e-mail notification** when a cheap fare becomes available to your favorite destination. Some will also tell you when fares to a particular destination are lowest.

TRAVEL PLANNING & BOOKING SITES

Keep in mind that because several airlines are no longer willing to pay commissions on tickets sold by online travel agencies, these agencies may either add a $10 surcharge to your bill if you book on that carrier—or neglect to offer those carriers' schedules.

The list of sites below is selective, not comprehensive. Some sites may have evolved or disappeared by the time you read this.

- **Travelocity** (www.travelocity.com or www.frommers.travelocity.com) and **Expedia** (www.expedia.com) are among the most popular sites, each offering an excellent range of options. Travelers search by destination, dates, and cost.

- **Orbitz** (www.orbitz.com) is a popular site launched by United, Delta, Northwest, American, and Continental airlines. (Stay tuned: At press time, travel-agency associations were waging an antitrust battle against this site.)

- **Qixo** (www.qixo.com) is another powerful search engine that allows you to search for flights and accommodations from some 20 airline and travel-planning sites (such as Travelocity) at once. Qixo sorts results by price.

- **Priceline** (www.priceline.com) lets you "name your price" for airline tickets, hotel rooms, and rental cars. For airline tickets, you can't say what time you want to fly—you have to accept any flight between 6am and 10pm on the dates you've selected, and you may have to make one or more stopovers. Tickets are nonrefundable, and no frequent-flier miles are awarded.

SMART E-SHOPPING

The savvy traveler is armed with insider information. Here are a few tips to help you navigate the Internet successfully and safely.

- **Know when sales start.** Last-minute deals may vanish in minutes. If you have a favorite booking site or airline, find out when last-minute deals are released to the public. (For example, Southwest's specials are posted every Tuesday at 12:01am central time.)

- **Shop around.** If you're looking for bargains, compare prices on different sites and airlines—and against a travel agent's best fare. Try a range of times and alternative airports before you make a purchase.

- **Stay secure.** Book only through secure sites (some airline sites are not secure). Look for a key icon (Netscape) or a padlock (Internet Explorer) at the bottom of your Web browser before you enter credit-card information or other personal data.

- **Avoid online auctions.** Sites that auction airline tickets and frequent-flier miles are the number-one perpetrators of Internet fraud, according to the National Consumers League.

- **Maintain a paper trail.** If you book an E-ticket, print out a confirmation, or write down your confirmation number, and keep it safe and accessible—or your trip could be a virtual one!

ONLINE TRAVELER'S TOOLBOX

Veteran travelers usually carry some essential items to make their trips easier. Following is a selection of online tools to bookmark and use.

- **Visa ATM Locator** (www.visa.com), for locations of PLUS ATMs worldwide, or **MasterCard ATM Locator** (www.mastercard.com), for locations of Cirrus ATMs worldwide.

- **Foreign Languages for Travelers** (www.travlang.com). Learn basic terms in more than 70 languages and click on any underlined phrase to hear what it sounds like. *Note:* Free audio software and speakers are required.

- **Intellicast** (www.intellicast.com) and **Weather.com** (www.weather.com). Gives weather forecasts for all 50 states and for cities around the world.

Tips Easy Internet Access Away from Home

There are a number of ways to check your e-mail, using any computer.

• Your **Internet Service Provider (ISP)** may have a Web-based interface that lets you access your e-mail on computers other than your own. Just find out how it works before you leave home. The major ISPs maintain local access numbers around the world so that you can go online by placing a local call. Check your ISP's website or call its toll-free number and ask how you can use your current account away from home, and how much it will cost. Also ask about the cost of the service before you leave home. If you're traveling outside the reach of your ISP, you may have to check the Yellow Pages in your destination to find a local ISP.

• You can open an account on a free, Web-based **e-mail provider** before you leave home, such as Microsoft's **Hotmail** (www.hotmail.com), **Yahoo! Mail** (http://mail.yahoo.com), or **Fastmail** (www.fastmail.fm). Your home ISP may be able to forward your home e-mail to the Web-based account automatically.

• Check out **www.mail2web.com**. This amazing free service allows you to type in your regular e-mail address and password and retrieve your e-mail from any Web browser, anywhere, so long as your home ISP hasn't blocked it with a firewall.

• Call your hotel in advance to see whether Internet connection is possible from your room. Usually only top-flight hotels in Peru have data modems in the rooms.

• In Peru, by far the easiest way to check your e-mail and surf the Web (usually your best source for current news) is to drop in at the Internet _cabinas_ (booths) that can be found in virtually every city and even small town. Connections are usually fast, and the service is as little as 75¢ per hour. Many Internet cabinas are starting to feature software programs such as Net2Phone, which allows you to call abroad through the Internet for ridiculously low prices. (Connections, however, aren't always perfect.)

• **Mapquest** (www.mapquest.com). This best of the mapping sites lets you choose a specific address or destination, and in seconds, it will return a map and detailed directions.

• **Cybercafes.com** (www.cybercafes.com) or **Net Café Guide** (www.netcafeguide.com/mapindex.htm). Locate Internet cafes at hundreds of locations around the globe.

• **Universal Currency Converter** (www.xe.net/currency). See what your dollar or pound is worth in more than 100 other countries.

11 Getting Around

Because of its size and natural barriers, including difficult mountain terrain, long stretches of desert coast, and extensive rain forest, Peru is complicated to get around. Train service is very limited, covering only a few principal tourist routes, and many trips take several days by land. Visitors with limited time tend to fly everywhere they can. Travel overland, though very inexpensive, can be extremely time-consuming and uncomfortable. However, for certain routes, intercity buses are your only real option.

BY PLANE

Flying to major destinations within Peru is the only practical way around the country if you wish to see several places in a couple weeks or less. Peru is a deceptively large country, and natural barriers make getting around rather difficult. Most major Peruvian cities can be reached by air, though not always directly. Some places in the jungle, such as Iquitos, can only be reached by airplane (or a very long and arduous boat ride). Flying to major destinations, such as Lima, Cusco, Arequipa, Puerto Maldonado, and Iquitos, is simple and relatively inexpensive. One-way flights to most destinations are between $59 and $89 (prices, in U.S. dollars, fluctuate according to season). Puno (and Lake Titicaca), however, require passengers to fly first to Juliaca before continuing by land the rest of the way (45km/28 miles)—a reality that prompts many to take a direct train or bus from Cusco to Puno.

Peru's carriers, some of which are small airlines with limited flight schedules, include **Aero Continente** (© 877/482-2501 in the U.S., or 01/242-4242; www.aerocontinente. net); **AeroCondor** (© 01/442-5215; www.aerocondor.com.pe); **LanPeru** (© 212/582-3250 in the U.S., or 01/ 213-8200; www.lanperu.com); **Taca Peru** (© 800/535-8780 in the U.S., or 01/213-7000; www.grupotaca. com); and **TANS** (© 01/213-6000; www.tansperu.com.pe).

LanPeru and Aero Continente are the only domestic airlines flying to most major destinations in Peru.

TANS flies to Cusco, Iquitos, and Pucallpa. AeroCondor flies to Cajamarca and Trujillo. Connections through Lima are often necessary, though many destinations are accessible directly from Arequipa and Cusco, and some routes may be limited to only several days a week. Both flight schedules and fares are apt to change frequently and without notice. One-way fares are generally half the round-trip fare. Flights should be booked several days in advance, especially in high season, and you should also make sure you get to the airport at least 45 minutes in advance, to avoid being bumped from a flight.

LanPeru and perhaps other Peruvian airlines are said to be studying the possibility of reinstating an air pass program, but for now, it remains merely a possibility.

BY TRAIN

The four tourist or passenger train routes operated by PeruRail (a private company owned by Orient-Express) are all very popular and scenic journeys. Because luggage theft has long been a problem on Peruvian trains, you should (if possible) purchase a premium-class ticket that limits access to ticketed passengers.

One of the popular journeys is the **Titicaca Route,** round-trip from Cusco to Puno, on the shores of Lake Titicaca; Inka-class (premium) service costs $30 one-way, and Tourist class costs $19 one-way. The **Blue Sky Route** runs round-trip from Puno to Arequipa; Inka class costs $30, Tourist $9. The **Valle de las Maravillas (Valley of Miracles) Route** is a new tourist train to Colca Canyon with the final segment to the canyon by minivan; it costs $25 one-way, $30 round-trip. By far the most popular train route in Peru, though, is the **Inka Route,** which serves Cusco and the Sacred Valley, traveling from the old Inca capital to Ollantaytambo and the world-famous ruins of Machu Picchu;

Combi or Carro? Getting Around in and Out of Town

Getting around Peru demands a mastery of terms that designate varied modes of transportation and a bewildering array of vehicles that aren't always easy to distinguish.

Within cities, travelers have several options. The most convenient and expensive are **taxis**, which function, for the most part, like taxis elsewhere in the world. However, taxis in Peru are wholly unregulated; in addition to registered, licensed taxis, you'll find "taxi" drivers who are merely folks with access to a two-bit car—usually rented for the purpose—and a taxi sticker to plunk inside the windshield. In Lima, this is overwhelmingly the case, and unregistered taxi drivers can be difficult to negotiate with for a fair price. There are no meters, meaning you have to negotiate a price before (not after) accepting a ride. In other cities, such as Cusco, taxis conform to standard pricing (S/2, or 50¢, within town), so taking cabs outside of Lima is a considerably less daunting proposition for most travelers.

Combis are vans that function as private bus services. They often race from one end of town to another, with fare collectors hanging out the door barking the name of the route. Combis also cover routes between towns. *Colectivos* are essentially indistinguishable from combis—they are vans that cover regular routes (such as between Cusco and Pisac), and they usually depart when they're full. Routes are often so popular, though, that colectivos leave regularly, as often as every 15 minutes, throughout the day.

For intercity transport, there is a similar slate of options. *Micros* are small buses, often old and quite colorful, that travel between cities. *Autobuses* (also called *buses* or *ómnibuses*) are large coaches for long-distance travel on scheduled intercity routes. Classes of buses are distinguished by price and comfort: *Económico* is a bare-bones bus with little more than a driver and an assigned seat; classes designated *especial* (or sometimes "Inka") have reclining seats, videos, refreshments, and bathrooms.

As if that complex web of terms weren't enough to get a handle on, there's an additional warning to heed: It's not uncommon to hear locals refer—loosely and confusingly—to buses as *carros* (which normally just means "car") and to colectivos as *taxis*.

Inka-class and Autovagón-class service cost $70 round-trip, and Tourist-class service costs $30 round-trip

Sadly, the spectacular high-altitude journey from Lima to Huancayo in the Andes is no longer in service for passenger travel.

There were no PeruRail train passes as of press time. For additional information, visit the **PeruRail** website at www.perurail.com or call ℭ **084/238-722** in Cusco or 054/215-640 in Arequipa.

BY BUS

Buses are the cheapest and most popular form of transportation in Peru—for many Peruvians, they are the only means of getting around—and they have by far the greatest reach. A complex network of private bus companies crisscrosses Peru, with numbers of competing lines covering the most popular routes. Many companies operate their own bus stations, and their locations, dispersed across many cities, can be endlessly frustrating to travelers. Luggage theft is an issue on many buses, and passengers should keep a watchful eye on carry-on items and pay close attention when bags are unloaded. Only a few long-distance buses have luxury buses comparable in comforts to European models (bathrooms, reclining seats, and movies). These premium-class ("Royal" or "Imperial" class) buses cost up to twice as much as regular-service buses, though for many travelers, the additional comfort and services are worth the difference in cost (which remains inexpensive).

For many short distances (such as Cusco to Pisac), *colectivos* (smaller buses without assigned seats) are the fastest and cheapest option.

Ormeño (© 01/472-1710 or 01/427-5679); **Cruz del Sur** (© 01/428-2570 or 01/424-1005); and **Civa** (© 01/426-4926) are among the bus companies with the best reputations for long-distance treks. Given the extremely confusing nature of bus companies, terminals, and destinations—which makes it impossible to even begin to list every possible option here—it is best to approach either a local tourism information office or travel agency (most of which sell long-distance bus tickets) with a destination in mind and let them direct you to the terminal for the best service (and if possible, book the ticket for you).

BY CAR

Getting around Peru by means of a rental car isn't the easiest or best option for the great majority of travelers. It is also far from the cheapest. Distances are long; the terrain is either difficult or unrelentingly boring for long stretches along the desert coast;

roads are often not in very good condition; Peruvian drivers are aggressive; and accident rates are very high. The U.S. State Department warns against driving in Peru, particularly at night or alone on rural roads at any time of day. A four-wheel-drive vehicle would be the best option in many places, but trucks and Jeeps are exceedingly expensive for most travelers.

However, if you want maximum flexibility and independence for travels in a particular region (say, to get around the Sacred Valley outside of Cusco, or to visit Colca Canyon beyond Arequipa) and you have several people to share the cost with you, a rental car could be a decent option. By no means plan to rent a car in Lima and head off for the major sights across the country; you'll spend all your time in the car. It is much more feasible to fly or take a bus to a given destination and rent a car there. The major international rental agencies are found in Lima, and a handful of international and local companies operate in other cities, such as Cusco and Arequipa. Costs average about $30 to $50 a day, plus 18% insurance, for an economy-size vehicle.

To rent a car, you need to be at least 25 years old and have a valid driver's license and passport. Deposit by credit card is usually required. Driving under the influence of alcohol or drugs is a criminal offense.

Major rental companies in Peru include **Avis** (© 01/575-0912, ext. 4155; www.avis.com); **Budget** (© 01/575-1674; www.budget.com); **Dollar** (© 01/444-3050); **Hertz** (© 01/575-1390; www.hertz.com); **InterService Rent a Car** (© 01/442-2256); **National Car Rental** (© 01/433-3750); and **Paz Rent a Car** (© 01/436-3941).

For mechanical assistance, contact the **Touring Automóvil Club del Perú** (Touring Club of Peru) in Lima at © **01/221-3225,** or in Cusco at 084/224-561.

12 Tips on Accommodations

A wide range of accommodations—including world-class luxury hotels in modern high-rise buildings and 16th-century monasteries, affordable small hotels in colonial houses, rustic rainforest lodges, and inexpensive budget inns—can be found in Peru. Midrange options have expanded in recent years, but the large majority of accommodations still court budget travelers and backpackers (outside Lima's hosting of international business travelers). During high season (June–Sept), and especially at times of national holidays and important festivals (Christmas, New Year's, Carnaval and Easter week, the week leading up to Inti Raymi, and Fiestas Patrias), advance reservations are recommended. This is especially true of hotels in the moderate and expensive categories in places such as Cusco and Machu Picchu.

Accommodations go by many names in Peru. *Hotel* generally refers only to comfortable hotels with a range of services, but *hostal* (or *hostales,* plural) is used for a wide variety of smaller hotels, inns, and pensions. (Note that "hostal" is distinct from the English-language term "hostel.") At the lower end are mostly *hospedajes, pensiones,* and *residenciales.* However, these terms are often poor indicators—if they are indicators at all—of an establishment's quality or services. Required signs outside reflect these categories: *H* (hotel); *Hs* (hostal); *HR* (hotel residencial); and *P* (pensión). The government's hotel-rating system, as in most countries, means that establishments are awarded stars for the presence of certain criteria—a pool, restaurant, elevator, and so on—more than for standards of luxury. Thus, it is not always true that the hotel with the most stars is necessarily the most comfortable or elegant. Luxury hotels are rare outside Lima and Cusco; budget accommodations are plentiful across the country, and many of them are quite good for the price. Some represent amazing values at under $30 a night for a double—with a dose of local character and breakfast, to boot.

Most published, or "rack," rates can be negotiated, and travelers can often get greatly reduced rates outside peak season simply by asking. This is especially true of jungle lodges, where published international prices differ greatly from the rate one might obtain on-site. Some hotels, especially at the upper end, quote room rates in U.S. dollars. Hotel taxes and service charges are an issue that has caused considerable grief in recent years, as most mid-to-upper-level hotels levied taxes of 18% and a service charge of an additional 10% to the bill. Legislation has been approved to do away with the service charge for foreign travelers (presentation of a passport is sufficient to have this charge dispensed with), but many hotels and their employees are still confused about its application. Many hotels—usually those at the mid- and lower ranges—simplify matters by including all taxes in their rates. Be sure to ask about taxes and service charges when you check in. Also note that at most budget and even many midrange hotels, credit cards are not accepted.

Safety is an issue at many hotels, especially at the lower end, and extreme care should be taken with regard to personal belongings left in the hotel. Leaving valuables lying around is asking for trouble. Hotels, except those at the lowest levels, should have safety deposit boxes. (Only luxury hotels have room safes.) Place your belongings in a carefully sealed envelope. If you arrive in a town without previously arranged accommodations, you should be at least minimally wary of taxi drivers and others who insist on showing you to a hotel. Occasionally, these will provide excellent tips, but, in general, they will merely be taking you to a place where they are confident they can earn a commission. A final precaution worth mentioning is the electric heater found on many showerheads. These can be dangerous, and touching them while functioning can prompt an unwelcome electric jolt.

The great majority of hotels in Peru are small and midsize independent inns; few international hotel chains operate in Peru. You'll find a Holiday Inn here, a Marriott, Best Western, or Orient-Express hotel there, but by and large, the chains you'll come into contact with are Peruvian chains. The most prominent, though they have only a handful of hotels each, are Sonesta, Libertador, and Don Carlos. Sonesta owns five Posadas del Inca hotels, which are 3- to 5-star hotels in the some of Peru's most trafficked locations (Lima, Cusco, the Sacred Valley, and Lake Titicaca). The hotels are extremely comfortable, decorated in similar schemes, and very good values. The Libertador hotels are elegant 4- and 5-star establishments, largely in historic buildings. Other Peruvian chains, such as Royal Inka and Don Carlos, have a few good 3-star properties but are, in general, more standard hotels.

TIPS FOR SAVING ON YOUR HOTEL ROOM

The **rack rate** is the maximum rate that a hotel charges for a room. It's the rate you'd get if you walked in off the street and asked for a room for the night. Hardly anybody pays these prices, however, and there are many ways around them.

- **Don't be afraid to bargain.** Most rack rates include commissions of 10% to 25% for travel agents, which some hotels may be willing to reduce if you make your own reservations and haggle a bit. Always ask whether a room less expensive than the first one quoted is available, or whether any special rates apply to you. You may qualify for corporate, student, military, senior citizen, or other discounts. Be sure to mention membership in AAA, AARP, frequent-flier programs, or trade unions, which may entitle you to special deals as well. Find out the hotel policy on children—do kids stay free in the room or is there a special rate?

- **Rely on a qualified professional.** Certain hotels give travel agents discounts in exchange for steering business their way, so if you're shy about bargaining, an agent may be better equipped to negotiate discounts for you.

- **Dial direct.** When booking a room in a chain hotel, compare the rates offered by the hotel's local line with that of the toll-free number. Also check with an agent and online. A hotel makes nothing on a room that stays empty, so the local hotel reservation desk may be willing to offer a special rate unavailable elsewhere.

- **Remember the law of supply and demand.** Resort hotels are most crowded and therefore most expensive on weekends, so discounts are usually available for midweek stays. Business hotels in downtown locations are busiest during the week, so you can expect big discounts over the weekend. Avoid high-season stays whenever you can: Planning your vacation just a week before or after official peak season can mean big savings.

- **Look into group or long-stay discounts.** If you come as part of a large group, you should be able to negotiate a bargain rate,

(Tips) Using a Cellphone on Your Trip

At this point, most wireless companies in North America do not provide roaming services overseas, which means it's still unlikely that you'll be able to use your own cellphone on your trip abroad. However, some telecommunications companies rent international cellphones that allow you to call from Peru. Renting a cellphone is much like renting a car: It comes fully equipped and ready to use—you just pick it up and go. Renting a phone before you leave home has its advantages:

• You know the phone number in advance to give to family and friends.

• The phone is delivered to you via Federal Express, UPS, or the like, and activated immediately.

• You can familiarize yourself with the phone before you leave home, instead of spending quality vacation time reading instructions.

• When you get home, you simply return the phone in the prepaid package provided for you.

• You can take the phone wherever you go; when you rent overseas, agencies bill in local currency and will not let you take the phone to another country.

Most wireless rental companies require a credit-card deposit and bill the customer at the end of the trip. Although prices vary widely, in general, using a rented cellphone is more expensive than using a telephone calling card but cheaper than calling direct from your hotel room. Most companies charge a basic rental fee (which may include activation and shipping fees) of $40 to $75, plus a per-minute rate for both outgoing and incoming calls (Nextel offers rates starting at $2.39 per min.). Know that if you plan to travel in different countries with different networks, you may need a separate phone for each. In addition, airtime rates vary from network to network and country to country. Bottom line: Shop around for the best deal.

A highly recommended wireless rental company is **InTouch USA** (© **800/872-7626**; www.intouchusa.com). Give them your itinerary, and they will tell you which wireless products and services you'll need. InTouch will also evaluate your own phone's international calling capabilities before you leave home. For this free evaluation, call © **703/ 222-7161** between 9am and 4pm.

because the hotel can then guarantee occupancy in a number of rooms. Likewise, if you're planning a long stay (at least 5 days), you may qualify for a discount. As a general rule, expect 1 night free after a 7-night stay.

• **Avoid excess charges.** When you book a room, ask whether the hotel charges for parking or telephone calls. Many hotels charge a fee just for dialing out on the phone in your room. Find out whether your hotel imposes a surcharge on local and long-distance calls. A pay phone, however inconvenient, may save you money, although many calling cards charge a fee when you use them on pay phones.

- **Consider a suite.** If you are traveling with your family or another couple, you can pack more people into a suite (which usually comes with a sofa bed), and thereby reduce your per-person rate. Remember that some places charge for extra guests.
- **Book an efficiency.** A room with a kitchenette allows you to shop for groceries and cook your own meals. This is a big money-saver, especially for families on long stays.
- Join hotel **frequent-visitor clubs,** even if you don't use them much. You'll be more likely to get upgrades and other perks.
- Many hotels offer **frequent-flier points.** Don't forget to ask for yours when you check in.

LANDING THE BEST ROOM

Somebody has to get the best room in the house. It might as well be you.

Always ask about a corner room. They're often larger and quieter, with more windows and light, and they often cost the same as standard rooms.

When you make your reservation, ask whether the hotel is renovating; if it is, request a room away from the construction. Ask about nonsmoking rooms, rooms with views, and rooms with twin, queen-, or king-size beds. If you're a light sleeper, request a quiet room away from vending machines, elevators, restaurants, bars, and discos. Ask for one of the rooms that have been most recently renovated or redecorated.

If you aren't happy with your room when you arrive, talk to the front desk. If they have another room, they may be willing to accommodate you. Join the hotel's frequent-visitor club; you may qualify for upgrades.

Here are some other questions to ask before you book a room:

- What's the view like? Cost-conscious travelers may be willing to pay less for a back room facing the parking lot, especially if they don't plan to spend much time in their room.
- Does the room have air-conditioning or just ceiling fans?
- Do the windows open?
- What is the noise level outside the room? If the climate is warm, and nighttime entertainment takes place alfresco, you may want to find out when showtime is over.
- What's included in the price? Your room may be moderately priced, but if you're charged for beach chairs, towels, sports equipment, and other amenities, you could end up spending more than you bargained for.
- Are airport transfers included in the price?
- If it's off-season, will any facilities be shut down while you're there?
- If it's off-season, what is the occupancy rate?
- What programs are available for kids?
- How far is the room from the beach?
- What is the cancellation policy?

13 Tips on Dining

Peruvian cuisine is incredibly varied and accomplished, for many travelers an exciting and delicious surprise. It is among the best and most diverse cuisines found in Latin America, and is one of the most important contributors to the wave of pan-Latino restaurants gaining popularity in many parts of the world. Peruvian cooking differs significantly by region, and subcategories mirror exactly the country's geographical variety: coastal, highlands, and tropical. The common denominator among them is a blend of indigenous and Spanish (or broader European) influences, which has evolved over the past 4 centuries. In addition to Peruvian cooking, visitors will also find plenty of international restaurants, including a particularly Peruvian variation, *chifas* (Peruvian-influenced Chinese food, developed by the large immigrant Chinese population), a mainstay among many non-Chinese Peruvians. Chifas are nearly as common as restaurants serving *pollo a la brasa* (spit-roasted chicken), which are everywhere in Peru. Traditional Peruvian coastal cooking is often referred to as *comida criolla*, and it's found across Peru.

Coastal preparations concentrate on seafood and shellfish, as might be expected. The star dish is ceviche, a classic preparation of raw fish and shellfish marinated (not cooked) in lime or lemon juice and hot chili peppers, served with raw onion, sweet potato, and toasted corn. Ceviche has been around since the time of some of Peru's earliest civilizations, though a traditional Andean argument over whether Peruvians or Ecuadorians should be credited with creating it persists. Cevicherías usually serve several types of ceviche as well as a good roster of other seafood. Other coastal favorites include *escabeche* (a tasty fish concoction served with peppers, eggs, olives, onions, and prawns), *conchitas* (scallops) and *corvina* (sea bass). Land-based favorites are *cabrito* (roast kid) and *ají de gallina* (a tangy creamed chicken and chili dish).

Highlanders favor a more substantial style of cooking. Corn and potatoes were staples of the Incas and other mountain civilizations before them. Meat, served with rice and potatoes, is a mainstay of the diet, as is trout (*trucha*). *Lomo saltado*, strips of beef mixed with onions, tomatoes, peppers, and french-fried potatoes and served with rice, seems to be on every menu. *Rocoto relleno*, a hot bell pepper stuffed with vegetables and meat, and *papa rellena*, a potato stuffed with veggies and then fried, are just as common (but are occasionally extremely spicy). Soups are excellent. In the countryside, you may see people in the fields digging small cooking holes in the ground. They are preparing *pachamanca*, a roast cooked over stones. It's the Peruvian version of a picnic; on weekends, you'll often see families outside Cusco and other places stirring smoking fires in the ground while the kids play soccer nearby. *Cuy* (guinea pig) is considered a delicacy in many parts of Peru, including the sierra, but its elevated status was never much apparent to me. It comes roasted or fried, with head and feet upturned on the plate.

In the Amazon jungle regions, most people fish for their food, and their diets consist almost entirely of fish such as river trout and *paiche* (a huge river fish). Restaurants feature both of these, with accompaniments including *yuca* (a root), *palmitos* (palm hearts) and *chonta* (palm-heart salad), bananas and plantains, and rice tamales known as *juanes*. Common menu items such as chicken and game are complemented by exotic fare such

Tips Dining on the Cheap

With the possible exception of Lima, it's possible for all but the most budget-conscious travelers to dine out in Peru's fanciest restaurants. In the first place, outside the capital, the top restaurants are generally not that fancy. Informal clothes and even outdoor duds such as hiking boots and fleece wear are perfectly acceptable. Second, prices for most dinner entrees are $10 or even less. And third, most of these upscale restaurants offer great-value fixed-price meals, often for not much more than $5.

as caiman, wild boar, turtle, monkey, and piranha fish.

Drinking is less of an event in Peru. Peruvian wines and beers can't really compare with superior examples found elsewhere on the continent (Chile and Argentina, predominantly). Yet one indigenous drink stands out: *pisco*, a powerful white-grape brandy. The pisco sour (a cocktail mixed with pisco, egg whites, lemon juice, sugar, and bitters) is effectively Peru's margarita: tasty, refreshing, and ubiquitous. Pisco is also taken straight. Peruvians everywhere drink *chicha*, a tangy, fermented brew made from maize and inherited from the Incas. Often served warm in huge glasses, it is unlikely to please the palates of most foreign visitors, though it's certainly worth a try if you come upon a small, informal place with the chicha flag flying in a rural village (literally—it means something akin to "fresh chicha available inside"). *Chicha morada*, on the other hand, is a nonalcoholic beverage, deep purple in color, prepared with blue corn. *Masato* is a beer made from yuca, typical of the Amazon region.

Among the more interesting dining customs—beyond the eating of guinea pig—is the lovely habit of offering a sip of beer or chicha before the meal to Pachamama, or Mother Earth. Many Peruvians still ritualistically thank the earth for its bounty, and they show their appreciation by spilling just a bit before raising the drink to their own mouths.

Restaurants range from the rustic and incredibly inexpensive to polished places with impeccable service and international menus. Set three-course meals are referred to by a variety of terms: *menú del día, menú económico, menú ejecutivo, menú de la casa,* and *menú turístico.* They are all essentially the same thing, and can sometimes be had for as little as $2. In general, you should ask about the preparation of many Peruvian dishes, as many are quite spicy. Informal eateries serving Peruvian cooking are frequently called *picanterías* and *chicherías.* Fancy restaurants may add a service charge of 10% and an additional tax of up to 18%. Less-expensive restaurants usually either charge a 5% tax or no additional tax or service charge.

Note: Many nicer restaurants will place a couple of small plates of cheese, sausage, olives, or other tidbits on your table to nibble on as you wait for your meal. In almost all cases, you will be charged for these items, called

 The Pisco Sour

Peru's pisco sour is the national drink of choice—something like an Andean margarita. You can get one virtually anywhere in the country, but to mix one at home, here's what you need:

1½ ounces pisco
1 teaspoon sugar
½ ounce Key lime juice
1 egg white
crushed ice
Angostura bitters

Blend the pisco with sugar and lime juice. Add ice and the egg white. Blend, pour into a small glass, and top with a few drops of Angostura bitters.

> **Tips Peruvian Cuisine Online**
>
> For more information on Peruvian cooking, check out **www.cocinaperuana. com**, which features a history of Peruvian cuisine, glossary, recipes, and a guide to restaurants in Peru.

a *cubierto,* or cover. Usually, it'll add S/6 to S/10 ($1.70–$3) to your bill. If you don't touch the stuff, in theory you shouldn't have to pay for it because you didn't order it, but many restaurants automatically tack on the charge and few are the customers that don't consider the cubierto part of the cost of eating out.

Dining hours are not much different from typical mealtimes in cities in North America or Great Britain, except that dinner (*cena*) is generally eaten after 8pm in restaurants. Peruvians do not eat nearly as late as Spaniards, and although lunch (*almuerzo*) is the main meal of the day, for most visitors it generally will not be the grand midday affair it is in Spain, unless you are dining at an outdoor *quinta,* where most locals linger over lunch for a couple hours.

Tipping is customary in most restaurants, but it's not obligatory. In general, you should tip about 10% of the bill. In some upper-echelon restaurants, a service charge of 10% and tax of 18% are included on the bill. Even if service is included, many customers also leave a small amount of additional change as a tip to the waiter. In very informal, budget restaurants, tipping is often not customary among Peruvians, though you might consider leaving some change after having what will surely have been a very inexpensive meal.

14 Tips on Shopping

Peru is one of the top shopping destinations in Latin America, with some of the finest and best-priced crafts anywhere. Its long traditions of textile weaving and colorful markets bursting with tourists have produced a dazzling display of alpaca-wool sweaters, blankets, ponchos, shawls, scarves, typical Peruvian hats, and other woven items. Peru's ancient indigenous civilizations were some of the world's greatest potters, and reproductions of Moche, Nasca, Paracas, and other ceramics are available. (Until recently, it was surprisingly easy to get your hands on the real thing, but that's no longer the case.) In some cities—especially Lima, Cusco, and Arequipa—antique textiles and ceramics are still available. Some dealers handle pieces that are 1,000 years old or more (and others simply claim their pieces are that old). However,

exporting such pre-Columbian artifacts from Peru is illegal.

Lima and Cusco have the lion's share of tourist-oriented shops and markets—particularly in Lima, you can find items produced all over the country—but other places may be just as good for shopping. Locals in Puno and Taquile Island on Lake Titicaca produce spectacular textiles, and Arequipa is perhaps the best place in Peru to purchase very fine, extremely soft baby-alpaca items. Handcrafted retablos from Ayacucho, depicting weddings and other domestic scenes, are famous throughout Peru and are available across the country. The Shipibo tribe of the northern Amazon produces excellent hand-painted textiles and decorative pottery. You'll also see items in the jungle made from endangered species—alligator skins, turtle shells, and the like. Purchasing these items is illegal, and it only encourages locals to further harm the natural environment and its inhabitants.

Baby alpaca and very rare vicuña are the finest woolens and are amazingly soft. Though merchants are happy to claim that every woven wool item in their possession is alpaca or baby alpaca, in fact much of what is sold in many tourist centers is anything but. Most, if not all, the very cheap ($5–$15) sweaters, shawls, hats, and gloves are made of acrylic or acrylic blends. If your new "alpaca" sweater stinks when it gets wet, it's llama wool. If you want the real thing—which is not cheap, but is much less expensive than you'd pay for alpaca of such fine

quality in other countries—visit one of the established chain stores in large cities (most have "alpaca" in the name). Arequipa is one of the finest centers for alpaca goods.

There are scores of general, look-alike *artesanía* shops in most tourist centers, and prices may not be any higher than what you'd find at street markets. At both stores and in open markets, bargaining—gentle, good-natured haggling over prices—is accepted and even expected. However, when it gets down to ridiculously small amounts of money, it's best to recognize that you are already getting a great deal on probably handmade goods and relinquish the fight over a few *soles*.

15 Suggested Itineraries

Unless you have at least 3 weeks or a month to spend in Peru, you probably won't get to see as much of the country as you'd like. It's large, and there are considerable geographic and transportation barriers that make zipping around Peru very difficult. A real danger is trying to do too much in a short period. Even on relatively short trips of 2 weeks or less, you have to take into account those hefty distances and complicated transportation routes, not to mention natural factors—such as jet lag and acclimatization to high altitude—that require most visitors to slow down.

A WEEK IN CUSCO & THE SACRED VALLEY In a single week, there's really only enough time to see the best of Inca Peru. Rest assured, though, that such an itinerary includes the absolute highlight of the country and a couple of the finest sights in all of South America. Arrive in **Lima** and spend a day at two of the best museums in the country, Museo de la Nación and Museo de Oro. Fly to **Cusco** the next day and spend 2 nights there, enjoying the beauty of

the ancient Inca capital and visiting the **Sacsayhuamán** ruins. Visit **Machu Picchu** on the fourth day (by train or helicopter), and the next day, take a quick tour of the principal **Sacred Valley** sights. Spend the night in Ollantaytambo or Urubamba before heading back to Cusco. The following day, return to Lima and spend your last day in the colonial center.

A 2-WEEK HIGHLIGHTS TOUR Even 2 weeks in Peru involves making several hard choices: Though it's tempting to try to hop around the country, distances and transportation don't really allow much of that in a short time. The first week could be spent as above, though it may be necessary to scale back on the Sacred Valley if you're intent on seeing another, very different part of the country.

During the second week, you'll have to choose. One option would be to do a short jungle excursion to **Puerto Maldonado** and **Tambopata** from Cusco (3–4 days) and then head south to **Lake Titicaca,** arranging an overnight stay at one of the lake's islands (2–3 days). From Puno (Lake Titicaca) you could travel by bus to Juliaca and then fly back to Lima. Alternatively, from Cusco you could head directly to Lake Titicaca (by train or bus) and, after visiting the city of Puno and the islands (3 days), head west to **Arequipa** and **Colca Canyon** to see the giant condors (3–4 days), before flying back to Lima. A third option would be to substitute the northern jungle for Arequipa. From Puno/Juliaca, fly north (through Cusco or Lima) to **Iquitos** and arrange a short jungle-lodge excursion (4–5 days total). Either of these last options requires about 4 days including transportation.

A 2-WEEK NATURE IMMER-SION Arrive in Lima and fly the next morning to **Cusco;** spend 2 or 3 days in the ancient Inca capital and acclimate yourself to the high altitude. Then do either the classic 4-day **Inca Trail** to Machu Picchu or the 2-day trek (if you do the latter, you'll have more time for other outdoors activities in the Sacred Valley, such as river rafting). Then choose a jungle lodge or camping excursion, either traveling by land and air to the **Manu Biosphere Reserve** or flying from Cusco to **Iquitos** in the northern Amazon. You'll need a minimum of 4 to 5 days for either (though many Manu trips are 7 days or longer), including transportation. If short on time, consider a jungle lodge tour to **Tambopata.** From Manu or Puerto Maldonado, you'll have to return to Cusco before flying on to Lima.

Hard-core trekkers could substitute hiking and mountain climbing in the **Cordillera Blanca** in place of a jungle excursion. For example, from Lima, you could travel by bus and spend 4 to 5 days trekking in the mountains and valleys outside of Huaraz. You could then return to Lima and spend the second week in Cusco and along the Inca Trail to Machu Picchu.

16 Recommended Reading

NONFICTION

The classic work on Inca history and the Spanish conquistadors is *The Conquest of the Incas* (Harvest Books, 1973) by John Hemming, a very readable narrative of the fall of a short-lived but uniquely accomplished empire. *Lost City of the Incas: The Story of Machu Picchu and Its Builders* (Atheneum, 1972), is the travelogue and still-amazing story of Hiram Bingham, the Yale academic who brought the "lost city" to the world's attention in 1911. Because it's out of print, you may have to uncover a copy in a used-bookstore, but Bingham's book makes for a very interesting read, especially after so many years of speculation and theory about the site.

The Incas and their Ancestors, by Michael Moseley (Thames and Hudson, 2001), is a good account of the Inca Empire and, importantly, its lesser-known predecessors. For most readers, it will serve as a good introduction to Peru's archaeology and the sites they will visit, though some people may find that it reads too much like a textbook. Illustrations include black-and-white photographs of Inca drawings and a few color photos. A terrific story of a recent archaeological find is *Discovering the Ice Maiden: My Adventures on Ampato* by Johan Reinhard (National Geographic Society, 1998). Reinhard's account of his discovery of a mummified Inca princess sacrificed 500 years ago on a volcano summit in southern Peru details the team's search and their race to save what is considered one of the most important archaeological discoveries in recent decades. The book contains excellent color photographs of the maiden who can now be viewed in Arequipa.

The Peru Reader: History, Culture, Politics, Orin Starn et al., ed. (Duke University Press, 1995), is one of the finest primers on Peru's recent history and political culture. It includes essays by several distinguished voices, including Mario Vargas Llosa.

Naturalists and birders may want to pick up *A Field Guide to the Birds of Peru* by James F. Clements (Ibis Pub Co., 2001), though it is perhaps not the comprehensive field guide a country as biologically diverse as Peru deserves. It is welcomed but simultaneously derided by many hard-core birders as incomplete and error-ridden. Many prefer *A Guide to the Birds of Colombia* by Steven Hilty and William Brown (Princeton University Press, 1986), probably the definitive regional guide (and covering many of the birds also found in Peru). Also of interest is *A Parrot Without a Name: The Search for the Last Unknown Birds on Earth* by Don Stap (University of Texas Press, 1991), an account of John O'Neill and LSU scientists documenting new species in the jungles of Peru.

Peru: The Ecotravellers' Wildlife Guide, by biologists David Pearson and Les Beletsky (Academic Press, 2000), is a 500-page handbook survey of Peruvian flora and fauna, including information about conservation, habitats, national parks, and reserves. It's a good introduction for readers ready to explore the Peruvian outdoors, from the Andes to the Amazon and other repositories of Peru's magnificent animal and plant life. The book is nicely illustrated and useful for identification purposes.

Peter Frost's *Exploring Cusco* (Nuevas Imágenes, 1999) is one of the best-detailed local guides, with excellent historical information and frank commentary by the author, a longtime Cusco resident, on the ancient Inca capital, the Sacred Valley and, of course, Machu Picchu. *Peru & Bolivia: Backpacking and Trekking,* by Hilary Bradt et al. (Bradt Publications, 1999), is a trusty guide, now in its third decade, of classic treks in Peru and Bolivia. Though it's in its seventh edition, with several new walks and treks added, some readers still find it out of date. Still, it's a good all-around guide for trekkers and walkers.

The Cloud Forest: A Chronicle of the South American Wilderness (Ingram, 1996) is a travelogue by Peter Matthiessen, who trekked some 10,000 miles through South America, including the Amazon and Machu Picchu. Matthiessen finds larger-than-life characters and ancient trails deep in the jungle, experiences that led to the author's fictional novel, *At Play in the Fields of the Lord* (Vintage Books, 1991). Set in the unnamed Peruvian jungle, it's a thriller about the travails of the missionary Martin Quarrier and an outsider, Lewis Moon, a mercenary who takes a much different tack while immersing himself in a foreign culture. Both are displaced outsiders whose lives have an irreversible impact on native Amerindian communities deep in the Amazon. The book was later made into an occasionally pretty but silly movie starring John Lithgow, Daryl Hannah, and Tom Beringer with a bowl-cut and face paint.

FICTION

The towering figure in contemporary Peruvian fiction is Mario Vargas Llosa, Peru's most famous novelist and a perennial candidate for the Nobel Prize, who was nearly elected the country's president back in 1990. It's difficult to choose from among his oeuvre of thoroughly praised works; *Aunt Julia and the Scriptwriter* (Penguin, 1995) is one of his most popular works, but it's without the heft of others, such as *The Real Life of Alejandro Mayta* (Noonday Press, 1998), a dense meditation on Peruvian and South American revolutionary politics that blurs the lines between truth and fiction, or *Death in the Andes* (Penguin, 1997), a deep penetration into the contemporary psyche and politics of Peru. Another side of the author is evident in the small erotic gem *In Praise of the Stepmother* (Penguin, 1991), a surprising and beautifully illustrated book. His powerful latest book, *The Feast of the Goat* (Farrar Straus & Giroux, 2001), about the Dominican dictator Rafael Trujillo, made the year-end best lists of many critics in 2001. Vargas Llosa may be a difficult and "heavy" writer, but he is an unusually engaging one.

César Vallejo, born in Peru in 1892, is one of Latin America's and the Spanish language's great poets. *Complete Posthumous Poetry* (University of California Press, 1980), in translation, and *Trilce* (Wesleyan University Press, 2000), a bilingual publication, are the best places to start with this great poet. Vallejo wrote some of the poems in *Trilce,* a wildly creative and innovative avant-garde work that today is considered a masterpiece of modernism, while in prison. Vallejo later fled to Europe and immersed himself in the Spanish Civil War.

 FAST FACTS: Peru

Addresses "Jr." doesn't mean "junior"; it is a designation meaning "Jirón," or street, just as "Av." (sometimes "Avda.") is an abbreviation for "Avenida," or avenue. Perhaps the most confusing element in Peruvian street addresses is "s/n," which frequently appears in place of a number after the name of the street. "S/n" means "sin número," or no number. The house or building with such an address simply is unnumbered.

Area Codes Lima, 01; Ica, Nasca, and Pisco, 034; Cusco, Sacred Valley, and Puerto Maldonado, 084; Puno/Lake Titicaca, 054; Arequipa, 054; Huaraz, Trujillo, and Cajamarca, 044; Chiclayo, 074; Iquitos, 094.

ATMs See "Money," earlier in this chapter

Business Hours Most stores are open from 9 or 10am to 12:30pm, and from 3 to 5 or 8pm. Banks are generally open Monday through Friday from 9:30am to 4pm, though some stay open until 6pm. In major cities, most banks are also open Saturday from 9:30am to 12:30pm. Offices are open 8:30am to 12:30pm and 3 to 6pm, though many operate continuously from 9am to 5pm. Government offices are open Monday through Friday from 9:30am to 12:30pm and 3 to 5pm.

Car Rentals See "Getting Around," earlier in this chapter.

Climate See "When to Go," earlier in this chapter.

Currency See "Money," earlier in this chapter.

Doctors & Hospitals Medical care is of a generally high standard in Lima, Cusco, and Arequipa, and adequate in other major cities, where you are likely to find English-speaking doctors. However, medical care is of a lesser standard in rural areas and small villages, where it is much less common to find an English-speaking physician. Many physicians and hospitals require immediate cash payment for health services, and they do not accept U.S. medical insurance (even if your policy applies overseas). You should check with your insurance company to see if your policy provides for overseas medical evacuation.

Documents See "Visitor Information" and "Entry Requirements & Customs," earlier in this chapter.

Driving Rules See "Getting Around," earlier in this chapter.

Drug Laws Until recently, Peru was the world's largest producer of coca-leaves, the base product that is mostly shipped to Colombia for processing into cocaine. Cocaine and other illegal substances are perhaps not as ubiquitous in Peru as one might think, though in Lima and Cusco, they are commonly offered to foreigners. (This is especially dangerous; many would-be dealers also operate as police informants, and some are said to be undercover narcotics officers themselves.) Penalties for the possession and use of or trafficking in illegal drugs in Peru are strict; convicted offenders can expect long jail sentences and substantial fines. Peruvian police routinely detain drug smugglers at Lima's international airport and land-border crossings. Since 1995, 3 dozen U.S. citizens have been convicted of narcotics trafficking in Peru. If arrested on drug charges, you will face protracted pretrial detention in poor prison conditions.

Coca leaves, either chewed or brewed for tea, are not illegal in Peru, where they're not considered a narcotic. The use of coca leaves is an ancient tradition dating back to pre-Columbian civilizations in Peru. You may very well find that mate de coca (coca-leaf tea) is very helpful in battling altitude sickness. However, if you attempt to take coca leaves back to your home country from Peru, you should expect them to be confiscated, and you could even find yourself prosecuted.

Drugstores For locations, consult a phone book's Yellow Pages under "Farmacias" and "Boticas." In Lima, large, multiservice pharmacies that are open 24 hours include **Farmacia Deza,** Av. Conquistadores 1140, San Isidro (© **01/440-3798**), and branches of the chain **Superfarma** (one is at Av. Benavides 2849; © **01/222-1575**).

Electricity All outlets are 220 volts, 60 cycles AC (except in Arequipa, which operates on 50 cycles) with two-prong outlets that accept both flat and round prongs. Some large hotels also have 110-volt outlets.

Embassies & Consulates The following are all in Lima: **U.S.,** Avenida La Encalada, block 17, Monterrico (© 01/434-3000); **Australia,** Víctor A. Belaúnde 147/Vía Principal 155, building 3, office no. 1301, San Isidro (© 01/222-8281); **Canada,** Libertad 130, Miraflores (© 01/444-4015); **U.K.** and **New Zealand,** Natalio Sánchez 125, 4th floor (© 01/433-8923); **South Africa,** Vía Principal 155, office no. 801, San Isidro (© 01/440-9996); and **Ireland,** Angamos Oeste 340, Miraflores (© 01/446-3878). The **United States** maintains a consulate in Cusco, at the Instituto Cultural Peruano-Norte Americano (ICPNA), Av. Tullumayo 125–127 (© 084/224-112); the **United Kingdom** also has a consulate in Cusco at Av. Pardo 895 (© 084/226-671).

Emergencies In case of an emergency, call the 24-hour **traveler's hot line** at © **01/574-8000** or the **tourist police** (in Lima, © **01/225-8698;** see "Fast Facts" in individual destination chapters for branch information). The general police emergency number is © **105.** The **Tourist Protection Service** can also assist in contacting police to report a crime; call © **01/ 224-7888** in Lima, or 0800/4-2579 toll-free from any private phone (the toll-free number cannot be dialed from a public pay phone).

Etiquette & Customs See "Etiquette & Customs" in Appendix A, "Peru in Depth."

Guides Officially licensed guides are available on-site at many archaeological sites and other places of interest to foreigners. They can be contracted directly, though you should verify their ability to speak English if you do not comprehend Spanish well. Establish a price beforehand. Many cities are battling a scourge of unlicensed and unscrupulous guides who provide inferior services or, worse, cheat visitors. As a general rule, do not accept unsolicited offers to arrange excursions, transportation, and hotel accommodations.

Holidays See "When to Go," earlier in this chapter

Information See "Visitor Information," earlier in this chapter.

Internet Access Public Internet booths, or *cabinas,* have proliferated throughout Peru. Most cities have several, if not dozens, to choose from, but few are of the cybercafe variety. Most are simple cubicles with terminals; occasionally, printers are available. The average cost for 1 hour is very inexpensive, usually less than $1. Many cabinas now feature software to make very inexpensive international phone calls via the Internet. Only the best hotels have modem lines in the rooms. Note that Internet locations open and close all the time. A partial but current list of sites (mostly in Lima) can be found at http://cybercaptive.com.

Language Spanish is the official language of Peru. The Amerindian languages Quechua (recently given official status) and Aymara are spoken primarily in the highlands. (Aymara is mostly limited to the area around Lake Titicaca.) English is not widely spoken but is understood by those affiliated with the tourist industry in major cities and tourist destinations. Most people you meet on the street will have only a very rudimentary understanding of English, if that. Learning a few key phrases of Spanish will help immensely. Check the glossary at the back of this book and consider picking up a copy of the *Berlitz Latin American Spanish Language* dictionary.

Legal Matters If you need legal assistance, your best bets are your embassy (which, depending on the situation, may not be able to help you much) and the **Tourist Protection Service** (© 0800/4-2579 toll-free, or 01/574-8000 24 hr.), which may be able to direct you to an English-speaking attorney or legal assistance organization.

Note that bribing a police officer or public official is illegal in Peru, even if it is a relatively constant feature of traffic stops and the like.

If a police officer claims to be an undercover cop, do not automatically assume he is telling the truth. Do not get in any vehicle with such a person. Demand the assistance of either your embassy or consulate, or of the Tourist Protection Service.

Liquor Laws A legal drinking age is not strictly enforced in Peru. Anyone over the age of 16 is unlikely to have any problems ordering liquor in any bar or other establishment. Wine, beer, and alcohol are widely available—sold daily at grocery stores, liquor stores, and in all cafes, bars, and restaurants—and consumed widely, especially in public during festivals. There appears to be very little taboo associated with public inebriation at festivals. Bars are open until midnight or later, while nightclubs and discos are often open until dawn.

Mail Peru's postal service is reasonably efficient, especially now that it is managed by a private company (**Serpost S.A.**). Post offices are open Monday through Saturday from 8am to 8pm; some are also open Sunday from 9am to 1pm. Major cities have a main post office and often several smaller branch offices. Letters and postcards to North America take between 10 days and 2 weeks and cost S/3.30 (95 ¢); to Europe, S/4.20 ($1.20). If you are purchasing large quantities of textiles and other hand-icrafts, you can send packages home from post offices, but it is not inexpensive—more than $100 for 10 kilograms (22 lb.), similar to what it costs to use DHL, where you're likely to have an easier time communicating. UPS is found in several cities, but for inexplicable reasons, its courier services cost nearly three times as much as DHL.

Maps Good topographical maps are available from the **Instituto Geográfico Nacional** (IGN), located at Av. Aramburú 1190, San Isidro, Lima (𝒞 01/ 475-9960 or 01/475-3030). Hiking maps are available from the **South American Explorers,** Piura 135, Miraflores, Lima (𝒞 **01/445-3306**).

Newspapers & Magazines In Lima, you will find copies (though rarely same-day publications) of the *International Herald Tribune,* the *Miami Herald,* and the odd European newspaper, as well as *Time, Newsweek,* and other special-interest publications. All may be at least several days old. Top-flight hotels sometimes offer free daily fax summations of the *New York Times* to their guests. Otherwise, your best source for timely news is likely to be checking in with news outlet websites. Outside Lima, international newspapers and magazines are hard to come by. Among local publications, look for *Rumbos,* a glossy Peruvian travel magazine in English and Spanish with excellent photography. If you read Spanish, *El Comercio* and *La República* are two of the best daily newspapers.

Police Peru has special tourist police forces (*Policía Nacional de Turismo*) with offices and personnel in all major tourist destinations, including Lima, Cusco, Arequipa, and Puno, as well as a dozen other cities. You are more likely to get a satisfactory response, not to mention someone who speaks at least some English, from the tourist police rather than from the regular national police (PNP). The number for the tourist police in Lima is 𝒞 **01/225-8698** or 01/225-8699. For other cities, see "Fast Facts" in individual destination chapters. Tourist police officers are distinguished by their white shirts.

Safety See "Insurance, Health & Safety," earlier in this chapter.

Smoking Smoking is extremely common in Peru, and it is rare to find a hotel, restaurant, or bar with nonsmoking rooms. However, there are now a few hotels (only at the 4- or 5-star levels) and restaurants with nonsmoking rooms, and the trend is growing, albeit slowly. There are nonsmoking cars on trains and most long-distance buses are also non-smoking.

Taxes A general sales tax (IGV), is added automatically to most consumer bills (18%). In some upmarket hotels or restaurants, service charges of 10% are often added. At all airports, passengers must pay a departure tax: $25 for international flights, S/12 or $3.40 for domestic flights, payable in cash only.

Telephone & Fax Peru's telephone system has been much improved since it was privatized and acquired by Spain's Telefónica in the mid-1990s. (There are now several additional players in the market, including Bell South.) It is relatively simple to make local and long-distance domestic and international calls from pay phones, which accept coins and phone cards (*tarjetas telefónicas*). Most phone booths display country and city codes and contain instructions in English and Spanish.

For local calls, you do not need to dial the area code (01 for Lima, 3 digits for all other cities); dial only the number. To make a long-distance call within Peru, dial the city code (including the zero) + telephone number. For international calls, dial 00 + country code + city code + telephone number. For information and directory assistance, dial ✆ **103**; for international dialing/operator assistance, dial ✆ **108**. Peru's country code is **51**.

Numbers beginning with 0800 within Peru are toll-free when called from a private phone (not from a public pay phone), but calling an 800 number in the States from Peru is not toll-free. In fact, it costs the same as an overseas call.

The easiest way to make a long-distance call is to purchase a phone card (maximum S/30, or $9). Many of these cards, purchased at newspaper kiosks and street vendors who sell nothing else, are called "Tarjeta 147." To use such a card, first rub off the secret number. Dial the numbers 1-4-7 and then dial the 12-digit number on your card. A voice recording will tell you (in Spanish only) the value remaining on the card and instruct you to dial the desired telephone number. It will then tell you how many minutes you can expect to talk with the amount remaining. You can also make international calls from Telefónica offices and hotels, though surcharges levied at the latter can be extraordinarily expensive. A new and very inexpensive way to make international calls is through Internet software such as "Net2Phone," which more and more Internet booths in Peru are featuring. Rates are as low as 20¢ per minute to the United States. Some cabinas even have private booths from which to talk. Reception, however, can be spotty.

Fax services are available at many hotels, but they are expensive, especially for international numbers ($3 per page and up). It is much easier to communicate by e-mail at Internet cabinas.

Time Zone Peru is 5 hours behind GMT (Greenwich mean time). Peru does not observe daylight saving time.

Tipping Most people leave about a 10% tip for the wait staff in restaurants. In nicer restaurants that add a 10% service charge, many patrons tip an additional 5% or a few coins for good service (because little if any of that service charge will ever make it to the waiter's pocket). Taxi drivers are not usually tipped unless they provide additional service. Bilingual tour guides should be tipped (about $1 per person for a short visit, $3 or more per person for a full day).

Toilets Public toilets are rarely available except in railway stations, restaurants, and theaters. Many Peruvian men choose to urinate in public, against a wall in full view, especially late at night; it's not recommended that you emulate them. Use the bathroom of a bar, cafe, or restaurant; if it feels uncomfortable to dart in and out, have a coffee at the bar. Public restrooms are labeled *WC* (water closet), *Damas* (Ladies), and *Caballeros* or *Hombres* (Men). Toilet paper is not always provided, and when it is, most establishments request that patrons throw it in the wastebasket rather than the toilet, to avoid clogging.

Water Visitors should drink only bottled water, which is widely available. Do not drink tap water, even in major hotels. Try to avoid drinks with ice. *Agua con gas* is carbonated; *agua sin gas* is still.

3

The Active Vacation Planner

The word "Peru" is derived from a word in Quechua signifying "land of abundance." There is little question that, in its distinct *costa, sierra,* and *selva* (coast, highlands, and jungle) regions, Peru is indeed blessed with an enormous variety of wilderness and some of the world's greatest and most diverse plant and animal species. It has been reported that Peru contains 84 of the known 104 biosystems in the world; more than 400 species of mammals and 300 species of reptiles; 50,000 plant species (among them the world's highest count of orchids, more than 3,000 kinds); and nearly 2,000 bird species, about 10% of the world's total. With desert sands, dense Amazon rain-forest canopy, amazing Andes peaks, and the world's deepest canyons, Peru is a country that definitely inspires travelers to get active and get outdoors.

Peru is perhaps the most diverse and best-equipped outdoors destination in South America. It is now rare to see visitors from abroad come to Peru with the intention of staying clean and dry in pressed slacks and loafers. Almost every gringo who sets foot outside of Lima is more properly outfitted in Gore-Tex water-repellent gear, fleece pullovers, hiking boots, and daypacks. However, in the minds of many nonspecialists, getting outside in Peru is still limited to easily reached jungle treks and lodges, day hikes in the valleys, and—if you're really adventurous—treks along ancient Inca trails.

Amazingly, given its natural abundance, Peru is still relatively new to the ecotourism game. Its infrastructure to receive large groups of ecotourists is not quite as developed as that of some other countries, such as Costa Rica. But Peru is quickly catching up, and tour operators, guides, and agencies, both local and international, are increasingly specializing in outdoor and active travel. The oldest jungle lodges in the Peruvian Amazon have been around for more than 30 years. Lodges, climbing and rafting expeditions, and birding and hiking trips all cater to environmentally aware travelers with deep interests in nature and seeing "the real Peru."

Whether you want to make active travel the sole focus of your trip or treat it as just an add-on, there are many different ways to approach it. This chapter lays out your options, from tour operators who run multiactivity package tours (and frequently include stays at eco-lodges) to the best spots in Peru to get outdoors (with listings of tour operators, guides, and outfitters that specialize in each) and an overview of the country's national parks and nature reserves. You'll also find a handful of tips on health and safety in the wilderness, what to bring, and educational and volunteer travel options for those with the time and desire to work towards the maintenance and preservation of Peru's natural wonders and gain a more in-depth understanding of Peru's culture and people.

1 Organized Adventure Trips

Because most travelers have limited time and resources, organized ecotourism or adventure travel packages, arranged by tour operators abroad or in Peru, are popular ways of combining cultural and outdoor activities. Bird-watching, horseback riding, rafting, and hiking can be teamed with visits to destinations such as Cusco, the Sacred (Urubamba) Valley and Machu Picchu, or Arequipa and Lake Titicaca.

Traveling with a group has several advantages over traveling independently. Your accommodations and transportation are arranged, and most (if not all) of your meals are included in the cost of a package. If your tour operator has a reasonable amount of experience and a decent track record, you should proceed to each of your destinations quickly without the snags and long delays that you might face if you're traveling on your own. You'll also have the opportunity to meet like-minded travelers who are interested in nature and active sports. Some group trekking trips include *porteros* or *arrieros* (porters or muleteers) who carry extra equipment. On some luxury treks of the Inca Trail, porters will even carry your backpack, so all you have to do is hike your lazy self up the mountain passes.

In the best cases of organized outdoors travel, group size is kept small (10–15 people), and tours are escorted by knowledgeable guides who are either naturalists or biologists. Be sure to inquire about difficulty levels when you're choosing a tour. While most companies offer "soft adventure" packages that those in decent but not overly athletic shape can handle, others focus on more hard-core activities geared toward very fit and seasoned adventure travelers.

See also the escorted tour operators listed in "Package Deals, Escorted Tours & Special-Interest Vacations," in chapter 2. Several operators offer adventure and outdoors components to their more standard Peru packages.

U.S. & INTERNATIONAL ADVENTURE TOUR OPERATORS

These agencies and operators specialize in well-organized and coordinated tours that cover your entire stay. Many travelers prefer to have everything arranged and confirmed before arriving in Peru—a good idea for first-timers and during high season (especially for travel to Cusco and its immediate environs, including the Inca Trail). Many of these operators are not cheap; 10-day tours generally cost upwards of $2,000 or more per person, and most do not include airfare to Peru.

Abercrombie & Kent (✆ 800/323-7308; www.abercrombiekent.com) is a premier luxury escorted tours company with brand-new South America programs. For outdoors combo trips in style, A&K offers the 9-day "Inca Adventure," with rafting on the Río Urubamba; for all Peru trips, you can add extensions to the Tambopata jungle or Colca Canyon. The website lists discounts on selected tours and dates.

Tips New Inca Trail Regulations

Trekkers could once do the Inca Trail on their own, but new regulations imposed by the Peruvian government to limit the environmental degradation and damage to the trail itself now require all trekkers to go with officially sanctioned groups. See the "New Inca Trail Regulations" box, in chapter 7, for more information.

Adventure Specialists (© 719/630-7687; www.gorp.com/adventur/ manu.htm) specializes in wildlife and birding adventures by dugout canoe in the Peruvian rain forest. Its trips include the Manu Biosphere Reserve and horse-supported Machu Picchu treks, as well as archaeological expeditions.

Amazonia Expeditions (© 800/262-9669; www.perujungle.com or www.peruandes.com) offers good-value, personalized, and flexible ecotourism trips to the Peruvian jungle and Andes. Trips of up to 7 days are all-inclusive (even laundry and tips are included). Jungle trips are to the Tahauyo Lodge (4 hr. from Iquitos) and the Tamshiyacu-Tahuayo Reserve.

Condor Journeys and Adventures ⚥ (© 01422/822-068; fax 01422/ 825-276) is one of the top U.K. agencies organizing package tours to Latin America. Condor offers a huge number of varied trips to Peru, including archaeology tours and lots of soft- and hard-core adventure and outdoor travel: hiking programs along Inca roads, horseback treks to Machu Picchu, rain-forest and white-water rafting in canyons and along the Apurímac and Urubamba, mountain-biking expeditions, and special, unusual programs such as "Mystical Peru" and hikes to Salcantay and Vilcabamba by llama.

GORP Travel (© 877/440-GORP or 877/591-9156; www.gorp.com), a self-styled "Guide to Outdoor Travel," is a wholesaler with an incredible range of options for adventure and more general travel throughout Peru and the world. It recently offered more than 60 outdoor-oriented vacations to Peru. A few are basic highlights trips, while others are cultural and language vacations or specialist adventures for very active and adventurous sorts. "Adventure Plus" membership ($59) gets you a 5% rebate on many trips, as well as other discounts.

International Expeditions (© 800/633-4734 or 205/428-1700; www. internationalexpeditions.com) features a number of Amazon cruises and jungle-lodge tours (including the most luxurious river cruises, run by Jungle Expeditions), as well as an interesting 9-day Machu Picchu Ecological Workshop, which has hands-on classes and culture visits. Visitors help with reforestation projects and participate in conservation programs and tree planting with local naturalists. An extension to a luxury jungle lodge is possible. The company offers five different Amazon trips, including a "Family Voyage" and an Amazon River cruise.

Journeys International (© 800/255-8735 or 734/665-4407; www.journeys-intl.com), offers small-group (4–12 people) natural history tours guided by naturalists. Trips include the 11-day "Inca Trail Trek & Amazon," featuring Peru highlights along with a rain-forest expedition to the Tambopata Nature Reserve; an 8-day "Amazon Wildlife Odyssey"; the 9-day "Amazon & Andes Odyssey," which includes the Tambopata Nature Reserve along with Cusco, Machu Picchu, and the Sacred Valley; an 8-day river cruise on the Amazon; and special Amazon and Inca trips for families.

Mountain Travel-Sobek (© 888/687-6235 or 510/527-8100; www. mtsobek.com) rates the level of difficulty of its trips and offers five itineraries to Peru, including the 10-day "Machu Picchu Adventure," with rafting on the Urubamba River and a 1-day hike on the Inca Trail, and "Hiking the Inca Trail, Cusco, and Sacred Valley." It also offers three options for mountaineers and committed trekkers: 15 days of strenuous trekking in Cordillera Blanca (mostly camping); a shorter 5-day (but still hard-core) trekking option in the same area; and a challenging 17-day trekking trip in the Cordillera Vilcabamba (half camping, half inns).

Overseas Adventure Travel (© 800/955-1925 or 617/876-0533; www. oattravel.com), offers natural history and "soft adventure" itineraries, with optional add-on excursions. Tours are limited to no more than 16 people and are guided by naturalists. All accommodations are in small hotels, lodges, or tent camps. The 17-day "Amazon Wilds & Galápagos" tour includes a short stay at a northern Amazon eco-lodge and a cruise around the Galápagos Islands.

Peruvian Andean Treks (© 800/683-8148 or 617/924-1974; www. andeantreks.com) offers adventure trips to the mountains and jungle throughout Peru. Its roster of reasonably priced trips for all levels include cloud-forest treks, llama trekking, trips to Manu and Tambopata, and highlands treks that combine white-water rafting or Amazon lodge stays.

Southwind Adventures (© 800/377-9463; www.southwindadventures. com) does high-end trips that include mountain biking in Manu, a 21-day Grand Andean Traverse trekking expedition, and options for bird-watching, rafting, and horse-packing.

Wildland Adventures ☆ (© 800/345-4453; www.wildland.com) is one of the finest international outdoor-tour companies with operations in Peru. It offers excellent special-interest trekking and rain-forest expedition programs. Wildland's programs are well designed, and guides are very professional. Trekkers can choose from the 9-day Cordillera Blanca trek or the more off-the-beaten-track 11-day Virgen del Carmen trek to Paucartambo, among several other well-designed trips.

Wilderness Travel (© 800/368-2794 or 510/558-2488; www.wilderness travel.com) specializes in 14-day outdoor group tours that are arranged with tiered pricing, meaning that the cost of the trip varies according to the size of group. Trips are graded according to difficulty. There are seven tours to Peru, including a llama trek in the Vilcabamba mountains, 16-day trek in the Cordillera Blanca, a Cordillera Huayhuash ice-range trek, and the unique Salcantay trail to Machu Picchu, with northern Amazon and Manu extensions as well as standard Peru highlights tours.

In addition to these companies, many environmental organizations regularly offer organized trips to Peru, including the **Nature Conservancy** (© 800/ 628-6860; www.tnc.org), which offers a riverboat Amazon voyage that visits the Nature Conservancy project in the Pacaya-Samiria National Reserve; the **Smithsonian Institute** (© 202/357-4700; www.si.edu), offering study tours that include a river cruise of the northern Amazon as well as a long and expensive trip down the Amazon, from Belém, Brazil to Pevas, Peru; and the **National Audubon Society** (© 800/274-4201 or 212/979-3066; www.audubon.org). A good resource for information on eco-travel is **Sacred Earth** (www. sacredearth.com), a loose consortium of "ethnobotanists" and eco-travelers that publishes an e-zine and has links to a half dozen featured trips and workshops to Peru, including Manu camping journeys and shamanistic "listening to the plants" tours of the northern Amazon.

PERUVIAN TOUR AGENCIES

Many tour companies based in the United States and elsewhere subcontract portions of their tours to established Peruvian companies. In some cases, independent travelers can benefit by organizing their tours directly with local companies. Prices on the ground can be much cheaper than contracting a tour abroad, but there are risks of not getting what you want when you want it. Also, the world of subcontracting can be byzantine, and even Peruvian travel agencies hire out adventure and outdoor specialists.

Local agencies offering adventure options abound, especially in Cusco, Arequipa, Huaraz, and Iquitos. These agencies can arrange everything from white-water rafting to day treks to horseback riding. Some tours may be held only when there are enough interested people or on fixed dates, so it's worthwhile to contact a few of the companies before you leave for Peru to find out what they might be doing when you arrive.

Class Adventure Travel (© 01/444-2220; www.cat-travel.com) is a well-run agency with offices in Lima and Cusco. Among its adventure offerings are rafting, trekking, and jungle tours.

Explorandes ℛ (© 01/445-0532 in Lima, or 084/238-380 in Cusco; www.explorandes.com) has been doing trekking and river expeditions in Peru for 25 years. One of the top high-end agencies for treks and mountaineering in Peru, it's reasonably priced and especially good for forming very small private groups. It offers a number of soft adventure trips (with stays in hotels and full- and half-day river trips) and an impressive lineup of real adventure, including cool, unique trips such as llama trekking to Chavín, a festival trek, rafting on the Apurímac River, and treks on southern peaks around Cusco—among many others. Amazon extensions are available.

InkaNatura Travel (© 888/287-7186 in the U.S. and Canada, or 084/251-173; www.inkanatura.com) is the Peruvian arm of Tropical Nature Travel. The company focuses on bird-watching, rain-forest lodges, and guided jungle expeditions, and it actively supports conservation efforts in the rain forest. Its specialist birding itineraries are in Manu as well as the northern Amazon. Custom trips for wildlife photography can also be arranged.

Peru Expeditions Overland (© 01/447-2057; www.peru-expeditions.com) is a Lima-based company run by Rafael Belmonte, an amiable fellow and dedicated cyclist. His company runs all kinds of cool trips across Peru, including treks, four-wheel-drive vehicle tours, and mountain biking, as well as more standard tours to destinations such as Arequipa, Cusco, and Colca Canyon.

SAS Travel Peru (© 084/237-292; www.sastravelperu.com) is one of the most popular agencies organizing outdoor travel for backpackers and budget-minded travelers in Cusco. Its roster includes a number of short treks in the Cusco area and a couple of longer, more challenging mountain treks lasting up to a week. Jungle treks are to Manu and Tambopata. SAS also offers white-water rafting, paragliding, climbing, mountain biking, and horseback riding.

2 Activities A to Z

The listings in this section describe the best places to practice particular sports and activities and includes the top tour operators and outfitters. If you want to focus on only one active sport during your trip to Peru, these companies are your best bets for quality equipment and knowledgeable service—but almost all of them will allow you to combine one activity with another, or engage in general cultural sightseeing.

BALLOONING & HANG GLIDING

In the mid-1970s, two foreigners constructed a balloon out of cotton and reed in an effort to prove that ancient cultures could have used balloons to design the mysterious Nasca Lines drawings in the southern desert sands. Too bad that didn't spark a wild interest in ballooning and hang gliding in Peru. So many parts of the country would be absolutely glorious to fly silently over: the Sacred Valley, the Nasca Lines, the valleys of the Callejón de Huaylas, the magnificent

Outdoor Adventures in Peru

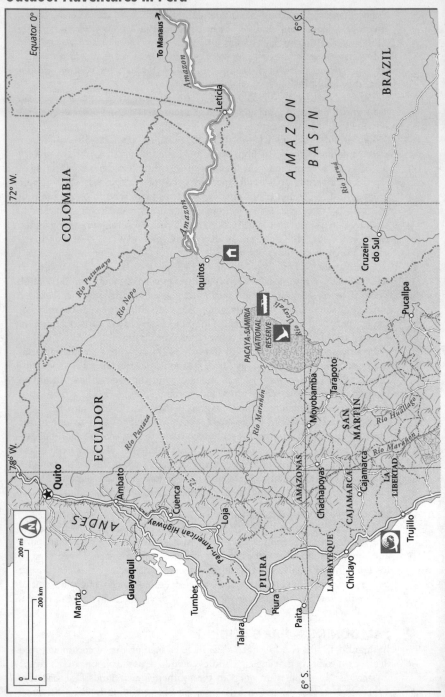

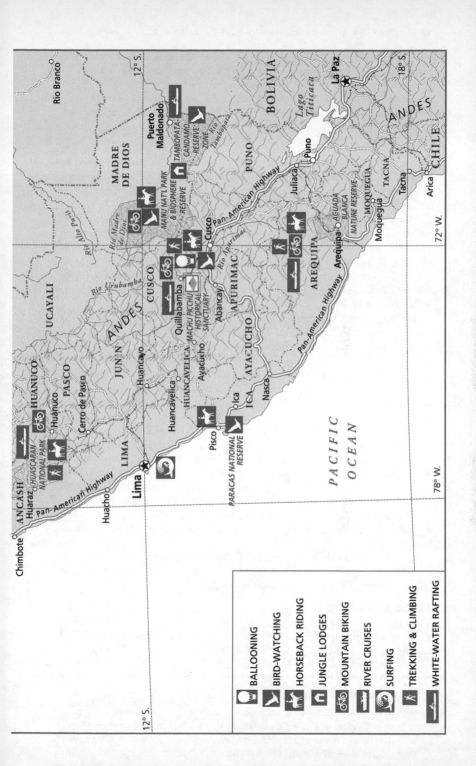

RÍO BRANCO
BOLIVIA
La Paz
12° S.
18° S.
Lago Titicaca
ANDES
CHILE
Puerto Maldonado
MADRE DE DIOS
PUNO
Puno
Juliaca
TAMBOPATA-CANDAMO RESERVE ZONE
Río Tambopata
Pan-American Highway
MANU NAT'L PARK & BIOSPHERE RESERVE
Río Madre de Dios
Cusco
Río Apurímac
AREQUIPA
AGUADA BLANCA NATURE RESERVE
MOQUEGUA
TACNA
Tacna
Arica
72° W.
Río Urubamba
CUSCO
Quillabamba
MACHU PICCHU HISTORICAL SANCTUARY
Abancay
APURÍMAC
Moquegua
Arequipa
ANDES
UCAYALI
PASCO
Cerro de Pasco
JUNÍN
Huancayo
Huancavelica
HUANCAVELICA
Ayacucho
AYACUCHO
Nasca
ICA
Ica
Pisco
PARACAS NATIONAL RESERVE
HUÁNUCO
Huánuco
ANCASH
Huaraz
HUASCARÁN NATIONAL PARK
Pan-American Highway
LIMA
Lima
Huacho
Chimbote
78° W.
PACIFIC OCEAN
12° S.
Río Alto Purús

BALLOONING
BIRD-WATCHING
HORSEBACK RIDING
JUNGLE LODGES
MOUNTAIN BIKING
RIVER CRUISES
SURFING
TREKKING & CLIMBING
WHITE-WATER RAFTING

91

pre-Columbian ruins, and the great canyons near Arequipa. Alas, the only out-fitter operating balloon flights in Peru is an U.S.-owned company, **Globos de los Andes** (© **084/232-352;** www.globosperu.com), and even it offers flights on an inconsistent basis. If you're interested, contact the company before your trip to Peru (and have other backup plans). Flights are generally May through August only.

BIRD-WATCHING

Peru is one of the greatest countries on earth for birders. The bird population in Peru is, incredibly, about 10% of the world's total. With nearly 2,000 species of resident and migrant birds identified throughout Peru, great bird-watching sites abound.

Manu Biosphere Reserve, believed to have the highest concentration of bird life on the planet, is legendary among birders. It boasts more than 1,000 species of birds. Cocks-of-the-rock, quetzals, toucanets, tanagers, and seven species of colorful macaws await patient birders. Some visitors have spotted as many as 500 species in relatively short visits to Manu. For specialists, the **Manu Wildlife Center** has the best reputation among birders, though also highly recommended is **Pantiacolla Lodge.**

The **Tambopata-Candamo Reserve Zone** is also extraordinary for birding and more accessible than Manu. The reserve, about a third the size of Costa Rica, claims more species of birds (around 600) and butterflies (more than 1,200) than any place of similar size. Both Tambopata and Manu are famous for their *collpas,* or salt licks, where hundreds of macaws, parrots, and other birds appear daily to feed. Nearer to Puerto Maldonado, good birding areas include the Sandoval and Valencia lakes, but they cannot compare to either of the major reserves.

In the northern Amazon, the **Pacaya-Samiria National Reserve** is home to more than 500 species of birds. The northern Amazon doesn't have quite the reputation that the varied cloud forests leading to Manu and the rest of the southeastern jungle do, though there is excellent birding in and around the protected Machu Picchu Sanctuary. **Machu Picchu Pueblo Hotel** organizes birding tours and has more than 100 species of birds on its property.

A handful of jungle lodges and river-cruise operators offer specialized birding options, but none is as complete as the trips offered by the specialist tour operators below.

Though Peru is one of the top birding destinations in the world, specialists complain about the lack of an essential field guide. See "Recommended Reading," in chapter 2, for a discussion on books about birding in Peru.

TOUR OPERATORS

Birding Peru (www.birdingperu.org) is a new tour operator based in Peru that offers birding trips to all regions of Peru, including the highlands, coasts, and rain forest. The outfitter will organize private birding trips, too. This company

---

Fun Fact **Butterflies**

Peru has become famous among bird-watchers, but naturalists who are fans of butterflies are in for an equal treat. Peru has the greatest diversity of butterflies in the world and the largest number of species: 3,700 (more than found in all of sub-equatorial Africa).

offers very little information about itself, so I suggest that you research it further by e-mailing the company before signing on for any of its services.

Field Guides (℃ 800/728-4953 or 512/263-7295; www.fieldguides.com) is a specialty bird-watching travel operator. It features five birding trips to Peru, including Manu Biosphere Reserve, Tambopata, Machu Picchu and the eastern slope of the Andes, the Amazon near the Peru–Brazil border, and a 24-day tour of the endemic-rich region of northern Peru. The 14-day tour of Manu costs $4,350 from Lima. Group size is limited to 14 participants.

InkaNatura Travel (℃ 888/287-7186 in the U.S. and Canada, or 084/251-173; www.inkanatura.com) offers birding tours to the Manu Biosphere Reserve, the endemic-rich region of northern Peru, and most other birding zones in Peru.

Wings (℃ 520/320-9868; www.wingsbirds.com) is a specialty bird-watching travel operator with more than 27 years of experience in the field. It promotes two trips to Peru: One is a 14-day journey to the Paracas Peninsula and high Andes lakes and forests; the other is a 19-day trip to Machu Picchu and the Manu Biosphere Reserve. Group size is usually between 6 and 18 people.

HORSEBACK RIDING

Lovers of horseback riding will find a few areas to pursue their interest. The best areas for treks on horseback are the Colca Canyon, near Arequipa, and the Callejón de Huaylas, the valley near the peaks of the Cordillera Blanca; a couple of local and international tour operators offer horse trekking in those areas. Outside that, your options are mostly limited to a few country hotels in Cajamarca, the Sacred Valley, and Colca Valley.

In the area around Pisco, horseback riding is available at **Ocucaje Sun & Wine Resort;** in Ica, at **Hotel Las Dunas.** On the outskirts of Cusco, the **Incatambo Hacienda Hotel** has horses, and beasts are available for walking between the ruins (Sacsayhuamán, Q'enko, Puca Pucara, and Tambomachay) just beyond Cusco. In the Sacred Valley, check out **Hotel Royal Inka Pisac, Sonesta Posada del Inca,** and **Posada del Inca Libertador;** in Ollantaytambo, you can usually arrange horseback riding along valley trails by asking around main square. In Arequipa, **El Lago Resort** has horses on the premises for rides around the area outside the city. The **Parador de Colca** has horses for treks in the Colca Valley and Canyon; local agencies in Arequipa that arrange horseback treks through the Colca Canyon include **Colca Trek** (℃ 054/224-578) and **Peru Trekking** (℃ 054/223-404). In Huaraz, try **Hotel Andino** or **Monttrek** (see below), which arranges good horseback mountain and valley treks. A number of country hotels just outside Cajamarca have horses for riding, including **Hotel Laguna Seca, Hotel Posada del Puruay, Hacienda San Vicente,** and **Hostal Portada del Sol Hacienda.** Finally, most people go to the jungle for bird-watching or canoe trips, but **Manu Expeditions** (℃ 084/226-671; www.manuexpeditions.com) organizes horseback riding from the Manu Wildlife Center.

TOUR OPERATORS

Adventure Specialists (℃ 719/630-7687; www.gorp.com/adventur/manu.htm) organizes horse-supported Machu Picchu treks, including the unique 8-day "Machu Picchu Pony Express."

Monttrek (℃ 044/721-124; www.monttrek.com) offers horseback riding and other adventure sports in the area around the Cordillera Blanca.

Southwind Adventures (© 800/377-9463; www.southwindadventures.com) offers horse-packing among its roster of adventure trips in Peru.

JUNGLE LODGES & TOURS

Nearly two-thirds of Peru is rain forest, and options for exploring it are myriad, from jungle lodges to independently guided treks to river cruises. The most important issue is choosing which major jungle destination fits best with your interest, time, and budget. Nearly all the international and Peruvian tour operators and wholesalers that do outdoor and adventure travel—for that matter, almost all agencies that handle travel to Peru—have some sort of jungle packages available. Some, of course, are more immersion-oriented than others. You can do a jungle add-on to a trip to Cusco or a full-scale jungle trek and cruise lasting 2 weeks or more. See the tour operators listed in "Organized Adventure Trips" (above), the packagers listed in "Package Deals, Escorted Tours & Special-Interest Vacations" (in chapter 2), and of course, the individual lodges and companies in chapter 9.

MOUNTAIN BIKING

Mountain biking is still in its infancy in Peru, though fat-tire options are growing fast. **Colca Valley** and **Canyon, Huaraz** and the **Callejón de Huaylas,** and the **Sacred Valley** are the major areas for off-road cycling. The **Manu jungle** is also good for hard-core biking. Several tour companies in those places rent bikes, and the quality of the equipment is continually being upgraded. If you plan to do a lot of biking and are very attached to your rig, bring your own. See individual destination chapters for rental listings.

My favorite mountain-biking spots are horse and mountain trails in the spectacular Callejón de Huaylas, which provide the kind of amazing climbing found in the Rockies of the western United States and mountain views that are second to none. Mountain bikers, along with other adventure sports fans, descend on Huaraz and the valley every June for its celebrated Semana del Andinismo. For gentler but also incredibly scenic trail riding, you can't beat the Sacred Valley.

TOUR OPERATORS & OUTFITTERS

In Huaraz and the Callejón de Huaylas, **Mountain Bike Adventures** (© 044/724-259; julio.olaza@terra.com.pe), run by Julio Olaza, and **Pony Expeditions** (© 044/791-642; www.ponyexpeditions.com), run by Alberto Cafferata, are the top two agencies for mountain biking. **Monttrek** (© 044/721-124; www.monttrek.com) also offers organized mountain-biking tours. **Peru Expeditions Overland** (© 01/447-2057; www.peru-expeditions.com) is run by a former top cyclist and offers mountain-biking trips in the Sacred Valley to Machu Picchu.

In Cusco, local outfitters **Amazonas Explorer** (© 084/236-826 or 084/225-284; www.amazonas-explorer.com), **Apumayo Expediciones** (© 084/246-018; www.cuscoperu.com/apumayo), **Eric Adventures** (© 084/228-475; www.ericadventures.com), and **Instinct Travel** (© 084/233-451; www.instinct-travel.com) offer 1- to 5-day organized mountain-biking excursions for novices and experienced single-trackers. **Manu Ecological Adventures** (© 084/261-640; www.cbc.org.pe/manu) and **Manu Nature Tours** (© 084/252-721; www.manuperu.com) offer mountain-biking add-ons to lodge stays and jungle treks, and **Southwind Adventures** (© 800/377-9463; www.southwindadventures.com) organizes trips that include mountain biking in Manu. In Arequipa, **Colca Trek** (© 054/224-578) and **Peru Trekking** (© 054/223-404) offer

Which Jungle? Comparing Piranhas & Monkeys

Choosing where to go in the Peruvian jungle is complicated. To begin, you need to define how much time and money you can spend, how you want to get there, and how much immersion—expeditions range from light to hard-core—you're interested in once there.

Cusco is the best base for excursions to the southern jungle, while eco-lodges and cruise trips in the northern jungle are accessible from Iquitos, to which most visitors fly. For many, the relative proximity of the southern Amazon basin to Cusco and the Sacred Valley makes a jungle experience in that part of the country all the more appealing.

Of the major jungle regions, the Manu Biosphere Reserve is the least touched by man. It is the most inaccessible zone and, therefore, also the most expensive for expeditions. Most visits require close to a week. But Manu also provides perhaps the best opportunities for viewing Amazon wildlife (especially birds). The Tambopata-Candamo Reserve Zone also offers excellent jungle experiences and wildlife, including easy access to the splendid macaw clay lick, with less expenditure of time and money.

Peru's northeastern jungle near Iquitos has suffered the most penetration by man and tour operators, having been accessible to travelers much longer than other parts of the Peruvian jungle. For travelers, though, the region is more convenient, with many more expeditions and lodges operating there, and prices are generally more affordable. Note, however, that the chances of phenomenal large mammal sightings, which are remote anywhere, are even slimmer in the northern Amazon. Travelers with limited time and budgets often fly to Iquitos (by far the most interesting jungle city in Peru) and hop on an inexpensive jungle lodge tour from there, although similarly reasonably priced tours are available from Puerto Maldonado in the south.

mountain biking in the Colca Canyon. See individual destination chapters for more information.

RIVER CRUISES

River cruises along the Amazon and its tributaries are one of the best ways to experience the Peruvian jungle. Cruises give travelers the option of floating luxury and good meals as well as the ability to stop in and see several different environments and river and jungle communities. Iquitos-based **Jungle Expeditions** (© 094/261-583; www.junglex.com), **Amazon Tours and Cruises** (© 094/233-931, or 800/423-2791 in the U.S. and Canada; www.amazontours.net), and **Paseos Amazónicos** (© 094/231-618; p-amazon@amauta.rcp.net.pe) all offer a variety of river cruises in the northern Amazon. **International Expeditions** (© 800/633-4734 or 205/428-1700; www.internationalexpeditions.com) is one of the most experienced tour operators organizing luxurious river cruises from the United States. The huge and remote **Pacaya-Samiria National Reserve** is one of the best, and up-and-coming, zones for cruises into pristine jungle and wetlands; see chapter 9 for details.

(*Fun Fact* **Whose Board Came First?**

Surfing is generally thought to have its origins in Polynesia or the South Sea Islands, but several historians claim that men first hopped aboard things not so dissimilar to modern surfboards in ancient Peru some 2,000 years ago. Textiles and pottery of pre-Columbian, north-coast civilizations depict men cruising waves on totora-reed rafts (though they were more likely fishermen in search of dinner than rad dudes out looking for point breaks).

SURFING

Peru has quietly become one of the world's top surfing destinations. It has 2,000km (1,200 miles) of Pacific coastline and huge possibilities for left and right reef breaks, point breaks, and monster waves, and boarders can hit the surf year-round. Northern beaches, in particular Puerto Chicama north of Trujillo, and Cabo Blanco, even farther north, draw surfers to some of the best waves in South America. There are also good surfing beaches south of Lima. The north is best from October to March, while the surfing in the south is good April through December and tops in May. Check out **www.a-styleadventures. com/english/surfing.htm** for information about surfing in northern Peru. Another good surfing site, with reports on water conditions and the best beaches up and down Peru, is **www.peruazul.com.pe**. For more details, see "Outdoor Activities & Spectator Sports" and "Side Trips from Lima," in chapter 4, and "Trujillo," in chapter 10.

TOUR OPERATORS

Tico Travel (© 800/493-8426; www.ticotravel.com) is an established expert on Costa Rica and Central America, now offering packages to Peru. One of its most interesting is a surfing tour, something it has a great deal of experience with in Costa Rica and Nicaragua. Tico also offers good-value, 4-day packages to Cusco, Cajamarca, Huaraz, and the Amazon, among other destinations, as well as 2-week "Best of Peru" packages and archaeological packages to northern Peru.

TREKKING & MOUNTAIN CLIMBING

Peru is one of the world's great trekking and mountain-climbing destinations, and its mountains and gorgeous valleys, ideal for everything from hard-core climbs to 6,000m (20,000-ft.) peaks to gentle walks through green valleys, are one of the country's calling cards. Experienced mountaineers, ice climbers, trekkers, and regular old athletic types and hikers beeline to Peru to experience the grandeur of the great Cordillera Blanca, the volcanoes and canyons around Arequipa, and of course, the Andes mountains in and around Cusco. The most celebrated trek, of course, is the Inca Trail to Machu Picchu—truly one of the world's most rewarding treks, provided the crowds don't get you down in high season.

Trekking circuits of varying degrees of difficulty lace the valleys and mountain ridges of Peru's sierra. Yet only a few have become popular, commercial trekking routes. Independent trekkers who like to blaze their own trail (metaphorically speaking—you should always stick to existing trails) have a surfeit of options in Peru for uncrowded treks.

Scores of outfitters, both international and local, organize a full run of mountain-climbing and trekking package tours. If you do outdoor travel in Peru, you should include soft trekking at a minimum, and many agencies specialize in trekking and climbing. Independent travelers can hook up with local agencies for tailored experiences. And travelers of all stripes can set out on easy treks in any of the areas above. There are details on accessible trekking in the destination chapters; see especially chapters 7, 8, and 10.

The best months for climbing are the dry season, between May and September (of those, June–Aug are perhaps best). In Huaraz, the Semana de Andinismo, held annually in June, attracts mountain climbers from around the world.

One of the best resources for hiking and climbing in Peru are the **South American Explorers** clubhouses in Lima and Cusco (© **01/445-3306** in Lima, or 084/245-484 in Cusco; www.samexplo.org). You have to become a member first for full access to their trail reports and other information, but if you're serious about trails and climbs in Peru, it's money well spent. You can join via their website or on the spot at a clubhouse. Another excellent resource in Huaraz is **Casa de Guías** (© **044/721-811**).

TOUR OPERATORS

For trekking, the most obvious candidates to organize trekking tours of Peru from abroad are **Mountain Travel-Sobek** (© 888/687-6235 or 510/527-8100; www.mtsobek.com), **Peruvian Andean Treks** (© 800/683-8148 or 617/924-1974; www.andeantreks.com), **Wildland Adventures** (© 800/345-4453; www.wildland.com), and **Wilderness Travel** (© 800/368-2794 or 510/558-2488; www.wildernesstravel.com). All have plenty of options, good guides, and levels of professionalism. One of the top Peruvian operators with a national reach is **Explorandes** (© 01/445-0532 in Lima, or 084/238-380 in Cusco; www.explorandes.com). For more information on all of these, see "Organized Adventure Trips," earlier in this chapter.

The local agencies listed in the chapters 7, 8, and 10 are the best places to turn if you want to organize some trekking and/or climbing once on the ground in Peru. There are also excellent local agencies specializing in experienced mountain-climbing expeditions in Arequipa, Huaraz, and Caraz. The best groups arrange a large number of area climbs and have equipment rental. Several have a 24-hour mountain-rescue service.

WHITE-WATER RAFTING

Peru, home to the origin of the mighty Amazon and great canyon rivers, has some stunning opportunities for white-water rafting. Whether you're a total novice or a world-class river runner, Peru has fantastic white water suited to your abilities. The rivers flowing through the **Colca** and **Cotahuasi canyons,** other rivers nearer Arequipa, and the Andean rivers of the **Urubamba Valley** stand out. A good adventurous experience is rafting in the Amazon jungle on the **Tambopata River.** There's also good white water on the **Río Santa** in the Callejón de Huaylas.

If you're just experimenting with river rafting, stick to Class II and III rivers. If you already know your way around a raft and paddle, there are plenty of Class IV and V sections to run. Hard-core runners come to Peru for some fantastic, multiday rafting trips to Class V and even Class VI rivers in remote canyons. The best months for rafting are May through September, when water levels are low. (During the rainy season, canyon rivers can be extremely dangerous.)

TOUR OPERATORS

A half dozen agencies in Arequipa, Cusco, and the Sacred Valley organize a range of local white-water opportunities. See chapters 6, 7, and 8 for more information.

Amazonas Explorer ℛ (www.amazonas-explorer.com; in U.S., booked through River Travel Center, annien@rivers.com) offers white-water-rafting tours, which can be combined with Inca Trail treks. Trips, which feature small groups, can be booked from abroad. Among its Peru trips are rafting the Río Apurímac, inflatable canoeing on the source of the Amazon (combined with trekking the Inca Trail), rain-forest rafting, and extreme Class IV to VI in Cotahuasi, the world's deepest canyon.

Earth River Expeditions (© 800/643-2784 in the U.S. and Canada; www.earthriver.com) does only one kind of trip: white-water rafting. Most of its trips are to Chile, though it offers a 12-day excursion to the Río Colca in July.

3 Peru's National Parks & Nature Reserves

Peru's extraordinary natural environment fortunately features a wealth of protected areas, wildlife reserves, and archaeological zones. Dozens of national parks and nature preserves make up a bit more than 10% of Peru. The majority of these national parks and nature reserves are undeveloped tropical forests, with few services or facilities available for tourism. Others, however, offer easier access to their wealth of natural wonders. The discussion below is not a complete listing of all of Peru's national parks and protected areas. Rather, it details the ones, including several of the largest and most biodiverse on the planet, that are the most accessible and most rewarding for visitors.

Many of them require visitor's permits, for a small fee. If you go with an organized tour, the tour operators almost always take care of the bureaucratic details and include the fees in their package price. See the listings of specialty tour operators in "Organized Adventure Trips," earlier in this chapter.

Peru's protected natural areas go by several names, according to distinct legal statutes and protections, in Spanish: *parques nacionales* (national parks), *reservas nacionales* (national reserves), *santuarios nacionales/históricos* (national or historic sanctuaries), and *zonas reservadas* (reserve zones), among others.

MANU NATIONAL PARK & BIOSPHERE RESERVE ℛℛ

Manu is probably the most famous national park in Peru. Covering nearly a million hectares, Manu National Park & Biosphere Reserve is the second-largest protected area in the country and one of the largest in South America. It is also thought to be the most biodiverse zone on earth. Created in 1973, the park reserve is on the eastern slopes of the Andes within the Amazon basin and comprises an extraordinary variety of habitats, including tropical lowland forest, mountain forest, and grasslands. The reserve zone contains the lower Manu River, the Río Alto Madre de Dios, and a number of beautiful oxbow lakes. About 1,000 bird species—about a quarter of all birds known in South America and 10% of all species in the world—and more than 200 species of mammals have been identified. Also found in the park are at least 13 endangered wildlife species, including black caimans, giant river otters, and ocelots. Botanists have claimed that Manu has a greater number of plant species than any other protected area on the earth.

Manu is superb for observing wildlife, but trips to Manu are lengthy and costly. Most trips bus travelers in and fly them out by light aircraft. There are very few lodges within the designated reserve and cultural zones, and access to the reserve zone is by organized tour. Independent visits are possible in the cultural zone only.

⌒ *Fun Fact* Giant Otters

One of the most fascinating creatures visitors have a chance of spotting in the southeastern Amazon basin in Peru is the giant otter (*Pteronura brasiliensis*), the largest of the 13 otter species in the world. Hunted for its pelt, it has landed on the World Conservation Union ignominious Red List of Endangered Species and has probably been eliminated in Argentina and Uruguay. It has recovered in Peru, but less than a couple hundred probably exist.

Giant otters today are primarily "hunted" by tourists and photographers. The large and very active animals are found in lakes and rivers of tropical lowlands, where they can rather easily be observed. Conservationists are concerned that otters in Manu and Tambopata, among other places, have suffered from human interference in the form of tourist canoes, which leads to long-term changes in behavior and decreases in reproduction. Less invasive observation towers and viewing platforms have been constructed in Cochas Otorongo and Salvador in the Manu Biosphere Reserve, and the Giant Otter Project of the Frankfurt Zoological Society (www.giantotters.com/rainforest) is overseeing monitoring and protection of the species in the Pacaya-Samiria National Reserve and the Manu and Bahuaja-Sonene national parks in southeastern Peru.

TAMBOPATA-CANDAMO RESERVE ZONE ⟡⟡

The Tambopata Reserve is more accessible and less restrictive than Manu. The park is made up principally of lowland forest along the Tambopata River. There are a number of lodges in and around the reserve, accessible from Puerto Maldonado. The lodges offer shorter stays but usually include naturalist-led expeditions to remote areas. Independent travel with a guide can also be arranged in Puerto Maldonado. Though Manu is more celebrated and probably more pristine, with greater species diversity, the flora and fauna that can be observed by most visitors at Tambopata are remarkably similar.

HUASCARAN NATIONAL PARK

Home to a chain of snowcapped mountains that comprise the longest tropical range in the world, the 161km (100-mile) Cordillera Blanca in the central Andes, Huascarán is a mecca for climbers and a host of outdoor and adventure travelers. Its scenery and offerings—mountain climbing, trekking, horseback riding, white-water rafting, fishing, and mountain biking, among others—are perhaps unequaled in the Americas. With 200 alpine lakes, 600 glaciers, spectacular mountain vistas, and nearby ancient pre-Columbian ruins, though, Huascarán is also a magnet for travelers who just want to appreciate the scenery with their eyes and not necessarily their legs and lungs.

Named for the highest peak in Peru, the park's altitude ranges from 2,500m to 6,768m (8,200–22,200 ft.) and includes more than 2 dozen snowcapped peaks above 6,000m (19,500 ft.). Huascarán is the second highest park in the South American Andes. Climbing and trekking opportunities range from expert to moderate, with the latter easily managed by anyone in good shape. Arrangements for manageable 2-day walks and 2-week camping hikes crisscrossing the formidable passes of the Cordillera can be easily arranged in Huaraz and Caraz.

For independent treks in the park, a permit must be obtained from the park office in Huaraz.

MACHU PICCHU HISTORICAL SANCTUARY

Machu Picchu is much more than the famous Inca ruins carved into a mountainside. The Machu Picchu Historical Sanctuary, named a UNESCO natural and cultural World Heritage Site in 1983, is a designated archaeological zone and 33,000-hectare preserve. International concern over environmental damage to Machu Picchu and the Inca Trail led the Peruvian government to introduce more stringent measures to protect the zone's natural heritage, including limits on the number of people allowed on the trail. Proposals that would severely compromise the natural environment, such as the building of cable cars to the ruins, have at least for now been defeated.

International environmental and conservation groups, such as World Parks Endowment, have been lobbying the Peruvian government to create a large Inca National Park and expand the protected area around Machu Picchu into the neighboring Vilcanota and Vilcambamba mountains, which would establish a major protected area.

PACAYA-SAMIRIA NATIONAL RESERVE 🐾🐾

The largest natural reserve in Peru, Pacaya-Samiria is one of the Amazon's (and the world's) richest wildlife habitats. Covering more than two million hectares of pristine rain forest and wetlands in the north-central Amazon region (about 322km/200 miles south of Iquitos), the reserve is difficult to penetrate during the rainy season (Dec–Mar). The reserve is full of rivers and lakes, and boasts some of the Amazon's most abundant species of flora and fauna.

Pacaya-Samiria is considerably less accessible than the jungle farther north, and is much less visited than Manu or Tambopata. Several tour operators now organize river cruises, canoe trips, and camping expeditions, and a couple of native communities are now promoting camping trips and immersion experiences. A permit from INRENA, the Peruvian parks authority, is required to enter the preserve.

PARACAS NATIONAL RESERVE 🐾

South of Lima, in the department of Ica on the southern coast, this peninsula is blessed with an abundance of marine wildlife and seabirds. About two-thirds of the 335,000-hectare reserve is ocean; the desert landscape is barren and rather absent of most plant life. The bird- and sea-lion-rich habitats of the Ballestas Islands, contained within the nature preserve, present excellent and very accessible opportunities for viewing wildlife up close.

4 Tips on Health, Safety & Etiquette in the Peruvian Wilderness

Though many outdoor travel itineraries in Peru require no special medications or vaccinations, there are special considerations for jungle travel. Additionally, acclimatization to the high altitude of the Andes is essential for anyone seeking to do trekking or climbing in the mountains.

For tropical travel in Peru, the Centers for Disease Control and Prevention recommends vaccinations against yellow fever, hepatitis A or immune globulin (IG), hepatitis B, typhoid, and booster doses for tetanus-diphtheria and measles, as well as pills for malaria. For more detailed information, see "Insurance, Health & Safety," in chapter 2.

While most tours and activities are extremely safe, there are risks involved in any adventure activity. The risks involved in mountain climbing, ice climbing, and white-water rafting are considerable. Know and respect your own physical limits and skills (or lack thereof) before undertaking any high-risk activity.

Be prepared for extremes in temperature and rainfall and wide fluctuations in weather. A sunny morning hike can quickly become a cold and wet ordeal, so it's a good idea to carry along some form of rain gear when hiking in the rain forest, bring sufficient protection against the cold at high altitudes, and have a dry change of clothing waiting at the end of the trail. Make sure to bring along plenty of sunscreen no matter where you travel. See "What to Bring," below, for more suggestions.

If you do any trekking or camping, exercise caution with the native species that live in natural habitats. Don't go poking under rocks or fallen branches: Snakebites are very rare, but don't do anything to increase the odds. If you do encounter a snake, stay calm, don't make any sudden movements, and *do not* try to handle it. The chance of getting bitten by a venomous snake is small; however, if you're bitten, wash out the bite and surrounding area very thoroughly (don't go Hollywood and try to suck out the venom). Because the bite may cause swelling, remove your jewelry. If symptoms persist, seek medical attention; the best way to demonstrate to a doctor what kind of snake bit you, of course, is to hand over the dead snake—certainly not always possible. Also beware of centipedes, scorpions, and spiders including tarantulas, brown recluses, and black widows. If you are bitten by a dog or another creature, such as a bat, there is a risk of rabies. Wash out the wound thoroughly with soap and water, and seek medical attention. For a detailed "disease risk analysis" and other precautions, take a look at **Travel Medicine**'s website at **www.travmed.com**.

Avoid swimming in jungle rivers unless a guide or local operator can vouch for their safety. Though white-water sections and stretches in mountainous areas are generally pretty safe, many rivers in the Amazon basin are home to contingents of crocodile and caiman populations.

Bugs and bug bites (and blisters) will probably be your greatest health concern in the Peruvian wilderness. Bugs are for the most part an inconvenience, although mosquitoes can carry malaria or dengue (see "Insurance, Health & Safety," in chapter 2, for more information). Strong repellent and proper clothing will minimize both the danger and inconvenience. On beaches, you may be bitten by sand fleas. These nearly invisible insects leave an irritating welt. Try not to scratch, as this can lead to open sores and infections.

However, in all probability, Peru's bounteous nature needs to be protected from visitors more so than visitors need to be protected from it. A fundamental component of enjoying nature is leaving the natural environment undisturbed. The responsible outdoor traveler's maxim is: Take nothing but memories (and photos), leave nothing but footprints. Do not cut or uproot plants or flowers. Pack out everything you pack in, and *never* litter. Leave places the way you found them. If you see garbage lying around in protected areas, pack it out, along with your own trash. Don't scratch your name or any other graffiti on trees or ancient monuments. On trails, bury your excrement far as possible from the trail. Over the years, too many insensitive trekkers along the Inca Trail, among other spots, did not follow this common-sense advice and did so much damage that international organizations such as UNESCO worried about the trail's survival.

To support local communities and appreciate what you have the rare opportunity to experience, it's a great idea to use (and adequately tip or pay) local guides and porters, and support locally owned businesses and artisans.

5 What to Bring

Outdoor and adventure travel in Peru requires some special gear, and it's a good idea to come prepared, as you're more likely to find a better selection of equipment, apparel, and other outdoor gear at home than you are in Peru. You can rent some equipment, such as crampons for ice climbing, but you'd be wise to bring most nontechnical items with you.

The most basic items for travelers to Peru who are doing any sort of light adventure, such as trekking or jungle lodge stays, are (already broken-in) **hiking boots** (it's not a bad idea to take them in a carry-on or wear them on the plane to avoid their loss), outdoor apparel such as **fleece pullovers,** and a **daypacks.**

Essential gear for almost all travelers to Peru includes

- a sun hat
- sunscreen
- cold-weather and water-repellent clothing
- light trekking shoes or boots
- several pairs of thick socks

Additional items for light adventure include

- good backpacking or climbing boots
- a base layer (thermal underwear or "wicking"-quality shirt)
- malarial pills (if traveling to jungle regions)
- insect repellent
- a pocketknife
- toilet paper
- a flashlight or headlamp
- a mosquito net
- a sleeping bag
- diarrhea medicine
- energy bars or other trail snack foods
- sports sandals or comfortable slides for post-climbing and trekking, or for river and wet-weather wear
- a water bottle or other portable hydration system
- a good internal-frame backpack

More stuff for hard-core adventure travel includes

- food supplies and cooking equipment
- a filter and/or water purification tablets
- a first-aid kit
- a compass and whistle
- a tent, camping stove, and cookware
- adequate fuel
- topographical maps of trails

6 Volunteer & Study Programs

Study and volunteer programs, including Spanish-language programs, are often a great way to travel in and experience a country with greater depth than most independent and package travel allows. Cultural immersion and integration with locals are the aims of many such programs, leading to a richer and more unique experience for many travelers.

Volunteering in particular often leads to greater culture sensitivity and cross-cultural learning experiences. Especially in a mostly poor country such as Peru, volunteers see up close the realities of the lack of running water and electricity, the relative absence of luxuries, and simple, home-cooked foods—not to mention local customs and traditions. These aspects of Peruvian life might be considerably more difficult to apprehend if staying in nice hotels and dining at upscale restaurants.

Most volunteer organizations are not-for-profit entities that charge participants to go abroad (to cover administrative and other costs), so volunteering isn't usually a way to get a free vacation. If you're concerned, though, ask about the cost breakdown for costs and field expenses. Any established, reputable volunteer organization should be willing to do this. Then you could always compare their costs to what traveling on your own would amount to.

Below are several institutions and organizations that work on humanitarian and sustainable development projects in Peru. Some international relief organizations, such as **Doctors Without Borders** (www.doctorswithoutborders.org) and **CARE** (www.care.org), accept volunteers to work crises and relief efforts. The devastating earthquake in southern Peru in 2001 was one such episode, which brought hundreds of volunteers to Peru.

VOLUNTEER PROGRAMS

Cross-Cultural Solutions (© 800/380-4777 or 914/632-0022; www.cross culturalsolutions.org) offers weeklong volunteer programs in Peru. The "Volunteer Abroad" section lists a number of opportunities for volunteering in Peru, including CARE, volunteer teaching, and environmental research. **Habitat for Humanity** (© 800/422-4828 or 229/924-6935, ext. 2549; www.habitat.org) and **Volunteers for Peace** (© 802/259-2759; www.vfp.org) also offer opportunities in Peru.

RESEARCH OPPORTUNITIES

Earthwatch Institute (© 800/776-0188 or 978/461-0081; www.earthwatch. org) has a unique mission: It sends travelers out to work in the field alongside scientists involved in archaeology and environmental conservation. There are three Peru research and education trips: You can join a 13-day excavation of a pre-Inca site, assist on research of Peruvian macaws, or document the biology of Andean rivers. But the trips are not all work; they're a way to see a fascinating slice of the country from an insider's—academic or conservationist—perspective.

SPANISH-LANGUAGE PROGRAMS

Local language schools, primarily located in Cusco and offering both short- and long-term study programs, often with home stays, are listed in chapter 6. **Study Abroad International** (www.studyabroadinternational.com) lists a number of Spanish-study programs in Cusco. **GORP Travel** (© 877/440-GORP; www. gorptravel.com) recently listed Spanish-study programs of short duration in Cusco; follow the "Education/Learning" link on the website for options.

4

Lima

Lima once ranked as the richest and most important city in the Americas and was considered to be the most beautiful colonial settlement in the region. Founded in 1535 by the conquistador Francisco Pizarro, the Spanish Crown's "City of Kings" quickly became the center of power and trade for the entire American viceregency that stretched from Quito to Santiago. Lima was home to some of the Americas' finest baroque and Renaissance churches, palaces, and mansions, as well as the continent's first university, founded in 1551. For 2 centuries, the capital also served as the headquarters of the Spanish Inquisition.

When Spain created a rival viceregency in Río de la Plata, which subsequently grew rich from silver mines, Lima quickly fell into decline. An earthquake decimated the city in 1746, leaving more than 4,000 dead and few buildings standing. Today, the capital of Peru is a sprawling, chaotic, and mostly unlovely metropolis, and many visitors dart through it as fast as possible—if not bypassing it altogether. Peru's blistering poverty is more apparent here than perhaps anywhere else: Depressing shantytowns called *pueblos jóvenes* lacerate the outer rings of the city. The despair of a large segment of the capital's largely migrant and *mestizo* population contrasts uncomfortably with the ritzy apartment and office buildings in the residential suburbs. And as if that weren't enough, for most of the year an unrelenting gray cloud called the *garúa* hangs heavily overhead, obscuring the coastline and dulling the city's appearance. The sun comes out in Lima only from December to April; the rest of the time, Lima makes London look like Lisbon. Lima has calmed down since the chaotic 1980s and '90s, when the city was the scene of carjackings, kidnappings, embassy takeovers, and strong-arm political maneuvers. But the city still feels schizophrenic; outer suburbs such as Barranco are relatively gentle oases, worlds apart from the congestion and grime of the rest of the city. Though middle-class Limeños from residential *barrios* are again venturing downtown along with foreign visitors, there are still plenty who consider central Lima off-limits.

For many visitors, Lima demands too much effort to sift beneath the soot and uncover the city's rewards, especially when such extraordinary treasures hover over the horizon in the Andes mountains and in the Amazon jungle. So why come to Lima except to beeline it to Cusco or elsewhere? If you skip Lima altogether, you'll miss a vital part of what is Peru today. With a population of eight million—about one-third Peru's population—and as the seat of the national government and the headquarters of most industry, Lima thoroughly dominates Peru's political and commercial life. The country's best museums, restaurants, and nightlife are here, and many of the classic colonial buildings in the old *centro* are slowly being refurbished.

Even if you have only a day or two for Lima, the city's art and archaeology museums serve as perfect introductions to the rich history and culture

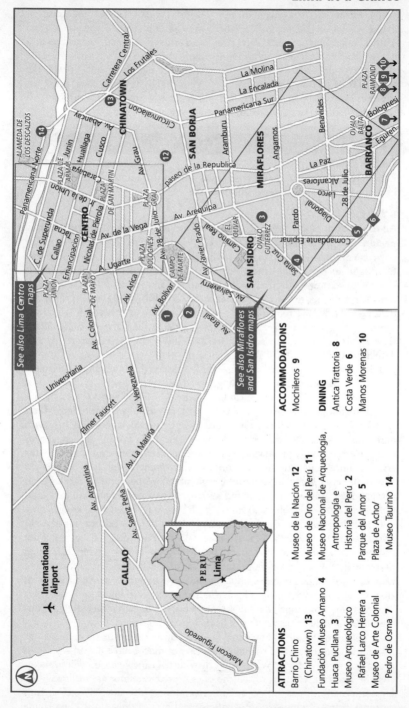

Lima at a Glance

International Airport ✈

CALLAO

Malecon Figueredo

Av. Argentina
Av. Saenz Peña
Av. Venezuela
Elmer Faucett
Universitaria
Av. La Marina
Av. Colonial
Av. Brasil
Av. Bolivar

PLAZA UNION
PLAZA 2 DE MAYO
PLAZA BOLOGNESI
A. Ugarte
Emancipacion
C. de Superunda
Callao
Tacna
Av. Arica
Av. Salaverry
Av. Javier Prado
CAMPO DE MARTE

ALAMEDA DE LOS DESCALZOS
Panamericana Norte
Av. Abancay
Carabaya
Junin
Huallaga
Cusco
PLAZA DE ARMAS
PLAZA DE SAN MARTIN
Jr. de la Union
Nicolas de Pierola
Av. de la Vega
Av. 28 de Julio - GRAU
Av. Grau

CENTRO

CHINATOWN

Carretera Central
Los Frutales
Circunvalacion

SAN BORJA
La Molina
La Encalada
Panamericana Sur
Aramburu
Angamos
Benavides

paseo de la Republica
Av. Arequipa
EL OLIVAR
Camino Real
OVALO GUTIERREZ

SAN ISIDRO
Santa Cruz
Comandante Espinar
Larco
Pardo
Diagonal
Alcantores
La Paz
28 de Julio

MIRAFLORES

OVALO BALTA
Eguren
Bolognesi
BARRANCO

PLAZA RAIMONDI

PERÚ
Lima ★

See also Lima Centro maps

See also Miraflores and San Isidro maps

ATTRACTIONS

Barrio Chino (Chinatown) **13**
Fundación Museo Amano **4**
Huaca Pucllana **3**
Museo Arqueológico
Rafael Larco Herrera **1**
Museo de Arte Colonial
Pedro de Osma **7**

Museo de la Nación **12**
Museo de Oro del Perú **11**
Museo Nacional de Arqueología,
Antropología e
Historia del Perú **2**
Parque del Amor **5**
Plaza de Acho/
Museo Taurino **14**

ACCOMMODATIONS

Mochileros **9**

DINING

Antica Trattoria **8**
Costa Verde **6**
Manos Morenas **10**

105

you'll encounter elsewhere in the country. Not to be missed are the Museo de la Nación, which traces the history of Peru's ancient civilizations; the Museo de Oro, bursting with thousands of gleaming artifacts from the Incas and their predecessors; and the Rafael Larco Herrera Museum, the world's largest private collection of pre-Columbian art. If you also squeeze in a tour of colonial Lima, dine at a great *criollo* restaurant, soak up some energetic nightlife, and browse the country's best shops, you may just come away from Lima surprised, if not exactly in love.

1 Orientation

ARRIVING

Lima is the gateway for most international arrivals to Peru; see "Getting There," in chapter 2, for more detailed information.

BY PLANE

All flights from North America and Europe arrive at Lima's **Aeropuerto Internacional Jorge Chávez** (© 01/575-0912), located 16km (10 miles) west of the city center. Lima is connected by air with all major cities in Peru; there are regular flights to Ayacucho, Cusco, Puerto Maldonado, Juliaca, Arequipa, Tacna, Cajamarca, Chiclayo, Trujillo, Pucallpa, Iquitos, Tarapoto, and Piura. The major domestic airlines are **Aero Continente** (© 877/482-2501 in the U.S., or 01/242-4242; www.aerocontinente.net), **AeroCondor** (© 01/442-5215; www.aerocondor.com.pe), **LanPeru** (© 212/582-3250 in the U.S., or 01/213-8200; www.lanperu.com), **Taca Peru** (© 01/213-7000; www.grupotaca.com), and **TANS** (© 01/213-6000; www.tansperu.com.pe).

The airport has a tourist information booth (in the international terminal only), two 24-hour currency-exchange windows, three banks, ATMs, a post office, and car-rental desks including **Avis** (© 01/575-0912, ext. 4155; www.avis.com), **Budget** (© 01/575-1674; www.budget.com), and **Hertz** (© 01/575-1390; www.hertz.com). The tourist information booth can help with hotel reservations. The arrival and departure terminals can be very congested, especially when long lines form to pay departure taxes, when a number of flights arrive at once, and early in the morning when many flights depart Lima for Cusco. Be very mindful of your luggage and other belongings at all times. To get through large groups of travelers and relatives all hovering about, you may need to forget about being polite and simply push your way through the crowd.

Domestic departures require payment of a S/12 ($3.50) exit tax; for international departures, the tax is $25. You must take your boarding pass to one of the booths in either terminal and stand in line to pay and receive a stamp indicating payment (in cash only) before proceeding to the departures area. Remember to reconfirm your flight at least 48 hours in advance and arrive at the airport with ample time before your flight. Flights are frequently overbooked, and passengers who have not reconfirmed their flights or who arrive later than (usually) 45 minutes before scheduled departure risk being bumped from the flight.

To get from the airport to Lima—either downtown or to suburbs such as Miraflores, San Isidro, and Barranco (the sites of most tourist hotels)—you can take a taxi or private bus. When you exit with your luggage, you will immediately be besieged with taxi offers; the ones nearest the door are invariably the most expensive. **Taxis** inside the security area at the international arrivals terminal charge around $20 to Miraflores and $15 to downtown Lima (Lima Centro). You can try bargaining or go just beyond the security area, where prices drop to about $10 to Miraflores and $8 to Lima Centro. The **Urbanito Airport shuttle service** (℃ **01/814-6932**) delivers passengers to the doors of their hotels. Stop by the desk in the international terminal; buses to downtown ($6) and Miraflores and San Isidro ($8) leave every half hour or so. The shuttle stops at the hotel of each passenger; at peak hours, if there are many passengers, this may not be the fastest way from the airport. Unless you're alone, it's also probably not the cheapest. Call a day ahead to arrange a pickup for your return to the airport. Private **limousine taxis** (*taxis ejecutivos,* or *remises*) also have desks in the airport; their fares range from $27 to $45 round-trip.

BY BUS

Lima is connected by bus to neighboring countries and all major cities in Peru. No central bus terminal exists, however; the multitude of bus companies serving various regions of the country all have terminals in Lima, making bus arrivals and departures exceedingly confusing for most travelers. Many terminals are located downtown, though several companies have their bases in the suburbs. Most bus terminals have nasty reputations for thievery and general unpleasantness; your best bet is to grab your things and hop into a cab pronto. Of the dozens of bus companies servicing the capital and points around the country, the largest with frequent service in and out of Lima are **Ormeño,** Av. Javier Prado Este 1059, San Isidro (℃ **01/472-1710** or 01/427-5679); **Cruz del Sur,** Paseo de la República 809, La Victoria (℃ **01/428-2570** or 01/424-1005); **Oltursa,** Coronel Inclán 131, 2nd floor, Miraflores (℃ **01/445-8141**); and **Civa** (℃ **01/426-4926**).

BY TRAIN

There is no longer train service between Lima and Huancayo, high in the Andes. Lima was the starting point of the Ferrocarril Central railroad, the highest railway in the world (reaching up to 4,781m/15,685 ft.). The full-day trip through the highlands to Huancayo was one of the Americas' most impressive train trips. No word as of press time on when or if service will be reinstated.

VISITOR INFORMATION

A 24-hour **tourist information booth** (℃ **01/574-8000**) operates in the international terminal at the Jorge Chávez International Airport. The municipal **Oficina de Información Turística** is helpful and well located a block off the Plaza de Armas at Los Escribanos 145 in Lima Centro (℃ **01/427-6080**). It's open Monday through Friday from 9am to 6pm, and Saturday and Sunday from 10am to 5pm. Two other offices are found in Miraflores: One is a small booth in Parque Central that's open daily from 9am to 9pm (but not always according to schedule); the other is at Av. Larco 770 (℃ **01/446-2649**), and it's open Monday through Friday from 8:30am to 5pm.

One of the best private agencies for arrangements and city tours as well as general information is **Fertur Perú,** Jr. Junín 211 and Azángaro 105, within the Hotel España (℃ **01/427-1958**). Another excellent spot for information and advice, particularly on outdoor and adventure travel in Peru such as trekking, mountaineering, and rafting, is the **South American Explorers,** Piura 135, Miraflores (℃ **01/445-3306;** www.samexplo.org). The clubhouse in Lima serves members (you can join on the spot) with a great library of maps, books, trail information, trip reports, and storage facilities. The Lima clubhouse is open Monday through Friday from 9:30am to 5pm (Wed until 8pm), and Saturday from 9:30am to 1pm. There's also a clubhouse in Cusco.

CITY LAYOUT

Lima is an exceedingly diffuse city, complicated to get around. The city center, known as Lima Centro, abuts the Río Rímac and the Rímac district across the river. The city beyond central Lima is a warren of ill-defined neighborhoods; most visitors are likely to set foot in only San Isidro, Miraflores, and Barranco, which hug the coast and the circuit of urban beaches leading to the so-called "Costa Verde." Major thoroughfares leading from the city center to outer neighborhoods are Avenida Benavides (to Callao); Avenida Brasil (to Pueblo Libre); Avenida Arequipa, Avenida Tacna, and Avenida Garcilaso de la Vega (to San Isidro and Miraflores); Paseo de la República (also known as Vía Expresa) and Avenida Panamá (to Miraflores and Barranco); and Avenida Panamericana Sur (to San Borja and south of Lima).

THE NEIGHBORHOODS IN BRIEF

Lima Centro Lima Centro is the historic heart of the city, where the Spaniards built the country's capital in colonial fashion. It has repeatedly suffered from earthquakes, fires, and neglect, so while it was once the continent's most important colonial city, stunning examples of the original town are less prevalent than one might expect. Much of Lima Centro is dirty, unsafe, crowded, and chaotic, though city officials are finally getting to much-needed restoration of the remaining historic buildings and have drastically upgraded police presence in the city center (making it just about as safe as anywhere in the city during the day). The great majority of visitors stay in outer suburbs rather than Lima Centro; most hotels are small *hostales* (inns) aimed at budget travelers and backpackers. The absolute heart of the Lima Centro is the Plaza de Armas, site of La Catedral (the Cathedral) and government palaces, and nearly all the colonial mansions and churches of interest are within walking distance of the square. Several of Lima's top museums are in **Pueblo Libre,** a couple kilometers southwest of Lima Centro, while **San Borja,** a couple kilometers directly

south of Lima Centro, holds two of the finest collections in all of Peru.

Miraflores & San Isidro San Isidro and Miraflores, the most exclusive residential and commercial neighborhoods where most tourist hotels are located, are farther south (5km–8km/3–5 miles) toward the coast. These districts are now the commercial heart of the city, having usurped that title from Lima Centro some years ago. San Isidro holds many of the city's top luxury hotels and a slew of offices and shopping malls. Miraflores is the focus of most travelers' visits to Lima; it contains the greatest number and variety of hotels, bars, and restaurants, as well as shopping outlets. A number of the city's finest hotels are along the malecón (boulevard) in Miraflores. Although San Isidro and Miraflores are middle-class neighborhoods, both are congested and not entirely free of crime.

Barranco Barranco, several kilometers farther out along the ocean, is a tranquil former seaside village that is the city's coolest and most relaxed district, now known primarily for its nightlife. It is where you'll find several of Lima's best restaurants, bars, and live-music spots, frequented by Limeños and visitors alike.

2 Getting Around

Navigating Lima is a complicated and time-consuming task, made difficult by the city's sprawling character (many of the best hotels and restaurants are far from downtown, spread among three or more residential neighborhoods), heavy traffic and pollution, and a chaotic network of confusing and crowded *colectivos* and unregulated taxis.

BY TAXI

Taxis hailed on the street are a reasonable and relatively quick way to get around in Lima. However, taxis are wholly unregulated by the government: All anyone has to do to become a taxi driver is get his hands on a vehicle—of any size and condition, though most are tiny Daewoo "Ticos"—and plunk a cheap TAXI sticker inside the windshield. Then he is free to charge whatever he thinks he can get—with no meters, no laws, and nobody to answer to except the free market. One has to counsel visitors to be a bit wary taking taxis in Lima, even though I personally have never had problems greater than a dispute over a fare. (If you're not fluent in Spanish, and even if you are but you have an obviously non-Peruvian appearance, be prepared to negotiate fares.) Limeños tell enough stories of theft and even the occasional violent crime in unregistered cabs to make hailing one on the street inadvisable for older visitors or for those with little command of Spanish or experience traveling in Latin America. If you hail a taxi on the street, taxi drivers themselves have told me, try to pick out older drivers; many contend that young punks are almost wholly responsible for taxi crime. If the issue of getting into quasi-official cabs makes you nervous, by all means call a registered company from your hotel or restaurant—especially at night (even though the fare can be twice as much).

Registered, reputable taxi companies include **Taxi Amigo** (✆ 01/349-0177), **Taxi Móvil** (✆ 01/422-7100), or **Taxi Seguro** (✆ 01/275-2020). Whether you call or hail a taxi, you'll need to establish a price beforehand—be prepared to bargain. Most fares range from $2 to $5. From Miraflores to downtown, expect to pay S/8 to S/10 ($2.25–$3); from Miraflores to San Isidro, about S/5 ($1.50); San Isidro to downtown, S/5 to S/7 ($1.50–$2); Miraflores to Museo de Oro, S/8 to S/10 ($2.25–$3); and Miraflores to Barranco, S/5 ($1.50).

BY BUS

Local buses are of two general types: *micros* (large buses) and *combis* or *colectivos* (minibuses or vans). Long-distance buses are usually called *ómnibuses.* For most visitors, micros and combis constitute an adventure and a challenge: Both types are quite crowded, have a reputation for pickpockets, and can be hailed at any place along the street without regard to bus stops. You pay a *cobrador* (money collector), who is usually hanging out the door barking destinations at would-be travelers, rather than the driver. Micros and combis are very inexpensive means of transportation. Routes are more or less identified by signs with street names placed in the windshield, making many trips confusing for those unfamiliar with Lima. Some do nothing more than race up and down long avenues (for example, TODO AREQUIPA means it travels the length of Av. Arequipa). For assistance, ask a local for help; most Limeños know the incredibly complex bus system surprisingly well. Though they sometimes seem to hurtle down the street, because they make so many stops, trips from the outer suburbs to downtown can be quite slow. Most micros and combis cost S/1 (30¢), slightly more after midnight and on Sunday and holidays. When you wish to get off, shout *Baja* (getting off) or *Esquina* (at the corner).

From Lima Centro to Miraflores, look for buses with signs in the windows indicating LARCO–SCHELL–MIRAFLORES (or some combination therein). From Miraflores to downtown Lima, you should hop on a bus headed along WILSON/TACNA. Buses to Barranco have signs that read CHORILLOS/HUAYLAS.

BY FOOT

Lima can be navigated by foot only a neighborhood at a time (and even then, congestion and pollution strongly discourage much walking). Lima Centro and Barranco are best seen by foot, and while large, Miraflores is also walkable. Between neighborhoods, however, a taxi or combi is essential.

 FAST FACTS: **Lima**

Airport See "Arriving," earlier in this chapter.

American Express The office at Jr. Belén 1040 (© **01/330-4485**) is open Monday through Friday from 9am to 5pm. There is another office with similar hours at Pardo y Aliaga 698, San Isidro (© **01/222-2525**). Both are housed with Lima Tours travel agencies; they will replace stolen or lost traveler's checks and sell American Express checks with an Amex card, but neither office will cash their own checks.

Babysitters Your best bet is to inquire at your hotel for babysitting services. Many of the higher-quality hotels offer babysitting; if yours doesn't, the concierge may be able to recommend a service.

Banks/Currency Exchange Peruvian and international banks with currency-exchange bureaus and ATMs are plentiful throughout Lima Centro and especially in the outer neighborhoods such as Miraflores, San Isidro, and Barranco, which are full of shopping centers, hotels, and restaurants. Money-changers, usually wearing colored smocks (sometimes with obvious "$" insignias), patrol the main streets off Parque Central in Miraflores and central Lima with calculators and dollars in hand.

Principal banks include **Banco Central,** Jr. Antonio Miró Quesada 441 (© 01/427-6250); **Banco Continental,** Av. Los Paracas s/n (© 01/436-1469); **Banco de Comercio,** Jr. Lampa 560 (© 01/428-9400); **Banco Wiese,** Jr. Cuzco 245 (© 01/428-6000); and **Citibank,** Miguel Dasso 121, San Isidro (© 01/442-5146).

Car Rentals See "Arriving," earlier in this chapter.

Dentists & Doctors The U.S. and British embassies (see "Embassies & Consulates," below) provide lists of English-speaking doctors, dentists, and other healthcare personnel in Lima. For dentists, you might also try contacting the **International Academy of Integrated Dentistry,** Calle Centauro 177, Urbanización Los Granados, Monterrico, Surco (© **01/435-2153**). Additionally, see "Hospitals," below.

Drugstores Two huge, multiservice pharmacies open 24 hours a day are **Farmacia Deza,** Av. Conquistadores 1140, San Isidro (© **01/440-3798**), and **Pharmax,** Av. Salaverry 3100, San Isidro, in the Centro Comercio El Polo (© **01/264-2282**). A chain with a number of storefronts across Lima is **Superfarma** at Av. Benavides 2849 (© **01/222-1575**) and Avenida Armendariz, Miraflores (© **01/446-3333**). These and other pharmacies have 24-hour delivery service. For additional locations, consult the Yellow Pages under "Farmacias" and "Boticas."

Embassies & Consulates **U.S.,** Av. La Encalada, block 17, Monterrico (© 01/434-3000); **Australia,** Víctor A. Belaúnde 147/Vía Principal 155, office 1301, San Isidro (© 01/222-8281); **Canada,** Libertad 130, Miraflores (© 01/444-4015); **U.K.** and **New Zealand,** Natalio Sánchez 125, 4th floor (© 01/433-8923).

Emergencies Call the **traveler's hot line** at © **01/574-8000** or the **tourist police** at © **01/225-8698** or 01/225-8699. The general **police** emergency number Is © **105**; for **fire,** dial © **116.**

Hospitals English-speaking medical personnel and 24-hour emergency services are available at the following hospitals and clinics: **Clínica Anglo-Americana,** Alfredo Salazar, block 3, San Isidro (© 01/221-3656); **Clínica San Borja,** Guardia Civil 337, San Borja (© 01/475-4000); **Maison de Sante,** Calle Miguel Adgouin 208-222, near the Palacio de Justicia (© 01/428-3000, emergency 01/427-2941); and **Clínica Ricardo Palma,** Av. Javier Prado Este 1066, San Isidro (© 01/224-2224). For an ambulance, call **Alerta Médica** at © 01/470-5000 or **San Cristóbal** at © 01/440-0200.

Internet Access Internet *cabinas* (booths) are everywhere in Lima. Rates are about S/2 to S/3 (50¢–75¢) per hour, and most are open daily from 9am to 10pm or later. Try **Telnet,** Jr. Camaná 315; **Internet Pardo,** Av. José Pardo 620; **Cybersandeg,** Jr. de la Unión 853, office 112; **Wamnet,** corner of Diez Canseco and Alcanfores, mezzanine, Miraflores; or **C@bin@s de Internet,** Diez Canseco 380, Miraflores.

Maps Tourist information booths give out free maps, but in a sprawling, confusing city such as Lima, they are inadequate for more than basic indications. Probably the best street map available is the "Lima 2000" map sold at bookstores and kiosks. Good topographical maps are available from the **Instituto Geográfico Nacional** (IGN), located at Av. Aramburú 1190, San Isidro (© **01/475-9960**). Hiking maps are available from the **South American Explorers,** Piura 135, Miraflores (© **01/445-3306**).

Newspapers & Magazines In Lima, you will find copies (though rarely same-day publications) of the *International Herald Tribune* and the *Miami Herald,* as well as *Time, Newsweek,* and other special-interest publications. Top-flight hotels sometimes offer free daily fax summations of the *New York Times* to their guests. Outside Lima, international newspapers and magazines are hard to come by. Among local publications, look for *Rumbos,* a glossy Peruvian travel magazine in English and Spanish with excellent photography. If you read Spanish, *El Comercio* and *La República* are two of the best daily newspapers.

Police The **Policía Nacional de Turismo** (National Tourism Police) has staff members that speak English and are specifically trained to handle the needs of foreign visitors. The main office in Lima is at Av. Javier Prado Este 2465, 5th floor, San Borja (next to the Museo de la Nación); contact the 24-hour hot line at © **01/225-8698** or 01/476-9879.

Post Office/Mail Lima's main post office (*Central de Correos*) is located on the Plaza de Armas at Camaná 195 (© **01/427-0370**) in central Lima. The Miraflores branch is at Petit Thouars 5201 (© **01/445-0697**); the San Isidro branch is at Calle Las Palmeras 205 (℡ 01/422-0981). A **DHL/Western Union** office is located at Nicolás de Piérola 808 (℡ 01/424-5820).

Restrooms The only public restrooms you're likely to find will be in airport and bus terminals, bars and restaurants, museums, and hotels. Sometimes it's easier to duck into a large hotel than into a restaurant.

Safety In downtown Lima and the city's residential and hotel areas, the risk of street crime remains high. Although carjackings, assaults, and armed robberies are not routine, they're not unheard of either. Armed attacks at ATMs have also occurred. Use ATMs during the day, with other people present. Public transportation on buses and combis are where most thefts occur. Be very careful with your belongings; leave your passport and other valuables in the hotel safe and use a money belt. Public street markets are also frequented by thieves, as are parks (especially at night), and the beaches in and around Lima. Taxis hailed on the street are considered dangerous by many residents of the city. Use telephone-dispatched radio taxis, especially at night. Ask your hotel or restaurant to call a cab, or call one from the list of recommended taxi companies (see "Getting Around," above).

Taxis See "Getting Around," above.

Telephone Lima's area code is 01. It need not be dialed when making local calls within Lima, but it must be dialed when calling Lima from another city. Telephone booths are found throughout the city; the principal Telefónica del Perú office, where you can make long-distance and international calls, is on Plaza San Martín (Carabaya 937) in Lima Centro (℡ 01/224-9355).

3 Where to Stay

Lima Centro has its share of hotels and budget inns, but most people head out to the residential neighborhoods of Miraflores, San Isidro, and, to a lesser extent, Barranco. These barrios have little in the way of sights, but they are more convenient for nightlife and shopping and probably safer, if not necessarily much quieter.

Hotel rates in Lima are the highest in the country, especially at the top end. There are plenty of midrange and budget choices, though few have the charm of affordable hostales in other cities. Unless otherwise noted, prices do not include taxes, service charges, or breakfast. Particularly at the top echelon, hotels tack on taxes and service charges to quoted rates, whereas most moderate and less-expensive inns quote rates that already include all taxes and service charges. Be on the lookout for any hotel that tries to charge you the 18% IGV (sales tax) on the basic room rate in addition to a 10% service charge. Foreigners and nonresidents with the passport to prove it should be exempted from the IGV (but not the service charges). Most hostales in Lima—unlike in Cusco, Arequipa, and a few other highland towns—do feature 24-hour hot water.

LIMA CENTRO
MODERATE
Gran Hotel Bolívar 🅡 *Value* Central Lima is filled with budget hostales for backpackers, but the area has few options for folks who want both a taste of old Lima and some comfort. This luxurious six-floor hotel, most of it nicely renovated, is probably the best-value upscale choice in central Lima (and a nice antidote to the extremely modern business hotels of the outer barrios). Since

Where to Stay & Dine in Lima Centro

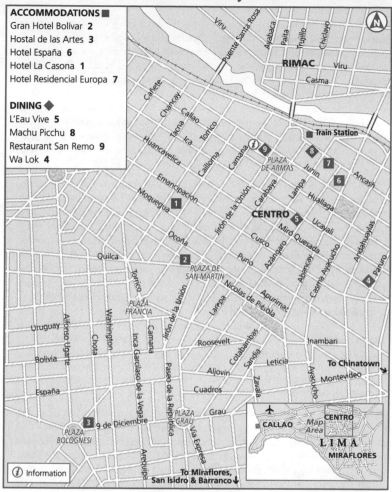

ACCOMMODATIONS ■
Gran Hotel Bolívar **2**
Hostal de las Artes **3**
Hotel España **6**
Hotel La Casona **1**
Hotel Residencial Europa **7**

DINING ◆
L'Eau Vive **5**
Machu Picchu **8**
Restaurant San Remo **9**
Wa Lok **4**

1924, it has occupied nearly a whole block on one side of handsome Plaza San Martín, just a 10-minute walk from the Plaza de Armas. Though it doesn't come close to the standards of Lima's finest new luxury hotels, the staff is very friendly and the public rooms couldn't be any grander. The lobby, where you can enjoy tea along with piano music, is crowned by an extraordinary stained-glass cupola. A grand staircase and neoclassical marble columns lead to the rooms. You can usually get an upgrade to a large junior suite, with a giant tile bathroom and late colonial–style furnishings, for the same price as a standard double (and probably less than the rack rate). The top floors aren't frequently filled, so ask for a room on either the second or third floor, which receive better upkeep. Though the Plaza San Martín itself isn't particularly dangerous, you should return by taxi to be safe.

Jr. de la Unión 958, Plaza San Martín, Lima. © 01/428-7672. Fax 01/428-7675. bolivar@terra.com.pe. 272 units. $90 double; $110–$250 suite. Rates include continental breakfast. MC, V. Covered parking. **Amenities:** 2 restaurants; cocktail lounge; coffee shop; concierge; 24-hr. room service; laundry service; 24-hr. medical service. *In room:* A/C, TV, minibar, hair dryer.

INEXPENSIVE

Hostal de las Artes *(Value)*   Located on the southern fringes of Lima Centro, a block from Plaza Bolognesi, this small Dutch-owned hostal is very friendly and well run—and one of the best budget bargains in town. It occupies an attractive, restored colonial-style house and has a pretty patio. It's safe, clean, and understandably very popular with backpackers and other value-conscious travelers. Some rooms could afford to be spruced up a bit, so if several are available, ask to see a couple on different floors. The hostal is also very gay-friendly. In case this one's full, the owners also operate a second, more basic hostal around the corner.

Jr. Chota 1460, Lima. ℭ 01/433-0031. Fax 01/428-5546. 18 units. http://arteswelcome.tripod.com. $9 per person double with shared bathroom; $6 per person, dormitory style. No credit cards. No parking. **Amenities:** Book exchange; luggage storage facilities; airport pickup available.

Hotel España *(Finds)*   Near the Convento de San Francisco and just 4 blocks from the Plaza de Armas, this extremely popular budget hostal has a funky flair and communal atmosphere. If you're looking to hook up with backpackers from around the globe and set off to explore Peru, you can't do better than Hotel España. It occupies a rambling colonial building chock-full of paintings, ceramics, faux Roman busts, plants, and even the occasional mummy and skull. A maze of rooms, most with shared bathrooms and some with odd numbers such as D3 and G2, are located up a winding staircase. The rooms themselves are simple, with concrete floors but bright wall colors. The leafy rooftop garden terrace, with views of San Francisco, is a good place to hang out and trade travel tales. Security is said to be a little lax, so store your stuff in the lockers. Hot water goes to the early bird. The place can be noisy and even a little nuts, but that's part of its charm.

Azángaro 105, Lima. ℭ 01/427-9196. Fax 01/428-5546. cmundonet@hotmail.com. 30 units (6 with private bathroom). $6 double with shared bathroom, $12 with private bathroom. No credit cards. No parking. **Amenities:** Cafe; laundry service; travel agency; traveler's message boards; book exchange; luggage storage facilities and lockers; nightly videos. *In room:* No phone.

Hotel La Casona   A decent budget option for those who want to be in the thick of Lima Centro's colonial quarter, within close range of churches and mansions, and about a 10-minute walk from the Plaza de Armas, La Casona is pleasant and friendly, built around an airy central courtyard. Rooms are basic, with high ceilings; a few are rather dismal and can be uncomfortably humid, so ask to see several. Many rooms come equipped with curious 1950s and '60s furniture and grandma-style big box TVs. In an attempt to compete with the more popular España and Europa hotels, it has converted a few rooms into "Backpacker's" dorm-style accommodations containing bathrooms.

Jr. Moquegua 289, Lima. ℭ and fax 01/426-6552. 40 units. S/30 ($9) double; S/12 ($3.50) per person in dorm rooms. Rates include taxes. No credit cards. Covered parking. **Amenities:** Restaurant; room service; communal TV room; luggage storage. *In room:* No phone.

Hotel Residencial Europa   This hotel is another grand old colonial mansion and shoestring traveler's favorite in the heart of Lima Centro. Though it has two interior courtyards, it has less character than Hotel España, and the rooms are a little dull and monastic, but the price can't be beat. There's a communal TV where you can catch up on sports scores and news (and cheesy Peruvian variety shows). The shared bathrooms have been known to be less than generous when it comes to hot water.

Jr. Ancash 376, Lima. ℭ 01/427-3351. 62 units. S/25 ($7) double with shared bathroom, S/35 ($10) with private bathroom. No parking. **Amenities:** Communal TV room. *In room:* No phone.

MIRAFLORES

VERY EXPENSIVE

Miraflores Park Plaza ⭐⭐⭐   Lima's most elegant hotel, the Park Plaza bathes business executives and upscale tourists in unsurpassed luxury. It hugs the malecón, the park-lined avenue that traces the Lima coastline. From the cozy, library-like lobby and handsome restaurant to the tastefully appointed, plush rooms (including marble and granite bathrooms most New Yorkers would give their left arms to live in), the hotel is a distinguished address from head to foot. All rooms are suites with comfortable king-size beds and sitting areas equipped with large televisions and VCRs, fax machines, two phone lines, and dataports. Many rooms have ocean views—at least for the few days of the year when you can see the coast in Lima.

Av. Malecón de la Reserva 1035, Miraflores, Lima. ℂ 01/242-3000. Fax 01/242-3393. www.mira-park. com/eng/index-ingles.html. 81 units. $270 deluxe double; $310–$650 suite. AE, DC, MC, V. Valet parking. **Amenities:** Restaurant; bar; cafe; small outdoor rooftop pool; exercise room and squash court; sauna; concierge; extensive business center and executive services; salon; 24-hr. room service; laundry service. *In room:* A/C, TV/VCR, fax, dataport, minibar, hair dryer.

EXPENSIVE

Best Western Embajadores ⭐   A reasonably priced hotel well located on a quiet residential street just 10 minutes from Parque Kennedy and the commercial nexus of Miraflores, this Best Western doesn't offer many surprises. The rooms could stand to be updated and soundproofed, but if you're looking for a convenient place to crash without dropping a lot of dough—and some of the other alternatives at this price point are full—it's not a bad 3-star option. The staff is very friendly and the hotel is well run, with a pretty good restaurant and bar, a small terrace-top outdoor pool and Jacuzzi, and conference facilities.

Juan Fanning 320, Miraflores, Lima. ℂ 01/242-9127. Fax 01/442-9131. www.bestwestern.com. 45 units. $98 double. AE, DC, MC, V. Covered parking. **Amenities:** Restaurant; bar; small outdoor rooftop pool; exercise room; Jacuzzi; game room; business center; 24-hr. room service; laundry service. *In room:* A/C, TV, minibar, safe.

Hotel Antigua Miraflores ⭐⭐⭐ *Kids* *Value*   This charming early-20th-century mansion, full of authentic Peruvian touches and color, calls itself "a hidden treasure in the heart of Miraflores." As many return visitors know, that's not just hype. Owned and operated by a North American who's a longtime resident of Lima, the house is elegant and tasteful, built around a leafy courtyard, and lined with colonial Peruvian art. The staff is exceptionally helpful and friendly. Rooms range from huge suites with large Jacuzzi bathtubs and kitchenettes to comfortable "colonial" double rooms with handcrafted furniture and good beds. Most bathrooms are quite luxurious, with colonial tiles, brass fixtures, and bathtubs. The public rooms look more like an art gallery than a hotel lobby. (The paintings are for sale.)

Av. Grau 350, Miraflores, Lima. ℂ 01/241-6116. Fax 01/241-6115. http://peru-hotels-inns.com. 35 units. $79–$89 double; $104 suite. Rates include taxes and a nice selection of traditional American and English breakfasts. AE, DC, MC, V. Free parking. **Amenities:** Restaurant; bar; small gym; Jacuzzi; room service; laundry service; e-mail facilities; airport transfers, safety deposit box. *In room:* A/C, TV, minibar, hair dryer.

Hotel & Suites Las Américas ⭐   A gleaming, modern high-rise hotel in the heart of Miraflores' top shopping and entertainment area, Las Américas caters to visiting business travelers with its ample and well-equipped rooms and suites. Rooms are nicely decorated in standard modern hotel decor, with separate sitting areas (very large in some suites); some rooms have nice views of the city and—on rare good days—the ocean. All suites have Jacuzzis. Ask about special discounts and upgrades; when the hotel isn't full, they are frequently available at significant reductions.

Av. Benavides 415 (at Av. Larco), Miraflores, Lima. (℃ **01/241-2820.** Fax 01/444-1137. www.hoteleslas americas.com. 151 units. $180 double; $200–$330 suites. Rates include breakfast buffet. AE, MC, V. Valet parking. **Amenities:** Restaurant; bar; piano bar; cafeteria; small outdoor swimming pool; small gym; sauna; business center; salon; room service; laundry service; casino; disco. *In room:* A/C, TV, dataport, minibar, safe.

JW Marriott Hotel & Casino 😿😿 *(Value)* Open since July 2000, this upscale business traveler's hotel isn't as luxurious as the exclusive Park Plaza or Swissôtel, but it's considerably more affordable, making it a very good value given the overall quality and dependability of the Marriott chain. It's a gleaming, ultramodern high-rise building hugging the coast and parks along the malecón, replete with glitzy ground-floor shops and a much-frequented casino. It seems to serve mostly short- and long-term business travelers from North and South America, but it's perfectly fine for leisure travelers and families. Children can be easily entertained at the outdoor pool or on the tennis court. Rooms are very well equipped and comfortable, with nice bathrooms, if without a whole lot of individual character. Inexpensive weekend rates are available, making the Marriott one of the best values in Lima.

Av. Malecón de la Reserva 615 Miraflores, Lima. (℃ **01/217-7000.** Fax 01/217-7002. www.marriott.com. 300 units. $145 deluxe double; $165 executive double; $185 junior suite. AE, DC, MC, V. Valet parking. **Amenities:** 2 restaurants; cafe; outdoor pool; health club; sauna; concierge; extensive business center and executive services; salon; 24-hr. room service; laundry service. *In room:* A/C, TV, dataport, minibar, hair dryer, safe.

Sonesta Posada del Inca 😿😿 The Miraflores branch of a chain with a handful of hotels across Peru (and several in Lima), this small modern hotel is efficient and professional. Centrally located just 2 blocks from Parque Central (Parque Kennedy), it's within easy walking distance of Miraflores' many nightclubs, restaurants, and shops. As they are across the chain, the well-appointed rooms are large with very comfortable beds, good-size bathrooms, and the familiar ochre-and-deep green color scheme with plaid bedspreads.

Alcanfores 329, Miraflores, Lima. (℃ **800/SONESTA,** 01/241-7688, or 01/222-4777. Fax 01/447-8199. www. sonesta.com/peru_miraflores. 28 units. $90 double; $120 suite. Rates include taxes, service charge, and breakfast buffet. AE, DC, MC, V. Free parking. **Amenities:** 24-hr. cafe and bar; fitness center (½ block from hotel); concierge; business center with fax and Internet access; 24-hr. room service; babysitting; laundry service; nonsmoking rooms. *In room:* A/C, TV, minibar, safe; hair dryer on request.

MODERATE

Hotel Colonial Inn On a busy avenue in Miraflores, flush with fast-food restaurants and stores galore, this oddly charming small hotel, a large yellow colonial building on a corner, is a surprising retreat for a modest price. Popular and often full, it's got lots of colonial flavor, from the masculine staircases and grand Spanish-style chairs and fireplace in the public rooms to the wood-beamed restaurant with copper pots hanging above the arches and armor on the walls. Carpeted rooms have interesting touches, such as their own arches above the beds, dark-wood ceilings, and lantern-like lamps. The tile bathrooms are a good size, with bathtubs; the suites have large Jacuzzis. The attached restaurant, La Tasca, has good-value fixed-price lunches.

Comandante Espinar 310, Miraflores, Lima. (℃ **01/241-7471.** Fax 01/445-7587. www.hotelcolonialinn.com. 37 units. $70 double. Rate includes taxes and breakfast buffet. AE, DC, MC, V. Limited street parking. **Amenities:** Restaurant; bar; room service; laundry service. *In room:* TV, minibar, safe.

Hotel La Castellana A nice-looking hacienda-style colonial house on a quiet street in Miraflores, this pleasant midrange option is comfortable and welcoming, even if the old-style and occasionally dingy accommodations don't live up to the promise of the inn's exterior or homey public rooms. The hotel features

Where to Stay & Dine in Miraflores

ACCOMMODATIONS ■
Best Western Embajadores **13**
Hostal Colonial Inn **1**
Hostal José Luis **17**
Hotel & Suites Las Américas **12**
Hotel Antigua Miraflores **5**
Hotel La Castellana **15**
Inkawasi Backpacker **3**
JW Marriott Hotel & Casino **19**
Miraflores Park Plaza **18**
San Antonio Abad **16**
Sonesta Posada del Inca **11**

DINING ◆
Antico Ristorante Italiano
  di Porto Rotondo **6**
Astrid y Gastón **10**
Café Café **7**
Café Suisse
  (La Tiendecita Blanca) **9**
El Señorío de Sulco **2**
La Trattoria di Mambrino **8**
Larco Pan Café **14**
Las Brujas de Cachiche **4**

an attractive courtyard and garden, which some rooms overlook; other rooms have colonial balconies and views of the street. All rooms have wall-to-wall carpeting and private bathrooms.

Grimaldo del Solar 222, Miraflores, Lima. © **01/444-4662.** Fax 01/446-8030. www.hotel-lacastellana.com. 40 units. $60 double. Rate includes taxes. AE, DC, MC, V. Limited street parking. **Amenities:** Restaurant; bar; limited business facilities with fax and e-mail access; 24-hr. room service; babysitting; laundry service; nonsmoking rooms. *In room:* TV, minibar, hair dryer, safe, ceiling fans, no phone.

San Antonio Abad 🟊 Named for a saint, this clean and very friendly neighborhood hotel aims high. Its goal is to be welcoming and comfortable, and it succeeds. The colonial building, near the commercial center of Miraflores and several parks, has a garden terrace, fireplace, and sitting room. The rooms, which are simply decorated but ample, have private bathrooms with hot water around the clock. Because of street noise (ever present in Lima), you might ask for a room with an interior courtyard view.

Av. Ramón Ribeyro 301, Miraflores, Lima. © **01/447-6766.** Fax 01/446-4208. www.hotelsanantonioabad.com. 24 units. $55 double; $120 suite. Rates include taxes and breakfast buffet. AE, DC, MC, V. Free parking. **Amenities:** Restaurant; bar; room service; laundry service; complimentary airport pickup; e-mail facilities; safety deposit box. *In room:* A/C, TV, minibar; hair dryer on request.

INEXPENSIVE

Hostal José Luis With only overgrown vegetation creeping over a high wall and no sign out front, this private youth-hostel-like B&B has operated on word-of-mouth for nearly 20 years. Deceptively large, with a capacity for nearly 60 guests, it's one of the cheapest places in Miraflores. It's secluded in a quiet residential part of the district, a 10-minute walk from Parque Central and its hubbub of nightlife and shops. As the name would indicate, there's a family feeling here, with cooking and laundry facilities. The common rooms are busy with furnishings and patterned wallpaper, but many rooms have bunk beds, dorm-room style. All have private bathrooms and 24-hour hot water.

Fransisco de Paula Ugarriza 727, Miraflores, Lima. © **01/444-1015.** Fax 01/446-7177. www.hoteljoseluis.com. 20 units. $12 per person. Rate includes taxes and breakfast. Limited street parking. **Amenities:** TV; fax and e-mail services. *In room:* No phone.

Inkawasi Backpacker 🟊 *(Kids)* Designed to appeal to backpackers, this pleasant bed-and-breakfast is a step up from most Peruvian hostales. It features an airy and comfortable homey atmosphere in a secure part of Miraflores, just a few blocks from shops, restaurants, banks, and cinemas. There are two fully equipped kitchens available to guests, an interior patio and garden, and a roof garden and barbecue area. All rooms have private bathrooms, and suites have a queen-size bed, desk, kitchenette with microwave, minibar, and cable TV. The inn is especially family-friendly; kids can enjoy a play area with toys and children's videos.

Alfredo Salazar 345, Miraflores, Lima. © and fax **01/422-7724.** www.inkawasi.com. 10 units. $10 per person, or $25–$35 double; $45 suite. Rates include taxes and continental breakfast. Use of kitchen $2 a day; extra bed $5; children's bed $2. Limited street parking. **Amenities:** TV/VCR in common room (some family videos available); fax; kitchen facilities; laundry service. *In room:* TV, minibar, and kitchenette in suites, no phone.

SAN ISIDRO
VERY EXPENSIVE

Country Club Lima Hotel 🟊🟊🟊 *(Kids)* This incredibly grand, lovely, and sprawling hacienda-style hotel, built in 1927 and wholly refurbished in 1998, is a swank and character-filled place to rest your head in Lima. Though it appears large, the hotel is in fact very cozy, friendly, and low-key. Rooms—all of which are suites, with separate work areas—are large and very luxurious, with tons of

Jugglers, dancers and an assortment of acrobats fill the street.

She shoots you a wide-eyed look as a seven-foot cartoon character approaches.

What brought you here was wanting the kids

to see something magical while they still believed in magic.

America Online Keyword: Travel

With 700 airlines, 50,000 hotels and over 5,000 cruise and vacation getaways, you can now go places you've always dreamed of.

Travelocity.com™
A Sabre Company
Go Virtually Anywhere.

"WORLD'S LEADING TRAVEL WEB SITE, 5 YEARS IN A ROW" WORLD TRAVEL AWARDS

Where to Stay & Dine in San Isidro

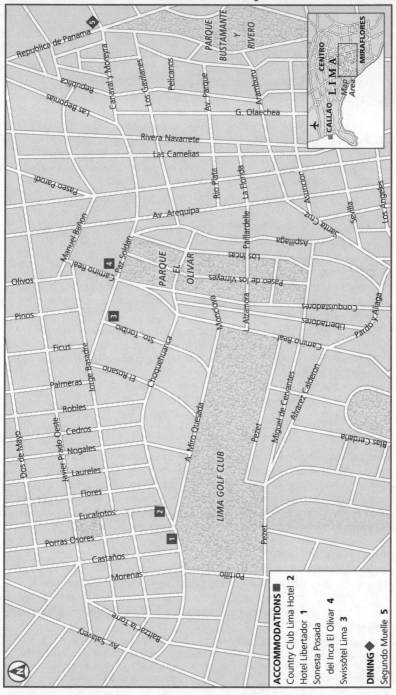

ACCOMMODATIONS ■
Country Club Lima Hotel **2**
Hotel Libertador **1**
Sonesta Posada
del Inca El Olivar **4**
Swissôtel Lima **3**

DINING ◆
Segundo Muelle **5**

Kids Family-Friendly Hotels

In Lima, you'll probably have to head to the suburbs if you're traveling with children. Lima Centro is just too crowded, polluted, and unsafe at night for the great majority of families to feel comfortable.

Country Club Lima Hotel (p. 118) For the family traveling in style, this historic and lovingly restored hacienda-style hotel will provide a memorable stay for both parents and children. Though it's full of antiques and elegant public rooms, there's plenty of room for the kids to run around. There are guest privileges at the excellent golf course and tennis club next door and a nice outdoor pool on the premises. Overall, it's a good value, too.

Hotel Antigua Miraflores (p. 115) More a large B&B than a hotel, this charming and low-key inn, a safe haven in the midst of busy Lima, is friendly and warmly decorated, and a good value. Suites have small kitchen facilities, ideal for fixing small meals for fussy eaters.

Inkawasi Backpacker (p. 118) Young backpacking families with kids in tow will find this very pleasant B&B a good, cheap place to park the group in Lima. It features two fully equipped kitchens (suites have kitchenettes with microwave), gardens, and a barbecue area, as well as a play area with toys and children's videos.

Sonesta Posada del Inca El Olívar (below) Though popular with business travelers, the El Olívar, which fronts a tranquil park, is also well positioned for families. Children will enjoy the outdoor rooftop pool, and if the price is a little high here, check out the more affordable Posada del Inca San Isidro, just a few blocks away. Guests there are free to use the pool and gym at El Olívar.

antiques and old-world appeal (though they don't skimp on modern conveniences). Many of the huge marble bathrooms have large Jacuzzis and separate showers. A member of The Leading Hotels of the World, it is ideal for just about anyone, including families, but especially perfect for stressed-out business travelers who've seen one too many blandly elegant hotels. Public rooms are very refined and inviting, with chandeliers and very high wood-beam ceilings, a close approximation of a local nobleman's estate. It's not surprising that they host frequent social functions. There's live music every Friday and Saturday evening in the elegant restaurant, and afternoon tea is served to the accompaniment of live piano music. Appropriately enough, the Country Club Hotel sits next to a golf course and tennis club (guest privileges included). The hotel is fairly priced for this kind of luxury and service; it also offers very good corporate rates, and packages are available.

Los Eucaliptos 590, San Isidro, Lima. © 01/611-9000. Fax 01/611-9002. www.lhw.com. 75 units. $220–$265 suite. AE, DC, MC, V. Valet parking. **Amenities:** 3 restaurants; bar; outdoor pool and sauna; fitness center; concierge; business center and meeting facilities; salon; 24-hr. room service; laundry service; nonsmoking rooms; guest privileges at Lima Golf Club across the street. *In room:* A/C, TV, dataport, minibar, safe.

Sonesta Posada del Inca El Olívar 🎄🎄 *Kids* *Value* The Sonesta chain's upscale property, aimed squarely at visiting business travelers, is El Olívar, named for the historic Olive Grove Park, which it faces. This seven-story hotel, opened in 1992, is well located for its dominant clientele, in a peaceful section of the San Isidro business district of the city. The rooms, a step up from the more rustic decor in the chain's other Posadas del Inca, are quite large, with beige marble bathrooms. Service is friendly and efficient, and the amenities outdo most hotels in the city. Business travelers on a tighter budget who nonetheless wish to stay in San Isidro should also check out the Sonesta Posada del Inca San Isidro, an easygoing 50-room sister property whose guests are allowed to use the pool and gym at El Olívar. It's located just a few blocks away at Av. Libertadores 490 (© 01/222-4373; $105 double, including taxes).

Pancho Fierro 194, San Isidro, Lima. © 01/221-2121. Fax 01/221-2141. www.sonesta.com. 134 units. $160–$190 double; $290–$700 suite. Rates include breakfast buffet. Children under 8 stay free in their parents' rooms. Weekend deals $99 per night. AE, DC, MC, V. Free parking. **Amenities:** 2 restaurants; cafe; cocktail lounge; bar; fitness center with rooftop outdoor pool and sun deck; golf privileges at nearby club; Jacuzzi; sauna; concierge; business and conference center with computers, fax and free Internet access; complimentary translation and typing; salon; massage; babysitting; 24-hr. valet and laundry service; airport pickup service; complimentary coffee/tea service; nonsmoking rooms. *In room:* A/C, TV/VCR w/pay movies, minibar, hair dryer, safe.

Swissôtel Lima 𝒜𝒜 One of Lima's most exclusive and sophisticated properties is this 5-year-old sparkling high-rise hotel. Formerly the Peruvian-owned Oro Verde, it takes its new pedigree (part of the international Swissôtel chain) very seriously: The hotel is very Continental classy. The lobby is awash in fine carpets, corridors are curiously lined with giant neoclassical columns, restaurants serve Swiss and Italian as well as Peruvian fare, and service is, of course, eminently efficient. Rooms are spacious and well appointed. Executive rooms include a work desk, two telephone lines, a coffee machine, a private executive lounge/board room, and cocktails (!). For business facilities, this property rivals the Marriott and Park Plaza, though I find the latter the most distinguished of the three.

Vía Central 150 (Centro Empresarial Real), San Isidro, Lima. © 01/421-4400. Fax 01/421-4422. www.swissotel.com. 244 units. $195–$330 double; $560–$1,200 suite. Rates include taxes and service charge. AE, DC, MC, V. Valet parking. **Amenities:** 3 restaurants; bar/lounge; cafeteria; small heated outdoor pool; fitness center; spa; sauna; concierge; business center with fax and Internet access, secretarial service; translations; salon; 24-hr. room service; laundry service; travel agency; nonsmoking rooms. *In room:* A/C, TV, safe.

MODERATE

Hotel Libertador 𝒜 *Value* Smack in the middle of the San Isidro financial district, the Libertador is relatively unassuming and tranquil, especially considering the more imposing and flashier hotels nearby. Still, that's its charm. It doesn't try too hard, but it gets the job done for guests that are both business travelers and tourists. Part of a five-member, very well-run Peruvian chain of upscale hotels, this midsize offering is handsomely decorated with modern art, some Kilim rugs, and bold colors—eschewing the typical blandness of business hotels—and has a nice top-floor restaurant and bar with good views. Quite a good value, especially if you can get an upgrade to a junior suite.

Los Eucaliptos 550, San Isidro, Lima. © 01/421-6666. Fax 01/442-3011. www.libertador.com.pe. 54 units. $80 double; $950–$235 suite. AE, DC, MC, V. Valet parking. **Amenities:** Restaurant; bar; gym; Jacuzzi; sauna; concierge; laundry service; Internet access. *In room:* A/C, TV, minibar.

BARRANCO
INEXPENSIVE

Mochileros 𝒜 *Value* The name means "backpackers," but this isn't your typical youth hostel. A great looking 1903 post-colonial mansion—once an evidently handsome theater—in the heart of Lima's most laid-back and bohemian district, Barranco. It has terrific communal rooms, painted in vibrant colors, with high ceilings. There are both large shared rooms and a handful of private doubles and singles. Shared bathrooms are outside the main building but have hot water all day. The on-site Irish Pub, Dirty Nelly's, is good fun and open every day but Sunday. (To locate this hotel, see the "Lima at a Glance" map on p. 105.)

Av. Pedro de Osma 135, Barranco, Lima. © 01/477-4506. Fax 01/247-6089. www.backpackersperu.com. 10 units. $10 per person in shared room; $30 double. Rates include breakfast. Free parking. **Amenities:** Restaurant; bar; TV lounge; bicycle rental; dining room and kitchen facilities; Internet access; lockers. *In room:* No phone.

4 Where to Dine

As one might expect, Lima presents the most cosmopolitan dining city in all of Peru, with restaurants of all budgets and a wide range of cuisines—from upscale seafood restaurants and *comida criolla* (coastal Peruvian cooking) to Chinese and plenty of Italian, French, and other international restaurants. Sometimes, there are entire streets and neighborhoods specializing in a single type of food. In Lima Centro you can visit the *chifas* of Chinatown, and in Miraflores, a pedestrian street off Parque Central is referred to as "Little Italy" for its scores of look-alike pizzerias and Italian restaurants.

Restaurants are, predictably, most crowded in the early evening, especially Thursday through Saturday. In the business districts of Miraflores and San Isidro, lunch can also get quite busy—at least in the nicer restaurants that are popular with local and international businessmen.

Fixed-price lunch deals are referred to below as *menús del día* (or simply *menú*). The majority of restaurants include all taxes and services in their prices, and your bill will reflect the menu prices. Others (including some upscale restaurants), however, separate taxes and services, and the bill can get pretty byzantine, especially when it comes to imported wine. You might see a subtotal, followed by a 10% service charge, a 20% "selectivo" wine tax, and an 18% IGV (general sales tax). It's crazy. Fortunately, the restaurants that do this are rare.

To locate restaurants in Lima Centro, Miraflores, and San Isidro, see the maps "Where to Stay & Dine in Lima Centro" (p. 113), "Where to Stay & Dine in Miraflores" (p. 117), and "Where to Stay & Dine in San Isidro" (p. 119).

LIMA CENTRO
MODERATE

L'Eau Vive ☆ *Finds* FRENCH/PERUVIAN If you're feeling obscenely rich in this impoverished country, you'll do a tiny bit of good and feel better by eating here. The restaurant, run by a French order of nuns, donates its proceeds to charity. In a colonial palace 2 blocks from the Plaza de Armas and across the street from one of Lima's most important mansions, Torre Tagle, it features several large dining rooms with high ceilings. If you come for the cheap lunch menú, though, you'll have to sit in the simpler front rooms. The "a la carte" dining rooms are considerably more elegant. Though the lunch menú is a deal, at night you get a pious show free with dinner: The nuns sing "Ave María" promptly at 9:30pm. The French menu includes items such as prawn bisque, trout baked in cognac, and grilled meats; it also incorporates some international dishes from around the globe—chiefly the many countries from which the order's nuns come.

Ucayali 370. © 01/427-5612. Reservations recommended on weekend nights. Main courses S/9–S/43 ($2.50–$12); menú del día S/8–S/12 ($1.25–$3.50). AE, DC, MC, V. Mon–Sat 12:30–3pm and 7:30–9:30pm.

Restaurant San Remo PERUVIAN On one of Lima Centro's more appealing streets, the tiny pedestrian passageway Los Escribanos near the Plaza de Armas, this efficient eatery has an attractive terrace with outdoor tables. Popular with local businessmen and travelers who trickle out of the tourism information office next door, it offers particularly good deals at lunch. The evening menu lists plenty of criollo and seafood plates from the Peruvian coast, including gourmet dishes with pre-Columbian influences. At lunch, though, most people sit down to more standard fare such as grilled trout and fettuccine Alfredo, served with a salad and beverage.

Los Escribanos 137–141. ℂ 01/427-9102. Reservations recommended on weekend evenings. Main courses S/10–S/28 ($3–$8); menú del día $6–$7. MC, V. Mon–Thurs 9am–9pm; Fri–Sat 9am–midnight.

INEXPENSIVE

Machu Picchu PERUVIAN   This extremely simple downtown restaurant is popular with budget travelers and folks on the way in or out of the San Francisco monastery, one of Lima Centro's top sights, across the street. It's a pleasant eating hall, with a long row of tables down one wall and more tables in back. Don't expect gourmet food, but you can be sure to get a very inexpensive, filling meal of Peruvian criollo standards such as *guiso* (stew) and *arroz con pollo* (chicken and rice), as well as a decent selection of fish and shellfish. The midday menú is ridiculously cheap.

Jr. Ancash 312. ℂ 01/427-9336. Reservations not accepted. Main courses S/7–S/19 ($2–$5.50); menú del día S/4.50 ($1.25). No credit cards. Daily 8am–10pm.

MIRAFLORES & SAN ISIDRO
VERY EXPENSIVE

Astrid y Gastón 🏵🏵🏵 PERUVIAN/INTERNATIONAL   Hidden discreetly behind a nonchalant facade on a busy side street leading to Parque Central is this warm and chic modern colonial dining room and cozy bar. The restaurant has high white peaked ceilings and orange walls decorated with colorful modern art, the products of local art students. At the back is an open kitchen where one of the owners, Gastón, can be seen cooking with his staff. The place is sophisticated but low-key, a description that could fit most of its clients, who all seem to be regulars. The menu might be called "criollo-Mediterranean"—Peruvian with a light touch. Try the spicy roasted kid or the excellent fish called *noble robado*, served in miso sauce with crunchy oysters. The list of desserts is nearly as long as the main-course menu. At evening's end, Astrid (the other member of the husband/wife team) often takes a seat and chats with customers at their tables.

Cantuarias 175, Miraflores. ℂ 01/444-1496. Reservations recommended. Main courses S/39–S/59 ($11–$17). AE, DC, MC, V. Mon–Sat 12:30–3:30pm and 7:30–midnight.

Las Brujas de Cachiche 🏵🏵 PERUVIAN (CRIOLLO)   The "Witches of Cachiche" celebrates 2,000 years of local culture with a menu that's a tour of the

---

⟨*Tips*⟩ Peruvian *Chifas*

Chinatown (Barrio Chino), southeast of the Plaza de Armas and next to the Mercado Central (beyond the Chinese arch on Jr. Ucayali), is a good place to sample the Peruvian take on Chinese food. These chifas, inexpensive restaurants with similar menus, are everywhere in the small but dense neighborhood. Among those worth visiting (generally open daily 9am–10pm or later) are **Wa Lok**, Jr. Paruro 864 (ℂ 01/427-2656), probably the best known in the neighborhood; **Salón Capon,** Jr. Paruro 864 (ℂ 01/426-9286), known for its dim sum; and **Salón China**, Jr. Ucayali 727 (ℂ 01/428-8350), which serves a good lunch buffet for S/30 ($9).

"magical" cuisines of pre-Columbian Peru. The chef even uses ancient recipes and ingredients. The extensive menu includes classic Peruvian dishes, such as *ají de gallina* (chili cream chicken), but concentrates on fresh fish and shellfish and fine cuts of meat with interesting twists and unusual accompaniments. Brujas de Cachiche sole is prepared with Asian and *criollo* (creole) spices and served with peas and bell peppers sautéed in soybean sauce. A steak in pisco-butter sauce is served with braised mushrooms. Among the excellent desserts, several continue the indigenous theme, such as *mazamorra morada* (purple corn pudding and dried fruit). The restaurant, in a sprawling old house with several warmly decorated dining rooms, is popular both night and day with well-heeled Limeños, expat businessmen and foreign government officials, and tourists. A lunch buffet is served Tuesday through Friday and Sunday from 11am to 4pm, and gastronomic festivals are frequent.

Jr. Bolognesi 460, Miraflores. ℂ 01/447-1883. Reservations recommended. Main courses S/30–S/62 ($9–$18); lunch buffet $33, including 2 glasses of wine. AE, DC, MC, V. Mon–Sat 1pm–midnight; Sun noon–5pm.

EXPENSIVE

El Señorío de Sulco ✿✿ PERUVIAN (CRIOLLO) Similar in purpose, style, and execution to Las Brujas de Cachiche, this elegant restaurant takes a thoughtful approach to traditional Peruvian cooking. Located at the northern extreme of the Miraflores district at the end of Avenida Pardo, the restaurant has several dining rooms, including a piano bar and an enclosed terrace that overlooks the coast. Many of the dishes come served in earthenware pots. Start with a *chupe de camarones,* a delicious soup of river shrimp, yellow potatoes, corn on the cob, milk, and cheese, or share a *ronda de ceviches,* a combo plate of sole, octopus, prawns, oysters, sea urchins, and scallops. For a main course, *huatia sulcana,* a dish of pre-Columbian origin, is beef stewed in a clay pot and smothered in aromatic herbs. The daily lunch buffet, with its almost overwhelming lineup of cold and hot plates, is the perfect way to sample a wide variety of Peruvian dishes, some spicier than others.

Malecón Cisneros 1470, Miraflores. ℂ 01/441-0389. Reservations recommended. Main courses S/28–S/55 ($8–$16). AE, DC, MC, V. Mon–Sat noon–midnight; Sun noon–5pm.

MODERATE

Antico Ristorante Italiano di Porto Rotondo ✿ ITALIAN A pretty yellow colonial house with an inviting library-like club bar off to one side, Porto Rotondo is a sophisticated retreat in the midst of Miraflores' hustle and bustle. Inside, you'll find deep red walls, black-and-white tile floors, and large mirrors. The menu focuses on classic and well-prepared Italian dishes: ravioli, risotto, gnocchi, and osso buco, as well as fresh fish. Some nights, there are many more people sitting at the bar than around the dining tables in the next room.

Recavarren 265, Miraflores. ℂ 01/447-9575. Reservations recommended. Main courses S/25–S/36 ($7–$10). MC, V. Daily noon–4pm and 8pm–midnight.

Café Suisse (La Tiendecita Blanca) (Kids) SWISS/INTERNATIONAL This classic old-style cafe, a Lima institution since 1937, is decorated with cool enamel doors and staffed by waitresses in folkloric red-and-white dresses. It's best known for its exquisite pastries, cakes, breads, and gourmet food shop, but "the little white store" is also a good little restaurant, perfect for lunch and even breakfast. Choose from fresh-baked quiches, *empanadas* (turnover pastries served stuffed or empty), and sandwiches, or go Swiss with a fondue for two. There's a daily lunch *menú de la casa* for $10. Of course, if you spot that long counter bursting with homemade desserts, you may be unable to resist spoiling your meal.

Av. Larco 111, Miraflores. ℭ **01/445-9797.** Reservations not accepted. Main courses S/19–S/34 ($5–$10). AE, DC, MC, V. Daily 8am–10pm.

La Trattoria di Mambrino *Kids* ITALIAN   One of Lima's most popular and enduring Italian eateries is this attractive bistro, owned by an Italian gentleman who makes the rounds on most evenings. Decorated in warm Roman tones, the restaurant is often packed with families and young couples. La Trattoria bakes its own delicious rustic bread—with a bit of olive oil, it's an appetizer in itself. Among the many excellent homemade pastas are several stuffed versions, such as the anglotti with three meats: rabbit, pork, and beef. There are daily specials such as ragout of rabbit over pappardelle, and stuffed peppers with prawns. Pizzas from the wood-burning oven and large fresh salads round out the menu.

Manuel Bonilla 106, Miraflores. ℭ **01/446-7002.** Reservations recommended. Main courses S/20–S/55 ($6–$16). AE, DC, MC, V. Daily 1–3:15pm and 8–11:15pm.

Segundo Muelle *Finds* SEAFOOD/CEVICHE   At the top of most people's lists of favorite Peruvian dishes is ceviche, and you won't have trouble finding a *cevichería* anywhere along the coast. Often, you have to choose between either very upscale or down-and-dirty versions. This informal, lunch-only place in San Isidro, popular with local office workers, is one of the most reasonable options in Lima for excellent fresh fish and ceviche plates without any fuss. Choose between a simple, almost cafeteria-style interior and an outdoor terrace. If you're new to ceviche, you can't go wrong with the *mixto* (white fish, octopus, prawns, snails, scallops, and squid). There is a long list of other fish dishes, including sole, salmon, seafood pastas, and various rice and seafood plates. Top off your meal with *chicha morada,* a purple-corn beverage made with pineapple and lemon—it's sweet and delicious. Kids plates are available for S/12 ($3.50). There's a second branch in San Isidro at Av. Conquistadores 490 (ℭ 01/421-1206).

Av. Canaval y Moreyra 605 (at the corner of Pablo Carriquirry), San Isidro. ℭ **01/224-3007.** Reservations not accepted. Main courses S/18–S/30 ($5–$8.50). MC, V. Daily noon–5pm.

INEXPENSIVE

Café Café SANDWICHES/COFFEE   A tried-and-true people-watching spot with a menu of 100-plus drinks and dozens of gourmet coffees, this agreeable two-story cafe, located just off the main park in Miraflores, is also ideal for a quick lunch or simple dinner. The predominantly young crowd drops by not only to meet up with friends and hang out at the outdoor tables, but also to sample inexpensive pizzas, salads (including a salad bar), or one of the 26 sandwiches. For folks in need of a real meal, there are also larger plates, including a fish of the day. It's also a good spot to have a quick and inexpensive breakfast.

Mártir Olaya 250, Miraflores. ℭ **01/445-1165.** Main courses S/8–S/34 ($2–$10). AE, DC, MC, V. Daily 8:30am–1:30am.

Larco Pan Café CAFE FARE   Sometimes in a foreign country—especially in a frenzied city like Lima—all you need is a cheap no-frills place where you can take a break and not have to deal with deciphering yet another menu. This cute little cafe, simple as can be, features a single daily *menú ejecutivo.* On the day I stopped by, pooped, they were offering a ceviche appetizer followed by fried fish, dessert, and fruit juice—all for about $2. If the set-lunch menú doesn't appeal to you, there are also pizzas, pastas, and sandwiches.

Av. Larco 1106, Miraflores. ℭ **01/445-3801.** Reservations not accepted. Most items under $4; menú del día S/8 ($2.25). Daily 8:30am–11pm.

(Kids) Family-Friendly Restaurants

Besides the restaurants listed below, families might head to "Little Italy," the restaurant row of pizzerias and pasta joints along a short pedestrian-only block leading off the Parque Kennedy (Parque Central) in Miraflores. There are a dozen places to choose from, most very popular with local families.

Antica Trattoria (p. 127) Just a couple blocks from Barranco's Municipal Park, where families hang out, this elegantly rustic Italian restaurant specializes in gourmet pizzas from wood-fired ovens. Adventurous palates will be tempted by unusual combinations, while kiddies who can't stand eggplant on their pie can have good old cheese pizza or spaghetti. The restaurant is divided up into several small dining rooms, perfect for families worried about an outburst from an overly tired kid.

Café Suisse (La Tiendecita Blanca) (p. 124) A longtime favorite old-style cafe from the 1930s, "the little white store" has great lunch options, including sandwiches, quiches, and a good-value menú de la casa for $10, and full breakfasts. The kids will be as tempted by the impressive lineup of homemade pastries, cakes, and breads as their parents will be. Waitresses are decked out in cute folkloric red-and-white dresses.

La Trattoria di Mambrino (p. 125) A very friendly Italian restaurant with some of the best pizzas in town, La Trattoria offers plenty of more sophisticated dishes for stressed-out parents who can't look at another slice of pizza. It's very popular with young Limeño families. The excellent home-baked rustic bread will tide over young ones who've been forced to eat later than they're accustomed to.

Manos Morenas (p. 127) Older kids who can stay up late should enjoy not only the authentic Peruvian cooking at this handsome 1900s house in a quiet part of Barranco, but also the nightly shows of costumed music and dance shows that are the restaurant's calling card. (Shows begin at 9pm Tues–Thurs, 10:30pm Fri–Sat.) It's the best option for families who want to drop in on a peña in Lima—others are much more of the nightclub variety—but the cover is a little stiff.

BARRANCO

To locate the following restaurants, see the "Lima at a Glance" map on p. 105.

VERY EXPENSIVE

Costa Verde ★★ *Overrated* SEAFOOD Any time a restaurant in Peru lists all prices in dollars, you know it's not going to be cheap. Costa Verde, perched on a promontory jutting out into the ocean along the "green coast" south of Miraflores, is probably as expensive a meal as you'll have in Peru, but it's also good enough to draw a decent number of Limeños celebrating special occasions. It draws a bigger share of foreigners, as evidenced by the touristy little national flags the hostess places on everyone's table. (I suggest telling her you're from Iceland or Zimbabwe, just to see how well stocked they are in miniature flags.) The restaurant is attractive enough, but it's the big-time seafood buffet that makes everyone's eyes bulge. There's a daily lunch buffet and also a huge gourmet dinner buffet ($60 a head—in Peru!), which the restaurant claims is registered in the *Guinness Book of Records.* The regular menu seems not to have changed in more than 3 decades of business, but you can't really argue with sea bass with wild mushrooms and morel sauce with scallop mousse, or basil and ricotta gnocchi with river shrimp in saffron sauce. Not in the mood for fish? Try the pork loin in beer-and-honey sauce. Sit in the glass-enclosed atrium—though it's rather devoid of character, you'll get to hear the sound of waves crashing against the shore. Then again, that may be the sound of your bank account crashing and burning.

Circuito de Playas (Playa Barranquito), Barranco. (C) 01/227-1244. Reservations recommended. Main courses $13–$29. AE, DC, MC, V. Daily 11am–midnight.

EXPENSIVE

Manos Morenas ✸✸✸ *(Kids* PERUVIAN (CRIOLLO)   In a beautiful early-1900s house on a quiet, leafy street in Barranco, this is one of the coolest restaurants in Lima. The name makes reference to the country's small but culturally potent Afro-Peruvian population and its traditions, influences crucial to both the menu and the lively, costumed music-and-dance shows that the restaurant has become famous for. The main dining room, in what was the house's interior patio, is very appealing, with handsome wood chairs and tables and art for sale on the elegant yellow walls. A nice bar greets you at the entrance in case you have to wait for a table. The kitchen, staffed by women dressed like the restaurant's logo of a black woman in a head wrap, creates excellent versions of Peruvian standards such as *lomo saltado, ají de gallina, tamalitos verdes* (green tamales), and *papa rellena* (stuffed potatoes). *Corvina Manos Morenas* is sea bass served with mashed potatoes, spinach, prawns, and a béchamel sauce. The restaurant charges a substantial cover (S/40, or $12) for the live shows, which are featured Tuesday through Thursday from 9pm to 1am, and Friday and Saturday from 10:30pm to 1am.

Av. Pedro de Osma 409, Barranco. (C) 01/467-0421. Reservations recommended. Main courses S/17–S/39 ($5–$11). AE, DC, MC, V. Mon–Sat 12:30–4pm and 7pm–1am.

MODERATE

Antica Trattoria ✸✸ *(Kids* *(Value* ITALIAN   This charming and laid-back Italian restaurant perfectly suits the surrounding neighborhood, which has large doses of both qualities. It has a number of small, separate dining rooms decorated with a rustic and minimalist masculinity: stucco walls, dark wood-beamed ceilings, country-style wood tables, and simple, solid chairs. The house specialty is gourmet pizza from the wood-fired ovens, but the menu has several tempting ideas to lure you away from pizza, such as homemade pastas and osso buco, or delicious *lomo fino a la tagliata* (beef buried under a mound of arugula). The relaxed environment makes this a great date place, as well as the perfect spot for dinner before stepping out to one of Barranco's live music or dance clubs.

San Martín 201, Barranco. (C) 01/247-5752. Reservations recommended. Main courses S/19–S/35 ($5.50–$10). AE, DC, MC, V. Daily noon–midnight.

5 What to See & Do

Many visitors to Lima are merely on their way to other places in Peru. But because everything goes through the capital, most people take advantage of layovers to see what distinguishes Lima: its colonial old quarter—once the finest in the Americas—and several of the finest museums in Peru, all of which serve as magnificent introductions to Peruvian history and culture.

Much of the historic center has suffered from sad neglect; the municipal government is committed to restoring the aesthetic value, but, with limited funds, it faces a daunting task. Today, central Lima has a noticeable police presence and is considerably safer than it was just a few years ago. A full day in Lima Centro should suffice; depending on your interests, you could spend anywhere from a day to a week traipsing through Lima's many museum collections, many of which are dispersed in otherwise unremarkable neighborhoods.

LIMA CENTRO: COLONIAL LIMA

Lima's grand **Plaza de Armas** ✿ (also called the Plaza Mayor, or Main Square), the original center of the city and the site where Francisco Pizarro founded the city in 1535, is essentially a modern reconstruction. The disastrous 1746 earthquake that initiated the city's decline leveled most of the 16th- and 17th-century buildings in the old center. The plaza has witnessed everything from bullfights to Inquisition-related executions. The oldest surviving element of the square is the central bronze fountain, which dates from 1651. Today, the square, while perhaps not the most beautiful or languid in South America, is still rather distinguished beneath a surface level of grime and bustle (and it has been named a UNESCO World Heritage Site). The major palaces and cathedral are mostly harmonious in architectural style and color. (The facades are a mix of natural stone and a once-bold yellow color now dulled by smog and mist.) On the north side of the square is the early-20th-century **Palacio del Gobierno** (Presidential Palace), where a changing of the guard takes place daily at noon. The **Municipalidad de Lima** (City Hall) is on the west side of the plaza. Across the square is **La Catedral**, rebuilt after the earthquake, making it by far the oldest building on the square, and next to the cathedral, the **Palacio Episcopal** (Archbishop's Palace), distinguished by an extraordinary wooden balcony.

A block north of the Plaza de Armas, behind the Presidential Palace, is the Río Rímac and a 17th-century Roman-style bridge, the **Puente de Piedra** (literally, "stone bridge"). It leads to the once-fashionable **Rímac** district, today considerably less chic—some would say downright dangerous—though it is the location of a few of Lima's best peñas, or live criollo music clubs. The **Plaza de Acho bullring,** once the largest in the world, and the decent **Museo Taurino** (Bullfighting Museum) are near the river at Hualgayoc 332 (✆ **01/482-3360**). The museum is open Monday through Friday from 9am to 3pm, and Saturday from 9am to 2pm. The ring is in full swing during the Fiestas Patrias (national holidays) at the end of July; the regular season runs October through December.

Five blocks southwest of Plaza de Armas is Lima Centro's other grand square, **Plaza San Martín.** Inaugurated in 1921, this stately square with handsome gardens was recently renovated. At its center is a large monument to the South American liberator, José de San Martín.

Lima's **Barrio Chino,** the largest Chinese community in South America (200,000 plus), is visited by most folks to get a taste of the Peruvian twist on traditional Chinese cooking in the neighborhood's chifas. For recommendations, see the "Peruvian *Chifas*" box on p. 123. The official boundary of Chinatown is the large gate on Jirón Ucayali.

THE TOP ATTRACTIONS

Convento y Museo de San Francisco ✿✿   Probably the most spectacular of Lima's colonial-era churches, the Convent of Saint Francis is a strikingly restored, yellow-and-white 17th-century complex that survived the massive earthquake in 1746. The facade is a favorite of thousands of pigeons, who rest

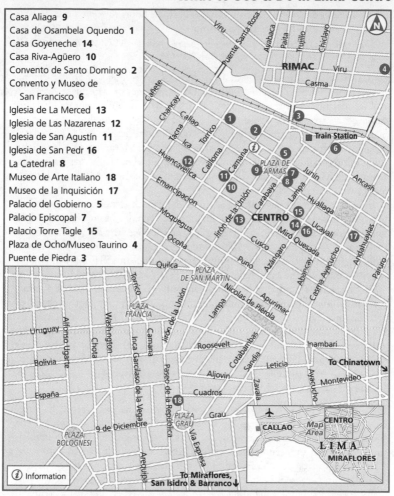

Casa Aliaga **9**
Casa de Osambela Oquendo **1**
Casa Goyeneche **14**
Casa Riva-Agüero **10**
Convento de Santo Domingo **2**
Convento y Museo de
  San Francisco **6**
Iglesia de La Merced **13**
Iglesia de Las Nazarenas **12**
Iglesia de San Agustín **11**
Iglesia de San Pedr **16**
La Catedral **8**
Museo de Arte Italiano **18**
Museo de la Inquisición **17**
Palacio del Gobierno **5**
Palacio Episcopal **7**
Palacio Torre Tagle **15**
Plaza de Ocho/Museo Taurino **4**
Puente de Piedra **3**

on rows of ridges that rise up the towers—so much so that, from a distance, it looks like black spots add an unexpectedly funky flavor to the baroque church. Cloisters and interiors are lined with beautiful *azulejos* (glazed ceramic tiles) from Seville; carved *mudéjar* (Moorish-style) ceilings are overhead. The mandatory guided tour takes visitors past the cloisters to a fine museum of religious art, with beautifully carved saints and a series of portraits of the apostles by the studio of Francisco Zurbarán, the famed Spanish painter. For many, though, the most fascinating component of the visit is the descent into the catacombs, which were dug beginning in 1546 as a burial ground for priests and others. (As many as 75,000 bodies were interred here before the main cemetery was built.) File past loads of bones—it's unknown how many levels down they go—and see a round well lined with perfectly laid skulls and femurs. Also of great interest are the church, outfitted with an impressive neoclassical altar, and a fantastic 17th-century library with 20,000 books, many of which date to the first years after Lima's foundation. A breathtaking carved Moorish ceiling over a staircase is a reconstruction of the original from 1625. Allow 1½ hours to see it all, including waiting time for an English-language tour.

Plaza de San Francisco (between Lampa and Ancash). No phone. Admission S/5 ($1.50) adults, S/2.50 (75¢) students. Guides available in English and Spanish. Daily 9am–4:45pm.

La Catedral ⭐ Lima's baroque cathedral, an enlargement of an earlier one from 1555, was completed in 1625. It suffered damages in earthquakes in 1687 and was decimated by the big one in 1746. The present building, though again damaged by tremors in 1940, is an 18th-century reconstruction of the early plans. Twin yellow towers sandwich an elaborate stone facade. Inside are several notable Churrigueresque (Spanish baroque) altars and carved wooden choir stalls, but the cathedral is best known for the chapel where Francisco Pizarro lies and a small **Museo de Arte Religioso** (Museum of Religious Art) housed in the rear of the church.

Immediately to the right after you enter the church is a chapel decorated in magnificent Venetian mosaics and marble. In case you don't know whose earthly remains are inside the tomb, letters in mosaic tiles over the arch of the chapel spell out FRANCISCO PIZARRO. The founder of Lima and killer of the Inca's emperor was himself assassinated in the Plaza de Armas in 1541, but his remains weren't brought to the cathedral until 1985. (They were discovered in a crypt in 1977.) Look closely at the mosaic on the far wall, which depicts his coat of arms, Atahualpa reaching into his coffer to cough up a ransom in the hopes of attaining his release, and other symbols of Pizarro's life. The museum has a few fabulous painted-glass mirrors from Cusco, a collection of unsigned paintings, and a seated sculpture of Jesus, with his chin resting pensively on his hand; it's as bloody a figure of Christ as you're likely to see. Allow about an hour for a visit.

Plaza de Armas. © 01/427-5980. Admission S/5 ($1.50) adults, S/3 ($1) students. Guides available in English and Spanish (voluntary tip). Mon–Sat 10am–5pm.

Museo de la Inquisición *Finds* This magnificent mansion across the street from the House of Congress once belonged to the family considered the founders of Lima, but it became the tribunal for the notorious Spanish Inquisition. Today, it is a museum that soberly addresses religious intolerance from the Middle Ages through colonial times. The handsomely restored house itself is worth a visit, because it's a fine peek at the elegant rooms of a prominent 16th-century colonial home (including the intricately carved ceiling of the Tribunal room). But its unfortunate history is plainly evident in the catacombs, which served as prison cells; on view are several instruments of torture. At least 32 Peruvians died here during the Inquisition, which persisted until 1820. The guided tour lasts about an hour.

Plaza Bolívar (Junín 548). © 01/427-5980. Free admission. Guided tours in English, Spanish, French, and Portuguese. Daily 10am–6pm.

COLONIAL CHURCH ROUNDUP ⭐⭐
Lima Centro has a number of fine colonial-era churches worth visiting. Most are open Monday through Saturday for visits, and most have free admission.

Directly south of La Catedral on Azángaro at Ucayal, **San Pedro** (© 01/428-3017), a Jesuit church that dates to 1638, is perhaps the best-preserved example of early colonial religious architecture in the city. The exterior is simple and rather austere, but the interior is rich with gilded altars and balconies. The bold main altar, with columns and balconies and sculpted figures, is particularly impressive. There are also some beautiful 17th- and 18th-century baroque *retablos* (gradines) of carved wood and gold leaf. A small museum of colonial art

is to the right of the entrance of the church, which is open Monday through Saturday from 10am to 1pm and 5 to 8pm.

Iglesia de La Merced, Jirón de la Unión at Miró Quesada (© **01/427-8199**), 2 blocks southwest of the Plaza de Armas, was erected on the site of Lima's first Mass in 1534. The 18th-century church has a striking carved baroque colonial facade. Inside, the sacristy, embellished with Moorish tiles, and the main altar are excellent examples of the period. The church also possesses a nice collection of colonial art. Yet it is perhaps most notable for the devoted followers of Padre Urraca, a 17th-century priest; they come daily in droves to pay their respects, praying and touching the large silver cross dedicated to him in the right-hand nave, and leaving many mementos of their veneration. The church is open Monday through Saturday from 8am to noon and 4 to 8pm.

Practically destroyed during an 1895 revolution, **San Agustín,** located at the corner of Jirón Ica and Jirón Camaná (© **01/427-7548**), is distinguished by a spectacular Churrigueresque facade, one of the best of its kind in Peru, dating to the early 18th century. San Agustín's official hours are Monday through Sunday from 8 to 11am and 4:30 to 7pm, but, in practice, it's frequently closed. The **Convento de Santo Domingo,** located at the corner of Conde de Superunda and Camaná, toward the River Rímac (© **01/427-6793**), draws many Peruvians to visit the tombs of Santa Rosa de Lima and San Martín de Porras. It is perhaps of less interest to foreign visitors, though it does have a very nice main cloister. It's open Monday through Saturday from 9am to 12:30pm and 3 to 6pm; admission costs S/3 ($1).

Las Nazarenas, at the corner of Huancavelica and Avenida Tacna on the northwest edge of the colonial center (© **01/423-5718**), has a remarkable history. It was constructed in the 18th century around a locally famous painting of Christ by an Angolan slave. Known as "El Señor de los Milagros," the image, painted on the wall of a simple abode (many slaves lived in this area on the fringes of the city), survived the massive 1655 earthquake, even though everything around it crumbled. People began to flock to the painting and soon the Catholic Church literally constructed a house of worship for it. Behind the altar, on the still-standing wall, is an oil replica, which is paraded through the streets on a 1-ton silver litter during the El Señor de los Milagros festival, which is one of Lima's largest and is held on October 18, 19, and 28 and November 1. Everyone wears purple during the procession. Las Nazarenas is open Monday through Saturday from 6am to noon and 5 to 8pm.

COLONIAL PALACE ROUNDUP 𝄞

The historic quarter of Lima, the old administrative capital of Spain's South American colonies, once boasted many of the finest mansions in the hemisphere. Repeated devastation by earthquakes and more recent public and private inability to maintain many of the superb surviving *casas coloniales,* however, has left Lima with only a handful of houses open to the public.

Casa Riva-Agüero, Camaná 459 (© **01/427-9275**), is an impressive 18th-century mansion with a beautiful green-and-red courtyard that now belongs to the Catholic University of Peru. It has a small folk-art museum in the restored and furnished interior. The house is open Tuesday through Saturday from 10am to 1pm and 2 to 7:30pm; admission costs S/2 (50¢). **Casa Aliaga,** Jr. de la Unión 224 (© **01/427-6624**) is the oldest surviving house in Lima, dating from 1535. It is also one of Lima's finest mansions, with an extraordinary inner patio and elegant salons, and it continues to be owned and lived in by descendants of the original family. The house can be visited only as part of a city tour

> **Tips Me Ama, No Me Ama, Me Ama . . .**
>
> A curious park along the ocean at the edge of Miraflores, much beloved by Limeños looking to score, the **Parque del Amor** (literally, "Love Park") is a cut-rate imitation of Antonio Gaudí's Parque Guell in Barcelona, Spain. It features good views of the sea (when it's not shrouded in heavy fog), benches swathed in broken-tile mosaics, and, most amusingly, a giant, grotesque statue of a couple making out—which is pretty much what everyone does nearby. Benches are inscribed with thickly sentimental murmurs of love such as *vuelve mi palomita.* If it's Valentine's Day, stand back.

($25) conducted exclusively by Lima Tours (© 01/424-5110). A worthy alternative if you don't want to spring for a guided tour is **Casa de Osambela Oquendo,** Conde de Superunda 298 (© 01/428-7919). The tallest house in colonial Lima, today it belongs to the Ministry of Education, and while it's still not officially open for visits, the caretaker, Lizardo Retes Bustamante, will show visitors around, including up four levels to the baby-blue cupola-mirador for views over the city. (The original owner built the house so he could see all the way to the port.) Next door is a 1770 house in a lamentable state; squatters inhabit it. The Osambela house has a spectacular patio, 40 bedrooms, and eight wooden balconies to the street, a sure sign of the owner's great wealth. It's open daily from 9am to 5pm; admission is free, but tips are accepted.

A couple blocks east of the Plaza de Armas at Ucayali 363 is **Palacio Torre Tagle,** the most famous palace in Lima and one of the most handsome in Peru. Today, the early 18th-century palace, built by a marquis who was treasurer of the Royal Spanish fleet, belongs to the Peruvian Foreign Ministry and, sadly, can no longer be visited by the public. Its exterior, with a gorgeous baroque stone doorway and carved dark-wood balconies, is very much worth a look (and you may get a peek inside the courtyard if a group of dark suits enters or leaves when you're passing by). Across the street from Torre Tagle, **Casa Goyeneche** (also called Casa de Rada) is another impressive 18th-century mansion, with distinct French influences; it's also not open to the public. Those with a specific interest in colonial architecture may also wish to have a look at the facades of **Casa Negreiros,** Jr. Azángaro 532; **Casa de las Trece Monedas,** Jr. Ancash 536; **Casa Barbieri,** Jr. Callao at Rufino Torrico; **Casa de Pilatos,** Jr. Ancash 390; and **Casa la Riva,** Jr. Ica 426.

THE TOP MUSEUMS

To locate the following museums, see the "Lima at a Glance" map on p. 105.

Museo Arqueológico Rafael Larco Herrera ⭐⭐   Founded in 1926, this is the largest private collection of pre-Columbian art in the world. It concentrates on the Moche dynasty, especially on its refined ceramics, with an estimated 45,000 pieces—including incredibly fine textiles, jewelry, and stonework from several other ancient cultures—all housed in an 18th-century colonial building. Rafael Larco Hoyle is considered the founder of Peruvian archaeology (he named the museum after his father); he wrote the seminal study *Los Mochicas* in 1938, though he succeeded in publishing only six chapters. (The rest has now been posthumously published.)

The Moche (A.D. 200–700), who lived along the northern coast in the large area near present-day Trujillo and Cajamarca, are credited with achieving one of

greatest artistic expressions of ancient Peru. The collection may be overwhelming to visitors who know little about the Moche, but one soon learns that the pottery gives clues to all elements of their society: diseases, curing practices, architecture, transportation, dance, agriculture, music, and religion. The Moche are also celebrated in the modern world for their erotic ceramics. The Sala Erótica is removed from the general collection, like the porn section in a video store. It's outdoors, downstairs, and across the garden. The Moche depicted sex in realistic, humorous, moralistic, religious, and—above all—explicit terms; the most common and even a few deviant practices are represented. If you're traveling with kids, expect giggles or questions about the ancient Peruvians' mighty phalluses. Plan on spending 2 hours to see it all.

Av. Bolívar 1515, Pueblo Libre. (© 01/461-1312. Admission S/20 ($6) adults, S/10 ($3) students. Private guides available in English and Spanish (tip basis, minimum S/10). Daily 9am–6pm. Take a taxi or the "Todo Brasil" colectivo to Av. Brasil and then another to Av. Bolívar. If you're coming from the Museo Nacional de Arqueología, Antropología e Historia del Perú (p. 134), walk along the blue path.

Museo de la Nación ☆☆☆ *Kids*   Peru's ancient history is exceedingly complicated—not to mention new territory for most visitors to the country. Indeed, Peru's pre-Columbian civilizations were among the most sophisticated of their times; when Egypt was building pyramids, people in Peru were constructing great cities. Lima's National Museum, the city's biggest and one of the most important in Peru, guides visitors through the highlights of overlapping and conquering cultures and their achievements, seen not only in architecture (including scale models of most major ruins in Peru) but also in highly advanced ceramics and textiles. The exhibits, spread over three rambling floors, are ordered chronologically—very helpful for getting a grip on these many cultures dispersed across Peru. They trace the art and history of the earliest inhabitants to the Inca Empire, the last before colonization by the Spaniards. In case you aren't able to make it to the archaeology-rich north of Peru, pay special attention to the facsimile of the Lord of Sipán discovery, one of the most important in the world in recent years. Explanations accompanying the exhibits are for the most part in both Spanish and English. Allow 2 to 3 hours for your visit.

Av. Javier Prado Este 2465, San Borja. (© 01/476-9878. Admission S/6 ($1.75) adults, S/3 ($1) seniors, S/1 (30¢) students. Tues–Sun 9am–5pm. Guides in several languages can be contracted. You can get here by colectivo along Av. Prado from Av. Arequipa, but it is much simpler to take a taxi from Lima Centro or Miraflores/San Isidro.

Museo de Oro del Perú ☆☆☆   The privately held Gold Museum is a gold mine in itself, drawing tourists in droves (and at one of the highest admission prices of any Peruvian museum). But most visitors concur that it's worth the crowds and the cost. The massive collection—assembled by one man, Miguel Mujica Gallo—of ceremonial objects, jewelry, and most of all, gold, from both the Incas and pre-Inca civilizations, glitters at every turn. Cases upon cases of the telling jewels and symbols of Peru's pre-Columbian history compete for your attention. But it's not just gold: There are hundreds, if not thousands, of exquisite tapestries on the second floor, masks, ancient weapons, clothing, several mummies, and an entire museum of military weaponry and uniforms from medieval Europe to ancient Japan. Frustratingly, visitors must purchase a rather expensive and not-altogether-well-done catalog to follow the exhibits, as explanatory plaques are scarce. Many famous items from the gold collection, such as the Tumi that has become a symbol of Peru, have been exhibited around the world. The entrance to the museum is lined with several chic souvenir boutiques, a cafe or two, and a bookshop. Allow several hours.

Av. Alonso de Molina 1100, Monterrico. ✆ 01/345-1292. Admission S/25 ($7) adults, S/10 ($3) students. Daily 11am–7pm. A taxi is the most direct way here; coming by colectivo involves taking at least 2 buses, along Arequipa to Av. Angamos and changing to one marked "Universidad de Lima," and asking the driver to let you off at the Museo de Oro.

Museo Nacional de Arqueología, Antropología e Historia del Perú

With such a mouthful of an official name, you might expect the National Museum of Archaeology, Anthropology and History to be the Peruvian equivalent of the Met. It's not (especially since much of the museum's huge collection remains in storage), but it's a worthwhile and enjoyable museum that covers Peruvian civilization from prehistoric times to the colonial and republican periods. There are ceramics, carved stone figures and obelisks, metalwork and jewelry, and lovely textiles. On view are early ceramics from 2800 B.C. in the central Andes, the great granite Tello Obelisk from the Chavín period, burial tombs, and mummies in the fetal position wrapped in burial blankets. There's also a selection of erotic ceramics from the Moche culture, but it's not nearly as extensive as that of the Museo Arqueológico Rafael Larco Herrera (p. 132). Individual rooms are dedicated to the Nasca, Paracas, Mochica, and Chimú cultures. Toward the end of the exhibit, which wanders around the central courtyard of the handsome 19th-century Quinta de los Libertadores mansion (once lived in by South American independence heroes San Martín and Bolívar), is a large-scale model of Machu Picchu with buttons that allows visitors to identify key sectors of the complex. Basic descriptions throughout the museum are mostly in Spanish, though some are also in English. Allow about an hour.

From the museum, you can follow a walking path along a painted blue line to the Rafael Larco Herrera Museum. It's about a mile away, or 20 minutes straight into traffic on Antonio de Sucre (make sure you turn at the Metro supermarket on Leguía Melendes).

Plaza Bolívar s/n, Pueblo Libre. ✆ 01/463-5070. Admission S/10 ($3) adults, S/5 ($1.50) students. Private guides available in English and Spanish (tip basis, minimum S/10, or $3). Tues–Sat 9:15am–5pm; Sun 10am–5pm. Take a taxi here, or take the "Todo Brasil" colectivo to Av. Vivanco and then a 15-min. walk.

OTHER MUSEUMS

To locate Fundación Museo Amano and Museo de Arte Colonial Pedro de Osma, see the "Lima at a Glance" map on p. 105. To locate Museo de Arte Italiano, see the "What to See & Do in Lima Centro" map on p. 129.

Fundación Museo Amano   This museum features a nice collection of artifacts belonging to a single collector, representing some of Peru's most important civilizations, including the Chimú and Nasca. The textiles and ceramics are among the best-displayed in Lima, and the collection really shows the strength of Chancay weaving (a culture from the northern coast), which you may not see a whole lot of elsewhere. You've really got to want to see the collection, though (and qualify, as restrictive as that sounds); it's open for limited hours and only by previous appointment to small groups. Allow about an hour or more.

Calle Retiro 160, Miraflores. ✆ 01/441-2909. Free admission (donations accepted). Mon–Fri 2–5pm by appointment and guided tour in Spanish. Take a taxi to the 11th block of Av. Angamos Oeste/Av. Santa Cruz.

Museo de Arte Colonial Pedro de Osma   This private museum, located in a historic Barranco mansion (Palacio de Osma), focuses on colonial Peruvian art from areas that were among the most distinguished cultural centers of the day, including Cusco, Arequipa, and Ayacucho. Like the Amano Museum, you'll need to call for an appointment, though you can also drop by and hope to get a guide with a sympathetic ear. Plan on spending an hour here.

Archaeological Sites in Lima

Lima is hardly the epicenter of pre-Columbian Peru, and few visitors have more than the museums featuring ancient Peruvian cultures on their minds when they hit the capital. Surprisingly, though, there are a handful of *huacas*—adobe pyramids—that date to around A.D. 500 and earlier interspersed among the modern constructions of the city. The archaeological sites are junior examples of those found in northern Peru, near Chiclayo and Trujillo. If you're not headed north, Lima's huacas, which have small museums attached, are worth a visit.

In San Isidro is **Huaca Huallamarca** (also called Pan de Azúcar, or "Sugar Loaf"), located at the corner of Avenida Nicolás de Rivera and Avenida El Rosario. The perhaps overzealously restored adobe temple of the Maranga Lima culture has several platforms and is frequently illuminated for special presentations. It's open Tuesday through Sunday from 9am to 5pm; admission is $1. Also in San Isidro is the **Huaca Juliana,** a pre-Inca mound dating to A.D. 400. It's at Calle Belén at Pezet and keeps the same hours as Huallamarca; admission is free. **Huaca Pucllana** is a sacred pyramid, built during the 4th century and still undergoing excavation, in Miraflores at the corner of calles General Borgoño (8th block) and Tarapacá, near Avenida Arequipa (✆ **01/445-8695**). It has a small park, a restaurant, and an artesanía gallery. From the pyramid's top, you can see the roofs of this busy residential and business district. It's open Wednesday through Sunday and Monday from 9am to 3pm; admission is free.

Unfortunately, these sites occasionally do not keep consistent hours, so you may find yourself staring through a chain-link fence if there's no one on hand to let you in.

Pedro de Osma 421, Barranco. ✆ 01/467-0141. Admission S/10 ($3) adults, S/5 ($1.50) students. Tues–Sun 10am–8pm. By colectivo from Av. Tacna to Barranco.

Museo de Arte Italiano   You probably didn't strap on your hiking boots on your way to Peru in expectation of a dose of Italian art, but that's what you'll find in this splendidly distinctive neoclassical building near the Centro. The explanation? The collection was a gift from Italy to Peru to commemorate the latter's centenary of independence. You'll find more reproductions of Italian masters than authentic works, though. Most of the art dates from the early 20th century, and the Italian collection is augmented by contemporary Peruvian works; allow about an hour to see it all. If nothing else, it's a good place to duck in when Lima's hectic pace, noise, and soot start to wear you down.

Paseo de la República 250, Centro. ✆ 01/423-9932. Admission S/3 (90¢) adults, S/2 (60¢) university students, S/1 (30¢) children. Mon–Fri 9am–4pm.

6 Especially for Kids

Lima isn't the most child-friendly city in the world, or in Peru, for that matter. Though Limeños, like all Peruvians, are very family-oriented, the city lacks a significant infrastructure for children and is unlikely to impress most people as an easygoing family destination. Still, families desperate to entertain little ones can find diversions during a short stay in Lima.

The most obvious place to start would be at the **Zoológico** and **Parque de las Leyendas** (Zoo and Legends Park), Av. La Marina s/n, block 24, (© **01/464-4282**). The park, in the San Miguel district between Centro and Callao, tries its best to represent Peru's three crucial geographical regions: *selva* (rain forest), *sierra* (highlands), and *costa* (coast). There are some good exotic Peruvian and South American fauna, such as condors, macaws, jaguars, llamas, and alpacas. The park has a playground with go-karts and some amusement park rides, and it's a good place for a picnic lunch. Kids kick a soccer ball around here on weekends. The zoo and park are open daily from 9am to 5pm; admission is S/6 ($1.75) for adults, S/3.50 ($1) for children 3 to 10.

The largest theme park in Peru is **Daytona Park,** within the Hipódromo de Monterrico (race track) at Av. El Derby s/n, door no. 4, Surco (© **01/435-6130**). It has go-karts, games such as Laser Quest, a skate park, and all kinds of video games. It's open daily from 11am to midnight.

Children's theater is occasionally staged at diverse locales, including the **Centro Cultural Ricardo Palma** (p. 140), **Satchmo** (p. 141), and the **Gran Parque de Lima,** near Plaza Grau between Vía Expresa and Avenida Garcilaso de la Vega. In Lima, consult the daily *El Comercio* newspaper or its website (www.elcomercioperu.com.pe) for additional information and events during your stay.

At least a couple of the city's finest museums should prove interesting, and perhaps even entertaining, to children of school age. The **Museo Rafael Larco Herrera** (p. 132) has a Fort Knox–like treasure trove of beautiful and curious little figures and statues from pre-Inca cultures, especially the Moche. The culture's famous erotic figures, sure to raise an eyebrow even among most adults, are conveniently kept in a separate room apart from the main collection; if you don't want to, you won't have to suffer through uncomfortable explanations of figures with phalluses swollen like baseball bats. The **Museo de la Nación** (p. 133) has excellent large-scale models of pre-Columbian ruins, including Machu Picchu and Chan Chan, a cool display of the important Lord of Sipán find, and great mysterious obelisks and totems from ancient Peruvian cultures. The **Museo de Oro** (p. 133), with its cases and cases of glittering gold, as well as weapons and armor (which may fascinate some little boys), isn't a boring old museum by any means. At the 16th-century **Convento de San Francisco** (p. 128), kids may enjoy the fantastic library, but they're sure to remember the spooky catacombs beneath the convent, full of artfully arranged bones.

Barranco, the most relaxed district in Lima, has a small but very enjoyable park, the **Parque Municipal,** where you'll often find families playing with their children. There's usually a group or two of alternative young people juggling torches or playing music for a few soles. At the **Gran Parque de Lima,** which Limeños consider an oasis in the midst of their rather unattractive city, there's a lagoon with paddleboats and lots of family-oriented activity on Sunday afternoon.

Tips **No Day at the Beach**

The beaches in and around Lima aren't good spots for children—they can't swim there, and the sands have bad reputations for crime. You'll be better off seeking a hotel with a pool if you're in Lima during the summer.

7 Organized Tours

Lima is a large, sprawling, and confusing city, so if you want to make quick work of a visit, an organized tour of the major sights may be the best option. Standard city tours are offered by innumerable agencies. Among the most dependable is **Lima Tours,** Belén 1040 (© **01/424-5110;** www.limatours.com.pe), which is the only organized tour with access to the Casa Aliaga, one of the most historic colonial mansions in Lima. A standard half-day tour of Lima Centro costs $25. Lima Tours also offers visits to Pachacámac, as part of its "Lima Arqueológica" tours, as well as highlights packages across Peru.

Lima Visión, Jr. Chiclayo 444, Miraflores (© **01/447-0482;** www.peruvision. com), offers 8-hour sightseeing tours of Lima, including a choice of excursions (for example, Pachacámac and the Museo de Oro) for $70. **Contacto Lima** (© **01/224-3854;** contactolima@tsi.com.pe) offers half-day city tours of "colonial and modern Lima" ($20), full-day tours ($70), museum tours ($25), and trail riding on Peruvian pacing horses, as well as tours to Nasca and Paracas, south of Lima. **Fertur Perú,** Jr. Junín 211 (© **01/427-1958;** http://ferturperu. tripod.com), with an office in the Hotel España, is a highly professional outfit with reasonably priced city tours and 4-day packages to sights across Peru.

Free short **walking tours** of Lima are frequently offered by the Municipalidad de Lima (Town Hall). For the latest schedule, call © **01/427-4848** or 01/427-6080, ext. 222.

Finally, though it sounds a bit uncomfortably close to those stag or bachelorette bus parties where everyone drinks their way across town dead set on making fools of their guest of honor, **El Bus Parrandero,** Av. Benavides 330, of. 101, Miraflores (© **01/445-4755;** www.busparrandero.com), is a colorful party bus promoting gregarious evening tours of Lima, with unlimited drinks, snacks, and live music. Tours are given Monday through Saturday from 8 to 11pm and 9pm to midnight; the ride costs $17.50 Monday through Wednesday, $20 Thursday through Saturday. If you've got your heart set on reliving (or continuing) your college days while you're in Lima, *¡adelante!*

8 Outdoor Activities & Spectator Sports

BEACHES   Though Lima is perched on the Pacific coast, Rio de Janeiro it's not. Still, several beaches in Miraflores and Barranco are frequented by locals, especially surfers, in the summer months. The beaches are unfit for swimming, however: The waters are heavily polluted and plagued by very strong currents. Worse, they're stalking grounds for thieves. While the beaches aren't that appealing in and of themselves, they might serve those with an interest in people-watching, as the sands are very much frequented by Limeños in the summer (Dec–Mar). Much nicer and cleaner beaches are located immediately south of Lima (see "Side Trips from Lima," below).

BICYCLING & JOGGING   Given Lima's chaotic traffic, jogging is best confined to parks. Probably the best area is the bicycling and jogging paths along the malecón in Miraflores, near the Marriott and Miraflores Park Plaza hotels. Contact the **Club de Bicicleta de Montaña** (Mountain Bike Club), Calle César Ortega s/n (© **01/872-4021**), which has information about routes near Lima and places to rent mountain bikes.

BULLFIGHTING   Bullfighting in Peru, less of a national craze than in Spain or Mexico, is held in July and in the main season from October to December at the 18th-century (and third oldest ring in the world) **Plaza de Acho,** Jr. Hualgayoc 332, in Rímac (© **01/315-5000** or 01/481-1467). Events are held Sunday afternoon. The *fiestas taurinas* bring matadors from Spain and take place at the same time as the Señor de los Milagros in October. Tickets, which range from about $20 to nearly $100 for a single event (depending on whether seats are in the shade or not), can be obtained at the box office at the bullring. They can also be purchased at **Farmacia Deza,** Av. Conquistadores 1140, San Isidro (© **01/440-3798**), or by phone from **Teleticket** (© **01/242-2823**). Inquire about advance tickets sending an e-mail to plazadeacho@peru.com.

GOLF Golf courses in Lima aren't open to nonmembers. Your best bet for golf is to stay at one of the exclusive hotels with golf privileges at the Lima Golf Club in San Isidro: **Country Club Lima Hotel** (p. 118) and **Sonesta Posada del Inca El Olívar** (p. 120).

PERUVIAN PACING HORSES Peruvian Paso horses (*caballos de paso*), which have a unique four-beat lateral gait, are considered by many to be the world's smoothest riding horse and also one of the showiest of all horse breeds. If you're already a fan of the breed, or just a fan of horses in general, seeing them on their home turf could be exciting. There are *concursos* (show events) scheduled at different times of the year; there's a big one in April (free admission). Information about exhibitions is available from the **Asociación Nacional de Caballos Peruanos de Paso,** Bellavista 549, Miraflores (© **01/444-6920** or 01/447-6331).

SOCCER Important league and national *fútbol* (soccer) matches are held at the venerable, 50-year-old **Estadio Nacional,** Paseo de la República, blocks 7–9, located just 5 minutes from the city center. Popular teams include Alianza Lima, Alianza Atlético, Universitario (known as "La U"), and Sporting Cristal. Tickets ($3–$25) for most matches can be purchased the same day at the stadium or from **Teleticket** (© **01/242-2823**).

SURFING Though several beaches in Miraflores and Barranco are popular with surfers in summer and are fine for beginners, the best beaches in southern Peru—Punta Hermosa, Punta Rocas (highly recommended), Cerro Azul, and Pico Alto (which is supposed to have the biggest waves)—are beyond Lima. Surfing in southern Peru is best April through December (and at its peak in May); surfers who hit the waves year-round usually do it in wet suits. Check out **www.wannasurf.com/spot/South_America/Peru/Lima** for specialist information, including a chart of southern beaches that specifies skill level and breaks. Information, equipment, boards (for sale only), and accessories are available at **O'Neills,** Av. Santa Cruz 851, Miraflores (© **01/242-4486**).

TENNIS The best-maintained outdoor tennis courts are at **Club Las Terrazas,** Malecón 28 de Julio 390, Miraflores (© **01/446-2620**), a private club that admits nonmembers ($5 per hr.). The courts are open daily from 7am to 6pm.

9 Shopping

The capital has the greatest variety of shopping in Peru, from tony boutiques to artisan and antiques shops. Shopping at markets in sierra villages or buying direct from artisans on Lake Titicaca are better experiences, certainly, but don't discount the fact that, unless you ship the loot home, you'll most likely have to bring it back to Lima anyway. In Lima, you can find traditional handicrafts from across Peru; prices are not usually much higher and the selection may be even better than in the regions where the items are made. One exception is alpaca goods, which are better purchased in the areas around Cusco, Puno, and Arequipa, both in terms of price and selection.

Miraflores is where most shoppers congregate, though there are also several outlets in Lima Centro and elsewhere in the city. Most shops are open from 9:30am to 12:30pm and 3 to 8pm. Most prices include an 18% sales tax, which, unfortunately, is only refundable on purchases made at the international departure lounge of Jorge Chávez International Airport.

ANTIQUES & JEWELRY

Look for silver jewelry and antiques along Avenida La Paz in Miraflores. *Platerías* and *joyerías* (silver and jewelry shops) worth a visit are **Ilaria,** Av. Larco 1325 (© 01/444-2347), and **El Tupo,** La Paz 553 (© 01/444-1511). Miraflores antiques shops include **El Almacén de Arte,** Francia 339 (© 01/445-6264), and **Porta 735,** Porta 735 (© 01/447-6158).

HANDICRAFTS & TEXTILES

Miraflores houses the lion's share of Lima's well-stocked shops, which overflow with handicrafts from around Peru, including weavings, ceramics, and silver. Several dozen large souvenir and handicrafts shops are clustered on and around Avenida Ricardo Palma (a good one is **Artesanías Miraflores,** no. 205) and Avenida Petit Thouars (try **Artesanía Expo Inti,** no. 5495). Handicrafts shops elsewhere in Miraflores include **Agua y Tierra,** Diez Canseco 298 (© 01/445-6980), and **Silvania Prints,** Diez Canseco 378 (© 01/242-0667). Alpaca sweaters and other items can be had at **Alpaca 111,** Av. Larco 671 (© 01/447-1623), **Alpaca Peru,** Diez Canseco 315 (© 01/241-4175), Mon Repos, Tarata 288 (© 01/445-9740), and **All Alpaca,** Av. Schell 375 (© 01/427-4704).

The best spot for handicrafts from around Peru in Lima Centro is the **Santo Domingo artesanía arcades** across the street from the Santo Domingo convent on Conde de Superunda and Camaná. For fine retablos and artisanship typical of Ayacucho (which produces some of Peru's most notable pieces), visit the **Museo-Galería Popular de Ayacucho,** Av. Pedro de Osma 116, Barranco (© 01/247-0599).

MARKETS & MALLS

Lima Centro's crowded **Mercado Central** (Central Market) is south of the Plaza Mayor, at the edge of Chinatown; you'll find just about everything there, but you should take your wits and leave your valuables at home. The **Feria Artesanal** (Artisans' Market, also called the Mercado Indio, or Indian Market) has a wide variety of handicrafts of varying quality, but at lower prices than most tourist-oriented shops in Lima Centro or Miraflores (quality may also be a bit lower than at those shops). Haggling is a good idea. The market is located at Avenida de la Marina (blocks 6–10) in Pueblo Libre; it's open daily from noon to 8pm.

There are small handicrafts markets, open late to catch bar and post-dinner crowds, in the main squares in both Miraflores and Barranco. The **Jockey Plaza Shopping Center** is a modern American-style shopping mall—the newest, biggest, and best in Lima—with department stores, restaurants, movie theaters, a supermarket, and some 200 exclusive shops. It's located next to the Jockey Club of Peru at Hipódromo de Monterrico, at the intersection of Javier Prado and Avenida Panamericana Sur in Surco. It's open daily from 11am to 9pm. **Centro Comercial Larco Mar,** in Miraflores along the malecón and Parque Salazar (near the Marriott hotel), is one of the swankest malls in Lima.

10 Lima After Dark

As the largest city in the country, with a population of immigrants from around the country and the most international flavor, Lima certainly has Peru's most varied nightlife scene. Whether you're into jazz, criollo, Latin, or rock music, you'll find it, along with discos of every flavor. The best after-dark scenes are in Miraflores and particularly Barranco.

THE PERFORMING ARTS

Lima's stunning **Teatro Municipal,** the pride of the local performing-arts scene and the primary locale for theater, ballet, opera, and symphony performances, burned to the ground in 1998. Since then, the National Symphony Orchestra and the National Ballet Company have performed at the **Museo de la Nación,** Avenida Javier Prado (℃ 01/476-9875). The 1940s-era **Teatro Segura,** Huancavelica 265 (℃ 01/426-7206) has picked up some of the slack for opera and music concerts. Frequent cultural events, including films and music recitals, are held every week at the **Centro Cultural Ricardo Palma,** Larco Herrera 770, Miraflores (℃ 01/446-3959) and the **British Council,** Calle Alberto Lynch 110, San Isidro (℃ 01/221-7552). The **Instituto Cultural Peruano Norteamericano,** located at the corner of Angamos and Arequipa in Miraflores (℃ 01/446-0381), hosts theater, jazz, classical, and folk music. See the daily newspaper *El Comercio* (www.elcomercioperu.com.pe/quehacer) or **www.decajon.com** for updated lists of live performing-arts events in Lima (in Spanish only).

Lima has a good theater scene, though as one might expect, nearly all plays are in Spanish. If you speak Spanish or are willing to give a Spanish play a try, two of Lima's best theaters are **Teatro Canout,** Av. Petit Thouars 4550, Miraflores (℃ 01/422-5373), and **Teatro Auditorio Miraflores,** Av. Larco 1036, Miraflores (℃ 01/447-9378). Tickets are available at the box offices.

BARS, LIVE MUSIC & CLUBS

BARS & PUBS

Freiheit, Lima 471, Miraflores, in front of Parque Kennedy (℃ **01/247-4630**) is a warmly decorated bar, in the style of a German tavern. The dance floor is separate from the bar area. There's a drink minimum on weekends. **O'Murphy's Irish Pub,** Shell 627, Miraflores (℃ **01/242-1212**), is a longtime favorite drinking hole. Of course, expect a pool table, darts, Guinness on tap, and Brits and Irishmen hoisting it. They also host live music on Thursday. **Son de Cuba,** Bulevar San Ramón 277, Miraflores (℃ **01/445-1444**), is on the pedestrian street called "Little Italy" by locals, but the club focuses on Caribbean rhythms and drinks Tuesday through Sunday. A trendy bar in Barranco is **Amnesia,** Bulevar Sánchez Carrión 153, just off the municipal square (℃ **01/477-9577**). It's open Thursday through Saturday.

LIVE MUSIC

My vote for best live-music club in Lima is **La Noche,** Bolognesi 307, Barranco (℃ **01/477-5829**). Despite its prosaic name, this sprawling multilevel club feels like a swank treehouse, with a great stage and sound system and good bands every night that run the gamut of styles (though it's frequently jazz), plus a hip mixed Limeño and international crowd. Monday-night jam sessions (no cover charge) are particularly good; otherwise, cover charges range from S/5 to S/15 ($1.50–$4).

Artsy **El Ekeko,** Av. Grau 266, Barranco (℃ **01/247-3148**), is a two-level place with live music Wednesday through Saturday. Most acts fall within the

Latin category—often Cuban. Cover charges range from S/10 to S/20 ($3–$6). **La Estación de Barranco,** Pedro de Osma 112 (© **01/247-0344**), is another nice place, housed in an old train station, with live music Tuesday through Saturday and a slightly more mature crowd (both locals and tourists). **Satchmo,** Av. La Paz 538, Miraflores (© **01/444-4957**), is a classy joint with a variable roster of live bands, including jazz combos—as the name would indicate. It's a good date spot. Cover charges range from S/20 to S/45 ($6–$13).

PEÑAS

You should check out at least one *peña,* criollo-music clubs that quite often inspire rousing vocal and dance participation, during your stay in Lima. Cover charges range from $1 to $10, depending on the act.

Caballero de Fina Estampa, Av. del Ejército 800, Miraflores (© **01/441-0552**), is one of the chicest peñas, with a large colonial salon and balconies. The cover charge is S/45 ($13). **De Rompe y Raja,** Manuel Segura 127, Barranco (© **01/247-3271**) is a favorite of locals. Look for the popular Matices Negros, an Afro-Peruvian dance trio. The cover is S/25 ($7). **Las Guitarras,** Manuel Segura 295, Barranco (© **01/479-1874**), is where locals go to play an active part in their peña. A cool spot, it's open Friday and Saturday only, with no cover charge and no credit cards accepted.

Brisas del Titicaca, Jr. Walkulski 168, the first block of Avenida Brasil in Lima Centro (© **01/332-1901**), is a cultural institution with "noches folklóricas" and some of the best shows in Lima. It's open Wednesday and Thursday from 8pm, and Friday and Saturday from 10pm. The excellent Barranco restaurant **Manos Morenas,** Pedro de Osma 409 (© **01/467-0421**), is a sophisticated peña with a $12 cover charge. Shows are given Tuesday through Thursday from 9pm onwards, and Friday and Saturday from 10:30pm until 2am or so. **Sachún,** Av. del Ejército 657, Miraflores (© **01/441-4465**), is a more accessible spot, favored by tourists and middle-class Limeños who aren't shy about participating with their feet and vocal chords. The cover charge ranges from S/25 to S/45 ($7–$13). **La Candelaria,** Bolognesi 292, Barranco (© **01/247-1314**), is a new, comfortable club celebrating Peruvian folklore. It's open Friday and Saturday from 9pm onwards; the cover is S/25 ($7).

DANCE CLUBS

Many of Lima's discos are predominantly young and wild affairs. Check out **Deja-Vu Trattoria & Bar,** Av. Grau 294, Barranco (© **01/247-3742**); the decor is based on TV commercials. It's a dancefest from Monday through Saturday; the music trips from techno to trance. **Kitsch,** Bolognesi 743, Barranco (no phone), is one of Lima's hottest bars—literally, sometimes it turns into a sweatbox—with over-the-top decor and recorded tunes that range from 1970s and '80s pop to Latin and techno. **Tequila Rocks,** Calle Diez Canseco 146, Miraflores (© **01/444-3661**), continues to be one of Lima's most popular discos, though it doesn't usually get going after 2am.

GAY & LESBIAN NIGHTLIFE

Though Peru as a whole remains fervently Catholic and many gay and lesbian Peruvians feel constricted in the expression of their lifestyle, Lima is the most progressive city in the country, with the most facilities and resources for gays and lesbians, including a significant number of nightclubs. Among the most popular are **Gitano 2,050** (no phone), Berlín 231, Miraflores, probably the best-known gay disco in the city, with two cruising balconies overlooking the dance floor;

Downtown Vale Todo, Pasaje los Pinos 160, Miraflores (© **01/444-6433**), currently the most popular club with go-go boys, occasional shows, and strippers; **Café Bar Kitsch,** Bolognesi 743, Barranco (no phone), a funky and highly original bar/disco that's also very popular with straights; and **Perseo Palace,** Av. Aviación 2514, San Borja (© **01/224-3731**), a lively disco with an eclectic soundtrack and large dance floor. All are open Wednesday through Saturday (Gitano 2,050 is open Sun as well); cover charges range from S/7 to S/25 ($2–$7). A gay-oriented combination sauna/gym/bar/video lounge is **Sauna Tivoli,** Av. Petit Thouars s/n, San Isidro (© **01/222-1705**). It's open daily from 2 to 10pm; the cover charge is S/25 ($7). There's more information on gay Lima and gay Peru on **http://gaylimape.tripod.com** and **www.sitiosgay.com.**

CINEMA

Most foreign movies in Lima are shown in their original language with subtitles. Art and classic films are shown at the **Filmoteca de Lima** in the Lima Museo de Arte, Paseo Colón 125, Lima Cercado (© **01/423-4732**), and **El Cinematógrafo,** Pérez Roca 196, Barranco (© **01/477-1961**). Commercial movie houses worth checking out include **Multicines Starvisión El Pacífico,** Av. José Pardo 121, near the roundabout at Parque Central, Miraflores (© **01/445-6990**); **Cinemark Perú Jockey Plaza,** Av. Javier Prado 4200 (© **01/435-9262**); and **UVK Multicines Larcomar,** Larcomar Centro Comercial Parque Salazar, Miraflores (© **01/446-7336**). Most theaters in the suburbs cost more than the ones in Lima Centro (S/10–S/15 or $3–$4.25, as opposed to S/4–S/8 or $1–$2.25), but they're more modern and better equipped. Several have special matinee prices and discounts on Tuesday. For a list of films *subtituladas* (with subtitles), consult the Friday edition of *El Comercio.* The term *doblada* means "dubbed."

CASINOS

Peruvians are big on casinos, and many of the larger upscale hotels favored by business travelers have casinos attached. Some of the better ones are **JW Marriott Hotel & Casino** (p. 116); **Grand Hotel Miraflores,** Av. 28 de Julio 151, Miraflores (© **01/447-9641**); **Country Club Lima Hotel** (p. 118); and **Sheraton Hotel & Casino,** Paseo de la República 170, Centro (© **01/433-3320**). Most casinos are open Monday through Thursday from 5pm to 2am, and Friday through Saturday from 5pm to 5am.

11 Side Trips from Lima

Most visitors to Lima, having seen the highlights of the colonial center and a few museums, head out on long-distance buses and planes to Cusco and Machu Picchu, Nasca, Arequipa, and north to the jungle. However, if you have time for an excursion or two closer to the Peruvian capital, consider the pre-Columbian ruins at Pachacámac or the attractive beaches south of Lima.

THE BEACHES
30–70km (20–45 miles) S of Lima

The best beaches easily accessible from Lima line the coast south of the city. Popular spots along the shadeless, arid desert landscape are El Silencio, Punta Hermosa (a good place for ceviche and fresh fish in any number of rustic seafood restaurants), Punta Negra, Santa María, and Pucusana. Probably the best bet is Pucusana, a small fishing village, though it's the farthest beach from Lima. The attractive beaches are very popular with Limeños during the summer months; on weekends, the southern coast is a long line of caravans of sun-seekers.

Note: Even though you can swim in the ocean at this distance from the capital, the currents are very strong, and great caution should be exercised. You should also be careful with your possessions, as thieves frequent these beaches. Finally, be forewarned that the beaches are only moderately attractive, certainly few peoples' idea of a tropical beach paradise.

GETTING THERE   Unless you have wheels, the best way to tour the beaches south of Lima is to hop on a combi, like Limeños do. Those marked "San Bartolo" (another one of the beaches) leave from Angamos and Panamericana Sur in Lima; others at Jirón Montevideo and Jirón Ayacucho in Lima Centro will also get you to the beaches. You'll have to tell the driver at which beach you want to get off (or hop off wherever a number of fellow bus travelers do), and then walk a mile or less down to the beach.

The ride costs S/3 to S/5 ($1–$1.50) and takes anywhere from 45 minutes to 2 hours. The beaches and their markers are as follows: El Silencio, Km 42; Punta Hermosa, Km 44; Punta Rocas, Km 45; Punta Negra, Km 46; San Bartolo, Km 52; Santa María, Km 55; and Pucusana, Km 65.

PACHACAMAC
31km (20 miles) S of Lima

The finest ruins within easy reach of Lima, **Pachacámac,** in the Lurín valley, was inhabited by several pre-Columbian cultures prior to the Incas. The extensive site, a sacred city and holy place of pilgrimage, includes plazas, adobe-brick palaces, and pyramidal temples, some of which have been rebuilt by the Peruvian government. It makes for an interesting visit, especially if you're not planning on heading north to the archaeological sites near Chiclayo and Trujillo.

The principal ceremonial center of the Peruvian coast, the earliest constructions date to the first century, though the site reached its apex during the Huari (or Wari) culture (10th c.). Pilgrims came to pay homage to the feared oracle and creator-god, Pachacámac, who was believed to be responsible for earthquakes and matters of state such as war. The Incas conquered the site in the 15th century, and it was one of the most important shrines in the Americas during their rule, though its ceremonial importance began to wane soon after. However, two of the most important structures on-site, the Temple of the Sun and the Acllahuasi (or Mamacuña) palace (where "chosen maidens" served the Inca), both date to the Inca occupation. Hernán Pizarro and his gold-hungry troops arrived in 1533 but were disappointed to find a paucity of riches. On the premises is a small museum of pre-Columbian artifacts, including textiles and the dual-personage carved wooden idol of Pachacámac, god of fire and son of the sun god.

The site (© 01/430-0168; http://wpro.com/pachacamac), which occupies a low hill, is large; allow at least a couple of hours to visit by foot (the visit from Lima can be completed in a half day). English-speaking guides are usually available for hire at the entrance if you do not arrive with a guide-led group. The site is open daily from 9am to 4pm. Admission is S/6 ($1.75) for adults, S/3 (75¢) for students, and S/1 (30¢) for children.

GETTING THERE   Pachacámac is about 45 minutes from Lima by car or bus. Combis (with signs reading "Pachacámac/Lurín") leave from Avenida Abancay and the corner of Ayacucho and Montevideo in Lima Centro. The most convenient way to visit—cheaper than hiring a taxi unless there are several of you—is by a half-day organized tour, offered by Lima Vision, Lima Tours, and other companies; see "Organized Tours," above. Most tours cost between $25 and $35 per person, including transportation and guide.

5

The Southern Coast

South of Lima along the coast, the hot and extraordinarily dry desert province of Ica—one of the most arid places on earth—contains one of Peru's most exotic, inscrutable sights: The Nasca Lines, huge pre-Columbian desert drawings, have raised many questions and given rise to wild theories about Peru's ancient past. The region forms part of the oldest geological strata in the country; fossils date back as far as the Tertiary or Quaternary eras. The Paracas and Nasca cultures that took root here (roughly speaking, 1300 B.C.–A.D. 700) were two of Peru's most advanced. Little was known about the two cultures until the 20th century, but they are acclaimed today for their exquisite textile weavings and ceramics, among the finest produced by pre-Columbian Peru.

Nasca is a small and unassuming town, recently rocked by a major earthquake that nearly leveled it. Indeed, it might go unnoticed were it not for the mysterious and mind-boggling Nasca Lines nearby. Nasca has several additional sites intimately tied to the ancient cultures that once settled and irrigated these desert lands, including remarkable stone aqueducts—evidence of advanced engineering—and an evocative burial ground. While the Nasca Lines reign as the undisputed highlight of the region, this stretch of arid coast and pampas south of Lima has other things to offer the visitor who's not in too much of a rush to roar on to Cusco, Arequipa, or Lake Titicaca.

Within easy reach of Nasca are the towns of Ica and Pisco and the nearby Reserva Nacional de Paracas (Paracas National Reserve), known for the Ballestas Islands, which locals liken to Ecuador's Galápagos Islands. That claim may be a slight exaggeration, but the maritime sanctuary, encompassing the Paracas Peninsula and a lovely bay with curious rock formations, swells with unusual flora and fauna, including thousands of sea lions, flamingos, and endangered Humboldt penguins. The dusty town of Pisco will sound familiar to anyone who's had a drink in a Peruvian bar or restaurant, since the country's famous cocktail, the pisco sour, is made with the white-grape brandy that shares its name with the town. The region's wineries (actually nearer to Ica) make Peru's best wines and, of course, pisco. Ica, the capital of the department, is a small, enjoyable town with stifling heat and several attractive churches, notable colonial mansions, and one of the better small museums in the country. The nearby Huacachina Lagoon is a beautiful green-and-blue oasis in the midst of the monochrome desert.

Although Paracas, Ica, and Nasca are all within easy striking distance of Lima, for those with limited time, a visit to the region may complicate moving on to other places in Peru. The only flights available from Lima are 1-day Nasca Lines overflights. Otherwise, you'll need to travel overland along the desert coast to get to the department of Ica, and by land again if you're headed to any of the

other major destinations in Peru. (For many travelers, that will mean returning to the capital and catching a flight.) The vast Carretera Panamericana (Pan-American Hwy.), a two-lane strip of asphalt that extends the length of Peru from the Ecuadorian border all the way down to Chile, slices through this section of the desert lowlands, and bus travel is direct, if not always visually stimulating. Many visitors move on by bus from Nasca to Arequipa and/or Lake Titicaca.

1 Pisco & the Reserva Nacional de Paracas

260km (162 miles) S of Lima

The first town of any size to the south of Lima, Pisco is also the first settlement beyond the beaches outside the capital that draws the attention of travelers. Yet that interest has little to do with the (rather lacking) attributes of the town and almost everything to do with the natural attractions in abundance at the nearby Ballestas Islands and Paracas National Reserve, just 22km (14 miles) from the center of Pisco. A few kilometers west of the Pan-American Highway, Pisco is a small port and fishing village of very modest interest (beyond the Moorish-inspired Municipal Palace) that sometimes serves as a base for those wishing to visit Paracas Peninsula and Bay without paying the higher prices commanded by the resort.

Fun Fact **El Libertador**

General José de San Martín—immersed in the continentwide campaign for independence from Spain and already having liberated Chile and Argentina—made landfall with an army of 4,500 men at Paracas in 1819 and established his headquarters in Pisco. Here began his legendary battle for Peru's independence, which he declared in Huacho in 1921. San Martín was subsequently named the "Protector of Peru" and went about constructing its new republican government.

ESSENTIALS
GETTING THERE

There are frequent buses up and down the coast from Lima to Arequipa with stops in between. From Lima, frequent buses normally take between 3 and 4 hours to reach Pisco. However, as the town is not directly on the Carretera Panamericana, not all coastal buses stop there. Be sure to confirm that the bus won't merely leave you on the side of the road en route to Ica (which would result in the hassle of getting a combi to town). **Ormeño** travels to and from Lima, Ica, Nasca, and Arequipa; in Lima, the office is located at Av. Carlos Zavala 177 (© 01/427-5679), and the Pisco office is at San Francisco 259, 1 block from the Plaza de Armas (© 034/522-058). **Soyuz Peru Bus** connects Pisco with Lima and Ica; you'll find an office in Lima at Av. Carlos Zavala 221 (© 01/428-6252) and in Pisco at Av. Ernesto R. Diez Canseco 41 (© 034/224-138). Bus terminals are located right in the center of town.

VISITOR INFORMATION

The **Municipality of Pisco office** at the Plaza de Armas (© 034/532-525) may be able to provide some rudimentary tourist information; a better bet is one of the travel agencies offering tours to Paracas and other places in the region. See "By Organized Tour" in "Getting Around," below.

FAST FACTS **Banco de Crédito,** Pérez Figuerola 162 (© 034/532-954), has a Visa-compatible ATM. You'll also find *cambistas,* or money exchangers, hovering around the Plaza de Armas.

If you need medical attention, go to **San Juan de Dios,** Av. San Juan de Dios 350 (© 034/532-332). In an emergency, you can reach the **police** at the Plaza de Armas on Calle San Francisco (© 034/532-165).

The **post office** at Calle Bolognesi 173 is open Monday through Saturday from 8am to 6pm. There's a **Telefónica del Perú** office at Calle Bolognesi 298; it's open daily from 9am to 6pm.

GETTING AROUND

The best way to get around Pisco itself is on foot, as anything of interest—hotels, restaurants, the cathedral—are only minutes from the Plaza de Armas. Taxis are readily available and cheap for any trip within the city (S/3–S/4, or $1). For transport to the Paracas National Reserve and other areas of interest, you can hire a taxi (less than S/17, or $5) or travel by bus. The most efficient way to see the highlights of the area is with a tour company, especially since there is no public transportation on the peninsula or within the reserve.

BY BUS Combis to the Ballestas Islands and Paracas National Reserve (marked EL CHACO–PARACAS) depart from the Pisco market on Fermín Tangus.

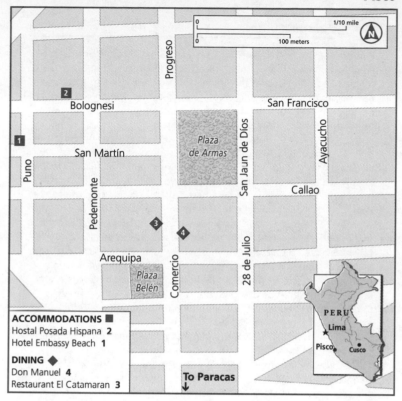

BY BOAT   Boat tours of the Paracas Bay and Ballestas Islands are available right on the El Chaco waterfront (S/35, or $10, per person) or by arranging an organized tour.

BY ORGANIZED TOUR   The following companies all offer packages to the Ballestas Islands and Paracas National Reserve (as well as tours to Tambo Colorado and Nasca): **Zarcillo Connections,** San Francisco 111 (© **034/536-543**); **Ballestas Travel Service,** San Francisco 249 (© **034/533-095**); and, near Ica, **Huacachina Tours,** Av. La Angostura 355, L-47, in front of the Hotel Las Dunas (© **034/256-582;** huacachinatours@computextos.com).

WHAT TO SEE & DO
RESERVA NACIONAL DE PARACAS
The Paracas Bay and Peninsula, along with the small Ballestas Islands, comprise the Paracas National Reserve, a place of gorgeous unpopulated beaches, strange desert vistas, and spectacular wildlife. Established in 1975, Paracas is the primary marine conservation center in Peru. The 14,504km² (5,600-sq.-mile) reserve, which can be visited year-round, is about two-thirds ocean, so don't come expecting to see a zoo-like array of plants and animals at every turn—except on the Ballestas, where several thousand sea lions, in addition to many other species, lie about in plain view.

Paracas Culture

Paracas may be best known for its great natural coastal beauty and wildlife, but the region is no less recognized (especially among archaeologists and historians) as the home of several advanced cultures that thrived in Peru before the Incas. The so-called *hombre de Santo Domingo* (Santo Domingo man), whose remains date to 7000 B.C., was found on the west shore of the Bay of Paracas.

Little was known about the Paracas culture, an ancient Amerindian civilization founded along the south-central coast more than 3,000 years ago, until 1925, when the Peruvian archaeologist Julio C. Tello discovered extraordinary burial sites, now referred to as the Paracas Necropolis, concealed by the desert sand dunes on the isthmus of the Península de Paracas. The arid climate and layers of sand had done wonders to protect extraordinary embroidered textiles—largely found within burial sites—that today are recognized as the finest representatives of pre-Columbian Peruvian woven art. The Paracas culture produced textiles of unrivaled color, technique, and design. The most exquisite examples of funereal textiles are found at Lima's Museo de la Nación (p. 133), but there are also fine pieces in Ica at the Museo Regional (p. 155) and at the Museo de Sitio Julio C. Tello within the Paracas National Reserve (p. 149).

Also found at the sites were skulls that reveal fascinating information about the Paracas social structure and notions of physical beauty. The Paracas employed methods to alter the shape of the skull, elongating it with weights and boards, to connote social status. Many of the skulls found in the Paracas Necropolis have stretched and sloped craniums. The Paracas people also practiced a crude form of brain surgery called trepanation. Like medieval physicians, who believed bloodletting aimed at the forehead was a cure-all, Paracas doctors surgically drilled holes in the skull to treat both physical trauma and, it seems, psychological disorders. The formation of scar tissue indicates that many of the patients actually survived the operations, though, of course, it's impossible to say how their physical or behavioral problems were affected.

The Paracas culture flourished from roughly 1300 B.C. to A.D. 200, but scholars are most knowledgeable about the late period of development, from 300 B.C. to A.D. 200. At the Paracas Necropolis, researchers discovered more than 400 funerary bundles, each consisting of a mummified priest or nobleman swathed in brilliantly woven and embroidered funeral tapestries. The large and exceptionally detailed, colorful weavings feature repetitive motifs of birds, fish, and other animals, revealing a keen sense of textile design and artistry.

Little is known about the disappearance of the Paracas culture around A.D. 200. Farther south along the coast, the Nasca culture reigned for about 5 centuries, itself eventually succeeded by the Huari and then Ica cultures, the last of which succumbed to the expanding Inca empire by the 15th century.

Exploring Paracas

What is not water in the Paracas National Reserve is hot and dry land, with no transportation to speak of except for independently hired taxis. For this reason, most tourists tend to visit the reserve as part of an organized tour. However, adventurous travelers with plenty of water, sunscreen, and stamina can get to know the peninsula and its rich marine birdlife on their own, camping far from other humans. Safety has become a concern in recent years, though, so camping alone is not a good idea.

Dirt roads crisscross the Paracas Peninsula, and a paved road goes around it, out toward Punta Pejerrey, near the Candelabro (see "Islas Ballestas," below). The dirt roads are the most interesting, reaching miniscule fishing villages such as attractive **Lagunillas** and a clifftop lookout point, **Mirador de los Lobos,** with views of the ocean and lots of sea lions. Across the isthmus from the Bahía de Paracas (and opposite Lagunillas) is a curious cave formation known as the **Cathedral,** a rocky outcrop that, with the assistance of wind and sea erosion, has taken on the appearance of a church tower. Sea otters populate the cave floor.

To hike around the peninsula, it's about 21km (13 miles) round-trip to the lookout point (5km/3 miles from the Tello Museum to Lagunillas). Begin at a turnoff left of the paved road beyond the museum. There are few facilities of any kind on the peninsula. You are allowed to camp on the beautiful beaches (where you may see no other humans, just pelicans and other birds), and there are a couple of seafood restaurants in Lagunillas.

Museo de Sitio Julio C. Tello   Named for the Peruvian archaeologist credited with uncovering many of the mysteries of the ancient Paracas culture, the Julio Tello Site Museum is located just past the entrance to the Paracas National Reserve, 5km (3 miles) from Paracas beach. It contains a small but instructive exhibit of ceramics and textiles that depict the evolution of the Paracas culture. The Paracas were experts at mummifying their dead; in the mummies, you can see the peculiar practices of cranial deformation and cranial trepanation, or brain surgery. The Paracas also admired trophy heads, and warriors often attached the heads of defeated foes to their armor to instill fear into their opponents.

Near the museum is the Paracas Necropolis (100 B.C.–A.D. 300), comprising the archaeological sites of Cabezas Largas and Cerro Colorado. First explored in the 1920s, it is the oldest discovered site in the region. Tello uncovered Paracas burial sites containing superb funerary cloths, skulls, and other artifacts—all key elements in his groundbreaking studies of the Paracas culture. However, there is very little to see today at the sites. About 270m towards the bay is a viewing tower, constructed to allow viewings of the dozens (or hundreds) of pink flamingos often gathered on the beach (usually July–Nov only).

Carretera Pisco, Puerto San Martín Km 27, Paracas. (€) 034/620-436. Admission S/3 (75¢) adults, S/1.50 (40¢) students and seniors, S/1 (30¢) children under 10. Daily 9am–5pm.

Fun Fact **A Bird-Watcher's Boon**

The Ballestas Islands are smack in the middle of the Humboldt Current, which flows 3,220km (2,000 miles) from Antarctica along the Pacific coastline. In the warm, shallow waters along the Peruvian coast, the current makes abundant growth of phytoplankton possible, which stimulates an ecological food chain that culminates in the largest concentration of birds on earth.

Islas Ballestas ⭐⭐

The primary focus of a visit to the reserve is a boat tour of the Ballestas (pronounced "bah-*yehs*-tahs") Islands. Though the islands can't possibly live up to the locals' touting of them as the "Peruvian Galápagos," the Ballestas do afford tantalizing close-up views (without allowing visitors on the islands) of the habitat's rich roster of protected species, including huge colonies of barking sea lions, endangered turtles and Humboldt penguins, red boobies, pelicans, turkey vultures, and red-footed cormorants. During the summer months (Jan–Mar), baby sea lions are born, and the community becomes even more populous and noisy. The wall-like, cantilevered islands are literally covered with birds; 110 migratory and resident sea birds have been documented, and the bay is a stopover point in the Alaska–Patagonia migration route. Packs of dolphins are occasionally seen slicing through the water, and less frequently, humpbacked whales and soaring Andean condors can also be glimpsed.

The islands are often referred to by locals as *las islas guaneras,* since they are covered in bird droppings. (*Guano* is the Quechua word for excrement.) The nitrogen-rich guano is harvested every 10 years and made into fertilizer. (A factory can be seen on the first island.) No humans other than the guano collectors—no doubt a contender for worst job title in the world—are allowed on the islands, and all the species in the reserve are protected by law, but in practice, there are no specially assigned police officers or boats available to enforce protection.

En route to the islands, boats pass the famous **Candelabro,** a giant candelabra-like drawing etched into a cliff overlooking the bay. The huge etching, 126m long and 72m wide (420 ft. by 240 ft.), looks as though it could be a cousin to the Nasca Lines, and it is similarly shrouded in mystery. Some believe it's a ritualistic symbol of the Paracas or Nasca cultures, while others contend that it dates only to the 18th or 19th century, when it served as a protective symbol and navigational guide for fishermen and sailors.

Most organized tours will take visitors from the San Andrés port to the El Balneario resort, a beach playground for upscale residents of Lima, and then on to Playa El Chaco, where boats leave for 1-hour tours of the Ballestas. You can also independently contract an island boat tour here from one of the 13 operators on the main street. Tours are $10 per person, and each boat has an English- or French-speaking guide on board. Most start early in the morning, between 7 and 8am. Visitors are not allowed to set foot on the islands, though boats get close enough for good viewing. Sweaters and windbreakers, hats, and sunscreen are essential.

Tips Organized Tours

Most people visit the Paracas National Reserve and Ballestas Islands as part of organized tours. Guides, transportation, and entrance fees are all included in the price. Those who prefer to visit the reserve on their own will need to pay an entrance fee upon entering the reserve (S/5, or $1.50, for adults and students 14 and older; free for children under 14). You can enter the reserve without a guide, but it's highly recommended that you contract one in order to get the most out of a visit, as much that is unique about the area—its climate and conditions, its migratory wildlife—is not always immediately obvious.

TAMBO COLORADO

An Inca fortress and probably the best-preserved ancient architectural complex on the southern coast, this outpost is thought to have been an administration checkpoint for Andean coastal migration. It was probably also where the Inca chieftain and his minions stayed for periods as he traveled back and forth between the Inca capital, Cusco, and coastal settlements. Unlike other archaeological sites where the characteristic vibrant colors have long faded, here at least some of the original red, white, and yellow walls are still preserved. (The name of the complex, *colorado,* refers to the red color of the walls.) Also unique in the Inca canon, the structures here were constructed not of neatly cut stone, but of materials that could be used for long-term construction given the lack of rain on the desert coast.

The complex contains a central plaza, storehouses, living quarters, and military installations. If you're headed to Cusco, you can be assured of seeing more impressive Inca sites, but Tambo Colorado is rewarding for archaeology fans and Inca completists.

The site is quite removed from Pisco—about 45km (26 miles) northeast. It lies about 5km (3 miles) outside the town of Humay, to which you can take a bus, but service is erratic. If you are intent on seeing Tambo Colorado, it's advisable either to go with an organized guided tour or hire a taxi, which will take you out to the site, wait for you, and return you to Pisco for $25 to $30. The site is open daily from 9am to 5pm; admission is S/5 ($1.50).

WHERE TO STAY
EXPENSIVE

Hotel Paracas ⋆ *(Kids*   The only hotel that lives up to the official billing of Paracas as a resort within the nature reserve, this is a large Mediterranean-style hotel on the bay and one of the best places to stay in the region. Airy and beachy, it has great views of the water. Rooms, furnished with bamboo appointments, have either bay or garden views, and all have small terraces. With three swimming pools, two tennis courts, a children's playground, water-skiing, and paddleboats, it's an especially good option for families. The hotel organizes its own Ballestas Islands visits, slightly more expensive than those down at El Chaco waterfront in Paracas, and they can arrange trips to the Nasca Lines as well. The hotel serves good buffet lunches, open to nonguests.

Av. Paracas 173, Paracas National Reserve, Pisco. ℂ and fax **034/545-100**, or ℂ 01/446-5079 in Lima. www.hotelparacas.com. 105 units. $90–$111 double; $149–$287 bungalows and suites. Rates include taxes. MC, V. **Amenities:** Restaurant; bar; 3 swimming pools; 2 tennis courts; children's playground; miniature golf; water-skiing and paddle boats. *In room:* A/C, TV.

MODERATE

El Mirador Hotel   El Mirador is very well situated near the sand dunes at the entrance to the nature reserve, about 16km (10 miles) south of Pisco. It has ample grounds and a nice terrace with sea views, as well as an appealing swimming pool. The well-furnished rooms are pretty nice, with carpeted floors and wood-beamed ceilings. If you want to be near the Paracas National Reserve, El Mirador is a better choice than the Embassy Beach.

Carretera Paracas Km 20, Paracas National Reserve, Pisco. ℂ and fax **034/665-016**, or ℂ and fax 01/ 423-8618 for reservations. http://accesoperu.com/mirador. 35 units. $40 double. Rate includes taxes and breakfast. MC, V. **Amenities:** Restaurant; bar; TV lounge; outdoor swimming pool; children's game room.

Hotel Embassy Beach This new and surprisingly modern three-star hotel, isn't located right on the beach, as its name might suggest—it's a 10-minute walk from both the center of Pisco and the sea. The rooms are very comfortable—almost luxurious for Pisco. This hotel rivals the Hotel Paracas for comfort and services.

Av. San Martín 1119, Pisco. © **034/532-568.** Fax 034/532-256. 40 units. Mon–Thurs $50 double; Fri–Sun $80 double. Rates include taxes. MC, V. **Amenities:** Restaurant; bar; nice outdoor swimming pool; game room. *In room:* TV, safe.

INEXPENSIVE

Hostal Posada Hispaña 🕊 *Value* This charming, colonial-style small hotel is managed by a Spanish couple from Cataluña. Recently renovated, the popular and good-value inn is clean and nicely decorated for the price; it's also only 1½ blocks from the Plaza de Armas. The rooms have loft spaces and bathrooms, and the hotel has a backyard garden.

Av. Bolognesi 236, Pisco. © and fax **034/536-363.** andesad@ciber.com.pe. 15 units. $20 double. Rate includes taxes. No credit cards. **Amenities:** Cafe; laundry service; kitchen access. *In room:* TV.

WHERE TO DINE

Pisco doesn't offer anything special in terms of restaurants, though the informal seafood eateries at the **El Chaco** waterfront in Paracas, where launches for the Islas Ballestas depart, are popular with travelers. In Pisco, there are several inexpensive cafes and pizzerias on or near the Plaza de Armas and a number of restaurants along the pedestrian boulevard (Comercio) with tourist *menús* (inexpensive set meals). For inexpensive mussels and ceviche, try the cevichería **Los Choritos Mágicos,** 28 de Julio 116 (© **034/534-158**). **Restaurant El Catamarán,** Jr. Comercio 166 (© **034/680-327**), serves the town's best pizzas and a very cheap menú. The most upmarket of the restaurants along the walkway, **Don Manuel,** Jr. Comercio 187 (© **034/532-035**), serves a variety of inexpensive full meals, including *churrasco* (grilled meats) and good fresh fish.

2 Ica

300km (186 miles) S of Lima

Capital of the department and surrounded by sand dunes, Ica is a surprisingly large and bustling colonial town, given the scorching desert sun its inhabitants have to contend with. Like Pisco, most of the principal attractions are located beyond the city. Ica is known primarily for its *bodegas,* wineries that produce a range of wines and pisco, the white-grape brandy that is the essential ingredient in the national drink, the pisco sour. Also welcome to travelers in the unrelentingly dry, sandy pampas of the department is the Huacachina Lagoon, a pretty oasis amid palm trees and dunes on the outskirts of Ica. In Ica proper is a small collection of interesting colonial mansions and churches, as well as the surprisingly excellent Museo Regional, with some splendid exhibits on the area's rich archaeological finds.

Ica was first settled as early as 10,000 years ago and then inhabited by a succession of advanced cultures including the Paracas, Nasca, Wari, and Ica civilizations. The Inca Pachacútec incorporated the Ica, Nasca, and Chincha valley territories in the 15th century, but by the mid–16th century, the Spaniards had arrived, and Jerónimo Luis de Cabrera founded the *Villa de Valverde del Valle de Ica,* which grew in importance as a commercial center focusing on wine and cotton production.

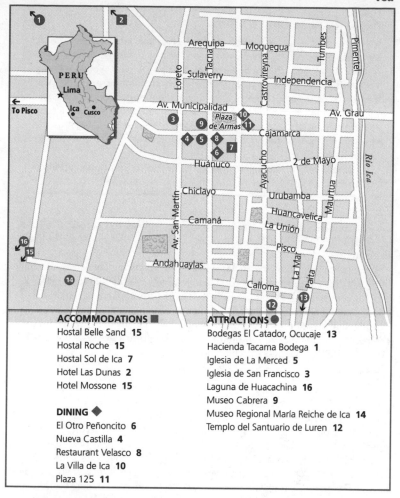

ACCOMMODATIONS ■

Hostal Belle Sand **15**
Hostal Roche **15**
Hostal Sol de Ica **7**
Hotel Las Dunas **2**
Hotel Mossone **15**

DINING ◆

El Otro Peñoncito **6**
Nueva Castilla **4**
Restaurant Velasco **8**
La Villa de Ica **10**
Plaza 125 **11**

ATTRACTIONS ●

Bodegas El Catador, Ocucaje **13**
Hacienda Tacama Bodega **1**
Iglesia de La Merced **5**
Iglesia de San Francisco **3**
Laguna de Huacachina **16**
Museo Cabrera **9**
Museo Regional María Reiche de Ica **14**
Templo del Santuario de Luren **12**

ESSENTIALS
GETTING THERE

There are frequent buses from Lima to Ica (4 hr.), which drop passengers in the center of town. Frequent service also connects Ica to Nasca (2 hr.) and Pisco (45 min.). **Cruz del Sur,** Avenida Paseo de la República, Lima (℃ **01/433-6765**), and **Ormeño,** Av. Carlos Zavala 177, Lima (℃ **01/427-5679**), travel between Lima, Pisco, Nasca, and Arequipa. **Soyuz-Peru Bus,** Av. Carlos Zavala 221, Lima (℃ **01/428-6252**), connects Ica with Lima and Pisco and is the fastest and best (with the most frequent departures) from either city.

VISITOR INFORMATION

Dirección de Turismo (MITINCI), Av. Jerónimo de Cabrera 426, Urbanización Luren (℃ **034/227-287**), is the main administrative office of the tourism ministry in Ica department, but it's a hike from the Plaza de Armas. Pay a visit only if you're in serious need of assistance.

Tips **No Wine Until It's Time**

Ica celebrates a wine harvest festival (*Festival Internacional de la Vendimia*) during early March. The second Friday of the month is a major holiday throughout the Ica department. Many activities take place in the vineyards, though around town there are concerts, handicraft fairs, Peruvian *caballos de paso* (step horses) shows, beauty pageants, and cockfighting. (Don't these last two always go together?) It's a great time to get your fill of pisco. The lovely maiden chosen as the Queen of the Festival gets to doff her shoes and squish grapes in a huge wine vat, to the titillation of all.

Another date to remember: July 25 is the **Día Internacional del Pisco** across Peru, and everybody gets drunk on a national scale.

FAST FACTS   **Banco de Crédito,** Av. Grau 109 at the corner of Callao (© **034/233-711**), has an ATM. You'll also find money exchangers on the Plaza de Armas.

For medical attention, go to **Hospital Félix Torrealva Gutiérrez,** Bolívar 1065 (© **034/234-450**), or **Hospital de Apoyo** (© **034/235-231,** or 034/235-101 for emergencies). If you need the **police,** their headquarters are located at Lambayeque, block 1 (© **034/224-553**).

You'll find a **post office** at Plaza de Armas (Libertad 119); it's open Monday through Saturday from 8am to 6pm. There's a **Telefónica del Perú** office at Jr. Huanuco 289 (© **034/217-247**); it's open daily.

GETTING AROUND

Ica is quite spread out, and getting around town will most likely involve taking inexpensive taxis, which flood the streets. (Most trips in town cost $2.) Taxis are especially useful in visiting the wineries located outside of town. There are also *ciclotaxis,* or bicycle rickshaws, which are cheaper still but less secure. Some visitors enjoy taking them out to Huacachina.

You can arrange Nasca Lines overflights from Ica, though it's considerably more common (not to mention cheaper) to do it in Nasca. If you want to do it from Ica, contact **AeroCondor,** Av. La Angostura 400, Hotel Las Dunas (© **034/256-820**), or **Inca Baths Tours,** Lima 171 on the Plaza de Armas (© **034/234-127**). For other organized tours, contact **Huacachina Tours,** Av. La Angostura 355, L-47, in front of the Hotel Las Dunas (© **034/256-582**), or **Pelican Travel & Service,** Independencia 156 and Lima 121 (© **034/225-211**).

WHAT TO SEE & DO
MUSEUMS

Museo Cabrera   A wildly idiosyncratic museum that specializes in purportedly ancient stones, this private unmarked collection is worth a visit if you prize the art of highly personal collecting. With more than 10,000 stones, including a series of fancifully engraved stones with depictions of primitive life (including dinosaurs), the collection makes an entertaining if almost assuredly fraudulent case for the nature of pre-Inca Peruvian civilizations. Dr. Javier Cabrera, a descendant of one of Ica's founders, claims that his stones prove the validity of his unique theories that an unprecedented advanced Stone Age culture flourished in Peru prior to the Inca Empire. Regardless of the truth, the stones were engraved by talented artisans, many of whom are still living today! A visit to this museum will be brief—in 15 or 20 minutes, you will have seen all you need to see.

Bolívar 170 (Plaza de Armas). © 034/2331-933. Admission only by guided tour, $5. Mon–Sat 9am–1pm and 4–8pm (though hours are not always maintained).

Museo Regional María Reiche de Ica *Finds* Ica's Regional Museum, founded in 1946 and frequently hailed as one of the best small museums in the country, houses a very good collection of intricate Paracas textiles, Nasca ceramics, mummies, fossils, deformed skulls, and trophy heads, as well as colonial and republican art. The well-organized collection also includes important pieces from the Huari, Ica, Chincha, and Inca civilizations, giving visitors an excellent primer on the region's rich history and archaeology. You'll find *quipus*, knotted strings used by the Incas who, in lieu of a writing system, made and maintained calculations, records, and historical notes with them, and a large scale model (1/500) of the Nasca Lines behind the museum. Allow about 45 minutes for a visit.

Jr. Ayabaca, block 8 s/n. © 034/234-383. Admission S/5 ($1.50) adults, S/2 (75¢) students. Mon–Sat 9am–6pm; Sun 9am–1pm. The museum is about a mile, or a 20-min. walk, from Ica's Plaza de Armas; you can also take bus 17 from the plaza to reach it.

BODEGAS (WINERIES)

Dispersed throughout the Ica countryside are some 85 traditional, artisanal wineries that produce pisco and regular table wines. Several of the larger bodegas welcome visits. The best way to visit the following, if you don't have your own transportation, is either to take a taxi or check with one of the travel agencies in town (see "Getting Around," above) about organized tours. Tours given on the premises of the wineries may be in Spanish only. Harvest time, from late February through April, is by far the best time to visit; at other times, the bodegas can be very quiet.

Bodega El Catador   Located in the Subtanjalla district 7km (4 miles) from Ica, this interesting bodega offers free tours and tastings. It has a small wine museum and a restaurant and tavern that often has live music. (The winery calls it a "discotheque.")

Fondo Tres Esquinas 102 (Carretera Panamericana Sur Km 296), Subtanjalla, Ica. © 034/403-295, or 034/403-427. Daily 8am–6pm.

Bodega Ocucaje   About 35km (24 miles) south of Ica, on the grounds of a colonial hacienda, this remote traditional winery is where the locally famous Vino Fond de Cave was born. The winery also operates an inn, the handsome Ocucaje Sun & Wine Resort (p. 157), with all-inclusive packages, sports, and winery tours.

Av. Principal s/n. © 034/408-001. S/10 ($3) per person. Mon–Fri 9am–noon and 2–5pm; Sat 9am–noon.

Bodegas Vista Alegre   Just 3km (nearly 2 miles) north of the center of Ica in the La Tinguiña district, this winery, founded in 1857 by the Picasso brothers, is one of the oldest and largest in Peru, well known for its pisco production. To get there on foot, walk on Avenida Grau from the Plaza de Armas, cross over the Ica River and turn left; the gate entrance to the colonial hacienda is impossible to miss.

Camino a La Tinguiña Km 2.5, Ica. © 034/232-919. Mon–Fri 9am–2pm.

Hacienda Tacama Bodega About 10km (6 miles) northeast of Ica, housed in a 16th-century colonial hacienda, this winery is known internationally. Despite the farm building's age—it's one of the oldest in the valley—the bodega uses modern technology. The vineyard is still irrigated, incredibly, by the amazing Achirana irrigation canal built by the Incas.

Camino a La Tinguiña s/n, Ica. © 034/228-395. Daily 9am–3pm.

COLONIAL CHURCHES & MANSIONS

Ica has several colonial churches and mansions of note, even though many have been felled by earthquakes over the years. The most important church to worshippers is the neoclassical **Templo del Santuario de Luren,** Calle Ayacucho at Piura, where the venerated image of the patron saint of the city, El Señor de Luren, is kept; during Holy Week and the third week of October, it is paraded around the city in well-attended processions. **Iglesia de La Merced** (also called La Catedral), on the southwest corner of the Plaza de Armas, is a late-19th-century colonial church with a handsomely carved altar. **Iglesia de San Jerónimo,** Cajamarca 262, is primarily of interest for its altar mural. **Iglesia de San Francisco,** though constructed in 1950, is notable for its stained glass; it's at Avenida Municipalidad at Avenida San Martín.

Among the most attractive of Ica's *casonas,* or colonial mansions, are the **Casona del Marqués de Torre** (today the Banco Continental) on the first block of Calle Libertad; **Casa Mendiola** on Calle Bolívar; **Casona Alvarado** at Cajamarca 178, a Greco-Roman imitation; and **Casona Colonial El Portón,** Calle Loreto 223.

OUTDOOR FUN

LAGUNA DE HUACACHINA If you stumble upon this gentle, beautiful oasis in the middle of the desert, surrounded by dunes and palm trees, you might think it's a mirage. Only 5km (3 miles) southwest of the center of Ica, Huacachina (pronounced "wah-kah-*chee*-nah") Lagoon is a great place to swim and relax if you're suffering from the heat, and there's a small resort village with a few hotels and restaurants. A boardwalk rings the lagoon. Locals contend that the sulfur-rich waters of the lagoon have curative medicinal properties. Kids can go sand boarding on the dunes (one of the restaurants and Hostal Rocha rent out boards) or paddleboat across the lagoon. Buses to Huacachina depart from the Plaza de Armas in Ica, or you can take an inexpensive taxi.

SAND BOARDING In the sand-dune-laden desert landscapes in southern Peru, surfing the dunes on sand boards and *areneros* (dune buggies) are popular sports. The largest sand dunes in South America, reaching a height of 2,000m (6,560 ft.), are just 8km (5 miles) from Nasca, and there are also really high dunes around the Huacachina Lagoon outside of Ica.

Sand boarding, a cross between downhill skiing and snowboarding on grainy stuff rather than white powder, is fairly easy to do. You can really build up some speed, and accomplished boarders can maneuver almost like they would on the slopes. It can be very hot, though, and tough going, as there aren't any lifts to transport you back up the dune. After a few spills, you'll be covered in sand. Accidents can occur, so it's best to get some instruction from a local or the outfit renting the boards.

Adrenaline-fueled adventure trips in buggies are available through local tours (information available at the **Hotel Paracas;** see p. 151) or at the 210m (700 ft.) dunes around the Huacachina Lagoon outside of Ica, where a restaurant and the Hostal Rocha rent out sand boards (about S/3, or $1, an hour; see p. 158).

For more information on the sport and competitions in Peru, see **www.peru boarding.com/Sandboarding**.

WHERE TO STAY

Most of the best hotel options lie beyond the center of Ica; the majority of those in town are rather unappealing budget choices that have inconsistent hot water.

EXPENSIVE

Hotel Las Dunas *Kids*   On the outskirts of Ica is this sprawling complex of white Mediterranean-style villas with pretty landscaped grounds, three swimming pools, and good sports opportunities, including horseback riding, golf, tennis, *frontón* (something like a cross between paddle tennis and jai alai), sand boarding, and volleyball. Rooms are large and nicely furnished, and most have garden views. A terrific new addition is the planetarium that provides a good introduction to the Nasca Lines (admission $5).

Av. La Angostura 400, Ica. ℂ and fax **034/256-224**, or ℂ 01/221-7020 for reservations. 106 units. Sun–Thurs $92 double; weekends $114 double. Rates include taxes and breakfast. AE, DC, MC, V. **Amenities:** Restaurant; cafeteria; bar; 2 swimming pools; small gymnasium; sauna; room service; conference room. *In room:* A/C, TV, minibar, safe; suites have Jacuzzis.

Hotel Mossone *Kids*   At the Huacachina Lagoon is a fancy, colonial-style hotel in a century-old mansion that was a luxurious resort hotel back in the 1920s. It has a pleasant pool, interior garden patio, and a restaurant veranda overlooking the lagoon. Rooms are elegantly furnished and have parquet floors. Although Las Dunas has more amenities and activities, the Mossone has more character and ambience, and the Huacachina Lagoon is an attraction in itself.

Balneario de Huacachina, Ica. ℂ **034/213-630**, or 01/261-0240 for reservations. Fax 034/236-137. reservas@derramajae.org.pe. 53 units. $71 double; $95–$116 suite. Rates include taxes. AE, DC, MC, V. **Amenities:** Restaurant; bar; outdoor swimming pool; room service; meeting rooms; safety deposit box. *In room:* TV.

MODERATE

Hostal Sol de Ica   This modern and fairly large place is centrally located and probably the best choice in town. Rooms aren't large, but they have private bathrooms and TV. There's also a pool on the premises.

Jr. Lima 265, Ica. ℂ **034/236-165**. 104 units. $40 double. Rate includes taxes and breakfast. MC, V. **Amenities:** Bar; outdoor swimming pool. *In room:* TV.

Ocucaje Sun & Wine Resort *Kids*   A lovely resort in the countryside about a half hour from Ica, Ocucaje is primarily a winery, but its hotel is popular among Limeños and other well-heeled guests with time to relax. Rooms are good-size and comfortably furnished. Sports options include tennis, volleyball, swimming, horseback riding, biking, and dune-buggy excursions. The hotel offers packages that include all meals, wines, and a tourist criollo show (2 nights, $100–$130 per person).

Carretera Panamericana Sur Km 336, Ica. ℂ **034/408-001**, or 01/444-4054 for reservations. Fax 034/408-003. www.ocucaje.com. 55 units. $65–$77 double. Rates include taxes and breakfast. Several meal plans and packages available. AE, DC, MC, V. **Amenities:** Restaurant; outdoor swimming pool; tennis courts; Jacuzzi; sauna; game room. *In room:* A/C, TV.

INEXPENSIVE

Hostal Belle Sand   Located a few kilometers north of Ica, this *hostal* (inn) has an outdoor pool with sun terrace, and sand boards for rent. The hostal is best suited for backpackers and sand boarders.

Av. Casuarinas B1-3, Residencial La Angostura. ✆ **034/256-039.** Fax 034/256-814. ecotourica@terra. com.pe. 21 units. S/60 ($17) double. No credit cards. **Amenities:** Cafeteria; bar.

Hostal Rocha *(Value* This small family-run inn is in a nice old house with large rooms and terraces with lagoon views. Rooms are more than adequate for the very low prices; some rooms have balconies. Popular with backpackers, the hostal has bikes and sand boards for rent.

Balneario de Huacachina, Ica. ✆ 034/222-256. 10 units. S/10 ($3) per person, shared bathroom; S/30 ($9) double with private bathroom. No credit cards. **Amenities:** Swimming pool.

WHERE TO DINE

Despite its size, Ica doesn't offer much in the way of fine dining. Most locals and visitors tend to gravitate toward the Plaza de Armas and the handful of sandwich shops, rotisserie-chicken places, and informal restaurants there.

Grab some snacks, breakfast, or a tourist set lunch, along with some local wines, at **La Villa de Ica,** Lima 139 at the Plaza de Armas (✆ **034/213-108**). **Plaza 125,** Lima 125 at the Plaza de Armas (✆ **034/211-816**), serves grilled meats, rotisserie chicken, and barbecue, as well as regional specialties, to a mixed crowd of families and young people. **El Otro Peñoncito,** Bolívar 422 (✆ **034/ 233-920**), is the nicest restaurant in the city center, with a hugely varied menu of criollo specialties and basic chicken, meat, and fish dishes, including some vegetarian plates. Sometimes, there's live music in the evenings. **Nueva Castilla,** Libertad 252 (✆ **034/213-140**), is a pretty nice restaurant serving Peruvian fare; there's a small patio. After dinner on weekends, the music is pumped up, and the restaurant becomes a disco of sorts. **Restaurant Velasco,** Libertad 137 (✆ **034/218-182**), is a popular cafeteria-style restaurant and bakery serving both Peruvian and international dishes at very affordable prices, as well as a selection of baked goods and other desserts and coffee.

3 Nasca

443km (275 miles) S of Lima

Nasca would just be a dusty little desert town of little interest were it not for the strange presence of massive, mysterious lines, etched into the sands of the pampas more than a millennium ago. Ancient peoples created a vast tapestry of "geoglyphs"—trapezoids and triangles, 70-odd animal and plant figures, and more than 10,000 lines—that have baffled observers for decades. They are so large, with some figures reaching dimensions of 300m (1,000 ft.), that they can only be appreciated from the air. Over the years, theorists have posited that they were signs from the gods, agricultural and astronomical calendars, or even extraterrestrial airports. Some believe the drawers of the lines must themselves have had the ability to fly, perhaps in hot-air balloons, over the designs below. The wildest theories, today discredited by all but fringe-dwelling true believers, prompted the old book and movie *The Chariots of the Gods.*

The town is named for the Nasca culture (300 B.C.–A.D.700), which succeeded the Paracas civilization along the southern desert coast. Little was known about the Nasca until the beginning of the 20th century. Today, the Nasca are renowned for their exquisitely stylized pottery, among the finest of preColumbian Peru. The small town of Nasca was devastated by a monstrous earthquake in 1996 and is just getting back on its feet. Most constructions in town were adobe, which crumbled and were replaced by hastily built concrete houses. The new construction adds to the dusty frontier feel of the town.

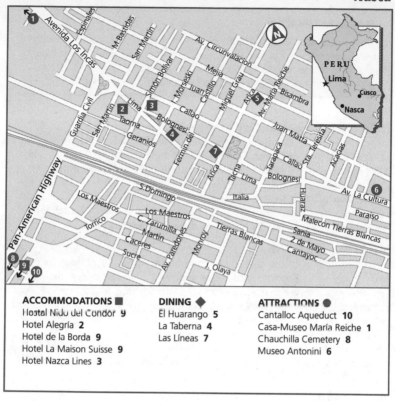

ACCOMMODATIONS ■
Hostal Nido del Condor **9**
Hotel Alegría **2**
Hotel de la Borda **9**
Hotel La Maison Suisse **9**
Hotel Nazca Lines **3**

DINING ◆
El Huarango **5**
La Taberna **4**
Las Líneas **7**

ATTRACTIONS ●
Cantalloc Aqueduct **10**
Casa-Museo María Reiche **1**
Chauchilla Cemetery **8**
Museo Antonini **6**

The surrounding desert is a strangely impressive place. Flying over the Nasca Lines, you see an unending expanse of craggy, dusty, origami-like folds in the sands, like deep wrinkles in a wizened face. Certainly nothing in the region equals the impact of a flight over the lines, but the town does have a couple of good museums and two archaeological sites that evoke the Nasca culture that flourished in the area.

ESSENTIALS
GETTING THERE
From Lima, **Cruz del Sur** buses (© 01/433-6765) pass through Nasca on the way to Arequipa; the trip to Nasca takes 7 to 8 hours. **Señor de Luren** buses (© 01/428-0630) also travel to Nasca from Lima. **Ormeño** (© 01/427-5679) makes the trip from Cusco (24+ hr.) and Arequipa (10 hr.), and like Cruz del Sur, returns to Lima. **Transportes Wari** (© 084/261-703) also makes the long journey between Cusco and Nasca (20–22 hr.).

VISITOR INFORMATION
The **Infotur** office, offering hotel and tourism packages and guide information, is on Callao 783. Tourist information can also be obtained from one of the travel agencies in town, though they are understandably more interested in selling tour packages.

Fun Fact **Say What?**

The Nasca people were evidently deeply rooted in the hot and painfully arid southern desert landscape that they inhabited in spite of numerous earthquakes and that they fought valiantly to farm. The word "Nasca" comes from the Quechua, *nanasca,* which means pain and suffering.

FAST FACTS   **Banco de Crédito** at avenidas Grau and Lima has an ATM with the Visa logo. For medical attention, go to **EsSalud,** María Reiche 308 (© 034/522-438), or **Hospital Apoyo,** Callao at Morsesky (© 034/522-586). The police are located next to the roundabout on Lima and Panamericana, near the Ormeño station.

The **post office** is located at Fermín de Castillo 379, between Callao and Bolognesi; it's open Monday through Friday from 9am to 5pm. The **Telefónica del Perú** office is on Lima 545; it's open daily from 8am to 10pm.

WHAT TO SEE & DO

Visitors who wish to see more than the Nasca Lines would probably benefit from arranging a group tour with one of the Nasca travel agencies, as the major archaeological sites are scattered about the valley and complicated to get to. For flights over the lines, it's sometimes best to simply go to the airport and purchase tickets directly from one of the charter airlines there. The following agencies all offer city and regional packages and information on the area: **Alegría Tours,** Jr. Lima 168 (© 034/832-440); **Nanasca Tours,** Lima 160 (© 034/522-917); **Nasca Travel,** Lima 438 (© 034/522-085); and **Nasca Trails,** Jr. Bolognesi 299 (© 034/522-858).

NASCA LINES ☆☆☆

The unique Nasca Lines remain one of the great enigmas of the South American continent. The San José desert, bisected by the great Pan-American Highway that runs the length of Peru, is more spectacularly marked by 70 giant plant and animal figures, as well as a warren of mysterious geometric lines, carved into the barren surface. Throughout the Nasca Valley, an area of nearly $1,000km^2$ (386 sq. miles), there are at least 10,000 lines and 300 different figures. Most are found alongside a 48km (30-mile) stretch of the Pan-American Highway. Some of the biggest and best-known figures are about 21km (13 miles) north of Nasca. Most experts believe they were constructed by the Nasca (pre-Inca) culture between 300 B.C. and A.D. 700, though predecessor and successor cultures—the Paracas and Huari—may have also contributed to the desert canvas. The lines were discovered in the 1920s when commercial airlines began flights over the Peruvian desert. From the sky, they appeared to be some sort of primitive landing strips.

As enigmatic as they are, the Nasca Lines are not some sort of desert-sands Rorschach inkblot; the figures are real and easily identifiable from the air. With the naked eye from the window of an airplane, you'll spot the outlines of a parrot, hummingbird, spider, condor, dog, whale, monkey with a tail wound like a top, giant spirals, huge trapezoids, and, perhaps oddest of all, a cartoonish anthropomorphic figure with its hand raised to the sky that has come to be known as the "Astronaut." Some figures are as much as 300m (1,000 ft.) long, while some lines are 30m (100 ft.) wide and stretch more than 9.5km (6 miles).

Questions have long confounded observers. Who constructed these huge figures and lines? And, of course, why? Apparently, the Nasca people, over many generations, removed hard stones turned dark by the sun to "draw" the lines in the fine, lighter colored sand. The incredibly dry desert conditions—it rains only about 50 centimeters a year on average—preserved the lines and figures for more than 1,000 years. Why the lines were constructed is more difficult to answer, especially considering that the authors were unable to see their work in its entirety without any sort of aerial perspective. The scientist who dedicated her life to study of the lines was a German mathematician, María Reiche. For 5 decades she lived austerely in the Peruvian desert and walked alone among the lines, taking painstaking measurements and making drawings of the site. She concluded that the lines formed a giant astronomical calendar, crucial to calculating planting and harvest times. According to this theory, the Nasca were able to predict the arrival of rains, a valuable commodity in such a barren territory. Other theories, though, abound. Nasca is a seismic zone, with 300 fault lines beneath the surface and hundreds of subterranean canals; an American scientist, David Johnson, proposed that the trapezoids held clues to subterranean water sources. Some suggest that the lines not only led to water sources, but that they were pilgrimage routes, part of the Nasca's ritual worship of water. Notions of extraterrestrials and the Nasca's ability themselves to fly over the lines have been dismissed by most serious observers.

An observation tower (*mirador*) stands beside the Pan-American Highway (about 19km/12 miles north of Nasca), but it only allows a vague and partial view of three figures: the hands, lizard, and tree. The view from the tower is vastly inferior to the overflight, but it's the best you'll be able to do if you can't take the stomach-turning dips and dives of the light-craft flights. (Only 10 min. into one recent flight, the four French travelers onboard with me were all tossing their *petits déjeuners* into the white plastic bags that had been thoughtfully provided.)

The small aircraft seat between three and five passengers. At latest count, seven small charter airlines offer flights over the lines from the small airport in Nasca. Flights cost between $35 and $50 and last 35 to 45 minutes. Pilots give

Tips Cahuachi & El Estaquería

The ruins of **Cahuachi,** an ancient adobe complex west of the Nasca Lines—said by some to be twice as large as Chan Chan, the massive city of the Chimú along the north coast—was the most important ceremonial and administrative center belonging to the Nasca culture. The site, in poor condition and in large part buried under sand, is still undergoing excavation. Because of ongoing work, only a handful of temples and pyramids may be visited, and only by guided tour. (The major agencies in Nasca usually offer the site as part of a group tour for around $10 per person.) Also on the premises is **El Estaquería,** a construction of rows of *huarango* trees, which probably marked important grave sites. The ruins are 30km (19 miles) from Nasca. The director of the Antonini Museum in Nasca has unearthed a spectacular collection of painted textiles, made with seven different dyes, at Cahuachi that he hopes to exhibit in a new museum some day in Nasca. Many of the finest examples of Nasca ceramics in existence were also discovered at Cahuachi.

Fun Fact **Nasca Culture**

The Nasca civilization is best known popularly for its artistry on a grand scale: those massive, and monstrously baffling line drawings on the desert floor of the coastal pampas. But among scholars, the culture is acclaimed for producing the most sophisticated ceramists of pre-Columbian Peru and ingenious engineers who irrigated their desert fields with hydraulic systems and aqueducts that carried underground water.

The Nasca succeeded the Paracas in the desert region south of present-day Lima. While the Paracas were extraordinary weavers and designers of textiles, the Nasca culture distinguished itself with highly artistic pottery. Their glazed ceramics featured vivid but earthy colors and symbolic motifs, and mineral-based pigments ensured lasting colors. Many of the stylized figures and lines on Nasca pottery closely echo the Nasca Lines, reinforcing theories about the latter's authorship.

---

very basic descriptions of the figures as they fly overhead. If you're interested in seeing the lines only, and you don't have time for the town of Nasca or the surrounding area, by far the most convenient—although certainly not the cheapest—way is as part of a 1-day round-trip package from Lima with Aero-Condor ($140 per person, minimum two people). For best visibility, try to go in the morning or late afternoon, but be prepared for conditions that frequently delay flights and, on occasion, make taking off impossible.

Light aircraft that operate Nasca Lines overflights from Nasca's María Reiche airport on Carretera Panamericana Sur Km 447 include: **AeroCondor,** Hostal El Nido del Cóndor (p. 164; © **034/522-402,** or 01/422-4214 in Lima); **AeroIca,** Hotel La Maison Suisse (p. 164; © **034/522-434**); and **Aeroparacas,** Jr. Lima 185 (© **034/521-027**).

OTHER NOTABLE SIGHTS NEAR NASCA

Cantalloc Aqueduct   About 4km (2½ miles) southwest of Nasca are very well-preserved stone aqueducts, part of a sophisticated subterranean system constructed by the Nasca to irrigate the fields in the pampas. There are 35 beautifully built Inca or pre-Inca aqueducts, or *puquios,* with surface air vents that form spirals descending to the water current. The canals, many S-shaped to slow down the flow of water, still function and are used by local farmers. Nearby, Los Paredones, ruins of an Inca trade center, is in poor shape, requiring a fertile imagination to conjure the activity that once reigned here.

Carretera Puquio–Cusco. Admission S/3. Daily 8am–5pm. To get here, you must come by taxi (S/15–S/20, or $4–$6, round-trip, including waiting time) or tour group (S/35, or $10, per person).

Casa-Museo María Reiche   The German mathematician María Reiche was the foremost expert on the Nasca Lines, earning her the nickname "Dame of the Desert." She dedicated most of her adult life to studying them, debunking the loonier theories about their purposes, and doing more than even the Peruvian government to publicize the lines' existence. Reiche died in 1998 at the age of 95. Today, the simple room where she worked and lived, which her tomb has been placed next to, has been converted into a small museum paying tribute to Reiche's life and the Lines, complete with maps, models, plans, and photos. The Casa-Museo (also variously referred to as Museo de Sitio María Reiche Newman and Museo Regional María Reiche) is located in the district called San Pablo, between Ica and Nasca. Allow a half hour to tour the museum.

Caserío la Pascana, Carretera Panamericana Sur Km 420 (27km/17 miles from Nasca), San Pablo. (✆ 034/234-383 or 034/522-428. Admission S/3 (90¢). Mon–Fri 9am–7pm; Sat 8:30am–6:30 pm; Sun 9am–1pm.

Chauchilla Cemetery ⚜ South of Nasca is a extensive valley of tombs from the Inca-Chincha period (1000–1400). It is a necropolis rather than a mere cemetery: Thousands of graves have been uncovered in the area. Only 12 underground tombs are exposed for visitors, though they present a rich picture of the ancient culture of the desert valley. One tomb holds only children, and others are populated with the remains of adults with thick, Rasta-like dreadlocks. The cemetery has been open to the public since only 1997, and only in the past year were the tombs covered with thatch roofs—which is why many skulls appear whitewashed from the blazing desert sun. The desert's very dry conditions helped preserve the mummies over the centuries. Fragments of textiles, feathers, and even bone are scattered about the site, clues to the cemetery's discovery by *huaqueros* (grave robbers) and how underfunded this project remains. Allow about 3 to 4 hours for travel time and viewing the necropolis.

Admission S/4 ($1). Daily 8am–5pm. Getting to Chauchilla is complicated; by taxi (S/30–S/40, or $8–$11, round-trip, including waiting time) or tour group (S/35, or $10, per person) are the only options.

Museo Antonini ⚜ *Kids* This excellent private archaeology museum, a labor of love inaugurated by an Italian foundation in 1999, addresses local Nasca culture with excellent exhibits that detail the process as well as the results of archaeological excavations in the area. On view are fine ceramics, trophy heads worn by warriors after beheadings to inspire fear among enemies, musical instruments, and a few well-preserved mummies. In the gardens out back is the Bisambra aqueduct, an ancient Nasca stone irrigation canal, as well as reproductions of tombs and scale models of the Nasca Lines. The director hopes one day soon to be able to open a new museum in Nasca to show off the world's greatest collection of painted textiles—made with seven different types of vegetable dyes—all uncovered from the huge adobe city of Cahuachi nearby. Plan to spend about an hour here.

Av. de la Cultura 600 (Bisambra), a 10-min. walk from the Plaza de Armas. (✆ 034/523-444. Admission S/10 ($3). Daily 9am–7pm.

WHERE TO STAY

There are plenty of low-end accommodations in Nasca and a handful of slightly more comfortable, if unspectacular, options in town and out by the airport. Look for a new hacienda hotel property, the **Hotel Hacienda Cantayo** (✆ **034/522-264;** fax 034/522-283; hotelcantayo@wayna.rcp). A large, renovated white hacienda with panoramic mountain views, it features a swimming pool, rooms with Balinese furniture, and a jogging track. Special activities for New Agers and spa services are planned.

MODERATE

Hotel Alegría The Alegría is the most popular hotel in town. It's a friendly place that operates a good travel agency and has loads of facilities and services for travelers. Some of the new, chalet-style rooms have air-conditioning. It also has a nice garden and free Internet access for guests.

Lima 168, Nasca. (✆ and fax 034/522-444. www.nazcaperu.com. 43 units. $35 double. Rate includes taxes, continental breakfast, and pre-arranged pickup from bus stop. DC, MC, V. **Amenities:** Restaurant; laundry service; safety deposit boxes. *In room:* A/C, TV.

Hotel de la Borda   This is an old hacienda with simple rooms around court-yards and a garden with bougainvillea. It could be a great place, but it looks and feels neglected. Still, plenty of people stay here (especially groups), and it's a tranquil setting. It's a few kilometers along a dusty road beyond the airport.

Carretera Panamericana Sur Km 447, Nasca. ℂ 034/522-576. 39 units. $45 double. Rate includes taxes and breakfast. MC, V. **Amenities:** Bar; outdoor pool; game room. *In room:* TV.

Hotel La Maison Suisse   Like the Nido del Cóndor (see below), this hotel is also across from the airport (and owned by AeroIca). It has slightly offbeat rooms with bamboo ceilings and frilly bedspreads. Suites have air-conditioning and huge Jacuzzis in the middle of the rooms, making them look a bit like porn sets. Continuing the theme, the bar is underground and has a huge glass window opening onto the pool for underwater views.

Carretera Panamericana Sur Km 447, Nasca. ℂ 034/522-434. 40 units. $55–$66 double; $105–$125 suite. Rates include taxes and breakfast. DC, MC, V. **Amenities:** Bar; outdoor pool. *In room:* TV, minibar; suites have A/C and Jacuzzi.

Hotel Nazca Lines *(Kids)*   The most upscale hotel in town, the Nazca Lines has a pretty courtyard with a good-size clean pool and tennis courts. The nice rooms have air-conditioning, old-style furnishings, and tile and iron accents. María Reiche lived here for many years in no. 130. There's a restaurant and planetar-ium, with Nasca Lines presentations, on the premises.

Jr. Bolognesi s/n, Nasca. ℂ 034/522-293. otorres@derramajae.or.pe. 34 units. $85 double. Rate includes taxes. DC, MC, V. **Amenities:** Restaurant; outdoor pool; tennis courts. *In room:* TV.

INEXPENSIVE

Hostal Nido del Cóndor   This hostal is directly across the road from the airport—very convenient for flights, less so for access to town—and is owned by AeroCondor. It's a relaxed place (if you don't mind the sound of propeller planes) with gardens, a pool, and a TV/video lounge. The rooms are very com-fortable with TV and fans—a good deal.

Carretera Panamericana Sur Km 447, Nasca. ℂ and fax 034/522-402. contanas@net.telematic.com.pe. 36 units. $20 double with private bathroom. Rate includes taxes and breakfast. DC, MC, V. **Amenities:** Restaurant; bar; TV lounge; outdoor pool; laundry service. *In room:* TV.

WHERE TO DINE

Your dining choices are rather limited in Nasca. Most people don't stay many nights, and they tend to eat at their hotels. Hotels with pretty decent restaurants include the Alegría, El Nido del Cóndor, and Nazca Lines, the last of which is a cut above (see above for reviews of all three hotels).

   Las Líneas, Jr. Arica 299-A (ℂ **034/522-488**), serves Peruvian fare such as ceviche and garlic chicken even though it looks like a Chinese restaurant. **El Huarango,** Jr. Arica 602 (ℂ **034/521-287**), is one of the better restaurants in Nasca, offering good value and a rooftop garden. **La Taberna,** Jr. Lima 321 (ℂ **034/521-411**), is a good restaurant with a varied international menu, live music on weekends, and the graffiti scrawlings of hundreds of international travelers who came before you. **Farita,** 388 Bolognesi (no phone), specializes in *chicharrones* (fried pork skins) and tamales.

6

CUSCO

The storied capital of the Inca dynasty and gateway to the imperial city of Machu Picchu, **Cusco** ✶✶✶ is one of the decided highlights of South America. Stately and historic, with stone streets and building foundations laid by the Incas more than 5 centuries ago, the town is also remarkably dynamic, enlivened by throngs of travelers who have transformed the historic center around the Plaza de Armas into a mecca of sorts for South American adventurers. Cusco is one of those rare places—perhaps like Bali, Kathmandu, or Prague—that seems able to preserve its unique character and enduring appeal despite its prominence on the international tourism radar.

Cusco looks and feels like the very definition of an Andean capital. It's a fascinating blend of pre-Columbian and colonial history and contemporary *mestizo* culture. The Incas made *Q'osqo* (meaning "navel of the world" in Quechua) the political, military, and cultural center of their empire, which stretched up and down the Andes, from Ecuador through Bolivia and all the way to Chile. Cusco was the empire's holy city, and it was also ground zero of the legendary Inca network of roads connecting all points in the empire.

The Spanish conquistadors knew it was essential to topple the capital city to take control of the region, a feat they ultimately accomplished after an epic battle at Sacsayhuamán. The Spaniards razed most Inca buildings and monuments, but in many cases found the structures so well engineered that they built upon the very foundations of Inca Cusco. Many perfectly constructed Inca stone walls, examples of unrivaled stonemasonry, still stand. After a devastating earthquake in 1650, Cusco became a largely baroque city.

The result is a city that showcases plainly evident layers of history. Cusco's highlights include both Inca ruins—such as Sacsayhuamán, a seemingly impregnable fortress on a hill overlooking the city, and Qoricancha, the Temple of the Sun—and colonial-era baroque and Renaissance churches and mansions. The heart of the historic center has suffered relatively few modern intrusions, and despite the staggering number of souvenir shops, travel agencies, hotels, and restaurants overflowing with visitors, it doesn't take an impossibly fertile imagination to conjure the magnificent capital of the 16th century.

Today, Cusco thrives as one of the most vibrant expressions of Amerindian and mestizo culture anywhere in the Americas. Every June, the city is packed during Inti Raymi, the celebration of the winter solstice and the sun god, a deeply religious festival that is also a magical display of pre-Columbian music and dance. Thousands trek out to Paucartambo for the riveting Virgen del Carmen festival in mid-July. Other traditional arts also flourish. Cusco is the handicrafts center of Peru, and its streets teem with merchants and their extraordinary textiles, many hand-woven using the exact techniques of their ancestors.

Tips **So Nice They Named It Twice**

"Cusco" refers to both the capital city and the department, or Cusco region, which includes the Sacred Valley, Machu Picchu, and other places covered in this and the following chapter.

Spectacularly cradled by the bold southeastern Andes mountains that were so fundamental to the Inca belief system, Cusco sits at a daunting altitude of 3,400m (11,000 ft.). The air is noticeably thinner here than in almost any city in South America, and the city, best explored on foot, demands arduous hiking up precipitous stone steps, leaving even the fittest of travelers gasping for breath. It takes a couple of days to get acclimatized before moving on from Cusco to explore the mountain villages of the Urubamba Valley (also known as the Sacred Valley), the Amazon basin, and, of course, Machu Picchu, but many visitors find Cusco so seductive that they either delay their plans to explore the surrounding region, or they add a few days to their trip to allow more time in the city. Increasingly, travelers are basing themselves in one of the lower-altitude villages of the Sacred Valley, but there is so much to see and do in Cusco that an overnight stay is pretty much required of anyone who hasn't previously spent time in the area.

Cusco's beautiful natural setting, colorful festivals, sheer number of sights—unparalleled in Peru—and facilities and services organized for travelers make it the top destination in Peru and one of the most exciting places in South America. It is loaded with good and, in many cases, embarrassingly cheap restaurants, *hostales* (inns), and lively bars that cater to enthusiastic crowds of young and old gringos outfitted with the latest in fleece wear, backpacks, and hiking boots. For the burgeoning crowd that comes to Peru to do justice to all that high-tech adventure gear, superb trekking, river-rafting, and mountain-biking opportunities abound throughout the Sacred Valley.

1 Orientation

ARRIVING

BY PLANE

In high season, flights arrive by the dozens from Lima, Arequipa, Puerto Maldonado, and La Paz, Bolivia, at **Aeropuerto Internacional Velasco Astete** (© 084/222-611), located 5km (3 miles) southeast of the historic center of Cusco. All major Peruvian airlines fly into Cusco, including **Aero Continente** (© 01/242-4242), **AeroCondor** (© 01/442-5215), **LanPeru** (© 01/213-8200), **Taca Peru** (© 01/213-7000), **Aviandina** (© 01/447-8080), and **TANS** (© 01/213-6000). A number of tour operators have booths in the arrivals terminal, and there is also a tourist information booth, an ATM, and currency exchange.

Transportation from the airport to downtown Cusco, about 20 minutes away, is by taxi or private hotel car. (A less-convenient *combi*, or small bus, passes outside the airport car park and goes to Plaza San Francisco; unless you have almost no baggage and your hotel is right on that square, it's not worth the few soles you'll save to take a combi.) Most hotels, even less expensive hostales, are happy

Cusco

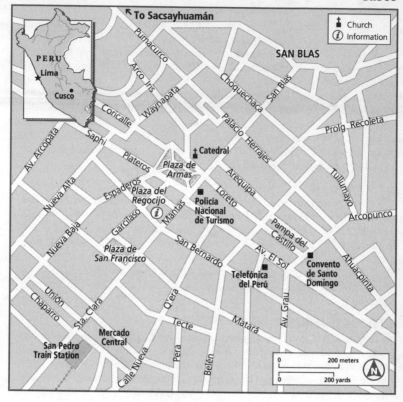

to arrange airport pickup. If you take a taxi, note that the fare is likely to drop precipitously if you merely refuse the first offer you get (likely to be S/15–S/20, or $4–$5.50). Taxi fare to Cusco is officially S/8 ($2.25) from the airport to the center, though you can often get one for S/5 ($1.50). When you exit with your luggage, you will be besieged with offers from taxi and tour-company representatives, many who will pretend to have your name on their "arrivals list" just to take you into town and try to score a commission from one of hundreds of tour operators. If you have arranged for your hotel to pick you up, be certain you are dealing with someone authorized by the hotel and who possesses your exact arrival information.

BY BUS

Buses to Cusco arrive from Lima, Arequipa, Puno/Juliaca, and Puerto Maldonado in the Amazon basin. The journey from Lima to Cusco takes 26 hours

Tips Breathtaking Views

If you fly to Cusco from Lima, ask for a seat on the left side of the plane, which by far affords the best views of the towering Andes—a spectacular sight sure to get you pumped for your visit to Cusco and Machu Picchu.

by land; from Puno, 9 to 10 hours; and from Arequipa, 12 hours. There is no central bus terminal in Cusco. Buses arrive either at a terminal on Avenida Pachacútec or (more commonly) at the newer Terminal Terrestre, at the end of Avenida El Sol (several kilometers from the city center). Buses from the Sacred Valley use small makeshift terminals on Calle Huáscar and Calle Intiqhawarina, off Tullumayo.

For service from Lima, contact the major companies including **Ormeño** (© 01/472-1710), **Cruz del Sur** (© 01/428-2570), **Oltursa** (© 01/445-8141), and **Civa** (© 01/426-4926). From Puno, the following offer daily service to Cusco: **First Class** (© 054/365-192), **Cruz del Sur** (© 054/622-626), and **Inka Express** (© 054/365-654). From Arequipa, your best bets are **Civa** (© 084/812-813) and **Cruz del Sur** (© 054/221-909).

BY TRAIN
There are two main PeruRail train stations in Cusco. Trains from Puno and Arequipa arrive at **Estación de Huanchaq,** Av. Pachacútec s/n (© **084/238-722** or 084/221-931), at the southeast end of Avenida El Sol. Trains from Ollantaytambo, Machu Picchu, and the Amazon jungle arrive at **Estación de San Pedro,** Calle Cascaparo s/n (© **084/221-352** or 084/221-313), southwest of the Plaza de Armas. Thieves operate in and around both stations, but visitors should be particularly cautious at San Pedro station, which is near the crowded Mercado Central.

VISITOR INFORMATION
As the top tourist destination in Peru, Cusco is well equipped with information outlets. There's a branch of the **Oficina de Información Turística** (© **084/ 380-145**) at the Velasco Astete Airport in the arrivals terminal; it's open daily from 6:30am to 12:30pm. The principal Oficina de Información Turística is located on Mantas 117-A, a block from the Plaza de Armas (© **084/263-176**). It's open Monday through Friday from 8am to 6pm, and Saturday from 9am to noon. It's very helpful and efficient, and it sells the essential *boleto turístico* (tourist ticket; see the box on p. 192). Another information office is located in the Terminal Terrestre de Huanchaq train station, Av. Pachacútec s/n (© **084/ 238-722**); it's open Monday through Saturday from 8am to 6:30pm.

South American Explorers has a recently opened office and club in Cusco at Choquechaca 188, no. 4 (© **084/245-484;** www.samexplo.org). The office stores luggage, maintains lists of trail reports for members, and has a library of useful information for trekking and mountaineering.

Tips Acclimatization
You'll need to take it easy for the first few hours or for even a couple of days in Cusco to adjust to the elevation. Drink plenty of water and do as the locals do: Drink *mate de coca,* or coca-leaf tea. (Don't worry, you won't get high or arrested, but you will adjust a little more smoothly to the thin air.) If that doesn't cure you, ask whether your hotel has an oxygen tank you can use for a few moments of assisted breathing. And if that doesn't do the trick, it may be time to seek medical assistance; see "Fast Facts," below.

> **Tips   Cusco = Cuzco = Q'osqo**
>
> Spanish and English spellings derived from the Quechua language are a little haphazard in Cusco, especially since there's been a linguistic movement to try to recuperate and value indigenous culture. Thus, you may see Inca written Inka; Cusco written Cuzco, Qosqo, or Q'osqo; Qoricancha as Coricancha or Koricancha; Huanchaq as Huanchac or Wanchac; Sacsayhuamán as Sacsaywaman; and Q'enko written Qenko, Kenko, or Qenqo. You're likely to stumble across others, with similar alphabetical prestidigitation, all used interchangeably.

CITY LAYOUT

The Incas designed their capital in the shape of a puma, with the head at the north end, at Sacsayhuamán (whose zigzagged walls are said to have represented the animal's teeth). This is pretty difficult to appreciate today; even though much of the original layout of the city remains, it has been engulfed by growth. Still, most of Cusco can be seen easily on foot, certainly the best way to take in this historic mountain city that is equal parts Inca capital, post-Conquest colonial city, and modern tourist magnet.

The old center of the city is organized around the stunning and busy Plaza de Armas, the focal point of life in Cusco. The streets that radiate out from the square—Plateros, Mantas, Loreto, Triunfo, Procuradores, and others—are loaded with travel agencies, shops, restaurants, bars, and hotels. The major avenue leading from the plaza southeast to the modern section of the city is Avenida El Sol, where most banks are located. The district of San Blas is perhaps Cusco's most picturesque barrio; the labyrinth-like neighborhood spills on cobblestone streets off Cuesta San Blas, which leads to crooked alleys and streets and view points high above the city.

Much of what interests most visitors is within easy walking distance of the Plaza de Armas. The major Inca ruins are within walking distance for energetic sorts who enjoy a good, uphill hike.

2 Getting Around

Getting around Cusco is straightforward and relatively simple, especially since so many of the city sights are in walking distance of the Plaza de Armas in the historic center. You will mostly depend on leg power and taxis to make your way around town.

BY TAXI

Unlike in Lima, taxis are regulated in Cusco and charge standard rates (although they do not have meters). Taxis are inexpensive (S/2, or 50¢, for any trip within the historic core during the day; S/3, or $1, after 10pm) and a good way to get around, especially at night. Hailing a cab in Cusco is considerably less daunting than in Lima, but you may still wish to call a registered taxi when traveling from your hotel to train or bus stations or the airport, and when returning to your hotel late at night. Licensed taxi companies include **Okarina** (© **084/247-080**) and **Aló Cusco** (© **084/222-222**). Taxis can be hired for return trips to nearby ruins or for half or full days. To the airport, taxis charge S/10 ($3) from the city center; to the distant Terminal Terrestre (bus station), they charge S/7 ($2).

> **Tips A Safety Note**
>
> Over the years, Cusco, which on the surface seems to be an easygoing if
> increasingly congested mountain city, has earned a reputation for being
> rather unsafe for foreign visitors, especially at night, when violent mug-
> gings have been known to occur on empty streets. Do not walk alone late
> at night; have restaurants and bars call taxis to transfer you to your hotel.
> Please refer to "Safety" in "Fast Facts: Cusco" (p. 172) for more details.

BY BUS

Most buses—called variously *colectivos, micros,* and *combis*—cost S/1 (30¢),
slightly more after midnight, on Sunday, and holidays. You aren't likely to need
buses often in the city, though the colectivos that run up and down Avenida El
Sol are a useful option for some hotels, travel agencies, and shopping markets.
A bus departs from Plaza San Francisco to the airport, but it isn't terribly convenient. Buses and combis are most frequently used to travel from Cusco
to towns in the Sacred Valley, such as Pisac, Calca, and Urubamba. Those buses
depart from small terminals on Calle Huáscar and Calle Intiqhawarina, off
Tullumayo.

BY TRAIN

The most popular means to visit Machu Picchu and the Sacred Valley sights is
by train. Trains to Ollantaytambo and Machu Picchu Pueblo (also called Aguas
Calientes) leave from **Estación de San Pedro,** Calle Cascaparo s/n (© **084/221-
352** or 084/221-313), southwest of the Plaza de Armas. Reservations for these
trains, especially in high season (May–Sept), should be made at least a day in
advance.

BY CAR

Renting a car in the Cusco region—more than likely to visit the beautiful Sacred
Valley mountain villages—is a more practical idea than in most parts of Peru.
Rental agencies include **Avis,** Av. El Sol 808 (© **084/248-800**), and **Localiza,**
Av. Industrial J-3, Urbanización Huancaro (© **084/233-131**). Rates range from
$40 per day for a standard four-door to $65 per day for a Jeep Cherokee four-
wheel-drive.

For information on driving around the Cusco department, and in case of
emergencies, contact the **Touring Automóvil Club del Perú,** Av. El Sol 349,
2nd floor (© **084/224-561**). The office is open Monday through Friday from
9am to 1pm and 3:30 to 7:30pm, and Saturday from 9am to 1pm.

BY FOOT

Most of Cusco is best navigated by foot, though because of the city's high
elevation and steep climbs, walking is demanding. Allow extra time to get
around and carry a bottle of water. You can walk to the major ruins just beyond
the city—Sacsayhuamán and Q'enko—but you should be rather fit to do so.

BY HELICOPTER

Visitors in a rush to visit Machu Picchu can get there from Cusco in a chopper
with **Helicusco,** Calle Triunfo 379, 2nd floor (© **084/227-283;** www.rcp.net.
pe/helicusco). For more information, see chapter 7, "Machu Picchu & the
Sacred Valley of the Incas."

FAST FACTS: **Cusco**

American Express There is an office at Av. El Sol 679 (© **084/243-229**), open Monday through Friday from 9am to 7pm, and Saturday from 9am to 1pm. They'll replace stolen or lost traveler's checks and sell American Express checks with an Amex card, but they do not cash their own checks. There's another American Express office within the travel agency **Lima Tours** at Portal de Harinas 177, Plaza de Armas (© **084/228-431**).

Airport See "Arriving" in "Orientation," earlier in this chapter.

Banks/Currency Exchange Most Peruvian and international banks with currency-exchange bureaus and ATMs are located along Avenida El Sol. Money-changers, usually wearing colored smocks, patrol the main streets off the Plaza de Armas and Avenida El Sol. Banks include **Banco Santander Central Hispano,** Av. El Sol 459; **Banco de Crédito,** Av. El Sol 189; and **Banco Continental,** Av. El Sol 366. The external ATMs nearest the Plaza de Armas are at Banco de Crédito (Visa/Plus); **Banco del Sur** (Visa/MasterCard), Av. El Sol 457; and **Banco Latino** (MasterCard), Av. El Sol 395. Several small casas de cambio, with similar rates to banks, operate out of travel agencies and shops on Plaza de Armas and Avenida El Sol.

Car Rentals See "Getting Around," earlier in this chapter.

Consulates **U.S.,** Av. Tullumayo 127 (© **084/224-112**); **U.K.,** Av. Pardo 895 (© **084/226-671**). Both are open daily from 9am to noon and 3 to 5pm.

Dentists/Doctors In an emergency, contact the **Tourist Medical Assistance (TMA),** Heladeros 157 (© **084/260-101**). It offers 24-hour emergency medical services, health information, and legal assistance.

Drugstores For locations, consult a phone book Yellow Pages under "Farmacias" and "Boticas."

Emergency For general emergencies and the **police,** call © 105. For the **tourist police,** call © 084/221-961. To report a **fire,** call © 103. In a medical emergency, go to **Hospital EsSalud,** Av. Anselmo Alvarez s/n (© 084/223-030), or contact **Tourist Medical Assistance** (© 084/260-101).

Hospitals English-speaking medical personnel is available at the following hospitals and clinics: **Hospital EsSalud,** Av. Anselmo Alvarez s/n (© 084/237-341); **Clínica Pardo,** Av. de la Cultura 710 (© 084/624-186); **Hospital Antonio Loren,** Plazoleta Belén s/n (© 084/226-511); **Hospital Regional,** Av. de la Cultura s/n (© 084/231-131); and **Clínica Paredes,** Lechugal 405 (© 084/225-265).

For **yellow-fever** vaccinations, try Hospital Antonio Loren on Tuesday or Hospital Regional on Saturday from 9am to 1pm.

Internet Access Internet *cabinas* are everywhere in the old section of Cusco. Rates are generally S/2.50 (70¢) per hour and S/1 (30¢) for 15 minutes. Most keep very late hours, opening by 9am and staying open until midnight or later. A few of the many cabinas around town include **Speed X,** Procuradores 50 and Tecsecocha 400; **@Internet,** Portal de Panes 123; and **Cyber-Planet,** Almagro 200. Several nightspots, including **Ukuku's** and **Mama Africa** (see "Cusco After Dark," later in this chapter) also have computers and Internet access, which is convenient if you got an e-mail address rather than a phone number from a cute guy or girl at the bar.

Language Schools For intensive Spanish courses, try **Escuela Amauta,** Suecia 480 (℃ **084/241-422;** www.amautaspanish.com), or **Academia Latinoamericana de Español,** Av. El Sol 580 (℃ **084/243-364**). Both schools are very popular with short- and long-term visitors to Cusco.

Laundry Two to try: **Easy Wash,** Ruinas 457 (℃ **084/238-124**), and **Totem Wash,** Saphi 726 (℃ **084/145-367**).

Maps The main tourist information office gives out free maps, and, for most visitors, these should be sufficient. (Cusco is easy to manage and a joy to wander around and even get lost in.) More detailed maps, and maps of the Inca Trail and other hiking trails in the Cusco region, are available at bookstores.

Police The **Policía Nacional de Turismo** (National Tourism Police) has an English-speaking staff that is specifically trained to handle needs of foreign visitors. The office is at Portal de Belén, Plaza de Armas (℃ **084/ 221-961**). You can also contact **Servicio de Protección al Turista** (Tourist Protection Bureau), Portal Carrizos 250, Plaza de Armas (℃ **084/252-974**); the staff is available daily from 8am to 8pm.

Post Office/Mail Cusco's main post office is located at Av. El Sol 802 (℃ **084/225-232**). It's open Monday through Friday from 8am to 1:30pm and 3 to 8pm, and Saturday from 8am to 1pm and 3 to 7pm.

A **DHL/Western Union** office is located at Av. El Sol 627-A (℃ **084/244- 167**). It's open Monday through Friday from 8:30am to 1pm and 3 to 7pm.

Restrooms You'll find public restrooms in the airport and at bus termi- nals, bars, restaurants, museums, and hotels. As many bars and restaurants as there are in Cusco, finding a bathroom shouldn't be a problem.

Safety Over the years, Cusco has earned a reputation for being rather unsafe for foreign visitors, especially at night, when violent muggings have been known to occur on empty streets. Most alarming are so-called "strangle muggings," in which thieves attack unsuspecting victims (usually on deserted streets), applying pressure to the neck and leaving the victim momentarily unconscious—giving themselves time enough to relieve the victims of their belongings. Though Cusco may appear laid-back and good-natured, it's a good idea to be at your most vigilant, especially in the neighborhoods of San Blas, in the side streets leading off the Plaza de Armas, near the Central Market, and at bus and train hubs. Try to always travel in groups (never walk alone late at night), and call a taxi to trans- fer you to your hotel from restaurants and bus and rail stations.

Taxis See "Getting Around," earlier in this chapter.

Telephone Cusco's area code is 084. The principal **Telefónica del Perú** office, for long-distance and international calls, is on Av. El Sol 382-6 (℃ **084/241-114**). It's open Monday through Saturday from 8am to 10pm.

Tour Operators & Travel Agencies Cusco is swimming in travel agencies— several hundred of all sizes, many apparently offering the exact same packages, compete for your attention. Only a few dozen have solid repu- tations, however, and many should be flat-out avoided. Do not contract any would-be travel agent on the street, and do not hand over money for a trip or package without visiting the outfit in its office. If you have any questions about an agency, particularly one not listed by name and recommended in this chapter, do not hesitate to inquire about its reputation in the Tourist Information Office.

For travel arrangements around Peru, as well as city tours and Sacred Valley, Machu Picchu, Inca Trail, and Amazon jungle trips, see the relevant sections below and in chapters 7 and 9.

3 Where to Stay

In recent years, lodgings of all shapes and sizes have really mushroomed in Cusco, now numbering in the hundreds. Most of the city's most desirable accommodations are very central—within walking distance of the Plaza de Armas. The San Blas neighborhood is also within walking distance, though many hotels and hostales in that district involve very steep climbs up the hillside. (The upside is that guests are rewarded with some of the finest views in the city.) Some visitors will wish to avoid hotels and inns too close to the Plaza de Armas; that zone's crowded bars and discos, many open until sunrise, tend to produce throngs of rambunctious and usually inebriated young people who stumble downstairs and howl at the moon or bellow at the people who just rejected them inside.

Advance reservations in high season in Cusco are essential, especially around the Inti Raymi and Fiestas Patrias festivals at the end of June and July, respectively. Outside high season, look for bargains, as hotel rates come down considerably. Hot water is an issue at many hotels, even those that swear they offer 24-hour hot showers. Many hotels and inns will arrange free airport transfers if you communicate your arrival information to them in advance.

Prices listed below are rack rates for travel in high season; unless otherwise noted, rates do not include taxes. During the low season (Nov–Apr), prices often drop precipitously, even at midrange inns and backpacker hostels—sometimes as much as 50%—as the glut of hotels fights for a much-reduced number of visitors.

Several of the hostales reviewed below are cozy, family-run places, but travelers looking for even greater contact with a Peruvian family might want to check out the very inexpensive inns belonging to the **Asociación de Casas Familiares** (Family Home Association), which operates a website (www.cusco.net/family house) with listings of guesthouses with one or more rooms available for short- or long-term stays.

NEAR THE PLAZA DE ARMAS
VERY EXPENSIVE

Hotel Libertador ✯✯✯   One of Cusco's top two hotels, the Libertador could just as easily be called the Conquistador. Directly across from the Inca Temple of the Sun and built on the foundations of the "Aclla Huyasi," where the Inca chieftain kept maidens, this elegant traditional hotel occupies a historic house once inhabited by none other than Francisco Pizarro. The handsome art- and antiques-filled hotel, just 4 blocks from the Plaza de Armas, is built around a dramatic colonial courtyard marked by perfect arches, terra-cotta tiles, and a Spanish-style fountain. The swank lobby has a massive pyramidal skylight and

> ### *Tips* No Sleeping In
>
> Most Cusco hotels have annoyingly early checkout times—often 9 or
> 9:30am—due to the deluge of early-morning flight arrivals to the city. At
> least in high season, hotels are very serious about your need to rise and
> shine, but you can always store your bags until later.

exposed Inca walls. Guest rooms are spacious and refined; furnishings have
rustic colonial touches, and the marble bathrooms are large and well equipped.
Many rooms have small terraces. But the Libertador perhaps most distinguishes
itself with extremely attentive and professional service. The fine but pricey
restaurant, Inti Raymi, is built around the edges of the courtyard and features a
nightly dance and music show.

San Agustín 400 (Plazoleta Santo Domingo 259), Cusco. © **084/231-961.** Fax 01/233-152. www.summit
hotels.com. 258 units. $205 deluxe double; $275–$325 suite. Rates include taxes. AE, DC, MC, V. **Amenities:**
Restaurant; coffee shop; fitness center; sauna; concierge; business center and executive services; salon;
24-hr. room service; laundry service; oxygen on request. *In room:* A/C, TV/VCR, minibar, hair dryer, safe; rooms
available with fax, PC, and dataport.

Hotel Monasterio 😊😊😊   Perhaps Peru's most extraordinary place to stay,
this beautiful hotel occupies the San Antonio Abad monastery, constructed in
1592 on the foundations of an Inca palace. An Orient-Express and Leading
Small Hotels of the World property, the Hotel Monasterio—converted into a
hotel only in 1995—exudes grace and luxury. While checking in, you relax in a
lovely hall while sipping coca-leaf tea. (Altitude-challenged guests can also
immediately hook up to an oxygen tank.) As much a museum as a hotel, it has
its own opulent gilded chapel and 18th-century Escuela Cusqueña art collection. Located on the Las Nazarenas square between the bohemian San Blas
district and the main square, the hotel makes fine use of two courtyards with
stone arches; one is set up for lunch, about as beautiful a setting as there is to be
found in Cusco. Rooms are impeccably decorated in both colonial and modern
styles; the accommodations off the first courtyard are more traditionally
designed and authentic feeling. For a special treat, consider one of the two-story
suites. The Tupay Restaurant is housed in the original vaulted refectory of the
monastery; early risers, many on their way to Machu Picchu, enjoy a terrific
breakfast buffet serenaded by Gregorian chants. There are travelers who prefer
the Libertador (see above) and have had reservations about the service at the
Monasterio, but, for me, the historic quarters and splendid grounds at the
Monasterio take the prize.

Calle Palacios 136 (Plazoleta Nazarenas), Cusco. © **084/241-777.** Fax 084/237-111. http://monasterio.orient-
express.com. 122 units. $205 deluxe double; $330–$410 suite. Rates include breakfast buffet. AE, DC, MC, V.
Amenities: 2 restaurants; cafe; bar; concierge; executive services and meeting rooms; 24-hr. room service;
laundry service; oxygen on request. *In room:* A/C, TV/VCR, minibar, hair dryer, safe.

EXPENSIVE

Hotel Don Carlos Cusco 😊   A modern high-rise hotel on Cusco's busiest
avenue, the Don Carlos, part of a Peruvian chain, appears to be more popular
with Peruvians than foreigners (which is a rarity in Cusco). Built around a
central courtyard, the hotel isn't exactly cutting edge or chic. Rooms are modern, with a purple-and-cream color scheme and rather ugly maroon-and-beige
bathrooms. Services are good and the facilities are fine, if not exciting.

Where to Stay in Central Cusco

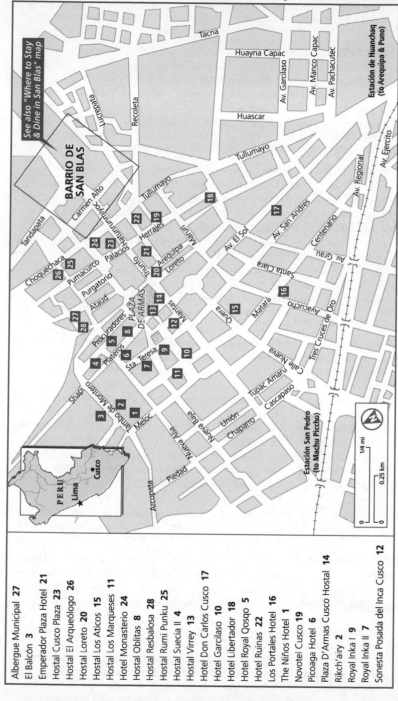

Albergue Municipal **27**
El Balcón **3**
Emperador Plaza Hotel **21**
Hostal Cusco Plaza **23**
Hostal El Arqueólogo **26**
Hostal Loreto **20**
Hostal Los Aticos **15**
Hostal Los Marqueses **11**
Hotel Monasterio **24**
Hostal Oblitas **8**
Hostal Resbalosa **28**
Hostal Rumi Punku **25**
Hostal Suecia II **4**
Hostal Virrey **13**
Hotel Don Carlos Cusco **17**
Hotel Garcilaso **10**
Hotel Libertador **18**
Hotel Royal Qosqo **5**
Hotel Ruinas **22**
Los Portales Hotel **16**
The Niños Hotel **1**
Novotel Cusco **19**
Picoaga Hotel **6**
Plaza D'Armas Cusco Hostal **14**
Rikch'airy **2**
Royal Inka I **9**
Royal Inka II **7**
Sonesta Posada del Inca Cusco **12**

175

Av. El Sol 602, Cusco. ☎ **084/226-207**, or 01/224-0263 for reservations. Fax 084/233-315. www.tci.net.
pe/doncarlos. 50 units. $110 double. Rate includes breakfast buffet. AE, DC, MC, V. **Amenities:** Restaurant;
bar; room service; laundry service. *In room:* TV, minibar, hair dryer, safe.

Hotel Ruinas ✵ It doesn't have a very auspicious name for a hotel, perhaps,
but Ruinas is a centrally located, clean, and modern hotel. However, it is overpriced given the somewhat plain, older-style rooms. Ask for a room with a view;
not many have one. What used to be a nice terrace with panoramic views is
being turned into a luxury suite.

Ruinas 472, Cusco. ☎ **084/260-644.** Fax 084/236-391. www.hotelruinas.com. 33 units. $125 double. Rate
includes taxes and breakfast buffet. AE, DC, MC, V. **Amenities:** Restaurant; bar; concierge; business facilities;
room service; babysitting; laundry service. *In room:* TV, minibar, hair dryer, safe.

Novotel Cusco ✵ Cusco's newest hotel, a member of the French Novotel
chain, is built around the guts of a 16th-century colonial building, but the
majority of rooms are in new sections. Opened in early 2001, the hotel is modern and dependable, with good services and amenities, though in most regards,
it's a notch below the city's two top-flight luxury hotels. Rooms are well
equipped and brightly colored, but are otherwise standard accommodations.
The hotel, a short distance from the Plaza de Armas, features a nice gardenside
restaurant serving French fare, and a warm bar with a fireplace.

Palacio San Agustín 239 (corner of Pasaje Santa Mónica), Cusco. ☎ **084/228-282.** Fax 084/228-855. www.
novotel.com. 99 units. $160 double. Rate includes taxes and breakfast. AE, DC, MC, V. **Amenities:** Restau-
rant/cafe; sauna; concierge; business facilities; salon; room service; babysitting; laundry service; safety deposit
box. *In room:* AC, TV, minibar, hair dryer.

Picoaga Hotel ✵ A very nice, more reasonably priced alternative to Cusco's
top two luxury hotels, Picoaga also occupies a historic building, in this case a
17th-century mansion that once belonged to a Spanish nobleman, the marquis
of Picoaga. Just minutes from the Plaza de Armas, the hotel is set around a lovely
arcaded courtyard—or at least one portion of it is. A newer wing is in a dated
and much less appealing modern section at the rear of the hotel. Ask for a room
in the front section overlooking the patio. Rooms there, about a third of
the total, are larger, have high ceilings, and are decorated with colonial-style
furniture and floral prints. Rooms are nice but certainly not over-the-top elegant. (Another tip: Request a room on the backside of the courtyard rather than
one facing the street, as traffic and street noise on Santa Teresa fires up promptly
at 5:39am.)

Santa Teresa 344, Cusco. ☎ **084/221-269.** Fax 084/227-691. www.picoagahotel.com. 70 units. $120 double;
$155 suites. Rates include breakfast buffet. AE, DC, MC, V. **Amenities:** 2 restaurants; fireplace bar; game
room; concierge; 24-hr. room service; laundry service. *In room:* A/C, TV, minibar, hair dryer, safe.

Royal Inka I & II ✵ These are sister hotels run by a very small chain of hotels
in Peru. Royal Inka I occupies a historic 19th-century house, built upon the
foundations of the Inca Pachacútec's palace, on a lively square just a block from
the Plaza de Armas. It's the smaller of the two hotels, but it has traditional
styling, a restaurant and popular bar, friendly service, and nice rooms. Some
accommodations have peaked and wood-beam ceilings that are a nice change
from the standard hotel room.

The nearby Royal Inka II is also in a 19th-century building, but it is the more
upscale and larger of the pair, with modern rooms around a nicely decorated,
plant-filled atrium with a huge mural. It also has a Jacuzzi and sauna. A restaurant and bar are in the atrium (there's also a restaurant/piano bar on the top

floor)—so if you're looking for peace and quiet, this may not be it. Of the two, I'd opt for the cheaper Inka I; it's a better value. Both places are popular with package tours.

Royal Inka I: Plaza Regocijo 299. Ⓒ **084/263-276.** Fax 084/234-221. www.royalinkahotel.com. 29 units. $64–$78 double. Royal Inka II: Santa Teresa 335. Ⓒ **084/231-067.** Fax 084/234-221. 65 units. $89–$95 double. Rates at both hotels include taxes and breakfast. AE, DC, MC, V. **Amenities:** Restaurant; bar; Jacuzzi, sauna, and massage (Royal Inka II only); salon; 24-hr. room service; laundry service. *In room:* A/C, TV, minibar, hair dryer, safe.

MODERATE

Emperador Plaza Hotel   A small, well-located, and impeccably clean and understated (some might say unexciting) hotel, the Emperador Plaza has excellent service and is a reliable, quiet choice just a block from the main square. The good-size rooms have wall-to-wall carpeting and fluffy, flowered bedspreads. The rooms with balconies are best. The green-and-white tile bathrooms are surprisingly large. A rooftop terrace, which could be fixed up better, has nice views.

Santa Catalina Ancha 377, Cusco. Ⓒ **084/261-733.** Fax 084/236-391. emperador@terra.com.pe. 20 units. $53 double. Rate includes taxes and breakfast buffet. AE, DC, MC, V. **Amenities:** Cafeteria; coffee shop; room service; laundry service. *In room:* TV, minibar, hair dryer, safe.

Hostal Cusco Plaza *Finds*   Sharing the same great square with the top hotel in Cusco, the Monasterio, this small, simple affair features a great central courtyard (with tables for breakfast) and simple decor, including nice parquet floors. A few of the rooms have spectacular views; no. 304 is by far the best, with huge windows and an arched ceiling.

Plaza Nazarenas 181, Cusco. Ⓒ **084/246-161.** Fax 084/263-842. 33 units. $65 double. Rate includes taxes and breakfast. AE, DC, MC, V. **Amenities:** Room service; laundry service; safety deposit box. *In room:* TV.

Hostal El Arqueólogo *Kids*   It takes a little effort to uncover this hostal, named for the profession responsible for discovering so much of Peru's pre-Columbian past and owned by a Frenchman who's a longtime resident of Cusco. Located down a stone alleyway and tucked behind the unprepossessing facade of a late-19th-century house just 5 minutes from the Plaza de Armas, it certainly doesn't jump out at you, but once inside, you'll find a lovely sunny garden—with ample space for kids to play—and rooms that run along a corridor overlooking the patio. Rooms are simply furnished but comfortable, and all have private bathrooms with 24-hour hot water. More rooms are being added in the colonial courtyard of an attached house. The French restaurant, La Vie en Rose, is fairly upscale and surprisingly good for an inn of this size. Also on-site is a large, efficient travel agency.

Ladrillos 425, Cusco. Ⓒ **084/232-569.** Fax 084/235-126. www.hotelarqueologo.com. 17 units. $40 double. Rate includes taxes and breakfast buffet. MC, V. **Amenities:** Restaurant; laundry service; safety deposit box; fax and e-mail services; kitchen; travel agency. *In room:* No phone.

Hotel Garcilaso   Just a block from the Plaza de Armas, this simple but attractive hotel, occupying a terrific colonial house, is a decent midrange alternative. Rooms aren't fancy, and the furnishings are a little outmoded, but they're nice enough. The pretty courtyard with bright blue balconies is a great place to have a drink and hang out away from busy Cusco. There are actually two Garcilaso hotels side-by-side; the accommodations in no. 2 are slightly larger.

Garcilaso 233–285, Cusco. Ⓒ **084/233-031.** Fax 084/222-402. hotelgarcilaso@hotmail.com. 54 units. $49 double. Rate includes taxes and breakfast. AE, DC, MC, V. **Amenities:** Restaurant; bar; coffee shop; room service; laundry service; safety deposit box. *In room:* TV.

Los Portales Hotel   A simple, airy hotel with wall murals of Andean scenes (even in the rooms) and a colonial-style staircase, Los Portales is comfortable and accessible. Rooms are nice enough, standard in both size and plain decoration for a midrange hotel; hot water is available 24 hours a day. Its major detraction is its location—it's on a very busy block a few streets removed from the more enjoyable action around the Plaza de Armas.

Matará 322, Cusco. Ⓒ and fax **084/222-391**. 33 units. $44 double. Rate includes taxes and breakfast. AE, DC, MC, V. **Amenities:** Restaurant; bar; room service; laundry service; safety deposit box. *In room:* TV and hair dryer on request for a fee.

Plaza D'Armas Cusco Hostal   This small, four-story hostal is very popular for one reason: location, location, location. It hugs a corner overlooking the Plaza de Armas, the lively hub of Cusco. If you want to be right in the thick of things, this reasonably priced place is a decent option, though the rooms are small and none have a view of the plaza (a few have views looking south). Still, the rooms are clean and pleasantly decorated, and the hostal is worth a look if you're more concerned about convenience than space.

Portal Mantas y Comercio 114, Cusco. Ⓒ **084/222-351**. Fax 084/247-130. www.peruhotel.com.pe. 29 units. $64 double. Rate includes taxes and continental breakfast. AE, DC, MC, V. **Amenities:** Coffee shop; laundry service; safety deposit boxes. *In room:* TV.

Sonesta Posada del Inca Cusco 🎯 *Value*   Like the rest of the hotels belonging to this small and very well-run Peruvian group, the Posada del Inca is extremely cozy, cheery, and a very good value. Best of all, it's sandwiched between the Plaza de Armas and Plaza Regocijo—about as centrally located as one can be in Cusco, without the additional all-night noise of being right on the plaza. Rooms are good-size and comfortable, with the chain's familiar yellow-and-dark-green color scheme and plaid bedspreads, and the homey lounge has a fireplace. Several rooms have excellent views of the city. Deals are often available ($80 double), including one with the possibility of staying 1 night at this hotel in Cusco and another at the chain's lovely place in the Urubamba Valley (in Yucay) for a slightly discounted rate.

Portal Espinar 142, Cusco. Ⓒ **084/227-061**. Fax 084/248-484. www.sonesta.com. 53 units. $100 double. Rate includes taxes and breakfast buffet. AE, DC, MC, V. **Amenities:** Cafe/restaurant; concierge; business facilities; room service; babysitting; laundry service; safety deposit boxes. *In room:* TV, minibar, hair dryer.

INEXPENSIVE

Albergue Municipal *Value*   On the way to Sacsayhuamán ruins, with enviable views over the top of Cusco, this youth hostel has a nice location away from the fray and none of the nasty institutional feel you find at most hostels. It has extremely clean dorm rooms with bunk beds, great sitting areas, and a nice cafeteria.

Kiskapata 240, San Cristóbal, Cusco. Ⓒ **084/252-506**. Fax 084/226-701. albergue@municusco.gob.pe. 11 units (64 beds). $5 per person, dorm room; $7 per person, double with shared bath. No credit cards. **Amenities:** Cafeteria; laundry; TV room; luggage storage; safety deposit boxes. *In room:* No phone.

Hostal Los Marqueses *Finds*   This 2-star hostal, housed in a mansion built in 1590, is loaded with colonial character. It's perfect for people who want a step up from a budget inn but not manufactured flavor. Rooms are huge and simply furnished; some beds and other furnishings are in definite need of updating, while others are cool colonial pieces. Yet one look at the magnificent arcaded courtyard, the breakfast room that looks like a 17th-century parlor, or the grand suite (no. 7) with a sitting room, canopy bed, carved wooden doors, and a huge dose of yesteryear, and this hostal is sure to appeal to travelers in search of the romantic side of Cusco. Discounts are available for 3- or 4-night stays.

Garcilaso 256, Cusco. ℰ **084/232-512.** Fax 084/227-028. marqueseshotel@hotmail.com. 30 units. $35 double. Rate includes taxes, continental breakfast, and airport pickup. No credit cards. **Amenities:** Laundry service; safety deposit boxes. *In room:* No phone.

Hostal Resbalosa *(Finds)*   A longtime favorite of backpackers, this inn is named for the street rather than any innate quality. ("Resbalosa" means "slippery.") The good-size rooms have hardwood floors, large windows, and immaculate bathrooms with pretty dependable hot water showers. There's a large rooftop terrace, perfect for sunning and just hanging out, enjoying the 180° views. The steep, pedestrian-only cobblestone street means you'll have to haul your pack up, but it's good training for the Inca Trail.

Resbalosa 394, Cusco. ℰ **084/240-461.** 20 units. S/25 ($7) double, S/30 ($9) double with private bath. No credit cards. **Amenities:** Laundry facilities. *In room:* No phone.

Hostal Rumi Punku *(Kids)* *(Finds)*   A glance at the name or address of this idiosyncratic family-owned hostal will give you an indication of its strong connection to Cusco's Inca roots. The massive portal to the street is a fascinating, original Inca construction of perfectly cut stones, once part of a sacred Inca temple. (The door is one of only three belonging to private houses in Cusco, and elderly residents of the city used to do the sign of the cross upon passing it.) Inside is a charming, flower-filled colonial courtyard with a cute little chapel and gardens along a large Inca wall. The clean bedrooms are ample, have hardwood floors, and are equipped with Norwegian thermal blankets. Hot water is available 24 hours a day. Breakfast is presently served in a cozy arched room, but the pleasant owner has big expansion plans, and she hopes to move the dining room to a top floor; if the city allows her to do it, it should have excellent views of the rooftops. The hostal is on the way up to Sacsayhuamán, but only a short walk from the Plaza de Armas. Rumi Punku, by the way, means "door of stone" in Quechua.

Choquechaca 339, Cusco. ℰ **084/221-102.** Fax 084/242-741. www.rumipunku.com. 24 units. $20–$30 per person. Rates include taxes and continental breakfast buffet. No credit cards. **Amenities:** Restaurant; laundry service; safety deposit box.

The Niños Hotel *★★★* *(Kids)* *(Value)*   The Dutch owners of the charming "Children's Hotel" have a story to tell, and it's an inspirational one. During just 4 short years in Peru, Jolanda van den Berg and her partner Titus Bovenberg have mounted a small empire of goodwill: They adopted 12 Peruvian street children, constructed an extremely warm and inviting hotel in the old section of Cusco that puts all its profits towards their foundation to care for needy children, built a learning center and restaurant for 125 such kids, and are in the process of creating a second center with athletic facilities and additional medical attention for another 125 disadvantaged youth of Cusco. The good news for travelers is that, should you be lucky enough to get a room here (reservations generally must be made about 6 months in advance), you won't have to suffer for your financial contribution to such an important cause. The hotel, in a restored colonial house just 10 minutes from the Plaza de Armas, is one of the finest, cleanest, and most comfortable inexpensive inns in Peru. The large rooms—named for the couple's adopted children—are very nearly minimalist chic, with hardwood floors and quality beds, and they ring a lovely sunny courtyard, where breakfast is served. The hotel also has 14 terrific apartments for

longer stays, which are ideal for small families, in the first of the children's learning and day-care facilities. Hot water is available around the clock.

Meloq 442, Cusco. © **084/231-424.** www.targetfound.nl/ninos. 20 units. $30 doubles with private bath,
$24 doubles with shared bath. Rates include taxes and continental breakfast. No credit cards. **Amenities:**
Restaurant/cafe; laundry service; book exchange. *In room:* No phone.

SAN BLAS
EXPENSIVE

Incatambo Hacienda Hotel 🏇 *(Kids)*   It's a long 3km (2½-mile) hike up to this
16th-century former hacienda (and it's not really walkable unless you're training
for the marathon), but the amazingly fresh air and country views may be worth
the trek. If you don't have time to stay overnight in the Urubamba Valley outside of Cusco, this is the next best thing. Reputedly once the home of the
conquistador Francisco Pizarro, it sits on 60 hectares (24 acres) of pine and
eucalyptus forest, just beyond the ruins of Sacsayhuamán. Rooms are simple and
woodsy, not nearly as luxurious as the house and location might lead you to
believe, and probably in need of updating. They are built around a Spanish-style
patio with a fountain, looking very much like the country estate it once was.
Guided horseback excursions are available, and the hotel has taxi service down
to Cusco from 6am to 10pm.

Carretera Cusco-Sacsayhuamán Km 2 (Fundo Llullipata), Cusco. © **084/221-918.** Fax 084/222-045. www.
hotelesdoncarlos.com/incatambo.html. 23 units. $88 double; $150 suite. Rates include taxes and breakfast
buffet. AE, DC, MC, V. **Amenities:** Restaurant; bar; 24-hr. room service; laundry service. *In room:* A/C, TV,
minibar, hair dryer, safety deposit box.

(Kids Family-Friendly Hotels

Hostal El Arqueólogo (p. 177)   A quiet inn with a sunny garden where
the kids can play and parents can relax and read. There's a very good
French restaurant and a travel agency on the premises, so you won't
have to troop all over town if you don't want to.

Hostal Los Aticos (p. 182)   The very inexpensive apartments have separate bedrooms and living rooms with sofa beds, plus kitchenettes.
Perfect for a family of four on a budget.

Hostal Rumi Punku (p. 179)   A family-owned hostal with a pretty,
flower-filled colonial courtyard, gardens, and a historic Inca wall.
There's plenty of room for the kids to run about behind the massive
Inca portal.

Incatambo Hacienda Hotel (below)   A country hotel on the edge of
Cusco, on 60 hectares (24 acres) of forest near the ruins of Sacsayhuamán. For the kids, there are guided horseback excursions.

The Niños Hotel (p. 179)   The very definition of a family-friendly
hotel, this one was built to allow Cusco street kids become part of a
family. Profits go to care for another 125 needy children. The restored
colonial house is one of the most charming and best-maintained small
inns around. Reserve well in advance. Families should inquire about
excellent-value apartments, at another location, for longer stays.

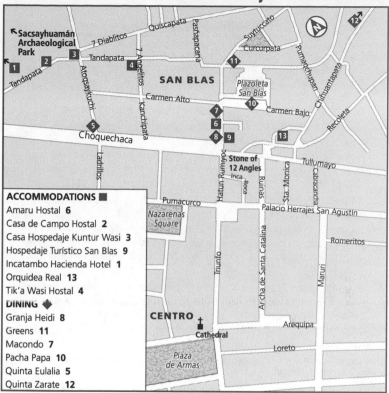

↖**Sacsayhuamán Archaeological Park**

Quiscapata

Pashapacana

7 Diablitos

Sinyturcato

Curcurpata

Tandapata

Tandapata

Atopsaykuchi

7 Angelitos

Kanchipata

SAN BLAS

Carmen Alto

Plazoleta San Blas

Pumachupan

Chihuantapata

Recoleta

Carmen Bajo

Choquechaca

Ladrillos

Hatun Rumiyoc

Inca

Roca

Stone of 12 Angles

Ruinas

Sta. Monica

Cabracancha

Tullumayo

Nazarenas Square

Pumacurco

Palacio Herrajes San Agustín

Romeritos

Triunfo

Ar.cha de Santa Catalina

Maruri

CENTRO

Cathedral †

Arequipa

Plaza de Armas

Loreto

ACCOMMODATIONS ■

Amaru Hostal **6**
Casa de Campo Hostal **2**
Casa Hospedaje Kuntur Wasi **3**
Hospedaje Turístico San Blas **9**
Incatambo Hacienda Hotel **1**
Orquidea Real **13**
Tik'a Wasi Hostal **4**

DINING ◆

Granja Heidi **8**
Greens **11**
Macondo **7**
Pacha Papa **10**
Quinta Eulalia **5**
Quinta Zarate **12**

MODERATE

Casa de Campo Hostal 🐒🐒 *Value*   Lodged in the hills of the traditional neighborhood San Blas, Casa de Campo means "country house," and the air up here, high above Cusco, has the freshness of country air. An organic complex, its chalet-style rooms appear to have sprouted one from the other. An exceptionally friendly and comfortable place, it's nonetheless not for everyone, especially not those who are tired of climbing the steps of Inca ruins. The climb up to the hotel is taxing enough, but once inside the gate, guests must use their remaining reserves to amble up several more flights of stone steps. Once there, though, you're rewarded with nice gardens and several terraces with unparalleled sweeping views of the city and surrounding mountains, as well as a cozy lounge with a large fireplace. Rooms are not overly large, but they have good firm beds and are rustically decorated, with exposed wood beams and thick wool blankets. (It's generally considerably cooler up here than just 15 min. down in Cusco.) One special room has a fireplace (for the same price as a regular room); another is like a cottage towering above the city. All rooms have 24-hour hot water. The staff will build a fire in the bar on request, and arrange a free city tour in Cusco. The owners also operate the Amauta Spanish-language school and Tertulia travel agency.

More Hotels & Hostales in Cusco

Despite the amazing number of accommodations strewn across the city, Cusco can get very crowded in high season; particularly if you're in town during the Inti Raymi festival (late June), July, and August, finding a place to rest your head can be headache inducing. Here are a few more recommended places to try (though a couple of them are often full):

Casa Hospedaje Kuntur Wasi   A tiny, family-run inn popular with Europeans, tucked up in the San Blas district. The small terrace has amazing views of Cusco. Rooms are plain, but they have pretty good beds, and there's laundry service. Tandapata 352, San Blas, Cusco. ℂ and fax **084/227-570.** S/30 ($9) double with shared bathroom, S/50 ($14) double with private bathroom.

El Balcón   A handsome early-17th-century colonial building with long balconies and excellent views of the city. The rooms are comfortable, and there's an inviting atmosphere throughout. Tambo de Montero 222, Cusco. ℂ **084/236-738;** fax 084/225-352. $50 double (breakfast included).

Hostal Loreto   Popular with many travelers for the original Inca stone walls featured in some rooms. The rooms can be very cold and dark, despite electric heaters. Still, it's just a few paces from Qoricancha, and all rooms have private baths with hot water. Loreto 115, Cusco. ℂ **084/ 226-352.** $40 double.

Hostal Los Aticos   A great option for families, these apartments have a separate bedroom and double bed, a living room with a sofa bed, a kitchenette, and a desk. There are also a handful of doubles. Excellent for long stays. Quera 253, Cusco. ℂ **084/231-710;** fax 084/231-388. $45 (up to four people); $30 double.

Hostal Oblitas   Just up the street from the Plaza de Armas, this small family-run hotel is homey and an excellent value. Breakfast is served in

Tandapata 296, San Blas, Cusco. ℂ **084/243-069.** Fax 084/244-404. www.hotelcasadecampo.com. 25 units. $35 double. Rate includes taxes, breakfast buffet, and airport pickup. AE, MC, V. **Amenities:** Restaurant; laundry service; safety deposit box; fax and e-mail services; kitchen; oxygen and heaters on request. *In room:* No phone in some rooms.

Orquídea Real 🖈 *Finds*   Hidden away along a narrow street wedged into the hill to San Blas, this tiny, unassuming inn has several surprises inside, beginning with some of the greatest views in Cusco and continuing to the rarity of a working fireplace in each room (a true benefit at this chilly elevation). The colonial building has original Inca walls and exposed wood beams, and the rustic accommodations are simply decorated in a cozy mountain lodge aesthetic. All rooms are oriented toward Cusco below, offering panoramic views; no. 20 is a suite with a little sitting room, available for the same price. There's hot water 24 hours a day. The company that owns the inn also offers a wide variety of all-inclusive package deals and tours in Cusco and across Peru (see its website).

Alabado 520, San Blas, Cusco. ℂ and fax **084/221-662,** or 01/444-3032 for reservations. www.orquidea. net. 11 units. $39–$44 double. Rates include taxes, continental breakfast, and airport pickup. AE, MC, V.

a dining room that will make you feel like you're staying at a Peruvian friend's house. Plateros 358A, Cusco. © and fax **084/223-871**. $33 double.

Hostal Suecia II   At the top of Procuradores, this friendly and consistently popular backpackers' inn is a notch above most others. It has comfortable rooms, an enclosed and covered courtyard, hot water, and nice beds. It's usually a great place to form Inca Trail groups. Tecsecocha 465, Cusco. © **084/239-757**. S/30 ($9) double with shared bathroom, S/50 ($14) double with private bathroom.

Hostal Virrey   If you're dying to be right on the Plaza de Armas, you can't do much better than this small inn. Two rooms have stunning views of classic Cusco. Portal Comercio 165, Cusco. © **084/221-771**; fax 084/235-349. $50 double.

Hotel Royal Qosqo   A popular little inn with a good vibe and a good location near the top of Procuradores. If you want to hang where the action is, this is one of your best low-rent bets. There's hot water from 6 to 10am only. Tecsecocha 2, Cusco. © and fax **084/226-221**. S/70 ($20) double with private bathroom, S/40 ($11) double with shared bathroom.

Rikch'airy   Nice basic rooms, laundry service, and a pretty garden with good views. This establishment has helpful English-speaking owners. Tambo de Montero 219, Cusco. © **084/236-606**. $12 per person.

Tik'a Wasi Hostal   A San Blas hostal with vehicular access—a rarity in this neighborhood—this attractive, newish inn has good services, a cafeteria, and comfortable carpeted rooms. TV lounge, 24-room service (another rarity among small hostales) and laundry services. Tandapata 491, San Blas, Cusco. © and fax **084/231-609**. $45 double.

Amenities: Cafeteria; laundry service; 24-hr. security guard. *In room:* TV, safety deposit box, working fireplace.

INEXPENSIVE

Amaru Hostal ℛ *(Finds*   A pretty colonial-Republican house in the midst of the San Blas artist studios and shops, this hostal has a lovely balconied patio, with a very nice garden area that tends to attract sunbathers and good views of Cusco. Rooms are very comfortable, attractively decorated, and a good value. Several have colonial-style furnishings and lots of natural light (ask to see several rooms if you can). Hot water is available around the clock. A very friendly and relaxed place.

Cuesta San Blas 541, San Blas, Cusco. © and fax **084/225-933**. www.cusco.net/amaru. 16 units. $25 double with private bath, $16 double with shared bath. Rates include taxes, continental breakfast, and airport pickup. No credit cards. Amenities: Coffee shop; laundry service; TV room; safety deposit box. *In room:* No phone.

Hospedaje Turístico San Blas ℛ   About halfway up the principal artery that wends its way up (and up) the artsy San Blas district is one of its most attractive inexpensive inns. Rooms are pretty spacious and warmly decorated. The airy colonial house has a glassed-in courtyard and a sun terrace with good views (and 24-hr. hot water). This inn is a nice step up from run-of-the-mill budget options in Cusco, and it's a good place to meet up with fellow travelers.

Cuesta San Blas 526, San Blas, Cusco. Ⓒ and fax **084/225-781.** www.cuscoperu.com/hostalsanblas. 20 units. $20 double with private bath, $14 double with shared bath. Rates include taxes, continental breakfast, and airport pickup. No credit cards. **Amenities:** Coffee shop; TV room; safety deposit box. *In room:* No phone.

4 Where to Dine

Visitors to Cusco have a huge array of restaurants and cafes at their disposal; eateries have sprouted up even faster than hostales and bars, and most are clustered around the main drags leading from Plaza de Armas. The large majority of them are economical, informal places favored by backpackers and adventure travelers—some offer midday three-course meals (*menús del día*) for as little as S/6 or S/7 (about $2)—though there are a number of upscale dining options as well, which tend to be excellent values. Calle Procuradores, which leads off the Plaza de Armas across from the Compañía de Jesús church, is sometimes referred to as "Gringo Alley," but it could just as easily be called "Restaurant Row" for the cheap eateries that line both sides of the narrow passageway. Many are pizzerias, and Cusco has become known for its wood-fired, crispy-crust pizzas.

Few restaurants in Cusco accept credit cards; many of those that do, especially the cheaper places, will levy a 10% surcharge to use plastic, so you're better off carrying cash (either soles or dollars). Top-flight restaurants often charge both a 10% service charge and 18% sales tax, neither of which is included in the prices listed below.

For restaurants in San Blas, see the "Where to Stay & Dine in San Blas" map on p. 181.

EXPENSIVE

El Truco ⊀ PERUVIAN   In a 17th-century *casona* that operated as a mint for the Spanish viceregency and later as a gambling house, combines good Peruvian cooking and *platos típicos* with a loud and lively peña show every night (8:30–10:30pm). The restaurant, virtually an institution now that it's been around for 40 years, has an attractive colonial interior and offers a daily lunch buffet of Peruvian specialties. At night, it's a la carte only. Dishes include pork tamales, roast pork, roast lamb, and stuffed rocoto peppers. The lively music-and-dance show, along with consistently good food, make El Truco very popular with upscale tour groups.

Plaza Regocijo 261. Ⓒ **084/232-441.** Reservations recommended. Main courses S/16–S/32 ($4.50–$9); daily lunch buffet $10. AE, DC, MC, V. Mon–Sat noon–11pm.

Inka Grill ⊀⊀⊀ PERUVIAN   A large and attractive modern two-level place right on the Plaza de Armas, popular with both young and old, the distinguished Inka Grill serves what might be called *nuevo andino* fare, and is one of Cusco's finest dining experiences. Start with a bowl of yummy *camote* (sweet potato) chips and green salsa. The best dishes are Peruvian standards such as sautéed alpaca tenderloin served over *quinua* (a grain) and *ají de gallina* (shredded chicken with nuts, cheese, and chili peppers), and desserts such as a coca-leaf crème brûlée. The extensive menu also includes a wide range of international dishes such as pizza, pasta, and risotto.

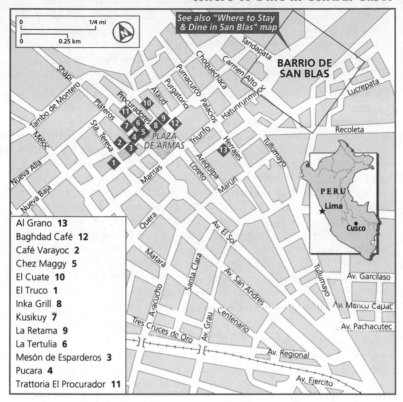

0   1/4 mi

0   0.25 km

See also "Where to Stay & Dine in San Blas" map

BARRIO DE SAN BLAS

PLAZA DE ARMAS

PERU

Lima

Cusco

Al Grano **13**
Baghdad Café **12**
Café Varayoc **2**
Chez Maggy **5**
El Cuate **10**
El Truco **1**
Inka Grill **8**
Kusikuy **7**
La Retama **9**
La Tertulia **6**
Mesón de Esparderos **3**
Pucara **4**
Trattoria El Procurador **11**

Portal de Panes 115. ☎ 084/262-992. Reservations recommended. Main courses S/18–S/45 ($5–$13). AE, DC, MC, V. Mon–Sat 11am–midnight.

La Retama 🎭🎭 *Kids* PERUVIAN/INTERNATIONAL Overlooking the Plaza de Armas from a huge second-floor space, La Retama is one of Cusco's most enduring favorites. The views and nightly folklore shows bring in the tour groups, of course, but the food is good enough to warrant a visit even by those who fear long tables with group leaders and interpreters. The menu focuses on classic Peruvian dishes, such as pink trout and king fish from Lake Titicaca, *seco de cordero* (lamb), *anticucho de lomo* (beef brochette), *cuy* (guinea pig), and trout ceviche. International dishes include chicken curry and trout Florentine. The restaurant's walls are lined with the art and handicrafts of Peru, and there's also a gift shop (see comment above about tour groups). The nightly folklore show begins at 8pm.

Portal de Panes 123, 2nd floor. ☎ 084/226-372. Reservations required. Main courses S/14–S/30 ($4–$8.50). AE, DC, MC, V. Mon–Sat noon–midnight.

Mesón de Espaderos PERUVIAN/INTERNATIONAL On one corner of the main square, the Mesón has excellent views from an attractive balcony overlooking the plaza (make a reservation or plan to dine quite early in the evening). The relaxed restaurant looks the part of a meat-eater's den, with stucco walls and dark-wood ceiling beams, and carnivores won't be disappointed. The menu is weighted toward excellent grilled meats and barbecue, including sausages, shish kebabs, chicken, pork, and, of course, guinea pig. But beef is king. A *parrillada* is a mixed grill. A standout among fish dishes is the grilled pink trout. There's also a good salad bar and a pretty decent wine list.

Espaderos 105, 2nd floor. © 084/235-307. Reservations recommended. Main courses S/18–S/35 ($5–$10). AE, DC, MC, V. Mon–Sat noon–11pm.

MODERATE

Greens ★★★ *Value* INTERNATIONAL In the heart of San Blas, on an atmospheric street just off the *plazoleta*, Greens is one of Cusco's most stylish and romantic restaurants. The intimate space has deep-green walls with modern art, an open kitchen, and a handful of candlelit tables mixed with hipster sofas near the fireplace for more informal dining. The soundtrack of laid-back dance beats, the creative and funky menu, and the reasonable prices appeal to a cool young crowd. The decor, presentation, and quality of the food are unusual in most parts of Peru; in fact, Tanya Miller, the restaurant's owner, previously worked in several London restaurants. On the menu, you'll find steak, chicken, and curries, all excellent. Try the beef tenderloin in red-wine-and-onion sauce, served with raisin rice, or the tropical chicken curry with bananas, peaches, and strawberries. On Sunday, the restaurant features a roast—by reservation only—that has become locally famous: chicken, potatoes, veggies, and homemade apple pie. Happy hour (2-for-1) is every evening from 6:30 to 7:30pm.

Tandapata 700, San Blas. © 084/243-820. Reservations recommended. Main courses S/10–S/24 ($3–$7). No credit cards. Daily noon–midnight.

Kusikuy ★ ANDEAN/INTERNATIONAL If you've resisted trying the Andean specialty that makes most foreigners recoil or at least raise an eyebrow, this could be the place to get adventurous. The restaurant's name in Quechua means "happy little guinea pig," so cuy *al horno* is, of course, the house dish. The rest of the menu focuses on other typical Peruvian dishes and adds stuff for gringos, such as pastas and basic chicken and meat dishes. It also serves a good-value lunch menú (which one day featured soup, chicken in red wine with rice, and pudding, plus juice). The good-looking restaurant on busy Plateros is warmly decorated with hardwood tables, black-and-white tile floors, and a mix of antiques and musical instruments from the Amazon.

Plateros 348. © 084/262-870. Reservations not accepted. Main courses S/12–S/38 ($3.50–$11). MC, V. Mon–Sat 8am–midnight.

Macondo LATIN AMERICAN/INTERNATIONAL This hip cafe/bar puts its claim to insider coolness on the door—the name is a reference to a banana plantation in García Márquez's *One Hundred Years of Solitude*. A recent addition to Cusco's dining scene, Macondo looks more like an artsy bar than a restaurant, and the soundtrack is generally trendy tropical rhythms. The cooking is nearly as funky and imaginative as the decor. Dishes are very well presented and served in generous portions; much of the menu echoes the laid-back tropical theme. *Juanes* are chicken, rice, and salsa wrapped in a Bijao leaf, and chicken kebabs are accompanied by peanut sauce, like a satay. You can also have alpaca mignon. Well-suited for the bohemian neighborhood of San Blas, this friendly cafe is also said by locals to be gay friendly.

Cuesta San Blas 571, San Blas. © 084/229-415. Reservations not accepted. Main courses S/15–S/30 ($4–$9). MC, V. Mon–Sat 8:30am–10pm; Sun 3–10pm.

Pucara PERUVIAN/INTERNATIONAL Just off the Plaza de Armas, this intimate, dimly lit restaurant has small wood tables, exposed wood beams, and

Cusco's *Quintas*

When the day warms up under a huge blue sky in Cusco, you'll want to be outside. Cusco doesn't have many sidewalk cafes, but it does have a trio of *quintas,* traditional open-air restaurants that are most popular with locals on weekends. These are places to get large portions of good-quality Peruvian cooking at pretty reasonable prices. Among the dishes they all offer are tamales, *cuy chactado* (fried guinea pig with potatoes), *chicharrón* (deep-fried pork, usually served with mint, onions, and corn), alpaca steak, *lechón* (suckling pig), and *costillas* (ribs). You can also get classics such as *rocoto relleno* (stuffed hot peppers) and *papa rellena* (potatoes stuffed with meat or vegetables). Vegetarian options include *sopa de quinua* (grain soup), fried yuca, and *torta de papa* (potato omelets). Quintas are open only for lunch (noon–5 or 6pm), and most people make a visit their main meal of the day. Main courses cost between S/15 and S/45 ($4–$13).

Pacha Papa (Plazoleta San Blas 120; © 084/241-318) is the newest quinta in Cusco, in a beautiful courtyard across from the small church in San Blas. In addition to Andean dishes, you'll find sandwiches. (The house specialty, cuy, must be ordered 1 day in advance). Alpaca steak is served in several varieties, including alpaca goulash and alpaca kebab (*anticucho de alpaca*).

Quinta Eulalia *Kids Finds* (Choquechaca 384; © 084/241-380) has been around since 1941, making it Cusco's oldest quinta. From a lovely colonial courtyard (only a 5-min. walk from the Plaza de Armas), there are views of the San Cristóbal district to the surrounding hills from the upper eating area. It's a great place on a sunny day, and the Andean specialties are reasonably priced.

Quinta Zárate *Finds* (Totora Paccha 763, at the end of Calle Tandapata; © 084/245-114), at the eastern end of town, has a lovely, spacious garden area with great views of the Cusco valley. Portions are very large, and the trout is a standout; try the ceviche de trucha (trout marinated in lime and spices). This quinta is pretty difficult to find; a taxi is recommended.

cloth lamps hanging low over the tables. As one of the first restaurants tourists stumble onto right off the main square, and as one of the better values in the historic center, it's generally packed. It has a few odd touches: On the walls are framed picture cutouts of the dishes, and the wait staff is a group of local women in yellow jackets and hairnet caps. But don't let that turn you off; it has a nice selection of traditional Peruvian and international dishes, including a tasty lomo saltado, several different soups, and a variety of white fish preparations.

Corner of Plaza de Armas and Plateros. © **084/222-027.** Reservations not accepted. Main courses S/12–S/28 ($3–$8). No credit cards. Mon–Sat 12:30–10pm.

INEXPENSIVE

Al Grano ASIAN   A quiet corner cafe, with lots of natural light and decorated with Andean textiles and featuring exposed Inca stonework, this little place

Kids Family-Friendly Restaurants

Finding a good restaurant for your family in Cusco shouldn't be too difficult; after all, backpackers on the cheap tend to eat a lot like kids: lots of pizza, pasta, and Mexican food. Almost all Cusco's restaurants are very informal affairs, often with plenty of noise and goings-on.

Chez Maggy (p. 189)   Maggy is where you go for the best pizza in Cusco, and if that's not appealing, families can also gorge on inexpensive homemade pasta and even Mexican food. If the kids aren't up for a night out, Chez Maggy will deliver for free.

El Cuate (p. 189)   If the kids are in need of a Mexican (or Tex-Mex) fix, El Cuate's the place. Enchiladas, tacos, and burritos are available on several high-value menús. Kids will feel right at home on the long, shared bench tables.

Granja Heidi (p. 189)   A cute, relaxed place serving super breakfasts and set-menu lunches. Heidi uses only fresh ingredients and farm products. Vegetarian and nonvegetarian choices are available, as well as superb desserts.

La Retama (p. 185)   Classic Peruvian cooking and a time-tested tourist show of Andina music and dance will keep the kids well fed and entertained.

La Tertulia (p. 190)   A fantastic spot for light meals and big carb breakfasts, including French toast and 16 types of crepes. There's a good-value menú and salad bar, as well as pizzas and sandwiches. La Tertulia donates S/1 of each breakfast buffet to a Peruvian orphanage.

Quinta Eulalia (p. 187)   A relaxing, traditional outdoor quinta, where Cusqueños bring their own families. There's a pretty colonial courtyard and great views of the hills from the upper eating area. A good place to try classic Peruvian dishes.

doesn't specialize in standard criollo fare, as you might expect. On the menu are items from Indonesia, India, Pakistan, and Sri Lanka, including chutneys, vegetarian curries, and lamb in spices and yogurt. Most dishes are pretty mild. There's a very cheap daily menú, served until 3pm, as well as daily specials. Al Grano also has a range of great baked goods for dessert (try the brownie or spice cake) and good coffee and tea. Locals report that the restaurant, while still dependable, was more carefully looked after a couple of years back.

Santa Catalina Ancha 398 (at San Agustín). (℃ 084/228-332. Reservations not accepted. Main courses S/6–S/18 ($1.75–$5); menú del día S/7.50 ($2). No credit cards. Mon–Sat 10am–9pm.

Baghdad Café PERUVIAN/INTERNATIONAL   Named for the 1988 German cult movie, and popular with gringos who know the reference, this cozy joint stands out for its phenomenal Plaza de Armas balcony, with unparalleled views of the square, the Compañía de Jesús church, and the mountain backdrop around Cusco. You'll have to jockey for a coveted table on the balcony, but once you score one, you're likely to linger (sometimes as a result of lazy service). The cafe has a decent lunch menú of platos típicos (stuffed peppers, ají de gallina, and alpaca steak) and things that go down well with a beer, such as soups and salads, pizzas, pastas, and sandwiches. It's a good spot for breakfast, too, and you can watch the city come to life.

Portal de Carnes 216. ℰ **084/239-949**. Reservations not accepted. Main courses S/10–S/20 ($3–$6). MC, V. Daily 8am–10pm.

Café Varayoc SWISS/CAFE FARE   This small and soothing cafe with great, subdued lighting is the perfect place to relax away from Cusco's constant hub-bub. Warm and charming, with a wood-beam ceiling and walls lined with masks and paintings of masks, it features excellent cakes and pastries, as well as a nice list of more substantial items for breakfast or a light lunch, or when you're not up to the confines of a restaurant with live shows and such for dinner. On the menu are crepes, Swiss fondues (the house specialty), sandwiches, pastas, and more elaborate dishes such as baked trout in wine-and-cheese sauce. It's especially nice in late afternoon for a great coffee or cappuccino and a diet-busting pastry or pie (try the cheesecake!), and it's conveniently located just off the Plaza de Armas. You'll see fellow travelers and a few locals reading or writing postcards.

Espaderos 142. ℰ **084/232-404**. Reservations not accepted. Main courses S/10–S/45 ($3–$13). AE, DC, MC. Daily 6am–1am.

Chez Maggy *Kids* ITALIAN/PERUVIAN   This bustling little joint, which has been around for 25 years and spawned a couple of branches in other parts of Peru, has a bit of everything, from trout and alpaca to homemade pastas to Mexican food, but most people jam their way in for the freshly baked pizzas made in a traditional wood-burning brick oven. They're some of the best in Cusco (even though every other restaurant in Cusco seems to be a pizzeria). Chez Maggy is usually packed in the evenings, and there's often live Andina music when roaming street musicians pop in to entertain diners. The restaurant is a long corridor with shared bench tables full of gringos—a good way to meet other travelers, because you'll be jockeying for elbow space with them. A second location is at Procuradores 344, better known as Gringo Alley. If you want a pizza on the terrace of your hostal, Chez Maggy will deliver for free.

Plateros 348. ℰ **084/234-861**. Reservations not accepted. Main courses S/12–S/30 ($4–$9). MC, V. Daily 6–11pm.

El Cuate *Kids* MEXICAN   I'm usually wary about trying out Mexican restaurants while traveling in countries other than Mexico, because they almost always serve a crummy imitation of Tex-Mex under a cheesy sombrero on the wall. But this animated hole-in-the-wall on "Gringo Alley" dishes out good-value, pretty authentic Mexican food for scores of backpacker types. El Cuate was Cusco's first Mexican restaurant, and its success has spawned several imitators who've felt compelled to add Mexican dishes to their Peruvian and Italian menus. But if you're sure you want Mexican, this is still the place to come. It has a number of bargain menús offering six courses for S/25 or S/15 ($7 or $4), or 5 items for just S/10 ($3), offered at lunch and dinner, and dishes such as *enchiladas suizas* (cheese enchiladas), Mexican soup, tacos, and burritos. With long bench tables, often shared, it's a jovial place.

Procuradores 386. ℰ **084/227-003**. Reservations not accepted. Main courses S/10–S/25 ($3–$7). MC. Daily 11am–midnight.

Granja Heidi *Kids* *Finds* HEALTH FOOD/VEGETARIAN   A healthy recent addition to the Cusco dining scene is this cute upstairs place in San Blas serving great breakfasts and very good-value menú meals. With a high ceiling and the airy, sun-filled look of an art studio, it's perfect for the neighborhood. Run by a German woman who has a farm of the same name outside Cusco, the restaurant features fresh ingredients and products, such as yogurt, cheese, and quiches, that taste like they came straight from the farm. The daily menú (served until 9:30pm) offers vegetarian and nonvegetarian choices and might start with pumpkin soup, followed by lamb or a veggie stir-fry, fruit salad, and tea. Don't pass on dessert, or you'll miss excellent home-baked cakes, such as the cheese-cake or the irresistible Nelson Mandela chocolate cake.

Cuesta San Blas 525, San Blas. ✆ 084/233-759. Reservations not accepted. Main courses S/7–S/20 ($2–$6); menú del día S/7.50 ($2). No credit cards. Daily 8am–9:30pm.

La Tertulia *(Kids (Value* BREAKFAST/CAFE FARE A classic Cusco spot for breakfast or other light meals, this little restaurant, up a tight spiral staircase from a travel agency, is a gringo hangout par excellence. The name means "discussion," which is fitting because people gather here to read newspapers and foreign magazines, and to exchange books and advice on hiking the Inca Trail and other far-flung adventures across South America. Many come to fuel up as early as 6:30am before setting out on one of those trips, and the superb break-fast buffet does the trick. It's all-you-can-eat eggs, fruit salads yogurt, granola, amazing homemade whole-meal bread, French toast, tamales, fresh juices, and coffee—truly the breakfast of champions and an excellent value. The breakfast menu also features 16 types of crepes. There's a set-lunch deal and a nice salad bar, as well as pizzas, sandwiches, and fondues. If you feel bad about stuffing yourself at breakfast, you can feel good about the fact that La Tertulia donates S/1 of each buffet to a Peruvian orphanage. You can also take salsa dance classes, but I wouldn't recommend trying it after breakfast.

Procuradores 44, 2nd floor. ✆ 084/241-422. Reservations not accepted. Main courses S/8–S/19.50 ($2–$6); breakfast buffet S/11.50 ($3). MC. V. Daily 7am–3pm and 5–11pm.

Trattoria El Procurador INTERNATIONAL This odd little place on restaurant row—where menu hawkers work the gringo crowds—is truly inter-national. It looks like the interior of an Indonesian bamboo hut, and the menu lists Mexican, Italian, and Peruvian criollo dishes. There's a cheap menú deal: 5 items for S/12 soles (that's an average of 70¢ per item), including a pisco sour. The food is only average, but if you're looking for something quick and dirty, pop in for the *rocoto relleno* (very spicy stuffed pepper) and *sopa de quinua* (a traditional grain-based soup).

Procuradores 351, 2nd floor. ✆ 084/232-302. Reservations not accepted. Main courses S/10–S/28 ($3–$8). No credit cards. Daily noon–10pm.

5 What to See & Do

The stately **Plaza de Armas** ✸✸, lined by arcades and carved wooden balconies and framed by the Andes, is the focal point of Cusco. After Machu Picchu, it is one of the most familiar sights in Peru. You will cross it, relax on the benches in its center, and pass under the porticoes that line the square with shops, restau-rants, travel agencies, and bars innumerable times during your stay in Cusco. The plaza—which was twice its present size in Inca days—has two of Cusco's foremost churches and the remains of original Inca walls on the northwest side of the square, thought to be the foundation of the Inca Pachacútec's palace.

What to See & Do in Cusco

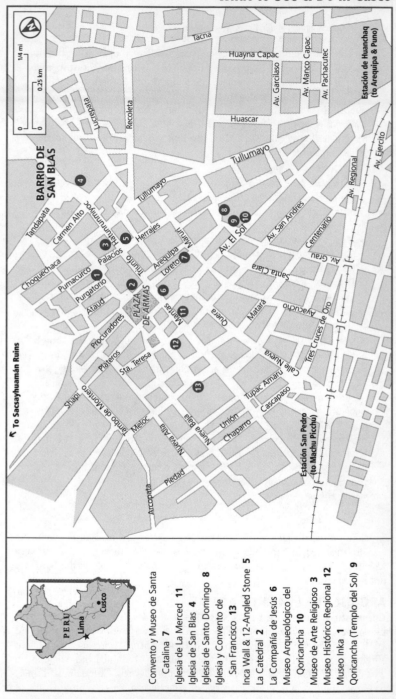

To Sacsayhuamán Ruins

BARRIO DE SAN BLAS

PLAZA DE ARMAS

Estación de Huanchaq
(to Arequipa & Puno)

Estación San Pedro
(to Machu Picchu)

Convento y Museo de Santa
  Catalina **7**
Iglesia de La Merced **11**
Iglesia de San Blas **4**
Iglesia de Santo Domingo **8**
Iglesia y Convento de
  San Francisco **13**
Inca Wall & 12-Angled Stone **5**
La Catedral **2**
La Compañía de Jesús **6**
Museo Arqueológico del
  Qoricancha **10**
Museo de Arte Religioso **3**
Museo Histórico Regional **12**
Museo Inka **1**
Qoricancha (Templo del Sol) **9**

PERU
Lima
Cusco

191

Value **Cusco's Boleto Turístico**

Cusco's municipal tourism office sells an excellent tourist ticket that is
your admission to 16 of the most important places of interest in and
around Cusco, including some of the major draws in the Sacred Valley
of the Incas. You cannot get into some churches and museums without it. The full ticket costs $10 for adults and $5 for students and
children, is valid for 10 days, and is available at the tourism office at
Mantas 117-A (② **084/263-176**). The boleto allows admission to the
following sights:

- **La Catedral** (p. 193)
- **Museo de Arte Religioso** (p. 196)
- **Iglesia de San Blas** (p. 195)
- **Municipal Palace Museum** (in the Palacio Municipal, Santa Teresa s/n
  ② 084/223-511)
- **Museo Arqueológico del Qoricancha** (p. 197)
- **Museo Histórico Regional** (p. 198)
- **Convento y Museo de Santa Catalina** (below)
- The **Inca ruins** of Sacsayhuamán, Q'enko, Puca Pucara, Tambo-
  machay, Pisac, Ollantaytambo, Chinchero, Pikillacta, and Tipón (see
  "Side Trips from Cusco," later in this chapter, and chapter 7, "Machu
  Picchu & the Sacred Valley of the Incas").

Not all of these sites are indispensable, and while you can buy a
partial ticket ($6) that allows entry to a handful of attractions, I don't
recommend it because chances are you'll want to see a combination of
all Cusco has to offer, even if you don't end up checking off absolutely
everything on your color-photo-coded boleto. Make sure that you
carry the ticket with you when you're planning to make visits, as
guards will demand to see it so that they can punch a hole alongside
the corresponding picture. Students must also carry their International
Student Identification Card (ISIC), as guards often demand to see that
ID to prove that they didn't fraudulently obtain a student boleto and
thus cheat the city out of 5 bucks.

Many principal sights within the historic quarter of Cusco and beyond the
city are included in the boleto turístico (see the box above), but a few very
worthwhile places of interest, such as the Qoricancha (Temple of the Sun), are
not included.

AROUND THE PLAZA DE ARMAS

Convento y Museo de Santa Catalina ☆☆   A small convent a couple of
blocks west of the Plaza de Armas, Santa Catalina was built between 1601 and
1610 on top of the Acllawasi, where the Inca emperor sequestered his chosen
Virgins of the Sun. The convent contains a museum of colonial and religious art.
The collection includes an excellent collection of Escuela Cusqueña paintings,
featuring some of the greatest works of Amerindian art—a combination of
indigenous and typically Spanish styles—in Cusco. The collection includes four
paintings of the Lord of the Earthquakes (El Señor de los Temblores) painted by

Amerindians. The interior of the monastery is quite beautiful, with painted arches and an interesting chapel with baroque frescoes of Inca vegetation. Other items of interest include very macabre statues of Jesus and an extraordinary trunk that, when opened, displays the life of Christ in 3-D figurines. (It was employed by the Catholic Church's "traveling salesmen," who were used to convert the natives in far-flung regions of Peru). The main altar of the convent church is tucked behind steel bars.

Santa Catalina Angosta s/n. ✆ 084/226-032. Admission included in boleto turístico. Daily 8am–6pm.

La Catedral   Built on the site of the palace of the Inca Viracocha, Cusco's cathedral is a beautiful religious and artistic monument, but until 2005, it will be undergoing massive restoration, and much of it is under wraps. The central nave looks like a construction site, entirely supported by wooden beams. Completed in 1669 in the Renaissance style, the cathedral possesses some 400 canvasses of the distinguished Escuela Cusqueña that were painted from the 16th to 18th centuries. There are also amazing woodcarvings, including the spectacular cedar choir stalls. The main altar—which weighs more than 401 kilograms (882 lb.) and is fashioned from silver mined in Potosí, Bolivia—features the patron saint of Cusco. To the right of the altar is a particularly Peruvian painting of the Last Supper, with the apostles drinking *chicha* (fermented maize beer) and eating cuy. The **Capilla del Triunfo** (the first Christian church in Cusco) is next door, to the right of the main church. It holds a painting by Alonso Cortés de Monroy of the devastating earthquake of 1650 and an altar adorned by the locally famous "El Negrito" (aka "El Señor de los Temblores," or Lord of the Earthquakes), a brown-skinned figure of Christ on the cross that was paraded

Ⓒ The Cusco School of Art

The colonial-era **Escuela Cusqueña**, or Cusco School of Art, that originated in the ancient Inca capital was a synthesis of traditional Spanish painting with local, mestizo elements—not surprising, perhaps, since its practitioners were themselves of mixed blood. Popular in the 17th and 18th centuries, the style spread from Cusco as far as Ecuador and Argentina. The most famous members of the school were Diego Quispe Tito, Juan Espinosa de los Monteros, and Antonio Sinchi Roca, even though the authors of a large majority of works associated with the school are anonymous. Most paintings were devotional in nature, with richly decorative surfaces. Artists incorporated recognizable Andean elements into their oil paintings, such as local flora and fauna, customs, and traditions—one depiction of the Last Supper has the apostles feasting on guinea pig and drinking chicha—and representations of Jesus looking downward, like the Indians who were forbidden to look Spaniards in the eye. Original Escuela Cusqueña works are found in La Catedral, the Convent of Santa Catalina, the Museum of Religious Art, and a handful of other churches in Cusco. Reproductions of original paintings, ranging from excellent in quality to laughable, are available across Cusco, particularly in the galleries and shops of the San Blas district.

The Magic of Inca Stones: A Walking Tour

Everywhere you walk, you'll see Cusco's dramatic **Inca walls** 𝒜𝒜𝒜, mammoth granite blocks so exquisitely carved that they fit together without mortar, like jigsaw puzzle pieces. The Spaniards razed many Inca constructions but built others upon the original foundations. (Even hell-bent on destruction, they recognized the value of good engineering.) Colonial architecture has, in many cases, not stood up nearly as well as the Incas' bold structures, which were designed to withstand the immensity of seismic shifts common in this part of Peru.

Apart from the main attractions detailed in this section, a brief walking tour will take you by some of the finest Inca constructions that remain in the city. East of the Plaza de Armas, **Calle Loreto** is one of the best-known Inca thoroughfares. The massive wall on the left-hand side, composed of meticulously cut rectangular stones, was once part of the Acllahuasi, or the "House of the Chosen Maidens," the Inca emperor's Virgins of the Sun. This is the oldest surviving Inca wall in Cusco, and one of the most distinguished. Northeast of the Plaza de Armas, off of Calle Palacio, is **Hatunrumiyoc**, a cobblestone street lined with impressive walls of polygonal stones. Past the Archbishop's Palace on the right side is the famed **12-angled stone** (now appropriated as the symbol of Cuzqueña beer), which is magnificently fitted into the wall. Originally, this wall belonged to the palace of the Inca Roca. While this large stone is impressively cut, the Incas almost routinely fitted many-cornered stones (with as many as 30, as seen at Machu Picchu, or even 44 angles) into structures. From Hatunrumiyoc, make your first right down another pedestrian alleyway, Inca Roca; about halfway down on the right side is a series of stones said to form the shape of a **puma,** including the head, large paws, and tail. It's not all that obvious, so if you see someone else studying the wall, ask him to point out the figure. Other streets with notable Inca foundations are Herrajes, Pasaje Arequipa, and Santa Catalina Angosta. Only a couple genuine Inca **portals** remain. One is at Choquechaca 339, and another is at Romeritos 402, near Qoricancha.

Not every impressive stone wall in Cusco is Inca in origin, however. Many are transitional period (post-Conquest) constructions, built by local masons in the service of Spanish bosses. Peter Frost's *Exploring Cusco* (available in local bookstores) has a good explanation of what to look for to distinguish an original from what amounts to a copy.

around the city by frightened residents during the 1650 earthquake (which, miracle or not, ceased shortly thereafter).

The entrance to the cathedral and ticket office, where you can purchase the boleto turístico, is actually at the entrance to the **Capilla de la Sagrada Familia,** to the left of the main door and steps.

Plaza de Armas (north side). No phone. Admission included in boleto turístico. Mon–Sat 10–11:30am and 2–5:30pm; Sun 2–5pm.

La Compañía de Jesús 🏛 Cater-cornered to the cathedral is this Jesuit church, which rivals the former in grandeur and prominence on the square (an intentional move by the Jesuits, and one that had Church diplomats running back and forth to the Vatican). Begun in the late 16th century, it was almost entirely demolished by the quake of 1650, rebuilt, and finally finished 18 years later. Like the cathedral, it was also built on the site of an important palace, that of the Inca Huayna Cápac (said to be the most beautiful of all the Inca rulers' palaces). Inside, it's rather gloomy, but the gilded altar is stunning, especially when illuminated. The church possesses several important works of art, including a picture of Saint Ignatius de Loyola, by the local painter Marcos Zapata, and the Cristo de Burgos crucifixion by the main altar. Also of note are the paintings to either side of the entrance, which depict the marriages of Saint Ignatius's nephews; one is the very symbol of Peru's mestizo character, as the granddaughter of Manco Inca weds the man who captured the last Inca, Tupac Amaru, the leader of an Indian uprising.

Plaza de Armas (east side). No phone. Free admission. Variable opening hours for visits; Mass schedule Mon–Sat 7am, noon, and 6pm; Sun 7:30, 11:30am, 6, and 7pm. Enter whenever open between Masses.

Museo Inka 🏛 *Kids* Housed in the impressive Admirals Palace, this museum contains artifacts designed to trace Peruvian history from pre-Inca civilizations and Inca culture, including the impact of the Conquest and colonial times on the native cultures. On view are ceramics, textiles, jewelry, mummies, architectural models, and an interesting collection—reputed to be the world's largest—of Inca drinking vessels (*qeros*) carved out of wood, many meticulously painted. The museum is a good introduction to Inca culture, and there are explanations in English. The palace itself is one of Cusco's finest colonial mansions, with a superbly ornate portal indicating the importance of its owner; the house was built on top of yet another Inca palace at the beginning of the 17th century. In the courtyard is a studio of women weaving traditional textiles. Allow 1½ to 2 hours to see the entire collection.

Cuesta del Almirante 103 (corner of Ataúd and Tucumán). ☎ 084/237-380. Admission S/5 ($1.50) adults, S/2 (50¢) students. Mon–Fri 8am–5pm; Sat 9am–4pm.

SOUTH & EAST OF THE PLAZA DE ARMAS

Barrio de San Blas 🏛🏛 Cusco's most atmospheric and picturesque neighborhood, San Blas, a short but increasingly steep walk from the Plaza de Armas, is lined with artists' studios and artisans' workshops, as well as a good number of tourist haunts. It's a great area to wander around—many streets are pedestrian-only—though you should exercise caution with your belongings, especially at night. The neighborhood also affords some of the most spectacular panoramic vistas in the city. In the small plaza at the top and to the right of Cuesta San Blas is the little white **Iglesia de San Blas** 🏛🏛, said to be the oldest parish church in Cusco (admission is by boleto turístico). Though a simple adobe structure, it contains a marvelously carved, Churrigueresque cedar pulpit. Some have gone as far as proclaiming it the finest example of woodcarving in the world; carved from a single tree trunk, it is certainly great. The pulpit comes with an odd story, and it's difficult to determine whether it's fact or folklore: It is said that the carpenter who created it was rewarded by having his skull placed within his masterwork (at the top, beneath the feet of St. Paul) upon his death. Also worth a look is the baroque gold-leaf main altar.

Museo de Arte Religioso (Palacio Arzobispal) On the corner of one of Cusco's most extraordinary streets, Hatunrumliyoc, a pedestrian alleyway lined with magnificent Inca stonemasonry (see "The Magic of Inca Stones: A Walking Tour" box on p. 194), the Museum of Religious Art is housed in a handsome colonial palace that previously belonged to the Archbishop of Cusco (and before that, it was the site of the palace of Inca Roca and then the home of a Spanish marquis). Inside is a nice collection of colonial religious paintings, notable for the historical detail they convey, but the extravagant old house—with its impressive portal and Moorish-style doors, balcony, carved-cedar ceilings, stunning stained-glass windows, and small chapel—is pretty nearly the main draw. Plan to spend about 1 to 2 hours here.

Corner of Hatunrumiyoc and Palacio. ℭ 084/225-211. Admission included in boleto turístico. Mon–Sat 8–11:30am and 3–5:30pm.

Qoricancha–Templo del Sol & Santo Domingo 𝕽𝕽𝕽 Qoricancha and Santo Domingo together form perhaps the most vivid illustration in Cusco of Andean culture's collision with Western Europe. Like the Great Mosque in Córdoba, Spain—where Christians dared to build a massive church within the perfect Muslim shrine—the temple of one culture sits atop and encloses the other. The extraordinarily crafted Temple of the Sun was the most sumptuous temple in the Inca Empire and the apogee of the Incas' naturalistic belief system. Some 4,000 of the highest-ranking priests and their attendants were housed here. Dedicated to worship of the sun, it was apparently a glittering palace straight out of El Dorado legend: Qoricancha means "golden courtyard" in Quechua, and in addition to hundreds of gold panels lining its walls, there were life-size gold figures, solid-gold altars, and a huge golden sun disc. The sun disc reflected the sun and bathed the temple in light. During the summer solstice, the sun still shines directly into a niche where only the Inca chieftain was permitted to sit. Other temples and shrines existed for the worship of lesser natural gods: the moon, Venus, thunder, lightning, and rainbows. Qoricancha was the main astronomical observatory for the Incas.

After the Spaniards ransacked the temple and emptied it of gold (which they melted down, of course), the exquisite polished stone walls were employed as the foundations of the Convent of Santo Domingo, constructed in the 17th century. The baroque church pales next to the fine stonemasonry of the Incas—and that's to say nothing about the original glory of the Sun Temple. Today, all that remains is Inca stonework. Thankfully, a large section of the cloister has been removed, revealing four original chambers of the temple, all smoothly tapered examples of Inca trapezoidal architecture. Stand on the small platform in the first chamber and see the perfect symmetry of openings in the stone chambers. A series of Inca stones displayed reveals the fascinating concept of male and female blocks, and how they fit together. The 6m (20-ft.) curved wall beneath the west end of the church, visible from the street, remains undamaged by repeated earthquakes and is perhaps the greatest example of Inca stonework. The curvature and fit of the massive stones is astounding.

After the Spaniards had taken Cusco, Francisco Pizarro's brother Juan was given the eviscerated Temple of the Sun. He died soon after, though, at the battle at Sacsayhuamán, and he left the temple to the Dominicans, in whose hands it remains.

Plazoleta Santo Domingo. ℭ 084/222-071. Admission S/4 ($1) adults, S/2 (50¢) students. Mon–Sat 8am–5pm; Sun 2–4pm.

Fun Fact **Hang a Right at Donkey Lips**

Cusco is littered with difficult-to-pronounce, wildly spelled street names that date to Inca times. In the bohemian neighborhood of San Blas, though, they're particularly colorful. Here's a primer of atmospheric street names and their literal meanings:

Atoqsayk'uchi Where the fox got tired
Tandapata Place of taking turns
Asnoqchutun Donkey lips
Siete Diablitos Seven Little Devils
Siete Angelitos Seven Little Angels
Usphacalle Place of sterility/place of ashes
Saqracalle Where the demons dwell
Pumaphaqcha Puma's tail
Cajonpata Place shaped like a box
Rayanpata Place of myrtle flowers
One to seek out: **P'asñapakana** Where the young women are hidden
And finally, one to avoid: **P'aqlachapata** Place of bald men

SOUTHWEST OF THE PLAZA DE ARMAS

Iglesia de La Merced ✦ Erected in 1536 and rebuilt after the great earthquake in the 17th century, La Merced ranks just below the cathedral and the La Compañía church in importance. It has a beautiful facade and lovely cloisters with a mural depicting the life of the Merced Order's founder. The sacristy contains a small museum of religious art, including a fantastic solid-gold monstrance swathed in precious stones. In the vaults of the church are the remains of two famous conquistadors, Diego de Almagro and Gonzalo Pizarro.

Calle Mantas s/n. ☎ 084/231-831. Admission S/3 ($1) adults, S/2 (50¢) students. Mon–Sat 8:30am–noon and 2–5pm.

Iglesia y Convento de San Francisco This large and austere 17th-century convent church, recently restored, extends the length of the square of the same name. It is best known for its collection of colonial art works, including paintings by Marcos Zapata and Diego Quispe Tito, both of considerable local renown. A monumental canvas (12 by 9m/40 by 30 ft.) that details the genealogy of the Franciscan family (almost 700 individuals) is by Juan Espinoza de los Monteros. The Franciscans also decorated the convent with ceiling frescoes and a number of morbid displays of skulls and bones. The church is worth a visit mainly for those with extra time in Cusco.

Plaza de San Francisco s/n. ☎ 084/221-361. Admission S/3 ($1) adults, S/2 (50¢) students. Mon–Sat 9am–4pm.

Museo Arqueológico del Qoricancha In three small rooms, this underground museum, across the garden from the Temple of the Sun and Santo Domingo, presents a decent collection of ceramics, metalwork, and textile weavings of Inca and pre-Inca civilizations, as well as a host of other archaeological finds. The museum pales in comparison to Qoricancha and the Museo Inka, however. Allow about a half hour, tops.

Av. El Sol (across the esplanade from Qoricancha). Admission by boleto turístico. Mon–Sat 9:30am–6pm.

Cusco Festivals

Cusco explodes with joyous celebration of both its Amerindian roots and Christian influences during festivals, which are crowded but splendid times to be in the city if you can find accommodations. It's worth planning your trip around one of the following fiestas, if possible.

Inti Raymi 🏵🏵🏵, the fiesta of the winter solstice (June 24 but lasting for days before and after), is certainly the star attraction. It's an eruption of Inca folk dances, exuberant costumes, and grand pageants and parades, including a massive one that takes over the stately Sacsayhuamán ruins overlooking the city. Inti Raymi is one of the finest expressions of local popular culture on the continent, a faithful re-enactment of the traditional Inca Festival of the Sun. Ultimately, there is the sacrifice of two llamas, one black and one white, by high priests to predict the fortunes of the coming year. Cusco's **Carnaval week,** with lots of music, dance, and processions of its own, is part of the buildup for Inti Raymi.

Semana Santa, or Easter week (late Mar/early Apr), is an exciting traditional expression of religious faith, with stately processions through the streets of Cusco, including a great procession led by El Señor de los Temblores (Lord of the Earthquakes) on Easter Monday. On Good Friday, booths selling traditional Easter dishes are set up on the streets.

In early May, the **Fiesta de las Cruces** (Festival of the Crosses), a celebration popular throughout the highlands, is marked by communities decorating large crosses that are then delivered to churches. Crucifix vigils are held on all hilltops that are crowned by crosses. Festivities, as always accompanied by lively dancing, give thanks for bountiful harvests. Early June's **Corpus Christi** festival 🏵 is another momentous occasion, with colorful religious parades featuring 15 effigies of saints through the city and events at the Plaza de Armas and the cathedral (where the effigies are displayed for a week).

On December 24, Cusco celebrates the **Santuranticuy Festival,** one of the largest arts-and-crafts fairs in Peru. Hundreds of artisans lay out blankets in the Plaza de Armas and sell carved Nativity figures and saints' images, in addition to ceramics and *retablos* (gradines). The tradition was begun by the Bethlehemite Order and Franciscan Friars.

A hugely popular Andean festival that attracts droves from Cusco and the entire region is the **Virgen del Carmen,** celebrated principally in Paucartambo (see "Side Trips from Cusco," later in this chapter) and with only a slightly lesser degree of exuberance in Pisac and smaller highland villages.

Museo Histórico Regional   The colonial home of Garcilaso de la Vega, a prominent historian of the Incas and colonial Cusco, is the appropriate setting for this museum, which presents a survey of Peruvian history from pre-Inca civilizations to the Inca and colonial periods. If you don't plan on visiting the bigger and better museums in Lima, this will serve as a good enough historical and archaeological overview of cultures such as the Chavín, Chancay, Moche, and Nasca. In addition to ceramics, textiles, and mummies, there's Cusco School art and colonial-era furniture. The museum isn't well labeled, though, so for some visitors, the handsomely rebuilt colonial mansion built around a pretty courtyard may ultimately prove more interesting. Plan to spend a couple of hours here if you have a keen interest in Peruvian history.

Plaza Regocijo, at the corner of Garcilaso and Heladeros. © 084/223-245. Admission included in boleto turístico. Mon–Sat 8am–5:30pm.

INCA RUINS NEAR CUSCO ✯✯✯

The best way to see the following set of Inca ruins just outside Cusco is as part of a half-day tour. The hardy may want to approach it as an athletic archaeological expedition: If you've got 15km (9¼ miles) of walking and climbing at high altitude in you, it's a beautiful trek. Otherwise, you can walk to Sacsayhuamán and nearby Q'enko (the climb from the Plaza de Armas is strenuous and takes 30–45 min.) and take a colectivo or taxi to the other sites. Alternatively, you can take a Pisac/Urubamba minibus (leaving from the bus station at Calle Intiqhawarina, off Av. Tullumayo, or Huáscar 128) and tell the driver you want to get off at Tambomachay, the ruins farthest from Cusco, and work your way back on foot. Some even make the rounds by horseback. You can easily and cheaply contract a horse at Sacsayhuamán, but don't expect a chance to ride freely in the countryside—you'll walk rather slowly to all the sites alongside a guide.

Visitors with less time in Cusco or less interest in taxing themselves may wish to join a guided tour, probably the most popular and easiest way of seeing the sites. Virtually any of the scads of travel agencies and tour operators in the old center of Cusco offer them. Some well-rated traditional agencies with a variety of programs include **Gatur Tour,** Puluchapata 140 (© **084/223-496**); **Milla Turismo,** Av. Pardo 689 (© **084/231-710;** millaturismo+@amauta.rep.net.pe); **SAS Travel,** Portal de Panes 143, Plaza de Armas (© **084/237-292;** www.sastravelperu.com); and **Top Vacations,** Portal Confiturías 265, Plaza de Armas (© **084/263-278**).

Admission to the following sites is by boleto turístico, and they are all open daily from 7am to 6pm. Guides, official and unofficial, hover around the ruins; negotiate a price or decide upon a proper tip. There are a handful of other Inca ruins on the outskirts of Cusco, but the ones discussed below are the most interesting.

These sites are generally safe, but at certain times of day—usually dawn and dusk before and after tour groups' visits—several ruins are said to be favored by thieves. It's best to be alert and, if possible, go accompanied.

Fun Fact Sexy Ruins

The pronunciation of Sacsayhuamán, like many Quechua words, proves difficult for most foreigners to wrap their tongues around, so locals and tour guides have several jokes that point to its similarity to the words "sexy woman" in English. You haven't really experienced Cusco until you've heard the joke a dozen times, from old men, guides, and little kids.

Inca Ruins near Cusco

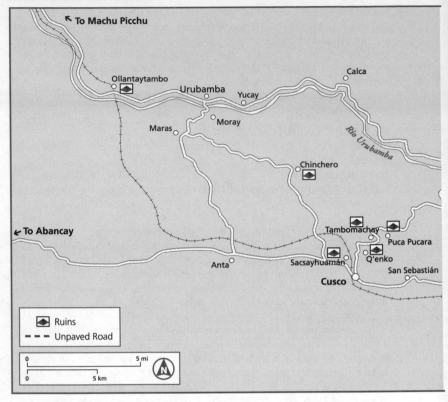

SACSAYHUAMAN ⭐⭐⭐

The greatest and nearest to Cusco of the ruins, Sacsayhuamán, a steep 30-minute (or longer) walk from the center, reveals some of the Incas' most extraordinary architecture and monumental stonework. Usually referred to as a garrison or fortress—because it was constructed with forbidding, castle-like walls—it was probably a religious temple, though most experts also believe it had military significance. The Inca emperor Pachacútec began the site's construction in the mid–15th century, though it took nearly 100 years and many thousands of men to complete it. Massive blocks of limestone and other types of stone were brought from as far as 32km (20 miles) away.

The ruins cover a huge area, but they constitute perhaps one-quarter of the original complex, which could easily house more than 10,000 men. Today, what survive are the astounding outer walls, constructed in a zigzag formation of three tiers. (In the puma-shaped layout of the Inca capital, Sacsayhuamán was said to form the animal's head, and the zigzag of the defense walls form the teeth.) Many of the base stones employed are almost unimaginably massive; some are 3.5m (12 ft.) tall, and one is said to weigh 300 tons. Like all Inca constructions, the stones fit together perfectly without aid of mortar. It's easy to see how hard it would have been to attack these ramparts with 22 distinct zigzags; the design would automatically expose the flanks of an opponent.

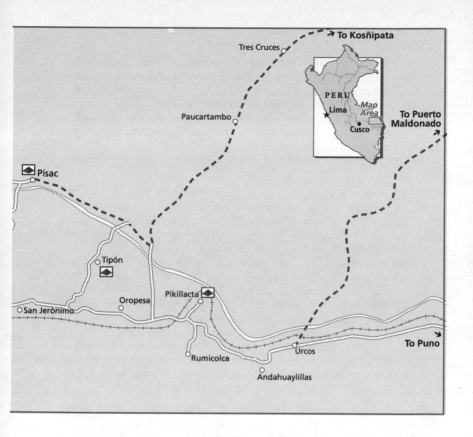

Above the walls are the circular foundations of three towers that once stood here; they were used for storage of provisions and water. The complex suffered such extensive destruction that little is known about the actual purposes Sacsay-huamán served. What is known is that it was the site of one of the bloodiest battles between the Spaniards and native Cusqueños. More than 2 years after the Spaniards had initially marched on Cusco and installed a puppet government, the anointed Inca (Manco Inca) led a seditious campaign that took back Sacsayhuamán and nearly defeated the Spaniards in a siege of the Inca capital. Juan Pizarro and his vastly outnumbered but superior armed forces stormed Sacsayhuamán in a horrific battle in 1536 that left thousands dead. Legend speaks of their remains as carrion for giant condors in the open fields here. After the defeat of the Inca troops, and the definitive Spanish occupation of Cusco, the Spaniards made off with the more manageably sized stone blocks from Sacsayhuamán to build houses and other structures in the city below.

The Inti Raymi festival is celebrated here annually, and it is truly a great spectacle—one of the finest in Peru (see the "Cusco Festivals" box on p. 198). A flat, grassy esplanade (where the main ceremony of the festival is celebrated) separates the defense walls from a small hill where you'll find the "Inca's Throne" and large rocks with well-worn grooves, used by children and oftentimes adults as slides. Nearby is a series of claustrophobia-inducing tunnels—pass through them if you dare.

(*Fun Fact* **Can't Leave Well Enough Alone**

The Peruvian authorities are notorious for messing with ancient Inca ruins, trying to rebuild them rather than let them be what they are: ruins. You'll notice at Sacsayhuamán and other Inca sites that unnecessary and misleading restoration has been undertaken. The grotesque result is that small gaps where original stones are missing have been filled in with obviously new and misplaced garden rocks—a disgrace to the perfection pursued and achieved by Inca stonemasons.

Night visits to the ruins are now permitted from 8 to 10pm. Under a full moon in the huge starlit Andean sky, Sacsayhuamán is so breathtaking that you'll instantly grasp the Incas' worship of the natural world, in which both the sun and moon were considered deities. If you go at night, take a flashlight and a few friends; security is a little lax, and assaults on foreigners have occurred.

Walking directions: There are a couple of paths up to the ruins from down-town Cusco. You can take Almirante, Suecia, or Plateros. Head northwest from the Plaza de Armas. Take Palacio (behind the cathedral) until you reach stairs and signs to the ruins; or at the end of Suecia, climb either Huaynapata or Resbalosa (the name means "slippery") until you come to a curve and the old Inca road. Past the San Cristóbal church at the top, beyond a plaza with fruit-juice stands, is the main entrance to the ruins. Plan to spend about an hour here for a brief run-through, up to 3 hours if you're really interested or a photogra-phy buff, or if you have kids who want to play on the slides and in the tunnels.

Q'ENKO ®

The road from Sacsayhuamán leads past fields, where, on weekends, Cusqueños play soccer and have cookouts, to the temple and amphitheater of Q'enko (*kehn*-koh), a distance of about a kilometer (half a mile). The ruins are due east of the giant white statue of Christ crowning the hill next to Sacsayhuamán; follow the main road, and you'll see signs for Q'enko, which appears on the right. A great limestone outcrop was hollowed out by the Incas and, in the void, they constructed a cave-like altar. (Some have claimed the smooth stone table inside was used for animal sacrifices.) Visitors can duck down into the caves and tunnels beneath the rock. You can also climb on the rock and see the many chan-nels cut into the rock, where it is thought that either chicha or, more salaciously, sacrificial blood coursed during ceremonies. Q'enko may very well have been a site of ritual ceremonies performed in fertility rites and solstice and equinox celebrations. Allow a half hour to tour the site, plus the time it takes you to get there.

PUCA PUCARA

A small fortress (the name means "red fort") just off the main Cusco–Pisac road, this may have been some sort of storage facility or lodge, or perhaps a guard post on the road from Cusco to the villages of the Sacred Valley. It is probably the least impressive of the sites, though it has nice views of the surrounding coun-tryside. From Q'enko, Puca Pucara is a 90-minute to 2-hour walk along the main road; allow a half hour for your visit.

TAMBOMACHAY

On the road to Pisac (and a short, signposted walk off the main road), this site is also known as *Los Baños del Inca* (Inca Baths). Located near a spring just a

short walk beyond Puca Pucara, the ruins consist of three tiers of stone platforms. Water still flows across a sophisticated system of aqueducts and canals in
the small complex of terraces and a pool, but these were not baths as we know
them—though ritualistic bathing may have taken place here—but most likely a
place of water ceremonies and worship. The exquisite stonework indicates that
the baños were used by high priests and nobility only. Plan on spending an hour
here.

6 Especially for Kids

Cusco is a blast to walk around, so entertaining the kids and finding suitable
restaurants and things to do shouldn't be a problem for most families. Kids old
enough to appreciate a bit of history may enjoy the well laid-out **Museo Inka,**
which will give them a good grounding in pre-Columbian civilizations and Inca
culture. Beside ceramics and textiles, it displays cool mummies and tiny hand-
painted Inca drinking vessels. You'll find Andean women weaving traditional
textiles in the courtyard.

Cusco resonates with remnants of the ancient capital; a walking tour with the
kids will take you past **Inca walls** with giant granite blocks that look like the
pieces of a giant jigsaw puzzle. Have the kids count the hand-cut angles in the
12-angled stone and find the outlines of the puma stone (see "The Magic of Inca
Stones: A Walking Tour" box on p. 194). Observing the walls will give you a
chance to impress your family with your knowledge of Andean history. Explain
that the Incas built these massive walls without mortar or cement of any kind
and with no knowledge of the wheel or horses, and that they constructed one of
the world's greatest empires, reaching from one end of South America to
another, without a written language and with runners who relayed messages to
rulers.

Another good activity for artistically inclined children is to pop into **artists'
studios** in the funky neighborhood of San Blas. Then walk—if you have the
energy—up to the ruins of **Sacsayhuamán.** There, you'll find more massive
stones and gorgeous views of the city and surrounding mountains, but kids will
really dig the huge rocks with slick grooves that make fantastic slides. There are
also some cool tunnels cut into stones nearby, which kids may enjoy much more
than their parents.

And, of course, the biggest family attraction of all lies beyond Cusco: Few are
the kids who aren't fascinated by the ruins of **Machu Picchu.** The easygoing
towns of the **Sacred Valley** are also great spots for families.

7 Shopping

Cusco is Peru's acknowledged center of handicraft production, especially hand-
woven textiles, and its premier shopping destination. Many Cusqueño artisans
still employ ancient weaving techniques, and they produce some of the finest
textiles in South America. Peru's top tourist draw overflows with shops stuffed
with colorful, enticing wares. From tiny one-person shops to large markets with
dozens of stalls, there are few better places to shop than Cusco for excellent-value
Andean handicrafts.

Items to look for (you certainly won't have to look too hard, as they're everywhere you turn) include alpaca-wool sweaters, shawls, gloves, hats, scarves, blankets, ponchos (in fact, there are so many cool and cheap cold-weather items here
that many people end up tossing the things they've brought for the chilly
nights), and antique blankets and textiles, beautiful but pricey; woodcarvings,

especially nicely carved picture frames; fine ceramics and jewelry; and Escuela Cusqueña reproduction paintings.

The barrio of **San Blas,** the streets right around the **Plaza de Armas** (particularly calles Plateros and Triunfo), and **Plaza Regocijo** are the best and most convenient haunts for shopping outings. Many merchants sell similar merchandise, so a bit of price comparison is always helpful. If sellers think you've just arrived in Peru and don't know the real value of items, your price is guaranteed to be higher. Although bargaining is acceptable and almost expected, merchants in the center of Cusco are confident of a steady stream of buyers, and, as a result, they are often less willing to negotiate than their counterparts in markets and more out-of-the-way places in Peru. Most visitors will find prices delightfully affordable, though, and haggling beyond what you know is a fair price, when the disparity of wealth is so great, is generally viewed as bad form.

ANTIQUES

Antigüedades y Artesanías Sayre at Triunfo 352-B (© **084/236-981**) and **Galería de Arte Cusqueño Antigüedades** at Plazoleta San Blas 114 (© **084/ 237-857**) have lots of different antiques, ranging from textiles to art and furniture. For a good selection of expensive antique Andean textiles, visit the small shop at Portal Comercio 173 on Plaza de Armas (© **084/233-484**); it appears to have no name, but the proud owner calls it **Tienda-Museo de Josefina Olivera.**

ART & HANDICRAFTS

For a general selection of *artesanía,* **Galería Latina,** Calle San Agustín 427 (© **084/246-588**), has a wide range of top-end antique blankets, rugs, alpaca-wool clothing, ceramics, jewelry, and handicrafts from the Amazon jungle in a large cozy shop near the Hotel Libertador. **Centro Artesanal Cusco** at end of Avenida El Sol, across from the large painted waterfall fountain and Hotel Savoy, is the largest indoor market of handicrafts stalls in Cusco, and many goods are slightly cheaper here than they are closer to the plaza. Other centers with stalls and similar goods are **Feria Artesanal Tesoros del Inca,** Plateros 334 (© **084/233-484**); **Centro Artesanal "Conde de Gabucha,"** Zetas 109 (© **084/248-250**); **Centro Artesanal El Inca,** San Andrés 218; **Centro Artesanal Sambleño,** Cuesta de San Blas 548; and **Feria Artesanal Yachay Wasi,** Triunfo 374.

San Blas is swimming with art galleries, artisan workshops, and ceramics shops. You'll stumble upon many small shops dealing in reproduction Escuela Cusqueña religious paintings and many workshops where you can watch artisans in action. Several of the best ceramics outlets are also here, and a small handicrafts market usually takes over the plaza on Saturday afternoon. Check out **Artesanías Mendivil,** known internationally for its singular saint figures with elongated necks but also with a nice selection of mirrors, carved wood frames, Cusco School reproductions, and other ceramics; it has locations at Plazoleta San Blas 619 (© **084/233-247**), Hatunrumíyoc 486 (© 084/233-234), and Plazoleta San Blas 634 (© 084/240-527). **Artesanías Olave,** the outlets of a high-quality crafts shop that does big business with tourists, are located at Triunfo 342 (© **084/252-935**), Plazoleta San Blas 100 (© 084/246-300), and Plazoleta San Blas 651 (© 084/231-835). **Juan Garboza taller** (workshop), Tandapata 676, Plazoleta San Blas (© **084/248-039**), specializes in pre-Inca-style ceramics. **Aqlla,** located at Cuesta de San Blas 565 and marked by a sign that says "Ethnic Peruvian Art" (© **084/249-018**), has great silver jewelry, folk and religious art, and fine alpaca items.

Several artists in the San Blas area open their studios as commercial ventures, though some of these can be fairly expensive for the opportunity to watch a painter paint. Look for flyers in cafes and restaurants in San Blas if you're interested.

Many, many shops in Cusco feature sheep's wool or alpaca *chompas,* or jackets, with Andean designs (often lifted directly from old blankets and weavings). **Artesanías Quipu Cancha,** Plateros 321 (*C* **084/223-369**), has by far the most stylish and best quality, but they're also the most expensive. These cool jackets, in alpaca and dozens of styles (they'll even custom-make one for you), are pretty much all they stock. For more upscale alpaca fashions, mostly sweaters and shawls, try the following stores: **Alpaca 3,** Calle Ruinas 472 (*C* **084/226-101**); **Alpaca Golden,** Portal de Panes 151 at Plaza de Armas and Zetas 109 at Plazoleta de Santo Domingo (no phone); **Alpaca 111,** Plaza Recocijo 202 (*C* **084/243-233**); or **Royal Alpaca,** Santa Teresa 387 (*C* **084/252-346**). **Werner & Ana,** a Dutch-Peruvian design couple, sell stylish clothing in fine natural fabrics such as alpaca. They have a shop on Plaza San Francisco 295-A at Garcilaso (*C* **084/231-076**).

CENTRAL MARKET

Cusco's famous, frenzied **Mercado Central** near the San Pedro rail station is shopping of a much different kind—almost more of a top visitor's attraction than a shopping destination. Its array of products for sale—mostly produce, food, and household items—is dazzling, and even if you don't come to shop, this rich tapestry of modern and yet highly traditional Cusco still shouldn't be missed. If you're an adventurous type who doesn't mind eating at street stalls (which are generally pretty clean), you can get a ridiculously cheap lunch for about $1. Don't take valuables (or even your camera) though, and be on guard, as the market is frequented by pickpockets targeting tourists. The market is open daily from 8am to 4pm or so.

JEWELRY

Ilaria deals in fine silver and unique Andean-style pieces and has two branches in Cusco (and several throughout Peru): one at Hotel Monasterio, Palacios 136 (*C* **084/221-192**), and another at Portal Carrizos 258 at the Plaza de Armas (*C* **084/246-253**). The contemporary jewelry designer **Carlos Chaquiras,** Triunfo 375 (*C* **084/227-470**), is an excellent craftsman; many of his pieces feature pre-Columbian designs. Another nice shop with silver items is **Platería El Tupo,** Portal de Harinas 181, Plaza de Armas (*C* **084/229-809**).

WOODWORK

Lots of shops have hand-carved woodwork and frames. However, the best spots for handmade baroque frames (perfect for your Cusco School reproduction or religious shrine) are **La Casa del Altar,** Mesa Redonda Lt. A near the Plaza de Armas (*C* **084/244-712**), which makes retablos and altars in addition to frames; and **Taller Cirilo León,** Córdoba del Tucumán 372 (no phone), where you can get frames made to order.

8 Cusco After Dark

Upon discovering an Andean city with such a pervasive, gentle Amerindian influence and colonial atmosphere, most first-time visitors to Cusco are surprised to find that it has such a rollicking nightlife. It's not as diverse as Lima's, but the scene, tightly contained around the Plaza de Armas, is predominantly young and rowdy, a perfect diversion from the rigors of trekking and immersion in Inca and colonial history. I have heard countless young backpackers from countries across the globe exclaim, in universal MTV lingo and with pisco sour in hand, "Cusco rocks!"

Perhaps the best part is that, even though the city is inundated with foreigners during many months of the year, bars and discos aren't just gringolandia outposts. Locals (as well as Peruvians from other cities, principally Lima, and other South Americans) usually make up a pretty healthy percentage of the clientele. Clubs are in such close range of each other—in the streets just off the Plaza de Armas and to a lesser extent in San Blas—that virtually everyone seems to adopt a pub-crawl attitude, bopping from one bar or disco to the next, often reconvening with friends in the plaza before picking up a free drink ticket and free admission card from one of the many girls on the square handing them out. It's rare that you'll have to pay a cover charge in Cusco.

For those who are saving their energy for the Inca Trail, there are less rowdy options, such as Andean music shows in restaurants, more sedate bars, and English-language movies virtually every night of the week. **Teatro Municipal,** Mesón de la Estrella 149 (© **084/221-847**), and **Centro Q'osqo,** Av. El Sol 684 (© **084/227-901**) occasionally schedule music concerts and dance performances. Check with the tourist information office for a schedule of events.

BARS & PUBS

In high season, bars are often filled to the rafters with gringos hoisting cheap drinks and trading information on the Inca Trail or their latest jungle or rafting adventure. Most bars are open from 11am or noon until 1 or 2am. Many have elongated or frequent happy hours offering half-price drinks, making it absurdly cheap to tie one on. (Travelers still adjusting to Cusco's altitude, though, should take it easy—alcohol can wipe you out if your body's not ready for it.)

One of the oldest pubs in town is **Cross Keys,** Portal Confiturías 233, Plaza de Armas, 2nd floor (no phone), owned by the English honorary consul and owner of Manu Expeditions. It's especially popular with Brits who can play darts or catch up on European soccer on satellite, and it's stuffed to the gills late at night. Pub grub is available if you can get an order in. **Los Perros,** Tecsecocha 436 (© **084/226-625**), is one of the coolest bars in Cusco, a funky lounge bar owned by an Australian-Peruvian couple. "The Dogs" has comfy sofas, good food and drinks (including hot wine), and a hip soundtrack, including live jazz on Sunday and Monday nights. The bar attracts a very international crowd, who take advantage of the book exchange and magazines.

Tips Raw Fish: A Cure for What Ails You

If you hang out so much and so late in Cusco that you wind up with a wicked hangover—which is even more of a problem at an altitude of 3,300m (11,000 ft.)—adopt the tried-and-true Andean method of reviving yourself. For once, the solution is not coca-leaf tea—it's ceviche that seems to do the trick. Something about raw fish marinated in lime and chili makes for a nice slap in the face. When I lived in Ecuador (a country that fights with Peru not only over boundaries, but for credit for having invented ceviche), late Sunday mornings at the cevichería were part of the weekly routine for pale-faced folks hiding behind sunglasses.

American-owned **Norton Rat's Tavern,** Loreto 115, next door to the La Compañía church (© **084/246-204**), is a rough-and-tumble bar, the type of biker-friendly place that you might find in any American Midwestern city. Nice balconies overlook the action below on the plaza. **Paddy Flaherty's,** Triunfo 124, Plaza de Armas (© **084/246-903**), is an Irish pub serving Guinness on draft. It's cozy, relaxed, and often crowded, with expats catching up on "football" (soccer, of course) and rugby. **Rosie O'Grady's,** Santa Catalina Ancha 360 near the Plaza de Armas (© **084/247-935**), is the other Irish tavern of note, considerably fancier digs in which to down your Guinness. There's live music Thursday through Saturday, and several happy hours throughout the day.

LIVE MUSIC

Live music is a nearly constant feature of the Cusco nightlife scene, and it's not all itinerant bands of altiplano musicians in colorful vests and sandals playing woodwind instruments. Not by a long shot. Live music tends to begin around 11pm in most clubs, and happy hours are generally from 8 to 9 or 10pm.

You can catch traditional Peruvian bands with a beat at Ukuku's and Rosie O'Grady's (see below), but for a traditional folklore music-and-dance show with panpipes and costumes—well, ponchos, alpaca hats, and sandals at a minimum—you'll need to check out one of the restaurants featuring nightly entertainment. In addition to **El Truco** (p. 184) and **La Retama** (p. 185), **Tunupa,** Portal Confiturías 233, 2nd floor (© **084/252-936**), has a pretty good traditional music-and-dance show, as well as a panoramic view of the Plaza de Armas.

By far the best place in Cusco for nightly live music is **Ukuku's,** Plateros 316, 2nd floor (© **084/227-867**). The range of acts extends from bar rock to Afro-Peruvian, and the crowd comes to get a groove on, jamming the dance floor. Often, the mix is half gringo, half Peruvian. If you're looking to pick up a Peruvian *chico* or *chica,* or at least practice your Spanish, it's one of the best spots in town. Ukuku's is open till the wee hours, and there's a room with computer terminals, 24-hour Internet access, and a pizza bar, as well as daily movies in the afternoon. Get your hands on a pass for free entrance so you don't get stuck paying a cover (though often it's not even necessary to have a pass; gringos often sail right in).

Kamikase, Plaza Regocijo 274, 2nd floor (© **084/233-865**), is the senior citizen of Cusqueño nightclubs, having been inaugurated before the tourist explosion, back in 1985. It's a cool and comfortable place, a two-level bar and a live music area with tables and funky decor. The music ranges from rock en español to reggae, and there are lots of locals—occasionally, Peruvians even outnumber gringos. (Imagine that!) There are nightly drink specials on things such as caipirinhas and mojitos. If you've imbibed one too many of those, you might want to take a breather before tackling the stairs to the street. I once had to carry a friend out, and it was a real challenge. The Irish pub **Rosie O'Grady's** (see "Bars & Pubs," above) also has live music—usually Peruvian, jazz, and blues—on weekends.

DANCE CLUBS

A pretty young crowd, both backpackers and young Peruvians, is lured to the discos by all the free drink cards handed out on the Plaza de Armas. **Mama Africa,** Espaderos 135, 2nd floor (© **084/241-979**), is like a multilevel all-inclusive nightclub; it's popular and often full and sweaty. There's occasional live music, and DJs spin a hot international dance mix of Latin, reggae, rock, and techno music for a mix of locals and fleece-clad gringos. There's also pizza and other good munchies, Internet facilities, and daytime movies. **Eko Club,**

Cafe Society

If you really just want to chill out and have a coffee, a glass of wine, or some dessert, drop into one of the city's comfortable cafes. The following are all good places for a light meal during the day, but at night they tend to take on some of that smoky Euro-cafe sheen, and travelers get all metaphysical about their treks through the Andes.

Café Ayllu, Portal de Carnes 208, Plaza de Armas (tel] 084/232-357) is a busy little place, drawing as many locals as gringos. It's known for its *ponche de leche* (a milky beverage, often served with a shot of pisco) and *lenguas* (a flaky pastry with *manjar blanco crème* in the middle). They also offer good breakfasts, sandwiches, and the mainstay, coffee. **Trotamundos,** Portal de Comercio 177, 2nd floor (© 084/232-387), has an excellent balcony on the main square, facing the cathedral. It also has an open fireplace, which is perfect for cold evenings. Here, you can enjoy good coffees and cakes, and a lively nighttime atmosphere. **La Tertulia,** Procuradores 44 (© 084/241-422), is more of a breakfast and lunch hangout, while **Café Varayoc,** Espaderos 142 (© 084/232-404), is a sophisticated place to read or get serious in the afternoon and at night. Varayoc serves excellent pastries and desserts, especially the cheesecake.

Away from the center, but well located if you're making the rounds of Manu travel operators, **Manu Café** is a chic rain-forest-style cafe, very swish for Cusco; it's attached to Manu Nature Tours at Av. Pardo 1046 (© 084/252-721). It serves excellent coffee (including imported roasts from around the world) and light meals, and there are racks of foreign newspapers for your perusal.

Plateros 334, 2nd floor (no phone), is the city's hottest dance club. The large dance floor throbs until dawn with a variety of rock, trance, and Euro-techno; for those who need a break, there's a laid-back lounge out back, good for a chair, a smoke, and a drink. **Up Town,** Suecia 302 (© 084/227-241), is Cusco's island resort disco on spring break. It offers free salsa, samba, and merengue dance classes (in English), and it's popular with locals. With two bars and a fleet of what seems like dozens of young girls enticing visitors with free drink cards, **Xcess,** Portal de Carnes 298 (© 084/240-901), swarms with one of Cusco's youngest and most frenetic crowds. Those who need to rest their hips can hang by the fireplace, catch a movie, or fortify themselves at the pizzeria.

CINEMA

There aren't many traditional cinemas in central Cusco, but there are a number of places showing movies, mostly to entertain international visitors in need of a break from trekking and sightseeing. Probably the best selection of films, ranging from classic to art house to children's flicks but mostly American, is found at **Peliclub Salón de Arte Cinema,** Tecsecocha 458 (© 084/246-442). Other screens showing movies, usually on a daily basis, are **Sunset Café** (above Hotel Royal Qosqo, on p. 183), Tecsecocha 2 (nightly videos); **Ukuku's,** Plateros 316 (daily at 5:30pm); and **Mama Africa,** Portal Belén 115, Plaza de Armas (daily at 4:30pm).

9 Side Trips from Cusco

Many visitors "do" Machu Picchu in a single day, taking a morning train out and a late-afternoon train back to Cusco. In my book, Machu Picchu is much too important and impressive a sight to relegate it to a day trip, but that's all many people have time for. The Sacred Valley villages and famed markets (especially Pisac and Chinchero) also constitute day trips for loads of travelers, but again, the area is so rich and offers so much for travelers with time to do more than whiz through it that the area—including Pisac, Urubamba, Ollantaytambo, Calca, Chinchero, and Moray—is treated separately in chapter 7, along with the great Inca ruins of Machu Picchu.

A Cusco-area **ruins hike,** either on foot or on horseback, of the Inca sites within walking distance of the capital—Sacsayhuamán, Q'enko, Puca Pucara, and Tambomachay—makes for a splendid daylong excursion (or half-day, if you make at least some use of public transportation or a taxi). For more information on the individual sites, see the "Inca Ruins near Cusco" section and map in "What to See & Do," earlier in this chapter.

Adventure travelers may wish to concentrate on other **outdoor sports,** including additional hikes, treks, mountain-biking excursions, and white-water rafting that can be done around Cusco. See the "Extreme Sacred Valley: Outdoor Adventure Sports" box in chapter 7.

PAUCARTAMBO
110km (69 miles) NE of Cusco

Most visitors who venture to very remote Paucartambo (and there aren't many of them) do so for the annual mid-July **Fiesta de la Virgen del Carmen** ⋆, one of Peru's most outrageously celebrated festivals (it lasts several days, and most attendees, be they villagers or foreigners, camp out because there is nowhere else to stay); see the "Cusco Festivals" box on p. 198 for more details. Yet the beautiful, small, and otherwise quiet mountain village might certainly be visited during the dry season (May–Oct), if you've the patience to venture way off the beaten track. A few travelers stop en route to Puerto Maldonado and the Manu Biosphere Reserve.

The peaceful colonial town, once a mining colony, has cobblestone streets and a lovely Plaza de Armas with white structures and blue balconies, but not a whole lot else—that is until it is inundated by revelers donning wildly elaborate and frequently frightening masks and drinking as if Paucartambo were the last surviving town on the planet. The colorful processions and traditional dances are spectacular, and a general sense of abandonment of inhibitions (senses?) reigns. *Mamacha Carmen,* as she's known locally, is the patron saint of the mestizo population.

Outside the festival, you might be able to get a simple bed at one of two small and very basic, inexpensive inns in town: the **Hostal Quinta Rosa Marina** and the **Albergue Municipal** (neither has a phone). During the festival, there's also a small office of tourist information on the south side of the plaza. More information on the celebrations is available from the main tourist office in Cusco (© 084/263-176).

Another 45km (28 miles) beyond Paucartambo is **Tres Cruces** (Three Crosses), sacred to the nature-worshipping Incas and still legendary for its mystical sunrises in the winter months. (May, June, and July are best.) Tres Cruces occupies a mountain ridge at the edge of the Andes, before the drop-off to the jungle. From a rocky outcropping at nearly 4,000m (13,200 ft.) above sea level, hardy travelers congratulate themselves (for having gotten there, as much as for the sight they've come to witness) as they gaze into the distance out over the dense, green Amazon cloud forest. The sunrise is full of intense colors and trippy optical effects (including multiple suns). Even for those lucky enough to have experienced the sunrise at another sacred Inca spot, Machu Picchu, it is truly a hypnotic sight.

GETTING THERE   Gallinas de Rocas minibuses leave daily for Paucartambo from Cusco's Avenida Huáscar, near Garcilaso (departure times vary; the journey takes 4–6 hr.). For the Virgen del Carmen festival (July 15–17), some small agencies organize 2- and 3-day visits, with transportation, food, and camping gear (or arrangements for use of a villager's bed or floor) included. Look for posters in the days preceding the festival. To get to Tres Cruces, see whether any Cusco travel agencies are arranging trips; otherwise, you'll either have to hire a taxi from Cusco or hitchhike from Paucartambo. (Ask around in town; some villagers will be able to hook you up with a ride.) Make sure you leave in the middle of the night to arrive in time for the sunrise.

TIPON
23km (14 miles) SE of Cusco

Rarely visited by tourists who are in more of a hurry to see the villages and Inca ruins of the Sacred Valley north of Cusco, the extensive complex of Tipón is nearly the equal of the more celebrated ruins found in Pisac, Ollantaytambo, and Chinchero. For fans of Inca stonemasonry and building technique, Tipón's well-preserved agricultural terracing is among the best created by the Incas and makes for a rewarding, if not easily accessible, visit. Peter Frost writes in *Exploring Cusco* (Nuevas Imágenes, 1999) that the terracing is so elaborately constructed that it may have been instrumental in testing complex crops, rather than used for routine farming. There are also baths, a temple complex, and irrigation canals and aqueducts that further reveal the engineering prowess of the Incas. The ruins are a healthy hour's climb (or more, depending on your physical conditioning) up a steep, beautiful path, or by car up a dirt road, and the uncluttered distant views are tremendous. The truly adventurous and fit can continue up above the first set of ruins to others perched even higher (probably another 2 hr. of climbing). During the rainy season (Nov–Mar), it's virtually impossible to visit Tipón.

GETTING THERE   Combis for "Urcos" leave from Avenida Huáscar in Cusco; request that the driver drop you off near Tipón, which is between the villages of Saylla and Oropesa. The site is 4km (2 miles) from the highway; it's open daily from 7am to 5:30pm. Admission is by the boleto turístico.

Tips **Jungle Adventure**

Cusco is the gateway to the southern Amazon region. If you're interested in a jungle expedition to Manu Biosphere Reserve and/or Tambopata Nature Reserve, don't miss chapter 9, "The Amazon Basin."

And Then There Were 12: The Inca Emperors

The Inca Empire, one of the greatest the Americas has ever known, had 12 rulers over its lifetime from the late 12th to the mid–16th century. The emperors, or chieftains, were called Incas; the legendary founder of the dynasty was Manco Cápac. The foundations of the palaces of the sixth and eighth leaders, Inca Roca and Viracocha Roca, respectively, are still visible in Cusco. Pachacútec was a huge military figure; the Inca responsible for creating a great, expansive empire. He was also an unparalleled urban planner; he made Cusco the capital of his kingdom, and, under his reign, the Incas built Qoricancha, the fortresses at Pisac and Ollantaytambo in the Sacred Valley, and mighty Machu Picchu. Huayna Cápac, who ruled in the early 16th century, was the last Inca to oversee a united empire. He divided the Inca territory, which by that time stretched north to Ecuador and south to Bolivia and Chile, between his sons, Huáscar and Atahualpa, which resulted in a disastrous civil war. Atahualpa eventually defeated his brother but was captured by Francisco Pizarro in Cajamarca and killed by the Spaniards in 1533, which led to the ultimate downfall of the Incas. The 12 Incas, in order:

1. Manco Cápac
2. Sinchi Roca
3. Lloque Yupanqui
4. Mayta Cápac
5. Cápac Yupanqui
6. Inca Roca
7. Yahuar Huácac
8. Viracocha Inca
9. Pachacútec
10. Tupac Inca
11. Huayna Cápac
12. Atahualpa

PIKILLACTA & RUMICOLCA
38km (24 miles) SE of Cusco

These pre-Inca and Inca ruins might go unnoticed by most were it not for their inclusion on the Cusco tourist ticket. Though the Cusco region is synonymous with the Incas, the Huari, and other cultures preceded them. **Pikillacta** is the only pre-Inca site of importance near Cusco. The Huari culture built the complex, a huge ceremonial center, between A.D. 700 and 900. The two-story adobe buildings, of rather rudimentary masonry, aren't in particularly good shape, though they are surrounded by a defensive wall. Many small turquoise idols, today exhibited in the Museo Inka in Cusco, were discovered at Pikillacta.

Less than a kilometer from Pikillacta, across the main road, is **Rumicolca,** an Inca portal—a gateway to the Valle Sagrado—constructed atop the foundations of an ancient aqueduct that dates to the Huari. The difference in construction techniques is readily apparent. The site was a travel checkpoint controlling entry to the Cusco Valley under the Incas.

GETTING THERE   Combis for "Urcos" leave from Avenida Huáscar in Cusco and drop passengers for Pikillacta near the entrance. Both sites are open daily from 7am to 5:30pm. Admission is by the boleto turístico.

7

Machu Picchu & the
Sacred Valley of the Incas

The Urubamba Valley, better known as *El Valle Sagrado de los Incas* or the Sacred Valley of the Incas, is an incomparably beautiful stretch of villages and ancient ruins spread across a broad plain and gentle mountain slopes northwest of Cusco. The magnificent ruins found from Pisac to Ollantaytambo and beyond—some of the finest not only in Peru but also in all of the Americas—are testaments to the region's ceremonial importance. The Incas built several of the empire's greatest estates, temples, and royal palaces between the sacred centers of Cusco and Machu Picchu, positioned like great bookends at the north and south ends of the valley.

Through the valley rolls the revered Río Urubamba (called the Willcamayu by the Incas; today, it is also called the Vilcanota in one section), a pivotal religious element of the Incas' cosmology. The Incas believed not only that the flow of the Urubamba was inexorably tied to the constellations and the mountain peaks, but also that the river was the earthbound counterpart of the Milky Way. With the river as its source, the fertile valley was a major center of agricultural production for the Incas, who grew native Andean crops such as white corn, coca, potatoes, and other fruits and vegetables in expansive fields and along spectacularly terraced mountain slopes.

Even though the villages of the Sacred Valley, stretching about 100km

(62 miles) from Pisac to Ollantaytambo, are highlights of most tourist itineraries, they remain starkly traditional. Quechua-speaking residents work the fields and harvest salt with methods unchanged since the days of the Incas, and market days—although now conducted to attract the tourist trade as well as intervillage commerce—remain important rituals.

Taken as a whole, the valley ranks as one of the standout attractions of Peru. Many visitors without a lot of time on their hands whip through the valley's highlights and markets on a daylong guided bus tour, sandwiching it between Cusco and Machu Picchu on the Inca itinerary. Seeing it blitzkrieg-style is certainly doable, but it can't compare to a leisurely pace that allows you an overnight stay or two in the valley and the chance to soak up the area's immense history, relaxed character, huge sky, stunning scenery, and, in the dry season, equally gorgeous spring-like weather. The valley is also about 300m (1,000 ft.) lower than Cusco, making it much more agreeable for those potentially afflicted with altitude-related health problems.

More and more visitors are now spending several days in the valley, even choosing to base themselves in Pisac, Urubamba, or Ollantaytambo rather than the regional capital, Cusco. Centrally located Urubamba has the greatest number of services geared toward visitors. The region now has some of the finest country-style hotels in Peru, especially geared

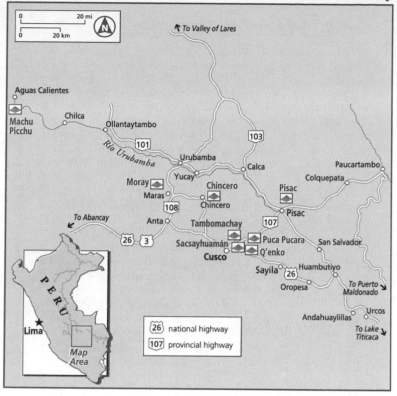

toward visitors who are looking for an easy pace or all the outdoor activities they can take advantage of (see the "Extreme Sacred Valley: Outdoor Adventure Sports" box, on p. 218). Several highlights of the Sacred Valley, such as the ruins of Pisac and Ollantaytambo, and the market town Chinchero, can be visited as part of the Cusco boleto turístico (see the "Cusco's Boleto Turístico" box, on p. 192, for complete details).

Beckoning at the end of the line, of course, is Machu Picchu. The greatest ruins in South America and a place

that retains its mystery, allure, and spectacular beauty despite its popularity, Machu Picchu is one of the most dramatic places on earth. The classic route to Machu Picchu is via the Inca Trail, a marvel of sensitive development and religious appreciation for nature. Hiking the trail requires 4 days (or 2 days along the shorter, less traditional path) of pretty tough trekking across mountain passes, but the experience is unforgettable. If you don't have time or interest in walking and camping, the train to Machu Picchu nearly rivals the trail for scenic beauty.

1 Pisac ★★

32km (20 miles) NE of Cusco

Pisac is a pretty, Andean village picturesquely situated at the eastern end of the valley. Though Pisac seems to be known principally for its Sunday artisans' market, a crowded but touristy but thoroughly enjoyable affair, it should be more

> *Tips* **Getting Around the Sacred Valley**
>
> Local buses (usually small combis or colectivos) are the easiest and cheapest way to get around the Sacred Valley. They are often full of local color if not much comfort. (Tall people forced to stand will not find them much fun.) Buses to towns and villages in the Sacred Valley—primarily to Pisac, Urubamba, and Chinchero—use terminals on Calle Huáscar and Calle Intiqhawarina, off Tullumayo, in Cusco. They leave regularly throughout the day, departing when full; no advance reservations are required. Fares range between S/1 and S/3 (25¢–$1).
>
> Nearly every Cusco travel agency offers a good-value, 1-day Sacred Valley Tour (as little as $15–$20 per person for a full-day guided tour), and most have English-speaking guides. The tours tend to coincide with market days (Tues, Thurs, and Sun) and generally include Pisac, Ollantaytambo, and Chinchero. An even better way to explore the Urubamba Valley, if you have the time, is to advance town by town toward Machu Picchu or vice versa, starting out from the great citadel and returning piecemeal toward Cusco. The first Sacred Valley visit on most itineraries is Pisac. *A caveat:* Though you will travel comfortably by chartered, air-conditioned bus and not have to worry about connections, you won't be able to manage your time at each place (indeed, you'll have precious little time in each place—only enough for a quick look around and visit to ruins or the local market).
>
> You can also hire a taxi for a daylong tour of the Sacred Valley—expect to pay about S/50 ($14)—or any of the valley towns.

widely recognized and visited for its splendid Inca ruins, which rival Machu Picchu. Perched high on a cliff is the largest fortress complex built by the Incas. The commanding distant views over a luxuriously long valley of green patchwork fields, from atop a mountain spur reached by a strenuous hike, are worthy of cliché: They are, quite literally, breathtaking.

ESSENTIALS
GETTING THERE
The bus trip from Cusco to Pisac takes 45 minutes to an hour. Colectivos drop passengers just across the river at the edge of town, a 3-block walk uphill from the main square (and market). From Pisac, buses return to Cusco and depart for other parts of the valley—Yucay, Urubamba (both a half-hour journey), and Ollantaytambo (1 hr.)—from the same spot.

While a taxi to Pisac on your own may cost S/35 ($10), it is often possible to go by private car for as little as S/3 (75¢) per person. Private cars congregate near the bus terminal and leave when they have three or four passengers; just get in and ask the price.

VISITOR INFORMATION
You're best off getting information on Pisac and the Sacred Valley prior to leaving Cusco at the helpful **Tourist Information Office,** Mantas 117-A, a block from the Plaza de Armas (© **084/263-176**). Cusco's **South American Explorers Club** (© **084/245-484**) is also an excellent source of information, particularly

on the Inca Trail and other treks, mountaineering, and white-water rafting in the valley. Inquire there about current conditions and updated transportation alternatives. Beyond that, the best sources of information are hotels.

Ideally, you should exchange much of the money you'll need in Cusco. If you don't feel safe doing that, your best bet is to exchange cash with small shops in Pisac. There's a post office on the corner of Comercio and Intihuatana.

WHAT TO SEE & DO
THE MARKET
Pisac's famed market draws many hundreds of shoppers on Sunday morning in high season, when it is without doubt one of the liveliest in Peru. (There are slightly less popular markets on Tues and Thurs as well.) Hundreds of stalls crowd the central square—marked by a small church, San Pedro el Apóstolo, and massive *pisonay* trees—and spill down side streets. Sellers come from many different villages, many of them remote populations high in the Andes, and wear the dress typical of their village. Dignitaries from the local villages usually lead processions after Mass (said in Quechua), dressed in their versions of Sunday finery.

The goods for sale at the market—sweaters, ponchos, and rugs—are mostly familiar to anyone who's spent a day in Cusco, but prices are occasionally lower on selected goods such as ceramics. While tourists shop for colorful weavings and other souvenirs, locals are busy buying and selling produce on small streets leading off the plaza. The market begins at around 9am and lasts until midafternoon. The market is so well-worn on the Cusco tourist circuit that choruses of, *"¿Foto? Propinita,"* (photograph for a tip) ring out among mothers or would-be mothers with tiny children in adorable local outfits. On nonmarket days, bustling Pisac becomes a very quiet, little-visited village with few activities to engage travelers.

THE PISAC RUINS 𝕣𝕣
The Pisac ruins are some of the finest, and largest, in the entire valley. Despite the excellent condition of many of the structures, little is conclusively known about the site's actual purpose. It appears to have been part city, part ceremonial center, and part military complex. It may have been a royal estate of the Inca emperor (Pachacútec). It was certainly a religious temple, and though reinforced with the ramparts of a massive citadel, the Incas never retreated here to defend their empire against the Spaniards (and Pisac was not, like Machu Picchu, unknown to Spanish forces).

The best but most time-consuming way to see the ruins is to climb the hillside, following an extraordinary path that is itself a slice of local life. Trudging along steep mountain paths is still the way most Quechua descendants from remote villages get around these parts; many people you see at the Pisac market will have walked a couple of hours or more through the mountains to get there. To get to the ruins on foot (about 5km/3 miles, or 90 min.), you'll need to be pretty fit and/or willing to take it very slowly. Begin the ascent at the back of

---

⌒Moments The Virgen del Carmen Festival
Pisac celebrates the Virgen del Carmen festival (July 16–18) with nearly as much enthusiasm as the more remote and more famous festival in Paucartambo (p. 209). It's well worth visiting Pisac during the festival if you are in the area.

Pisac's main square, to the left of the church. The path bends to the right through agricultural terraces. There appear to be several competing paths; all of them lead up the mountain to the ruins. When you come to a section that rises straight up, choose the extremely steep stairs to the right. (The path to the left is overgrown and poorly defined.) If an arduous trek is more than you've bargained for, you can hire a taxi in Pisac (easier done on market days) to take you around the back way. (The paved road is some 9.5km/6 miles long.) If you arrive by car or colectivo rather than by your own power, the ruins will be laid out the opposite of the way they are described below.

From a semicircular terrace and fortified section at the top, called the **Quorihuayrachina,** the views south and west, of the gorge and valley below and agricultural terraces creeping up the mountain slopes, are stunning. Deeper into the nucleus, the delicately cut stones are some of the best found at any Inca site. The most important component of the complex, on a plateau on the upper section of the ruins, is the **Templo del Sol** (Temple of the Sun), one of the Incas' most impressive examples of masonry. The temple was an astronomical observatory. The **Intihuatana,** the so-called "hitching post of the sun," resembles a sundial but in fact was an instrument that helped the Incas to determine the arrival of important growing seasons rather than to tell the time of day. Sadly, this section is now closed to the public, due to vandals who destroyed part of it a few years ago. Nearby (just paces to the west) is another temple, thought to be the **Templo de la Luna** (Temple of the Moon), and beyond that is a ritual bathing complex, fed by water canals. Continuing north from this section, you can either ascend a staircase path uphill, which forks, or pass along the eastern (right-hand) edge of the cliff. If you do the latter, you'll arrive at a tunnel, which leads to a summit lookout at 3,400m (11,200 ft.). A series of paths leads from here to defensive ramparts (**K'alla Q'asa**), a ruins sector called **Qanchisracay,** and the area where taxis wait to take passengers back to Pisac.

In the hillside across the Quitamayo gorge, at the backside (north end) of the ruins, are hundreds of dugout holes where *huaqueros* (grave robbers) have ransacked a cemetery that was among the largest known Inca burial sites.

The ruins are open daily from 7am to 5:30pm; admission is by Cusco's boleto turístico (p. 192). Note that to explore the ruins thoroughly by foot, including the climb from Pisac, you'll need at least 4 hours. Most people visit Pisac as part of a whirlwind day tour through the valley, which doesn't allow enough time either at the market or to visit the ruins. Taxis leave from the road near the bridge and charge around S/10 ($3) to take you up to the ruins.

WHERE TO STAY

If either of the two places below are full or beyond your budget, check out either of these inexpensive, basic inns in town: **Hospedaje Buho,** Intihuatana 642/Camino Ruinas (© **084/203-001**), on a side street near the main square, with rooms (even a few with private bathrooms) around a central patio and an artesanía shop; or **Kinsa Cocha Hospedaje,** Arequipa 307 (© **084/203-101**), a family-run place with clean dorm rooms near the main plaza.

Hostal Pisaq *Finds* Owned by a friendly Peruvian-American couple, this small, pleasant B&B is a good option in town. Warm and cozy, and located right on the main square in Pisac, it has murals hand-painted by the owners, a sauna, and an attractive courtyard with flowers. It also operates a small bar/restaurant with good pizza from a wood-burning oven and home-cooked meals. Rooms, full of Andean textiles, are nicely decorated for the price.

Plaza Constitución 333, Pisac. (✆) and fax **084/203-062**. hotelpisaq@terra.com.pe. 11 units. $20 double with shared bathroom, $26 with private bathroom. No credit cards. **Amenities:** Restaurant; bar; sauna. *In room:* No phone.

Hotel Royal Inka Pisac ⊛ The best place to stay in Pisac is about a 15-minute walk from the village along the road up to the Inca ruins. The hotel, which sprawls around a pretty mustard-colored hacienda, has a surprising array of facilities and activities, including a tennis court, indoor pool, Jacuzzi, sauna, massage, horseback riding, and mountain-bike rentals. Rooms are ample and comfortable; some have fireplaces. The hotel is ideal for those wishing to spend time at Pisac's ruins and as a base for exploring the Sacred Valley—as a slightly cheaper alternative to hotels in Urubamba/Yucay. It's popular with groups, though in off-season, it can get a little lonely.

Carretera Pisac Ruinas Km 1.5 s/n, Pisac. (✆) and fax **084/203-064**. www.royalinkahotel.com. 86 units. $78 double. Rate includes taxes and breakfast buffet. AE, DC, MC, V. **Amenities:** Restaurant; bar; indoor swimming pool; tennis court; sauna; bike rental; room service; massage; laundry service; horseback riding. *In room:* TV, minibar, safe.

WHERE TO DINE

For eats in Pisac, check out **Samana Wasi,** Plaza Constitución 509 (no phone), which serves good, inexpensive trout dishes straight from the river. The restaurant also has a couple of basic rooms for rent. There's also an excellent, traditional-style **bakery** on Mariscal Castilla 372 (no phone), a short walk from the plaza. It serves excellent vegetarian *empanadas* (stuffed pastries) and breads from adobe ovens—snacks that prove extremely popular on market days. **Restaurant Inti Wasi,** a restaurant about a mile beyond the city limits on the main road to Calca ((✆) **084/203-047**), serves good lunches, including fresh fish, to tourist groups on bus tours through the Sacred Valley. If you're not on an organized tour, it's still a good place for lunch, though it's a bit out of the way.

2 Urubamba ⊛ & Yucay

78km (48 miles) NW of Cusco

Centrally located Urubamba is the busiest of the Sacred Valley towns, if only because it's the best equipped to handle visitors. While the town itself doesn't have a whole lot more than a handsome main plaza and magnificent mountain scenery to offer, several of the best hotels in the region are located between it and Yucay, about 3km (2 miles) down the road. Together, the two towns form a fine base from which to explore the Sacred Valley region.

ESSENTIALS
GETTING THERE

To Urubamba, a 2-hour bus ride from Cusco, you can either go via Pisac or via Chinchero (a slightly more direct route). Buses arrive at **Terminal Terrestre** (no phone), the main bus terminal, about a kilometer (a half mile) from town on the main road to Ollantaytambo, just beyond and across from the Incaland Hotel. Buses from the Urubamba terminal depart for Cusco and Chinchero (1 hr. away), as well as Ollantaytambo (30 min. away). Combis for other points in the Sacred Valley depart from the intersection of the main road at Avenida Castilla. To continue on to Yucay, just a couple of kilometers down the road, catch a mototaxi or a regular taxi in Urubamba or a colectivo along the highway (headed east, the opposite direction of the bus terminal from town).

Extreme Sacred Valley: Outdoor Adventure Sports

Peru has become a star on South America's burgeoning adventure and extreme sports travel circuit, a far cry from the days when just traveling to Peru was adventure enough. These days, many gringos in Peru have Gore-Tex boots on their feet and adrenaline rushes on their minds.

The Cusco–Sacred Valley region is one of the best in Peru—and the whole of South America—for white-water rafting, mountain biking, trekking, hang gliding, and paragliding. The most popular outdoor activity in Cusco is, of course, hiking the Inca Trail to Machu Picchu, but there are scores more trekking and other adventure opportunities. River runs are extremely popular, and justifiably so: Peru has some of the world's wildest rivers, and even for beginners, rafting is a sport that ripples with excitement.

Many tour operators in Cusco organize adventure trips, some lasting a single day and others multiday camping trips focusing on one or more extreme sports. Participants range from novices to hard-core veteran adventure junkies; no experience is required for many trips, but be sure you sign up for a program appropriate for your level of interest and ability. Extreme sports being what they are, I suggest you thoroughly check out potential agencies and speak directly to the guides, if possible. Hunting for bargains in this category is not advisable; quality equipment and good, English-speaking guides are fundamental for safety considerations.

White-Water Rafting: There are some terrific Andean river runs near Cusco, ranging from mild class II to moderate and world-class IV and V, including 1-day Urubamba River trips (Huambutío–Pisac and Ollantay-tambo–Chillca), multiday trips to the more difficult Apurímac River, and for hard-core rafters, the Tambopata (10 days or more) in the Amazon jungle. Recommended agencies include **Amazonas Explorer,** P.O. Box 722, Cusco (✆ **084/236-826** or 084/225-284; www.amazonas-explorer.com); **Apumayo Expediciones,** Garcilaso 265, office no. 3, Cusco (✆ **084/ 246-018;** www.cuscoperu.com/apumayo); **Eric Adventures,** Plateros 324, Cusco (✆ **084/228-475;** www.ericadventures.com); **Instinct Travel,** Procuradores 50, Cusco (✆ **084/233-451;** www.instinct-travel.com); **Loreto**

VISITOR INFORMATION

You should pick up information on the Sacred Valley prior to leaving Cusco, either at the helpful main **Tourist Information Office,** Mantas 117-A, a block from the Plaza de Armas (✆ **084/263-176**), or from Cusco's **South American Explorers Club** (✆ **084/245-484**). In Urubamba, you may be able to scare up some limited assistance at Av. Cabo Conchatupa s/n; in Yucay, try the office of Turismo Participativo, Plaza Manco II, 103 (✆ **084/201-099**).

FAST FACTS   If you need cash, you'll find ATMs on either side of the main road to Yucay from Urubamba. For medical assistance, go to **Centro de Salud,** Av. Cabo Conchatupa s/n (✆ **084/201-334**), or **Hospital del Instituto Peruano de Seguridad Social,** Av. 9 de Noviembre (✆ **084/201-032**).

Tours, Calle del Medio 111, Cusco (© **084/236-331**); **Mayuc,** Portal Confiturías 21, Cusco (© **084/232-666**; www.mayuc.com); and **Sacred Valley Adventures,** Convención 117, Urubamba (© **084/201-207**).

Trekking: Too many highland-trekking adventures are offered to fully describe here. In addition to the groups listed in "Inca Trail Tour Agencies" (p. 242), which organize Inca Trail and other regional treks, the following companies handle a wide variety of trekking excursions: **Apu Expeditions,** Portal Comercio 157, Cusco (© **084/652-975**); **Aventours,** Av. Pardo 545, office no. 6, Cusco (© **084/224-050**; www.aventours.com); **Manu Expeditions,** Av. Pardo 895, Cusco (© **084/226-671**; www.manuexpeditions.com); **Mayuc,** Portal Confiturías 21, Cusco (© **084/232-666**; www.mayuc.com); and **Peruvian Andean Treks,** which is based in Watertown, MA (© **800/683-8148** or 617/924-1974; www.andeantreks.com/peru.htm).

Mountain Biking: Mountain biking is just really beginning to catch on in Peru, and tour operators are rapidly expanding their services and equipment. Cusco's nearby ruins and the towns, villages, and gorgeous scenery of the Sacred Valley (and the Manu jungle for more adventurous excursions) are the best areas. **Amazonas Explorer, Apumayo Expediciones, Eric Adventures, Instinct Travel** (for contact information, see "White-Water Rafting," above), and **Manu Ecological Adventures,** Plateros 356 (© **084/261-640**; www.cbc.org.pe/manu), offer 1- to 5-day organized mountain-biking excursions ranging from easy to rigorous.

Hot-Air Ballooning & Paragliding: Less extreme, but no less enjoyable, are sports that get you soaring high above Cusco. **Globos de los Andes,** Arequipa 271 (© **084/232-352**; www.globosperu.com), has been on-again and off-again in the last couple years, but it's the only outfit organizing such trips. If you've got the money (ballooning isn't cheap no matter where you do it) and you want aerial panoramas of the Sacred Valley, Inca ruins, and the majestic Andes, contact Globos to verify current flight programs. You might also check around Cusco for posters advertising tandem paraglide flights over the Sacred Valley.

Urubamba has one of the best Internet cabinas in all of Peru, with a good supply of machines and fast connections. **Academia Internet Urubamba,** established with the help of an American exchange student, is 2 blocks northeast of the Plaza de Armas, on the corner of Jirón Belén and Jirón Grau. If you need a post office in Urubamba, you'll also find one on the Plaza de Armas.

WHAT TO SEE & DO

The main square of Urubamba, the **Plaza de Armas,** is attractively framed by a twin-towered colonial church and pisonay trees. Dozens of mototaxis, a funky form of local transportation not seen in other places in the valley (and only a couple of other places in Peru), buzz around the plaza in search of passengers. Worth visiting in town is the beautiful home workshop of **Pablo Seminario,** a ceramicist whose whimsical work features pre-Columbian motifs and is sold throughout Peru. The grounds of the house, located at Berriozábal 111 (© 084/ 201-002; www.ceramicaseminario.com), are a minizoo, with llamas, parrots, nocturnal monkeys, falcons, rabbits, and more. The workshop is open Monday through Saturday from 10am to 6pm.

A groovy bar in Urubamba is **Inti Killa,** Av. Grau 708 (no phone), which sounds as though it could be named for a Peruvian rap star. About a block from the main square, the bar/club has good dance beats, a large dance floor separate from the bar and a lounge area, and good pitchers of pisco sours.

Yucay is a pleasant and quiet little village with extraordinary views of the surrounding countryside. The Spaniards "bequeathed" the land to their puppet Inca chieftain, Sayri Tupac, who built a palace here. Inca foundations are found around the attractive **main plaza,** and some of the best agricultural terracing in the valley occupies the slopes of mountains around the village.

Very worthwhile side trips from Urubamba and Yucay are the ancient Inca salt pans of Maras or the Inca site at Moray; see "Beyond Urubamba," below, for additional information.

WHERE TO STAY

A cheaper alternative to the more upscale hotels reviewed below is the pleasant and very good-value **Hostal Y'llary,** Plaza Manco II, 107 (© 084/226-607 or 084/201-112). With nice, large rooms and gardens for a relatively modest price ($30 double), it occupies a section of the same 18th-century hacienda as the much fancier Posada del Inca (see below). The **Willka T'ika Guesthouse,** on the road to Ollantaytambo (© 084/201-181), is a small inn with cottages and a lovely garden setting. Closely associated with New Age and yoga- and meditation-related tourism, it accepts only special-interest group lodgings with Magical Journey Tours and others groups (see "Package Deals, Escorted Tours & Special-Interest Vacations," in chapter 2, "Planning Your Trip to Peru").

EXPENSIVE

Sonesta Posada del Inca Sacred Valley 𝄞𝄞 *(Kids)*   This handsome ranch-style hotel is one of the best in the valley. Originally a monastery in the late 1600s and then a hacienda, it is now a colonial-village-like complex with great character, mountain views, and relaxed comfort. Converted into a hotel in 1982, the grounds feature a chapel brought in whole from a provincial town, nice gardens, a good restaurant, and a cool little museum with ancient ceramics and textiles. There are mountain bikes for guests' use. Room 115 in the old section is a nice loft space, while room 312 has fantastic windows and superior views. Couples should inquire about the "Romance and Adventure" packages.

Plaza Manco II de Yucay 123, Yucay. © **084/201-107,** or 01/222-4777 for reservations. Fax 084/201-345. www.sonesta.com/peru_yucay1. 69 units. $115 double. Rate includes breakfast buffet. AE, DC, MC, V. **Amenities:** Restaurant; fireplace lounge; bicycles; room service; laundry service; horseback riding. *In room:* TV, minibar, safe.

MODERATE

Hotel San Agustín Monasterio de la Recoleta *(Finds)*   Close to Urubamba, just off the main road, is this charming and rustic hotel inhabiting parts of 16th-century Franciscan monastery. Less polished and luxurious than the Posada del Inca hotels, it has far simpler rooms and more limited services. Ask for a room in the old part of the convent and climb up to the bell tower above the old chapel for great views of the valley.

Recoleta s/n, off the main Urubamba–Ollantaytambo road. ℂ **084/201-420,** or 01/222-4777 for reservations. Fax 084/201-004. riviera@telematic.edu.pe. 25 units. $70 double. Rate includes taxes and breakfast. AE, DC, MC, V. **Amenities:** Restaurant; swimming pool; room service; laundry service; safety deposit boxes. *In room:* TV.

Incaland Hotel & Conference Center *(Kids)*

Though it sounds as though it's part of a theme park where you'd find a Machu Picchu roller coaster, this sprawling, English-owned complex is a very comfortable and relaxed place to hang out in the Sacred Valley. It has nearly 11 hectares (26 acres) of beautifully landscaped gardens, a (chilly) Olympic pool, stupendous mountain views, river access, and spacious, bungalow-style rooms. There are llamas and alpacas on the grounds, as well as horses for hire. The hotel even courts New Agers, who come to Peru to celebrate the Incas' naturalistic beliefs, by offering spiritual seminars and meditation activities.

Av. Ferrocarril s/n, Urubamba. ℂ and fax **084/201-071,** or ℂ 01/222-0852 for reservations. 65 units. $75 double. Rate includes taxes and breakfast buffet. AE, DC, MC, V. **Amenities:** Restaurant; bar; indoor swimming pool; tennis courts; room service; laundry service; horseback riding. *In room:* TV, minibar, safe.

Posada del Inca Libertador *(Value)*

The same dependable chain that operates the excellent Incaland Hotel (above) has a smaller historic inn across the road. A lovely colonial house more recently converted into a hotel, it is named for a famous guest: Simón Bolívar, the great liberator of Peru, who stayed in room 136 in 1825. Rooms are spacious, well decorated, and set around a traditional courtyard. Room 141 is a coveted attic, nearly always rented but worth inquiring about nonetheless. Gardens lead down to the Urubamba River. Both of the two Sonesta Sacred Valley hotels are happy to organize adventure activities in the Sacred Valley, including rafting, mountain biking, horseback riding, and excursions to the salt pans of Maras or the Inca site at Moray.

Plaza Manco II de Yucay 104, Yucay. ℂ **084/201-116,** or 01/222-4777 for reservations. Fax 084/201-608. www.sonesta.com. 39 units. $85 double. Rate includes breakfast buffet. AE, DC, MC, V. **Amenities:** Restaurant; room service; laundry service; horseback riding. *In room:* TV, minibar, safe.

WHERE TO DINE

The best restaurant in Urubamba, and the entire Sacred Valley for that matter, is **La Casa de la Abuela**, Bolívar 272 (ℂ **084/622-975**), a charming and sprawling house a couple of blocks from the Plaza de Armas. Specializing in pizzas from a wood-burning oven, pastas, and tasty home-cooked Peruvian dishes, the restaurant has terra-cotta walls, several dining rooms, and an inviting living room/bar area. It looks and feels like someone's house, and in fact, it is the house of the friendly owner's great-grandmother. People flock here for the Carnaval fiestas and *noches criollas,* which feature peña music.

Che Mary, Plaza de Armas (ℂ **084/201-280**), is a funky two-story pub/restaurant with a single corner balcony upstairs. It features good soups and sandwiches, as well as ceviche and grilled or garlic trout; there are also vegetarian dishes. At night, it's more hip-music pub than restaurant.

On the main road going toward Yucay, **Quinta Los Geranios,** Av. Cabo Conchatupa s/n (ℂ **084/201-093**), is a good open-air restaurant, set around a garden. It gets hit midday with tour buses but still manages to concoct fine versions of Peruvian standards such as *rocoto relleno* (stuffed hot peppers) and a number of indigenous soups. The three-course lunch menú is a good value. A similar tourist-group restaurant across the street is **El Maizal,** Av. Cabo Conchatupa s/n (ℂ **084/201-054**); it offers a buffet lunch and has both indoor and outdoor seating.

> **Tips   Chicha Here, Get Your Warm Chicha**
>
> Throughout the valley, you'll see modest homes marked by long poles with red flags (or red balloons). These chicha flags indicate that home-brewed fermented maize beer, or chicha, is for sale inside. Served in huge tumblers for next to nothing, tepid chicha is definitely an acquired taste.

BEYOND URUBAMBA
SALINERAS DE MARAS

About 6km (4 miles) down the main road toward Ollantaytambo (northwest of Urubamba) is the amazing sight of the **Salineras de Maras** 𝆊𝆊—thousands of individual, ancient salt pans that form unique terraces in a hillside. The mines, small pools thickly coated with crystallized salt like dirty snow, have existed in the same spot since Inca days and are still operable. Families pass them down like deeds and continue the backbreaking and poorly remunerated tradition of salt extraction (crystallizing salt from subterranean spring water).

GETTING THERE   To get to the salt pans, take a taxi (S/5, or $1.50) to a point near the village of Tarabamba; you can either have the taxi wait for you or hail a combi on the main road for your return. From there, it's a lovely 4km (2-mile) walk under a huge sky and along a footpath next to the river. There are no signs; cross the footbridge and bend right along the far side of the river and up through the mountains toward the salt pans. As you begin the gentle climb up the mountain, stick to the right path to avoid the cliff-hugging and only inches-wide trail that forks to the left.

MORAY

Among the wilder Inca sites you'll come across are the enigmatic concentric ring terraces found in Moray. Unique in the Inca oeuvre, the site is not ruins of a palace or fortress or typical temple, but what almost appears to be a large-scale environmental art installation. Three main sets of rings, like bowls, are set deep into the earth, forming strange sculpted terraces. The largest of the three has 15 levels. Viewed from the air, I'm pretty certain they would prompt a sense of intrigue much like the Nasca Lines, but they're just as cool to walk around while you contemplate their ancient functions (something you can't do at Nasca). Most likely, the site was an agricultural development station where masterful and relentlessly curious farmers among the Incas tested experimental crops and conditions. The depressions in the earth (caused by erosion) produced intense microclimates, with remarkable differences in temperature from top to bottom, that the Incas were evidently studying. Given the rings' peculiar forms, however, it's difficult to discount other, more spiritually inclined purposes.

GETTING THERE   Unfortunately, Moray, removed from the main road that travels from Urubamba to Chinchero, is not easy to get to, with no public transportation of any kind, so it tends to draw only very committed travelers and Inca completists. The most convenient option would be to take a taxi from either Urubamba or Chinchero; the driver would have to wait for you, since there's nothing nearby, so the trip is sure to set you back at least $50. Another option is to take a colectivo or bus that climbs up to Chinchero from Urubamba (or vice versa), getting off on the road to the village of Maras. (Make sure you ask the driver for the *desvío a Maras*.) From that point, you'll need to hike along the

road about 4km (2 miles) to Maras and then walk along an 8km (5-mile) trail to the site, for a total of at least 3 hours. Occasionally, a car or taxi will pass, but don't count on it. If you do go to Moray, it's possible to add on to your hike by walking another 7km (4 miles) along a trail down to the Salineras de Maras. The only people you'll likely see along the trail are workers from the salt pans, as many of them walk back and forth from Moray to work (as if their work weren't grueling enough).

CHINCHERO 🖈

Popular among tour groups for its bustling Sunday market, Chinchero is spectacularly sited and much higher than the rest of the valley and even Cusco; at 3,800m (12,500 ft.) and far removed from the river, technically Chinchero doesn't belong to the Urubamba Valley. It has gorgeous views of the snowy peak of Salcantay and the Vilcabamba and Urubamba mountain ranges in the distance. Sunset turns the fields next to the church—where child shepherds herd their flocks and grown men play soccer without goal posts—gold against the deepening blue sky.

Though it may once have been a great Inca city, except on the main market day, Chinchero remains a graceful, traditional Andean Indian village. Its 15,000 inhabitants represent as many as 12 different indigenous communities. The main points of interest, in addition to the fine market, are the expansive main square, with a handsome colonial church made of adobe and built on Inca foundations, and some Inca ruins, mostly terraces that aren't quite as awe-inspiring today as their counterparts in Ollantaytambo and Pisac.

In the main plaza is a formidable and famous Inca wall composed of huge stones and 10 trapezoidal niches. The foundations once formed the palace of the late-15th-century Inca Tupac Yupanqui. The early-17th-century church has some very interesting, if faded, frescoes and mural paintings. It isn't open all that frequently, but some of the best frescoes are outside under the porticoes.

The market is made up of two marketplaces: one at the square in front of the church, focusing on handicrafts, and the other, consisting mainly of produce, at the entrance to town. Chinchero's market is one of the best places in the entire valley for Andean textiles and common goods such as hats, gloves, and shawls. Even on Sunday, it feels slightly more authentic than the one at Pisac. Sellers continue to wear traditional garments, and even the kids seem less manipulative in pleading for your attention and soles. Midweek (especially Tues and Thurs) there are usually a number of sellers who set their wares on blankets around the main square, and you'll have a better chance at bargaining then.

Through the terraces to the left of the church is a path leading towards a stream and to some finely sculpted Inca masonry, including stone steps, water canals, and huge stones with animal figures.

GETTING THERE   Colectivos leave every half hour or so from Tullumayo in Cusco for Chinchero (a 90-min. journey). Buses also leave every 20 minutes or so from the Terminal Terrestre in Urubamba. Entrance to Chinchero—officially just the market and church, but in practice to the whole town, it seems—is by Cusco boleto turístico. Nearly everyone visits Chinchero on a half-day visit from either Cusco or Urubamba, and there's not much else in the way of infrastructure to detain you, though there are a handful of inexpensive restaurants on the main road where the bus drops you off for lunch. One serving pretty good Andean specialties is **Abarrotes Bar Restaurant,** Av. Mateo Pumacahua 143 (© **084/306-052**). There's nowhere of note to stay the night unless you camp.

3 Ollantaytambo ★★★

97km (60 miles) NW of Cusco; 21km (13 miles) W of Urubamba

A tongue twister of a town, this gentle, lovely little place at the northwestern end of the Sacred Valley is affectionately called Ollanta (oh-*yahn*-tah) by locals. Plenty of outsiders who can't pronounce it fall in love with the town, too. The scenery around Ollantaytambo is some of the loveliest in the region. The snow-capped mountains that embrace the town frame a much narrower valley here than at Urubamba or Pisac, and both sides of the gorge are lined with Inca *andenes,* or agricultural terraces. Most extraordinary are the precipitous terraced ruins of a massive temple-fortress built by the Inca Pachacútec. Below the ruins, Ollantaytambo's old town is a splendid grid of streets lined with adobe brick walls, blooming bougainvillea, and perfect canals, still carrying rushing water down from the mountains. Except for the couple of hours a day when tour buses deposit large groups at the foot of the fortress (where a handicrafts market habitually breaks out to welcome them), the town is remarkably quiet.

Ollantaytambo is one of the best spots to spend the night in the Sacred Valley, especially if you want to be able to wander around the ruins alone in the early morning or late afternoon, before or after the groups take them over.

ESSENTIALS
GETTING THERE
BY TRAIN   The only spot in the Sacred Valley you can get to by train is Ollantaytambo, which lies midway on the Cusco–Machu Picchu route. All trains traveling to Aguas Calientes (Machu Picchu) from Cusco stop first at Ollantaytambo (a 90-min. ride). Trains depart Cusco from **Estación San Pedro,** Calle Cascaparo s/n (© **084/221-352** or 084/221-313), and arrive in Ollantaytambo 90 minutes later. The train station in Ollantaytambo is a long 15-minute walk from the main square. The train is the only option for travelling from Ollantaytambo to Machu Picchu other than the Inca Trail. For more information on traveling to Machu Picchu, see "Machu Picchu & the Inca Trail," later in this chapter.

BY BUS   To get to Ollantaytambo from Cusco, you'll need to change buses at the terminal in Urubamba. Buses drop passengers at the Plaza de Armas in the old town, about a kilometer (a half mile) from the ruins. The train is a simpler option from Cusco if you don't plan on intermediate stops in the valley.

From Ollantaytambo, buses for Cusco depart from Avenida Estación, the main street leading away from the rail terminal. For Urubamba, colectivos depart from the Plaza de Armas.

BY TAXI   Taxis between Ollantaytambo and Cusco generally charge $20 each way.

VISITOR INFORMATION
You're best off getting information on the Sacred Valley prior to leaving Cusco, either at the helpful main **Tourist Information Office** (© **084/263-176**) or at Cusco's branch of the **South American Explorers Club** (© **084/245-484**). In Ollantaytambo, try the **CATTCO** museum, located off Calle Principal (no phone), for assistance.

Your best bet for exchanging cash in Ollantaytambo is with small shops. If you need medical assistance, go to **Centro de Salud,** Calle Principal (© **084/ 204-090**). The **post office** is located on the Plaza de Armas.

WHAT TO SEE & DO
FORTRESS RUINS ᴿᴿ

The Inca elite adopted Ollantaytambo, building irrigation systems and a crowning temple designed for worship and astronomical observation. The ruins represent one of the Inca Empire's most formidable feats of architecture. Rising above the valley and an ancient square (Plaza Mañaraki) are dozens of rows of stunningly steep stone terraces carved into the hillside. They appear both forbidding and admirably perfect. The Incas were able to successfully defend the site against the Spanish in 1537, protecting the rebel Manco Inca after his retreat here from defeat at Sacsayhuamán. The complex was in all probability more a temple than a citadel to the Incas.

The upper section—reached after you've climbed 200 steps—contains typically masterful masonry of the kind that adorned great Inca temples. A massive and elegant doorjamb indicates the principal entry to the temple; to its left is a series of 10 niches. On the next level are six huge, pink granite blocks, amazingly cut, polished, and fitted together; they appear to be part of rooms never completed. On the stones, you can still make out faint, ancient symbolic markings in relief. Across the valley is the quarry that provided the stones for the structure; a great ramp descending from the hilltop ruins was the means by which the Incas transported the massive stones—thousands of workers essentially dragged them around the river—from several kilometers away.

A footpath wends up the hill behind an outer wall of the ruins to a clearing and a wall with niches that have led some to believe prisoners were tied up here— a theory that is unfounded. Regardless of the purpose, the views south over the Urubamba Valley and of the snowcapped peak of Verónica are outstanding.

The ruins are open daily from 7am to 5:30pm; admission is by Cusco's boleto turístico. To see the ruins in peace before the tour buses arrive, plan on getting to them before 11am. Early morning is best of all, when the sun rises over mountains to the east and then quickly bathes the entire valley in light.

At the bottom of the terraces, next to the Patacancha River, are the **Baños de la Ñusta** (Princess Baths), a place of ceremonial bathing. Wedged into the mountains facing the baths are granaries built by the Incas (not prisons, as some have supposed). Locals like to point out the face of the Inca carved into the cliff high above the valley. (If you can't make it out, ask the guard at the entrance to the ruins for a little help.)

OLD TOWN ᴿᴿ

Below the ruins and across the Río Patacancha is the finest extant example of the Incas' masterful urban planning. Many original residential *canchas,* or blocks, each inhabited by several families during the 15th century, are still present; each cancha had a single entrance opening onto a main courtyard. The finest streets of this stone village are directly behind the main square. Get a good glimpse of community life within a cancha by peeking in at **Calle del Medio** (Chautik'ikllu St.), where a couple of neighboring houses have a small shop in the courtyard and their ancestors' skulls are displayed as shrines on the walls of their living quarters. The entire village retains a solid Amerindian air to it, unperturbed by the crowds of gringos who wander through it, snapping photos of children and old women. It's a starkly traditional place, largely populated by locals in colorful native dress and women who pace up and down the streets or through fields absentmindedly spinning the ancient spools used in making hand-woven textiles.

On the edge of the old town, 2 blocks northwest of the Plaza Mayor, is an enjoyable and well-presented but not indispensable **CATCO** (Centro Andino de

> **Tips Sacred Valley Festivals**
>
> The traditional Andean villages of the Sacred Valley are some of the finest spots in Peru to witness vibrant local festivals celebrated with music, dance, and processions. Among the highlights are Christmas, **Día de los Reyes Magos** (Three Wise Men, Jan 6), **Ollanta-Raymi** (celebrated in Ollantaytambo the week after its big brother, Cusco's Inti Raymi, during the last week of June), and Chinchero's **Virgen Natividad** (Sept 8), the most important annual fiesta in that village. The **Fiesta de las Cruces** (Festival of the Crosses, May 2–3) is celebrated across the highlands with enthusiastic dancing and the decoration of large crosses. Pisac celebrates a particularly lively version of the **Virgen del Carmen** festival held in Paucartambo (July 16).

Tecnología y Cultural de Ollantaytambo) **Ethnographic and History Museum,** a museum of ethnographic and historical exhibits in the Antiguo Parador Casa del Horno, just off Calle Principal. It's small, but informative, with interesting exhibits on local artisanship, archaeology, culture, and costume; plan to spend up to an hour here. It's open Tuesday through Sunday from 10am to 1pm and 2 to 4pm; admission is S/5 ($1.50).

Ollantaytambo is an excellent spot in the valley for gentle or more energetic walks around the valley and into the mountains, as well as horseback riding. You can rent slow-moving horses for S/10 ($3) per hour from José Luis in a shop on the main square.

WHERE TO STAY

In addition to the hotels below, budget travelers gravitate toward **Hostal Las Orquídeas** (© 084/204-032), which has clean and simple rooms with a shared bathroom around a courtyard for $20; and **Hostal La Ñusta,** Carretera Ocobamba (© 084/204-032), a clean and friendly place with good views from the balcony. Rooms are $10 per person with shared bathroom. Also worth a look if the town is getting full is **Hostal Muna Tika,** Av. Estación s/n (© and fax 084/204-111; tika@latinmail.com), with pleasant, simple double rooms for $25. Seven of the nineteen rooms have private bathrooms; the others are S/50 ($14) per person.

EXPENSIVE

Hotel Pakaritampu 𝕣𝕣   On the road from the train station to town, this new hotel is quite upscale for unassuming Ollantaytambo. With beautiful gardens, great views, and cozy touches such as a fireplace lounge and a library, it retains a lived-in country feel, even though it's only a couple of years old. Rooms are very tasteful, with sturdy, comfortable furnishings, and there's a nice restaurant/bar. It's owned by one of Peru's best-known athletes, an Olympic volleyballer.

Av. Ferrocarril s/n, Ollantaytambo. © 084/204-020. Fax 084/205-105. www.pakaritampu.com. 20 units. $99 double. Rate includes taxes and breakfast. AE, DC, MC, V. **Amenities:** Restaurant; bar; TV lounge; laundry service; safety deposit box; Internet access.

MODERATE

El Albergue 𝕣   This is a rustic and homey hostal owned by a longtime American resident of Ollantaytambo. It has large, comfortable, and nicely—if austerely—furnished rooms with excellent beds, great gardens, a wood-fired sauna, three Labrador retrievers roaming the grounds, and a spot right next to the train

to Machu Picchu. It's frequently full—Inca Trail groups come through regularly—even though it's more expensive than other budget accommodations in town. You can't miss the hostal; it's right next to the train terminal, and painted on the wall is the name of the proprietor in capital letters: Wendy Weeks.

Av. Estación s/n (next to the railway station platform), Ollantaytambo. Ⓒ and fax **084/204-014.** www.bed42.com/elalbergue. 6 units. $30 double with shared bathrooms. Rate includes taxes and breakfast. No credit cards. **Amenities:** Cafe; sauna; laundry service. *In room:* No phone.

Hostal Sauce   Sandwiched between the main square of the village and the CATCO museum, this modern and comfortable free-standing building has a smattering of very clean, nicely equipped rooms, a chimney lounge, and a small restaurant. Some rooms have superb views of the ruins. The inn's name, which may strike some English speakers as a little odd, refers to the *sauce* tree out front.

Ventiderio 248, Ollantaytambo. Ⓒ **084/204-044.** Fax 084/204-048. 8 units. $69 double ($10 discount if paying cash). Rate includes taxes and breakfast. V. **Amenities:** Restaurant; fireplace bar; laundry service.

WHERE TO DINE
Kusicoyllor, Plaza Araccama s/n (Ⓒ **084/204-103**) is a cool cafe/bar right next to ruins, so you might expect it to be a tad touristy and overpriced. It is, but it's still a nice, cozy place. It serves standard Peruvian and predominantly Italian dishes and offers a fixed-price $7 menú. Breakfast is especially good, making it a fine stop after an early-morning tour of the ruins.

   Restaurant El Mirador, Convención s/n (no phone) touts its foremost feature upfront in the name: its fantastic lookout spot over the old town and across to the Ollantaytambo ruins. A rustic, outdoor quinta-style restaurant that is pretty much like being invited to the family picnic (the menu is delivered orally, and your server could be any member of the family), this is a great place for a simple lunch of *lomo saltado* or a basic chicken dish. You'll be tempted to sit for hours drinking beer, gazing at the mountains, and toasting your good fortune of having time to relax on your own in Ollantaytambo.

   Bar-Restaurant Tunupa, Av. Estación s/n (no phone) is an inexpensive family-run terrace joint between the main plaza and the ruins, and it has a very agreeable open-air atmosphere. It serves breakfast, lunch, and dinner; has a surprisingly wide-ranging menu; and enjoys great views of the ruins. **El Alcázar Café,** Calle del Medio (Ⓒ **084/204-034**), is an informal but reliable little place mostly open for lunch only; you can pick up a snack or the midday menú. You can also get a good home-cooked meal at the hostal by the train station, **El Albergue** (p. 226). Other cheap restaurants, such as **Bar Ollantay** and **Fortaleza,** ring the main square.

4 Machu Picchu ⟨★⟨★⟨★ & the Inca Trail ⟨★⟨★⟨★
120km (74 miles) NW of Cusco

The Incas hid Machu Picchu so high in the clouds that it escaped destruction by the empire-raiding Spaniards, who never found it. It is no longer lost, of course—and you can zip there by high-speed train and helicopter as well as trek there along a 2- or 4-day trail—but Machu Picchu retains its perhaps unequaled aura of mystery and magic. No longer overgrown with brush, as it was when it was discovered in 1911 by the Yale archaeologist and historian Hiram Bingham with the aid of a local farmer who knew of its existence, from below it is still totally hidden from view. The majestic setting the Incas chose for it remains unchanged: The ruins are nestled in towering Andes mountains and are

Hiking Trails in the Sacred Valley

Energetic travelers with a fierce desire to get outdoors and exercise their legs in the Sacred Valley can do much more than the standard ruins treks and even the Inca Trail, though the latter is certainly the best known and, perhaps, most rewarding trek in the area (if not in all Peru). Other trails are considerably less populated, so if you're looking for isolation in the Andes, give some of the following treks a try.

The entire valley is virtually made for treks, but Ollantaytambo and Yucay are particularly excellent bases for treks into the lovely, gentle hillsides framing the Urubamba Valley. The Cusco office of the South American Explorers Club (© 084/245-484) is very helpful with trip and trail reports for members.

- **Km 82 of the Inca Trail:** Whether or not you're planning to do the Inca Trail, hiking the section from Km 82 to Km 88 is a nice addition to the classic or miniroute. By staying to the north (or railroad) side of the Río Urubamba, you'll pass several good ruins sites, including Salapunku and Pinchanuyoq, finally reaching the Inca bridge at Km 88.

- **Pumamarca ruins:** You can reach the small but well-preserved Inca ruins of Pumamarca by a pretty trek along the banks of the Río Patacancha, which takes you through tiny villages. The walk from Ollantaytambo takes about 5 hours round-trip. To get there, take the road that leads north out of Ollanta along the Patacancha. After it crosses the river, it turns into a footpath and passes the village of Munaypata. Veer left toward the valley and terracing, then sharply to the right (northeast), toward the agricultural terraces straight ahead.

- **Pinculluna:** The mountain looming above Ollantaytambo makes for an enjoyable couple hours trek up, past Inca terracing. However, the trail isn't very clearly marked in sections, so it might be worthwhile to ask around town for a guide.

- **Huayoccari:** Adventurous trekkers in search of solitude should enjoy the 2-day hike (one-way) from Yucay to the small village of Huayoccari, which passes some of the valley's loveliest scenery: from the Inca terraces along the San Juan river ravine to Sakrachayoc and ancient rock paintings overlooking caves. After camping overnight, trekkers continue to the Tuqsana pass (4,000m/13,100 ft.) and descend to Yanacocha Lake before arriving at Huayoccari.

frequently obscured by mist. When the early morning sun rises over the peaks and methodically illuminates the ruins row by row, Machu Picchu leaves visitors as awestruck as ever.

The great majority of visitors to Machu Picchu still do it as a day trip from Cusco, but many people feel a few hurried hours in the presence of the ruins at peak hours, shared with throngs of people tagging along in guided tours, simply do not suffice. By staying at least 1 night, either at the one hotel just outside the grounds of Machu Picchu or down below in the town of Aguas Calientes (also called Machu Picchu Pueblo), you can remain at the ruins later in the afternoon after most of the tour groups have gone home, or get there for sunrise—a dramatic sight.

The base for most visitors, Aguas Calientes is a tiny, classic tourist trade town, where weary backpackers rest up and celebrate their treks along the Inca Trail over cheap eats and cheaper beers. Some additional good hikes in the area draw outdoor enthusiasts, but most people head immediately back to Cusco after a couple of days in the area.

ESSENTIALS
GETTING THERE
BY TRAIN The 112km (69-mile) train journey from Cusco to Machu Picchu is spectacular. It zigzags up Picchu Mountain and then through lush valleys hugging the Urubamba River, with views of snowcapped Andes peaks in the distance. There are three tourist trains from Cusco to Machu Picchu, taking between 3 and 5 hours to make the trip. The colorful but crowded and occasionally dangerous local train is no longer an option for foreign tourists. The tourist trains, all of which now belong to Orient-Express, depart from **Estación San Pedro**, at Cascaparo s/n in Cusco (© **084/221-352**), and arrive at **Estación Machu Picchu Pueblo** in Aguas Calientes. Tickets may be purchased in Cusco at Estación San Pedro and **Estación Huanchaq**, Av. Pachacútec s/n (© **084/ 238-722**). For the best views, sit on the left side of the train. Travelers based in other parts of the Sacred Valley before heading to Machu Picchu can go by train from Ollantaytambo (a 70-min. journey).

The Económico, or as it's commonly called, the "Backpacker" train, is the slowest and least expensive tourist train. It departs Cusco at 7:30am and arrives in Aguas Calientes at 11:25am. It returns at 4:35pm, arriving in Cusco at 8:50pm ($25 one-way, $30 round-trip). The fastest train, the Autovagón, serves a snack and beverage and leaves Cusco at 6am, arriving in Machu Picchu at 9:25am. The same-day departure is at 3pm, arriving in Cusco at 6:40pm (adults $50 one-way, $70 round-trip; children $25 one-way, $35 round-trip). The top-of-the-line Inka Class train is perhaps a tad more comfortable, and it serves breakfast. It leaves Cusco at 6:10am and pulls into Machu Picchu at 10am. The return departs Machu Picchu at 3:20pm and arrives in Cusco at 7:15pm (adults $50 one-way, $70 round-trip; children $25 one-way, $35 round-trip).

Passengers traveling to Machu Picchu from Ollantaytambo or vice versa should board the Ferrostal (round-trip $55 adults, $30 children) or Backpacker Cerrojo (round-trip $25adults and students) train. It departs from Ollantaytambo at 6:30, 9:30am, and 3:35pm, arriving in Aguas Calientes at 7:40, 10:40am, and 4:55pm. Returning to Ollantaytambo, the train leaves at 8am, 2:05, and 5:20pm.

Tips The Train to Machu Picchu

Train schedules have changed with alarming frequency in the past few years, according to season and, it seems, the whims of some scheduler, so it would be smart to verify hours and fares before you go at your hotel (if you're staying in one of the better ones with good service and informed personnel), the Tourist Information Office in Cusco, or on the PeruRail website (www.perurail.com). Especially in high season, it's wise to make your reservation a day (or more) in advance.

Estación Machu Picchu Pueblo, the new train station in Aguas Calientes, is on the river side of the tracks, just beyond the market stalls of Avenida Imperio de los Incas. Porters from Machu Picchu Pueblo Hotel and other inns greet the trains upon arrival each morning.

BY HELICOPTER   If you're in a huge hurry to get to Machu Picchu (who isn't?) or if you just have money to burn, **Helicusco** ferries the impatient and well-heeled by helicopter daily from Cusco. It's a far cry from the Inca Trail: The flight takes 25 minutes. The views over the Urubamba Valley are not as spectacular as you might think because visibility is limited, and the helicopters are not allowed to fly over Machu Picchu itself. They leave Cusco each morning at 8:30am and return at 3pm; the trip costs $90 one-way to Machu Picchu, $100 one-way back to Cusco, or $170 round-trip. Children under 2 pay 10% of the fare; children 2 to 12, 50%. Rates are for the flight only and do not include transportation to the ruins, entrance fees, or guided tours. If you're interested, contact Helicusco at Triunfo 379, 2nd Floor, Cusco (© **084/227-283;** www.rcp.net.pe/helicusco).

BY BUS   You can't travel from Cusco to Machu Picchu by bus, but unless you walk the Inca Trail—or ascend the slope to the ruins from the town of Aguas Calientes by foot—you will have to take one of the frequent shuttle buses that leave from down by the railroad tracks. The buses wend their way up the mountain, performing exaggerated switchbacks for 15 minutes before suddenly depositing passengers at the entrance to the ruins. Cost is $9 round-trip. There's no need to reserve in advance; just purchase your ticket at the little booth in front of the lineup of buses, at the bottom of the market stalls. Buses begin running at 6:30am and come down all day, with the last one descending at dusk. Some people choose to purchase a one-way ticket up and walk down (30–45 min.) to Aguas Calientes.

BY FOOT   The celebrated **Inca Trail** (Camino del Inca, or Camino Real) is almost as famous as the ruins themselves, and the trek is rightly viewed as an attraction in itself rather than merely a means of getting to Machu Picchu under your own power. There are two treks: one that takes 4 days (43km/26 miles) and another shorter and less demanding route that lasts just 2 days. The trails begin outside Ollantaytambo (at Km 82 of the Cusco–Machu Picchu railroad track); you can return to Cusco or Ollantaytambo by train. See "Hiking the Inca Trail," later in this section, for more details; many new regulations have been introduced in the past couple years.

VISITOR INFORMATION

Strangely enough, given the overwhelming tourist interest in Machu Picchu, there is no real source of tourist information in Aguas Calientes. In truth, though, little info is necessary. The town is straightforward enough, and all the hotels and inns should be able to deal with any questions you might have.

FAST FACTS   There are no banks in Aguas Calientes. To exchange money (cash or traveler's checks), try **Gringo Bill's Hostal** at Colla Raymi 104, just off the main square. Shops and restaurants along the two main streets, Avenida Imperio de los Incas and Avenida Pachacútec, buy dollars from gringos in need at standard exchange rates.

You'll find the **police** on Avenida Imperio de los Incas, down from the railway station (© **084/211-178**).

There are ridiculously expensive (for Peru, at S/8, or $2.25, per hr.) Internet cabinas with painfully slow connections at the **Café Internet** on Avenida

Endangered Machu Picchu

Machu Picchu survived the Spanish onslaught against the Inca Empire, but in the last few decades it has suffered more threats to its architectural integrity and pristine Andean environment than it did in nearly 500 years of existence. UNESCO recently threatened first to add Machu Picchu to its list of endangered World Heritage Sites and then withdraw that status unless stringent measures were taken by the Peruvian government to protect the landmark ruins.

In 2001, a film company shooting a TV ad for a Peruvian beer sneaked equipment into the site and irreparably damaged the stone Intihuatana atop the ruins. Additionally, developers planned to build cable cars that would run from Aguas Calientes to Machu Picchu to facilitate access. The plan, endorsed by the government, would have quadrupled the number of visitors and created an eyesore among the majestic peaks that surround the ruins. Fortunately, those ill-conceived plans were finally scuttled. Responding to the pressure from UNESCO, foreign governments, and watchdog groups, the Peruvian government also introduced measures to clean up the historic Inca Trail and restrict access to it. In a unique debt-swap initiative, the government of Finland traded 25% of Peru's outstanding debt (more than $6 million) for conservation programs.

The 2001 World Monuments Watch list of the 100 Most Endangered Sites in the World included Machu Picchu, but in 2002, the site was removed from the notorious list in recognition of the government's more stringent regulations on the Inca Trail and the suspension of the cable-car plan.

Imperio de los Incas, a block away from the main square on the railroad tracks. **Gringo Bill's Hostal** on Colla Raymi 104 also has Internet access. There's a **post office** on the corner of Manco Cápac at Avenida Imperio de los Incas. The **Telefónica del Perú** office is at Av. Imperio de los Incas 132.

PERU'S TOP ATTRACTION: MACHU PICCHU ✸✸✸

Since its discovery in 1911 and initial exploration by an American team of archaeologists from Yale during the next 4 years, the ruins of Machu Picchu have resonated far beyond the status of mere archaeological site. Reputed to be the legendary "lost city of the Incas," it is steeped in mystery and folklore. The unearthed complex, the only significant Inca site to escape the ravenous appetites of the Spanish conquistadors in the 16th century, ranks as the top attraction in Peru, arguably the greatest in South America, and for my money, one of the world's most stunning sights. Countless glossy photographs of the stone ruins, bridging the gap between two massive Andean peaks and swathed in cottony clouds, just can't do it justice. I distinctly remember seeing pictures of Machu Picchu in a textbook when I was 5 years old and dreaming that someday I would go there. When I did, for the first time in 1983, the glorious city of the Incas more than lived up to all those years of expectation.

Invisible from the Urubamba Valley below, Machu Picchu lay dormant for more than 4 centuries, nestled nearly 2,400m (8,000 ft.) above sea level under

We Call It Choclo: Foods of the Incas

Wondering what the Incas cultivated on all those amazing, steeply ter-raced fields that so elegantly grace the hillsides? Sure, they grew *papas* (potatoes) and *coca* (coca leaves), but corn was perhaps the Incas' most revered crop. Though corn was important throughout the Americas in pre-Columbian times, the Inca empire raised it to the level of a sacred state crop. Corn was a symbol of power, and the Incas saved their very best lands for its cultivation. The *choclo* of Cusco and the Sacred Val-ley was considered the finest of the empire. It is still an uncommon delight: huge, puffy, white kernels with a milky, sweet taste, it's best enjoyed in classic corn-on-the-cob style, boiled and served with a hunk of mountain cheese.

Pachamanca is a classic sierra dish perfected by the Incas. The word is derived from "Pachamama," or Mother Earth, in Quechua. A pachamanca is distinguished by its underground preparation. Several types of meat, along with potatoes, chopped ají (hot pepper), herbs, and cheese are baked in a hole in the earth over hot stones. Banana leaves are placed between the layers of food. The act of cooking underground was symbolic for the Incas; they worshipped the earth, and to eat directly from it was a way of honoring Pachamama and giv-ing thanks for her fertility. Peruvians still love to cook pachamancas in the countryside.

Quinua, which comes from the word that means "moon" in Quechua (another central element in the Inca cosmology) was the favored grain of the Incas. The grain, which expands four times its original volume when cooked and contains a greater quantity of pro-tein than any other grain, remains central to the Andean diet. Most often seen in *sopa a la criolla,* it is often substituted for rice and incor-porated into soups, salads, and puddings.

thick jungle and known only to a handful of Amerindian peasants. Never mentioned in the Spanish chronicles, it was seemingly lost in the collective memory of the Incas and their descendants. The ruins' unearthing, though, raised more questions than it answered, and experts still argue about the place Machu Picchu occupied in the Inca Empire. Was it a citadel? An agricultural site? An astronomical observatory? A ceremonial city or sacred retreat for the Inca emperor? Or some combination of all of these? Adding to the mystery, this complex city of exceedingly fine architecture and masonry was constructed, inhabited, and deliberately abandoned all in less than a century—a mere flash in the 4,000-year-history of Andean Peru. Machu Picchu was very probably abandoned even before the arrival of the Spanish, perhaps as a result of the Incas' civil war. Or perhaps it was drought that drove the Incas elsewhere.

Bingham erroneously thought Machu Picchu to be the lost city of Vil-cabamba, the last refuge of the rebellious Inca Manco Cápac (see "Bingham, the 'Discoverer' of Machu Picchu," on p. 240). Machu Picchu, though, is not that lost city (which has been discovered, deeper in the jungle at Espíritu Pampa). Most historians believe that the Inca Pachacútec, who founded the Inca Empire

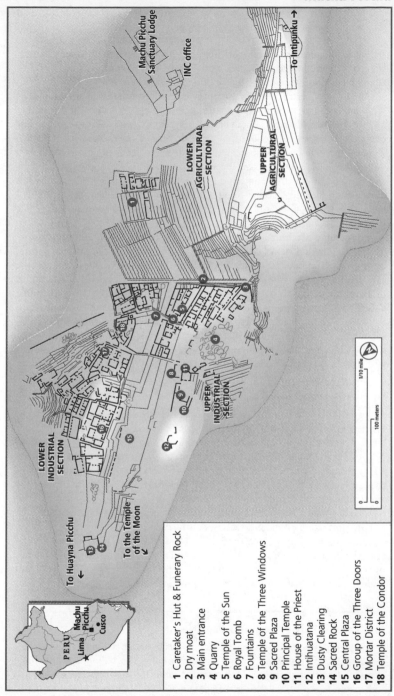

Machu Picchu
Sanctuary Lodge

INC office

To Intipunku →

LOWER
AGRICULTURAL
SECTION

UPPER
AGRICULTURAL
SECTION

UPPER
INDUSTRIAL
SECTION

LOWER
INDUSTRIAL
SECTION

To Huayna Picchu
↓

To the Temple
of the Moon
↓

1/10 mile

100 meters

PERU
Lima
Machu
Picchu
Cusco

1 Caretaker's Hut & Funerary Rock
2 Dry moat
3 Main entrance
4 Quarry
5 Temple of the Sun
6 Royal Tomb
7 Fountains
8 Temple of the Three Windows
9 Sacred Plaza
10 Principal Temple
11 House of the Priest
12 Intihuatana
13 Dusty Clearing
14 Sacred Rock
15 Central Plaza
16 Group of the Three Doors
17 Mortar District
18 Temple of the Condor

and built most of the greatest and most recognizable of Inca monuments, had
the complex constructed sometime in the mid-1400s, probably after the defeat
of a rival group in 1438. Machu Picchu appears to have been both a ceremonial
and agricultural center. Never looted by the Spaniards, many of its architectural
features remain in excellent condition—even if they ultimately do little to
advance our understanding of the exact nature of Machu Picchu.

One thing is certain: Machu Picchu is one of the world's great examples of
landscape art. The Incas revered nature, worshipping celestial bodies and more
earthly streams and stones. The spectacular setting of Machu Picchu reveals just
how much they reveled in their environment. Steep terraces, gardens, and granite and limestone temples, staircases, and aqueducts seem to be carved directly
out of the hillside. Forms echo the very shape of the surrounding mountains,
and windows and instruments appear to have been constructed to track the sun
during the June and December solstices. Machu Picchu lies 300m (1,000 ft.)
lower than Cusco, but you'd imagine the exact opposite, so nestled are the ruins
among mountaintops and clouds.

Appreciating Machu Picchu for its aesthetic qualities is no slight to its significance. The Incas obviously chose the site for the immense power of its natural
beauty. They, like we, must have been in awe of the snowcapped peaks to the
east, the rugged panorama of towering, forested mountains and the sacred cliff
of Putukusi to the west, and the city sitting gracefully like a proud saddle
between two huge *cerros,* or peaks. It remains one of the most thrilling sights in
the world. At daybreak, when the sun's rays creep silently over the jagged
silhouette, sometimes turning the distant snowy peaks fiery orange, and then
slowly, with great drama, cast brilliant light on the ruins building by building
and row by row, it's enough to move some observers to tears and others to
squeals of delight.

VISITING THE RUINS

At least 1,000 visitors a day visit the ruins, and from May through the end of
September, far more than that; 400,000 people visited Machu Picchu in 2000.
Though you've got to arrive early or stay late for a bit of splendid Inca isolation,
Machu Picchu's huge numbers of visitors are rarely overwhelming. The place is
large enough to escape most tour group bottlenecks, though people fearful of
the crush should plan to arrive before 11am and/or stay past 3pm. Perhaps the
worst time to visit is from July 28 to August 10, when Peruvian national holidays land untold groups of schoolchildren and families at Machu Picchu.

For information on the shuttle buses to the ruins, see "Getting There," above.

The ruins are open from dawn to dusk: The first visitors, usually those staying
at the hotel or arriving from the Inca Trail, enter at 6am. Everyone is ushered out
by 6pm. The entrance fee is $20 (students pay half price with an ISIC card). Sec-
ond-day admission, if you have your entrance ticket from the previous day, is half

---

Fun Fact Not a Woman's World

For years, the world thought Machu Picchu had been almost entirely
populated by the Inca's chosen "Virgins of the Sun." Bingham and his
associates originally reported that more than three-quarters of the human
remains found at the site were female. Those findings have been dis-
proved, however; the sexual makeup of the inhabitants of Machu Picchu
was no different than anywhere else in society: pretty much 50/50.

> **Tips One-Stop Package Visits to Machu Picchu**
>
> Machu Picchu packages that include round-trip train fare between Cusco and Aguas Calientes, shuttle bus and admission to the ruins, a guided visit, and sometimes lunch at Machu Picchu Sanctuary Lodge for same-day visits, can be purchased from travel agencies in Cusco. They generally run between $90 and $110; it's worth shopping around for the best deal (but make sure the packages you're comparing include the same components). Try **Gatur Tour,** Puluchapata 140 ((C) **084/223-496), Milla Turismo,** Av. Pardo 689 ((C) **084/231-710),** or any of the tour agencies listed later in this section that organize Inca Trail treks. Packages that include overnight accommodations at the ruins or in Aguas Calientes can also be arranged.

price. You will be given an official Institute of National Culture map of the ruins, which gives the names of the individual sections, but no detailed explanations. The numbers indicated in brackets below follow our own map, "Machu Picchu," on p. 233. English-speaking guides can be independently arranged on-site. Most charge around $15 for a private 2-hour tour. Individuals can sometimes hook up with an established group for little more than $2 per person.

INSIDE THE RUINS

After passing through the ticket booth, you can either head left and straight up the hill, or go down to the right. The path up to the left takes you to the spot above the ruins, near the **Caretaker's Hut** and **Funerary Rock** [1], that affords the classic postcard overview of Machu Picchu. If you are here early enough for sunrise (6:30–7:30am), by all means do this first. The hut overlooks rows and rows of steep agricultural terraces (generally with a few llamas grazing nearby). In the morning, you may see exhausted groups of trekkers arriving from several days and nights on the Inca Trail. (Most arrive at the crack of dawn for their reward, a celebratory sunrise.)

From this vantage point, you can see clearly the full layout of Machu Picchu, which had clearly defined agricultural and urban zones; a long **dry moat** [2] separates the two sectors. Perhaps a population of 1,000 lived here at the high point of Machu Picchu.

Head down into the main section of the ruins, past a series of burial grounds and dwellings and the **main entrance to the city** [3]. A section of stones, likely a **quarry** [4], sits atop a clearing with occasionally great views of the snowcapped peaks (Cordillera Vilcabamba) in the distance (looking southwest).

Down a steep series of stairs is one of the most famous Inca constructions, the **Temple of the Sun** [5] (also called the Torreón). The rounded, tapering tower has extraordinary stonework, the finest in Machu Picchu: Its large stones fit together seamlessly. From the ledge above the temple, you can appreciate the window perfectly aligned for the June winter solstice, when the sun's rays come streaming through at dawn and illuminate the stone at the center of the temple. The temple is cordoned off, and entry is not permitted. Below the temple, in a cave carved from the rock, is a section traditionally called the **Royal Tomb** [6], even though no human remains have been found there. Inside is a meticulously carved altar and series of niches that produce intricate morning shadows. To the north, just down the stairs that divide this section from a series of dwellings called the **Royal Sector,** is a still-functioning water canal and series of interconnected **fountains** [7]. The main fountain is distinguished both by its size and excellent stonework.

Back up the stairs to the high section of the ruins (north of the quarry) is the main ceremonial area. The **Temple of the Three Windows** [8], each trapezoid extraordinarily cut with views of the bold Andes in the distance across the Urubamba gorge, is likely to be one of your lasting images of Machu Picchu. It fronts one side of the **Sacred Plaza** [9]. To the left, if you're facing the Temple of the Three Windows, is the **Principal Temple** [10], which has masterful stonework in its three high walls. Directly opposite is the **House of the Priest** [11]. Just behind the Principal Temple is a small cell, termed the **Sacristy,** renowned for its exquisite masonry. It's a good place to examine how amazingly these many-angled stones (one to the left of the doorjamb has 32 distinct angles) were fitted together by Inca stonemasons.

Up a short flight of stairs is the **Intihuatana** [12], popularly called the "hitching post of the sun." It looks to be a ritualistic carved rock or a sort of sundial, and its shape echoes that of the sacred peak Huayna Picchu beyond the ruins. The stone almost certainly functioned as an astronomical and agricultural calendar (useful in judging the alignment of constellations and solar events and, thus, the seasons). It does appear to be powerfully connected to mountains in all directions. The Incas built similar monuments elsewhere across the empire, but most were destroyed by the Spaniards (who surely thought them to be instruments of pagan worship). The one at Machu Picchu survived in perfect form for nearly 5 centuries until 2001, when authorities allowed filming of a Cuzqueña beer commercial here, and the crew sneaked in a 1,000-pound crane, which fell over and chipped off the top section of the Intihuatana. All to sell more beer!

Follow a trail down through terraces and past a small plaza to a **dusty clearing** [13] with covered stone benches on either side. Fronting the square is a massive, sculpted **Sacred Rock** [14], whose shape mimics that of Putukusi, the sacred peak that looms due east across the valley. This area likely served as a communal area for meetings and perhaps performances.

To the left of the Sacred Rock, down a path, is the gateway to **Huayna Picchu,** the huge outcrop that serves as a dramatic backdrop to Machu Picchu. Though it looks forbidding, it can be climbed by anyone in reasonable shape. The steep path up takes most visitors about an hour or more, though some (including me) have ascended the peak in less than 25 minutes. Guards at a small booth require visitors to sign in and out. (The path is open 7am–1pm, and you must return before 3pm, or they'll come looking for you.) At the top, you'll reach a platform of sorts, which is as far as many get, directly overlooking the ruins. Others who've come this far and are committed to reaching the apex continue on for a few more minutes, up through a tight tunnel carved out of the stone, to a rocky perch with 360° views. There's room for only a handful of hikers up there, and the views are so astounding that many are tempted to hang out

---

Tips Be the Early Bird

It's probably best to ascend Huayna Picchu, the peak that looms as a postcard backdrop to Machu Picchu, early in the morning (by 9 or 10am). Arrive for sunrise, look around for an hour or two, and then hit the trail to avoid the thick parade of single-file climbers later in the day. The sun isn't as harsh early, either, so not only will you not bake as much, but also your photos will be better.

for hours—so new arrivals may need to be patient to win their place on the rock. The views of Machu Picchu below and the panorama of forested mountains are quite literally breathtaking.

Ascending Huayna Picchu is highly recommended for energetic sorts of any age. (I've seen octogenarians climb the path at an enviable clip.) In wet weather, you may want to reconsider, though, as the stone steps can get very slippery and become very dangerous.

Returning back down the same path (frighteningly steep at a couple points) is a turnoff to the **Temple of the Moon,** usually visited only by Machu Picchu completists. The trail dips down into the cloud forest and then climbs again, and is usually deserted. Cleaved into the rock at a point midway down the peak and perched above the Río Urubamba, it almost surely was not a lunar observatory, however. It is a strangely forlorn and mysterious place of caverns, niches, and enigmatic portals, with some terrific stonework, including carved thrones and an altar. Despite its modern name, the temple in all likelihood had to do with worship of the Huayna Picchu mountain spirit. The path takes about 1 to 1½ hours roundtrip from the detour.

Passing the guard post (where you'll need to sign out), continue back into the main Machu Picchu complex and enter the lower section of the ruins, separated from the spiritually oriented upper section by a **Central Plaza** [15]. The lower section was more prosaic in function, mostly residential and industrial. Eventually, you'll come to a series of cells and quarters, called the **Group of the Three Doors** [16] and the **Mortar District** or Industrial Sector [17]. By far the most interesting part of this lower section is the **Temple of the Condor** [18]. Said to be a carving of a giant condor, the rock above symbolizes the great bird's wings. You can actually crawl through the cave at the base of the rock.

For those who haven't yet had their fill of Machu Picchu, the climb up to **Intipunku** (Sun Gate) is well worth it. The path just below the Caretaker's Hut [1] leads to the final pass of the route Inca Trail hikers use to enter the ruins. The views from the gateway, with Huayna Picchu looming in the background, are spectacular. Two stone gates here correspond to the all-important winter and summer solstices; on those dates, the sun's rays illuminate the gates like a laser.

For a more detailed guide of the ruins and Machu Picchu's history, Peter Frost's *Exploring Cusco* (Nuevas Imágenes, 1999), available in Cusco bookstores, is quite excellent.

HIKING THE INCA TRAIL ✸✸✸

At its most basic, the Inca Trail (Camino del Inca) was a footpath through the Andes leading directly to the gates of Machu Picchu. Contrary to its image as a lone, lost, remote city, Machu Picchu was not isolated in the clouds. It was the crown of an entire Inca province, as ruins all along the Inca Trail attest. Machu Picchu was an administrative center in addition to its other putative purposes. That larger purpose is only comprehensible to those who hike the ancient royal route and visit the other ruins scattered along the way to the sacred city.

Tips **Come Prepared**

Take a bottle of water in a knapsack to Machu Picchu (not to mention a good sun hat and sunscreen), no matter how long you plan to stay. It gets very warm, the sun is incredibly strong at this elevation, and there's nowhere to go for refreshment (and few places to find shade) besides the hotel at the entrance.

More than that, though, the Incas conceived of Machu Picchu and the great trail leading to it in grand artistic and spiritual terms. Hiking the Inca Trail—the ancient royal highway—is hands-down the most authentic way to visit Machu Picchu and get a clear grasp of the Incas' overarching architectural concept and supreme regard for nature. As impressive as Machu Picchu itself, the trail traverses a 325km^2 (125-sq.-mile) national park designated as the Machu Picchu Historical Sanctuary. The entire zone is replete with extraordinary natural and man-made sights: Inca ruins, exotic vegetation and animals, and dazzling mountain and cloud-forest vistas.

Today, the Inca Trail—which, as part of the Machu Picchu Historical Sanctuary, has been designated a World Heritage natural and cultural site—is the most important and most popular hiking trail in South America, followed by many thousands of ecotourists and modern-day pilgrims in the past 3 decades. Its popularity in recent years led to concerns among environmentalists and historians that the trail was suffering potentially irreparable degradation. The National Institute of Culture (INC) and the Ministry of Industry, Tourism, Integration, and International Trade (MITINCI), reacting to pressure from groups such as UNESCO (which threatened to rescind Machu Picchu's World Heritage Site status), instituted far-reaching changes in practices in 2001 designed to limit the number of visitors and damage to Machu Picchu and the Inca Trail; see the "New Inca Trail Regulations" box on p. 245.

There are two ways to walk to Machu Picchu: either along a fairly arduous, 4-day/3-night path with three serious mountain passes, or as part of a more recently opened and more accessible 2-day/1-night trail. You can hire porters to haul your packs or suck it up and do it the hard way, but, in contrast to past years, when independent hikers could embark on the trail on their own, you must now go as part of an organized group arranged by an officially sanctioned

---

Tips An Athletic Binge at Machu Picchu

For most visitors, simply touring Machu Picchu in the hot sun is taxing enough. A couple of hours at the ruins are like an afternoon on the Stair-Master. But fitness junkies can make a whole trekking day out of a visit to Machu Picchu (especially those who've arrived by train and are looking with envy or awe at others who trekked the Inca Trail).

Your first mission should be to walk the 8km (5 miles) up the hillside from Aguas Calientes: The shuttle bus is for wimps! After you've spent a few hours climbing up and down the ruins, climb the peak of **Huayna Picchu**. (Be careful to record your time against the known record, 22 min.) After the steep ascent to the top, take the detour on the way back down to **Templo de la Luna** (Temple of the Moon). That will get you a total of an additional 2 hours walking and climbing. Need more? Head off in the opposite direction, above the Caretaker's Hut, to **Intipunku** (the Sun Gate), the route into the ruins for Inca Trail hikers. That should get you an extra 45 minutes or hour of workout time. More still? If it's still early in the day, you could even continue on to **Huiñay Huayna,** an enchanting, small set of Inca ruins that are the last ruins along the Inca Trail. The path, through cloud forest, is narrow and beautiful, and takes most determined hikers close to 2 hours from Intipunku. (Be sure to leave yourself time to get back to Machu Picchu.)

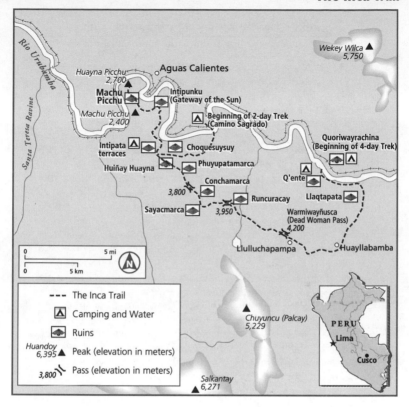

tour agency (at last count, 29 agencies, most in Cusco, were allowed to sell Inca Trail packages).

Even with the new regulations, hiking the Inca Trail, beautiful and mystical as it is for most, is not a silent, solitary walk in the clouds laid out only for hard-core hikers. Though you'll either join up with others in a group or form your own, at least in high season you will contend with groups walking the trail both in front and behind you. Some will invariably be noisy student groups.

PREPARING FOR YOUR TREK

The classic **4-day route** is along hand-hewn stone stairs and trails through sumptuous mountain scenery and amazing cloud forest, past rushing rivers and dozens of Inca ruins. The zone is inhabited by rare orchids, 419 species of birds, and even the indigenous spectacled bear. The trek begins at Qorihuayrachina near Ollantaytambo—more easily described as Km 88 of the railway from Cusco to Aguas Calientes. The 43km (27-mile) route passes three formidable mountain passes, including the punishing "Dead Woman's Pass," to a maximum altitude of 4,200m (13,700 ft.). Most groups enter the ruins of Machu Picchu at sunrise on the fourth day, although others, whose members are less keen on rising at 3:30am to do it, trickle in throughout the morning.

The **2-day version** of the trail is being promoted by authorities as the Camino Sagrado del Inca, or "Sacred Trail," though it might also be called the Camino "Lite." It is a reasonable alternative to the classic trail if time or fitness

Bingham, the "Discoverer" of Machu Picchu

Hiram Bingham is credited with the "scientific discovery" of Machu Picchu, but in fact, when he stumbled upon the ruins with the aid of a local campesino, he didn't know what he'd found. Bingham, an archaeologist and historian at Yale University, had come to Peru to satisfy his curiosity about a fabled lost Inca city. He led an archaeological expedition to Peru in 1911, sponsored by Yale University and the National Geographical Society. Bingham was in search of Vilcabamba the Old, the final refuge of seditious Inca Manco Cápac and his sons, who retreated there after the siege of Cusco in 1537.

From Cusco, Bingham and his team set out for the jungle through the Urubamba Valley. The group came upon a major Inca site, which they named Patallacta (Llaqtapata), ruins near the start of the Inca Trail. A week into the expedition, at Mandorpampa, near today's Aguas Calientes, Bingham met Melchor Arteaga, a local farmer. Arteaga told Bingham of mysterious ruins high in the mountains on the other side of the river and offered to guide the expedition to them. In the rain, Bingham climbed the steep mountain with Arteaga. Despite his grandiose claims, the ruins were not totally overgrown, as a number of campesinos were farming among them.

In *The Lost City of the Incas,* Bingham writes: "I soon found myself before the ruined walls of buildings built with some of the finest stonework of the Incas. It was difficult to see them as they were partially covered over by trees and moss, the growth of centuries; but in the dense shadow, hiding in bamboo thickets and toggled vines, could

are lacking. The path rises only to an elevation of about 2,750m (9,075 ft.) and is a relatively easy climb to Huiñay Huayna and then down to Machu Picchu. The minitrail begins only 14km (8 miles) away from Machu Picchu, at Km 104, and it circumvents much of the finest mountain scenery and ruins. Groups spend the night near the ruins of Huiñay Huayna before arriving at Machu Picchu for sunrise on the second day.

Either way you go, it is advisable to give yourself a couple of days in Cusco or a spot in the Sacred Valley to acclimatize to the high elevation. Cold- and wet-weather technical gear, a solid backpack, and comfortable, sturdy, broken-in hiking boots are musts (also needed: sleeping bag, flashlight, and sunblock). Above all, respect the ancient trail and its environment. Whatever you pack in, you must also pack out. You should also choose your dates carefully. The dry season (June–Sept) is the most crowded time on the trail, but it's excellent in terms of weather. May is perhaps best, with good weather and low numbers of trekkers. Other months are simply too wet for all but the hardest-core trail vets.

For the classic 4-day Inca Trail, the most common and economical service—pooled standard-class treks—range between $150 and $250 per person, including entrance fees ($50) and return by tourist ("Backpacker") train ($25). Independent trekkers join a mixed group of travelers; groups tend to be between 12 and 16 people (maximum 20) with guaranteed daily departures. The cost includes a bus (or train) to Km 88 to begin the trek, an English-speaking guide, be seen here and there walls of white granite ashlars most carefully cut and exquisitely fitted together . . . I was left truly breathless."

Bingham was convinced that he'd uncovered the rebel Inca's stronghold, Vilcabamba. Yet Vilcabamba was known to have been hastily built—and Machu Picchu clearly was anything but—after the conquest, and most accounts had it lying much deeper in the jungle. Moreover, the Spaniards were known to have ransacked Vilcabamba, and there is no evidence whatsoever of Machu Picchu having suffered an attack. Despite these contradictions, Bingham's pronouncement was accepted for more than 50 years. The very name should have been a dead giveaway: Vilcabamba means "Sacred Plain" in Quechua, hardly a description one would attach to Machu Picchu, nestled high in the mountains.

In 1964, the U.S. explorer Gene Savoy discovered what are now accepted as the true ruins of Vilcabamba, at Espíritu Pampa, a several-days' trek into the jungle. Strangely enough, it seems certain that Hiram Bingham had once come across a small section of Vilcabamba, but he dismissed the ruins as minor.

The Machu Picchu ruins were excavated by a Bingham team in 1915. A railway from Cusco to Aguas Calientes, begun 2 years earlier, was finally completed in 1928. The road up the hillside to the ruins, inaugurated by Bingham himself, was completed in 1948. Bingham died still believing Machu Picchu was Vilcabamba—even though he'd in fact uncovered something much greater—and more mysterious.

tents, mattresses, three daily meals, and porters that carry all common equipment. Tips for porters or guides are extra. Personal porters, to carry your backpacks and other personal items, can be hired for about $50 for the 4 days.

Premium-class services generally operate smaller group sizes (usually a maximum of 10 trekkers), and you generally get an upgrade on the return train. Prices for pooled premium-class group treks range between $250 and $350 per person (and up). Private premium-class treks (for small groups of your own formation) are also available from many operators; prices go up to $1,000 per person for guided treks for one or two people only.

The entrance ticket for the 2-day Camino Sagrado, purchased in Cusco, is $25 for adults or $15 for students. Basic pooled service (maximum 16 trekkers) costs about $100 per person (including the entrance fee). There is no premium-class services for the 2-day trek.

Do not purchase Inca Trail (or, for that matter, Machu Picchu or any other tour) packages from anyone other than officially licensed agencies, and be careful to make payments (and get official receipts) at the physical offices of the agencies. If you have questions about whether an agency is legitimate or is authorized to sell Inca Trail packages, ask for assistance at the main tourism information office in Cusco.

Prices vary for Inca Trail packages based on services and the quality and experience of the agency, and prices may come down if an agency needs to fill slots.

Cerro Victoria: A New Inca City

Since the demise of the Inca Empire, rumors, clues, and fabulous tales of a fabled lost Inca city stuffed with gold and silver have rippled across Peru. The tales prompted searches, discoveries, and, often, reevaluations. Machu Picchu wasn't the lost city Hiram Bingham thought it was—Vilcabamba the Old was the last refuge of the Incas. The search continues, and incredibly, new discoveries continue to occur. First, it was Choquequirao in the 1990s. Then, just as this book was going to press, a team organized by National Geographic announced the discovery of yet another lost Inca city.

Led by Peter Frost, a group of explorers uncovered the ruins of a large settlement that may have been occupied by the Incas long before they'd built a continent-spanning empire. Among the ruins are tombs and platforms, suggestive of an important burial site and sacred rites. There are also indications that the site, 35km (22 miles) southwest of Machu Picchu in the Andes, was an entire city. On Cerro Victoria, the ruins cover 6km² (2¼ sq. miles) and occupy a spectacular mountaintop location with panoramic views of the Vilcabamba range's snowcapped peaks, which were considered sacred by the Incas. Archaeologists, already claiming that Cerro Victoria is one of the most important sites found in the Vilcabamba region since it was abandoned by the Incas nearly 500 years ago, have high hopes that the ruins will help them piece together the Inca Empire from beginning to end.

In general, however, you get what you pay for. Rock-bottom prices will probably get you a guide who speaks little English, food that is barely edible, camping equipment on its last legs, and a large, rowdy group. Especially important is the ability of an agency to guarantee departure even if its target number of travelers is not filled. Student discounts, generally 15% to 25%, are applied by all operators. Be sure you're carrying a valid International Student Identity Card (ISIC).

INCA TRAIL TOUR AGENCIES

With the new regulations introduced in 2001, only officially sanctioned travel agencies are permitted to organize group treks along the Inca Trail. With the higher-end agencies, it is usually possible to assemble your own private group, with as few as two hikers. Budget trekkers will join an established group. In addition to cost, hikers should ask about group size (15 or fewer is best), the quality of the guides and their English-speaking abilities, the quality of food preparation, and porters and equipment. You should also make certain that the agency guarantees daily departures, so that you're not stuck waiting in Cusco for a group to be assembled.

Recommended agencies, which score high on those criteria, include

- **Andean Life,** Plateros 341 (© **084/249-410;** www.andeanlife.com). Relatively new, reputable midrange company, offering both pooled basic and premium private treks. Good guides.
- **Big Foot Tours,** Plateros 335 (© **084/222-123;** sylviagamez@yahoo.com). A popular budget agency.

- **Explorandes,** Av. Garcilaso 316-A (© **084/238-380;** www.explorandes. com). One of the top high-end agencies and the most experienced in treks and mountaineering across Peru. Especially good for forming very small private groups.
- **Inca Explorers,** Suecia 339 (© **084/239-669;** www.incaexplorers.com). One of the better agencies offering midrange, comfortable Inca Trail treks. Porters carry hikers' packs, and groups are small (including private group treks).
- **Mayuc,** Portal de Confiturías 211, Plaza de Armas (© **084/232-666;** www.mayuc.com). Especially good for pampered Inca Trail expeditions (porters carry all packs); aims to be low-impact. Smaller groups.
- **Q'Ente,** Plateros 325, 2nd floor (© **084/238-245;** fax 084/222-535; www.qente.com). Receives very high marks from budget travelers. Very competitively priced, with responsible good guides.
- **SAS Travel Peru,** Portal Panes 143, Plaza de Armas (© **084/237-292;** fax 084/225-757; www.sastravelperu.com). Established agency serving budget-oriented trekkers. Very popular, responsible, and well organized.
- **United Mice,** Plateros 351 (© **084/221-139;** unitedmi@terra.com.pe). Started by one of the trail's most respected guides, this is another of the top agencies organizing affordable midrange treks.

DAY-BY-DAY: THE CLASSIC 4-DAY INCA TRAIL TREK
The following is typical of the group-organized 4-day/3-night schedule along the Inca Trail.

DAY 1   Trekkers arrive from Cusco, either by train, getting off at the midway stop, Ollantaytambo, or Km 88, or by bus at Km 82, the preferred method of transport for many groups. (Starting at Km 82 doesn't add an appreciable distance to the trail.) After crossing the Río Urubamba (Vilcanota), the first gentle ascent of the trail looms to Inca ruins at **Llaqtapata** (also called Patallaqta, where Bingham and his team first camped on the way to Machu Picchu). The path then crosses the Río Cusicacha, tracing the line of the river until it begins to climb, until it reaches the small village (the only one still inhabited along the trail) of **Huayllabamba**—a 2- to 3-hour climb. Most groups spend their first night at campsites here. Total distance: 10 to 11km (6–7 miles).

DAY 2   Day 2 is the hardest of the trek. The next ruins are at **Llullucharoc** (3,800m/12,540 ft.), about an hour's steep climb from Huayllabamba. **Llulluchapampa,** an isolated village that lies in a flat meadow, is a strenuous 90-minute to 2-hour climb through cloud forest. There are extraordinary valley views from here. Next up is the dreaded Abra de Huarmihuañusqa, or **Dead Woman's Pass,** the highest point on the trail and infamous among veterans of the Inca Trail. (The origin of the name—or who the poor victim was—is anybody's guess.) The air is thin, and the 4,200m (13,700-ft.) pass is a killer for

---

Tips Plan Ahead for the Inca Trail
The new restrictions on the numbers permitted on the Inca trail in 2002 have limited most tour operators in Cusco to a single group of trekkers per day. Some dates sell out as much as a year in advance (especially end of May and weekend and holidays June–Aug). It's never too early to book your organized tour if you know the dates you'll be in Cusco.

most: a punishing 2½-hour climb in the hot sun, which is replaced by cold winds at the top. It's not uncommon for freezing rain or even snow to meet trekkers atop the pass. After a deserved rest at the summit, the path descends sharply on complicated stone steps to **Pacamayo** (3,600m/11,900 ft.), where groups camp for the night. Total distance: 11km (7 miles).

DAY 3   By the third day, most of the remaining footpath is the original work of the Incas. (In previous sections, the government has "restored" the stonework with a heavy hand.) En route to the next mountain pass (1 hr.), trekkers encounter the ruins of **Runcuracay**. The circular structure (the name means "basket-shaped") is unique among those found along the trail. From here, a steep 45-minute to 1-hour climb leads to the second pass, **Abra de Runcuracay** (3,900m/12,700 ft.), and the location of an official campsite just over the summit. There are great views of the Vilcabamba mountain range. After passing through a naturally formed tunnel, the path leads past a lake and a stunning staircase to **Sayacmarca** (3,500m/11,550 ft.), named for its nearly inaccessible setting surrounded by dizzying cliffs. Among the ruins are ritual baths and a terrace view point overlooking the Aobamba Valley, suggesting that the site was not inhabited but instead served as a resting point for travelers and as a control station.

The trail backtracks a bit on the way to **Conchamarca,** another rest stop. Here, the well-preserved Inca footpath drops into jungle thick with exotic vegetation, such as lichens, hanging moss, bromeliads, and orchids, and some of the zone's unique bird species. After passing through another Inca tunnel, the path climbs gently for 2 hours along a stone road, toward the trail's third major pass, **Phuyupatamarca** (3,800m/12,540 ft.); the final climb is considerably easier than the two that came before it. This is a spectacular section of the trail, with great views of the Urubamba Valley. Some of the region's highest snowcapped peaks (all over 5,500m/18,150 ft.), including Salcantay, are clearly visible, and the end of the trail is in sight. The tourist town of Aguas Calientes lies below, and trekkers can see the backside of Machu Picchu (the peak, not the ruins).

From the peak, trekkers reach the beautiful, restored Inca **ruins of Phuyupatamarca.** The ancient village is another one aptly named: It translates as "Town above the Clouds." The remains of six ceremonial baths are clearly visible, as are retaining-wall terraces. A stone staircase of 2,250 steps plummets into the cloud forest, taking about 90 minutes to descend. The path forks, with the footpath on the left leading to the fan-shaped **Intipata terraces.** On the right, the trail pushes on to the extraordinary ruins of **Huiñay Huayna,** which are actually about a 10-minute walk from the trail. Back at the main footpath, there's a campsite and ramshackle trekker's hostel offering hot showers, food, and drink. The grounds are a major gathering place for trekkers before the final push to Machu Picchu, and for some, they're are a bit too boisterous and unkempt, an unpleasant intrusion after all the pristine beauty up to this point

---

Tips Howling at the Moon

For a truly spectacular experience on the Inca Trail, plan your trip to depart 2 or 3 days before a full moon. Locals say the weather's best then, and having your nights illuminated by a full or near-full moon, especially for the early rise and push into Machu Picchu on the last day, is unforgettable.

New Inca Trail Regulations

For decades, individuals trekked the Inca Trail on their own, but hundreds of thousands of visitors—as many as 75,000 a year—left behind so much detritus that not only was the experience compromised for most future trekkers, but the very environment was also placed at risk. The entire zone has suffered grave deforestation and erosion. The Peruvian government, under pressure from international organizations, has finally instituted changes and restrictions designed to lessen the human impact on the trail and on Machu Picchu itself:

- All trekkers are now required to go accompanied by a guide and group.
- Entrance fees for both the trail and ruins have tripled ($17–$50 for adults, $9–$25 for students).
- The overall number of trekkers permitted on the trail has been significantly reduced.
- Only professionally qualified and licensed guides are allowed to lead groups on the Inca Trail. (The maximum size of each group is 16 tourists, and groups larger than 9 trekkers must hire an additional guide to accompany the group.)
- The maximum load porters can carry has been limited to 44 pounds. Additionally, all companies must pay porters the minimum wage (about $30).
- Tourists are no longer permitted to travel on the local train from Aguas Calientes to Machu Picchu (or vice versa).

These changes have cut the number of trekkers on the trail in half (a maximum of 500 is allowed to begin the trail each day) and made reservations virtually essential in high season. Otherwise, you may arrive in Cusco only to find the Inca Trail fully booked during your stay. Guarantee your space on the trail by making a reservation at least 1 week in advance. At least in high season (June–Sept), it is extremely difficult to simply show up in Cusco and book a reservation for the Inca Trail within days. Travelers willing to wing it *may* still find available spots, perhaps even at discounted rates, but it seems to me too large a risk to take if you're really counting on doing the Inca Trail.

The key changes for travelers are that it is no longer possible to go on the trail independently and no longer dirt cheap to walk 4 days to Machu Picchu. The good news is that the trail is more organized and hope for its preservation is greater.

on the trail. Though closest to Machu Picchu, the Huiñay Huayna ruins, nearly the equal of Machu Picchu, were only discovered in 1941. Its name, which means "Forever Young," refers not to its relatively recent discovery, but to the perpetually flowering orchid of the same name, which is found in abundance nearby. The stop was evidently an important one along the trail; on the slopes around the site are dozens of stone agricultural terraces, and 10 ritual baths, which still have running water, awaited travelers. Total distance: 15km (9 miles).

(Tips **Shunning the Masses**

Though the Peruvian government has adopted new measures to restrict the numbers of trekkers along the world-famous Inca Trail, exclusive it no longer is. Though it remains a spectacular trek, in high season, it's tough to find the solitude and quiet contemplation such a sacred path deserves. Hard-core trekkers are turning to other, less accessible trails to keep a step ahead of the masses. If you're one who wants to go where few others do, talk to one of the trek tour agencies (such as Q'ente) about **Choque-quirao,** another "lost" Inca city only truly unearthed in the past decade. It takes 5 days to get there over an arduous trail, but when you get back to Cusco, you can be sure that not everyone in the coffeehouse will have the same bragging rights.

DAY 4   From Huiñay Huayna, trekkers have but one goal remaining: reaching Intipunku (the Sun Gate) and descending to Machu Picchu, preferably in time to witness the dramatic sunrise over the ruins. Most groups depart camp at 4am or earlier to reach the pass at Machu Picchu and arrive in time for daybreak, around 6:30am. Awaiting them first, though, is a good hour-to-90-minute trek along narrow Inca stone paths, and then a final killer: a 50-step, nearly vertical climb. The descent from Intipunku to Machu Picchu takes about 45 minutes.

Having reached the ruins, trekkers have to exit the site and deposit their backpacks at the entrance gate near the hotel. There, they also get their entrance passes to Machu Picchu stamped; the pass is good for 1 day only. Total distance: 7km (4 miles).

AGUAS CALIENTES (MACHU PICCHU PUEBLO)

Renamed Machu Picchu Pueblo by the Peruvian government—one can only guess so as not to confuse tourists—Aguas Calientes is quite literally the end of the line, a gringo outpost of *mochileros* (backpackers) outfitted in the latest alpaca and indigenous weave fashions designed to tempt them. Hats, gloves, sweaters—they are walking (if unshaved) advertisements for Peruvian artisanship. Making it Peru's own Kathmandu, the trekkers hang out for a few days after their great journey to Machu Picchu, sharing beers and tales, and scoring a final woven hat or scarf to wear as a trophy back home.

There's not much else to do in Aguas Calientes, to be honest. The town has *baños termales,* or outdoor **thermal baths**—the source of the town's name—that are a 10-minute climb up Avenida Pachacútec. Many visitors find them a bit hygienically challenged and not overly attractive, but they're popular with folks who've completed the Inca Trail and are in desperate need of muscular relaxation (not to mention a bath). The one pool with freezing mountain water can be tremendously restorative if you've just finished a long day at the ruins. The springs are open from 5am to 9pm; admission is S/5 ($1.50). Leave your valuables locked up at the hotel.

Adventurous sorts not yet exhausted from climbing may want to climb the sacred mountain **Putukusi** (✦), which commands extraordinary distant views across the river to the ruins of Machu Picchu. The trail begins on the right side of the railroad just out of town. (A signpost reads KM 111.) Veer to the right up stone steps and get ready for an athletic feat, struggling up vertical ladders with missing steps until you reach a clearing and series of stone-carved switchbacks.

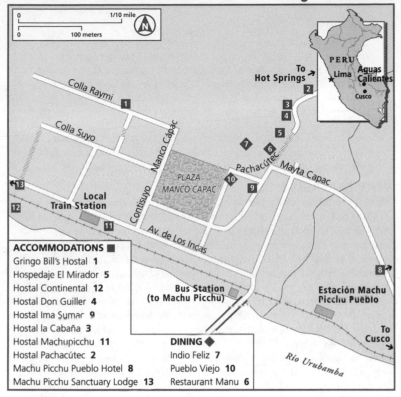

Aguas Calientes

To Hot Springs

PERU
Lima Aguas Calientes
Cusco

Colla Raymi
Colla Suyo
Manco Cápac
Contisuyo
PLAZA MANCO CAPAC
Pachacútec
Mayta Capac
Av. de Los Incas
Local Train Station

Bus Station (to Machu Picchu)

Estación Machu Picchu Pueblo

To Cusco

Río Urubamba

ACCOMMODATIONS ■
Gringo Bill's Hostal **1**
Hospedaje El Mirador **5**
Hostal Continental **12**
Hostal Don Guiller **4**
Hostal Ima Sumar **9**
Hostal la Cabaña **3**
Hostal Machupicchu **11**
Hostal Pachacútec **2**
Machu Picchu Pueblo Hotel **8**
Machu Picchu Sanctuary Lodge **13**

DINING ◆
Indio Feliz **7**
Pueblo Viejo **10**
Restaurant Manu **6**

At the top, Machu Picchu is nestled like an architectural model between its two famous peaks. The trek up takes about 75 minutes; the descent, 45 minutes. Gazing across the valley at the ancient Inca city? Priceless. But, unless they've repaired the trail by the time you get to Aguas Calientes, it's only for fit climbers.

Another good trail, particularly for bird-watchers, is the short trail to **Mandor Ravine** and a waterfall found there. From the railroad tracks, walk downstream (beyond the old train station) until you come to the ravine (about 3km/2 miles). A short climb takes you to the waterfall.

WHERE TO STAY

It's usually only the very fortunate—those who not only plan far ahead but who also have healthy bank accounts—that have the option of staying at the one upscale hotel next to the ruins. For the rest of us, below the ruins in Aguas

---

Fun Fact **Racing the Trail**

It may take mere mortals 4 days to reach Machu Picchu along the Inca Trail, but professional crazies—marathon runners and Eco-Challenge types—compete every year to race the trail. The winner typically covers the 43km (27 miles) of mountainous terrain in less than 8 hours. No camping necessary.

Tips **About Tipping**

At the end of the Inca Trail, guides, cooks, and especially porters expect—and fully deserve—to be tipped for their services. They get comparatively little of the sum hikers pay to form part of the group, and they depend on tips for most of their salary, like wait staff in American restaurants. Tip to the extent that you are able.

Calientes, there are scores of *hostales* (inns) aimed at the grungy backpacker crowd, a couple of midrange options, and one self-styled eco-lodge that's perfect for bird-watchers who want to take it easy. Sorry, no camping within Machu Picchu.

VERY EXPENSIVE

Machu Picchu Sanctuary Lodge 🐒🐒   Back in the 1970s, the Peruvian government built a temporary hotel on the top of the mountain just steps from the entry to Machu Picchu as a way to show the ruins off to international movers and shakers. As the ruins grew in popularity as a destination, the hotel was rewarded with a begrudged permanence. Today, the hotel stands as the only dramatic alteration to the ruins' isolated setting. Formerly a rather plain but overpriced modern hotel—as the only one perched right next to the ruins, it pretty much charged what it wanted—the rustic inn was recently taken over by Orient-Express Hotels (which also manages the Hotel Monasterio in Cusco, the city's nicest) and transformed into a luxury lodge in 2001. Rooms are not especially large, but they now have a good deal of Peruvian character, with some lovely antiques, and the hotel claims that one-third of them have views of the ruins site (and just as impressive, astounding vistas of the surrounding Andes). It's still hard not to decry the hotel as an absurd and unwelcome modern intrusion in this mystical and sacred place, but it's here to stay. And who can blame travelers for wanting to stay as close to Machu Picchu as possible, waking up to see the sun rise over the ruins and, at night, gazing at the stars from an elevation of 2,400m (8,000 ft.)? Not me, much as I wish it weren't there. And not the scores of wannabe patrons, who must reserve 3 months in advance during high season (May–Sept). The steep buffet lunch ($20) is open to all visitors.

Machu Picchu (next to the ruins). © **084/246-419.** Fax 084/246-983. www.orient-express.com. 33 units. $275–$285 double, $335 suite. Rates include taxes but not breakfast. AE, DC, MC, V. **Amenities:** Cafeteria; restaurant; snack bar; room service; laundry service. *In room:* TV, minibar, hair dryer, safe.

EXPENSIVE

Machu Picchu Pueblo Hotel 🐒🐒   This hotel is easily the best place to stay if you can't get into the Machu Picchu Sanctuary Lodge (or don't want to pay its exorbitant prices). It's also the best place for naturalists who want to get a glimpse of some of the extraordinary bird- and plant life in this part of the Machu Picchu Historical Sanctuary. This rustic 10-year-old hotel, a compound of Spanish colonial, tile-roofed *casitas* (bungalows), is craftily set into lush gardens, and it offers orchid tours, bird-watching, and guided ecological hikes. The spectacular grounds (5ha/13 acres of cloud-forest garden beside the Vilcanota River with a tea plantation and more than 100 species of birds and 250 species of butterflies); large, comfortable rooms (reasonably priced junior suites have fireplaces and small terraces); and a pretty, spring-water pool make this a great place to relax while taking in the grandeur of Machu Picchu. Especially popular with an older set, the only strike against it is that it sits about a 10-minute, inconvenient walk along the railroad tracks from Aguas Calientes' restaurants and bars—but that's the price to pay for a superior natural setting.

Av. Imperio de los Incas (Km 10 Línea Férrea Cusco, Quillabamba). ℭ 084/211-032, or 084/245-314 for reservations. Fax 084/211-124. www.inkaterra.com.pe. 86 units. $155 double, $173–$201 suite. AE, DC, MC, V. **Amenities:** Cafe; restaurant; bar; swimming pool; room service; laundry service; naturalist activities; campsite. *In room:* Hair dryer (some rooms have fireplaces).

MODERATE

Gringo Bill's Hostal ⚘   Gringo Bill's, established by an American expat, is a backpacker's institution that's been around since the early 1980s, when Machu Picchu began to take off. I first stayed here in 1983, at a time when there were very few other options. Tucked into the hillside behind the left-hand corner of the Plaza de Armas, the cheery and plant-filled hostal has a great vibe, with a cool patio, a lounge bar with a fireplace where travelers hang out watching videos, and a pretty good restaurant. The comfortable and clean rooms have good beds, and many have great views of the Upper Amazon tropical rain forest from bedroom windows and balconies. Throughout the inn are trippy cosmic murals, painted by the Cusco artist Gonzalo Medina. Visitors headed to Machu Picchu or out on treks can pick up bagged lunches to go. A stay of 2 or 3 nights will earn you a 10% discount, but some backpackers still find it comparatively expensive for budget travel.

Colla Raymi 104, Plaza de Armas, Aguas Calientes. ℭ 084/211-046, or 084/241-545 for reservations. Fax 084/211-046. www.machupicchuperu.com. 86 units. $30–$40 double with shared bathroom. Rates include taxes and continental breakfast. MC, V. **Amenities:** Restaurant; bar; laundry facilities; book exchange; Internet access (S/5, or $1.50, per hr.); currency exchange; luggage storage; safety deposit box. *In room:* No phone.

Hostal Machupicchu   Across from the police station and, in true frontier fashion, right on the train tracks (better than it sounds—a balcony on the other side overlooks the Vilcanota River, and the hostel's in perfect position for barhopping), this midsize hotel is one of the best midrange options in Aguas Calientes. Restored and redecorated in 1999, it has very clean, well-furnished, and airy rooms, some painted in funky colors. Its sister hotel next door, the Presidente, has 28 rooms and is pretty similar, but is slightly costlier.

Av. Imperio de los Incas s/n, Aguas Calientes. ℭ 084/211-212. Fax 084/212-034. presidente@terra.com.pe. 24 units. $35 double with shared bathroom. Rate includes taxes and continental breakfast. MC, V. **Amenities:** Cafe; bar; laundry facilities; luggage storage; safety deposit box.

INEXPENSIVE

Hostal Continental (*Value*   One of the best dirt-cheap hostales along the main drag and railroad tracks, this basic hotel is very tidy (it was refurbished in 2001), and you won't lack for hot water. Rooms aren't large, but they have style, and the beds are pretty decent for a budget backpacker's delight. It used to have great river views, but new boomtown construction has sadly done away with them. Extras include a library.

Av. Imperio de los Incas 177, Aguas Calientes. ℭ 084/244-598. presidente@terra.com.pe. 12 units. $10 double with shared bathroom. Rate includes taxes and continental breakfast. No credit cards. **Amenities:** Laundry service. *In room:* No phone.

WHERE TO DINE IN AGUAS CALIENTES

Scores of small and friendly restaurants line the two main drags (okay, the only two real streets) in Aguas Calientes, Avenida Imperio de los Incas and Avenida Pachacútec. Many are fairly generic, serving decent, cheap menús and pizzas from wood-fired ovens. If you're just looking for pizza, **El Fogón de las Mestizas** and **Chez Maggy** (both on Av. Pachacútec), **Incawasi, Inti Killa, Pizzería**

Tips   More Places to Crash in Aguas Calientes

Aguas Calientes fits the classic definition of a tourist town: It basically exists to accommodate gringos on their way up to or down from Machu Picchu. The town is little more than two main streets crammed with basic hostels, restaurants, and bars. But in the winter months (June–Aug), it gets very crowded, and finding accommodations can be a little complicated if you're the backpacker type arriving on the fly. In addition to the choices reviewed in this section, you may also wish to check out the following, which are all pretty decent, clean, and moderately priced (ranging from S/20, or $6, per person to S/7.50, or $25, for a double room with private bathroom):

• **Hostal Don Guiller,** Av. Pachacútec 136 (© 084/211-128)
• **Hostal Ima Sumac,** Av. Pachacútec 173 (© 084/211-021)
• **Hostal la Cabaña,** Av. Pachacútec 20 (© 084/211-048)
• **Hostal Pachacútec,** Av. Pachacútec s/n (© 084/211-061)
• **Hospedaje El Mirador,** Av. Pachacútec 135 (© 084/211-194)

Su Chosa, and **Pachamama** (all on Av. Imperio de los Incas) are all dependable. Menú hawkers, often the children of the cook or owner, will try to lure you in with very cheap menú deals.

For lunch during visits to the ruins you have two choices: the overpriced buffet lunch at Machu Picchu Sanctuary Lodge or a sack lunch. I recommend the latter (pick one up at Gringo Bill's or assemble one from the breakfast buffet of your hotel).

EXPENSIVE

Indio Feliz *Value* PERUVIAN/FRENCH   A restaurant named "The Happy Indian" may not sound too P.C., especially for a place that sits at the foot of a city abandoned by the Incas sometime before the Spanish invaded, but this is Aguas Calientes's best restaurant. An attractive and friendly two-level place with lots of plants, it's usually jam-packed with gringos, save the backpacker set. Even though its fixed-price menú is a great value, the restaurant qualifies as distinctly upscale in this ramshackle town. Nearly everyone opts for the three-course menú, because ordering a la carte will only get you basically the same thing at higher prices. Starters include quiche Lorraine and *sopa a la criolla* (Peruvian grain-based soup); the standout among main courses is the lemon or garlic trout. The ginger chicken is also quite nice, as are the desserts.

Lloque Yupanqui 112 (down an alley to the left off Av. Pachacútec). © 084/211-090. Reservations recommended in high season. Main courses S/16.50–S/29.50 ($5–$9); fixed-price menú S/37.50 ($11). MC, V. Daily noon–midnight.

INEXPENSIVE

Pueblo Viejo PERUVIAN   One of the more animated spots on restaurant row (right at the beginning, off the plaza), Pueblo Viejo is fairly large but simple and cozy, with live Andean music and a roaring fire. It specializes in grilled meats, and it draws plenty of backpackers and families for the low-priced fixed menús: Choose from vegetarian, menú de la casa, and menú turístico versions. Good pizza and a few outdoor tables.

Av. Pachacútec s/n. © **084/211-193**. Reservations not accepted. Main courses S/4.50–S/16 ($1.25–$4.50). MC, V. Daily noon–midnight.

Restaurant Manu _(Value)_ PERUVIAN/PIZZA   At the top end of restaurant row, toward the hot springs, Manu—named for the great Amazon reserve—is a relaxed and friendly spot with a nice terrace and gardens. With a vaguely tropical look and feel, it's just as good a place to hang out and sip pisco sours as it is to have lunch or dinner. If a group comes in, it can get pretty animated. Almost everyone seems to order pizzas baked in the wood-fired oven, but the menu also features lots of international and Peruvian items, including homemade pastas, baked trout, and grilled chicken.

Av. Pachacútec 139. © **084/211-101**. Reservations not accepted. Main courses S/5–S/20 ($1.50–$6). MC, V. Daily 10am–10pm.

8

Southern Peru

Southern Peru ranks just behind Cusco and the Sacred Valley on the visitors' circuit. The mountainous desert landscapes are some of Peru's most distinctive, and the region is a beacon to outdoors enthusiasts who enjoy hiking and river running. The deep sapphire waters and islands of Lake Titicaca, the world's highest navigable body of water at nearly 4,000m (13,200 ft.) above sea level, are one of the world's unique sights. The volcanoes and canyons near Arequipa hold tremendous trekking and sights such as the elusive Andean condor, one of the world's great birds, which at one celebrated spot passes directly over the heads of spectators every morning.

As cities go, Puno is not one of Peru's most interesting or attractive, though its position on the banks of Lake Titicaca and the creative partying at folkloric festivals couldn't be more spectacular. Arequipa is a stunning and sophisticated city. A colonial town built mostly of white volcanic stone and framed by three snowcapped volcanoes, it is one of the prettiest in the country. The elegant historic center feels very different from the rest of Peru. Within the thick walls of the Santa Catalina monastery, one of Peru's great sights, you almost feel as though you were in southern Spain rather than southern Peru.

1 Puno & Lake Titicaca

388km (241 miles) S of Cusco; 297km (184 miles) NE of Arequipa; 1,011km (627 miles) SE of Lima

Puno, founded in the late 17th century following the discovery of nearby silver mines, is a messy, ramshackle town that draws numbers of visitors wholly disproportionate to its innate attractions. A mostly unlovely city on a high plateau, it has one thing going for it that no other place on earth can claim: Puno hugs the shores of fabled Lake Titicaca, the world's highest navigable body of water, a sterling expanse of deep blue at 3,800m (12,540 ft.) above sea level. South America's largest lake, Titicaca is also the largest lake in the world above 2,000m (6,560 ft.). It straddles the border of Peru and Bolivia; many Andean travelers move on from Puno to La Paz, going around, or in some cases over, Lake Titicaca.

Before leaving Puno, though, almost everyone hops aboard a boat to visit at least one of several ancient island-dwelling peoples that seem to have materialized straight out of the pages of *National Geographic*. A 2-day tour takes travelers to the Uros Floating Islands, where Indian communities consisting of just a few families construct tiny islands out of totora reeds, and two inhabited natural islands, Amantaní and Taquile.

To many Peruvians, Lake Titicaca is a mystical and sacred place. Manco Cápac, the original Inca chieftain believed to be a direct descendant of the Sun, is said to have risen from the lake's waters along with his sister to found the Inca Empire. The Uros Indians may remain on their floating islands because they believe themselves to be lake people by birth, the very descendants of the royal siblings.

Though dry and often brutally cold, Puno is known for its warmly celebrated festivals. In fact, the unassuming town, with a population of people descended from both the Aymara and the Quechua, is reputed to be the capital of Peruvian folklore. Its traditional fiestas, dances, and music are, without argument, among the most vibrant in Peru.

ESSENTIALS
GETTING THERE
BY PLANE   Puno does not have an airport; the nearest is **Aeropuerto Manco Capac** (© 054/322-905) in Juliaca, about 45km (28 miles) north of Puno. **Aero Continente** (© 01/242-4242; www.aerocontinente.net), **LanPeru** (© 01/213-8200; www.lanperu.com), and **TANS** (© 01/213-6000; www.tansperu.com.pe) fly daily from Lima and Arequipa to Juliaca; flights range from $59 to $89, one-way. Flights from Cusco to Juliaca were recently suspended, so be sure to check whether they have been reinstated by the time you are ready to travel. Tourist buses run from the Juliaca airport to Puno (a 1-hr. trip), depositing travelers on Jirón Tacna.

BY BUS   Road service to Puno from Cusco has been greatly improved in recent years, and many more tourists now travel by bus, which is faster and cheaper than the train, and the terrific views during the day are pretty much the same. Most buses drop passengers at Melgar, a few short blocks from downtown.

From Cusco, Executive- or Imperial-class buses make the trip in less than 7 hours. **Imexso,** Av. El Sol 818 (© **084/240-801;** $14), and **First Class,** Calle Garcilaso 210, office 106 (© **084/240-408;** $25), operate buses with videos and English-speaking tour guides. **Inka Express,** Calle Saphy 478 (© **084/ 241-706**), has daily 8am departures of regular-class service between Cusco and Puno (10 hr.). **Cruz del Sur,** Av. Pachacútec 510 (© **084/812-813**) has night service to Puno (10 hr.). Regular-class buses are as cheap as S/12 ($3.50), but they are uncomfortable, have no restrooms or videos, and are potentially dangerous.

From Arequipa to Puno, buses generally travel all night, leaving around 5 or 6pm and arriving at 5am. Two companies that make the trip are **Cruz del Sur,** Nuevo Terrapuerto (© **054/427-375**), and **Ormeño,** Av. San Juan de Dios 657 (© **054/218-885**). The trip between Puno and Arequipa by bus continues to be tortuous, 12 hours of winding mountain roads—it's about the same as the train, but cheaper.

BY TRAIN   The Titicaca Route journey from Cusco to Puno, along tracks at an altitude of 3,500m (11,500 ft.), is one of the most scenic in Peru, though it is slow (9–10 hr. and prone to late arrivals) and has a reputation for being unsafe. Trains to Puno leave from Cusco's **Estación Wanchaq,** Av. Pachacútec s/n (© **084/238-722**) and arrive at **Estación La Torre** (© **054/351-041**), on the outskirts of downtown Puno, a short taxi ride or long walk to most hotels. Service to Puno is Monday, Wednesday, Friday, and Saturday, departing at 8am and arriving at 6:30pm. Inka class costs $30, one-way; Tourist (Turismo) class, $19. All trains stop in Juliaca en route.

Service from Arequipa to Puno (10–11 hr.) departs Sunday at 9pm, arriving at 7:35am; Wednesday at 7am, arriving at 5:30pm; and Saturday at 8am, arriving at 6pm. Inka class costs $30, one-way; Tourist class, $8.50. In high season, purchase your tickets at least 2 days in advance; it may be simpler and more convenient to purchase them directly from a travel agent. Trains stop near Colca Canyon en route.

On the trains themselves, but especially at rail stations, travelers are advised to pay close attention to their belongings, even going so far as to lock them to luggage racks. The routes have earned a reputation as havens for thieves; for this reason, safer Inka-class seats are recommended.

VISITOR INFORMATION
A small and poorly equipped tourist information office is located at Pasaje Lima 549 (© **054/363-337**), the pedestrian-only main drag of Puno. There, you can pick up a map and get a couple of hints on sights in town. However, you're better off going to one of the travel agencies that organizes Lake Titicaca–area trips, such as **All Ways Travel** or **Edgar Adventures** (see "Organized Tours," later in this chapter), for information on Puno's most important attractions, all of which lie beyond the city.

Tips Take it Easy
Puno's elevation of 3,300m (10,900 ft.) is nearly as high as Cusco, and unless you've already spent time in the Andes, you'll almost certainly need to rest for at least a day to acclimatize. See "Insurance, Health & Safety," in chapter 2, for more information on how to address altitude sickness.

Puno

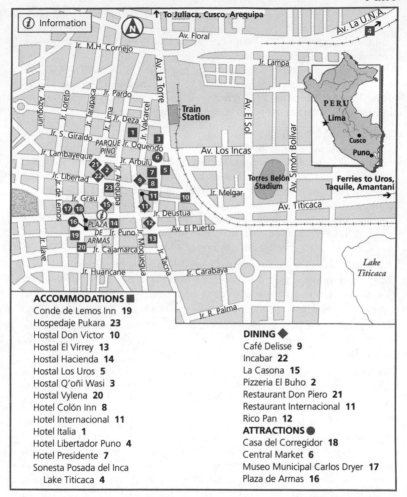

FAST FACTS You'll find banks and ATMs located along Jirón Lima (aka Pasaje Lima), just before the tourist information office; banks include **Banco Continental** at Lima 400 and **Banco de Crédito** on the corner of Jirón Lima and Jirón Grau. Money-changers can generally be found along Jirón Tacna, where most bus stations are located, and at the market near the railway and Avenida de los Incas.

For those crossing into Bolivia, the **Bolivian Consulate** is located at Jr. Arequipa 120 (© **054/351-251**). North Americans, Europeans, New Zealanders, and Australians do not need a visa to enter Bolivia, but the border is a historically problematic one (it was closed for more than a month in 2001), so you may need to check on the status of the crossing before traveling to Bolivia.

In a medical emergency, go to **Clínica Puno,** Jr. Ramón Castilla 178–180 (© **054/368-835**), or **Hospital Regional Puno,** El Sol 3 (© **054/369-696**). The **tourist police** are located at Jr. Deustua 538 (© **054/357-100**).

Pretty fast Internet connections are available at **Qoll@internet,** Jr. Oquendo 340 (on Parque Pino). It's open Monday through Saturday from 8am to midnight, and Sunday from 3 to 9pm. Rates are S/2 (60¢) per hour. Other Internet cabinas with comparable rates are located along Pasaje Lima.

Puno's main **post office** is located at Moquegua 267 (© **054/351-1410**). It's open Monday through Friday from 8am to 6pm, and Saturday from 8am to 1pm. The **Telefónica del Perú** office is on Lima 439 (© **054/369-180**). An international calling center is also found on Parque Pino.

GETTING AROUND

Few visitors spend a whole lot of time in Puno, and the little getting around that needs to be done in town is either on foot or by taxi to your hotel. The small downtown area is pretty easily managed on foot, though several of Puno's nicest hotels lie several kilometers away, on the banks of Lake Titicaca. The port is only about 10 blocks east from the Plaza de Armas in the center of town. The main pedestrian thoroughfare, Jirón Lima, connects the Plaza de Armas to Parque Pino.

Visits to Lake Titicaca and its islands, as well as the ruins on the outskirts of town, are most conveniently done by organized tour.

BY TAXI   Taxis are inexpensive and plentiful, easily hailed on the street, and best used at night and to get back and forth from the hotels on the banks of Lake Titicaca. Most trips in town cost no more than S/3 (75¢). Taxis can also be hired for return trips to nearby ruins or for half or full days.

BY FOOT   Puno is small enough to get around almost entirely on foot, unless you're staying out at one of the upscale hotels on the shores of Lake Titicaca several kilometers from the center of town.

BY BOAT   You can independently hire boats at Puno harbor to take you out on Lake Titicaca, but most travelers sign up for economical organized tours to the islands (see "Organized Tours," later in this chapter).

WHAT TO SEE & DO

Puno itself is a rather bleak and unimpressive place if you don't count its enviable geography. The main attractions in Puno are outside the city: the communities of Lake Titicaca and the ancient Sillustani ruins. What there is to see in Puno doesn't delay most visitors for more than a half day or so. However, if you stumble upon one of Puno's famously colorful festivals, you may want to linger.

PUNO HIGHLIGHTS

The large **Catedral,** on the west side of the Plaza de Armas at the end of Jirón Lima, is the focal point of downtown Puno. The 18th-century baroque church is large, but no great shakes; the elaborate exterior is much more impressive than the spartan, spacious, chilly interior. Also on the main square at Deustua 576 is the **Casa del Corregidor,** purportedly Puno's oldest house, with an impressive Spanish balcony. Nearby, the **Museo Municipal Carlos Dryer,** Conde de Lemos 289, is the town's principal (but small) museum. It has a decent selection of pre-Inca ceramics and textiles, as well as mummies with cranial deformations, but the collection is not very well illuminated. The museum is open Monday through Friday from 7:30am to 3:30pm; admission is S/2.50 (75¢).

For a view of Lake Titicaca and a vantage point that makes Puno look more attractive than it really is, climb the steep hill to **Huajsapata Park,** about 10 minutes southwest of the main square. On top is a blazing white statue of Manco Cápac, the legendary first Inca and founder of the empire. Back down

Puno & Lake Titicaca Festivals

Official travel literature rarely tires of labeling Puno the folkloric capital of Peru. Its festivals, celebrated with spectacularly vibrant pre-Columbian dances and costumes, certainly rank among the most spectacular in the country. Festivals in Puno are not just colorful, they're usually wild affairs. (Excessive imbibing seems to be as important a ritual as singing or dancing.) Locals zealously guard their ancestral traditions and cultural expressions, which are known for their unusual variety, singular choreography, and lilting altiplano music. The local cultures are responsible for registering more than 360 dances in the National Institute of Culture.

Foremost among local festivals is the **Festival de la Virgen de la Candelaria** (or Candlemas), held during the first 2 weeks of February. The celebration of Puno's patron saint brings bands and more than 200 groups of dancers from villages and towns all over the region. The festival owes its origins to ancient rituals linked to agricultural cycles and harvests. Festivities blend traits associated with the dominant native local groups: the sobriety of the Quechua people and the *joie de vivre* of the Aymara. The principal Candlemas dance is the *diablada,* or devil dance. Dancers, wearing spectacular costumes and grotesque masks, play panpipes and make offerings to Pachamama, or Mother Earth. You'll see terrifying devil masks with twisted horns and angelic, sequined "suits of lights." Official functions are held in the stadium, while more popular exercises are on the streets of Puno. The more informal events are a real highlight for most observers. Festival dances are divided clearly between two historical epochs: pre-Columbian dances, celebrated on Saturday, and the post-Columbian dances, which take place on Sunday. On Monday is a grand 12-hour Folkloric Parade throughout Puno. Street dancing is observed every day of the week, so even if you miss the first couple of days, you're sure to get a healthy dose of the Virgen de la Candelaria.

Puno Week, celebrated during the first week of November, remembers Manco Cápac, who according to legend, rose from the waters of Lake Titicaca to found the Inca Empire. A major procession leads from the shores of the lake to the town stadium. Dances and music pervade the city, and things sometimes get pretty wild, with plenty of people staggering and falling down drunk by the end of the evening.

Puno is also well known for its pre-Lenten **Carnaval** celebrations (late Feb–early Mar). Not quite the same as Brazil's hedonistic party, Carnaval is celebrated with native dances, lots of drinking, and water bombs.

Other lively festivals in and around Puno and Lake Titicaca, worthy of planning your trip around, include **San Juan de Dios** (St. John), March 7 and 8; **Fiesta de las Cruces Alasitas,** May 8; **San Juan, San Pedro, and San Pablo** (St. John, St. Peter, and St. Paul) June 24 to 29; and **Apóstol Santiago** (St. James), July 25, which is the most enthusiastically celebrated day on Isla Taquile.

below, Jirón Lima is a pedestrianized mall that runs from the Plaza de Armas to pretty **Parque Pino,** a relaxed square populated by locals just hanging out. Puno's seedy **central market** is 2 blocks east of here, and it spills across several streets. While unattractive, it's a realistic look at the underbelly of the Peruvian economy. Beyond the railroad tracks is a **mercado de artesanía** targeting tourists with all kinds of alpaca and woven woolen goods, often much cheaper those than found in Cusco and other cities. (Try on those sweaters, though; they rarely seem to fit as well as you'd expect.)

LAKE TITICACA 𝔸𝔸𝔸

Lake Titicaca has long been considered a sacred place among indigenous Andean peoples. The people who live in and around the lake consider themselves descendants of Mama Qota, or Sacred Mother, and they believe that powerful spirits live in the lake's depths. According to Andean legend, Lake Titicaca was the birthplace of civilization. Viracocha, the creator deity, lightened a dark world by having the sun, moon, and stars rise from the lake to occupy their places in the sky.

Worthy of such mystical associations, Lake Titicaca is a dazzling sight. Its deep azure waters seemingly extend forever across the altiplano, under the monstrously wide sky at an elevation of more than 3,800m (12,540 ft.). The lake covers more than 8,500km^2 (3,282 sq. miles); it is 176km (109 miles) long and 50km (31 miles) wide. The sun is extraordinarily intense at this altitude, scorching off 600m^3 of water per second. Daybreak and sunset are particularly stunning, as the sun sinks low into the horizon.

Massive Titicaca, the world's highest navigable body of water, has been inhabited for thousands of years. Totora-reed boats roamed the lake as early as 2500 B.C. Titicaca's islands—both man-made and natural—are home to several communities of Quechua and Aymara Indians, groups with remarkably different traditions and ways of life. Visiting them and staying overnight on one of the islands if you can is one of the certain highlights of Peru and one of the most unique experiences in South America.

The most convenient way to visit is by an inexpensive and well-run guided tour, arranged by one of several travel agencies in Puno (see "Organized Tours," later in this chapter). While it is possible to arrange independent travel, the low cost and easy organization of group travel don't encourage it. Even if you were to go on your own, you'd inevitably fall in with groups, and your experience wouldn't differ radically. You can go on a half-day tour of the Uros Floating Islands or a full-day tour that includes Taquile Island, but the best way to experience Lake Titicaca's unique indigenous life is to stay at least 1 night on either Taquile or Amantaní, preferably in the home of a local family.

Tips A Ship to Visit

Nowadays, fleets of tourist boats set out daily for the floating and natural islands of Lake Titicaca. The oldest ship to ply the world's highest navigable waterway, the **Yavarí,** built in 1862 in Birmingham, England, today sits inactive on the shore of the lake. The restored ship, which was originally shipped as a kit to Arica (and then carried by mule for more than 6 years to Lake Titicaca), has been converted into a small museum and bar. The ship is owned by a foundation, Asociación Yavarí. To arrange a free visit with Captain Carlos Saavedra and his crew, call ℭ **054/369-329** or stop by the ship on most afternoons.

Lake Titicaca

Uros Floating Islands (Las Islas Flotantes) ⚓

As improbable as it sounds, the Uros Indians of Lake Titicaca live on floating "islands" made by hand from totora reeds that grow in abundance in the shallow waters of the lake. This unique practice has endured since the time of the Incas, and today, there are some 45 floating islands in the Bay of Puno. The islands first came into contact with the modern world in the mid-1960s, and their inhabitants now live mostly off tourism.

Many visitors faced with this strange sight conclude that the Uros can't possibly still live on the islands, that it must be a show created for their benefit. True, they can seem to be little more than floating souvenir stands; the communities idly await the arrival of tourist boats and then seek to sell handmade textiles and reed-crafted items while the gringos walk gingerly about the springy islands—truly an odd sensation—photographing houses and children. Yet the islands and their people are not just a show. A couple hundred Uros Indians continue to live year-round on the islands, even if they venture to Puno for commercial transactions. The largest island, Huacavacani, has not only homes but also a floating Seventh-Day Adventist church, a candidate for one of the more bizarre scenes you're likely to find in Peru. Others have schools, a post office, and souvenir shops. Only a few islands are actually set up to receive tourists. The vast majority of the Uros people live in continual isolation and peace, away from camera lenses.

The Uros, who fled to the middle of the lake to escape conflicts with the Collas and Incas, long ago began intermarrying with the Aymara Indians, and many

---

Fun Fact **Say What?**

The undeniably exotic name "Titicaca" may cause giggles among some schoolchildren, though the name isn't derived from Spanish but from the local languages Aymara and Quechua. To locals, Titicaca may mean "Sacred Lake," but *titi* means "cat" in Aymara, while *caca* means "the sacred rock on the island of the sun" in Quechua.

---

have now converted to Catholicism. Fishers and birders, the Uros live grouped by family sectors, and entire families live in one-room tent-like thatched huts constructed on the shifting reed island that floats beneath. They build modest houses and gondolas with fanciful animal-head bows out of the reeds, and they continually replenish the fast-rotting mats that form their fragile islands. Visitors might be surprised, to say the least, to find some huts outfitted with televisions powered by solar panels (which were donated by the Fujimori administration after a presidential visit to the islands). For a fee, locals will take visitors on short rides from one island to another in the reed boats, but you should consider it a contribution to the community: At $2 a head for a 5-minute jaunt, it's hardly the best deal in Peru.

GETTING THERE   Inexpensive tours (normally S/15, or $4, per person) that go only to the Uros Islands last about 3 hours and include hotel pickup, an English-speaking guide, and motorboat transportation to the islands. Unless you're unusually pressed for time, it's best to visit the Uros as part of a wider tour to the natural islands of Amantaní or Taquile. You can go on your own by catching a *lancha* (small boat) at the port. Depending on how many people you or the skipper is able to assemble, the cost will usually be between S/5 and S/10 ($1.50–$3) or even up to S/15 ($4), the cost of a guided tour.

Taquile Island (Isla Taquile) 🏵🏵
Life on the natural islands of Lake Titicaca is more authentic feeling and less overtly dependent on tourism than on the man-made islands. Taquile is a fascinating and stunningly beautiful island about 4 hours from Puno. The island is narrow, only a kilometer (half mile) wide, but about 6km (3 miles) long. It rises to a high point of 264m (870 ft.), and the hillsides are laced with formidable Inca stone agricultural terraces. The island is a rugged ruddy color, which contrasts spectacularly with the blue lake and sky. Taquile is littered with Inca and pre-Inca stone ruins.

The island is as serene as the views. Taquile has been inhabited for 10,000 years, and life remains starkly traditional; there's no electricity and no vehicles, and islanders (who number slightly more than 1,000) quietly go about their business. Taquile natives, of whom there are still about 3,000 or so, allow tourists to stay at private houses (in primitive but not uncomfortable conditions), and there are a number of simple restaurants near the central plaza. Though friendly to outsiders, the Quechua-speaking islanders remain a famously reserved and insular community. Their dress is equally famous: Taquile textiles are some of the finest in Peru. Men wear embroidered, woven red waistbands (*fajas*), and embroidered wool stocking caps that indicate marital status—red for married men, red and white for bachelors. Women wear layered skirts and black shawls over their heads. Taquile textiles are much sought-after for their hand-woven quality, but they are considerably more expensive than mass-produced handicrafts in other parts of

Peru. Along with agriculture, textiles are the island's main source of income. There's a cooperative shop on the main plaza, and laid-back stalls are set up during festivals and the high season of tourist travel (June–Aug). Locals are usually more reluctant to haggle than are artisans in other parts of Peru. (Often they simple refuse to bargain.) There's very little of the noise and activity that's present at most Peruvian markets.

If you are lucky enough to catch a festival on the island, you will be treated to a festive and stubbornly traditional pageant of color, with picturesque dances and women twirling in circles, revealing as many as 16 layered, multicolored skirts. (Easter, Fiesta de Santiago on July 25 and Aug 1–2, and New Year's are the best celebrations.) Any time on the island, though, is a splendid, unique experience—especially once the day-trippers have departed and you have the island and incomparable views of the blue waters framed by stone archways virtually to yourself. Taquile then seems about as far away from modernity and "civilization" as one can travel on this planet. On top of the island on a clear night, under a carpet of stars, Taquile is even more magical.

Access to the island from the boat dock is either by a long path that wends around the island or by an amazing 533-step stone staircase that climbs to the top, passing through two stone arches with astonishing views of the lake. Independent travelers sign in and pay a nominal fee. Those wishing to stay the night can arrange to be put up in a family house. If you stay, expect to rough it a bit without proper showers. Many islanders do not speak Spanish, and English is likely to be met with blank stares.

GETTING THERE   The only feasible way to visit Taquile is as part of an organized tour, which is both inexpensive and convenient. Most single-day tours of the Uros and Taquile islands depart early in the morning and stop at the islands of Uros for a half hour en route. For most visitors, a day trip, which allows only an hour or two on the island and 8 hours of boat time, is too grueling and insufficient to appreciate the beauty and culture of Taquile Island. A 2- or 3-day visit, with time to spend the night on either Taquile or Amantaní, is preferable.

Amantaní Island (Isla Amantaní) &&

Amantaní, a circular island located about 4½ hours from Puno (and about 2 hr. from Taquile), is home to a very different, although equally fascinating, Titicaca community. Also handsomely terraced and home to farmers, fishers, and weavers, in many ways Amantaní is even more rustic and unspoiled than Taquile. It is a beautiful but barren and rocky place, with a handful of villages composed of about 800 families and ruins clinging to the island's two peaks, Pachatata and Pachamama (Father Earth and Mother Earth). The island presents some excellent opportunities for hikes up to these spots, with terrific views of the lake and the sparsely populated island landscape. The agricultural character of the island is perhaps even more apparent than on Taquile. Long, ancient-looking stone walls

---

Tips Don't Be a Lone Wolf

Going on your own to the Titicaca islands is possible, but boats wait for a sufficient number of passengers—meaning you'll go with a group anyway, and without the benefit of an English-speaking guide. Plus, the savings going independently are minimal (only a couple dollars), and you won't get hotel pickup and drop-off, as you do with organized tours.

mark the fields and terraces of different communities, and cows, sheep, and alpacas graze the hillsides.

The islanders, who for the most part all understand Spanish, are more open and approachable than natives of Taquile. The highlight of a visit to Amantaní is an overnight stay with a local family. Not only will the family prepare your simple meals, but you will also be invited to a friendly dance in the village meeting place. For the event, most families dress their guests up in local outfits—the women in layered, multicolored, embroidered skirts and blouses, and the men in wool ponchos. Though the evening is obviously staged for tourists' benefit, it is low-key and charming rather than cheesy.

Amantaní islanders also make lovely hand-woven textiles, particularly the show-stopping black shawls embroidered with seven colors. The main festival on Amantaní, Fiesta de la Santa Tierra, is on the third Thursday in January, when the population splits in two—half at the Temple of Pachamama and the other half at the Temple of Pachatata (a perfect illustration of their dualistic, male/female belief system). Other good festivals are the anniversary of Amantaní (Apr 9, lasting 3 days) and Carnaval (in Feb or Mar).

Amantaní is best visited on a tour that allows you to spend the night (visiting the Uros Islands en route) and travel the next day to Taquile. Tour groups place groups of four or five with local families for overnight stays. The tour price normally includes accommodations, lunch, and dinner on the first day and breakfast the following morning.

It's a good idea to bring small gifts for your family on Amantaní, because they make little from stays and must alternate with other families on the island. Pens, pencils, and batteries all make good gifts.

GETTING THERE   The only feasible way to visit Amantaní is by organized tour. Almost all tours that go to Amantaní also visit the Uros and Taquile islands, stopping en route at Uros and spending the night on Amantaní before visiting Taquile the following day.

OTHER ATTRACTIONS NEAR PUNO
Sillustani Ruins ⍟
On the outskirts of Puno are mysterious pre-Inca ruins called *chullpas* (funeral towers). The finest sit on the windswept altiplano on a peninsula in Lake Umayo at Sillustani, 32km (20 miles) from Puno. The Colla people—a warrior tribe that spoke Aymara—buried their elite in giant cylindrical tombs, some as tall as 12m (40 ft.) The stonemasonry is exquisite (many archaeologists and historians find them more complex and superior even to Inca engineering), and the structures form quite an impression on such a harsh landscape.

The Collas dominated the Titicaca region before the arrival of the Incas. After burying their dead along with foodstuffs, jewels, and other possessions, the towers were sealed. Dress warmly for your visit here, as the bitter gusts make the wind of a wintry day on Lake Michigan look like a gentle spring breeze.

GETTING THERE   By far the best way to visit Sillustani is by guided tour, usually in the afternoon around 2 or 2:30pm (see "Organized Tours," below). Tours are inexpensive and very convenient. Going on your own generally isn't worth it because the site is a pain to reach, and once there, you've no guide to explain the significance of the ruins. If you insist, though, catch a "Juliaca" colectivo from downtown Puno and request to be let off after about 20 minutes, at the fork in the road that leads to Sillustani (DESVIO PARA SILLUSTANI). From that point, it's 15km (9 miles) and a half hour farther away, but colectivos aren't frequent. To return, you're best off trying to hitch a ride back to Puno. In other words: Take the guided tour.

Chucuito: Fertility Temple

Eighteen kilometers (11 miles) south of Puno, on a small promontory on the southern shore of Lake Titicaca, Chucuito, a small Aymara town, is one of the oldest in the altiplano region. The town, capital of the province during colonial times, has a lovely main square and a colonial church, **Nuestra Señora de La Asunción** (built in 1601). Chucuito was also the primary Inca settlement in the region. Near another colonial church, **Santo Domino,** is a most curious construction dating to pre-Columbian times and the town's main attraction: **Inca Uyo** is composed of dozens of large, mushroom-shaped phallic stones, most a few feet high, which were erected, apparently, as part of fertility rituals. The anatomically correct stones, which until a few years ago were kept in a sterile museum, leave little doubt as to what their creators were getting at. Some point up at the sun god, Inti, while others are inserted into the ground, directed at Pachamama, or Mother Earth. At the center of the ring, lording over the fertility temple, is the king phallus. Local guides tell tales of the exact rituals during which virgins purportedly sat for hours atop the phalluses to increase fertility. The stones may predate the Incas, but some contend that they are fake. Spanish missionaries did everything in their power to destroy all symbols and structures they considered pagan, and it does seem odd that they would have constructed two churches nearby but left this temple intact.

If you find yourself drawn to the stones at Inka Uyo, you can stay the night at **Las Cabañas de Chucuito,** a comfortable International Youth Hostel at Jr. Tarapaca 153 (© and fax **054/351-276;** lodgecabanas@hotmail.com). It has bungalows with private bathrooms for $7 per person and a nice setting by the lake. Also worth a look is the **Chucuito Resort Hotel,** Carretera Panamericana Sur Km 17 (© **054/622-208;** fax 054/352-108). The hotel has good views of Lake Titicaca and nice carpeted rooms.

GETTING THERE   "Acora" colectivos leave from Puno's Avenida El Sol. The ride to Chucuito costs S/1 (30¢) and takes 15 to 20 minutes; tell the driver you want to get off at Chucuito, which lies about halfway between Chimú and Acora.

ORGANIZED TOURS

Most travel agencies in Puno handle the conventional tours of Lake Titicaca and Sillustani, along with a handful of other ruins programs. Two of the best agencies are **All Ways Travel,** Jr. Tacna 234 (© **054/355-552;** awtperu@terra.com.pe), which is run by the friendly and very helpful Victor Pauca and his daughter Eliana, with progressive cultural trips in addition to the standard tours; and **Edgar Adventures,** Jr. Lima 328 (© **054/353-444;** edgaradventures@terra.com.pe), which is run by a Peruvian husband/wife team. Both agencies can arrange bus and air travel as well, including travel to Bolivia. Another agency worth checking out for travel arrangements is **Highland Travel Experts,** Jr. Tacna 273 (© **054/365-737;** hightravel@latinmail.com).

Uros Islands half-day trips cost about $4 per person. Uros Islands and Taquile Island full-day trips cost $8 to $10 per person. Uros, Taquile, and Amantaní trips, lasting 2 days and 1 night, cost $12 per person. Sillustani and Chucuito tours, usually 3 hours long, cost $5 per person each.

> **Tips** **Seek Help**
>
> Wherever you're headed from Puno, if you're traveling by bus, it's advisable to visit a travel agent to make bus reservations because a confusing number of bus companies and services travel in and out of Puno. See "Organized Tours," above.

SHOPPING

Though it has few nice shops on the order of Lima, Cusco, or Arequipa, Puno is one of the better places to load up on inexpensive woolen and alpaca goods, including hats, gloves, scarves, shawls, and blankets. They are cheaper here than in those cities, though you may not encounter the quality found at some upscale shops. The **open-air market** just beyond the railroad tracks (between Jr. Melgar and Av. Titicaca) has a couple dozen stalls specializing in alpaca and woolen goods. There is a cluster of souvenir and clothing shops along **Jirón Lima,** the pedestrian mall.

WHERE TO STAY

Puno doesn't exactly overflow with good hotel options. The majority continues to be geared toward the budget-backpacker crowd; even the best of those are very basic, and many are dingy, noisy dives with fleeting hot water. If you're looking at the bottom end, check the place out first, and ask to see a couple of rooms. If you don't mind relying on taxis to get back and forth and can afford to spend a bit more, the best options are on the banks of Lake Titicaca. Outside high season (June–Sept), most hotels and *hostales* (inns) are more than willing to bargain.

EXPENSIVE

Hotel Libertador Puno 🦊   Ensconced in serenity and splendid isolation on the shore of a small island 5km (3 miles) from Puno, overlooking the expanse of Lake Titicaca, this hotel takes full advantage of its privileged location. Part of the luxury Libertador chain (formerly the state-owned Hotel de Turistas), the hotel's rooms are spacious if a little bland, and about half have panoramic views of the lake. Service is excellent, and the large, white-block hotel has soaring ceilings, but it doesn't have as much character as the less expensive Posada del Inca, which has views that are almost as good. The hotel is linked to the mainland by a causeway, and the only way back and forth to Puno is by taxi.

Isla Esteves s/n, Lake Titicaca. ✆ 054/367-780. Fax 054/367-879. www.libertador.com.pe. 123 units. $145 deluxe double; $215–$240 suite. Rates include breakfast buffet. AE, DC, MC, V. **Amenities:** Restaurant; bar; fitness center; sauna; concierge; 24-hr. room service; laundry service; disco. *In room:* A/C, TV, minibar, hair dryer, safe.

Sonesta Posada del Inca Lake Titicaca 🦊🦊 (*Kids*)   Like the Libertador, the Posada is perched on the shores of Titicaca, 5km (3 miles) from downtown Puno, but it fits more sensitively into its enviable surroundings. The newest hotel in Puno, it is imaginatively designed, with warm colors and Peruvian touches, including bright modern art and folk artifacts. Rooms are large and comfortable, outfitted in the chain's familiar bright colors, and bathrooms are also large and nicely equipped. The restaurant and many rooms look over the lake; other rooms have views of the mountains. The relaxed lobby has a cozy fireplace. Service is friendly, and the staff can arrange visits to Titicaca's islands. Children will enjoy the miniversion of a floating lake community on the grounds by the lake.

Conquicentenario 610, Sector Huaje, Lake Titicaca. ✆ **054/363-672.** Fax 054/364-111. www.sonesta.com/ peru_puno. 62 units. $82 double. Rate includes breakfast buffet. AE, DC, MC, V. **Amenities:** Restaurant; cocktail lounge; concierge; business center; 24-hr. room service; laundry service. *In room:* A/C, TV, minibar, hair dryer, safe.

MODERATE

Conde de Lemos Inn   The fact that it is family-owned may qualify it to be called an "inn," I suppose, but this weirdo-modern midsize hotel just off the Plaza de Armas really wants to be a high-style midrange hotel in a town with little style itself. Maybe that's why it comes off as such an oddity. The exterior is all concrete and glass, though done on the cheap, and the interior is a hodgepodge of floral patterns and green and white—like a hotel you might expect to find in Abu Dhabi. Still, if you can't spring for the Libertador or the Posada del Inca, and the Hotel Colón is full, the Conde de Lemos has probably the next-best amenities and service in Puno. That's not saying a whole lot, but all in all, the hotel's not a bad deal. Rooms are decent size, and four have glassed-in terraces with views of the back of the cathedral. (*Note:* The hotel had just 11 rooms when I visited, but the owners promised that the ongoing construction would more than triple its size.)

Jr. Puno 675–681, Puno. ✆ and fax **054/369-898.** condelemosinn@punonet.com. 11 units. $52 double. Rate includes taxes and breakfast. AE, DC, MC, V. **Amenities:** Restaurant; bar; room service; laundry service; Internet access. *In room:* TV, minibar, safe.

Hospedaje Pukara   Right around the corner from Puno's main drag, this friendly little hostal is often filled with backpackers. Rooms are on the small side for a midrange hostal, but they're clean and have private bathrooms and good hot-water showers. The inn has an attractive rooftop breakfast restaurant and the lobby area has a cool, huge mural.

Jr. Libertad 328, Puno. ✆ and fax **054/368-448.** pukara@terra.com.pe. 14 units. $40 double. Rate includes taxes and American breakfast. AE, DC, MC, V. **Amenities:** Restaurant; bar; room service; laundry service. *In room:* TV.

Hostal Hacienda   Built around a pair of sunny courtyards on a busy downtown street, this cheerful midsize hotel is pleasant and does its best to impersonate a hacienda-style inn. Rooms are simple, carpeted, and nice enough. A project continually expanded over the past few years, half the hotel's rooms were newly constructed at the end of 2001. Request one of the newer accommodations, as they have much-improved bathrooms (with tubs) and double beds.

Jr. Deustua 297, Puno. ✆ and fax **054/356-109.** hacienda@latinmail.com. 40 units. $53 double. Rate includes taxes and continental breakfast. MC. **Amenities:** Restaurant; cafe; bar; concierge; laundry service. *In room:* TV.

Hotel Colón Inn ⭐ *(Value*   A small and charming Belgian-owned hotel (but affiliated with Best Western) in the heart of Puno, the Colón inhabits a 19th-century republican-era building on a corner. Built around an airy, sky-lit, colonial-style lobby, it has three floors of good-size and comfortably appointed, carpeted rooms with desks and marble bathrooms. The cozy top-floor pub is advertised for its panoramic views, but in reality, all you can see are the tops of concrete buildings. The two restaurants, Sol Naciente and Pizzeria Europa, are a couple of the better places in Puno for lunch or dinner.

Calle Tacna 290, Puno. ✆ and fax **054/351-432.** www.titicaca-peru.com. 21 units. $53 double. Rate includes taxes and breakfast buffet. AE, DC, MC, V. **Amenities:** 2 restaurants; bar; room service; laundry service; Internet access (S/5, or $1.50, per hr.). *In room:* TV, minibar, safe.

Hotel Italia   A modest little hotel in the midst of Puno's hubbub, the Italia is homey and well maintained, and it has an attractive small restaurant and

Tips Additional Hostales

If you arrive in Puno during festival time and there's a crunch on affordable accommodations, try these modest hotels and budget-backpacker places:

Hostal Don Víctor   Located near the railroad tracks, this hostal is clean and well maintained. The 12 rooms have private bathrooms, and some have pretty decent views of Lake Titicaca. Melgar 166 (© 054/366-087). S/50 ($14) double.

Hostal El Virrey   Similar to Hotel Internacional (below), El Virrey has pretty clean rooms with private bathrooms, TV, and hot water. Some rooms even have views of Titicaca. Tacna 510 (© 054/354-495). S/75 ($21) double.

Hostal Q'oñi Wasi   Located across from the train station, this hostal has simple rooms with twin beds, private bathrooms, and electric showers. It also has a decent little breakfast room. Av. La Torre 119 (© 054/353-912). S/25 ($7) double.

Hotel Internacional   This hotel is a more upscale choice. It's a modern block with nice clean rooms and sitting areas with TVs, as well as good views of the lake. All rooms have private bathrooms. There's also a good restaurant on the ground floor. Libertad 161, at the corner of Moquegua (© 054/352-109; fax 054/355-632; www.puno-peru.com). S/75 ($21).

breakfast room. The rooms are clean, decent-size, and, for the most part, tastefully decorated, though many are marred by scary circular fluorescent lights. The staff is very friendly and helpful. An unusual feature for a small, moderately priced hotel: free porn on channel 39 (more a feature of local cable than of this otherwise modest hotel, I'm guessing).

Jr. Teodoro Valcarcel 122, Puno. © and fax **054/352-521**. hitalia@hotelesonline.net. 21 units. $38 double. Rate includes taxes and continental breakfast. MC. **Amenities:** Restaurant; cafe/bar; concierge; laundry service. *In room:* TV.

INEXPENSIVE

Hostal Los Uros   Los Uros is one of the more popular Puno hostales targeting backpackers, representing a decent value at the low end. The very basic rooms are clean, beds are pretty decent, the place is quiet, and if you get chilly, the staff will dole out extra wool blankets. About half the rooms have a private bathroom; the rest have shared bathrooms. Your best bet for hot water is in the evening. Breakfast is available at the simple cafeteria.

Jr. Teodoro Valcarcel 135, Puno. © **054/352-141**. 14 units. $10 double with private bathroom, $8 with shared bathroom. Rates include taxes. No credit cards. **Amenities:** Cafeteria. *In room:* No phone.

Hostal Vylena   About a block and a half away from the Plaza de Armas, on the south (left) side of the square where few tourists tend to tread, is this curious little inn. It's dressed up like Grandma's house, sort of (if you were Peruvian and came from Puno, that is), with wood paneling and homey details. There's a sitting room, and the sun-filled, carpeted rooms have simple decor. All rooms have private bathrooms. For a simple step up from dingy backpacker dives, it's a bargain.

Jr. Ayacucho 505, Puno. © **054/351-292**. Fax 054/351-292. www.orake.com/vylena. hostalvylena@hotmail. com. 9 units. S/65 ($19) double. Rate includes taxes. No credit cards. **Amenities:** Cafeteria; room service; laundry service. *In room:* TV, no phone.

Hotel Presidente   This basic budget hotel isn't anything special—in fact, it's pretty nondescript—but it's cheap and clean (a relative term at this level in Puno), with firm beds and hot water (supposedly around the clock). All rooms have private bathrooms. Attached is a nice cafe, where breakfast is served.

Jr. Tacna 248, Puno. © and fax **054/356-109**. 25 units. S/35 ($10) double. Rate includes taxes. No credit cards. **Amenities:** Cafeteria; laundry service; TV on request. *In room:* No phone.

WHERE TO DINE

Chilly, drab Puno isn't a place for fine dining. It's better suited for pizzas from wood-fired ovens and simple, straightforward Peruvian cooking. On those scores, it succeeds. Besides, at this altitude, it's not a great idea to overindulge in eating or drinking. Most of Puno's more attractive restaurants, popular with gringos, are located on the pedestrian-only main drag, Jirón Lima. In addition to those listed below, check out the two restaurants at Hotel Colón Inn (p. 265).

MODERATE

Apu Salkantay PERUVIAN/INTERNATIONAL   A cozy, two-level lodge-like place that seems to attract more people for drinks next to the fireplace-stove, this Quechua-named restaurant is open for all meals of the day. The menu has standard offerings such as soups, pizza from the wood-burning stove, pastas (spaghetti, lasagna, and so on), and basic fish (kingfish and trout), but they also serve up Peruvian specialties such as *cuy* (guinea pig) and alpaca steak with quinoa rice. Deftly targeting tourists, the cafe/bar also has Internet facilities. The daily *menú* (inexpensive set meal) includes a soft drink, bread, and main course.

Jr. Lima 357. © **054/363-955**. Reservations not accepted. Main courses S/17–S/22 ($5–$6); menú del día S/22 ($6). DC, MC, V. Daily 9am–10pm.

Incabar ⭐ NOUVEAU PERUVIAN/INTERNATIONAL   Awfully stylish and downright funky for rough-around-the-edges Puno, this new lounge bar and restaurant aims high (again, by Puno standards). The menu is much more creative and flavorful—even if dishes don't always succeed—than other places in town, with interesting sauces for lake fish and alpaca steak and artful presentations. For a recent meal, I had a spinach-and-tomato-cream soup and *atraveza-dos de pollo*—chicken rolls marinated in sesame, ginger, and garlic, served with pineapple, peppers, and rice. There are two inexpensive fixed-price menús daily. Incabar is also a good place to hang out, have a beer or coffee, and write post-cards; the back room has comfortable sofas. Breakfast is also served.

Jr. Lima 356. © **054/368-865**. Reservations recommended. Main courses S/12–S/17 ($3.50–$5); menú del día S/15–S/20 ($4–$5.75). DC, MC, V. Daily 9am–10pm.

La Casona ⭐ *(Value* PERUVIAN/INTERNATIONAL   Puno's best and most popular eatery calls itself a "museum-restaurant." In a town like Puno, with relatively few attractions, that's fair enough. La Casona ("big house") has traditional, rather old-style Spanish charm, with lace tablecloths. The three dining rooms are filled with antiques and large religious canvasses, but it retains a decidedly informal appeal. Its specialty is Titicaca lake fish, such as trout and kingfish (*pejerrey*), served La Casona–style, which means with a kitchen-sink preparation of rice, avocado, ham, cheese, hot dog, apple salad, french fries, and mushrooms. Chicken and beef are prepared the same way. If that's a little overwhelming for you, go with the simple trout served with mashed potatoes. In the evening, make a point about asking for the menú del día, which is offered but not advertised; it's a great deal (essentially half price). Service can be a little slow, but there's not much to do in Puno anyway.

Jr. Lima 517. ✆ 054/351-108. Reservations recommended. Main courses S/12–S/32 ($3.50–$9); menú del día S/13 ($3.75). DC, MC, V. Daily 9am–10pm.

Restaurant Don Piero PERUVIAN/INTERNATIONAL   A longtime standard of Pasaje Lima, the pedestrian boulevard at the heart of Puno, Don Piero now seems a little stale. It still cranks out the same standard Peruvian and international fare in large portions as it always has, but the nondescript, midrange place doesn't appeal much to backpackers, and more interesting new competition has cropped up on the street for more discriminating palates. Outside on slow days, bow-tied waiters looking bored halfheartedly appeal to tourists to come in. The menu has barbecued chicken and a long list of Peruvian favorites such as *palta rellena* (avocado stuffed with chicken salad) and *lomo saltado* (beef strips with french fries, onions, and peppers).

Jr. Lima 348-364. ✆ 054/351-766. Reservations not accepted. Main courses S/15–S/34 ($4–$9). DC, V. Daily 11am–10pm.

Restaurant Internacional PERUVIAN/INTERNATIONAL   This austere two-level place has about as much personality as its ho-hum name. But it's actually one of the better restaurants in town and is pretty popular among locals and out-of-towners. Service can be indifferent and ambience is distinctly lacking, but the wide range of midpriced meals, including pasta and pizza in addition to trout and standard preparations of chicken and steak, draws regulars. Breakfast is also served.

Libertad 161 (at the corner of Moquegua). ✆ 054/352-502. Reservations not accepted. Main courses S/12–S/20 ($3.50–$6). DC, V. Daily 8:30am–10:30pm.

INEXPENSIVE

Café Delisse PERUVIAN/VEGETARIAN/BREAKFAST   If you're disappointed that not enough restaurants in Peru's more touristy areas look and feel authentically Peruvian, this is the place for you. Sure it's a bit dumpy, but you wanted authenticity, right? A corner cafe room carved out of someone's house and decorated with textiles draped over the tables, it's an informal, family-operated place that has a surprisingly encyclopedic handwritten menu of mostly vegetarian items. Breakfast options are plentiful, including omelets, pancakes, and lots of mixed juices. Veggie main courses include all manner of Chinese dishes and tofu stuff, and there are also ceviche, pizzas, fish . . . the menu goes on and on, and you wonder how Mom (or whoever's back in the kitchen) can possibly crank out such a variety of items. Ridiculously cheap menús, but pretty basic grub. It's best for breakfast before heading out on Lake Titicaca.

Moquegua 200. No phone. Reservations not accepted. Main courses S/2–S/18 (50¢–$5); menú del día S/5–S/8 ($1.50–$2.25). DC, MC, V. Daily 7am–10pm.

Pizzería El Buho *(Value* PIZZA/ITALIAN   A cozy little place with red-checked tablecloths, a high vaulted ceiling, a wood-burning oven/chimney warming nearby tables, and a lofty perch upstairs, the "Owl Pizzeria" feels like a spot where you'd duck in from the cold at a ski lodge. It's extremely popular with both gringos and locals, and it serves the best pizza in Puno. The menu also lists

Traveling to Bolivia

Plenty of travelers make their way across the Andes to Puno not only to visit Lake Titicaca but also to continue on to Bolivia, which shares a border with Peru. Several travel agencies (see "Organized Tours," earlier in this chapter) in Puno sell packages and bus tickets to Bolivia.

The most common and scenic route is from Puno to La Paz via **Yunguyo** and **Copacabana.** You get dropped off at the border and then pick up a colectivo or taxi shuttle across, where you go through Customs and passport control. If going on your own, you'll need to catch another colectivo to Copacabana, just over a half hour away. The trip to La Paz takes 7 or 8 hours by bus. Buses also go to La Paz via **Desaguadero.** You can also go by a combination of overland travel and hydrofoil or catamaran, a unique but very time-consuming journey (13 hr.).

At the border, visitors get an exit stamp from Peru and a tourist visa (30 days) from Bolivia. Foreigners are commonly tapped for phony departure and entry fees; resist the officials' blatant attempts at corruption.

For more information about Bolivia, pick up a copy of *Frommer's South America.*

a good number of pastas, such as cannelloni, fettuccine, and lasagna, and a handful of thick cream-based soups, but I swear I've never seen anyone have anything other than pizza.

Jr. Lima 347. ✆ 054/363-955. Reservations not accepted. Main courses S/8–S/12 ($2.25–$3.50); pizzas S/8–S/22 ($2.25–$6). DC, V. Daily 4:30–10:30pm.

Rico Pan CAFE/BAKERY   You know what to expect at a small cafe and bakery with a name like "Tasty Bread," and Rico Pan doesn't disappoint. Drop by for inexpensive sandwiches, pastries, and cakes. It also serves very good coffees, including espresso and cappuccino, and is a good spot for breakfast or for stockpiling goodies for boat trips on Titicaca.

Moquegua 330, Puno. ✆ 054/354-179. Reservations not accepted. Main courses S/4–S/10 ($1–$3). No credit cards. Daily 7am–11pm.

PUNO AFTER DARK

There's not a whole lot happening in Puno after dark; the city's nightlife consists of a handful of bars and discos strung along the pedestrian mall, Jirón Lima. **Positive Vibrations** (no. 345) and **Apu Salcantay** (no. 425) are among the bars worth a stop for some decent music and hot drinks to warm up. **La Hostería** (no. 501) and **Ekeko's** (no. 355) often have live bands, and the latter has a large-screen TV showing soccer or videos, and a small dance floor. **Kusillo's Pub,** Libertad 259 (✆ 054/351-301), has a nightly happy hour and reggae, jazz, and blues, as well as occasional folklore shows.

2 Arequipa ★★

1,020km (632 miles) S of Lima; 521km (323 miles) S of Cusco; 297km (184 miles) SW of Puno

The southern city of Arequipa, the second largest in Peru, may be the most handsome in the country. Founded in 1540, it retains an elegant historic center constructed almost entirely of *sillar* (a porous, white volcanic stone), which gives the city its distinctive look and the nickname *la ciudad blanca,* or the white city. Colonial churches and the sumptuous Santa Catalina convent gleam beneath palm trees and a brilliant sun. Ringing the city are three delightfully named snowcapped volcanic peaks: El Misti, Chachani, and Pichu Pichu, all of which hover around 6,000m (20,000 ft.).

Arequipa has emerged as a favorite of outdoors enthusiasts who come to climb volcanoes, raft on rivers, trek through the valleys, and above all, head out to Colca Canyon—twice as deep as the Grand Canyon and the best place in South America to see giant condors, with their legendary wingspan, soar overhead. Suiting its reputation as an outdoor paradise, Arequipa has weather that is Southern California–perfect: more than 300 days a year of sunshine, huge blue skies, and low humidity. Arequipa looks very much the part of desert oasis.

The commercial capital of the south, Arequipa not only looks but also feels very different from the rest of Peru. Arequipeños have earned a reputation as aloof and distrusting of centralized power in Lima. Relatively wealthy and home to prominent intellectuals, politicians, and industrialists, Arequipa has a haughty air about it—at least to many Peruvians who hail from less distinguished places.

As beautiful and confident as it is, Arequipa has not escaped disaster. The latest devastating earthquake (which registered 8.1 on the Richter scale) struck the city, and other points farther south, in June 2001. Though international reports painted a picture of a city that had caved in on itself, thankfully, that wasn't the case. Poorly constructed housing in some residential districts was destroyed, but the colonial core of the city survived intact. The major structure damaged, the cathedral on the Plaza de Armas, is already undergoing repair, its asymmetry of towers no doubt a serious aesthetic offense in this stately city.

ESSENTIALS
GETTING THERE
BY PLANE   There are daily flights to Arequipa from Lima, Juliaca, and Cusco on **Aero Continente** (© 01/242-4242; www.aerocontinente.com), **LanPeru** (© 01/213-8200; www.lanperu.com), and **TANS** (© 01/213-6000; www.tansperu.com.pe). Flights from Lima and Cusco range from $59 to $79 one-way.

Aeropuerto Rodríquez Ballón (© 054/443-464 or 054/443-458) is about 7km (4 miles) northwest of the city. From the airport to downtown hotels, transportation is by taxi ($3–$5) or shared colectivo service (about $2 per person).

BY BUS   The main **Terminal Terrestre** is about 4km (2 miles) from downtown Arequipa; nearby is a newer station, **Nuevo Terrapuerto.** Most long-distance buses leave from the Nuevo Terrapuerto. A huge number of bus companies travel in and out of Peru's second city from across the country. From Lima (a 16-hr. ride), recommended companies include **Ormeño** (© 01/472-1710), **Cruz del Sur** (© 01/428-2570), **Civa** (© 01/428-5649), and **Oltursa** (© 01/476-9724). For service from Puno (10–12 hr.) and Juliaca, contact **Cruz del Sur** (© 054/622-626), **Civa** (© 054/426-563) and **Julsa** (© 054/331-952). **Ormeño** travels to Arequipa from Puno (Av. Titicaca 318, © 054/352-321) as well as Cusco (Plaza Tupac Amaru 114, © 084/228-712). Other options from Cusco (12–15 hr.) are **Civa** (© 084/812-813) and **Cruz del Sur** (© 084/233-383). From Chivay/Colca Canyon (3–4 hr.), call **Reyna** (© 054/426-549) and **Cristo Rey** (© 054/213-094).

BY TRAIN   The Arequipa rail station is 8 blocks south of the city center, at Av. Tacna y Arica 201 (© **054/215-640**). The PeruRail ticket office is open

Monday through Friday from 6:30 to 10:30am and 2 to 6pm, and Saturday and Sunday from 8am to noon and 3 to 6pm.

You can travel by train to Arequipa from Puno/Juliaca or Cusco (which requires a 1-night stopover in Puno), but not from Lima. Trains from Puno, which are less frequent and more expensive than buses, are part of the Blue Sky (Southern) PeruRail route. Service from Puno to Arequipa is Sunday (departing at 7am, arriving at 5pm), Monday (departing at 9:30am, arriving at 7:30pm), and Thursday (departing at 7am, arriving at 5:30pm). Trains stop near Colca Canyon en route. Inka-class seats cost $30, one-way; Tourist class (local), $8.50. In high season, reserve your tickets at least 2 days in advance and/or purchase them the day before traveling; it may be simpler and more convenient to purchase them directly from a travel agent.

Beware: On the trains themselves, and especially at rail stations, travelers are advised to pay very close attention to their belongings, even going so far as to lock them to luggage racks. The route between Arequipa and Puno has earned a reputation for thieves; more exclusive and safer Inka-class seats are recommended.

VISITOR INFORMATION

There's a **tourist information booth** at the Aeropuerto Rodríquez Ballón (© 054/444-564), open Monday through Friday from 9am to 4pm. There's also a very helpful office on the Plaza de Armas across from the cathedral at Portal de la Municipalidad 112 (© 054/211-021); it's open daily from 8am to 6pm. You can also get information and maps from the **tourist police,** Jerusalén 315 at the corner of Ugarte (© 054/239-888).

FAST FACTS You'll find ATMs located in the courtyards of the historic Casa Ricketts at San Francisco 108, now the offices of **Banco Continental.** Other banks in the historic center include **Banco Latino** at San Juan de Dios 112, and **Banco de Crédito** at General Morán 101. Money-changers can generally be found waving calculators and stacks of dollars on the Plaza de Armas and major streets leading off the main square. There are several casas de cambio near the Plaza de Armas; one is **Arequipa Inversiones,** Jerusalén 109.

The general emergency number in Arequipa is © 105. If you need the police, call the **Policía Nacional** (national police) at © 054/254-020, or **Policía de Turismo** (tourist police) at © 054/239-888. For fire emergencies, call © 116. If you need medical attention, go to **Clínica Arequipa,** Avenida Bolognesi at Puente Grau (© 054/253-416), which has good service and English-speaking doctors. You can also try **Hospital General,** Peral s/n (© 054/231-818), and **Hospital Regional Honorio Delgado,** Av. Carrión s/n, a kilometer south of the Plaza de Armas (© 054/238-465).

Arequipa has plenty of Internet cabinas. Most are open daily from 8am to 10pm, charge S/2 per hour, and have Net2Phone or other programs that allow very cheap Web-based international phone calls. Two of the cheapest and fastest cabinas are **La Red,** Jerusalén 306B (© 054/286-700) and **TravelNet,** Jerusalén 218 (© 054/205-548). Only slightly more expensive and open a bit later, **Catedral Internet** is on the pedestrian mall just behind the cathedral (© 054/220-622).

The main **post office** is located at Moral 118 (© 054/215-246); it's open Monday through Saturday from 8am to 8pm, and Sunday from 9am to 2pm. A **DHL** office is located at Santa Catalina 115 (© 054/220-045); it's open Monday through Friday from 8:30am to 7:30pm, and Saturday from 9am to noon. **Telefónica del Perú** offices are located at Alvarez Thomas 209 (© 054/281-112)

(Tips A Note About Safety

Arequipa has earned a reputation as one of Peru's more unsafe cities, at least in terms of pickpocketing, though locals continue to talk about tourist robberies and even "strangle muggings." I found some citizens to be quite alarmist. Several people were outspoken about what you should carry on your person (nothing of value, including a camera) and how to conduct yourself (be on guard at all times), even in the daytime, when plenty of police patrol the streets in the old quarter. I've never had a problem in Arequipa, but I do think that late at night, you should be especially cautious when exiting bars and restaurants in the historic center, and you should leave your daypack and other unnecessary belongings in your hotel. Some taxi drivers in Arequipa also warn about their colleagues who set tourists up for ambushes. They suggest either calling for a cab or getting into taxis with older drivers because most of the crimes have been perpetrated by younger drivers.

---

and Av. Los Arces 200B, in the Cayma district (© **054/252-020**). They're open Monday through Friday from 8:30am to 6pm, and Saturday from 9am to 1pm.

GETTING AROUND

Arequipa is compact, and most of its top attractions can easily be seen on foot and with an occasional taxi. The historic center is built around the stately Plaza de Armas, marked by the cathedral on the north flank and porticoed buildings on the other three sides. Most sites of visitor interest, including most hotels and restaurants, are found in the blocks immediately north of the plaza. A few blocks west of the main square is the Río Chili and, beyond it, the residential neighborhood Yanahuara and La Recoleta monastery. Two bridges, Puente Grau and Puente Bolognesi, lead from the center to these areas.

BY TAXI   Taxis are inexpensive and plentiful, easily hailed on the street, and best used at night. Most trips in town cost no more than S/3 (75¢). To call a taxi at night, try **Taxi Seguro** (© 054/450-250), **Taxi Sur** (© 054/465-656), **Master Taxi** (© 054/220-505), or **Ideal Taxi** (© 054/288-888).

BY CAR   A car isn't necessary in Arequipa unless you wish to explore the countryside, especially Colca and/or Cotahuasi canyons, independently. Try **Lucava Rent-a-Car,** Aeropuerto Rodríquez Ballón (© 054/650-565) and Centro Comercial Cayma no. 10 (© 054/663-378); and **Avis,** Aeropuerto Rodríquez Ballón (© 054/443-576), and Palacio Viejo 214 (© 054/282-519).

WHAT TO SEE & DO
PLAZA DE ARMAS ℛ

Arequipa's grand Plaza de Armas, an elegant and symmetrical square of gardens and a central fountain lined by arcaded buildings on three sides, is the focus of urban life. It is one of the loveliest main squares in Peru, though its profile suffered considerable damage when the great earthquake of 2001 felled one of the cathedral's two towers and whittled the other to a delicate pedestal. The 17th-century neoclassical **Catedral,** previously devastated by fire and other earthquakes, is likely to remain closed for several years to repair the damage (it was almost entirely enveloped by wooden scaffolding in late 2001), though it remains an impressive sight, occupying one entire side of the main square.

What to See & Do in Arequipa

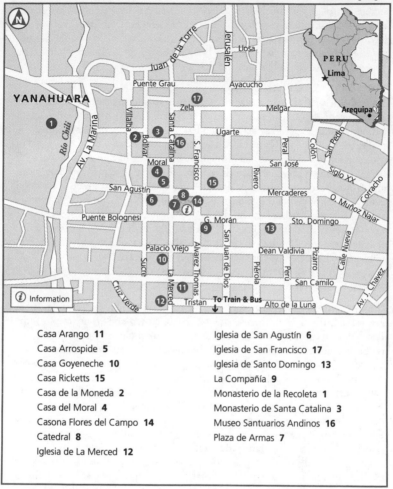

Casa Arango **11**
Casa Arrospide **5**
Casa Goyeneche **10**
Casa Ricketts **15**
Casa de la Moneda **2**
Casa del Moral **4**
Casona Flores del Campo **14**
Catedral **8**
Iglesia de La Merced **12**

Iglesia de San Agustín **6**
Iglesia de San Francisco **17**
Iglesia de Santo Domingo **13**
La Compañía **9**
Monasterio de la Recoleta **1**
Monasterio de Santa Catalina **3**
Museo Santuarios Andinos **16**
Plaza de Armas **7**

    La Compañía ⊛, just off the plaza at the corner of San Francisco and Morán, opposite the cathedral, is a splendid 17th-century Jesuit church with an elaborate (Plateresque) facade carved of sillar stone. The magnificent portal, one of the finest in Peru, shows the end date of the church's construction, 1698, more than a century after work began on it. The interior holds a handsome carved-cedar main altar, bathed in gold leaf, and two impressive chapels: the Capilla de San Ignacio, which has a remarkable painted cupola, and the Capilla Real, or Royal Chapel. Painted murals in the sacristy feature a jungle motif in brilliant colors. Next door to the church are the stately Jesuit cloisters, of stark sillar construction, now housing upscale boutiques (enter on Calle Morán). Climb to the top for good views of the city's rooftops and distant volcanoes. The church is open Monday through Saturday from 9am to noon and 3 to 7pm; admission is free.

    On the east side of the plaza at Portal de Flores 136 is the **Casona Flores del Campo** (✆ **054/244-150**), the oldest house in Arequipa. Begun in the late 1500s but not finished until 1779, today it is in deplorable condition, having suffered through earthquakes and a lack of funds that have left it barely standing. If you don't mind crawling through rubble, enter at your own risk to see a few interesting period details, such as the double-arched patio and leather ties made from llama skin, still holding beams together after all these years. The house is open to the public daily from 10am to 5pm.

MORE ATTRACTIONS

Casa del Moral 🏛 An extraordinary mestizo baroque mansion, built at the beginning of the 18th century by a Spanish knight and nicely restored with period detail in 1994, Casa del Moral offers one of the best windows onto colonial times in Arequipa. Named for an ancient mulberry tree—the *moral* found in the courtyard—the home is also distinguished by a magnificent stone portal with heraldic emblems carved in sillar. Handsome furnishings, carved wooden doors, and Cusco School oil paintings decorate large salons, built around a beautiful courtyard, the largest of the colonial residences in the city. Look for 17th-century maps that depict the borders and shapes of countries quite differently from their usual representations today. A second courtyard, painted cobalt blue, was used as the summer patio. Climb to the rooftop for a great view of Arequipa and the surrounding volcanoes. Visits are by guided tour (at no extra cost).

Calle Moral 318 (at Bolívar). ℂ 054/210-084. Admission S/5 ($1.50) adults, S/3 (75¢) students. Mon–Sat 9am–5pm; Sun 9am–1pm.

Monasterio de la Recoleta 🏛 A 10-minute walk from the Plaza de Armas across the Chili River, distinguished by its tall brick-red-and-white steeple, is the Recoleta convent museum. Founded in 1648 and rebuilt after earthquakes, the peaceful Franciscan convent contains impressive cloisters with sillar columns and lovely gardens; today, just four of the original seven remain. The convent museum includes several collections. In one room is a collection of pre-Inca culture artifacts, including funereal masks, textiles, and totems; in another are mummies and a series of paintings of the 12 Inca emperors. At the rear of the convent is a small Amazonian museum, stocked with curious items collected by Franciscan missionaries in the Amazon basin. The missionaries were understandably fascinated by prehistoric-looking fish, crocodiles, piranhas, and the clothing of indigenous communities. These souvenirs pose an interesting contrast to the Dominicans' fine library containing some 20,000 volumes, including rare published texts from the 15th century. Guides (tip basis) are available for 1-hour tours in English, Spanish, and French.

Recoleta 117. ℂ 054/270-966. Admission S/5 ($1.50) adults, S/3 (75¢) students, free for seniors. Mon–Sat 9am–noon and 3–5pm.

Tips Photo Op

One of the best views in Arequipa is from the *mirador* (lookout point) on Avenida del Ejército, in the tranquil suburb of Yanahuara just across Puente Grau. Next to a small plaza, a series of sillar stone arches beautifully frames the snowy peak of El Misti. Across from the mirador is the small church of Yanahuara, also built of sillar in the mid–18th century and featuring a splendid baroque carved facade and bell tower. A good way to visit the mirador is to combine it with lunch at Sol de Mayo (p. 284), just a few blocks south.

House Tour: Arequipa's Colonial Mansions

Arequipa possesses one of the most attractive and harmonious colonial nuclei in Peru. Several extraordinary seigniorial houses were constructed in white sillar stone. They are predominantly flat-roofed, single-story structures, a construction style that has helped them withstand the effects of frequent earthquakes that would have toppled less-solid buildings. Most of these houses have attractive, though small, interior patios and elaborately carved facades. Best equipped for visitors is the recently restored **Casa del Moral** (p. 274), but several others are worth a look, especially if you have an interest in colonial architecture.

Just off the main square at San Francisco 108, **Casa Ricketts** (also called Casa Tristán del Pozo), a former seminary and today the offices of Banco Continental, is one of the finest colonial homes in Arequipa. Built in the 1730s, its beautiful portal, perhaps Arequipa's finest expression of colonial civil architecture, has delicate representations of the life of Jesus. Inside are two large, beautiful courtyards, with gargoyle drainage pipes.

On the other side of the cathedral at the corner of Santa Catalina 101 at San Agustín, **Casa Arróspide** (also called Casa Iriberry), from the late 18th century, is one of the most distinguished sillar mansions in the city. Now the Cultural Center of San Agustín University (© **054/204-482**), its several *salas* host temporary exhibits of contemporary art and photography; you'll also find an art shop and nice little cafe with a terrace and great views over the top of the cathedral.

Other colonial houses of interest include **Casa Arango,** a squat and eclectic 17th-century home located on Consuelo at La Merced; **Casa Goyeneche,** La Merced 201, today the offices of Banco de Reserva; and **Casa de la Moneda,** Ugarte at Villaba.

Monasterio de Santa Catalina ★★★   Arequipa's stellar and serene Convent of Santa Catalina, founded in 1579 under the Dominican order, is the most important and impressive religious monument in Peru. Santa Catalina is not just another church complex; it is more like a small, labyrinthine village, with narrow cobblestone streets, plant-lined passageways, and pretty plazas, fountains, chapels, and cloisters. Tall, thick walls, painted sunburned orange, faded blue, and brick red, hide dozens of small cells where more than 200 sequestered nuns once lived. Built in 1569, the convent remained a mysterious world unto itself until 1970, when local authorities forced the sisters to install modern infrastructure, a requirement that led to opening the convent for tourism. Today, only 30 cloistered nuns remain, out of sight of the hundreds of tourists who arrive daily to explore the huge and curious complex.

Santa Catalina feels like a small village in Andalusia, Spain, with its predominantly *mudéjar* (Moorish-Christian) architecture, intense sunlight and shadows, and streets named for Spanish cities. In all, it contains three cloisters, six streets, 80 housing units, a square, an art gallery, and a cemetery. Though the nuns entered the convent having taken vows of poverty, they lived in relative luxury, having paid a

The Discovery of Juanita, the Ampato Maiden

The mummy of the teenage Inca maiden now christened Juanita is one of the most important archaeological finds of the last few decades in the Americas. The first frozen female found from the pre-Columbian era in the Andes, her body, packed in ice and thus not desiccated like most mummies, preserved a wealth of information about her culture and life.

Juanita was discovered at the summit of the Ampato volcano in September 1995 by the American anthropologist Dr. Johan Reinhard, the *National Geographic* explorer-in-residence. She immediately became news around the world. Reinhard, who had spent 2 decades looking for clues in the volcanoes of the western Andes near Arequipa, was working on a project co-sponsored by Arequipa's Catholic University of Santa María and was accompanied by Carlos Zárate, a locally famous mountaineer who for years has run one of the best mountain-climbing-expedition tour companies in Peru. Juanita had been remarkably preserved in ice for more than 500 years, but hot ashes from the eruption of the nearby Mount Sabancaya volcano melted the snowcap on Ampato and collapsed the summit ridge, exposing what had been hidden for centuries. Reinhard and Zárate at first saw only the feathers of a ceremonial Inca headdress. It took the two men 2 days to descend the peak with the 80-pound mummy, fighting against time to conserve her frozen body and get her back to Arequipa and the Catholic University labs.

Juanita was selected by Inca priests to be sacrificed as an appeasement to Ampato, whose dominion was water supply and harvests. The offering was almost certainly a desperate plea to stave off drought and starvation. Reinhard and his team later discovered two additional mummies, a girl and a boy, several thousand feet below the summit—probably companion sacrifices leading to the more important sacrifice of the princess on Ampato's summit.

The mummy's incredibly well-preserved corpse allows scientists to examine her skin, hair, blood, internal organs, and even the contents of her stomach. Her DNA makeup is being studied. Juanita was dressed in

dowry to live the monastic life amid servants (who outnumbered the nuns), well-equipped kitchens, and art collections. Today, the convent has been nicely restored, though it retains a rustic appeal. Visitors are advised to wait for an informative guided tour (in English and other languages), though it's also fun just to wander around. Among the convent's highlights are the Orange Tree Cloister, with mural paintings over the arches; Calle Toledo, a long boulevard with a communal *lavandería* at its end, where the sisters washed their clothes in halved earthenware jugs; the 17th-century kitchen with charred walls; and the rooms belonging to Sor Ana, a 17th-century nun at the convent who was beatified by Pope John Paul II and is on her way to becoming a saint. Visitors can enter the choir room of the church, but it's difficult to get a good look at the main chapel and its marvelous painted cupola. To see the church, slip in during early morning Mass (daily at 7:30am); the cloistered nuns remain secluded behind a wooden grille.

Santa Catalina 301. © 054/229-798. Admission S/15 ($4.25). Daily 9am–5pm (last entry 4pm).

superior textiles from Cusco, clues to her probable nobility. Incredibly important was the fact that the ceremonial site was undisturbed, with all ritual elements in place, allowing anthropologists to essentially recreate the ceremony.

The peak of Apu Ampato was sacred to the Incas, and only priests were allowed to ascend to it. It is most extraordinary that the Incas were able to climb 6,000m (20,000-ft.) peaks without the assistance of oxygen or other modern climbing equipment. Juanita's transfer and sacrifice there, at the age of 13 or 14, was part of an elaborate ritual. Having first met with the Inca emperor in Cusco, she must have known her fate: an imminent journey to meet the mountain gods so revered by the Incas. Sacrifice was the greatest honor bestowed upon an individual. Led up the frozen summit by priests, in sandals and surely exhausted, she was probably made to fast and may have been given drugs or an intoxicating beverage before she was killed by a swift blow to her right temple. Scientists at Johns Hopkins University in Baltimore examined the mummy with a CT scan that revealed a crack in the skull, just above the right eye, and internal bleeding.

More than 100 sacred Inca ceremonial sites have been found on dozens of Andes peaks, though no mummies have been uncovered in the frozen condition of Juanita. Anthropologists believe that there may be hundreds of Inca children entombed in ice graves on the highest peaks in South America from central Chile to southern Peru. The Incas believed that they could approach Inti, the sun god, by ascending the highest summits of the Andes. The mountain deities they believed to live there were considered protectors of the Inca people. Sacrifices were frequently responses to cataclysmic events: earthquakes, eclipses, and droughts.

Juanita and many of the ritualistic elements found at the ceremonial site are now exhibited at the Museo Santuarios Andinos (see below). More information about the Mount Ampato expedition can be found in the June 1996 edition of *National Geographic*.

Museo Santuarios Andinos ⭐⭐⭐   The Museum of Andean Sanctuaries has a number of fascinating exhibits, including mummies and artifacts from the Inca Empire, but it is dominated by one small girl: Juanita, the Ice Maiden of Ampato. The victim of a ritualistic sacrifice by Inca priests high on the volcano Mount Ampato and buried in ice at more than 6,000m (20,000 ft.), "Juanita" was discovered in almost perfect condition in 1995 after the eruption of a volcano melted ice on the peak. Juanita's remarkable preservation has allowed researchers to gain great insights into Inca culture by analyzing her DNA. Today, she is kept in a glass-walled freezer chamber here (as she has been since 1998), less a mummy than a frozen body nearly 600 years old. Displayed nearby are some of the superb doll offerings and burial items found alongside the corpse. Guided visits are mandatory.

Santa Catalina 210. © 054/200-345. Admission S/15 ($4.25) adults, S/5 ($1.50) students, free for seniors. Mon–Sat 9am–6pm; Sun 9am–3pm.

SHOPPING

Arequipa is perhaps the number-one spot in Peru—better even than Cusco and Lima—to shop for top-quality baby alpaca, vicuña, and woolen goods. Though many items are considerably more expensive than the lesser-quality goods sold in other parts of Peru, in Arequipa you'll find nicer designs and export-quality knit sweaters, shawls, blankets, and scarves. In many parts of Peru, what is sold as alpaca or baby alpaca is often a mix of alpaca and synthetics. Many of the finest pure alpaca woven items in Peru come from Arequipa. The city also produces very nice leather goods, and there are several excellent antiques shops featuring colonial pieces and even older items (remember, though, that these antiques cannot legally be exported from Peru; see "Entry Requirements & Customs," in chapter 2, for regulations).

ALPACA GOODS   Three general areas are particularly good for alpaca items. One is the **cloisters** next to La Compañía church (p. 273), where you'll find several alpaca boutiques and outlets. Another good place is **Pasaje Catedral,** the pedestrian mall just behind the cathedral, and a third is **Calle Santa Catalina.** Shops with fine alpaca items include **Millma's Baby Alpaca,** Pasaje Catedral 177 (© 054/205-134); **Baby Alpaca Boutique,** Santa Catalina 208 (© 054/206-716); **Anselmo's Souvenirs,** Pasaje Catedral 119 (no phone); and an outlet store of the chain **Alpaca 111,** Calle Zela 212 (© 054/223-238).

ANTIQUES   Calle Santa Catalina and nearby streets have several antiques shops. I found lots of items I wished I could have taken home at the following three stores: **Curiosidades,** Zela 207 (© 054/952-986); **Alvaro Valdivia Montoya's** two shops at Santa Catalina 204 and Santa Catalina 217 (© 054/229-103); and **Arte Colonial,** Santa Catalina 312 (© 054/214-887).

BOOKS   A good bookstore with art books and English-language paperbacks is **Libería El Lector,** San Francisco 221 (no phone).

HANDICRAFTS   There is a general handicrafts market (*mercado de artesanía*) with dozens of stalls in the old town jail, next door to the Plazuela de San Francisco (between Zela and Puente Grau). For handmade leather goods, stroll along Puente Bolognesi, which leads west from the Plaza de Armas, and you'll find numerous small stores with handbags, shoes, and other items.

WHERE TO STAY

Arequipa has an ample roster of hotels and *hostales* (inns) at all levels. A number of them occupy historic houses in the old quarter, within very easy walking distance of major sights, restaurants, and bars. Even budget travelers can do very well in Arequipa—it's a very good place for a significant step up in comfort and style (but not price) from the usual backpacker dregs. The area north of the

Where to Stay & Dine in Arequipa

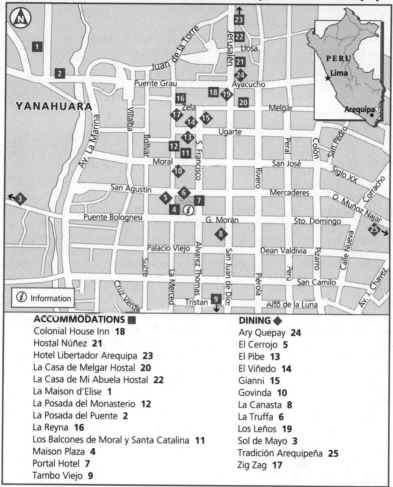

ACCOMMODATIONS ■
Colonial House Inn **18**
Hostal Núñez **21**
Hotel Libertador Arequipa **23**
La Casa de Melgar Hostal **20**
La Casa de Mi Abuela Hostal **22**
La Maison d'Elise **1**
La Posada del Monasterio **12**
La Posada del Puente **2**
La Reyna **16**
Los Balcones de Moral y Santa Catalina **11**
Maison Plaza **4**
Portal Hotel **7**
Tambo Viejo **9**

DINING ◆
Ary Quepay **24**
El Cerrojo **5**
El Pibe **13**
El Viñedo **14**
Gianni **15**
Govinda **10**
La Canasta **8**
La Truffa **6**
Los Leños **19**
Sol de Mayo **3**
Tradición Arequipeña **25**
Zig Zag **17**

Plaza de Armas is nicer, less chaotic, and less commercial than the streets south of the square.

EXPENSIVE

El Lago Resort ⚐ The only problem with this beautiful country resort hotel is that it's out in the country, and too far removed from the historic center of Arequipa for most people's tastes. In the area out by the old windmill in Sabandía, guests have to hop a taxi or a 45-minute bus each time to town. If you've just come from Lima, though, and need a break, this former Holiday Inn is perfect for some real R & R. Set on a small man-made lake (*el lago*) amid farm fields with fantastic views of the gentle countryside and amenities such as a large pool, Jacuzzi, fireplaces, and horseback riding, it's a super place to kick back. The rooms are large and comfortable, standard upscale accommodations, with king-size beds and large bathrooms. It has a very good restaurant on the premises, which draws lots of Arequipeños, and service is very professional. The resort is family-owned; the sons run the Cusipata travel agency and organize excellent white-water-rafting and trekking trips.

Camino al Molino s/n, Sabandía, Arequipa. © **054/448-383.** Fax 054/448-344. ellagoresort@terra.com.pe. 52 units. $97 double; $144 suite; $250 bungalow. Rates include taxes, continental breakfast, and airport transfer. AE, DC, MC, V. **Amenities:** Restaurant; bar; large outdoor pool; Jacuzzi; concierge; 24-hr. room service; laundry service. *In room:* A/C, TV, minibar, safe.

Hotel Libertador Arequipa *★★* *(Kids)* Arequipa's swankest hotel within reach of the historic center is in this handsome, sprawling 1940s colonial-style building. In the midst of quiet Selva Alegre, the largest park in Arequipa, the midsize hotel, recently renovated and part of a small upmarket Peruvian chain, is about a 15-minute walk from the main square. It maintains a colonial theme throughout, with soaring ceilings, historical murals, and older-style dark-wood period furnishings in expansive, elegantly appointed rooms. Accommodations, equipped with marble bathrooms, are about as large as you're likely to find. The hotel has a lovely, large outdoor pool among nice gardens and tall palm trees. Families will appreciate the outdoor recreation and game area for children.

Plaza Bolívar, Selva Alegre, Arequipa. © **054/215-110.** Fax 054/241-933. www.libertador.com.pe. 88 units. $115 deluxe double; $174 suite. Rates include taxes. AE, DC, MC, V. **Amenities:** 2 restaurants; bar; large outdoor pool; fitness center; Jacuzzi; sauna; concierge; 24-hr. room service; laundry service. *In room:* A/C, TV, minibar, safe.

La Maison d' Elise *★* *(Finds)* This small gem of a hotel is hidden behind a nondescript, rather unappealing facade. Across from the park on the other side of Puente Grau, just beyond the historic center, this 10-year-old hotel is like a small Mediterranean village. Ochre and white villas are clustered around courtyards ripe with cactus and colorful flowering plants. Double rooms are very large and comfortably furnished; matrimonial suites have a lower-level sitting room. There are also apartments with private terraces. The hotel has a small pool with a rock waterfall, and a notable and nicely decorated restaurant. Deals are sometimes available. The hotel is less luxurious overall than the Libertador (see above), but it's got a quirkier charm and is much more affordable.

Av. Bolognesi 104, Yanahuara, Arequipa. © **054/256-185.** Fax 054/271-935. mdelisehotel@terra.com.pe. 88 units. $74 double; $82–$100 suite. Rates include taxes. AE, DC, MC, V. **Amenities:** 2 restaurants; bar; swimming pool, room service; laundry service. *In room:* A/C, TV, safe.

La Posada del Puente *★* Tucked beneath the overpass (Puente Grau) leading from Arequipa's historic center to the countryside, this curious little hotel sports fabulous gardens, where llamas graze near the banks of the Río Chili, and terrific views of the El Misti volcano in the distance. The inn's modern salmon-colored and whitewashed Mediterranean look, complete with an ornate plaza, sculpted fountain and circular staircase leading down to the restaurant, are a little surprising to find beneath a bridge. Rooms are small and outfitted in modern, feminine pastel-and-white furnishings, with brown tiled bathrooms and arched ceilings. All have small balconies or terraces to take advantage of the views. Suites are huge and very posh, more tastefully decorated in warm woods, and equipped with huge Trinitron TVs.

At the corner Puente Grau at Av. Bolognesi 101, Arequipa. © **054/253-132.** Fax 054/253-576. www.posadadelpuente.com. 24 units. $70 deluxe double; $105–$179 suite. Rates include taxes. AE, DC, MC, V. **Amenities:** Restaurant; bar; room service; laundry service. *In room:* A/C, TV, minibar, safe.

Portal Hotel *★* The best thing about this large hotel right on the Plaza de Armas is its location (unless you've got a room facing the square and need total quiet). While it's perfectly located to allow you to see and do everything in Arequipa with ease, it's an uncomfortable step back into the 1970s. The place looks very "casino," with brown and orange furnishings, Las Vegas–style lights, and mirrors. The lobby opens to game rooms with slot machines on either side, and there's a karaoke disco in-house that's called—I swear—"Dady-O." The staff isn't terribly friendly, but the rooms are comfortable enough if you need a retro brown fix; some have nice little terraces under the porticoes with plaza views. There's also a nice little rooftop pool with flower beds.

Portal de Flores 116, Plaza de Armas, Arequipa. ℂ 054/215-530. Fax 054/234-374. reserva@portalhotel. com.pe. 51 units. $80 standard double; $93 deluxe double; $115 presidential suite. Rates include taxes. AE, DC, MC, V. **Amenities:** 2 restaurants; bar; outdoor rooftop pool; sauna; concierge; room service; laundry service; disco. *In room:* A/C, TV, minibar, safe.

MODERATE

La Casa de Melgar Hostal 🌟🌟 *(Finds* A spectacular colonial house made of white sillar, this charming, small hotel is one of the nicest in Peru and one of the best values. Just 3 blocks from the Plaza de Armas, the great and lovingly restored 18th-century mansion—the former residence of the Bishop of Arequipa—has massive thick walls, three courtyards, and gardens, and is decorated in original colonial colors, rich brick red and blue. The ample rooms have good beds. Some rooms—especially those on the ground floor that have high vaulted brick ceilings—exude colonial character; if the hotel isn't full, ask to see a couple. The staff is very friendly. Breakfast is served in the neat little cafe next door in one of the courtyards. Advance reservations are a must in high season.

Melgar 108, Cercado, Arequipa. ℂ and fax **054/222-459.** lacasademelgar@terra.com.pe. 23 units. $35–$45 double. Rates include taxes and breakfast. V. **Amenities:** Restaurant; bar; laundry service; communal TV room; safety deposit boxes.

La Casa de Mi Abuela Hostal 🌟 One of the friendliest and best-run small hotels in Peru, "my grandmother's house" is tucked behind a security gate but welcomes everyone with open arms and an easygoing atmosphere. An organic place that has grown from a tiny B&B operation into a very popular 50-room hotel, it is still family-run. Today, it's a self-contained tourism complex and miniresort, with a restaurant, live-music peña bar, free (but limited) Internet access, book exchange, travel agency, and beautiful, relaxing gardens with views of El Misti. Some rooms have roof terraces, others balconies. Many rooms are plainly decorated and cramped, but the hostal is still a very good deal given the level of services, facilities, and security. The hostal is about a 10-minute walk (6 blocks) north of the main square; it's often filled, so make advance reservations. Nice breakfasts in the garden (extra charge).

Jerusalén 606, Cercado, Arequipa. ℂ **054/241-206.** Fax 054/242-761. 50 units. $44 double. Rate includes taxes. DC, MC, V. **Amenities:** Restaurant; bar; pool; game room; laundry service; travel agency; library. *In room:* TV, minibar, safe.

La Posada del Monasterio From the outside and a few steps into the entrance, this looks like a real winner. It's set within gorgeous 17th-century colonial digs across the street from the Monasterio de Santa Catalina, and you'd expect to find great antiques in rooms full of period character. Unfortunately, the rooms are a disappointment, rather cheaply done with modern, flowery decor. They're perfectly fine if you don't feel misled by the luxurious courtyard and art-filled lobby. There's a nice rooftop terrace with views overlooking Santa Catalina, good service, and plenty of amenities. The hotel seems to draw a disproportionate number of Italians and other Europeans.

Santa Catalina 300, Arequipa. ℂ **054/247-353.** Fax 054/283-076. 26 units. $57 double. Rate includes taxes, breakfast, and airport transfer. MC, V. **Amenities:** Restaurant; bar; safety deposit boxes. *In room:* TV, minibar.

Maison Plaza This small, modest, and quirky hotel has an enviable location overlooking the Plaza de Armas. The lobby, up a flight of stairs, is a surprise with an impressive stone vaulted ceiling and religious art. Rooms are clean and pleasant, carpeted but otherwise unadorned, and the beds are just okay. Single rooms are tiny. The breakfasts are pretty substantial.

Portal de San Agustín 143, Arequipa. ℂ 054/218-929. Fax 054/218-931. arequipa@planet.com.pe. 17 units. $35 double. Rate includes taxes, breakfast buffet, and airport transfer. MC, V. **Amenities:** Restaurant; safety deposit boxes. *In room:* TV, minibar.

INEXPENSIVE

Colonial House Inn *(Finds* A rambling 200-year-old house—continually owned by the same family—in the old quarter, this friendly, eclectic inn is perfect for backpackers or budget travelers in search of some local flavor. It has a great rooftop terrace with good views; nice large rooms, all with private bathroom; a comfortable covered patio; a library and book exchange; and good breakfasts in a little cafe area.

Puente Grau 114, Arequipa. ℂ and fax 054/223-533. casos@ec-red.com. 7 units. $12 double. Rate includes taxes. No credit cards. **Amenities:** Restaurant; laundry service; safety deposit boxes.

Hostal Núñez *(Value* This pretty, colonial inn is very attractive and affordable—and thus popular. Friendly and family-owned, it's on a street in the old quarter loaded with travel agencies. Rooms are ample and have hardwood floors and cable TV, and they're decorated with actual color schemes, a rarity at these prices. Public rooms are very congenial and loaded with plants. A huge rooftop terrace has excellent views of the city, and there are other unusual amenities at this level: a salon on-site, a city tour desk, and laundry service. Breakfast on the terrace is a great perk. Couples or friends sharing a room are best off: Singles are pretty small.

Jerusalén 528, Arequipa. ℂ and fax 054/218-648. http://usuarios.tripod.es/Hostal_Nunez. 7 units. S/60 ($17) double with private bathroom. Rate includes taxes. No credit cards. **Amenities:** Cafeteria; salon; laundry service; safety deposit boxes. *In room:* TV.

La Reyna *(Value* One of the most popular backpacker budget inns in town, La Reyna is smack in the middle of the historic center, just a block from the famed Santa Catalina monastery and paces away from plenty of bars and restaurants. The hostal's many rooms feed off a labyrinth of narrow staircases that climb up three floors to a roof terrace, a popular spot to hang out and write postcards and plan hiking expeditions, or to veg out and stargaze late at night. There are simple, rock-bottom dormitory rooms for zero-budget travelers and a couple of rooftop casitas that, though basic in their decoration, have private bathrooms and their own terraces with awesome views of the mountains and the monastery below—something akin to backpacker penthouse suites. (No. 20 is worth reserving if you can.) The hostal, though a little haphazardly run, organizes lots of canyon treks and volcano-climbing tours, and even offers Spanish classes.

Zela 209, Arequipa. ℂ 054/286-578. Fax 054/286-578. 20 units. S/24 ($7) double with shared bathroom, S/35 ($10) double with private bathroom; S/12 ($3.50) per person in shared rooms. Rates include taxes. No credit cards. **Amenities:** Laundry service; kitchen facilities.

Los Balcones de Moral y Santa Catalina *(Value* An inviting small hotel with a big name, this new inn is very comfortable and well furnished, a nice step up from budget hostales. In the heart of the old quarter, it's only a couple of blocks from the Plaza de Armas. One-half of the house is colonial (first floor); the other is republican, dating from the 1800s. The house is built around a colonial patio with a nice, sunny terrace. Furnishings are modern, with wallpaper and firm beds. Eleven of the good-size rooms have large balconies with nice views of the city and hardwood floors; the other rooms are carpeted and less desirable (though quieter). All have good tiled bathrooms.

Moral 217, Arequipa. © 054/201-291. Fax 054/222-555. www.losbalconeshotel.com. 17 units. S/90 ($26) double. Rate includes taxes. MC, V. **Amenities:** Restaurant; laundry service; safety deposit boxes. *In room:* TV.

Tambo Viejo (Value) This budget hostal, occupying an old colonial family home, is a 15-minute walk south of the Plaza de Armas, but it's popular and usually full of backpackers drawn by good word-of-mouth about the tranquil and genial atmosphere. There are rooms with shared and private bathrooms, a big garden with sun terraces and volcano views, a cafe serving veggie breakfasts and other meals, book exchange, a TV lounge, and hot water all day.

Av. Malecón Socabaya 107, Arequipa. © 054/288-195. Fax 054/284-747. tamboviejo@yahoo.com. 20 units. $20 double with private bathroom, $15 double with shared bathroom. Rates include American breakfast and taxes. DC, V. **Amenities:** Cafe; laundry service; TV lounge; safety deposit boxes; travel agency.

WHERE TO DINE

Arequipa is one of the best dining towns in Peru. It has no chic, luxuriously appointed 5-star places, but the historic center and zones just beyond its limits are very well stocked with great-value casual restaurants. Even the best restaurants are surprisingly affordable, within reach of most travelers. Arequipeño cooking is famous throughout Peru, and several restaurants specialize in traditional regional specialties, a couple of them with fabulous outdoor seating and excellent views of the volcanoes.

MODERATE

Ary Quepay (★) PERUVIAN   A relaxed, rustic restaurant with a garden-like dining room under a bamboo roof and skylights, decorated with lots of plants and native tapestries and instruments, Ary Quepay specializes in traditional Peruvian cooking. Starters include *choclo con queso* (corn on the cob with cheese), stuffed avocado, and *sopa a la criolla* (with beef, noodles, and eggs). Mains are classic: *rocoto relleno* (stuffed peppers), *adobo* (pork stew with ají), and *escabeche de pescado* (spicy fish stew). There are a number of dishes for vegetarians and good breakfasts, juices, and milkshakes. In the evenings, there's often live folkloric music.

Jerusalén 502. © 054/672-922. Main courses S/10–S/25 ($3–$7). DC, MC, V. Daily 8am–10pm.

El Cerrojo PERUVIAN/INTERNATIONAL   There are, predictably, scores of restaurants ringing the main square, and a couple are plain tourist traps. On one side, upstairs along a very long balcony that extends practically the length of one side of the Plaza de Armas, this restaurant is probably the best of the bunch, and the views of the square are brilliant. The lengthy menu offers *platos típicos* of Peruvian cooking, of course, as well as well-prepared meats (rabbit and pork chops) and fish dishes such as grilled shrimp, *corvina* (sea bass), and ceviche. But plenty of people come just for the views and simple fare such as pizza and pasta. You can count on getting serenaded by a peripatetic band of Peruvian musicians, just like you can count on getting accosted by the restaurant's advertising gals handing out free drink cards every time you pass under the arches of this side of the square.

Portal San Agustín 111. © 054/201-842. Main courses S/14–S/30 ($4–$8.50). AE, DC, MC, V. Daily noon–midnight.

El Pibe (Finds) ARGENTINE/GRILLED MEAT   Hopping on the Argentine-steak bandwagon, this new "asado bar" specializes in Argentina-style grilled meats, complete with nightly shows of tango and Latin American folklore. It's a nifty little place, with sillar stone walls and simple wooden tables and chairs. Meat eaters can sink their bicuspids into *asados* (roasts) of beef, lamb, ribs, pork, chorizo, and chicken, served up with the requisite *chimichurri* sauce. Argentines and wannabes can even go for *molleja de res* (sweetbreads), *morcilla* (blood sausage), and kidneys. There are several goods salads and a terrific bargain *menú turístico* for S/22 ($6), enough meat for most people to share. El Pibe is more focused on grilled meats than its main competition, El Viñedo (see below), which tries to be more things to more people.

Ugarte 210. © **054/206-260.** Reservations recommended on weekends. Main courses S/12–S/30 ($3–$9). AE, DC, MC, V. Daily noon–midnight.

El Viñedo ☆ ARGENTINE/GRILLED MEAT   Hard to say whether this Argentine restaurant would satisfy the purist carnivore instincts of my friends from Buenos Aires, but for Peru, this rustic yet refined restaurant is a winner. It does a good enough job with its *parrilladas* (mixed grills) to convince this gringo. There are also "Argentine" pizzas (topped by ingredients such as grilled chorizo and served on wood boards) and pastas, which Argentines adore. The interior is sprawling, cozy, and candlelit, with a tango music soundtrack, a half dozen separate dining rooms, and a garden courtyard that a waiter told me is perfect for couples. Though the ceilings are bamboo and the walls wood-paneled, waiters wear white gloves and tuxedo shirts. A bonus for those who can only eat so much meat: a free salad bar. The wine list may not earn the restaurant's name ("the Vineyard"), but it's pretty good for Peru, if a little expensive. Connected to the restaurant is El Jayari, a restaurant serving Peruvian dishes (and sharing the same chef and kitchen).

San Francisco 319-A. © **054/205-053.** Reservations recommended on weekends. Main courses S/10–S/25 ($3–$7). AE, DC, MC, V. Daily 1pm–midnight.

Gianni *(Kids)* ITALIAN   A very popular, amiable trattoria on Arequipa's restaurant row, this bustling little place with red-and-white-checked tablecloths is often filled with more locals and families than gringos—always a good sign. In fact, there are usually about as many kids knocking back pizza as young people having a beer and a bite before heading to one of the bars and dance clubs within a 2-block radius. There's seating on the second floor above the bar, or downstairs under a vaulted ceiling. Gianni's serves up standard but well-prepared Italian fare such as gnocchi, ravioli, cannelloni, lasagna, as well as trout and other fish and steaks. Service is fast and friendly.

San Francisco 304. © **054/287-138.** Reservations recommended. Main courses S/9–S/24 ($2.50–$7). DC, MC, V. Mon–Sat 6pm–1am.

La Truffa ☆ *(Value)* ITALIAN   A charming little restaurant tucked behind the cathedral on a pedestrian-only pasaje lined with alpaca boutiques and a couple of cafes, La Truffa (the truffle) is decorated like someone's cozy house, with oil paintings and local artifacts. The menu specializes in homemade pastas and good pizzas, but it's also a great place to get well-prepared fish dishes such as *delicia de corvina* (sea bass served with cheese, shrimp, and mushrooms). There are only a handful of tables in two rooms, and it's popular with gringos and locals, so don't be surprised if you have to wait.

Pasaje la Catedral 111. © **054/242-010.** Reservations recommended. Main courses S/12–S/27 ($3–$8). DC, MC, V. Mon–Sat 11am–11pm.

Sol de Mayo ☆☆☆ *(Value)* PERUVIAN   A 5-minute taxi ride from the *centro* in Yanahuara, the city's nicest residential neighborhood, this longtime stalwart (which has been around for more than a century) is the standard-bearer for Arequipeño cooking. A favorite of upscale locals and tourists alike, it is perhaps the most delightful of the city's restaurants. The colonial tables are set around the edges of a breezy, picture-perfect courtyard with thick grass, geraniums, cactus, a small pool and cascading waterfall, and strolling altiplano musicians. There are also indoor dining rooms inside the brick-red and yellow sillar stone building, but nothing beats eating outdoors here. Peruvian specialties are Sol de Mayo's calling card: *chicharrón de chancho* (fried pork), ostrich, fresh shellfish, and a tantalizing lineup of ceviches. Starters include a yummy mixed salad of *choclo* (white corn), tomato, and avocado. Good pisco sours are a must to start off your meal. Even for budget-oriented backpackers, this would be the place in Arequipa to splurge, even though splurging in southern Peru means no more than $10 to $15 a head.

Jerusalén 207, Yanahuara. ℂ 054/254-148. Reservations recommended. Main courses S/12–S/30 ($3.50–$8.50). AE, DC, MC, V. Daily11am–10pm.

Tradición Arequipeña ⟨ℛℛ⟩ ⟨*Value*⟩ PERUVIAN   It's a few kilometers outside town on a busy avenue in the district called Paucarpata, so you'll need to grab a taxi to get to this classic open-air restaurant. Elegantly set amid beautiful gardens and stunning views of snowcapped El Misti from the upper deck, it's only open for lunch (though you could also squeeze in an early dinner at 5 or 6pm). Most encouraging is how popular it is not only among tourists but also among locals. In fact, it's the restaurant that seems most highly recommended to foreigners by Arequipeños. It serves large portions of classic Peruvian dishes, such as cuy, adobo, and ceviche, but they're more carefully prepared here than in many other comida típica restaurants. A good starter is combination fried cheese and fried yuca with picante sauce and salsa verde. The prices are very affordable for such an elegant place.

Av. Dolores 111, Paucarpata. ℂ 054/426-467. Reservations recommended on weekends. Main courses S/8–S/32 ($2–$9). AE, DC, MC, V. Daily noon–7pm.

Zig Zag ⟨ℛℛ⟩ PERUVIAN/GRILLED MEAT   One of my favorite restaurants in Arequipa, this place is both chic and comfortable, equally welcoming to families and young people on dates. It's also unique: The house specialty is stone-grilled ostrich. The owners have a farm with 4,000 ostriches, and they educate their customers about ostrich as a healthy alternative to other meats. Inside the handsome, leather-bound menu is a chart that shows how low in cholesterol, calories, and fat the great bird is. (Alpaca is healthier still.) Try the ostrich carpaccio in lemon, or ostrich stone-grilled with Swiss-style hash browns (or get any other meat, such as lamb, beef, or alpaca, prepared in a similar fashion). Other favorites are fondues and pastas. Big-time meat eaters should order the *"piedra criolla"* (stone-grilled chorizo, beef, lamb, pork, hearts, intestines, and gizzards with potatoes and chimichurri sauce), a world-class bargain for just S/27 ($8). The two-level restaurant plays hip music, has attentive service, and features sillar walls and vaulted ceilings. A couple of the tables upstairs are perched on a ledge overlooking attractive Plazuela San Francisco.

Zela 210. ℂ 054/206-020. Reservations recommended. Main courses S/12–S/30 ($3.50–$8.50). AE, DC, MC, V. Daily 6pm–midnight.

INEXPENSIVE

Govinda ⟨*Value*⟩ VEGETARIAN/INDIAN   A good all-around vegetarian restaurant, Govinda—part of a chain across Peru, with the original in London—has a pleasant outdoor garden dining area and good-value menús and dishes. It serves vegetarian Italian, Asian, and Peruvian items, as well as pizzas, pastas, soups, salads, and yogurt dishes, a nice reprieve from many travelers' overdose of chicken, pork, and alpaca in Peru. The daily menús are very cheap, though the self-service buffet is not all-you-can-eat and its lineup of vegetarian dishes isn't the most creative you've ever seen. It's a good place for breakfast, with muesli, brown bread, fruit salads, and juices.

Santa Catalina 120. ✆ **054/285-540.** Reservations not accepted. Main courses S/5–S/15 ($1.50–$4.25); menú del día S/6–S/15 ($1.75–$4.25); buffet S/10.50 ($3). No credit cards. Daily 7am–9:30pm.

La Canasta SANDWICHES/BREAKFAST A charming bakery and lunch and breakfast nook, hidden away inside the courtyard of a massive colonial mansion on a heavily trafficked street, La Canasta has only a couple of tables on the patio. You can get pizzas, empanadas (stuffed pastries), sandwiches, and hamburgers, as well as freshly baked baguettes and croissants, part of some of the best breakfasts you're likely to come across in Peru.

Jerusalén 115. ✆ **054/287-138.** Reservations not accepted. Main courses S/3–S/6 (75¢–$1.75). No credit cards. Mon–Sat 7am–8:30pm.

Los Leños (Value) PIZZERIA This is a charming cave of a pizza place, where diners share long wooden tables and where the footprints of many hundreds of travelers carry on in the graffiti that cover every square inch of stone walls up to a vaulted ceiling. It looks and feels like a college tavern. The house specialty is pizza from the wood-fired oven; among the many varieties, the Leños house pizza is a standout: cheese, sausage, bacon, ham, chicken, and mushrooms. Those who've had their fill of pizza can opt for other standards, such as lasagna and a slew of other pastas. Los Leños opens early; choose from among 20 different "American breakfasts."

Jerusalén 407. ✆ **054/289-179.** Reservations not accepted. Main courses S/6–S/13 ($1.75–$3.75); menú del día S/6–S/15 ($1.75–$4.25); buffet S/10.50 ($3). No credit cards. Daily 7am–11pm.

AREQUIPA AFTER DARK

Arequipa has a pretty hopping nightlife in the old quarter, with plenty of bars, restaurants, and discos catering both to gringos and locals. Sunday through Wednesday is usually pretty quiet, with things heating up on Thursday night.

Las Quenas, Santa Catalina 302 (✆ **054/281-115**) is a peña bar and restaurant featuring live Andean music Monday through Saturday from 9pm to midnight and special dance performances on Friday and Saturday nights. It's a cozy little place that serves pretty good Peruvian dishes. You can also catch peña music at **El Tuturutu,** Portal San Agustín 105 (✆ **054/201-842**), a restaurant on the main square. Another spot for folkloric music is **La Troica,** Jerusalén 522 (✆ **054/ 225-690**), a tourist-oriented restaurant in an old house.

As for pubs and bars, **Siwara,** Santa Catalina 210 (✆ **054/626-218**) is a great-looking beer tavern that spills into two patios in the building of the Santuarios Andinos museum, across from the Santa Catalina monastery. Fashionable young people spill out of **La Leña,** Zela 202 (no phone), a pub with good music and drinks, until the wee hours. Another good spot for a drink is **Montréal Le Café Art,** Santa Catalina 300B (no phone), which features live music Wednesday through Saturday and has happy hours between 5 and 11pm. **La Casa de Klaus,** Zela 207 (✆ **054/203-711**), is a simple and brightly lit tavern popular with German, British, and local beer drinkers.

For a little more action, check out **Forum Rock Café,** San Francisco 317 (✆ **054/202-697**), a huge place that is equal parts restaurant, bar, disco, and concert hall. It sports a rain-forest theme, with jungle vegetation and "canopy walkways" everywhere. Live bands (usually rock) take the stage Thursday through Saturday. The upstairs grill has great panoramic views of the city. Just down the street, **Déjà Vu,** San Francisco 319 (© **054/221-904**), has a good bar with a mix of locals and gringos, a lively dance floor, and English-language movies on a big screen every night at 8pm. It also has a spectacular rooftop terrace, which is a good spot for dinner or even breakfast after a long night partying. **Kibosh,** Zela 205 (© **054/626-218**), is a chic, upscale pub with four bars, wood-oven pizza, a dance floor, and live music Wednesday through Saturday (ranging from Latin to hard rock).

SIDE TRIPS FROM AREQUIPA

Easy day trips from Arequipa include jaunts to the suburbs of **Paucarpata** and **Sabandía,** in the countryside surrounding the city. But the excursions of primary interest to visitors—for many, the main reason for a visit to Arequipa—is **Colca Canyon,** where the highlight is **Cruz del Cóndor,** a lookout point where giant South American condors soar overhead; see "Colca Valley," below, for more information. The region around Arequipa is unimaginably blessed by nature. It has soaring, active volcanoes, perfect for experienced mountaineers and trekkers; the two deepest canyons in the world, Colca and Cotahuasi; and chilly rivers that lace the canyons. The opportunities for trekking, rafting, and mountaineering expeditions through the valley are some of the finest in Peru. Out in the desert are ancient petroglyphs at **Toro Muerto.**

Tour agencies have mushroomed in Arequipa, and most offer very similar city and countryside (*campiña*) trips. Going with a tour operator is economical and by far the most convenient option for visitors with limited time and patience—public transportation is poor and very time-consuming in these parts. Of the many agencies that crowd the principal streets in the old quarter, only a handful of tour operators in Arequipa are well run, and visitors need to be careful when signing up for guided tours to the valley. Avoid independent guides who don't have official accreditation.

THE SUBURBS

Paucarpata, 7km (4 miles) southeast of Arequipa, is a pretty little town surrounded by Inca-terraced farmlands and El Misti volcano in the distance. About a kilometer down the road, the peaceful village of **Sabandía,** is where many Arequipeños visit on weekends for country-style restaurants. For out-of-town visitors, the highlight of the village is a large stone *molino,* or water-powered mill, from the early 17th century. There are several nice colonial estates in the surrounding countryside. One of the nicest is **La Mansión del Fundador,** a handsome colonial mansion in the suburb of **Huasacache,** 10km (6 miles) from Arequipa. The house, once the property of the founder of Arequipa, Don García Manuel de Carbajal, is nicely outfitted with original antique paintings and furnishings. It's open daily from 9am to 5pm; admission is S/10 ($3).

GETTING THERE   You can catch a Sabandía colectivo from San Juan de Dios or Independencia, a few blocks from the Plaza de Armas, but it's much simpler to take a taxi (S/7–S/10, or $2–$3). The molino is on the same road as the **El Lago Resort** hotel (p. 279), a good spot for lunch.

TORO MUERTO

About 3 hours from Arequipa, near the town of Corire, is **Toro Muerto,** touted as the world's largest field of petroglyphs. Whether it is in fact the world's largest number of petroglyphs in one place is hard to say; many contend that other places have more. But the site is certainly exceptionally big, unique, and fascinating: Carved on hundreds of volcanic boulders, the glyphs lie scattered in an area at least a couple kilometers long. Most historians believe that they were created by the Huari culture more than 1,000 years ago (and perhaps added to by subsequent peoples such as the Incas).

The enormous scale and the beautiful desert setting, more so than the individual drawings, is what most impresses about the site. The carvings comprise somewhat crude animal, human, and geometric representations. Though some estimates claim that there are 6,000 engraved stones at Toro Muerto, there are many more stones that are not carved, so walking among the boulders in the sand and under a hot desert sun in search of the engraved stones requires considerable effort. The site draws very few tourists. Its distance from Arequipa and the difficulty getting there (and, no doubt, the competing popularity of Colca Canyon) preclude many groups from going to Toro Muerto.

GETTING THERE   General-service tour agencies in Arequipa arrange group trips to Toro Muerto. You could also hire a taxi from Arequipa at a cost of $35 to $40.

3 Colca Valley (★(★(★

165km (102 miles) N of Arequipa

Mario Vargas Llosa, the Peruvian novelist and most famous Arequipeño, described Colca as "The Valley of Wonders." That is no literary overstatement. Colca is one of the most scenic regions in Peru, a land of imposing snowcapped volcanoes, artistically terraced agricultural slopes, narrow gorges, arid desert landscapes and vegetation, and remote traditional villages, many visibly scarred by seismic tremors common in southern Peru.

The Colca River, one of the sources of the mighty Amazon, slices through the canyon, which remained largely unexplored until the mid-1970s, when rafting expeditions descended to the bottom of the gorge. Reaching depths of 3,400m (11,220 ft.)—twice as deep as the Grand Canyon—*el Cañón del Colca* forms part of a tremendous volcanic mountain range more than 100km (62 miles) long. Colca Canyon, though, is no longer considered the world's deepest; Cotahuasi, at the extreme northwest of the Arequipa department, has wrested that honor away. Among the region's great volcanoes, several of which are still active, are Mount Coropuna (6,425m/21,200 ft.), Peru's second-highest peak, and Mount Ampato (6,310m/20,800 ft.), where a sacrificed Inca maiden, known to the world as Juanita, was discovered frozen in 1995 (see "The Discovery of Juanita, the Ampato Maiden" box, on p. 276).

Dispersed across the Colca Valley are 14 colonial-era villages, which date to the 16th century and are distinguished primarily by their small but often richly decorated churches. Local populations in the valley, descendants of the Collaguas and Cabanas, pre-Inca ethnic communities, preserve ancient customs and distinctive traditional dress. They speak different languages and can be distinguished by their hats; some women wear hats with colored ribbons, others have elaborately embroidered and sequined headgear. Colca villages are also celebrated for their vibrant festivals, as authentic as any in Peru, throughout the year. The valley's meticulous agricultural terracing, even more extraordinary and extensive than the Inca terraces seen in the Sacred Valley near Cusco, were first cultivated more than 1,000 years ago.

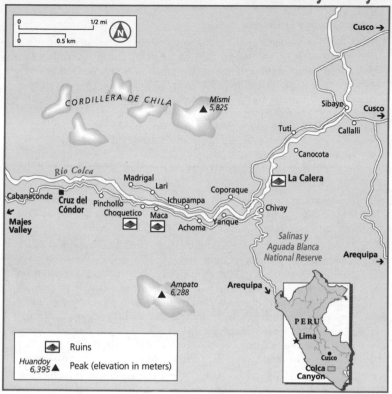

Travelers are now spending more time in the Colca Valley, lapping up its extraordinary beauty, quiet traditional life, and opportunities for outdoor adventure sports, but the number-one draw remains the almost ineffable wonder of seeing majestic, giant condors soar overhead at Cruz del Cóndor lookout point over Colca Canyon. The best time to visit Colca is during the dry season, May through November.

ESSENTIALS

GETTING THERE

Colca Valley is a long half-day trip from Arequipa along dusty roads that climb steadily, passing the Aguada Blanca National Reserve en route. The great majority of visitors to the Colca Valley and the canyon do so on guided tours, arranged in Arequipa.

BY ORGANIZED TOUR Conventional travel agencies offer day trips to Cruz del Cóndor, leaving at 3 or 4am, with brief stops at Chivay before returning to Arequipa—an awful lot to pack into a single day, especially at a high altitude. Expect to pay $15 to $20 per person. Two-day tours are much more enjoyably paced and cost $35 to $50, depending on hotel arrangements. Other campiña tours offered by many agencies include the Toro Muerto petroglyphs; Mejía lagoons, a bird sanctuary; Laguna Salinas, a saltwater lagoon populated by flamingos; Aguada Blanca Nature Reserve; and the remote Valley of the Volcanoes, a lunar landscape located more than 13 hours from Arequipa. The

---

> ### ⌒Tips The Air Up There
>
> The road from Arequipa to the Colca Valley climbs impressively, reaching 4,800m (15,800 ft.) at the Patapampa lookout point. The air is very thin at this altitude, and breathing is not at all easy. The main town in the valley, Chivay, sits at an altitude of nearly 3,600m (12,000 ft.), and nights can be brutally cold. Travelers who haven't yet spent time in either Cusco or Puno/Lake Titicaca should take it easy for a couple of days in Arequipa before heading out to Colca. *Soroche,* or acute mountain sickness, is common. See "Insurance, Health & Safety," in chapter 2, for additional information on how to combat it.

---

best all-purpose agencies in Arequipa are **Giardino Tours,** Jerusalén 604-A (© **054/241-206**); **Santa Catalina Tours,** Santa Catalina 219 (© **054/ 216-994**); and **Illary Tours,** Santa Catalina 205 (© **054/220-844**).

BY TRAIN   It is possible to get within reach of Colca Valley and Colca Canyon by train, but it's not very convenient. The Arequipa-Puno rail line stops at Sumbay, 97km (60 miles) from Arequipa and another 67km (42 miles) from Chivay. Travelers must arrange local valley transport, so relatively few people visit Colca this way, though the train would permit you to visit Colca on the way from Arequipa to Puno (or vice versa) without backtracking to Arequipa. From Arequipa to Sumbay, service is Sunday at 9pm, Wednesday at 7am, and Saturday at 8am; returning to Arequipa, the train leaves Monday at 4pm, Thursday at 1:30pm, and Sunday at 1:30pm. The cost is $25 one-way, $30 round-trip.

BY BUS   Local buses travel from Arequipa to Cabanaconde (6 hr.), near Cruz del Cóndor, with stops in Chivay (4 hr.). Two companies that make these runs are **Reyna,** Terminal Terrestre, Arequipa (© **054/426-549**), and **Cristo Rey,** San Juan de Dios 510, Arequipa (© **054/213-094**); the ride costs S/15 ($4).

VISITOR INFORMATION
There's a small tourist information office on the Plaza de Armas in Chivay. It's open daily in the afternoon and should be able to provide hiking information. You can also pick up information in Arequipa from the tourist information office or one of the travel agencies that organize Colca trips.

WHAT TO SEE & DO
CHIVAY & CABANACONDE
Chivay, though the valley's main town, is a sleepy little place that not long ago got on just fine without electricity. The indigenous locals here are Collaguas, and the women wear tall white hats adorned with colorful ribbon bands. For most travelers on their way to Cruz del Cóndor and other spots in the valley, Chivay amounts to little more than a stopover. For those adhering to a leisurely pace, though, Chivay, which benefits from an extraordinarily scenic natural setting, can be an enjoyable place to hang out. The attractive, low-key Plaza de Armas is the focus of attention in town, and the site of several restaurants and hostales. Most visitors hit the soothing and clean **La Calera hot springs** while in town. They're easy to get to, just a 4km (2-mile) walk or a colectivo ride from town, and inexpensive (S/5, or $1.50); they're open daily from 9am to 8pm.

The tiny, reserved village of **Cabanaconde,** the last town in the Colca Valley, is a couple of hours from Chivay. Some stay here because it is within walking

distance 15km (9 miles) of the Cruz del Cóndor lookout point, and it's well positioned for other hikes in the canyon and throughout the valley. The views of the canyon are tremendous, and short walks take you to excellent vantage points overlooking some of the most brilliant agricultural terracing in the area. The locals are descendants of the Cabanas people, and they maintain traditional dress and customs. Women wear hats embroidered with flowers and wide skirts.

CRUZ DEL CONDOR ✿✿

Cruz del Cóndor, or Condor Cross, about 50km (32 miles) west of Chivay, is a lookout point fast growing in fame. At a spot 1,200m (3,960 ft.) above the canyon river, crowds gather, zoom lenses poised, to witness a stunning wildlife spectacle. Beginning around 9am, Andean condors—the largest birds in the world, with wingspans of 3.5m (11½ ft.)—begin to appear, circling far below in the gorge and gradually gaining altitude with each pass, until they literally soar silently above the heads of awestruck admirers. Condors are such immense and heavy creatures that they cannot lift off from the ground; instead, they take flight from cliff perches. Each morning, from around 9 to 10am or later, condors both young and mature glide and climb theatrically before heading out along the river in search of prey. To witness the condors' majestic flight up close (the feathers at the end of their wings spread like fingers) is a mesmerizing sight, capable of producing goose bumps on even the most jaded travel-

> **Fun Fact Say What?**
> The Colca Valley is named after the *colcas,* or warehouses, that the Incas once carved out of the canyon walls and used to stored grain. The sealed vaults are about 1m (3 ft.) in diameter and constructed of straw and mud.

ers. On my last trip to Colca, I saw at least 2 dozen condors take off over the canyon, and a guide I spoke with claimed he once saw 54 in a single morning; some visitors will inevitably have less luck. The condors return late in the afternoon, but fewer people attend the show then.

INDEPENDENT HIKING IN COLCA

Those looking to spend some quality hiking time in the valley and canyon can get to the region by public transportation or rental car from Arequipa and go out on their own. The largest number of inexpensive hotel accommodations is in Chivay. You can also camp throughout the canyon and valley, with the exception of Cruz del Cóndor.

The region is loaded with excellent hikes that can be done independently if you have suitable gear and camping equipment. Unless you're an experienced hiker, however, it's best to go with a guide (see "Tour Agencies for Rafting, Trekking & Mountaineering Expeditions," below).

Among the best hikes is a **4-hour descent into Colca Canyon** from the Cruz del Cóndor lookout. Because of the arduous, lengthy 6-hour climb back out, most travelers who do this hike end up camping down below near the Sangalle oasis with palm trees and water suitable for swimming. Hikes down to the canyon floor require good physical conditioning and preparedness (plenty of water, food, sunscreen, and so on). The trails are quite difficult in sections, and the altitude complicates the trek—the drop is more than 1,000m (3,300 ft.). An even longer and more demanding hike is to the village of **Tapay,** beginning at

A Typical Guided Tour of Colca Valley

Most organized tours of the region are very similar if not identical. The road that leads out of Arequipa and into the valley, bending around the El Misti and Chachani volcanoes, is poor and unbearably dusty. It passes through the **Laguna Salinas** and **Aguada Blanca Nature Reserve,** where you'll usually have a chance to see rare vicuñas, llamas, and alpacas from the road. The altiplano landscape is barren and bleak. Most tours stop at volcano and valley lookout points along the way before heading to Chivay.

The gateway to the region, a little more than 3 hours from Arequipa, is **Chivay,** the valley's main town on the edge of the canyon. This easygoing market town lies at an altitude of 3,600m (11,880 ft.). From here, many organized tours embark on short hikes above the canyon and visit the wonderfully relaxing hot springs of **La Calera** near Chivay (p. 290). Evening visits to the hot springs allow visitors to bathe in open-air pools beneath a huge, starry sky; artificial light in the valley is almost nonexistent. Charming colonial villages in the valley often visited by tours include Yanque, Coporaque, Maca, and Lari. Most 2-day tours head out early the following morning for **Cruz del Cóndor** to see the Andean condors begin to circle around 9am.

Organized tours generally include transportation, an English-speaking guide, hotel accommodations in Chivay or a nearby village (with breakfast), and park entrance fees to Colca and Cruz del Cóndor. Additional meals are extra.

Cabanaconde and following a good trail from the oasis via the Río Colca (about 6 hr. each way). The path is very steep.

Less taxing hikes are possible simply walking from one village to another in the region. From **Chivay** to **Yanque** along the main road is about 7km (4 miles). You can continue from Yanque to the villages of **Achoma** (another 7km/4 miles), **Maca** (12km/7 miles), and **Pinchollo** (10km/6 miles). From there, on the way to Cabanaconde it's about an hour to the **Colca Geyser** (Hatun Infiernillo).

EXTREME COLCA VALLEY: RAFTING, TREKKING & VOLCANO CLIMBS

The countryside around Arequipa, laced with canyons and volcanoes, is one of the best in Peru for outdoor adventure travel. Trails crisscross the Colca Valley, leading across mountain ridges, agricultural terraces, and curious rock formations, and past colonial towns and fields where llamas and vicuñas graze. The most common pursuits are river running, treks through the canyon valleys, and mountain climbing on the volcanoes just beyond the city. Many tour agencies in Arequipa offer conventional 2- and 3-day visits to Colca Canyon, as well as longer, more strenuous treks through the valley and to Cotahuasi Canyon. Some of the most interesting (but most time-consuming and difficult) expeditions combine rafting and trekking. Your best bet for organizing any of these activities is with one of the tour operators mentioned below; several in Arequipa focus solely on eco- and adventure tourism.

RIVER RAFTING

The rivers and canyons around Arequipa pose some excellent river-running opportunities for both novices and experts. The best months for rafting are May through September, when water levels are low. (In the rainy season, when water levels are high, the canyon rivers can be extremely dangerous.) The most accessible rafting, suitable for first-timers, is on the **Río Chili,** just 15 minutes from downtown. It offers Class-III and -IV runs, and is a great way to get your feet wet during a half-day trip. Year-round runs of similarly moderate difficulty and scenic beauty can be arranged on day trips to the **Río Majes** (the Río Colca beyond the gorge). Rafting in Cotahuasi and Colca canyons is serious stuff for confident rafters; while there are 3-day rafting trips to Colca (about $125) for those with moderate experience, longer, 10- to 12-day trips to either canyon are the goal of serious white-water runners. The **Río Colca** (Class IV–V) is extremely technical, though some upriver sections are less dangerous and difficult. **Río Cotahuasi** was only first explored in 1994; it has 120km (75 miles) of Class-IV and -V rapids (and some Class VI). A few agencies offer annual trips that combine trekking with hard-core white-water rafting in Cotahuasi. These trips are expensive ($2,000 and up) and lengthy, usually 12 to 14 days total.

MOUNTAIN & VOLCANO CLIMBING

At the foot of the western Andes, Arequipa is ideally positioned for a variety of ascents—many of them not technically challenging—to volcano summits and mighty Andes peaks. Climbers in good physical condition can bag 5,000m (16,400-ft.) summits on ascents of 2 days or less. The best months for climbing are July through September, although some peaks can be climbed year-round. Climbers should be sufficiently acclimatized prior to making any ascents; if you've spent several days in Cusco or Puno before arriving in Arequipa (and are in good physical shape), you should be fine. Adventure travel operators in Arequipa provide logistical support, porters, and guides, but you must provide your own sleeping bag and boots. Be sure to ask plenty of questions about weather conditions, equipment, and experience before setting out with any guide.

El Misti, a nearly 6,000m (20,000-ft.) volcano, dominates the Arequipa landscape from a distance of about 20km (12 miles). The most popular climb among both locals and visitors, Misti is a demanding 2- or 3-day trek with few technical challenges. It is suitable for inexperienced climbers accompanied by professional guides. Most climbers stay the first night at the base camp Nido de Aguilas (Eagle's Nest) and reach the summit after about 7 hours of climbing on the second day. Arequipa's other major volcano, **Chachani** (6,075m/20,050 ft.), also presents an excellent and technically straightforward climb, a good opportunity for inexperienced climbers to brag about reaching a 6,000m (20,000-ft.) summit.

The Colca Valley has a number of peaks that draw serious climbers, including the **Ampato** volcano (6,288m/20,750 ft.), a 3- or 4-day climb, and the **Hualca Hualca** glacier (6,025m/19,880 ft.). **Coropuna** (6,425m/21,200 ft.), perhaps the most stunning mountain in the Cotahuasi Valley, requires a couple of days of travel from Arequipa to begin the difficult climb.

TOUR AGENCIES FOR RAFTING, TREKKING & MOUNTAINEERING EXPEDITIONS

The best general agencies in Arequipa ("Getting There," above) arrange entry-level rafting and trekking itineraries. Almost all are located on just two streets in Arequipa, Jerusalén, and Santa Catalina, so it's pretty simple to browse up and down and get a feel for an agency.

> **Tips Cañón del Cotahuasi**
>
> Reputedly the deepest canyon in the world, Cotahuasi (3,354m/11,068 ft.
> at its deepest point) was only recently explored by rafting teams. As entic-
> ing as trekking or rafting in the world's deepest canyon no doubt is to
> many, the effort required to get to Cotahuasi is substantial. It's a full 12 to
> 15 hours from Arequipa by bus, more than 400km (250 miles) on pretty
> difficult roads. While some adventurers do go independently, trekking or
> rafting in the Cotahuasi is much better and more safely organized by a
> professional outfit such as Zárate Aventuras (see "Tour Agencies for Raft-
> ing, Trekking & Mountaineering Expeditions," below).

Cusipata Viajes y Turismo, Jerusalén 408-A (© **054/203-966**), is the local specialist for Chili and Colca rafting and kayaking (including courses), and its guides—three brothers—frequently subcontract out to other agencies in Are-quipa. **Apu Expediciones,** Portal Comercio 157, Cusco (© **084/652-975**), arranges rafting trips to Majes and Colca, among other adventure options. **Apumayo Expediciones,** Garcilaso 265, Cusco (© **084/246-018**; www.cusco peru.com/apumayo), is good for long trekking/rafting expeditions to Cotahuasi and Colca, as is **Amazonas Explorer,** Zela 212, Arequipa (© **054/ 212-813**; www.amazonas-explorer.com), an international company that organ-izes hardy multisport trips to Cotahuasi and Colca, which can be combined with tours to Cusco, the Inca Trail, and Machu Picchu. **Ideal Tours,** Urbanización San Isidro F-2, Vallecito (© **054/244-433**), handles Chili and Majes rafting, as well as Colca and other standard tours. **Colca Trek,** Jerusalén 401-B (© 054/ 224-578), and **Peru Trekking,** Jerusalén 302-B (© 054/223-404), are two other Arequipa outfits that offer canyon treks of 3 to 5 days or more and a num-ber of other adventure activities, such as horseback riding, mountain biking, rafting, and climbing.

For hard-core mountain climbing, one agency stands out. **Zárate Aventuras,** Santa Catalina 204, no. 3 (© **054/263-107**; www.mundomail.net/zarate) is run by Carlos Zárate, perhaps the top climbing guide in Arequipa (a title his dad held before him). He can arrange any area climb and has equipment rental and a 24-hour mountain-rescue service. Climbing expedition costs are (per person) El Misti, $50; Chachani, $70; and Colca Canyon, $75.

WHERE TO STAY & DINE

Most agencies offering 2- and 3-day trips to Colca Canyon put passengers up at modest hotels in Chivay. If you can afford to step up a notch from budget accommodations, the following country-style inns in and around the canyon are the most comfortable and atmospheric in Colca. Though they're not luxurious, they are by far the best choices if offered by tour operators or if you're traveling to Colca independently.

Albergue El Mirador de los Collaguas, Piura s/n, Yanque (© and fax 054/448-383; www.rci.com), is a small country inn within easy walking dis-tance of Yanque's attractive plaza. There are thermal baths on the premises; rooms, in small adobe bungalows, cost $65 double. The inn features a nice restaurant, La Casa Nostra, with a wood-burning stove and good alpaca steak and trout dishes. Giardino Tours (p. 290) books its Colca tour guests at the newest country inn in the Colca Valley, **Albergue La Casa de Mama Yacchi** ✵,

Coporaque (© **054/241-206;** www.lacasademamayacchi.com). Located just outside the village of Coporaque, it has very comfortable rooms, great views, a fireplace lounge, and an attractive rustic restaurant featuring good local preparations. It's owned by the same folks that run La Casa de Mi Abuela Hostal in Arequipa. Rooms cost $48 double. **Colca Lodge** ⚘, about 10km (6 miles) from Chivay (© **054/212-813;** www.colca-lodge.com), is a comfortable, eco-style hotel with adobe, stone, and thatched-roof architecture, solar power, and its own private thermal baths. The views of the valley are excellent. The hotel also has a comfortable lodge-style restaurant serving lunch and dinner. The lodge's 29 rooms cost $60 to $70 double. Plenty of travelers rave about **Parador de Colca** ⚘⚘, Fundo Curiña, Yanque (© **054/288-440;** paradordelcolca@terra. com.pe). Swedish-owned and perched on the lip of the canyon, it's a rustic ranch-style eco-lodge with solar energy and a breakfast terrace with gorgeous valley views of gardens, terraced fields, and the river. The rooms have loft spaces and private patios with fire pits overlooking the canyon. The lodge also offers horseback riding. The seven rooms start at $70 double.

Other options include more modest inns in Chivay and Cabanaconde. If you want to spend the night in Chivay and don't have a pre-arranged hotel, there are several simple hostales with hot-water showers. One of those that's on most organized tour itineraries is **Colca Inn,** Av. Salaverry 307 (© **054/521-088;** colcainn@perutravel.org). It has carpeted rooms with the look of a mountain lodge; doubles cost $34. **Hostal Anita,** Plaza de Armas 607 (© **054/521-114**), is friendly and offers basic rooms built around a pleasant garden courtyard for about $5 per person. **Rumi Llaqta Lodge,** Huayna Cápac s/n, near the main square (© **054/521-098**), is probably the nicest inn in Chivay. The charming, small, stone bungalows have thatched roofs. Rooms are comfortable and nicely decorated, but not overly large. There's a nice restaurant with a wood-burning stove and, frequently, folkloric music for entertainment. Rooms cost $59 double. The best bet for a meal in Chivay is probably **Casablanca,** Plaza de Armas 705 (© **054/521-019**), which serves a good-value menú, alpaca, and a handful of vegetarian dishes.

There are just a few hostales in Cabanaconde. **Hostal Valle del Fuego,** Calle Grau, 1 block from the plaza (© **054/280-367**), is very basic and cheap, but it's clean and it has solar-powered showers. The owners also operate a restaurant in town with a dinner menú for S/7 ($2). **La Posada del Conde,** Calle San Pedro at Calle Bolognesi (© **064/440-197;** pdelconde@yahoo.com) is a slight step up with private bathrooms. Rooms in both inns cost less than $10 double, and the staff can provide hiking information and guide contacts.

9

The Amazon Basin

Nearly two-thirds of Peru is Amazon rain forest, which thrives with some of the richest biodiversity on the planet. Covering 6,475,000km^2 (2.5 million sq. miles), the Amazon basin represents 54% of all remaining rain forest on the planet. This vast, largely impenetrable region, with the smallest human population in the country and few towns of any size, clearly is not the Peru of great pre-Columbian civilizations and Inca ruins. For the traveler, it stands in stunning contrast to rugged Andean peaks and arid desert coasts. The humid frontier towns of the jungle, well past stages of oil and rubber boom and now hell-bent on ecotourism, are worlds apart from the historic cities Cusco and Arequipa and the modern madness of Lima.

Many naturalists and biologists believe that Peru's Amazon rain forest holds the greatest diversity in the world. It teems with a staggering roster of life: 400 species of mammals, 2,000 species of fish, 300 reptiles, 1,700 birds, and more than 50,000 plants. Recent studies have shown a region just south of Iquitos to have the highest concentration of mammals anywhere in the world.

Not surprisingly, jungle ecotourism has exploded in Peru, as it has in several other Latin American countries. Peru's jungle regions are now much more accessible than they once were—which is both a good and a bad thing, of course—and there are more lodges and eco-options than ever. Still, accessibility is a crucial factor in jungle trips: The more remote a lodge or camping trek, and the more pristine and unspoiled

the environment, the more it's going to cost you to get there in terms of time and money. Rivers define life in the jungle even more so than do the forests; for both locals and visitors, almost all transport along the vast river system that stretches across the whole of eastern Peru is by dugout canoe, motorboat, or large riverboats (*lanchas*).

The southern Amazon region, which extends to the Bolivian and Brazilian borders, is concentrated in the Madre de Dios department, the least populated area in Peru. While accessible by land from Cusco, it is an exceedingly difficult route. Most travelers fly to Puerto Maldonado (the gateway to the Tambopata Nature Reserve) and travel overland to the Manu Biosphere Reserve, returning by small aircraft.

The gateway to the northern Amazon basin is Iquitos. An example of how huge the Amazon is: Iquitos lies nearly 3,220km (2,000 miles) from the mouth of the great Río Amazonas, the second-longest river in the world. Other than an arduous journey by boat, the only way to get to Iquitos is by airplane (usually from Lima). The northern Amazon reaches all the way to Peru's borders with Colombia and Brazil.

The best time to visit the Amazon is during the dry season, May through November. During the rainy season in the southern Amazon, parts of the jungle are flooded and impassable. The northern jungle does not have a rainy season per se, and travel there is less restricted during the winter; many lodges remain open year-round.

The Amazon Basin

However, water levels can rise from 7.5m (25 ft.) to more than 15m (50 ft.) from December through May, and some jungle villages become flooded. Many naturalists find high-water months to be best for wildlife observation.

1 The Southern Amazon Jungle

Cusco is the gateway to the southern jungle and some of Peru's finest and least spoiled Amazon rain forest. The area has been less penetrated by man than has the northern Amazon; the southern jungle was largely unexplored until expeditions into the remote rain forest were undertaken in the 1950s. Two of Peru's top three jungle zones—and two of the finest in South America—dominate the southeastern department of Madre de Dios. The region's two principal protected areas, the Manu Biosphere Reserve (Parque Nacional Manu) and the Tambopata-Candamo Nature Reserve (Zona Reservada Tambopata-Candamo),

---

Fun Fact **The Mighty Amazon**

The Amazon River begins as a small stream on the peak of El Nevado Mismi in the southern Andes glaciers and flows all the way to the Atlantic ocean—a distance of nearly 6,440km (4,000 miles), making it the second-longest river in the world (after the Nile). The Amazon contains 20% of the world's fresh water.

---

are both excellent for jungle expeditions, though they differ in terms of remoteness and facilities.

Manu, one of the largest protected natural areas in the Americas, remains complicated and time-consuming to visit; expeditions last a minimum of 4 or 5 days (and most are a week or more), involve both overland and air (not to mention river) travel, and are expensive. Access is easiest from Cusco, though it involves a day's travel overland (or a half-hour flight), followed by a couple of days by boat.

Travelers without the time or budget to reach Manu often find Tambopata a most worthy alternative: Its wildlife and jungle vegetation are nearly the equal of Manu in some parts. Most lodges in Tambopata are easier to get to and cheaper than those in Manu, although a couple require up to 12 hours of travel by boat from Puerto Maldonado. The jungle frontier city of Puerto Maldonado, which is the capital of Madre de Dios department and just a half-hour flight from Cusco, is the jumping-off point to explore Tambopata.

In travel packages to both destinations, round-trip airfare from Cusco to Puerto Maldonado or Boca Manu (the gateway to the Manu Biosphere Reserve) is usually extra. Cheaper tours travel overland, stay at lesser-quality lodges (or primarily at campsites), and may travel on riverboats without canopies. Independent travel to Tambopata and two-way overland travel to either are options only for those with a lot of time and patience on their hands. Independent travelers not only find it complicated to enter many parts of the jungle, but they are also not permitted to enter the most desirable section of Manu, the Reserve Zone. Organizing a trip with one of the lodges or tour operators listed below is highly recommended, both in terms of access and convenience. Do not purchase any jungle packages from salesmen on the streets of Cusco; their agencies may not even be authorized to enter restricted zones, and last-minute "itinerary changes" are likely.

Dry season (May–Nov) is the best time for southern jungle expeditions—during the rainy season, rivers overflow and mosquitoes gobble up everything in sight. Be careful to note when a tour operator's fixed departures leave (some are every Wed, others every Sun, and so on).

PUERTO MALDONADO

Formerly a prosperous rubber town, Puerto Maldonado is a humid, busy, and fast-growing place, a frontier market town that has gone through several phases of boom and bust, as have most jungle outposts. After the rubber boom came the game hunters and loggers. Today, the town's primary industries continue to be based on exploiting the rain forest that surrounds Puerto Maldonado: gold prospecting and Brazil-nut harvesting. For most travelers, Puerto Maldonado is merely a gateway to the jungle, and groups booked on Tambopata package tours often blow through town with little notice. For some visitors, it's a stiflingly hot one-horse (and motor-scooter) town, but the frontier atmosphere, which

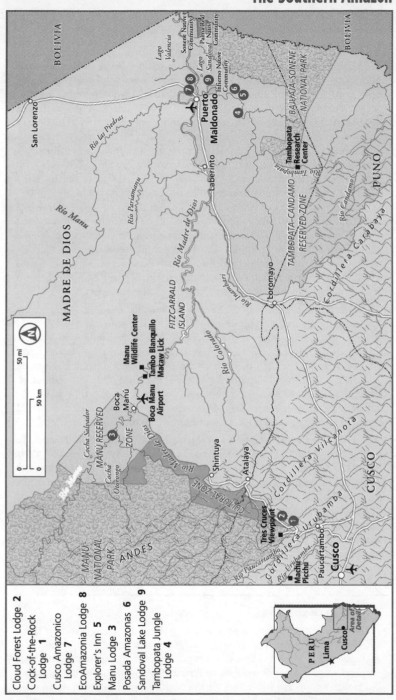

The Southern Amazon

BOLIVIA

BOLIVIA

San Lorenzo

Río las Piedras

MADRE DE DIOS

Río Manu

Río Pariamanu

Sonene Native Community

Lago Valencia

Palma Real

Lago Sandoval

Puerto Maldonado

Sandoval Native Community

Infierno Native Community

7 **8**

9

6

5

4

Tambopata Research Center

BAHUAJA-SONENE NATIONAL PARK

PUNO

Laberinto

Río Madre de Dios

Río Inambari

TAMBOPATA-CANDAMO RESERVED ZONE

Río Tambopata

Río Candamo

Cordillera Carabaya

Manu Wildlife Center

Tambo Blanquillo Macaw Lick

FITZCARRALD ISLAND

Río Colorado

toromayo

Río Manu

Cocha Salvador

MANÚ RESERVED

Boca Manú

Boca Manu Airport

Río Madre de Dios

3

ZONE

Cocha Otorongo

Río Manu

Shintuya

Atalaya

CULTURAL ZONE

Cordillera Vilcanota

CUSCO

MANÚ NATIONAL PARK

ANDES

Tres Cruces Viewpoint

2

1

Cordillera Vilcabamba

Cusco

Río Paucartambo

Paucartambo

Río Urubamba

Machu Picchu

N

50 mi

50 km

0

0

Cloud Forest Lodge **2**

Cock-of-the-Rock Lodge **1**

Cusco Amazonico Lodge **7**

EcoAmazonia Lodge **8**

Explorer's Inn **5**

Manu Lodge **3**

Posada Amazonas **6**

Sandoval Lake Lodge **9**

Tambopata Jungle Lodge **4**

PERU

Lima

Cusco

Area of Detail

continues to draw dreamers from across Peru, proves interesting to others, at least for a day or two before pushing on into the jungle.

ESSENTIALS

GETTING THERE   The **Aeropuerto Internacional Padre Aldamiz Puerto Maldonado** (© 084/571-531) is 8km (5 miles) outside of the city. Flights arrive from Cusco and Lima on **TANS** (© 01/213-6000; www.tansperu.com.pe), **AeroCondor** (© 01/442-5215; www.aerocondor.com.pe), and **Aero Continente** (© 01/242-4242; www.aerocontinente.net). Health Ministry nurses are on hand to vaccinate visitors against yellow fever. If you've been vaccinated, be sure to carry your card. To get from the airport to town, the best bet is a *motocarro* (a motorcycle rickshaw), which costs S/5 to S/7 ($1.50–$2).

Hardy budget travelers looking for a new warrior experience can travel by truck between Puerto Maldonado and Cusco. The journey takes at least 3 days in the dry season and up to 10 days in wetter conditions, and the route traverses more than 500km with zero comfort to speak of; it's certainly one of the worst (if not *the* worst) roads in Peru connecting two points of obvious interest. It costs about $10 or $15 and will provide you with stories for months, but you will definitely suffer for the privilege. Trucks leave from Plaza Tupac Amaru in Cusco and arrive in Puerto Maldonado at the Mercado Modelo on Calle Ernesto Rivero. Trucks call out for passengers. Take the challenge at your own risk.

VISITOR INFORMATION   In Puerto Maldonado, there's an office of the **Ministerio de Industria y Turismo** (MITINCI) at Fitzcarrald 411 (© 084/571-164), and a small booth at the airport can give limited information on the city and jungle lodges. Most visitors leave for the southern jungle from Cusco, so if you spend a few days there, it's worthwhile to pick up information on Puerto Maldonado and the rest of the jungle at the main **Tourist Information Office** at Mantas 117-A, a block from the Plaza de Armas (© 084/263-176). Anyone traveling to Manu or Tambopata with an organized expedition should be able to get all the necessary information from the tour organizer.

FAST FACTS   Banks on the Plaza de Armas include **Banco de la Nación,** Jr. Carrión 233 (© 084/571-064), and **Banco de Crédito,** Arequipa 334 (© 084/571-001). Only Banco de Crédito changes traveler's checks. There are also casas de cambio along Puno. Credit cards are not widely accepted in Puerto Maldonado, so you should plan on bringing cash for incidentals if you've already booked a lodge or tour program.

The **Bolivian consulate** is on the Plaza de Armas (Calle Loreto). For exit stamps to travel to Bolivia via Puerto Heath (a trip of 3–4 days by boat), visit the **Immigration Office** at 26 de Diciembre 356, a block from the Plaza de Armas. It's open Monday through Friday from 9am to 1pm.

Tips Take the Shot

Yellow-fever vaccinations are more than a wise idea before visiting the jungles of southeastern Peru. Even though the only reported outbreaks of yellow fever in the last couple of years have been in the northern Amazon around Iquitos, local authorities in Puerto Maldonado insist on making sure that visitors are protected. At the airport arrival terminal, travelers without documentation of valid yellow-fever shots will be administered one by Health Ministry nurses. Carry your vaccination records with you.

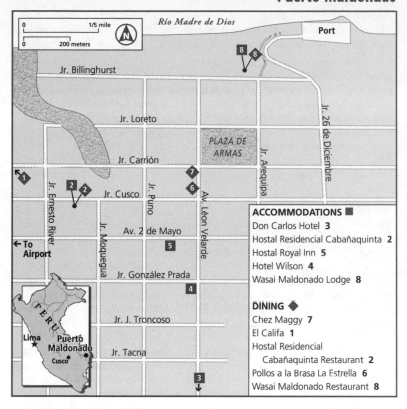

For medical attention, go to **Hospital Santa Rosa,** Cajamarca 171, at Velarde (© **084/571-127**). The **police** can be found at Carrión 410 (© **084/571-022**). The **post office** is located on Velarde 675 (© **084/571-088**). There's a **Telefónica del Perú** office at Puno 670 (© **084/571-600**).

GETTING AROUND　Quick, easy, and cheap, motocarros are everywhere; most rides in town cost S/2 (75¢). Ferries cross the Río Tambopata if you just want to cruise across the river; you'll have to negotiate the price, but expect to spend S/15 to S/20 ($4–$6) per person.

WHAT TO SEE & DO NEAR PUERTO MALDONADO

Good jungle experiences, with possibilities of some fauna sightings and attractive walks in primary and secondary forest, are within easy reach of Puerto Maldonado. However, your experience will be vastly improved if you go farther from the city, particularly for stays of 3 days or more at one of the lodges discussed below. Still, a couple of easy and inexpensive day trips from the regional capital—vastly better than comparable close-in trips from Iquitos—can be arranged.

LAGO SANDOVAL　Sandoval Lake is about an hour by boat from Puerto Maldonado. Even if you don't stay at either of the lodges here (see "Tambopata Tour Operators & Lodges," below), this pretty and serene oxbow lake makes a good day trip downriver from Puerto Maldonado. It boasts a surprising diversity of wildlife, including macaws, parrots, herons, kingfishers, caimans, turtles, and even a family of giant otters that can frequently be spied in the lake. The best way to get here is to catch a canoe or motorboat at the port. You'll then have to walk a couple kilometers along a path through the jungle, but it's a beautiful hour-long trek.

LAGO VALENCIA It takes about 2 hours by lancha (or several hours by motorized canoe) to reach this large lake about 64km (40 miles) from Puerto Maldonado. Along the way, you'll pass gold panners on the banks of the Madre de Dios River and native settlements of the Ese'eja communities. At the lake, the best thing to do is go for a trek through the forest to get a sense of the extraordinary jungle flora here, including huge Tahuari trees, and native species of birds, such as hoatzins (large, strange birds with claws at the ends of their wings), herons, cormorants, and pink flamingos. There are caimans and turtles in the lake.

WHERE TO STAY & DINE

Most people stay overnight in Puerto Maldonado only as long as it takes them to arrange a trip to the jungle. In town, there are only a couple of decent and comfortable hotels, in addition to about a dozen very basic hostels.

The best place to stay in Puerto Maldonado is **Wasai Maldonado Lodge** ⋆, Jr. Guillermo Billinghurst (© **084/572-290;** www.wasai.com). Though it's only a block from the main square in town, this inn is built much more like a jungle lodge, with 6 of the 18 bungalows on stilts. The location is quite beautiful, overlooking the Madre de Dios River. The spacious bungalows are cabin-like paneled rooms with refrigerators, private bathrooms with hot water, air-conditioning (or fan), and TV. The small swimming pool even has a little waterfall. The lodge restaurant, the best and most upscale in town, is in a gazebo that sits above the riverbank; on the second floor is a new bar with good river views. The bungalows with river views cost $48; others, $20. Ecotours and jungle expeditions with stays at the Wasai Tambopata Lodge and Research Center, 120km (74 miles) upriver on the Río Tambopata, can be arranged (4 days/3 nights, $291).

Don Carlos Hotel, Velarde 1271 (© **084/571-029;** www.hotelesdon carlos.com), sits above the banks of Tambopata River about 5 blocks south of the center of town and is surrounded by native flora. Smaller, more rustic, and more low-key than the chain's other hotels, this inn nonetheless has a host of services and amenities, including a restaurant, laundry, 24-hour room service, an outdoor swimming pool, and air-conditioning. The 15 rooms aren't anything special, but they're a pretty good value at $26 double. **Hostal Residencial Cabañaquinta,** Cusco 535 (© **084/571-063**), is a comfortable inn with basic but pretty decent rooms, a nice garden, and one of the better restaurants in town. Double rooms cost $25.

At the low end, **Hostal Royal Inn,** Av. Dos de Mayo 333 (© **084/571-048**), is a well-maintained and modern midsize hostel in the town center. Some have complained that it can get pretty noisy. The 30 rooms with private bathrooms are S/35 ($10) double. **Hotel Wilson,** Av. Gonzales Prada 355 (© **084/ 571-086**), is a budget inn that plays host to backpackers on the cheap, but it's a little down-at-the-mouth. The basic rooms with shared showers and others with their own cold-water showers are less than $10 double.

In addition to the hotel restaurants at Wasai, Don Carlos, and Cabañaquinta, there are a slew of basic eateries, chifas, and cafes clustered near the Plaza de Armas and lining León de Velarde, the main street. **Chez Maggy,** Plaza de

> **Fun Fact Native Foods**
>
> Local jungle dishes worth a try include *patarashca,* a steamed river fish wrapped in banana leaves; *timbuche,* a thick soup made with local fish; and *tacacho,* or bananas cooked over coals and served with fried pork and chopped onions. Locals also eat *motelo* (turtle soup served in its shell) and *muchangue* (turtle eggs with steamed bananas), but, given that river and sea turtles are endangered species protected by Peruvian law, it seems especially criminal for gringos to indulge this custom. *Mazato* is a local beverage of fermented yuca, bananas, and milk.

Armas (© **084/571-082**), is a decent pizzeria. **El Califa,** Piura 266 (© **084/ 571-119**), serves local jungle cuisine and Peruvian meals at lunch. Grilled and rotisserie chicken, always a good bet in Peru, can be had at **Pollos a la Brasa La Estrella,** Velarde 474.

TAMBOPATA NATURE RESERVE 🐾🐾
650km (403 miles) NE of Cusco

Upstream from Puerto Maldonado, the Tambopata Nature Reserve (officially called the Tambopata-Candamo Reserve Zone, or TRZ) is a massive tract of humid subtropical rain forest in the department of Madre de Dios. The Peruvian government prohibited hunting and logging in the area in 1977 and created the Tambopata-Candamo Reserve Zone in 1990. Nearly one-third the size of Costa Rica, Tambopata has more species of birds (595) and butterflies (more than 1,200) than any place of similar size on earth.

Visits to jungle lodges owned by tour operators in Tambopata are generally more accessible, both in terms of cost and travel time, than Manu. Although mankind's imprints are slightly more noticeable here, the area is one of superb environmental diversity, with a dozen different types of forest and some gorgeous oxbow lakes. Environmentalists claim that the TRZ's great diversity of wildlife is due to its location at the confluence of lowland Amazon forest with three other ecosystems. There are at least 13 endangered species found here, including the jaguar, giant otter, ocelot, harpy eagle, and giant armadillo.

The Tambopata macaw clay lick (Collpa de Guacamayos) within the reserve is one of the largest natural clay licks in the country and one of the wildlife highlights of Peru. Thousands of brilliantly colored macaws and parrots arrive daily at the cliffs to feed on mineral salts.

Most visitors prebook tours to Tambopata in Cusco, although one could easily arrange a lodge visit by stopping in the local offices of travel agents and tour operators in the center of Puerto Maldonado or at the airport. Access to the Tambopata Reserve is by boat from Puerto Maldonado. Packages begin with 2-day/1-night arrangements, but 3-day/2-night packages are better. Lodge stays generally allow visitors to see a large variety of trees, plants, and birds, but sightings of wild mammals, apart from monkeys and otters, are rare. Species such as jaguars and tapirs seldom show their faces.

Lodges are located predominantly either along the Río Tambopata, which extends south of Puerto Maldonado, or the Río Madre de Dios, east of the city. The forest around the Río Tambopata is generally better for wildlife viewing, with greater primary forest.

> ⓘ **Tips** **¡Que Frío!**
>
> The weather in the Madre de Dios region is usually extremely hot and sticky, as you would expect. But the southern jungle's proximity to the Andes produces periodic cold spells called *friajes*, which originate in the South Pole, from June through August. When they hit, friajes drop the temperature to 9°C (48°F) for a period of 2 or 3 days.

TAMBOPATA TOUR OPERATORS & LODGES
South of Puerto Maldonado: Along Río Tambopata

- **Peruvian Safaris (Explorer's Inn)** 🐾🐾, Plateros 365, Cusco (ⓒ **084/235-342**), and Fitzcarrald 136, Puerto Maldonado (ⓒ **044/572-078**; www.peruviansafaris.com). About 3 hours upriver from Puerto Maldonado, at the edge of the Tambopata Reserve Zone, **Explorer's Inn** is a comfortable, professionally run 25-year-old lodge that hosts both tourists and scientists. The inn is excellent for fauna, particularly jungle birds. (It's probably the top spot in Tambopata for birding.) Established in 1976, the complex has seven thatched-roof bungalows and 30 rooms with private bathrooms. The lodge has a good network of nearly 32km (20 miles) of trails, including several to nearby oxbow lakes. Guides are Peruvian and international biologists (or biologists in training). Prices range from $180 for 3 days/2 nights to $495 for 5 days/4 nights.

- **Rainforest Expeditions** 🐾🐾, Portal de Carnes 236, Cusco (ⓒ **877/905-3782** in the U.S., or 084/232-772), and Jr. Arequipa 401, Puerto Maldonado (ⓒ **084/571-056**; www.perunature.com). This 10-year-old ecotourism company promotes tourism with environmental education, research, and conservation. It operates two Tambopata lodges. The large and nicely outfitted **Posada Amazonas** lodge, about 2 hours upriver from Puerto Maldonado, is owned jointly with the Ese'eja indigenous community and promotes some cultural interaction with the group. Posada Amazonas is good for reasonably priced, introductory nature tours. It has an eagle nest site and an observation tower. Prices range from $190 for 3 days/2 nights to $370 for 5 days/4 nights. The smaller and more spartan **Tambopata Research Center** is also more remote (8 hr. upriver from Puerto Maldonado), located near the famed Tambopata macaw clay lick, and better for in-depth tours and wildlife sightings. It's the place to go to see flocks of colorful macaws. Prices are $590 for 5 days/4 nights to $889 for 7 days/6 nights. (In longer programs, lodging for 2 or 3 nights is at the Posada Amazonas.)

- **Tambopata Jungle Lodge** 🐾, Suecia 343, Cusco (ⓒ and fax **084/245-695**; www.tambopatalodge.com). A private reserve lodge 4 hours from Puerto Maldonado, this place has 24km (15 miles) of trails, including trails to lake systems on the opposite bank of the Tambopata River. The lodge consists of individual two-bedroom cabins with porches, hammocks, and private bathrooms. Superior rooms have solar-powered lighting and hot water. There are several trails nearby and good organized jungle treks, and the lodge organizes overnight trips to the Tambopata macaw clay lick. Prices range from $180 for 3 days/2 nights to $530 for 5 days/4 nights. Macaw clay lick programs are the more expensive of the two; additional days at the *collpa* (clay lick) can be arranged for $80 per day. Programs at the Tambopata Jungle

Lodge are available through **Peruvian Andean Treks,** Pardo 705, Cusco (© **084/225-701;** www.andeantreks.com).

East of Puerto Maldonado: Along the Río Madre de Dios

Lodges nearer to Puerto Maldonado are generally cheaper and, of course, less time-consuming to get to than those deeper in the Tambopata Nature Reserve. Because they are located in secondary jungle and not nearly as remote, they best serve as introductory visits to the Amazon. The forest along the Madre de Dios is generally not as pristine as that found along the Tambopata River. The following lodges are several of the best that are easily accessible from Puerto Maldonado (as little as a half hour by boat).

- **Sandoval Lake Lodge** _(Value_, run by InkaNatura Travel, Plateros 361, 2nd floor, Cusco (© **888/287-7186** in the U.S., or 084/251-173; www. inkanatura.com). This lodge, located on high bluffs overlooking lovely Sandoval Lake and surrounded by thick forest, is perhaps the best option close to Puerto Maldonado. Getting to the lodge is itself fun; after walking (or riding in a bicycle rickshaw) a couple kilometers through secondary forest, you hop aboard a canoe and paddle along a canal and then across the lake. The spacious facility consists of a large main dining room and lounge and two wings of rooms; about half have private bathrooms. In the lake environs are significant concentrations of birds and even giant otters. Monkeys, caimans, and macaws can often be seen. Extensions to visit the Tambopata macaw clay lick and camp nearby can be arranged. A 2-day/1-night stay costs $140; 3 days/2 nights, $180.

- **Cusco Amazónico Lodge,** J.C. Tello C-13, Urbanización Santa Mónica, Cusco (© **084/235-314,** or 01/422-6574 in Lima). Featuring a large main house and 43 bungalows, this rustic lodge is 15km (9 miles) down the Madre de Dios. Rooms have private bathrooms and terraces with hammocks. There's a good system of trails nearby. A 3-day/2-night stay costs $160.

- **EcoAmazonia Lodge,** booked through Andean Life, Plateros 341, Cusco (© **084/221-491;** www.andeanlife.com/ecoamazonialodge.htm). About an hour by boat from Puerto Maldonado, this large lodge with long rows of basic bungalows has trails that lead to a canopy-viewing platform. It's a friendly and comfortable place surrounded by 10,000 hectares (25,000 acres) of forest, and it offers _ayahuasca_ ceremonies (see the "Trippin' Amazon Style" box, on p. 323). Rates run from $40 per day.

MANU BIOSPHERE RESERVE ★★★
242km (150 miles) NE of Cusco

Manu, a UNESCO World Biosphere Reserve and World Heritage Site, certainly doesn't lack for distinctions and accolades. The Biosphere Reserve encompasses the least accessible and explored jungle of primary and secondary forest in Peru,

---

Fun Fact What's an Oxbow Lake?

An oxbow lake is a natural lake formed by the normal shifting of river waters, which have fashioned a new streambed in the riverbanks. The old riverbed fills with water and forms a lake. Oxbow lakes, which can be very large and stocked with fish, are so named because they are shaped like an old-fashioned U-shaped yoke.

Tips **Birds, Plants? Check. Jaguars? Good Luck.**

Peru's Amazon jungle regions have some of the greatest recorded biodiversity and species of plants and animals on earth. However, you will be disappointed if you go expecting a daily show of *Wild Kingdom*. An expedition to the Amazon is not like a safari to the African savanna. Many mammals are extremely difficult to see in the thick jungle vegetation, and though the best tour operators employ guides skilled in ferreting them out, there are no guarantees. Even in the most virgin sections and after devoting several patient days to the exercise, you are unlikely to see many large mammals, especially the rare species such as tapirs, jaguars, and giant otters. If you bag even a single sighting, your jungle expedition would be considered a roaring success. In Manu and Tambopata, you are much more likely to see plenty of jungle birds (including fabulous macaws), butterflies, insects, and some monkeys, though some groups are fortunate enough to see a tapir or a family of otters. Travelers with a thing for birds and botany are likely to be the most amply rewarded.

---

and is about as close as you're likely to come to virgin rain forest anywhere in the world. In fact, it's so remote that not only did the Spaniards, who found their way to virtually every corner of Peru except Machu Picchu, never enter the jungle, but also the Incas, who created an empire that stretched from Ecuador to Chile, never conquered the region, either. The forest wasn't really penetrated until the late 1800s, when rubber barons and loggers set their sights on it. Peru declared it a national park in 1973.

Only slightly smaller than the Pacaya-Samiria National Reserve (see the "Into the Wild: Farther Afield from Iquitos" box, on p. 324), Manu is one of the largest protected areas in South America, with just under two million hectares (more than four million acres). Its surface area of varied habitats includes Andes highlands, cloud forests, and lowland tropical rain forests. The park encompasses an area of almost unimaginable diversity, climbing as it does from an altitude near sea level to elevations of 3,500m (11,550 ft.).

A single hectare of forest in Manu may have 10 times the number of species of trees that a hectare of temperate forest in Europe or North America has. Manu, which contains the highest bird, mammal, and plant diversity of any park on the planet, offers visitors perhaps their best opportunity for viewing wildlife that has been pushed deep into the rain forest by man's presence. It boasts nearly 1,000 species of birds, 1,200 butterfly species, 20,000 plants, 200 species of mammals, and 13 species of primates. Species in danger of extinction include the spectacled bear, giant armadillo, and cock-of-the-rock.

Birders thrill at the prospect of glimpsing bird populations that account for 10% of the world's total, more than found in all of Costa Rica. Hugely prized among wildlife observers are giant river otters, parrots, and macaws at a riverbank clay lick, preening and bright red cocks-of-the-rock, and lumbering lowland tapirs gathering at a forest clay lick. Scientists estimate that perhaps 12,000 to 15,000 animal species remain to be identified. Manu is also home to dozens of native Amerindian tribes, some of which have contact with the modern world and others that remain secluded.

Going with a group tour to Manu is the only realistic way to visit the park, and only a handful of travel agencies in Cusco are authorized to organize excursions to the Manu Biosphere Reserve. Visitors can enter two of three separate zones of the reserve. Access to the uninhabited Reserve Zone, up the Manu River northwest of Boca Manu, is by permit and with accompaniment by an authorized guide only. The other sector of the park, the Cultural Zone, is home to traditional nomadic groups, but the zone is open to all visitors; many tour operators in Cusco offer tours to lodges. Traveling independently to the Cultural Zone is possible, but extremely demanding and time-consuming—too much so for all but the hardiest eco-adventurers with tons of time. The third and largest zone (it occupies 3.7 million ha/9.1 million acres, or about three-fourths of the entire reserve), the Manu National Park, is off-limits to everyone but native peoples and researchers with special government permission.

Most trips to Manu visit jungle trails and lakes Cocha Salvador and Cocha Otorongo. Both are uniquely endowed with wildlife, including several types of caimans and wild monkeys. Cocha Otorongo is home to a prized, endangered group of giant otters. Virtually all tours make stops at key observation piers, platforms, and towers for wildlife viewing. Many longer Manu trips include visits to a macaw clay lick.

Getting to Manu is itself an eco-adventure. Overland access to the Manu Reserve Zone from Cusco (from Puerto Maldonado is much more difficult) is a stunning (and stunningly beautiful) 2-day journey through 4,000m (13,120 ft.) mountains and cloud forest before descending into lowland rain forest. The scenery along the narrow road, full of switchbacks and great panoramic views of glaciers and the eastern Andes, is so extraordinary that many lodges and tour operators travel overland and return to Cusco by small aircraft (a 25-min. flight from Boca Manu). The trip passes through Paucartambo (see chapter 6, "Cusco") and travels along roads whose steep descents are thrilling—though unsettling to some travelers—on the way to high jungle. Bus or plane travel to Boca Manu is followed by up to a couple of days of river travel to lodges, campsites, and principal points of interest in the reserve. Because Manu is so isolated and access so restricted, reserve visits are expensive and plainly beyond the scope of most budget travelers ($500–$1,500 per person or more for a 5- to 8-day trip). Most visits to Manu require about a week.

MANU TOUR OPERATORS

Just 10 tour companies are permitted to run organized expeditions to the Reserve Zone, and they are limited to 30 travelers each per week. The best of the firms listed below are closely involved with conservation and local development programs. The least expensive expeditions are those that bus travelers in and out or return by small plane. Land travel is time-consuming, but an excellent opportunity to experience the diverse terrain and types of forest that comprise Manu.

⌒ *Tips* **Manu Tour Considerations**

The best deals are usually available by arranging your trip on-site in Cusco rather than your home country. However, doing so carries some risks. Your chosen tour operator may not have space available. Another warning worth heeding is that of previous travelers who've gone to Manu but had their returns delayed (by weather conditions and mechanical and other mishaps) by several days. It's wise to schedule a Manu expedition in the middle of your trip, with a few buffer days before your scheduled departure.

Tips **All Alone in the Forest . . . With a Few Good Friends**

As remote and huge as the Manu Reserve Zone is, don't expect to find yourself enveloped and alone in the quiet of the jungle during high season. The few lodges and tour operators with a presence in the zone are very busy during the months of June, July, and August, and travelers' contact with each other may greatly outdistance their contact with species native to the rain forest. This is the case despite the official limits of 30 travelers per agency per week. (If all 10 agencies have full loads, that's still 300 people traveling many of the same waterways and racing to arrive first at primary observation points.)

Note that most companies operate with fixed departure dates only in the dry season, from May through November. The prices below do not include air transportation.

Most of the tour operators below post detailed itineraries and information about their Manu trips on their websites.

- **InkaNatura Travel,** Plateros 361, 2nd floor, Cusco (✆ **888/287-7186** in the U.S., or 084/251-173; www.inkanatura.com). A joint owner of the **Manu Wildlife Center,** it arranges stays there and elsewhere in the area, including trips to new tented camps. A 6-day/5-night trip costs $1,299. Specialist birding programs are available, as well as Tambopata expeditions. InkaNatura also operates **Cock-of-the-Rock Lodge,** which is owned by a local conservation group. The lodge, located in the Selva Sur Nature Reserve, is named for the preening birds and their lek (mating ground) just a short walk away. Located on the road from Cusco to Manu, near the switchback road that leads from the Andes to cloud forest, at an elevation of 1,600m (5,000 ft.), the small lodge is very well positioned for birding in that habitat. A 2-day/1-night trip costs $540; 3 days/2 nights, $720; 4 days/3 nights, $875.

- **Manu Ecological Adventures,** Plateros 356, Cusco (✆ **084/261-640;** www.cbc.org.pe/manu). This 6-year-old agency offers some of the most affordable trips, ranging from 5 days/4 nights (in and out by plane, $724) to 8 days/7 nights (overland, $550), with 2 nights in open-air lodges and the rest in campsites. A 4-day visit to the Cultural Zone only is $300 (overland).

- **Manu Expeditions** *,* Av. Pardo 895, Cusco (✆ **084/226-671;** www.manuexpeditions.com). The longest established operator in the Manu Biosphere Reserve has been organizing rain-forest tours for nearly 2 decades. The company is owned by the British Honorary Counsel in Cusco, a respected ornithologist. It offers stays at the **Manu Wildlife Center,** of which the group is part owner, and at a safari camp facility deep within the Manu Biosphere Reserve. The Wildlife Center is the best lodge in Peru for birding and is well positioned for wildlife viewing of all types, including the elusive lowland tapir, with nearly 48km (30 miles) of trails nearby. There are a couple of canopy viewing platforms nearby. Maximum group size is 10; minimum, 4. The company has three basic programs: 4-, 6-, and 9-day tours, ranging from $1,200 to $1,600 per person. The programs with safari camping components are especially recommended. It also specializes in birdwatching tours and horse treks.

- **Manu Nature Tours** 🐾, Av. Pardo 1046, Cusco (© **084/252-721;** www. manuperu.com). A very professional outfit with 15 years experience in Manu—it was one of the first to send expeditions to the reserve—Manu Nature Tours operates the well-known and comfortable **Manu Lodge,** the oldest lodge within the Reserve Zone (4-, 5-, and 8-day trips, $1,532–$1,879), which overlooks a 2km (1¼-mile) oxbow lake; and the new but refreshingly small **Cloud Forest Lodge,** adjacent to a 120m (400-ft.) waterfall in the Cultural Zone (2- and 3-day trips, $309–$465; 7-day combined camping, $710). The agency claims the oxbow lake is one of the best spots anywhere in the jungle to view giant river otters. Add-on options include mountain biking, river rafting, and tree canopy climbs, and extensions to visit the macaw clay lick are also possible. The office in Cusco is attached to a Patagonia outdoor gear shop and a rain-forest cafe, in case you needed any reassurance of their commitment. The agency is also expanding its activities to include trekking programs in the southern and central highlands, as well as more traditional tourist trips throughout Peru.
- **Pantiacolla,** Plateros 360, Cusco (© **084/238-323;** www.pantiacolla.com). An initiative of a Dutch biologist and local conservationist, the agency is one of the most conservation-oriented agencies organizing trips to Manu, and its programs are slightly more affordable than others of similar quality. The company operates the small **Pantiacolla Lodge** at the edge of the Manu National Park. It's favored by budget travelers and good for birders. Prices range from $725 for 5 days to $765 for 9 days.

Other reputable Manu tour companies and lodges whose programs are worth looking into in greater detail, especially for budget travelers, include:

- **Expediciones Vilca,** Saphi 456 and Plateros 363, Cusco (© **084/251-872;** www.cbc.org.pe/manuvilca). Vilca has been organizing Manu expeditions for a decade, with trips that split time between lodges and campsites. It has earned a sturdy reputation among budget-minded travelers.
- **Mayuc,** Portal de Confiturías 211, Plaza de Armas, Cusco (© **084/ 232-666;** www.mayuc.com). Mayuc is a traditional tour operator with programs across Peru, plus good budget-camping programs to Manu.
- **SAS Travel,** Portal de Panes 143, Plaza de Armas, Cusco (© **084/237-292;** www.sastravelperu.com). This well-run and popular all-purpose agency offers varied programs to both Manu and Tambopata and stays at various lodges.

2 Iquitos & the Northern Amazon ⭐⭐

1,860km (1,150 miles) NE of Lima

Iquitos, the gateway to the northern Amazon, is Peru's largest jungle town and the capital of its largest department, Loreto, which occupies nearly a third of the national territory and is nearly the size of Germany. Though you must fly to get here—unless you have a week to kill for hot and uncomfortable river travel—the pockets of jungle down- and upriver from Iquitos are the most accessible of the Peruvian Amazon basin. Some of the best jungle lodges in the country, some of which are entering their fourth decade of ecotourism, are located just a few hours by boat from Iquitos. Because the region is the most trafficked and developed of the Peruvian Amazon, costs are lower for most jungle excursions than they are in the more exclusive Manu Biosphere Reserve.

The most important port city of the Amazon lies at the confluence of the Nanay and Itaya rivers. The city was founded in 1754 by Jesuit missionaries, although some continue to claim it was actually not founded until nearly a century later. The city's proximity to South America's greatest rain forest and its isolation from the rest of Peru have created a unique tropical atmosphere. In the late 1860s and '70s, pioneering merchants got rich off the booming rubber trade and built ostentatious mansions lined with glazed tiles along the river. Iquitos rivaled Manaus in Brazil for leadership of the rubber trade. The city went from boom to bust, though oil exploration, shipping, logging, and other export trade would later revive and sustain the city's fortunes. Today, tourism is quite evidently among the Iquitos's most important industries.

Iquitos is far from the grand port of old. The modern city of nearly a half million is composed of descendants of original ethnic groups such as the Yaguas, Boras, Kukama, and Iquitos, as well as significant populations of immigrant groups from Europe and Asia. Those great homes along the malecón are now faded monuments to the city's glory days, and just blocks from the main square lies the fascinating Belén district, where families live in a squalid pile of ramshackle wooden houses on the banks of the river. Some are propped up by spindly stilts, while others float, tethered to poles, when the river rises 6m (20 ft.) or more.

The Belén district looks distinctly Far Eastern, and Iquitos has more in common with steamy tropical Asian cities than the highlands of Peru. Like a South American Saigon, the air is waterlogged and the streets buzz with unrelenting waves of motorcycles and motocarros. Locals speak a languid, mellifluous Spanish unmatched in other parts of the country, and pretty prostitutes loll about the Plaza de Armas. Locals dress not in alpaca sweaters and shawls, but flesh-baring tank tops and short skirts.

Iquitos has a relaxed, intoxicating feel that's likely to detain you for a couple of days at least. But for most visitors, the lure of the Amazon rain forest is the primary attraction. Virgin rain forest, though, is hard to find. To lay eyes on exotic wildlife, such as pink dolphins, caimans, and macaws, you have to get far away from Iquitos, at least 80km (50 miles) out and onto secondary waterways. Options for rain-forest excursions include lodge visits, river cruises and, for the adventurous, independent guided treks.

Tips Malaria & Yellow Fever in Northern Peru

According to the Centers for Disease Control and Prevention, epidemic malaria rapidly emerged in the northern Amazon in the 1990s. Peru has the second highest number of malaria cases in South America (after Brazil), with the majority of cases from the Loreto department. From 1992 to 1997, malaria increased 50 times in Loreto, a rate more than 10 times greater than the rest of the country. Malaria around the city of Iquitos accounts for the greatest number of cases in Loreto.

In June 2001, the Peruvian Ministry of Health also reported an outbreak of yellow fever in the Loreto department in three districts, including Iquitos. Eight cases of yellow fever were confirmed, with two deaths.

These outbreaks should not deter most travelers from visiting the Amazon of northern Peru, but they should emphasize the need for proper vaccinations and medication prior to (and during) traveling to the region. See "Insurance, Health & Safety," in chapter 2, for more information.

The Northern Amazon

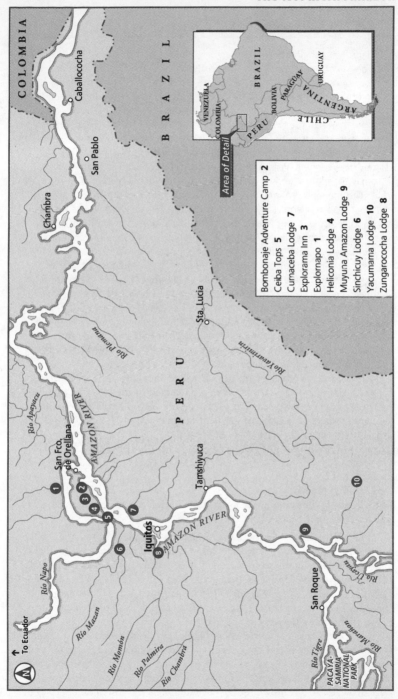

COLOMBIA

Caballococha

San Pablo

Chambra

BRAZIL

Area of Detail

VENEZUELA
BRAZIL
COLOMBIA
PERU
BOLIVIA
PARAGUAY
URUGUAY
ARGENTINA
CHILE

Bombonaje Adventure Camp **2**
Ceiba Tops **5**
Cumaceba Lodge **7**
Explorama Inn **3**
Explornapo **1**
Heliconia Lodge **4**
Muyuna Amazon Lodge **9**
Sinchicuy Lodge **6**
Yacumama Lodge **10**
Zungarococha Lodge **8**

Sta. Lucia

Río Pichimína

Río Yavarimírím

P E R U

San Fco. de Orellana

AMAZON RIVER

Río Apayacu

Tamshiyuca

1 **2**
3
4
5 **7**
Iquitos **8** *AMAZON RIVER*
6

9

10

San Roque

Río Napo

To Ecuador

Río Mazán

Río Momón

Río Palmira

Río Chambira

Río Tigre

Río Ucayali

Río Marañón

PACAYA-SAMIRIA
NATIONAL
PARK

N

311

Manu Bird-Watching & the Macaw Clay Lick

Manu has a mythic reputation among birders. And it should: It has the highest concentration of birdlife on the planet. In addition to its many thousands of species of plants, more than a dozen species of monkeys, and hundreds of mammals, the Manu Biosphere Reserve contains some 1,000 species of birds, including seven species of colorful macaws. That's more than half the bird species in all of Peru—one of the top countries in the world (along with Colombia and Indonesia) for recorded bird species within its borders—more species than are found in all of Costa Rica, and one of every nine birds in the world! The forests of the western Amazon enjoy the highest density of birds per square mile of any on earth.

The immense variety of birds is due to the diversity of altitudinal zones, habitats, and ecosystems spread across Manu, which encompasses cloud forest, and upper and lowland tropical forest. In addition, Manu shimmers with vastly different types of forests, lakes, and microclimates. From the Andes Mountains surrounding Cusco, the road to Manu plummets an amazing 4,000m (13,120 ft.) down to the dense tropical forests of the Amazon basin. For every 1,000m (3,280 ft.) of change in elevation, the indigenous bird life changes just as dramatically. The twisting road near the Cock-of-the-Rock Lodge has been called "the best road in the world" by one of the world's leading bird-tour companies.

In visits of just 2 to 3 weeks in Manu, dedicated birders have recorded a staggering 500 species. Birders can expect to come into contact with quetzals, toucanets, tanagers, and the famed, blazing-red Andean cocks-of-the-rock at their numerous leks. Others of certain interest to birders, among many dozens more, are the blue-headed macaw, white-cheeked tody-tyrant, bamboo antshrike, and Manu antbird. On river-banks, expect daily sightings of giant macaws and other parrots, while

ESSENTIALS
GETTING THERE

Water-locked Iquitos can only be reached by airplane or boat, and for most travelers, air is the only practical option.

BY PLANE Iquitos's **Aeropuerto Francisco Secada Vigneta** (© 094/ 260-151) was until relatively recently an international airport, receiving flights from Miami, but those were suspended in 1999. **Aero Continente** (© 01/ 242-4242; www.aerocontinente.net), **Aviandina** (© 01/242-4242 or 01/484- 1177), and **TANS** (© 01/213-6000; www.tansperu.com.pe) fly daily from Lima and from Pucallpa and Tarapoto, other cities in the Loreto department. Flights from Lima cost between $59 and $69.

The airport is usually chaotic when flights arrive, with dozens of representatives of tour operators and countless touts and con men competing for your attention. Do not let anyone take your bags, and don't let anyone you don't know hop in a cab with you. Definitely wait before even discussing Amazon lodge packages. To downtown Iquitos, an automobile taxi costs about S/10 ($3); a motocarro, S/7 ($2). If a taxi driver offers to take you for less, he will certainly take you directly to a hotel where he can earn commission, not where you mixed-feeding flocks containing dozens of different types of birds—a defense against predators—soar overhead.

One of the most rewarding birding experiences in Tambopata or Manu is the spectacle of hundreds of macaws and other birds feeding at a *collpa,* or clay lick. Many birds and mammals (such as tapirs) supplement their diets with minerals found in clay, which is loaded with minerals and salts. Early in the morning, parrots gather in trees above the river. They then descend in large numbers and feed at the clay. Gorgeously colored and noisy macaws arrive next. Visitors often view the scene from a small catamaran. **Blanquillo Macaw and Parrot Lick,** the subject of a 1994 *National Geographic* report and subsequent TV special on macaws, is the most famous collpa in Manu. Collpa viewings are during the dry season only and are best from July through September; macaws do not feed at the clay licks during the month of June, for reasons unknown.

All the Manu tour operators focus to some extent on birding, of course, but for specialists, the **Manu Wildlife Center,** jointly owned by Manu Expeditions, itself run by a well-known ornithologist, is perhaps best suited for enthusiastic birding in Manu. Also recommended by birders is **Pantiacolla Lodge,** where birders have recorded 500 birds in a month's time.

Birders and would-be birders should check out **Birding Peru** (www.birdingperu.org) for specialist bird-watching trips to Peru, as well as **Ornifolks** (www.ornifolks.org). **WorldTwitch** (http://worldtwitch. virtualave.net) has helpful links to birding lodges, tour operators, and organizations throughout Peru, as well as the Americas and the Caribbean.

necessarily want to go. (The difference may be a lot more than the few soles you save on the taxi fare.) City buses (S/0.50, or 15¢) are available outside the gates of the airport on the main road (they travel along Ocampo/Tacna/Grau), but unless you have a very manageable backpack as your only luggage, it's not worth the hassle.

BY BOAT   Arriving by boat is an option only for those with the luxury of ample time. It takes about a week when the river is high (and 3–4 days in the dry season) to reach the capital city of Loretos upriver along the Amazon from Pucallpa or Yurimaguas.

To travel to Colombia or Brazil by boat, your best bet is by river cruise, though as of early 2002, trips to Manaus had been suspended. The Iquitos port, Puerto Masusa, is about 3km (2 miles) north of the Plaza de Armas. See "Cruises," on p. 324, for more details.

VISITOR INFORMATION

A municipal **tourism information booth** (© 094/235-621) is at the arrivals terminal baggage claim at the airport. It maintains a chart of hotels and costs, and the staff is happy to dispense information (and frequently opinions) about the various jungle-tour and lodge operators.

One of Peru's most helpful and controversial tourism information offices is on the north side of the Plaza de Armas at Napo 226 (© **094/235-621**). The English-speaking staff has free maps and lists of all recommended hotels and tour operators (including photo albums of lodges). The office is run, oddly enough, by an expat Texan who has taken it as his mission to straighten out the confusing offers of unofficial guides and lodge operators. (Er, it's a jungle out there.) His shoot-from-the-hip approach to tourism information has angered a number of local officials and business people, but visitors are the beneficiaries. The office is open Monday through Saturday from 8am to 8pm, as well as occasional Sunday mornings.

FAST FACTS   ATMs and banks are located along Putumayo and Próspero, on the south side of the Plaza de Armas. Two banks that exchange traveler's checks and cash are **Banco de Crédito,** Putumayo 201 at Próspero, and **Banco Continental,** Sargento Lores 171. Money-changers can usually be found hanging around the Plaza de Armas and along Putumayo and Próspero, but calculate the exchange beforehand and count your money carefully.

If you're looking to cross into Brazil or Colombia, the **Brazilian consulate** is located at Sargento Lores 363 (© **094/232-081**), and the **Colombian consulate** is at Callao 200 (© **094/231-461**). You should make contact with their embassies in Lima or even at home before traveling to Peru. For questions about border-crossing formalities for jungle travel to and from Brazil and Colombia, visit or call the **Migraciones** office at Malecón Tarapacá 382 (© **094/235-371**).

In an emergency, call © **105.** You can also call **Cruz Roja** (Red Cross) at © **094/241-072** for medical emergencies, and © **094/267-555** for fire emergencies. For medical attention, go to one of the following hospitals or clinics: **Clínica Ana Stahl,** Av. la Marina 285 (© **094/252-535**); **EsSalud,** Av. la Marina 2054 (© **094/250-333**); or **Hospital Regional,** Av. 28 de Julio s/n, Punchana (© **094/251-882**). The **tourist police** office is located at Sargento Lores 834 (© **094/242-081**). There's also a **Tourist Protection Service** office at Huallaga 311 (© **094/243-490**).

Most Internet cabinas in Iquitos stay open late, and rates are about S/2 (60¢) per hour. One to try is **Estación Internet,** Fitzcarrald 120 (© **094/223-608**). Several other cabinas are located near the Plaza de Armas, particularly on Próspero and Putumayo. The small cabina (no name) next to the entrance to the Casa de Fierro is pretty dependable.

Iquitos's **post office** is located at Arica 403, on the corner of Morona (© **094/231-915**); it's open Monday through Friday from 8am to 6pm and Saturday from 8am to 3pm. The **Telefónica del Perú** office is at Arica 276; it's open Monday through Friday from 9am to 6pm.

GETTING AROUND

Iquitos is for all practical purposes an island city, defined by water—not just the mighty Amazon, which borders it to the west, but also a complex network of smaller rivers and streams, as well as a series of lakes just outside the city. The riverfront along the Amazon is a long boulevard, Malecón Tarapacá, with a pedestrian walkway that has recently been extended and much improved. It reaches all the way from the focal point of downtown, restaurants and bars near the Plaza de Armas, to the shabby but picturesque Belén district. Próspero is the main avenue of communication from the main square to residential zones south.

ATTRACTIONS ●
Barrio de Belén
(market & port) **21**
Casa de Fierro **12**
Iglesia Matriz **11**
Lago Moronacocha &
Santo Tomás **19**
Malecón Tarapacá **13**
Museo Amazónico **15**
Parque/Laguna de
Quistococha **20**
Plaza de Armas **8**
Puerto Bellavista/Río Nanay **2**

ACCOMMODATIONS ■
El Dorado Plaza Hotel **9**
El Huaralino **16**
Hospedaje El Sitio **18**
Hospedaje La Pascana **3**
Hotel Acosta **10**
Hotel Amazon Garden **1**
Hotel Victoria Regia **17**
Real Hotel Iquitos **7**

DINING ◆
El Nuevo Mesón **4**
Fitzcarraldo **5**
Montecarlo **6**
Regal (Casa de Fierro) **12**
Restaurant Gran Maloca **14**

ⓘ Information

0 _____ 200 meters
0 _____ 200 yards

BY MOTOTAXI & TAXI Motocarros are everywhere in Iquitos; if you don't mind the noise and wind in your face (and aren't worried about accidents), it's a great way to get around. In-town fares are S/1.50 (40¢). Regular car taxis are only slightly less ubiquitous; most trips in town cost S/2 (60¢).

BY BUS *Combis* and *ómnibuses* (buses) travel principal routes, but are much less comfortable and not much less expensive than more convenient motocarros. The fare is S/0.50 (15¢).

BY MOTORCYCLE If you want to travel around town as Iquiteños do, rent a small *moto,* or motorcycle. Try **Visión Motos,** Nauta 309 (ⓒ **094/234-759**). Rates are about $40 per day or $5 per hour.

BY FOOT Though the city is spread over several square miles, the core of downtown Iquitos is compact and easy to get around on foot, and even Belén is easy to walk to. Some hostels and hotels are a distance from the main square, though, requiring at least the occasional use of inexpensive motocarros.

The Amazon in Danger

Could the vast Amazon rain forest disappear from the face of the Earth during our lifetimes? Some scientists now maintain that the forest itself—not to mention the many thousands of plant, animal, bird, and insect species that call it home—is in imminent danger of extinction. A new mathematical model by an American researcher, presented at a 2001 Geology Society conference in Scotland, suggests that the destruction of Amazonian rain forests could be irreversible in as few as 10 years, and forecasts the whole-scale destruction of Brazil's rain forest in 40 or 50 years.

Peru, the origin of the great Amazon River, boasts some of the largest and most biologically diverse rain forests in the world. The country counts 84 of 103 existing ecosystems and 28 of the 32 climates on the planet among its remarkable statistics. Peru has 72 million hectares (178 million acres) of natural-growth forests—70% in the Amazon jungle region—that comprise nearly 60% of the national territory. But Peru is losing nearly 300,000 hectares (more than 700,000 acres) of rain forest annually. In other Amazon basin countries, the picture is even bleaker. Half the world's known plant and animal species live in rain forests, but according to the World Resources Institute, more than 100 species become extinct in the world every day due to tropical deforestation. The destruction of their habitats is estimated at 81,000 hectares (200,000 acres) each day—an area larger than New York City. Less than 50 years ago, 15% of the earth's land surface was rain forest. Today, that total has been reduced to a mere 6%.

The primary threats to Peru's tropical forests are deforestation caused by agricultural expansion, cattle ranching, logging, oil extraction and spills, mining, illegal coca farming, and colonization initiatives. Deforestation has shrunk territories belonging to indigenous peoples and wiped out more than 90% of the population. In the southern Amazon's Madre de Dios department, 3 decades of gold prospecting have pushed isolated Mashco-Piros, Amahuaca, Yaminahuas, and Yora tribes to the edge of extinction. Along with the threats to communities comes cultural extinction: Knowledge of plants and natural medicines, traditional ways of life, and even languages are lost. In Peru's Amazon jungle, new languages are being discovered even as others become extinct. Once-isolated communities in the jungle spoke up to 150 languages; today, only 57 survive and 25 of them are in danger of extinction, according to the Summer Institute of Linguistics.

Governments in developing countries have traditionally been reluctant to adopt tough measures to halt deforestation, bowing to the need for "economic development" and offering inducements to industry and extraction practices that have ranged from rubber extraction to logging and oil drilling. Slash-and-burn clearing of land, unproductive farming, and overhunting by marginalized people living in and around the jungle have further denuded the landscape of vegetation and animals.

Can anything be done to save the Amazon and its people, plants, and animals? Leaving the rain forests intact, with their wealth of nuts, fruits, oil-producing plants, and medicinal plants, has greater economic value than destroying them for unsustainable short-term interests. More than six times as much can be earned from sustainable harvests of fruit, cocoa, timber, and rubber from the rain forest tract than commercial logging produces. Slash-and-burn practices, which involve no preparation of the land and no safeguards to make its yield sustainable, destroys the land's capacity to produce: A plot can be burned just twice before a farmer must abandon it and search for another, uncultivated piece of land.

For most of the 20th century, Peru gave carte blanche to oil and gas exploration by multinationals in the Amazon basin, and the government looked the other way with regard to invasive gold mining in Indian communities. However, Peru has done a slightly better job of setting aside tracts of rain forest as national park reserves and regulating industry than have some other Latin American and Asian countries. The Manu Biosphere Reserve, the Tambopata-Candamo Reserve Zone, and the Pacaya-Samiria National Reserve are three of the largest protected rain-forest areas in the world, and the government regulates entry of tour groups. Peru augmented the Bahuaja-Sonene National Park, which was created in 1996, by 809,000 hectares (two million acres) in 2001. INRENA, Peru's Institute for Natural Resource Management, enforces logging regulations and reseeds Peru's Amazon forests. A handful of international and Peruvian environmental and conservation groups, such as ProNaturaleza, Conservation International, and the Rainforest Action Network are active in Peru, working on reforestation and sustainable forestry projects.

What about ecotourism initiatives in the rain forest? Do visitors to lodges in primary forest and jungle trekkers add to the threats facing native communities and species or do they in some way ensure their protection? Many conservationists have mixed feelings about promoting ecotourism in endangered habitats. Responsible tourism has the potential to educate people about the rain forest and its threats and may spur much-needed activism. The income produced by ecotourism is vital to local communities—many of whom are increasingly dependent upon tourists to buy their handicrafts or to lead on treks into the jungle—and to countries, as an incentive to protect the very things tourists come to see. A small handful of lodges in the rain forest have successfully integrated local tribes into the running of the lodges. But mankind's heavier imprints in the jungle are, of course, a potentially grave threat, pushing species and native communities ever farther from their natural habitats.

The lodges and tour operators I've recommended for travel in the Amazon all profess to practice responsible, low-impact tourism. Please do your utmost to follow suit. If you witness a tour group or lodge practicing unsafe ecotourism, by all means report it to either **INRENA** (© **01/224-3298**) or **PromPerú** (© **01/224-3279**; www.promperu.org), or to the tourist information offices in Cusco (© **084/263-176**) or Iquitos (© **094/235-621**).

For additional information on threatened species, visit the **World Conservation Union**'s website at www.iucn.org and check out its "Red Book" list. Another excellent resource is the **World Rainforest Information Portal** (www.rainforestweb.org). For information about the struggles of and threats to indigenous peoples, visit the **Survival International** website at www.survival-international.com.

Tips **Biblioteca Amazónica**

The Iquitos municipal library, Biblioteca Amazónica, is a handsome public space inhabiting an old rubber baron's mansion and overlooking the malecón and Río Amazonas. The reading room features lots of carved wood and colorful tiles. If a visit to the Amazon has whetted your appetite for old maps or information on the jungle, you can find them here. It has the largest collection of historical documents on the Amazon basin in Peru. Malecón Tarapacá 354, 2nd floor (© 094/242-353). Open Monday through Friday from 9am to noon.

WHAT TO SEE & DO
IN IQUITOS

The **Plaza de Armas,** while perhaps not Peru's most distinguished, is, as always, one of the focal points in town. It is marked by the early-20th-century, neo-Gothic **Iglesia Matríz** (parish church), built in 1919. Many of the church's most attractive elements, such as the tower, were later additions. Across the square stands the **Casa de Fierro,** or Iron House, which was designed by Gustave Eiffel for the 1889 Paris Exhibition. The walls, ceiling, and balcony are plastered in rectangular sheets of iron. Said to be the first prefabricated house in the Americas, it was shipped unassembled from Europe and built on-site where it currently stands.

One block back from the plaza, facing the Amazon River, the riverfront promenade **Malecón Tarapacá** was recently enlarged and improved with fountains (one a giant pink dolphin), benches, and street lamps, making it the focus of Iquitos urban life. The malecón is lined with several exquisite 19th-century mansions, relics from the rubber heyday, lined with Portuguese glazed tiles, or *azulejos.* The most spectacular is probably **Casa Hernández,** no. 302–308. Other houses worth checking out along the boulevard are **Casa Fitzcarrald,** Napo 200–212, an adobe house belonging to a famed rubber baron; **Casa Cohen,** Próspero 401–437; **Casa Morey,** Brasil, on the first block off the malecón; and the **Logia Unión Amazónica,** Nauta 262.

The **Museo Amazónico,** Malecón Tarapacá 386 (© 094/231-072), has occasionally interesting exhibits of Amazon folklore and tribal art, and a curious collection of 76 Indian statues made of fiberglass but fashioned as if they were bronze. Reportedly, some of the mothers whose children served as models for the works freaked out when they were covered in plaster for the moulds, thinking the children would be buried alive. The museum building, which dates to the mid–19th century, is a nicely restored example of the malecón's period mansions. The museum is open Monday through Friday from 9am to 1pm and 3 to 7pm, and Saturday from 9am to 1pm. Admission is S/3 (85¢).

The waterfront **Barrio de Belén** ✿✿, about a 15-minute walk south along the malecón, is Iquitos's most unusual quarter. Known for its sprawling, colorful, and odiferous open-air market, where you'll find a bounty of strange and wonderful Amazon fish, fauna, and fruits, Belén's residential district is a seedy and extremely poor but endlessly fascinating shantytown. Houses are constructed above the waters of the Amazon, and when the river is high, transportation is by canoe. Visitors are free to walk about in dry season (or, for much of the year, to take a locally arranged canoe trip) and see the houses—some on stilts, others floating during the rainy season—but you should go in a group and during the day only. It's an atmospheric and photogenic place, akin to Calcutta—you'll see scrappy kids tumbling out of clapboard houses and playing with pet monkeys, and a few houses proudly outfitted with cable TV and other modern conveniences—but exercise some caution and restraint if walking around the area with expensive camera equipment. Most residents of the neighborhood, while perhaps puzzled at foreigners' interest in the aesthetics of their dilapidated streets, are more than approachable for photos if you ask respectfully. The animated market, which extends over several blocks, is itself a wild place to visit, with all sorts of extraordinary exotic items for sale, including potions used by faith healers, *paiche* fish, and yummy Amazonian fruits such as *maracuyá* (passion fruit), *aguaje, cocona,* and others. Look for the stands set up with blenders, cranking out fruit juices and smoothies (*refrigerios* and *jugos*).

ATTRACTIONS NEAR IQUITOS

PUERTO BELLAVISTA & RIO NANAY   This Río Mañon port and suburb, a couple kilometers from downtown at the northern edge of Iquitos, has a pretty white-sand beach (Playa Nanay) enjoyed by locals and safe for swimming during summer months. It's also a good spot to hire a boat and cruise down to the confluence of the Amazon and Nanay rivers, where you can appreciate the difference in water colors (muddy brown and black), passing beaches, and a handful of local communities—among them the Boras and Yaguas—along the way. To get there, take a colectivo marked "Bellavista/Nanay," which leaves from points along Próspero.

PARQUE/LAGUNA DE QUISTOCOCHA   A resort complex about 13km (8 miles) south of Iquitos, the Quistococha Lagoon and Tourist Park has a nice beach and swimming area. It's mostly a spot for local families to hang out on weekends. There are picnic grounds, paddleboats, an aquarium, a walking path around the lagoon, and a zoo with exotic jungle animals and fish, including monkeys, serpents, jaguars, and pumas. A fish hatchery is populated by giant paiche fish. There's a restaurant on the grounds, as well as informal food stalls set up near the entrance to the park. To get there, you can take a 20-minute ride in a motocarro (about $3) or catch a colectivo marked "Quistococha" (S/2, or 60¢) on the corner of Moore and Bermúdez.

LAGO MORONACOCHA & SANTO TOMAS   Southwest of Iquitos, the lake at Moronacocha is little more than a place to relax at a couple of bars by the water, though locals head out there to swim and water-ski. Another 16km (10 miles) or so south of Moronacocha is another lake complex, Rumococha, and the small fishing village of Santo Tomás, known for its pottery artisans. It also has a lake (Lago Mapacocha) and resort-like activities, such as paddleboats and dugout canoes. To get there, board a colectivo marked "Aeropuerto" on Tacna/Grau; ask to be let off at the turnoff to Santo Tomás. There are colectivos

---

(*Fun Fact* Our Fish Is Bigger Than Your Fish

The Amazon is known for the piranha, that weird little fish with tiny teeth and a huge reputation, but it's not the only unique fish in the rivers of the rain-forest region. The Amazon paiche fish, which you'll find on restaurant menus throughout the zone, can grow up to 3m (9 ft.) long and weigh up to 113kg (250 lb.).

waiting at the intersection that ferry people back and forth to Santo Tomás. You can also get there by motocarro; the 20-minute ride is about $4.

SHOPPING IN IQUITOS

The most intriguing shopping option is the Belén open-air market (see above), though it's likely you'll find more to photograph and smell than actually buy. For local artisans' goods, there aren't many options; try **Centro Artesanal Anaconda,** the sparsely populated market downstairs from the malecón, or **Mercado Artesanal,** the larger market with wooden outdoor stalls selling hammocks, woodcarvings, and paintings on Avenida Quiñones, on the way out to the airport (about 3km/2 miles from downtown). Unlike most markets in Peru, here many of the sellers are also the craftspeople behind the work. Some of the best crafts, including textiles and pottery, come from the Shipibo Indian tribe of the Amazon.

Art Gallery Camu-Camu, Trujillo 498 (℃ **094/253-120**), showcases the work of the most famous local artist, Francisco Grippa, whose colorful paintings evoke Amazonian themes, including jungle flora and fauna. Grippa's exuberant and expressive style, known in the United States and Europe, has been labeled "grippismo." He uses local materials, including a canvas made from tree bark. The gallery is open daily from 10am to 1pm and 4 to 7pm. Tour groups often visit the Grippa's home/gallery in Pevas, the oldest town in the Peruvian Amazon, about 150km (90 miles) downriver from Iquitos.

JUNGLE TOURS, LODGES & RIVER CRUISES

The mighty Amazon reaches widths of about 4km (2½ miles) beyond Iquitos, and the river basin contains 2,000 species of fish (among them everyone's favorite, piranhas), 4,000 species of birds (including 120 hummingbirds), native mammals such as anteaters, tapirs, marmosets, and pink dolphins, and 60 species of reptiles, including caimans and anacondas.

Ecotourism is the primary draw for visitors to Iquitos, and the giant Amazon river system just beyond the city holds a wealth of natural wonders: rustic jungle lodges, canopy walks, and opportunities for bird-watching, piranha fishing, visits to Indian villages, and wildlife spotting (as well as less-standard activities, such as shaman consultations and ayahuasca drug ceremonies). Your options for exploring the jungle are **lodge stays,** which include jungle activities such as treks and canoe excursions; **river cruises;** or more adventurous **camping treks** with private guides. Most people head for lodges of varying degree of rusticity and distance from Iquitos. The jungle is immense and most parts of it are inaccessible. Immersing yourself in anything resembling pristine jungle is both costly and time-consuming.

Don't expect to spend your time in the jungle checking off a lengthy wildlife list of sightings; no matter where you go, your opportunities for viewing more than a couple of species of birds, fish, and mammals will be severely limited. You'll see lots of birds and if you're lucky, perhaps a few monkeys, caimans, and pink dolphins. (For deeper and more adventurous treks into the jungle, see the "Into the Wild: Farther Afield from Iquitos" box, on p. 324, and "Independent Guides," later in this section.)

For a quick and simple experience, you can stay at a lodge only an hour or two (within a 50km/31-mile radius) by boat from Iquitos, in secondary jungle. You're likely to see more fauna and have a more authentic experience in primary rain forest, but you'll have to travel much farther (beyond a radius of 80km/50 miles; up to 4 hr. by boat) and pay quite a bit more for the privilege. Generally speaking, you must trade comforts for authenticity. Very short trips (2–3 days) are unlikely to produce much in the way of wildlife, though you can still expect enjoyable contact with the Amazonian habitat. A true foray into virgin jungle, far from the heavy footsteps of thousands of guides and visitors before you, requires at least a week of demanding camping and trekking. Hard-core eco-types may wish to contract private guides to go deep into the *selva* and camp. (Ask at the tourism information office for a list of licensed, official guides; they also have a list of blacklisted guides.)

Prices for lodges and tours vary tremendously. For conventional lodges con-tracted in Iquitos, lodge tours average around $40 to $50 and $100 or more per person per day for lodges located farthest from the city. Some budget lodges offer bargain rates, as little as $25 to $30 a day (though in most cases you get what you pay for), and independent guides may charge as little as $15 a day. Costs are directly related to distance from Iquitos; the farther away, the more expensive they are. Costs include transportation, lodging, buffet-style meals, and guided activities (beverages extra).

Be careful: There are lots of look-alike lodges and tours. Lodges and eco-tourism companies come and go, and everyone's competing for your dollars. Hustlers, con artists, and all manner of disreputable touts abound in Iquitos, and you need to exercise a certain amount of caution before handing over money for a promised itinerary. The local tourism office works hard trying to ferret out guides, tours, and lodges with bad reputations. The office has photo albums of lodges and a thick book of travelers' comments, with pages and pages of frank opinions on virtually every lodge and tour. If you're making a tour deci-sion on the ground in Iquitos, it's a good idea to visit the office first for the most up-to-date information.

Most jungle lodges feature either individual rustic thatched-roof bungalows or main buildings with individual rooms; beds with mosquito netting; communal dining areas; hammock lounges; covered plank walkways; toilets; and either hot- or cold-water sinks and showers. A few lodges have extras such as swimming pools, lookout towers, canopy walkways, and electricity. Guests are taken on guided day- and nighttime excursions, including jungle walks, piranha fishing, and canoe and motorboat trips to spot birds, caimans, and dolphins. Many lodges offer artificial, even cheesy, visits with local Indian tribes, staged for your pleasure, and some host ayahuasca rituals (see the "Trippin' Amazon Style" box, on p. 323).

⟨ *Tips* Eco-nomizing

Though the prices of some lodges may seem steep to backpackers accus-tomed to dropping $8 to $10 for a place to sleep in other parts of Peru, getting by on $40 to $50 a day or a little more is really a pretty decent bar-gain, considering that food, river transportation, English-speaking guides, fishing and wildlife trips and treks, and shelter are all included. That said, you can almost certainly get a better deal when signing up with a lodge or tour on the ground in Iquitos by going door-to-door to the sales offices and comparing programs and prices than you would contracting one in Lima or from your home country prior to stepping foot in Peru. Especially during the off-season, lodges are willing to negotiate. However, you risk not getting the tour you want when you want it. For many travelers, the extra hassle and uncertainty may not be worth the dollars saved. Prices quoted on websites and through travel agents may be quite negotiable if you contact operators directly, depending on season and occupancy levels.

JUNGLE LODGES

The following are tour operators and lodges with good reputations. The list is not by any means exhaustive; there are dozens more agencies and lodges, but reports on many of them are less than stellar.

- **Cumaceba Lodge,** Putumayo 184, Iquitos (℃ 094/232-229; www. manguare.com.pe/cumaceba). This is one of the better budget lodges, though the company uses freelance "pirates" to snare customers and has received complaints for their sales tactics. The lodge has shared bungalows 36km (22 miles) downriver from Iquitos on the shores of the Río Amazonas. It also operates the rustic **Bombonaje Adventure Camp,** located 85km (53 miles) downriver from Iquitos, for more adventurous trips of 4 days minimum. A 2-day/1-night trip costs $85 per person; 3 days/2 nights, $125. Discounts may be offered.

- **Explorama Tours** 𝕮𝕮, Av. la Marina 340, Iquitos (℃ 094/252-530, or 800/707-5275 in the U.S. and Canada; www.explorama.com). The longest-established jungle-tour company in Iquitos and owned by an American, Explorama operates three lodges and a campsite, ranging from 160km (100 miles) to 40km (25 miles) downriver from Iquitos. The company has perhaps the best reputation of any in the field, bolstered by good guides, very good facilities and food, and a range of flexible activities. The company's first lodge, **Explorama Inn** (80km/50 miles from Iquitos), is large and attractive, with two long wings and a lovely restaurant/bar and communal area. Explorama owns the jungle's most luxurious lodge, **Ceiba Tops** (40km/25 miles from Iquitos), a jungle resort hotel with air-conditioning, a spectacular pool with a slide, and a Jacuzzi. There are trails nearby, and boats can take you out onto the river for dolphin-spotting and fishing, but Ceiba Tops is much more about relaxing in style surrounded by jungle. Near **Explornapo** (the Explorama lodge deepest in the jungle), there's a splendid **canopy walkway** 𝕮, one of the longest in the world. At a height of 36m (115 ft.) and a rambling length of 500m (a third of a mile), it alone is one of the highlights of a visit to this part of the Peruvian Amazon. It's possible to mix and match lodges; a popular plan for many travelers is several days at Explornapo (or more adventurous still, the rustic Explortambos campsite) followed by a couple days of relative luxury at Ceiba Tops. Prices range from $200 for a 2-day/1-night stay at Ceiba Tops to $285 for a 3-day/2-night stay at Explorama Lodge. The 8-day/7-night lodge combination program costs $1,100 per person ($1,400 for single). There's no price discounting, but specials are offered.

- **Heliconia Lodge,** Ricardo Palma 242, Iquitos (℃ 094/231-959; www. heliconialodge.com.pe), and **Zungarococha Lodge,** Próspero 574, Iquitos (℃ 094/235-132). Owned by the same group that manages the Acosta and Victoria Regia hotels in Iquitos, Heliconia is a good midrange, resort-like choice with nice facilities, located 80km (50 miles) downriver from Iquitos. Zungarococha is a jungle resort hotel with a pool accessible by land, only 15km (9 miles) downriver from Iquitos. A 3-day/2-night stay at Heliconia costs $240; Zungarococha costs about $60 a day. Package programs with stays at either the Victoria Regia or Acosta in Iquitos are available.

- **Muyuna Amazon Lodge,** Putumayo 163-B, Iquitos (℃ 094/242-858; www.muyuna.com). Muyuna is a small and attractive bungalow lodge located 120km (74 miles) upriver from Iquitos, on the black waters of the Yanuyacu River. With attractive, rustic bungalows, it's friendly and very popular with young travelers. In fact, it's one of the best budget options, with good service and food. The facilities may be a little nicer at the

Heliconia, but the atmosphere for backpackers is probably better here. A 4-day/3-night stay costs $225.

- **Paseos Amazónicos,** Pevas 246, Iquitos (© **094/231-618;** p-amazon@ amauta.rcp.net.pe). This company operates three well-run lodges, **Tambo Amazónico, Sinchicuy,** and **Yanayacu.** The farthest, Tambo Amazónico, is 180km (112 miles) upriver from Iquitos on the Yarapa River; the other two are much closer and focus on quick in-and-out tours. The Sinchicuy (30km/20 miles from Iquitos) is one of the oldest-established lodges in the zone. Yanayacu lodge is 60km (38 miles) from the city. The company is honest and professionally run, and offers good and clean budget- to midrange standard tours in rustic shared lodges. The lodges are offered by several Peruvian and international travel agents and tour operators. Adventurers may be interested in the company's camping trips to the Pacaya-Samiria National Reserve, one of the best opportunities to rough it and catch glimpses of Amazonian wildlife (see the "Into the Wild: Farther Afield from Iquitos" box, on p. 324). A 4-day/3-night stay at Tambo Amazónico Lodge costs $295. Sinchicuy day visits cost $70; a 3-day/2-night stay costs $170; and a combination 4-day/3-night Sinchicuy-Yanayacu trip costs $237. A 4-day/3-night camping expedition to Pacaya-Samiria costs $545.

- **Yacumama Lodge** 禽禽, Sargento Lores 149, Iquitos (© **094/235-510,** or 800/854-0023 in U.S. and Canada; www.yacumama.com). Yacumama is an American-owned first-class lodge with a gorgeous main house, private bungalows, solar power, and eco-sensitive flush toilets deep in the Amazon— 186km (110 miles) upriver on Río Yarapa (a tributary of the Río Ucayali). It's located on an excellent 7,000-hectare (17,300-acre) forest reserve with a cool 10-story canopy tower; the treetop perspective is nearly as spectacular as Explorama canopy walkway, though you miss the possibility of walking above the trees. The lodge's hammock room overlooks the river. In operation since 1993, Yacumama has built a solid reputation with its environmentally sound engineering, good jungle treks, and possibilities for dolphin sightings. The company offers Machu Picchu/Cusco program extensions. A 4-day/3-night stay costs $750; discounts may be available in Iquitos.

- **Yacuruna Lodge,** Pevas 225, Iquitos (© **094/223-801;** www.yacuruna. com). Close to Iquitos (45km/28 miles downriver, on the Yanuyacu), this

---

Fun Fact Trippin' Amazon Style

Several Amazon lodges offer ayahuasca ceremonies, which involve the privilege of taking a natural hallucinogenic potion prepared by an "authentic" Indian shaman, at $15 a shot. It's the local version of taking peyote with Don Juan, but at some joints, it teeters on the edge of spring break at the ecolodge. Ayahuasca is an authentic ritual and herbal drug with deep roots in local communities. A shaman boils diverse Amazonian plants and roots for up to 6 hours, and the resulting potion can indeed be very hallucinogenic. It is taken as part of a cleansing ritual, to purify the body and mind. The ceremony is not to be taken lightly, though some lodges seem to do just that, for the sake of selling a cool Amazon experience. Reports circulate about some travelers losing their minds, but it's hard to say if they should be taken seriously. At a minimum, ayahuasca is a cultural practice that should be respected and not abused by gringos.

Into the Wild: Farther Afield from Iquitos

The opportunity for spectacular wildlife sightings and experiencing how locals truly live in the Amazon are severely diminished in most areas where the jungle lodges are located. For primary rain forest and more authentic native villages, you have to be willing to rough it more than traditional lodges force you to. However, as jungle tourism in Peru continues to grow, several midrange and luxury cruise operators are now organizing river cruises to one of Peru's greatest jungle zones with an almost unimaginable biodiversity.

About 300km (190 miles) south of Iquitos, a couple days removed by boat and sandwiched between the Marañón and Ucayali rivers, is the **Pacaya-Samiria National Reserve** 𝕽𝕽, the largest protected area in Peru and one of the most pristine in the world. Established in 1982, it contains 2,080,000 hectares (5,100,000 acres) of thick, untouched rain forest and wetlands. Incredibly, that accounts for 1.5% of Peru's total surface area. Riddled with rivers and 85 lakes, it's huge and daunting, and should only be explored with an experienced guide. Some of the Amazon's finest and most abundant wildlife resides in the reserve, such as pink dolphins, macaws, black caimans, spider monkeys, and giant river turtles. The reserve's numbers are staggering: It is home to 539 species of birds, 101 species of mammals, 256 kinds of fish, and 22 species of orchids. Guides typically take visitors by dugout canoe from **Lagunas** (upstream from Iquitos) through the reserve. Villages on the outskirts of the reserve worth visiting are **San Martín de Timpishia** and **Puerto Miguel.** To enter the reserve, officially you need permission from INRENA, the Peruvian parks authority. Contact its office in Iquitos (Pevas 350; ℂ 094/231-230) or in Lima (Los Petirrojos 355, Urbanización El Palomar, Lima; ℂ 01/224-3298) for additional information. You'll need a minimum of 4 or 5 days to do the trip from Iquitos. Jungle Expeditions, Amazon Tours and Cruises, and Paseos Amazónicos all organize Pacaya-Samiria National Reserve river cruises and, in the case of the latter, camping trips (for contact information, see "Jungle Lodges," above, and "Cruises," below).

new lodge is a good budget option with a reputation for undercutting others. If you arrive in Iquitos without a tour and want a quick and cheap option for a couple of days, you might be able to sign on for $30 a day.

CRUISES

Riverboat cruises down the Amazon and along its tributaries don't allow you to see much in the way of fauna or pristine jungle, though you will likely spot lots of birds and dolphins. Cruises are best for people who don't want to rough it too much and like the romance of traveling the Amazon by boat, though varying degrees of rusticity and luxury are available. Many cruises stop off at reserves for jungle walks and visits to local villages. Some of the best cruises are those to the Pacaya-Samiria National Reserve; see "Into the Wild: Farther Afield from Iquitos," above, for details.

The Cocamas native community at San Martín de Tipishca in the northern edge of the Pacaya-Samiria National Reserve now have a young American woman working with them as an interpreter and are reaching out to travelers who want an experience of close contact with the people of an Amazon village. Reports are that the trips are extremely professional in character. Contact Virginia Blum, care of her office at Piura 1072 in Iquitos (© 094/251-185; virginiablum@yahoo. com). The community charges $40 per day per person, plus the $19 permit to enter the preserve. Trips usually last 4 to 5 days and are limited to groups of 12 to 15 people (though as few as 2 people can arrange a trip). Other, less involved visits to local native communities, such as the Huitotos, Boras, and Yaguas, can also be arranged. Inquire about independent trips at the tourism office on the Plaza de Armas in Iquitos.

Another option for down-and-dirty exploration of Amazon culture and sights is to cruise the rivers not on (relatively) pampered boats that take tourists out to lodges, but aboard the **three-decked riverboats** that form the transportation backbone of the region, ferrying people back and forth from villages on Amazon tributaries to Iquitos and other towns. The boats are rough going, stuffed with animals and densely packed families and their household goods, and almost entirely absent of comforts. You should take along plenty of bottled water, a hammock, and foodstuffs such as fruit and canned items. Journeys may last several days, but slinging yourself into a hammock on the top deck and floating slowly down the Huallaga or Ucayali will certainly win points among your friends when it comes to regaling them with vacation heroics. For budget travelers, it's a perfect antidote to high-priced lodges and river cruises: It's virtually impossible to spend more than $10 a day, including transportation.

For more details about how to organize trips to Pacaya-Samiria or simple river transport along the rivers, contact the helpful folks at the tourist information office on the Plaza de Armas in Iquitos for up-to-the-minute suggestions. See also "Independent Guides," below, for information on treks with independent guides.

- **Amazon Tours and Cruises,** Requena 336, Iquitos (© **094/233-931,** or 800/423-2791 in the U.S. and Canada; www.amazontours.net). This American-owned company has been active in the northern Amazon for almost 40 years. Its midlevel cruises have good service and are aboard an older, air-conditioned fleet that is not as nice nor as expensive as Jungle Expeditions (see below), the leader in upscale river cruises. Amazon Tours operates specialist tours targeting birders, sport fishers, and other travelers (even wild-mushroom/shamanistic voyages) in conjunction with specialty travel operators. It offers 3- and 6-night Río Amazonas cruises, and may again be offering 9- and 11-night monthly cruises to Manaus (Brazil) by the time you read this. A 6-night cruise costs $1,395; a 9-night cruise to Manaus will set you back $1,995 (per person, double occupancy). May offer discounts.

• **Jungle Expeditions** 𝒜𝒜, Av. Quiñones 1980, Iquitos (© **094/261-583;** www.junglex.com). Jungle Expeditions focuses on prearranged luxury river cruises on its fleet of six beautiful and elegant ships. Food, service, and accommodations are all top shelf. Ships cruise upriver along the Río Ucayali. Trips start at $995 for a 4-day/3-night program with lodge accommodations and range from $1,500 (7 days) to $2,698 (8 days) per person for riverboat expeditions. The lodge program includes stays at a couple of Explorama lodges and a visit to the ACEER canopy walkway (see "Explorama Tours," above). Because Jungle Expeditions only accepts passengers through its Lima booking office (© 01/241-3232) or the U.S.-based International Expeditions (© 800/633-4734; www.internationalexpeditions.com), which offers programs with Cusco and Machu Picchu extensions and all-inclusive packages from Miami, you'll have to plan ahead. No price discounting.

INDEPENDENT GUIDES

For travelers who want to get away from the lodges and groups and riverboats, more flexible independent treks into the jungle are the way to go. You'll see more fauna and especially flora than will other travelers, and you'll get to visit native communities that aren't merely putting on a show for your benefit. You'll rough it in varying degrees (everything from eating rice and beans cooked over an open fire and cans of tuna to fresh-caught fish straight from the river, to camping in makeshift sites along the way). To immerse yourself in the dense Amazonian jungle, you need an experienced, reliable wilderness guide. Scores of independent guides operate in the jungle around Iquitos and scout for tourists in the city. Their quality and professionalism varies tremendously, however, and many plainly are not to be trusted. Several guides in Iquitos have criminal records for robbing the very tourists that entrusted themselves to them.

Because you're going to be spending all your time in the jungle with the guide, depending on him to lead you, communicate with you, cook for you, and build good campsites, selecting a competent guide is of the utmost importance. Most guides are "extralegal"; only a couple of guides in Iquitos are officially licensed to operate as full-fledged independent jungle guides (though possessing a license, an expensive bureaucratic requirement out of reach of most guides, isn't the only determination). No matter what you hear from other travelers, if you're thinking about hiring a guide for a solo or small-group trek into the jungle, visit the tourism information office in Iquitos before exchanging monies; ask for the office personnel's recommendations and take a look at the review books of comments about guides. Rates depend on the number of travelers and length of trips; they can range from $35 to $40 a day per person to more than $100 per day.

Carlos Grandez is one (unlicensed) guide who gets good reviews. An unassuming gentleman in his late 60s, he is nonetheless fearless when it comes to jungle expeditions and has nearly 4 decades of experience with local communities and hard-core jungle living. Grandez was introduced to me as the "Dr. Doolittle of the Peruvian Jungle," and everyone reports that you are in good hands with him, but his English skills are almost nil. Some people with little grasp of Spanish have gotten along fine, resorting to primitive hand signals and a few shared words (which seems like part of the adventure), but this could be a problem in the event of an emergency. Contact Carlos at Alfonso Ugarte 531 in Iquitos (© **094/263-998;** carlosgrandez@hotmail.com). Another guide with an outsized reputation is **Richard Fowler,** an American ex-military sort who leads hard-core wild-man treks (he calls them survival-oriented "*Deliverance* tours" and "*Apocalypse Now* tours") through the Chinchilejo Expeditions company

(**©** **094/937-325**). Past trekkers have learned to scalp, eaten monkey-head soup, and witnessed monkey-head shrinking. It's not for the tame, though Fowler can also let up and arrange somewhat more easygoing tours of the jungle. Not that he wants to, you understand.

WHERE TO STAY

For many visitors, Iquitos amounts to little more than a way station on their journey to the Amazon. As a result, the city has many fewer good hotels than its environs have attractive jungle lodges. Things are improving, though, and Iquitos finally got its first 5-star hotel a couple years back. Midrange hotels are more expensive than similarly equipped hotels in many other parts of the country, but discounts are frequently available at most top-level and midrange hotels.

All but the cheapest *hostales* (inns) will usually arrange for a free airport transfer if you pass on your arrival information ahead of time. Even so, be careful whom you tell at the airport that you're expecting a certain hotel to pick you up; always make sure the driver already knows your name before going anywhere with him.

EXPENSIVE

Hotel El Dorado Plaza ⚜   With a privileged place on the Plaza de Armas, the El Dorado Plaza has filled a gaping hole in the Iquitos hotel scene—the city never before had a bona fide 5-star hotel. A modern high-rise building, with a soaring lobby, a good restaurant, and an excellent outdoor pool, this is clearly the finest hotel in town. Rooms are large and nicely outfitted, if not quite at the upper-echelon levels found in Lima or Cusco. Guests have either a view of the main square or of the pool. The hotel has quickly become popular with foreigners who come to Iquitos for top-of-the-line jungle tours. The staff is very friendly and helpful. Deals are frequently available—occasionally as much as half the rack rate.

Napo 258, Plaza de Armas, Iquitos. **©** **094/222-555**. Fax 094/224-304. www.eldoradoplazahotel.com. 65 units. $130 double. Rate includes breakfast buffet. AE, DC, MC, V. **Amenities:** Restaurant; 2 bars; coffee shop; excellent outdoor pool; fitness center; Jacuzzi; sauna; concierge; 24-hr. room service; laundry service. *In room:* A/C, TV, minibar, hair dryer, safe.

MODERATE

Hostal Jhuliana   This friendly and good little midrange hotel is stocked with amenities including a nice pool and restaurant, as well as 24-hour room service (a rarity at this price). Rooms are comfortable and carpeted, with hot-water showers and minibars. It's comparable to the other hotels in this price range, but it's a step below the Victoria Regia, which is a better value though a bit more expensive.

Putumayo 521, Iquitos. **©** and fax **094/233-154**. 20 units. $50 double. Rate includes taxes and breakfast. MC, V. **Amenities:** Restaurant; bar; cafe; swimming pool; 24-hr. room service; laundry service. *In room:* A/C, TV, minibar.

Hotel Acosta   The lower-priced sister hotel of the Victoria Regia (see below), the Acosta underwent a head-to-toe renovation in 2001. The carpeted rooms have been upgraded slightly, an improvement on decent-size and attractively, if not luxuriously, outfitted accommodations. The major drawback is the noisy street corner location of the hotel—motocarros zoom by incessantly. Still, the hotel remains a good value, and it's well run by a small, family-owned chain of Iquitos hotels and jungle lodges.

Corner of Calvo de Araújo and Huallaga s/n, Iquitos. **©** **094/231-761**, or 01/421-9195 for reservations. Fax 094/442-4338. 30 units. $35 double. Rate includes taxes and breakfast. AE, DC, MC, V. **Amenities:** Restaurant; bar; small business center with Internet access (for a small fee); laundry service. *In room:* A/C, TV, minibar, safe.

Hotel Amazon Garden About 10 blocks removed from the action northwest of the Plaza de Armas, this neat, small hotel is housed in a private home in a residential part of town. Owned by the operator of Amazon Tours and Cruises, it's a comfortable, relaxing place to stay away from the considerable noise and hubbub of the malecón and the main square. The hotel has a nice pool, but rooms are a little nondescript. Some rooms may be pretty humid, so check out a couple first if possible.

Pantoja 417 (at Yavarí), Iquitos. © **094/236-140**, or 800/423-2791 in the U.S. Fax 094/231-265. www. amazontours.net. 14 units. $45 double. Rate includes taxes and breakfast. MC, V. **Amenities:** Swimming pool; small gym; laundry service. *In room:* A/C, TV, hair dryer.

Real Hotel Iquitos *(Value)* The former (and formerly grand) state-owned Hotel de Turistas is now a curious hotel with a unique appeal to those who shy away from perfectly run, internationally flavored chain hotels. Part of a Peruvian group with a half dozen hotels spread across the country, this midsize entry seems larger and emptier than it is. Some of the rooms are surprisingly expansive, and a few have enviable balconies overlooking the malecón and the river. If you score such a room (ask to see a few first), you'll have yourself a deal (no. 312 is huge and has its own terrace). They're simply furnished, though with some unique touches, such as red curtains and green walls—kind of cool in an offbeat way—though I admit it's not the place for folks in search of great air-conditioning and top-shelf service. No other hotel, though, can boast these river views—and the Amazon is why you came to Iquitos, isn't it? Interior rooms, with no view and considerably smaller, are half as expensive as the larger accommodations.

Malecón Tarapacá s/n, Iquitos. © and fax **094/231-011**. 54 units. $45 double with view; $23 double without view; $80 suite. Rates include continental breakfast. MC, V. **Amenities:** Restaurant; bar; laundry service. *In room:* A/C, TV.

Victoria Regia *(Value)* An extremely comfortable and friendly midsize hotel, the Victoria Regia—named for the lily found throughout the Amazon—is the choice of both independent travelers and business execs with long-term affairs to attend to in Iquitos. A modern block hotel on a busy residential street about 10 minutes from the main square, the hotel's rooms, with air-conditioning that really cranks, are built around an attractive indoor pool and are only a notch below the Hotel El Dorado Plaza in terms of comfort. The Victoria Regia is part of a small, local, family-owned chain of hotels, which includes the Hotel Acosta and the Heliconia and Zungarococha Lodges.

Av. Ricardo Palma 252, Iquitos. © **094/231-983**. Fax 094/232-499. www.victoriaregiahotel.com. ventas@ heliconialodge.com.pe. 45 units. $60–$70 double; $70–$90 suite. Rates include breakfast buffet. AE, DC, MC, V. **Amenities:** Restaurant; bar; covered swimming pool; small business center with Internet access (for a small fee); laundry service. *In room:* A/C, TV, minibar, hair dryer; safe.

INEXPENSIVE

Hospedaje El Sitio In the midst of several of the city's busiest streets, El Sitio—its name means, plainly, "the place" or "site"—doesn't aspire to much more than good, clean budget accommodations. Rooms are simple, cheap, and humid, though they have ceiling fans, private bathrooms, and cable TV. Rooms on the bottom floor are somewhat larger than those upstairs.

Ricardo Palma 541, Iquitos. © **094/234-932**. Fax 094/233-466. pascana@tsi.com.pe. 20 units. $10 double. Rate includes taxes. No credit cards. **Amenities:** Cafeteria; 24-hr. room service. *In room:* TV.

Hospedaje La Pascana *(Value)* One of the better budget inns in Iquitos, the Pascana is a friendly, small place with rooms built around a long, plant-lined and open-air courtyard. Rooms are very simple, but not uncomfortable, and they have fans rather than air-conditioning. The place is quiet and peaceful, and just a 2-minute walk from the malecón and the Plaza de Armas—reasons why it's often full and popular with small budget-level groups. Don't expect much hot water at this price, though you probably won't care in the sweltering heat.

Pevas 133, Iquitos. © 094/231-418. Fax 094/233-466. pascana@tsi.com.pe. 18 units. $14 double. Rate includes taxes and continental breakfast buffet. No credit cards. **Amenities:** Cafeteria; communal TV room; book exchange.

Hostal Ambasador   Associated with Hostelling International, this small hotel is an especially good value for HI members. A centrally located, modern white block, it has well-maintained rooms with good amenities (such as a restaurant with 24-hr. room service) and private bathrooms. For most backpackers used to bargain-basement hostels, this is a definite step up—it may be a good place to crash after a few days in the wild.

Pevas 260, Iquitos. © 094/233-110. Fax 094/231-618. paseosiqt@meganet.com.pe. 25 units. $30–$40 double; discounts for HI members. Rates include taxes. MC, V. **Amenities:** Bar/cafe; 24-hr. room service; laundry service. *In room:* A/C, TV.

WHERE TO DINE

Easygoing restaurants in Iquitos are a good place to sample dishes straight out of the Amazon, such as paiche, hearts of palm salad, and *juanes* (rice tamales made with minced chicken, pork, or fish, prepared with black olives and egg, wrapped in *bijao* leaves). Although protected species are not supposed to appear on menus, they often do. You might want to think twice before encouraging restaurateurs by ordering turtle-meat soup or alligator. If you venture into the Belén market, be prepared for even more exotic foodstuffs, such as monkey and lizard meat.

EXPENSIVE

Montecarlo 🌟🌟 *Value*   INTERNATIONAL/PERUVIAN   The exterior of this new restaurant in Iquitos, behind the cheesy, glittering gold lights of a casino, doesn't look too auspicious. Yet upstairs from the gaming tables is an elegant restaurant that produces the most refined dining in this jungle city. It's perhaps the only place where you'll sit down to a full set of silver, and wine and water glasses. The decor goes for a 5-star treetop look, with ferns, wood-beamed ceilings, jungle murals, and a little Disneyesque Indian hut in the corner. Yet Montecarlo, which opened in early 2001 and looked to be expanding into the neighboring building at last visit, serves exquisitely prepared seafood and jungle specialties such as turtle stew and tropical gator (though I hate to report these items on menus). If you can't bear to bite into an endangered species, try the *pescado a la diabla,* lightly fried John Dory fish drenched in squid and shrimp and topped with a spicy ginger and tomato sauce; hearts of palm stuffed with shrimp; or daily specials such as *cazuela de pescado y marisco* (fish and seafood casserole). There are also some appetizing steaks and pastas.

Napo 140, 2nd floor. © 094/232-246. Reservations recommended. Main courses S/17–S/32 ($5–$9). AE, DC, MC, V. Daily noon–3:30pm and 6pm–midnight.

Regal (Casa de Fierro)   INTERNATIONAL/PERUVIAN   In the famed Iron House on the Plaza de Armas, this British pub and hangout is also a reputable restaurant exuding a desultory colonial atmosphere. There are great views from the wraparound iron balcony, with its slowly rotating old-style ceiling fans, overlooking the plaza. It's a good place to try local dishes such as paiche, served any number of ways, or the house specialty, *Regal lomo fino* (beef tenderloin in port-wine sauce, served with salad, Greek rice, a peach stuffed with Russian salad, and fries). The food may not hold up to the general ambience, and it's a tad overpriced, so you might opt just to kick back with the expat Brits around the bar for a pint.

Putumayo 182, 2nd floor, Plaza de Armas. © 094/222-732. Reservations recommended. Main courses S/16–S/30 ($4.50–$8.50). AE, DC, MC, V. Daily noon–10pm.

Restaurant Gran Maloca *(Value* PERUVIAN/AMAZONIAN   One of Iquitos's most celebrated traditional restaurants, located in a grand, tile-covered (and air-conditioned!) 19th-century house, Gran Maloca serves both jungle dishes and standard upscale fare. Try Amazon-style venison (with cilantro, coconut, and yuca), tropical alligator, or less risky items such as filet mignon, tenderloin with mushroom risotto, or chicken a la Maloca (chicken breast stuffed with ham and baked in white wine). The split personality of the restaurant is present in the decor: The would-be formal trappings and pastel color scheme coexist with a large collection of colorful butterflies adorning the walls. (If you like those, wait until you get a load of the framed Amazonian bugs, tarantulas, and other creepy crawlers in the bathrooms.) Gran Maloca serves a good-value (meaning cheap), three-course daily lunch special for just S/12 ($3.50).

Sargento Lores 170. © 094/233-126. Reservations recommended. Main courses S/18–S/30 ($5–$8.50). AE, MC, V. Daily noon–10pm.

MODERATE

El Huaralino *(Finds* PERUVIAN   A lunch-only affair worth seeking out, this family-oriented place is in the heart of the Iquitos commercial district, about 15 minutes from the Plaza de Armas. More popular with locals than tourists, the pleasant, airy restaurant with stucco walls and yellow trim serves Peruvian *comida criolla.* Excellent, large-portion dishes include paiche fish served with salad and rice and beans, *pato de ají* (spicy duck), guinea pig, and asado (grilled meats). The service is personal and very friendly. The only thing to detract from an easygoing meal here is the inevitable, incessant noise of passing mototaxis. (The restaurant is open to the street.)

Huallaga 490. © 094/233-126. Reservations not accepted. Main courses S/14–S/20 ($4–$6). AE, DC, MC, V. Daily 11am–5pm.

El Nuevo Mesón PERUVIAN   Open to the passing parade of people, souvenir sellers, and curious locals on the malecón, this lively restaurant is a good place for an introduction to regional specialties and the city itself. If you come on a weekend night, you'll be entertained not only by altiplano musicians inside, but also by all kinds of locals hovering about the sidewalk tables, some gawking at your meal (several kids jostled for the rights to my leftovers at last visit). Service can be a little haphazard, but most dishes are pretty well prepared. Try regional dishes such as the regional favorite *pescado a la loretana* (fish filet with yuca, fried bananas, and palm-heart salad), and freakier fare such as alligator crisps with fried yuca or curried turtle. There are steaks, *mariscos* (shellfish), and a long list of fish, dominated by *dorado* (a kind of flaky white catfish) served in a variety of styles, such as "poor boy," with potatoes, salad, bananas, eggs, and rice.

Malecón Tarapacá 153. © 094/231-837. Reservations recommended for groups. Main courses S/15–S/26 ($4–$7.50). MC, V. Daily noon–midnight.

Tips Amazonian Delicacies

Throughout South America, the Amazon region is famed for its exotic fruits. In Iquitos, check out stands around the Plaza de Armas for natural fruit juices and ice creams made from stuff hard to get at home, such as aguaje, maracuyá, and cocona.

Tips **Chifas in Iquitos**

To some observers, there's something distinctly Asian about hot, humid, and motorcycle-crazed Iquitos. Waves of Chinese immigrants came as laborers to Iquitos throughout the 20th century, which is the biggest reason why there are so many chifas in town. Eating Chinese food at the edge of the Amazon instead of exotic jungle fruits and fish may not be your first impulse in Iquitos, but chifas are plentiful and reasonably priced—perfect fallback dining options. Try **Wai Ming,** San Martín 464 at Plaza 28 de Julio (© **094/234-391**); **Chifa Chong,** Huallaga 165 (no phone); **Hueng Teng,** Nauta at Pucallpa (no phone); and **Chifa Can Chau,** Huallaga 173 (no phone). Others chifas, cheaper still, line Avenida Grau near Plaza 28 de Julio.

Fitzcarraldo INTERNATIONAL   This popular joint right on the malecón has a diverse menu to appeal to travelers of all stripes and appetites. You can go light, choosing from a number of salads such as *chonta* (palm-heart salad) with avocado and tomato, or regular dinners including pescado a la loretana or even turtle in ginger sauce with yuca. There are also pizzas, sandwiches, and hamburgers for the less adventurous. The restaurant is a convivial place in an open-air house (which once belonged to a British rubber company) featuring updated colonial touches and views of the Amazon, with good music, sidewalk tables, and underpowered ceiling fans.

Napo 100 (at Malecón Tarapacá). © **094/243-434.** Reservations recommended for groups. Main courses S/6–S/38 ($1.75–$11). MC, V. Daily noon–midnight.

INEXPENSIVE
Ari's Burger   A quintessential gringo hangout right on the Plaza de Armas, this brightly lit fast-food joint is open to the street on two sides—great for people-watching. It seems nearly every visitor to the city hits Ari, called "Gringolandia" by locals both for its clientele and American-style menu, at least once for a burger and fries, ice cream, or fresh-squeezed juice or a milkshake. It's open late and is very popular with folks after rounds at the bars and discos.

Próspero 127 (at the corner of Napo). No phone. Reservations not accepted. Main courses S/3–S/18 ($1–$5). MC, V. Daily 8am–3am.

IQUITOS AFTER DARK
More locals than gringos usually make it to the coolest spot in Iquitos, **Café-Teatro Amauta,** Nauta 250 (© **094/233-366**), a bar-cum-theater with great bohemian flavor and a romantic interior with thick, red curtains framing a small stage that opens to sidewalk tables. Calling itself "El Rincón de los Artistas," (Artists' Corner) it supports live Peruvian, Latin, and Amazon music Monday through Saturday from 10pm until 3am. Try some of the funky *aguardientes* ("fire waters") made from Amazonian herbs. Along the malecón are a couple of lively bars with good views of the river. **Arandú Bar,** Malecón Tarapacá 113 (© **094/243-434**), is particularly hopping, a good place for sharing a pitcher of sangria and loud rock-and-roll. Locals hang out at **Noa-Noa,** Pevas 298 at Fitzcarraldo (© **094/232-902**), a disco and rock bar near the Plaza de Armas. When the two-level dance floor is happening, the smoke machines crank and the sound system pumps out salsa and Latin rock.

Northern Peru

Northern Peru is vastly under appreciated; in fact, most of the region is virtually unknown to foreigners who travel to Peru. The few travelers who get to know the north are mainly those with a specific interest in ancient Peruvian cultures, or hikers and adventurous travelers looking to get out into the country, beyond the reach of the majority of gringos who trod well-beaten paths in the Andes and southern Peru. If you make it to this part of Peru, you may be in for the not unwelcome treat of being one of the few.

You wouldn't know it from the paucity of foreign visitors, but the northern coastal desert of Peru holds some of the country's greatest archaeological treasures: Chan Chan, the great adobe city of the Chimú civilization; 1,500-year-old Moche temples; and the royal tomb that brought the great Lord of Sipán to the world's attention in 1987—Peru's very own King Tut. Northern beaches draw surfers to some of the best waves off South America, and nestled in the sierra is one of the country's most charming and beautiful mountain towns, Cajamarca, a mini-Cusco of the north.

Where gringos of a particular ilk and style of outdoor performance gear do make it in significant number is the Cordillera Blanca, which holds some of the most beautiful peaks in South America and some of the finest trekking on the continent. Huaraz is the primary base for excursions into the valleys and mountain ranges of the northern Andes. For years, the destination has been favored principally by sports and adventurer travelers, especially hardcore hikers, but the range of activities is opening up and appealing more and more to other travelers who also want a taste of Peru's great outdoors.

1 Trujillo

561km (348 miles) N of Lima; 200km (124 miles) S of Chiclayo; 298km (185 miles) SW of Cajamarca

Trujillo, the capital of La Libertad department, is the third-largest city in Peru and one of only two of commercial importance on the entire north coast. Yet the town, founded in 1534 by Diego Almagro on the orders of Francisco Pizarro, retains the Spanish colonial feel of a much smaller town. Locals saunter along the grandly laid-out plaza, and the downtown area is an attractive grid with streets lined by elegant, pastel colonial mansions embellished by wrought-iron window grilles.

The importance of this area greatly predates the arrival of the Spaniards, however, and Trujillo is celebrated mostly for a collection of pre-Columbian sites that abound on the outskirts of the city. Looming in the desert are five major archaeological sites, including two of the richest ensembles of Moche temples and ruins of the Chimú culture in Peru. Chan Chan, a monumental adobe complex of royal palaces covering more than 52km^2 (20 sq. miles), is the primary draw for visitors, but archaeological tours also visit the fascinating Temples of

the Moon and Sun (Huacas del Sol y de la Luna), built by the Moche culture around A.D. 500. Though several of these sites have been partially restored, they still require some imagination to conjure a sense of their immensity, the busy daily activity, and the grandeur of the ceremonies once held there.

Near Trujillo is Huanchaco, a laid-back beach resort that serves as a virtual bedroom community for many visitors. Ideally positioned for ruins visits, it's also a lot less hectic and has a good roster of cheaper small hotels, budget *hostales* (inns), and seaside seafood restaurants.

ESSENTIALS
GETTING THERE
BY PLANE   Aero Continente (© **01/242-4242;** www.aerocontinente.net) and **AeroCondor** (© **01/442-5215;** www.aerocondor.com.pe) fly daily to Trujillo from Lima and Cajamarca. Flights from Lima cost between $59 and $69. Aero Continente also flies from Chiclayo. Flights arrive at the **Aeropuerto Carlos Martínez de Pinillos** on Carretera Huanchaco in the Huanchaco district (© **044/525-102**). The airport is about 20 minutes northwest of downtown.

To downtown Trujillo, a taxi costs as little as S/10 ($3) if you bargain, though most drivers start by charging S/17 to S/20 ($5–$6). Huanchaco–Trujillo buses and colectivos pass in the general direction of the airport, but at a distance of about a mile from the entrance, making public transportation to and from the airport impractical for anyone with luggage.

BY BUS   Like most big cities, Trujillo is serviced by several domestic bus companies from Lima and most major points along the north coast and northern highlands. Many long-distance buses travel at night only. There is no central bus station in Trujillo. Most individual company terminals are near downtown, located to the northwest by the Estadio Mansiche, to the southwest near Avenida España, or to the east near Avenida El Ejército.

The major companies making the 8-hour trip from Lima are **Ormeño** (© 01/427-5679), **CIVA** (© 01/428-5649), **Cruz del Sur** (© 01/225-6163), and **Oltursa** (© 01/475-8559). For the 6-hour trip from Cajamarca, **Transportes Línea** (© 044/245-181 in Trujillo, or 044/823-956 in Cajamarca) has two classes of service, *económico* and *especial,* which is slightly faster, a bit more comfortable, and a tad more expensive than económico class. Transportes Línea (© 074/233-497) is also the major company for the 3-hour journey from Chiclayo and the 8-hour journey from Huaraz. **ITTSA** (© 044/222-541) runs from Lima, Chiclayo, and Piura.

VISITOR INFORMATION

A small and friendly (though not very well-equipped) tourist information office belonging to the **Cámara Regional de La Libertad** is located at Independencia 628, 1 block north of the Plaza de Armas (© 044/938-922). The office is open Monday through Saturday from 9am to 6pm. It has free maps, and the staff can advise you on the easiest way to visit Chan Chan and the other major archaeological sites beyond the city.

FAST FACTS   Banks that exchange traveler's checks and cash and have ATMs are **Banco de Crédito,** Jr. Gamarra 562 (© 044/242-360); **Banco Latino,** Jr. Gamarra 572 (© 044/243-461); and **Banco Continental,** Pizarro 620, in the colonial Casa de la Emancipación. **Interbanc,** located at Pizarro and Gamarra, has a Cirrus/Plus ATM. Money-changers can usually be found hanging about the Plaza de Armas or along Gamarra.

In case of emergency, call © **105.** The helpful **tourist police** are located at Independencia 630, in the Casa Ganoza Chopitea (© 044/291-705). For complaints, you can also call the **Tourist Protection Service** at © 044/204-146.

If you need medical attention, you're likely to find English-speaking doctors at **Clínica Peruana-Americana,** Av. Mansiche 702 (© 044/231-261). Other hospitals are **Hospital Regional,** Av. Mansiche 795 (© 044/231-581), and **Hospital Belén,** Bolívar 350 (© 044/245-281). In Huanchaco, a clinic (*posta médica*) is located at Atahualpa 437 (© 044/461-547).

For Internet access, two cabinas to try are **Cibercafé Internet,** Manuel María Izaga 716 (© 044/228-729), and **Deltanet/Telecom,** Orbegoso 641 (© 044/ 294-327). Both charge about S/2 to S/2.50 (60¢–70¢) per hour.

Trujillo's **post office** is located at Independencia 286 (© 044/245-941); it's open Monday through Saturday from 8am to 8pm. A **DHL/Western Union** branch is at Almagro 579 (© 044/203-686). The **Telefónica del Perú** office is at Pizarro 561; it's open Monday through Saturday from 8am to 8pm. A *locutorio* (public calling place) is located at Gamarra 454.

GETTING AROUND

Downtown Trujillo is a grid of relatively short blocks ringed by Avenida España. At the heart of the centro is the Plaza de Armas, and the main sights are all nearby on the major streets leading off the square. Getting around the small centro is thus best managed on foot. However, you'll need to take either a taxi or a

Trujillo

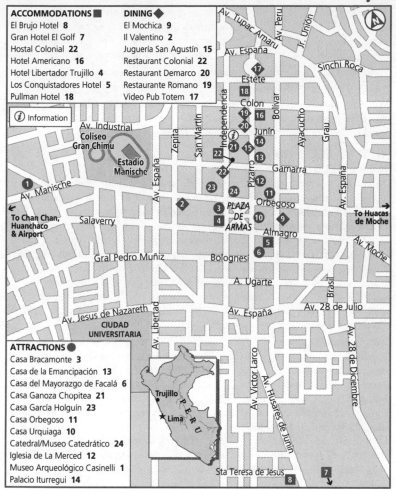

ACCOMMODATIONS ■
El Brujo Hotel **8**
Gran Hotel El Golf **7**
Hostal Colonial **22**
Hotel Americano **16**
Hotel Libertador Trujillo **4**
Los Conquistadores Hotel **5**
Pullman Hotel **18**

DINING ◆
El Mochica **9**
Il Valentino **2**
Juguería San Agustín **15**
Restaurant Colonial **22**
Restaurant Demarco **20**
Restaurante Romano **19**
Video Pub Totem **17**

ⓘ Information

ATTRACTIONS ●
Casa Bracamonte **3**
Casa de la Emancipación **13**
Casa del Mayorazgo de Facalá **6**
Casa Ganoza Chopitea **21**
Casa García Holguín **23**
Casa Orbegoso **11**
Casa Urquiaga **10**
Catedral/Museo Catedrático **24**
Iglesia de La Merced **12**
Museo Arqueológico Casinelli **1**
Palacio Iturregui **14**

public bus to visit the major archaeological sites outside Trujillo, or the beach-side suburb, Huanchaco.

Confusing as can be are Trujillo's street names: Nearly every street and avenue has two names and two corresponding signs, one a smaller printed version and the other a fancier painted sign. Most maps go by the smaller, printed name, which is what I give in this chapter.

Several *urbanizaciones,* or residential districts, lie just beyond Avenida España. Urbanización El Recreo, where several resort-style hotels are located, is just west of Av. 28 de Julio. Chan Chan is just 5km (3 miles) northwest of the city, on the way to the airport and Huanchaco. The Huacas de Moche are 8km (5 miles) south of town beyond the Carretera Industrial.

BY TAXI Taxis, all uniformly painted black and yellow, are plentiful in Trujillo. Most in-town fares, inside the Avenida España ring, are about S/3 (85¢). A taxi ride to Chan Chan costs S/10 ($3); to Huanchaco, S/10 ($3). You can hire taxis by the hour (S/15, or $4–$5) or by the day ($25–$35) to tour archaeological sites in the environs of Trujillo. Be sure to negotiate or ask first in the tourist office to determine the going fares, as price gouging is not uncommon in Trujillo. Official taxis are identified by a coat of arms of the city.

BY BUS   Combis and ómnibuses cost S/0.50 (15¢). Somewhat rickety buses will take you to Huanchaco for S/1 (30¢).

BY CAR   Should you wish to rent a vehicle to make trips to Chan Chan and other sites, or even to travel around the northern region, try **Global Car Rental,** Ecuador 122, oficina 201, Urbanización El Recreo (© **044/295-548**).

WHAT TO SEE & DO
IN TRUJILLO

Trujillo has an impressive collection of elegant colonial and republican-era houses (*casas antiguas*) and baroque churches, as well as one of Peru's odder museums of ancient ceramics. A tour of Trujillo rightly begins with the graceful **Plaza de Armas,** where vendors hang out and families in their Sunday finery pose for pictures in front of the Libertad monument. On the square is the **Catedral,** built in the mid–17th century but rather sober and uninteresting, though it has a **Museo Catedrático** (© **044/235-083**) with silver and gold chalices and bishops' vestments. The plaza is ringed by colorful examples of fine colonial-era mansions, including the one that is now home to the Hotel Libertador. Trujillo's pastel-colored colonial buildings are distinguished by their ornamental wrought-iron window grilles, unusual in Peru.

Casa Ganoza Chopitea 🔎   Better known in Trujillo as La Casa de los Leones (House of the Lions) because of the lions crowning the main door, this 17th-century house is one of the most splendid of the colonial era. Opposite the San Francisco church, the entrance is loaded with baroque and rococo details, including river stones (*canto rodado*) on the ground. A *concha venera,* or welcoming shell, is placed above the door. Inside the house, you'll pass through the Salón de Varones (Men's Hall), with a high wooden ceiling, followed by the Salón de Damas (Women's Hall). Look for the curious air holes in the latter— they go all the way to the roof to allow fresh air to circulate.

Jr. Independencia 630. No phone. Free admission. Mon–Fri 9am–1pm and 3–5pm.

Casa Orbegoso 🔎   This huge yellow-and-brown, mid-18th-century house, once the property of former president Luis José de Orbegoso, stretches around the block and has its own plaza facing the San Agustín church. In the entrance are Moorish-Christian mural paintings that were buried beneath successive baroque, rococo, and finally neoclassical murals. Inside are some original furnishings and mural paintings that can still be seen around the lower sections of

---

Tips Guided Tours

Agencies offering standard city and archaeological tours include **Guía Tours,** Jr. Independencia 580 (© **044/245-170**); **Chacón Tours,** Av. España 106 (© **044/255-212**); **Consorcio Turístico del Norte,** Jr. Pizarro 478 (© **044/205-645**); and **Trujillo Tours,** Diego de Almagro 301 (© **044/ 233-091**). Most standard tours cost $12 to $15 per person. Tours to El Brujo are generally $25 to $30.

<Fun Fact **Freedom U**

The general known as El Libertador, Simón Bolívar, founded Trujillo's Libertad University in 1824, during his post-independence stay in the city.

---

some rooms. The front part of the house still belongs to descendants of the original owners. Orbegoso, who fought alongside Bolívar in the War of Independence, is buried in a mausoleum in the house.

Orbegoso 553. ℂ 044/234-950. Free admission. Mon–Sat 9am–1pm and 4–7pm.

Casa Urquiaga (Casa Calonge) ℛ   This grand colonial mansion, royal blue with white window grilles, conserves the 18th-century desk of Simón Bolívar, who lived here for 2 years after proclaiming Peru's independence in 1824. The home, with three lovely interior courtyards, is one of Trujillo's most magnificently restored and most historic. It hosted the first viceroy of Peru in 1604 and was the headquarters of the first bank in Trujillo. The dining room features spectacular French porcelain, and, throughout, there are beautiful chandeliers and mirrors. In a second patio is an exhibit of Moche and Nasca ceramics. Look for the gold Chavín necklaces and several Chimú ornamental pieces, also in gold. Today, the mansion is owned by the Banco Central.

Jr. Pizarro 446, Plaza de Armas. No phone. Free admission; passport or other identification required. Mon–Fri 9:15am–3:15pm.

Iglesia de La Merced   On a small square set back from the street and next to the Corte Superior de Justicia (itself worth a peek), La Merced, one of Trujillo's most impressive churches, dates to 1636. It is especially notable for the colorful carved figures in relief around the cupola, including alternating series of small angels and cherubs supporting the top section—perhaps 100 in all. Inside, the church is salmon and white, with white stone arches. At the rear, apparently jammed into the organ loft, is a massive rococo pipe organ.

Jr. Pizarro 550. No phone. Free admission. Daily 8am–6pm.

Iglesia y Monasterio El Carmen   This lovely church and monastery, founded in 1724 and occupying an entire city block, has the most important collection of colonial art in Trujillo. Its Carmelite museum (Pinacoteca Carmelita) possesses 150 baroque and rococo paintings, the majority of them from the 17th and 18th centuries, as well as paintings of the Quito Art School. The final room shows the process of restoration of paintings, though explanations are in Spanish only. The church's central gilded altar is marvelous. The main *retablo* (gradine) was created by Master Fernando Collado de la Cruz, a free black Peruvian. Floral murals in soft pastels line each side of the church. The monastery has two cloisters (and 10 cloistered nuns) and contains a fair portion of the convent's art collection, but it cannot be visited.

Jr. Bolívar (at Colón). ℂ 044/233-091. Admission S/3 (75¢) adults, children S/1 (30¢). Mon–Sat 9am–1pm.

Museo Arqueológico Casinelli *(Finds)*   One of the most curious places you'll ever see a selection of fine ceramics is this private museum, about a 10-minute walk from the Plaza de Armas, housed in a dumpy space beneath a Mobil gas station. What are the odds of a gas-station and car-wash owner devoting all his money, time, and attention to assembling and displaying one of the largest private collections of ancient ceramics? Going on 40 years of existence, with dreams

> ### *Tips* Casas Antiguas
>
> Besides the colonial and republican houses that allow visitors, other houses worth a look from outside (and occasionally inside, if they're public buildings) are the bright yellow **Casa de la Emancipación** (now Banco Continental), Pizarro 610, where independence from Spain was proclaimed on December 29, 1820; **Casa Bracamonte,** Independencia 441; **Casa Lynch,** on the Plaza de Armas opposite the cathedral; **Casa Aranda,** Bolívar 621; **Casa del Mayorazgo de Facalá,** Pizarro 314; and **Casa García Holguín,** Independencia 527 on the Plaza de Armas.

of greater recognition and expansion, Señor Casinelli's superb collection of the Moche, Nasca, Chavín, Huari, and Chimú cultures (among others) holds about 4,000 pieces (though only 2,000 can be displayed "for lack of space and lack of support from the Peruvian government") and spans more than 2,500 years. There are some excellent examples of all those cultures displayed on pressboard shelves, including, behind a wall meant to protect innocent eyes, the famed erotic ceramics of the Moche. (You may have to ask the old guy to open the case, a feeling akin to asking the pharmacist for condoms.) Casinelli owns the gas station upstairs and has an architect's model of the much larger museum, along with a 3-star hotel, he'd like someday to build (but since he's now in his 80s, that dream is growing dim). Guided tours are in Spanish only.

Av. Nicolás de Piérola 607 (at intersection of Huanchaco and Carretera Panamericana). © 044/246-110. Admission S/5 ($1.50). Daily 9am–12:30pm and 3–6:30pm (on Sun, opens a half hour later both in the morning and afternoon).

Museo de Arqueología de la Universidad Nacional de Trujillo   This small university museum concentrates on pre-Columbian objects unearthed in the areas around Trujillo. Rooms are dedicated to items found at the Huacas del Sol y de la Luna. The museum is only worth a visit if you have extra time on your hands. Plan to spend 45 minutes here, tops.

Jr. Junín 682 (corner of Jr. Ayacucho). © 044/249-322. Admission S/5 ($1.50). Mon 9:30am–2pm; Tues 9:15am–1pm and 3–7pm; Sat–Sun 9:30am–4pm.

Palacio Iturregui   This bright yellow mansion, an excellent example of neoclassical civil architecture that dates to the 19th century, is home to the Club Central, Trujillo's traditional social club. Though it continues to be members-only, visitors can tool around for a view of an only slightly dilapidated exclusivity. The two-story mansion, with a large central courtyard, is outfitted with window grilles, thin columns, and Italian marble statues. Upstairs is a small museum containing Moche ceramics. Members in semiformal dress still drop by for lunch or dinner at the club, followed by a game of cards.

Jr. Pizarro 688. © 044/234-212. Admission (guided tour) S/5 ($1.50). Mon–Sat 8–11am (before 10am, ring bell for entrance).

HUANCHACO

Huanchaco, 12km (7 miles) northwest of Trujillo, is a tranquil and traditional fishing village now doubling as pretty low-key resort. On summer weekends, though, it gets jumping with folks from Trujillo and vacationing Peruvians. Huanchaco is a very good alternative to Trujillo as a base for exploring the archaeological sites of the Chimú and Moche (and a day's visit to the capital city is easily accomplished from Huanchaco).

The town's fishing character is apparent in the long jetty that juts out over the water and the pointy handcrafted boats called *caballitos del mar* (or *caballitos de totora*), for which Huanchaco has become famous and which remain the photogenic vessel of choice for fishers. These small boats, made of bound totora reeds, have been used by fishermen for more than 1,000 years, since the reign of the Moche. The area around Huanchaco is one of the few places in Peru where this ancient sea vessel tradition has not disappeared from use. When not out on the water, they're parked on the beach in groups like slender tepees.

Besides a stroll on the beach and visit to Huanchaco's pleasant artesanía market, there's not too much to see or do. A 16th-century colonial church clings to a cliff, but it's a long walk uphill from town. More than anything else, Huanchaco's easy pace and proximity to the sea are its main attractions. It has several agreeable resort hotels, seafood restaurants, and nice stretches of beach. The big waves here attract local surfers and a few board-carrying tourists, though the biggest and best waves are at **Puerto Chicama** (also known as Malabrigo), about 80km (50 miles) farther up the coast. Waves there can be ridden up to a half mile, and it's the site of the largest left-hand wave in the world. (Another good spot in the far north is **Cabo Blanco,** about 110km/68 miles south of Tumbes.) La Casa Suiza hostal (p. 346) rents out body boards.

To get there, pick up a Huanchaco bus (S/1, or 30¢) along Independencia in Trujillo; the buses go along the first part of the beach before turning on Los Ficus. You can get to Puerto Chicama by colectivos, which depart hourly from the Terminal Interurbano on Calle Santa Cruz in Trujillo; the journey takes about 90 minutes.

ARCHAEOLOGICAL SITES NEAR TRUJILLO

Chan Chan 🏛️🏛️ One of the most important archaeological sites in Peru, though in its present state it may not seem as "complete" to the layman observer as some of the Inca stone ruins in the highlands, Chan Chan is an enormous adobe city in the Moche valley, just 5km (3 miles) from Trujillo. The great capital of the Chimú empire, which stretched some 966km (600 miles) along the northern coast of Peru from Lima to the Ecuadorian border, is the largest complex of its kind from pre-Columbian America. The urban Chimú were the chief state in Peru prior to the continental conquest of the Inca Empire. Begun around 1300, it reaches all the way from Huanchaco port to Campana Mountain, an area covering more than 25km^2 (9½ sq. miles) of desert floor. First excavated in the mid-1960s, the crumbling mud city was once home to perhaps as many 60,000 inhabitants. In all, the UNESCO Cultural Mankind Heritage Monument comprises more than a dozen citadels and a maze of living quarters, thick defensive walls, ramps, plazas, gardens, workshops, warehouses, narrow streets, a huge reservoir, a royal cemetery, and pyramidal temples. Nine palaces were the personal domains of Chimú chieftains; when one died, he was buried in an elaborate ritual in the palace and a new royal compound was built for his successor. These were almost certainly overflowing with gold and silver riches,

---

Tips **Catch Some** *Ondas*

Check out **www.a-styleadventures.com/english/surfing.htm** for more information about surfing in northern Peru. If you can read Spanish, another good surfing site is **www.peruazul.com.pe**.

and were later ransacked not by the Incas but by the Spaniards and subsequent *huaqueros* (grave robbers, or treasure hunters). The fragile buildings themselves have fallen victim to erosion caused by recurring El Niño floods; in 1986, Chan Chan was listed on World Heritage Sites in Danger due to both physical erosion and acts of continued pillaging.

The Chimú kingdom began around 1000 and reached its apex in the 15th century, before succumbing to the Incas in 1470 and 1471, after more than a decade of resistance. Today, one can only imagine what this massive complex looked like and the sophisticated society that once inhabited it. Unfortunately, there are no written records or documents that aid our understanding of the establishment of the city or reconstruct the daily activities that took place there. Long walls are embellished with friezes of geometric figures, stylized birds and fish, ocean motifs, and mythological creatures—though some might be considered a bit too impeccably restored. There are no doors or arches in the entire complex, and there are no stairs—only ramps.

There are four main sites at Chan Chan, all spread out over a large area that requires either a lot of walking or a couple taxi rides. The principal complex, named the **Tschudi Palace** for a 19th-century Swiss explorer, has been partially restored, and a walking tour is indicated by painted arrows. The royal palace was home to a noble population of 500 to 1,000. The first area of interest is a ceremonial courtyard decorated with aquatic-themed friezes. The original walls were 18m (60 ft.) high. Just beyond the courtyard are walls with interesting friezes of fish and seabirds. The most fascinating component of the palace is the large area known as the Sanctuary, whose walls are textured like fishing nets. Although Chan Chan contains the ruins of an additional eight royal compounds, none has been restored like Tschudi, and very little can be seen or understood from viewing them.

The **Museo de Sitio de Chan Chan,** along the road back toward Trujillo, has a small collection of ceramics from Chan Chan and some exhibits about the nature of the city and its history. The museum is equipped with a new auditorium and models of Chan Chan; an audio and light presentation is given in English as well as Spanish. The museum is at least a 20-minute walk from Tschudi Palace.

Huaca Esmeralda and Huaca Arco Iris are two smaller pyramidal temples that are rather removed from the main palace. They are included in the Chan Chan ticket, but one must go to either the museum or Tschudi Palace first. **Huaca Esmeralda** is in the Mansiche district, midway between Chan Chan and Trujillo (several blocks behind the church, to the right). The huaca consists of a couple

---

Tips Chan Chan Crime Report

Chan Chan is spread out over several kilometers, and some visitors walking alone among the component parts have reported robberies and attacks. To be safe, stick to the main paths between the major sites and avoid wandering along smaller paths in the open fields around Tschudi Palace. Chan Chan is just a couple of kilometers from the beach, but the route to the water has a very bad reputation and should be avoided; too many reports of muggings and worse have been registered over the years to risk it. There have also been crime reports in the neighborhoods around Huaca Arco Iris and Huaca Esmeralda; it's best to take a taxi there from the Museo de Sitio de Chan Chan.

> **Fun Fact The Peruvian Rat Dog**
>
> Near the Chan Chan site museum, or elsewhere in northern Peru, you may spot a peculiar smooth, black-skinned creature, often with blotches. This less-than-blessed creature is the *biringo*, or Peruvian hairless dog. Ancient and—to my Labrador-loving tastes—ugly as all get out, these dogs were kept by several of the pre-Inca cultures of the region, and they're still around and kept as pets. These dogs are hot to the touch, and it is said that ancient nobles kept them as portable heaters. The Lambayeque and Chimú not only domesticated the animal, though; they also made it part of their diets. Eeuww.

platforms and some friezes that have not yet been restored; though less impressive than others, at least visitors get a clear chance to see original reliefs.

Huaca Arco Iris (the Rainbow Temple, also called Huaca El Dragón), lies in the La Esperanza suburb a couple kilometers from Trujillo, west of the Pan-American Highway. It is in much better condition than Huaca Esmeralda, having only been excavated in the 1960s, and its well-conserved rainbow-shaped friezes are fascinating. Some have interpreted the central motif to be that of a dragon. Outer walls have reliefs of snakes and peculiar lizards. The fairly large structure has several ramps, and visitors can climb to platforms at the top of the temple.

To visit all the sites, you'll need the better part of a day. Many people choose to break up the visit over 2 days. A visit can begin at either Tschudi Palace or at the Museo de Sitio, transferring between them by bus or taxi, then going to the adjunct temple sites by taxi.

Valle de Moche. (Huaca El Arco Iris: Jr. Pedro Murillo 1681, La Esperanza, Trujillo, Panamericana Norte). Admission S/10 ($3); ticket is good for 48 hr. and all 4 sites of the complex. Guides are available at the entrance to Tschudi Palace for S/20–S/30 ($6–$9) per group. Daily 9am–4pm. Catch the Huanchaco bus (S/1, or 30¢) on Av. España (at the corner of Independencia/Ejército) and ask to be let off at the turnoff to Chan Chan. Occasionally, there are taxis waiting here; otherwise, walk nearly a mile down a dirt road to the left, to the Tschudi Palace. For the Museo de Sitio, catch a bus returning to Trujillo. Taxis from Trujillo cost about S/10.50 ($3). Because transportation among the 4 sites is not always available, it might be worthwhile to contract a taxi to take you to the sites and wait for you.

El Brujo 🐾 Difficult to get to and explore without a private guide, the remote Moche complex of El Brujo nonetheless makes a very worthwhile visit for those intrigued by what they've seen at Chan Chan and the huacas near Trujillo. Because it is so little explored—until recently it was closed to the public—many visitors enjoy El Brujo even more than those other sites. (Because of ongoing excavations, some groups are reportedly still occasionally turned away.)

El Brujo lies in the Chicama Valley, about 60km (36 miles) north of Trujillo along the coast, or 1½ hours by car. A number of cultures developed in the Chicama Valley region since the pre-ceramic period, and at least one of the three temples here, **Huaca Prieta,** is about 5,000 years old. Oddly enough, it's essentially a giant, prehistoric garbage dump—not much to see for nonspecialists, but containing a wealth of nonbiodegradable information for archaeologists researching the ancient people of the same name. (The Huaca Prieta civilization inhabited the area from around 3500–2200 B.C.) The main temple of interest at El Brujo is **Huaca Cao,** a leveled-off pyramid with terrific and huge multicolored friezes—some of the finest in northern Peru. They depict figures of warriors, priests, and sacrificial victims. Nearby, **Huaca Cortada** has some cool and menacing figures in high relief, brandishing a knife in one hand and a recently decapitated head in the other.

Near Magdalena de Cao, Valle de Chicama. Admission S/20 ($6). Daily 9am–4pm. Several tour agencies in Trujillo organize excursions to El Brujo; be sure to ask about the status of current admissions policy at the site. Private guides that frequently take individuals and small groups are Michael White and Clara Luz Bravo (© 044/243-347). Ask at the Tourism Information Office (© 044/938-922) about other guides.

Huacas de Moche ★   About 8km (5 miles) south of Trujillo in the desert Valle de Moche, this complex of Moche ruins is enigmatic from a distance. Two imposing rounded-off and weathered adobe pyramids, partially eroded, sit in a dusty open field at the foot of Cerro Blanco. Built by the Moche people around A.D. 500, they are about 7 centuries older than the ruined city of Chan Chan. The two masses constituted a religious center and an urban settlement.

The first pyramid, the **Huaca del Sol** (Temple of the Sun), is nearly 20m (70 ft.) high, though it was once bigger by perhaps two-thirds, and it was very likely the largest man-made structure in the Americas in its day. Heavy rains of the El Niño phenomenon, and the Spaniards' diversion of the nearby Moche River, precipitated the erosion. It is said to have been built by 250,000 men and 140 million adobe bricks. The pyramid once surely was composed of multiple staircases and platforms. The *huaca* (pyramid) remains unexcavated, and it looks very fragile, as though a major rainstorm could easily take it out. Though signs warn visitors against climbing on the ruins (NO ESCALAR), plenty do climb up to the top along steep trails. Additional foot traffic only furthers the erosion, though, and the views are equally good from the Huaca de la Luna across the way. Some visitors inevitably find this lumpen mass a bit of a disappointment, just a massive mound of muddy earth; if you find yourself in that camp, hurry over to the neighboring huaca.

Across the open field, where burials sites have been found and living quarters were once erected, is the smaller but more interesting **Huaca de la Luna** (Temple of the Moon). It is better preserved than the Temple of the Sun and has been excavated; many of the most important finds took place only in the last decade, and excavations are ongoing. The structure consists of five independent levels, with no communication among them—perhaps a result of the fact that the huaca was constructed in major phases over 600 years. Inside the adobe walls (at the top of an entrance ramp) are polychromatic friezes of large rhomboids, featuring a repeated motif of the fearsome anthropomorphic figure Ai-Apaek, known as *El Degollador* (the decapitator god), and several secondary figures. The yellow, red, white, and black designs are quite remarkable; the god is said to have the hair of the sea and eyes of an owl. From the top of the Huaca de la Luna, there are excellent views of Huaca del Sol and the surrounding countryside. Near the ticket booth, where you can arrange for a guide, is a small refreshment stand and souvenir shop.

Valle de Moche. © 044/291-894. Admission S/5 ($1.50); cost includes a Spanish- or English-speaking guide (tip expected). Daily 9am–4pm. Catch the yellow "Campiña de Moche" colectivo (S/1, or 30¢) on Suárez (at Av. Los Incas), several blocks northeast of the Plaza de Armas. Otherwise, you can take a taxi there for about S/17.50 ($5). In high season, you won't have to have the driver wait, as there are frequent buses and taxis returning to Trujillo. If there are few people around, however, you can usually get the driver to wait an hour or so to take you back to Trujillo for around S/35 ($10) round-trip.

SHOPPING

Trujillo doesn't have much to interest potential shoppers, unless you need eyeglasses; Calle Bolívar is loaded with opticians. For a taste of what shopping means to most Trujillo natives, check out the sprawling **street *mercado*** that

Moche Culture

Anyone who has spent time in a small museum room crammed with the famed erotic ceramics of the Moche culture might feel we know almost too much about this ancient civilization, certainly more than plenty of people are comfortable seeing depicted on vases and other vessels. But our knowledge isn't limited to their sexual mores. The Moche, who inhabited the northern coastal desert of Peru from A.D. 100 to 700, left detailed information about their entire civilization in their finely detailed ceramics, which are some of the finest produced in pre-Columbian Peru. The apogee of the Moche society was A.D. 500–600.

The Moche are, along with the contemporary Nasca people from the desert coast south of Lima, the best-documented culture of the Classical period. Though they possessed no written language, their superior painted pottery presents evidence of nearly all elements of their society, from disease and dance to architecture, transportation, agriculture, music, and religion. The Moche (also referred to as "Mochica," though the latter term is losing some currency) were a strictly hierarchical, elite-dominated society that developed into a theocracy. They were also one of the first true urban cultures in Peru. Religious temples or pyramids, called huacas, were restricted to nobles, warriors, and priests; common citizens—farmers, artisans, fishers, and slaves—lived in areas removed from the temples.

The finest selection of Moche ceramics in the country is at the Museo Arqueológico Rafael Larco Herrera (p. 132) in Lima, the largest private collection of pre-Columbian art in the world. The founder of the museum is the author of the classic study *Los Mochicas.*

operates daily along Avenida Los Incas. It's one of the more unruly (and headache-inducing) markets in Peru, with vendors struggling to be heard over the incessant sounds of car horns. The market stretches across several blocks and spreads out into the street, selling an unending variety of vegetables, fish, and household items; there are even carts full of charcoal.

Most visitors will be better off shopping in Huanchaco. **Artesanía del Norte,** Los Olivos 504 (© **044/461-220**), has some of the coolest exclusive ceramics designs in Peru. They'll ship pieces to your home if you can't limit yourself to just one. The *mercado de artesanía* fronting the beach in Huanchaco has a number of stalls and is also an excellent place for jewelry, including pieces made with the sought-after blue stone, lapis lazuli.

WHERE TO STAY

Visitors have the option of staying in downtown Trujillo, which has a nice colonial feel to it but can be rather noisy and harried, or staying in the less expensive and more relaxed beachside town of Huanchaco, just 12km (7 miles) away, where there are several laid-back resort hotels and some good budget hostales. Because the focus of many travelers' attentions is Chan Chan, which is located northwest of the city towards Huanchaco, staying beachside is a very practical option.

DOWNTOWN TRUJILLO
Expensive
Gran Hotel El Golf *(Kids)*   This modern resort hotel, the largest in the north of Peru, is built around a large circular swimming pool and is located close to a golf country club in one of the most upscale residential districts of Trujillo (5 min. from the Plaza de Armas). Rooms are spacious, as are bathrooms, but I wouldn't call them luxurious. It's like a 3-star establishment posing as a 5-star property. The hotel doesn't have the character of the Hotel Libertador on the main square, which beats it with its location and historic building. The Golf's two-story units overlook the pool and nice gardens. For those (particularly families) looking for some relaxation and space for the kids to run around in, it's not a bad bet. Additional distractions include tennis courts, a spa, children's games, and nearby beaches.

Los Cocoteros 500, Urbanización El Golf, Trujillo. **©** **044/282-515.** Fax 044/282-231. 120 units. $108 double. Rate includes taxes and breakfast buffet. AE, V. **Amenities:** Restaurant; bar; outdoor pool; nearby golf course with privileges; fronton and tennis courts; concierge; business center; 24-hr. room service; laundry service. *In room:* A/C, TV, minibar, hair dryer, safe.

Hotel Libertador Trujillo *(Kids)*   The top place to stay in Trujillo is right on the Plaza de Armas, in a beautiful salmon-colored colonial mansion with a courtyard patio and a nice pool with palm trees and lots of vegetation. The place has a fair amount of colonial elegance and flavor. Unusual for a place with such amenities, it's a fair deal, too. Rooms are not spectacularly luxurious, but they are certainly comfortable and well outfitted with somewhat-dated furnishings. Rooms on the interior are quieter and have views of the pool. Other rooms look out onto the busy but pretty plaza, and some have small balconies that are perfect for people-watching (but be prepared for the trade-off: street noise until late). The hotel has a handsome bar, a good restaurant, and both dry and steam saunas. On Sunday, there's a big-time brunch starting at noon, with both Peruvian and international foods (S/29, or $8, adults; half price for children).

Jr. Independencia 48, Plaza de Armas, Trujillo. **©** **044/232-741,** or 01/442-995 for reservations. Fax 044/235-641. www.libertador.com.pe. 78 units. $87 double. Rate includes taxes and breakfast buffet. AE, DC, MC, V. **Amenities:** Restaurant; bar; excellent outdoor pool; sauna; concierge; 24-hr. room service; laundry service. *In room:* A/C, TV, minibar, hair dryer, safe.

Moderate
El Brujo Hotel   In the La Merced residential district about 8 blocks south of the Plaza de Armas, this modern hotel resembles a small shopping mall from the outside. Inside, it's clean if not especially brimming with character. It has the look of a Peruvian business traveler's hotel. Rooms are functionally decorated, with (occasionally brightly colored) wall-to-wall carpeting, full-length curtains, and patterned bedspreads (the kind with that annoying sheen).

Santa Teresa de Jesús 170, Urbanización La Merced, Trujillo. **©** and fax **044/223-322.** www.perunorte.com/elbrujohotel. 24 units. $75 double with A/C; $60 double without A/C. Rates include taxes and breakfast. No credit cards. **Amenities:** Cafeteria; bar; room service; Internet access (for a small fee); safety deposit boxes. *In room:* A/C in some units; TV.

Los Conquistadores Hotel *(Value)*   On a busy street just a couple blocks from the Plaza de Armas, this modern and very clean midsize independent hotel is a nice surprise. With handsome public rooms set way back from the street and its hubbub, it has a very welcoming atmosphere and good service. All of the quiet rooms are large and carpeted, with pretty standard modern hotel decor and good beds decked out in flowery bedspreads. Suites are especially large, with separate sitting areas. Walk-in discounts are frequently available. In this price range, Los Conquistadores is your best bet.

Diego de Almagro 586, Trujillo. ℂ **044/244-505**. Fax 044/235-917. conquistadores@computextos.com.pe. 50 units. $73 double. Rate includes taxes and continental breakfast. AE, DC, MC, V. **Amenities:** Restaurant; bar; business center and meetings hall; room service; laundry service; safety deposit boxes. *In room:* A/C, TV.

Pullman Hotel *(Value)*   Well-located, on the pedestrian-only section of Jirón Pizarro next to the Plazuela El Recreo, this modern midsize hotel isn't a bad place to set down your bags for a short stay in Trujillo. The comfortable rooms are a decent size, with shiny parquet floors and white dorm-style refrigerators. Suites have large separate sitting areas with couches and overstuffed chairs; they're an excellent value. Since it's not on a street overrun with honking taxis, it tends to be pretty quiet. The Pullman is one of the few hotels in Peru that offers massage service (a steal at only S/25, or $7, per hr.)—for weary travelers, it's reason enough to camp out here. Another nod toward relaxation is the large interior terrace.

Jr. Pizarro 879, Trujillo. ℂ and fax **044/203-624**. www.perunorte.com/hotelpullman. 50 units. $30 double; $43 suite. Rates include taxes and continental breakfast. MC, V. **Amenities:** Restaurant; cafeteria; bar; conference room; room service; massage; laundry service; safety deposit boxes. *In room:* A/C, TV, minibar, fridge, dataport.

Inexpensive

Hostal Colonial *(Value)*   My taxi driver turned me on to this small Belgian-owned hotel, and for once, the driver wasn't just trawling for a commission—he was right. A handsome and recently restored colonial house just a block from the Plaza de Armas, it is an excellent value. Some of the rooms are a bit plain, though large. The rooms looking over the interior patio are best; a couple of them have balconies with chairs. If you don't mind a bit of street noise, the rooms facing the street are also good bets. Attached to the hotel is a genial little cafe that's a good, cheap place for lunch.

Jr. Independencia 618, Trujillo. ℂ **044/258-261**. Fax 044/223-410. hostcolonialtruji@latinmail.com. 24 units. S/60 ($17) double. Rate includes taxes and breakfast. No credit cards. **Amenities:** Restaurant; room service; safety deposit boxes. *In room:* TV.

Hotel Americano   This formerly grand hotel is a shadow of its former self, but fans of faded splendor—better put, lovers of down-in-the-chops decadence—may find themselves at home here. The huge hotel has a few hints of its bygone elegance and grand architecture (now totally uncared for) in the lobby, such as cool reliefs—if you squint hard enough. The rooms, though, are pretty dingy. Floorboards are in bad shape, the fluorescent lighting stinks, and the place feels abandoned. It's a shame, because if it were restored and kept up, it would look like an early-20th-century North African hotel straight out of *The English Patient*. Comparatively, the Hostal Colonial or any of the hostales in Huanchaco are a much better value. Then again, staying at the Americano might have its own peculiar value for some travelers, inexplicably drawn to places in free-fall decline.

Jr. Pizarro 764, Trujillo. ℂ **044/241-361**. 120 units. S/35 ($10) double with bathroom and hot water; S/16 ($4.50) without bathroom. Rate includes taxes. No credit cards. *In room:* No phone.

HUANCHACO
Moderate

Hostal Bracamonte *(Kids)*   A miniresort tucked behind a high gate and a couple of blocks' walk from the beach, this relaxed hostal has a bit of a motel atmosphere. Rooms and bungalows are positioned around a large pool. Perfect for families, the hotel has a playground and gardens for kids to run around, as well as several terraces, a barbecue grill area, and a game room. Bungalows have room for three or four guests each. Rooms have a beachy, unadorned feel, with tile floors but comfortable beds. Overall, it's a pretty good, if not outstanding, value, and it's an especially welcome retreat for those traveling with children.

Jr. Los Olivos 503, Huanchaco. ℂ and fax **044/461-266.** www.huanchaco.net/hostalbracamonte. 40 units. S/85 ($24) double; S/125–S/145 ($36–$41) bungalows. Rates include taxes. AE, DC, MC, V. **Amenities:** Restaurant; cafeteria; bar; outdoor swimming pool; game room; conference room; library and video rentals; Internet access (for a fee). *In room:* A/C, TV.

Huanchaco Hostal This attractive and friendly hostal, facing the Plaza de Armas in Huanchaco and just a couple minutes' walk from the beach, has rooms with plenty of light and terra-cotta floors. Rooms aren't especially large, but they're nicely decorated with iron headboards and solid wood furnishings. Public rooms are decorated with lots of ceramics and local paintings and have nice sitting areas. Among the amenities are a very nice pool in a courtyard garden setting, a game room with pool table, a TV room, and a souvenir shop.

Jr. Víctor Larco 287, Huanchaco. ℂ **044/461-272.** Fax 044/461-688. www.solui.com/huanchacohostal. 24 units. $28 double. Rate includes taxes and breakfast. AE, DC, MC, V. **Amenities:** Bar; outdoor swimming pool; game room. *In room:* A/C, TV.

Huanchaco International Hotel *(Kids)* This Belgian-owned modern beach resort hotel, positioned right on the beach on the road to Huanchaco, is a welcoming place, especially for families. Popular with vacationing Peruvians, it has a huge pool, yellow and white bungalow accommodations dotting the property, and gardens with sea views. Breakfast is served on a terrace overlooking the beach. Rooms are large and very clean; many of the little house-like bungalows are attractively positioned up stone steps. If you're staying for a few days, ask about package deals that include area visits.

Autopista a Huanchaco Km 13.5, Playa Azul, Huanchaco. ℂ **044/461-754.** Fax 044/461-753. www. perunorte.com/huanchacoint. 40 units. $45 double; $55 bungalows. Rates include taxes and breakfast. Packages available for longer stays. AE, DC, MC, V. **Amenities:** Restaurant; bar; cafe; large outdoor swimming pool; solarium; car-rental desk; conference room; laundry service; Internet access and fax; safety deposit boxes. *In room:* TV.

Inexpensive

Casa Hospedaje Los Ficus *(Value)* A good option if nearby La Casa Suiza is full, this very friendly, family-run 3-year-old hostal occupies a large, modern home. It has a relaxed atmosphere and good-value, though not terribly large, rooms. Guests have kitchen privileges. It's very clean and safe, with a large, relaxing courtyard, and it's located just a block from the beach.

Los Ficus 516, Huanchaco. ℂ and fax **044/461-719.** www.huanchaco.net/losficus. 8 units. S/32 ($9) double. Rate includes taxes and breakfast. No credit cards. **Amenities:** Breakfast room; kitchen; common room with TV and videos. *In room:* No phone.

Hostal Caballito de Totora A beachy three-story inn on a palm-tree-lined seafront, this place has been around for 25 years. It has a small and cozy courtyard with plants, a small pool, and good views of the ocean from a rooftop terrace or from the few rooms with balconies. Rooms are in three blocks and range from suites to an apartment that sleeps six people. The owners, Elvira and Walter, promote local culture with dance and music performances at a nearby restaurant/nightclub.

La Rivera 219, Huanchaco. ℂ **044/461-154.** Fax 044/461-004. totora@terra.com. 18 units. $36–$50 double. Rates include taxes. No credit cards. **Amenities:** Restaurant; cafeteria; bar; outdoor swimming pool. *In room:* TV.

La Casa Suiza *(Finds)* A favorite of backpackers for more than 20 years, this inn run by a Swiss-Peruvian family—still referred to as "Heidi's house" by longtime vets—is an extremely friendly place to hang out and meet up with other travelers. The large and comfortable rooms are simply adorned, but the star at this hostal is the great rooftop terrace, where guests line-dry their laundry and write in their journals. The terrace is topped by a tile table and glowing red Swiss lamp. There's a cable TV room, a book exchange, and Internet access (and even a laser printer). Would-be surfers are well cared for here; the hostal has gear (including wet suits and boards) for rent. Breakfast is prepared by Wendy, a Swiss woman who's practically an institution at this friendly joint. Most rooms are shared, though three have private bathrooms.

Los Ficus 516, Huanchaco. (©) and fax 044/461-719. www.huanchaco.net/losficus. 8 units. $10 double with private bathroom; $4 per person in shared room with shared bathroom. Rates include taxes. No credit cards. **Amenities:** Breakfast room; TV room; free limited Internet access; book exchange. *In room:* No phone.

WHERE TO DINE

Dining out is a pretty low-key affair in Trujillo. Even though it's Peru's third-largest city, it doesn't have many sophisticated restaurants. Most visitors enjoy eating out in Huanchaco, which has one excellent luxury restaurant and a number of simple seafood places along the beach.

TRUJILLO
Moderate

El Mochica ☆ PERUVIAN   The one restaurant that everyone in Trujillo recommends is a bit of a surprise. From the outside, it looks to be a pretty sophisticated joint, as it's housed within a beautiful colonial building with an impressive carved-wood balcony. Inside, though, the dining room is a little jarring, with white plastic chairs and a large TV blaring videos in the front room but waiters dressed in black tie. A second room has a bar and a stage for live music on weekends. Still, despite the inauspicious surroundings, El Mochica produces very well-prepared and good-value criollo cooking and classic dishes such as roasted guinea pig and *parrilladas* (mixed grilled meats), in addition to fresh fish such as *corvina* (sea bass).

Bolívar 462. (©) 044/293-441. Reservations recommended for live music on weekends. Main courses S/8–S/24 ($2.25–$7). AE, DC, MC, V. Daily 8pm–1am.

Il Valentino ☆ ITALIAN   Across from Trujillo's jam-packed Cine Primavera is the city's classiest-looking restaurant. An attractive, somewhat Mediterranean-style place, it has yellow walls and arched doorways, subdued lighting, and tables on two levels with tablecloths and fake flowers. The menu is dominated by pizzas and pastas of the upscale variety, plus a few steaks. It's perfectly located for dinner before or after a movie (Cine Primavera shows films in their original language), though service here can be a bit slow, so I recommend going to the movie first and having dinner afterwards.

Orbegoso 224. (©) 044/246-643. Reservations recommended on weekends. Main courses S/15–S/26 ($4–$7). AE, DC, MC, V. Tues–Sun noon–11pm.

Restaurante Demarco *(Value* ITALIAN/INTERNATIONAL   A pleasant cafe-style restaurant, which resembles an ice cream parlor crammed with small tables and ceiling fans, Demarco has something for just about everyone and every time of day. From a good breakfast selection to sandwiches, pizza, pastas, and other Italian fare, as well as excellent cakes and ice creams, it draws a consistent crowd of locals. The extensive menu also has criollo specialties such as *asado de res con puré y arroz* (roast beef with mashed potatoes and rice), *churrasco con tacu tacu* (grilled meats served with rice and beans), and the classic *lomo saltado* (strips of beef with onions, tomatoes, and french fries over rice). It has a daily lunch *menú* (inexpensive set meal), but is just as good for a midafternoon snack or late dessert.

Pizarro 725. ✆ **044/234-251.** Reservations not accepted. Main courses S/12–S/24 ($3.50–$7); menú del día S/5–S/10 ($1.50–$3). AE, DC, MC, V. Daily 8am–midnight.

Restaurante Romano ITALIAN/INTERNATIONAL   Located on one of the city's main thoroughfares, this uncomplicated and cheery restaurant is a good, easygoing place for pizzas, rice dishes, salads, and omelets, as well as more substantial items such as steak, pork loin, and filet mignon with mushrooms. There are also homemade pastas, including ravioli, lasagna, and cannelloni. The weekday set-price menu is a very good value; it might be a tuna and vegetable salad to start, followed by baked chicken with rice and mashed potatoes, plus juice and bread. Romano is open for breakfast and has a nice selection of desserts and excellent coffees, including cappuccino and espresso. It's very popular with local regulars, especially at lunch. Waiters bring the food through the front door, which looks odd, as if they are going out to the street to fetch your meal. (The kitchen is around the other side of the restaurant.)

Pizarro 747. ✆ **044/252-251.** Reservations recommended. Main courses S/9.50–S/21 ($2.50–$6); menú del día S/6–S/10 ($1.75–$3). AE, DC, MC, V. Daily 8am–midnight.

Inexpensive

Jugería San Agustín JUICE BAR/SNACKS   This cafeteria-style "juice bar" may not be the first place you'd think of for a meal, but you can get a perfectly acceptable and cheap menú (Mon–Fri) for just S/5 ($1.50), as well as a host of sandwiches, roasted chicken, and grilled meats. And of course, there are fresh-squeezed tropical juices. (I'd pop in daily for maracuyá.) There's another branch in Trujillo at Bolívar 522.

Pizarro 691. ✆ **044/259-591.** Reservations not accepted. Main courses S/4–S/16 ($1–$4.50); menú del día S/5 ($1.50). AE, DC, MC, V. Daily 8pm–1am.

Restaurant Colonial PERUVIAN   This cute and relaxed cafe, with just six tables, is attached to the Hostal Colonial. It has floor-to-ceiling wall murals of colonial Trujillo and Moche motifs from Las Huacas and other sites in the area. It offers simple Peruvian fare, but it's perfect for a great midday menú (just S/4, or $1), which might include a soup or *papa a la huacaína* (boiled potato with a creamy cheese sauce) and a main course of *churrasco* (barbecued meats) or *arroz con pollo* (chicken and rice). The menu also has pork, Chinese-style fried rice, spaghetti, and omelets, as well as three breakfast options.

Jr. Independencia 618. ✆ **044/258-261.** Reservations not accepted. Main courses S/8–S/12 ($2–$3.50); menú del día S/4 ($1). No credit cards. Daily 8am–9pm.

Video Pub Totem PERUVIAN   Admittedly, the name would seem to indicate that this joint is anything but a restaurant. I don't know that it is a *restaurant*, exactly; it's a small one-man operation on the Plazuela Recreo, a laid-back eatery frequented by locals who drop in for a beer, a game of cards, and maybe a home-cooked meal. There's no name outside, no menu as such, and only a few wooden tables; it looks more like a small drinking hall (but not a "video pub"). Ramiro, the gregarious owner, will tell you what he's got cooking on that particular day. You can usually count on a huge portion of lomo saltado, soup, or perhaps a baked chicken dish. Most of all, he makes a mean (and spicy) ceviche. If you feel like hanging out in the square, Ramiro will deliver your beer to you there.

Pizarro 922. No phone. Reservations not accepted. Main courses S/6–S/7 ($1.75–$2); menú del día S/3–S/4. No credit cards. Daily 11am–9pm.

HUANCHACO

Moderate

Club Colonial ☆☆☆ BELGIAN/FRENCH   A romantic and magnificently inviting restaurant occupying a renovated 1790s mansion on a quiet square, this is one of the most refined places to dine in northern Peru. Enter through a small courtyard and stunning Art Nouveau stained-glass doors. The warm dining salon is straight ahead, and off to the right is a small bar with well-chosen cafe tables and chairs. The colorful decor lives up to the restaurant's name and reeks of French colonial atmosphere. Walls are bright blue, orange, red, and yellow, and the place is brimming with large mirrors, antiques, fresh flowers, and dark wood. It looks like some cool expat's house. The menu is an interesting mix of Peruvian and Franco-Belgian items. Starters include excellent salads, ceviches, and homemade pastas. Main courses include French brochette in three sauces, cordon bleu, and pork loin with curry pineapple sauce. But for my money, the stars are the exquisitely prepared fish dishes, such as *corvina a la vasca* (Basque-style sea bass) and lobster. There are even Belgian classics such as waterzooi. Desserts, such as crêpes Suzettes and crêpes Suchards (with ice cream and chocolate), are also outstanding. Service lags in comparison to the food and surroundings, but you're unlikely to care. After you've dined, wander out to the garden courtyard past the bar to see the 12 penguins and two small caimans. Club Colonial is more expensive than other restaurants in northern Peru, but is definitely worth it.

Grau 272. © 044/461-015. Reservations recommended. Main courses S/10–S/35 ($5–$10). AE, DC, MC, V. Daily noon–10pm.

Inexpensive

El Peñón *Value* SEAFOOD   Huanchaco, a fishing village, is rightly famous for its fresh fish. And there are few better places to plunge into the local catch than this casual and comfy place, one of the first tourist-oriented restaurants in Huanchaco. It couldn't be simpler: white plastic chairs, tables with green tablecloths, and the roar of the sea. (There is also indoor seating, but the best spot is on the small terrace.) Located right across the street from the surf, the family-run restaurant is a favorite of locals, and the amiable owner seems to know everyone. Try one of the excellent ceviches, seafood omelets, or main courses such as *arroz con mariscos* (shellfish rice), *calamares* (squid), or *pulpo* (octopus).

Corner of Av. Víctor Larco and Raymondi. © 044/461-549. Reservations recommended in high season. Main courses S/6–S/20 ($1.75–$6). DC, MC, V. Daily noon–10pm.

El Piccolo ITALIAN/INTERNATIONAL   A very simple and inexpensive family-run eatery, El Piccolo (which also runs a surf and art shop) is a good place for pastas, pizzas, salads, and other cafe fare. It's a favorite hangout of backpackers from up the street at La Casa Suiza. The owners, with German and French backgrounds, attend to a crew of international visitors in their native languages.

Los Abetos 142. © 044/461-451. Reservations not accepted. Main courses S/3–S/14 ($1–$4). No credit cards. Daily 11am–11pm.

La Barca SEAFOOD   A popular, homey little place with basic tables and chairs and very little fuss, "The Boat" serves up very good and reasonably priced fresh seafood dishes, as well as some criollo standards. I'd stick to the fish: succulent ceviche, *langostinos* (prawns), or *cangrejo* (crab). There's a daily set menú Monday through Friday, and on Saturday evening, there's a piano bar. There's a second, similar branch at Av. Víctor Larco 514, just a couple blocks away, facing the beach.

Jr. Unión 209. © 044/461-549. Reservations recommended in high season. Main courses S/6–S/22 ($1.75–$6). DC, MC, V. Daily noon–10pm.

TRUJILLO AFTER DARK

Trujillo is pretty quiet except on weekends, when it springs to life. A few night-clubs and peñas are clustered in the centro, but most of the hopping discos that go all night are very local and young affairs, on the outskirts of the city. Trujillo has a surprising roster of casinos and movie houses (including two multiplexes showing recently arrived English-language films), and those are as good as any destination for an evening out.

Las Tinajas, Pizarro 383 (© **044/296-272**), with a balcony overlooking the Plaza de Armas, is a pretty chic and popular bar with a downstairs disco, good for drinks midweek. On weekends, it features live rock and pop; the cover is S/5 ($1.50). **El Estribo,** San Martín 810, is a lively and large open music hall with peña music and Mariah Carey wannabes occasionally performing. The cover charge is S/7 ($2). **La Canana,** San Martín 791 (© **044/232-503**), is another nearby peña with a good restaurant and live music and dancing on weekends. The cover is usually about S/10 ($3).

Luna Rota, at América Sur 2119 in the Santa María district at the end of Huayna Cápac (© **044/228-877**), is an all-in-one complex with a thumping disco for teenagers, a pub, and a casino for slightly more mature folks. The cover in the disco and pub is S/7 to S/10 ($2–$3).

Cine Primavera, Orbegoso 239 near the Plaza de Armas (© **044/241-277**), has first-run American and European films in their original languages, and draws long lines of moviegoers. Among the collection of casinos along Orbegoso and Pizarro is **Casino Solid Gold,** Orbegoso 554 (© **044/207-662**). Open daily 24 hours, it has cocktail waitresses in flashy short skirts and a low-rent Vegas feel to it; its cheesy theme is "Chan Chan Lost World."

2 Chiclayo

770km (477 miles) N of Lima; 200km (124 miles) N of Trujillo; 235km (146 miles) NW of Cajamarca

Though it's Peru's fourth-largest city, with a population of just under half a million, Chiclayo would be just another busy commercial town, generating little notice among travelers were it not for the city's strong associations with Peru's ancient cultures. The primary draw is Chiclayo's proximity to the archaeological sites Sipán and Túcume, two of the most important related to the Moche and Lambayeque cultures, and the Museo Brüning, which houses one of the country's most remarkable finds of the past several decades: the tomb of the Lord of Sipán.

Chiclayo is a modern and relatively new city. Though it was founded in the mid–16th century, most of its real development dates to the late 1800s and early 1900s. (The Parque Principal, or main square, didn't come into existence until 1916.) Today, Chiclayo is a sprawling, bustling place; the city itself holds little interest for most visitors. Frankly, most people come here to get out of town. The capital of the Lambayeque department, Chiclayo calls itself "La Ciudad de la Amistad"—the City of Friendship. There's no real reason for such a distinction as far as I can see, but why not? It's not Peru's prettiest, biggest, or most fascinating city, but it is an agreeable, down-to-earth place.

Nearby Lambayeque, where the Museo Brüning is located, was once the more important of the two towns. Today, that is true only from the traveler's perspective. It is a slow-moving, rather dilapidated town with a smattering of interesting colonial buildings, none of which is particularly well-restored or open to visitors. Except for the draw of the Lord of Sipán, the town lives in the shadow of Chiclayo's ever-growing commercial importance.

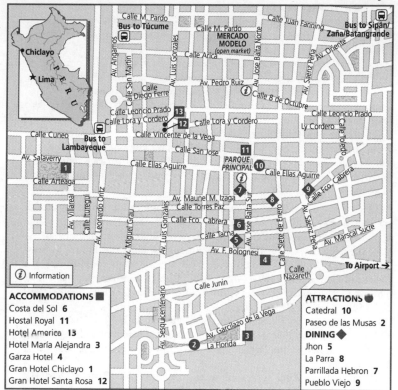

Chiclayo
Lima

Bus to Túcume
Calle M. Pardo
Calle M. Pardo
Calle Juan Fanning
**Bus to Sipán/
Zaña/Batangrande**
MERCADO
MODELO
(open market)
Calle Arica
Av. Pedro Ruiz
Calle 8 de Octubre
Calle Diego Ferre
Calle Leoncio Prado 13
Calle Leoncio Prado
Calle Lora y Cordero 12
Calle Lora y Cordero
Ly Cordero
Calle Vincente de la Vega
**Bus to
Lambayeque**
Calle Cuneo
Calle San José
Av. Salaverry
11
Calle Elías Aguirre
PARQUE
PRINCIPAL 10
Calle Elías Aguirre
Calle Arteaga
1
7
Av. Maunel M. Izaga
9
Calle Torres Paz
8
Calle Fco. Cabrera
6
Calle Tacna
5
Av. F. Bolognesi
4
Av. Marscal Sucre
To Airport →
Calle Nazareth
Calle Junín
i Information
Calle Garcilazo de la Vega
2
La Florida
3

ACCOMMODATIONS ■
Costa del Sol **6**
Hostal Royal **11**
Hotel America **13**
Hotel María Alejandra **3**
Garza Hotel **4**
Gran Hotel Chiclayo **1**
Gran Hotel Santa Rosa **12**

ATTRACTIONS ●
Catedral **10**
Paseo de las Musas **2**
DINING ◆
Jhon **5**
La Parra **8**
Parrillada Hebron **7**
Pueblo Viejo **9**

ESSENTIALS
GETTING THERE
BY PLANE **Aero Continente** (© 01/242-4242; www.aerocontinente.net)
and **Aviandina** (© 01/447-8080) fly daily from Lima to Chiclayo; flights cost
around $69. **LanPeru** (© 01/213-8200; www.lanperu.com) flies from Trujillo.
There are also flights north to and from Piura, and occasional charter flights
from Cajamarca.

Flights arrive at **Aeropuerto José Quiñones González,** Av. Bolognesi s/n
(© 074/233-192), just 2km (1 mile) east of downtown. To the center of
Chiclayo, a taxi costs S/3 to S/4 ($1).

BY BUS Chiclayo is serviced by several domestic bus companies from Lima
and most major points along the north coast and northern highlands. Many
long-distance buses travel at night only. There is no central bus station in Chiclayo; most companies have their own terminals at offices on Avenida Bolognesi,
5 blocks south of the Parque Principal.

The major carriers making the 8-hour trip from Lima are **Ormeño** (© 01/
427-5679), **CIVA** (© 01/428-5649), **Cruz del Sur** (© 01/225-6163), and
Oltursa (© 01/475-8559). **Transportes Línea** (© 044/245-181, or
044/261-482) and **ITTSA** (© 044/222-541) make the 3-hour trip from
Trujillo to Chiclayo, as do a number of colectivos and combis. Transportes Línea
is also the major carrier from Huaraz (© 074/233-497) and Cajamarca.

VISITOR INFORMATION

Chiclayo has two accessible tourist information kiosks, but they are run not by the municipal government but by two related restaurants. One is on the Parque Principal, or the main plaza. Another is on Avenida José Balta Sur (at Manuel María Izaga), in front of the Hebrón restaurant. Both kiosks give out maps of the city and the area, and they'll give you some basic information about how to get around. And they'll put in a plug for barbecue chicken to boot.

The official tourism information office is the **Ministry of Industry and Tourism** (MITINCI), at Sáenz Peña 838 (© 074/233-132); it's a large, bureaucratic office of little assistance to most travelers looking for general information. **Sipán Tours,** 7 de Enero 772 (© 074/229-053), is more amiable and willing to dispense information without giving you the hard sell for package tours (but if you're interested, they're the most reputable agency in town offering city and archaeological tours).

FAST FACTS   Most banks are clustered around the Parque Principal, including **Banco de Crédito,** José Balta 630, and **Interbanc,** Elías Aguirre 680. Money-changers usually hang around in front of banks.

In an **emergency,** call © 105. The helpful **tourist police** are located at Sáenz Peña 830 (© 074/236-700). For medical attention, go to **Hospital Las Mercedes,** González 635 (© 074/237-021); **Clínica Lambayeque,** Vicente de la Vega 415 © 074/237-961); or **Clínica Santa Cecilia,** González 668 (© 074/237-154).

For Internet access, try **Sic@n Internet,** Vicente de la Vega 204 (© 074/227-668), or **Efenet,** Elías Aguirre 181 (no phone). There are also Internet cabinas clustered around the Parque Principal and on Manuel María Izaga near Avenida Balta.

Chiclayo's **post office** is located at Elías Aguirre 140 (© 074/237-031), about 6 blocks from the Parque Principal. It's open Monday through Saturday from 8am to 8pm. The **Telefónica del Perú** office is behind the cathedral at Elías Aguirre 631 (© 074/232-225).

GETTING AROUND

Chiclayo is a busy and fairly congested city. The center of town is, as always, the Plaza de Armas—though in Chiclayo it more often than not goes by the name Parque Principal. About 4 blocks north of the main square is the other focal point in the city, the Mercado Modelo, a sprawling, spirited open street market with stalls spread across several blocks. The main axis in town is Avenida José Balta, which runs north to south and extends on either side of the Parque Principal (with designations "Sur" and "Norte"). Lambayeque is 12km (7 miles) due west of Chiclayo, the airport and Sipán to the east of Chiclayo.

Walking around the centro is easy enough, but you'll need public or private transportation to get to Lambayeque or the major archaeological sites.

BY TAXI   Inexpensive mototaxis buzz about downtown, as do regular taxis. You can hire the latter by the hour ($6) or by the day ($30–$35) to tour archaeological sites or to visit Lambayeque. A round-trip taxi ride to Túcume from Chiclayo costs between $15 and $20.

BY BUS   Combis and ómnibuses are most useful for getting to Lambayeque and several archaeological sites outside of Chiclayo. There are several terminals around the city serving different destinations. The fare is about S/0.50 to S/1 (15¢–30¢).

BY CAR   If you want to rent a car to make trips to Lambayeque, Sipán, Túcume, and other sites, try **Chiclayo Rent a Car** in the Gran Hotel Chiclayo at Av. Federico Villarreal 115 (© **074/237-512**). They have four-wheel-drive vehicles available.

WHAT TO SEE & DO

IN CHICLAYO

A brief look around Chiclayo should be sufficient. Start at the **Parque Principal,** the attractive and overwhelming focal point of life in the city. People camp out on park benches and slurp on ice cream cones, shoeshine boys scurry from one pair of scuffed-up loafers to the next, and pigeons flutter from treetops to sidewalks to rooftops. The white, twin-domed neoclassical **Catedral** that dominates the square dates to 1869. About 10 long blocks south of the plaza, the **Paseo de las Musas** is an attractive park area rather inexplicably outfitted with neoclassical statuary of mythological figures.

The fascinating **Mercado Modelo** ⟲, 5 blocks north of the Parque Principal, is one of Peru's most raucous open street markets. Open daily from dawn to dusk, it carries virtually everything under the sun, but it's famed for the section of small stalls crammed with the elixirs and potions of shamans and faith healers. The so-called *mercadillo de brujas* (witches' little market), near Calle Arica, is redolent with exotic spices and drying herbs, wild with visual overload: hanging shells, small altarpieces and bottles filled with hooves and claws, snakeskins, miniature desiccated crocs, claws, skunks, and fish eggs. Echoing throughout are the distinctive come-ons of vendors. The city of stalls is about as close as you'll get to India or Morocco in Peru, but it's nonetheless a primer on the country's extensive informal economy. You'll find luggage, natural Viagra substitutes, baskets, guitars, hats, calf brains, children's clothes, vats of peanut butter, stuffed animals, shops of canned goods that look like someone's pantry, machetes, and butcher knives. There are dozens of beauty salons under wooden ceilings, and shoe and electronics repair headquarters.

LAMBAYEQUE

The modern **Museo Arqueológico Brüning** (see below) is the undisputed highlight of this small, quiet, and dusty town that was once considerably more important than Chiclayo but has long since been overtaken by it. A few clues to Lambayeque's former status are evident in a number of colonial houses and the baroque **Iglesia de San Pedro,** a large and impressive yellow-and-white church built in 1700 and located on the main square. It's worth a look inside for the impressive mural paintings on the ceiling of the central nave and the cupola. Columns are painted to look like real marble, which I suppose they do if you squint hard enough. The rest of the church is done up in pastel hues of green, blue, and yellow.

On the corner of Dos de Mayo and San Martín is Lambayeque's other building of import, **Casa de la Logia** (also known as Casa Montjoy). Erected in the 16th century, it claims the longest balcony in Peru, a pretty wooden wraparound structure 67m (220 ft.) long. The house can only be viewed from the exterior.

Lambayeque really only springs to life on market day, Sunday. Otherwise, there's little to detain visitors. If you're looking for a bite to eat after visiting the Brüning Museum, check out Dos de Mayo, where there are several cevicherías and other restaurants.

Museo Arqueológico Brüning ⟲⟲⟲   This modern museum, named for a German-Peruvian collector, holds one of Peru's most spectacular exhibits. The

(Value) A Modest Discount

A combination discount boleto is available to visit the Museo Arqueológico Brüning and archaeological sites of Túcume and Sipán for S/15 ($4.25), rather than the separate admission price of S/21 ($6). Okay, so that's not a huge savings, but it's worthwhile just the same if you're certain you'll be visiting all three sites. Combo boletos are available at any of the participating locations.

Lord of Sipán, discovered in 1987, ranks as one of the most important archaeological discoveries in Peru of the past 50 years. Unearthed at the Huaca Rajada at Sipán, the multilevel royal funeral tomb of El Señor de Sipán, a Moche royal figure buried more than 1,700 years ago, was remarkable for its undisturbed, methodical layers and wealth of ceremonial ornaments and treasures that provided key clues to Moche culture. Buried along with the king, who was presumed to be a sort of living deity, were companions joining him on his journey to the afterlife: a Moche warrior, a priest, three female concubines, a dog, two llamas, a child, 212 food and beverage vessels, and a guard with a copper shield, gold helmet, and amputated feet—symbolic of his everlasting protection over the king's tomb.

This outstanding discovery dominates the Brüning Museum, which was inaugurated in 1966 but never attained such acclaim and importance until the arrival of the Lord of Sipán (after a stint at Lima's Museo de la Nación) a few years ago. The Brüning was completely remodeled in 1994 to accommodate its star exhibit, which occupies two floors and several rooms of the museum. The collection also includes some 1,500 items from the Lambayeque, Moche, Chavín, Vicus, and Inca civilizations. Some pieces date back 10,000 years; the stunning, darkened **gold room** holds 500 gleaming jewels and ornamental objects of the Sicán culture.

The rooms dedicated to the Lord of Sipán are one of the most impressive and unforgettable sights under a roof in Peru—a revelation for visitors who've visited several of the archaeological sites in northern Peru and been disappointed to find little more than difficult-to-decipher, colossal piles of clay. The spectacular Sipán finds articulate the grandeur and achievements of pre-Inca cultures and help us comprehend their religious beliefs, social structure, and sophistication. Rather than merely using one's imagination to reconstruct what surely were magnificent, meticulously ordered societies, we get to see the proof. On display from the main funerary chamber—amazingly, never looted—are headdresses, garments, and breastplates of gold, silver, and precious stones that tell an intricate story of power and rank. Several pieces, such as the royal necklace of 20 peanuts, half gold and half silver, are stunning. Other tombs uncovered and recreated here are those of the priest, the mythical "Bird-Man" and top-ranking religious official, and the *Viejo Señor de Sipán* (or Old Lord of Sipán), a Moche spiritual dignitary whose death preceded that of the newer lord's and whose remains were found buried farther below.

The Brüning Museum is one of the best organized and best designed in Peru, an eminently worthy resting place for this monumental discovery.

Av. Huamachuco (block 7), Lambayeque. ℂ **074/282-110.** Admission S/7 ($1.50), students S/1 (30¢). Guides available for S/10 ($3). Daily 9am–5:30pm. Colectivos to Lambayeque depart Chiclayo from the corner of Av. Angamos and Vicente de la Vega and pass right in front of the Brüning Museum about a half hour later. The main plaza is a couple blocks from the museum (across the street).

ARCHAEOLOGICAL SITES NEAR CHICLAYO

Batán Grande   The Batán Grande archaeological complex is a set of ruins from the Sicán culture that comprises some 50 adobe pyramids. Here, archaeologists discovered a network of tombs from the middle Sicán period (A.D. 900–1000). Some of the finest pre-Columbian artifacts in Peruvian museums were found here, including a nearly 7-pound gold Tumi (ceremonial knife) figure and an estimated 90% of all gold pieces from the Lambayeque civilization. Set amid a large nature reserve of mesquite forest (El Bosque Seco de Pómac), there's an on-site interpretation center for visitors, but the pyramids are not as established on the tourist circuit as are those at Túcume.

Located 57km (35 miles) SE of Chiclayo, and 5km (3 miles) NE of Túcume. ℂ 074/201-470. Admission S/7 ($1.50) adults, S/2.50 (70¢) students. Guides available for S/10 ($3). Daily 7am–4pm. Colectivos leave from the Terminal de Epsel at the corner of Av. Oriente and Nicolás de Piérola in Chiclayo, a somewhat unsavory area. It's more convenient to visit Batán Grande by organized tour; contact Sipán Tours at ℂ 074/229-053.

Templo de Sipán   The site where the Lord of Sipán was discovered in 1987, this Moche burial ground 35km (22 miles) from Chiclayo was overlooked by archaeologists for decades. Grave robbers, who'd beaten scientists to countless other valuable sites in Peru, had just begun to loot the ones here, tipping off Peruvian archaeologist Dr. Walter Alva to the presence of the tomb in time to save it. The Sipán sarcophagus held greater riches than any other found to date in Peru and, today, is recognized as one of the most outstanding of the Americas. The twin adobe pyramids, connected by a platform, held five royal tombs. The most elaborate was that of El Señor de Sipán; deeper still was the tomb of an older spiritual leader, now referred to as El Viejo Señor. The remains of both are exhibited at the Museo Arqueológico Brüning. Near the original site, Huaca Rajada ("Cracked Pyramid"), is a small site museum with photos of the excavations and some replicas of tombs. Though it's interesting to see where the tombs were found, and the views from the top of the large pyramid across from the Sipán excavation site are excellent, Templo de Sipán is no substitute for the splendor of jewels and ornaments now housed at the Museo Arqueológico Brüning.

Complejo Arqueológico de Huaca Rajada, Sipán. ℂ 074/800-048. Admission S/5 ($1.50). Guides available for S/7 ($2). Daily 8am–6pm. Colectivos leave from the Terminal de Epsel at the corner of Av. Oriente and Nicolás de Piérola in Chiclayo, a somewhat unsavory area, and take about 45 min.

Túcume   Located 33km (20 miles) north of Chiclayo, this magnificent, massive complex of 26 adobe pyramids (not for nothing do locals call it "El Valle de las Pirámides") was constructed by the Sicán civilization around A.D. 1000 and developed over a period of nearly 500 years. The site was settled and enlarged by the Chimú culture in the 14th century and, finally, occupied by the Incas. Túcume was the most important elite urban center of the region and is considered the last great capital of the Lambayeque culture.

You can wander freely around the maze of courtyards and pyramids and even scale several of them, which are still being excavated and together present an enigmatic desert ensemble. Walking around sites such as these is almost more evocative of what a contemporary archaeologist's life is like than of the lives of those ancient cultures that lived there. The Túcume complex's stunning size, more than a mile long in each direction (a total of 81 acres), is more impressive than any individual structure. The pyramid toward the back of the complex, known as **Huaca Larga,** is reputed to be the largest adobe brick structure in South America. It measures (even after erosion) 700m (2,296 ft.) long, 280m (918 ft.) wide, and 30m (98 ft.) high. A massive platform with several patios and courtyards connected by ramps and corridors, the huaca has walls covered in red, white, and

The Sicán Civilization

The Sicán culture (often designated the Lambayeque civilization, refer-ring to the region where it grew to prominence) developed on the north coast of Peru in the 7th century following the collapse of the Moche civilization. A sophisticated culture whose economic mainstay was agriculture, the Sicán specialized in irrigation engineering. The society reached its apogee between 900 and 1100 and established religious and administrative headquarters at Batán Grande in the Pómac forest, near the Leche River. The site there is known as the "Temple of the Moon" in the ancient local dialect, Muchik. Around 1100, the Sicán abandoned Batán Grande, which they appeared to set fire to, and moved their capital across the valley to El Purgatorio, a hill in the midst of what are now the Túcume ruins. There, they built a splendid urban center, the most important in the region, but the civilization was eventually conquered by the Chimú in 1375.

black murals. Archaeologists have uncovered evidence of the three major stages of construction in Huaca Larga, from the original Lambayeque to Chimú, whose "Temple of the Mythical Bird" dates to 1375, and finally an Inca structure built on top of the Chimú building at the end of the 15th century. Inside the Inca room was a burial tomb, where 22 bodies were discovered, including a local ruler and warrior, interred along with 2 other males and 19 females.

An interestingly conceived site museum exhibits photographs of the excavations and discusses the involvement of a Norwegian explorer, the late Dr. Thor Heyer-dahl, who sought to connect ancient Peruvian culture to that of Polynesia. (He sailed a balsa-wood craft called the *Kon Tiki* from Peru to the Polynesian islands.) Heyerdahl was the director of the 1989 to 1994 Túcume Project, which carried out excavations at the site. Also on-site are a handicrafts-and-ceramics workshop and a snack shop. You'll often find women cooking out in the open on the grounds.

Complejo Arqueológico, Caserío La Raya, Campo. © **074/422-027**, or 074/800-052 site museum. Admission S/7 ($1.50) adults, S/2.5 (70¢) students. Guides available for S/10 ($3). Daily 8am–4:30pm. Colectivos leave from Av. Angamos between Naturaleza and Pardo in Chiclayo (a 45-min. ride), though they leave travelers a good mile or so from the site. Look for a taxi or mototaxi, or walk along the road. A good idea is to visit the Museo Arqueológico Brüning in the morning and head out to Túcume in the afternoon. Buses leave for Túc-ume from very near the museum in Lambayeque; the ticket office can indicate exactly where. Tell the driver you'll be getting off at Túcume.

Zaña   Ruins of an entirely different sort, this 16th-century ghost town was once an important and wealthy colonial outpost, loaded with churches and monaster-ies. On the fast track toward becoming the Peruvian capital, it underwent a tur-bulent period of slave rebellion and pirate attacks. Wealthy families fled to Lambayeque city, and Zaña was soon after wiped out by a massive flood in 1720. The overflowing Río Zaña caused such structural damage that the population abandoned the city. Today, it's a curious sight of ornate columns, church arches, and the remains of the once-grand Gothic Convento de San Agustín (as well as three other convents). A small, inhabited village (also called Zaña) is nearby.

46km (29 miles) SE of Chiclayo. Colectivos leave from the Terminal de Epsel on the corner of Av. Oriente and Nicolás de Piérola in Chiclayo, a somewhat unsavory area. Numerous tour agencies also include Zaña in organized outings, probably the most efficient way of visiting the town; try Sipán Tours at © 074/229-053.

NEARBY BEACHES: PIMENTEL & SANTA ROSA

Pimentel is a beach resort 14km (9 miles) west of Chiclayo, with a nice-enough beach that's very popular in summer and a small fishing community that still employs the caballitos de mar (totora-reed boats) seen in Huanchaco, near Trujillo. Just 6km (4 miles) south of Pimentel is **Santa Rosa,** a more attractive beach and fishing village with totora-reed and gaily painted wooden fishing boats. It has a handful of good seafood restaurants. Both beaches are low-key and a good antidote to touring archaeological sites.

Buses and colectivos run from Vicente Vega and Angamos in Chiclayo to Pimentel. In summer, they continue along a "circuito de playas" to Santa Rosa, Puerto Etén, and Monsefú, none of which are spectacular.

WHERE TO STAY

Chiclayo is hardly brimming with good, interesting hotel options. The best among the bunch are merely functional. Travelers used to a high level of comfort and style won't find much to their liking in Chiclayo, and the paucity of good hotels extends down to the budget level.

EXPENSIVE

Gran Hotel Chiclayo 𝄞   Several blocks removed from the heart of downtown, Chiclayo's largest and most luxurious hotel is a modern, concrete block with mainstream corporate style. Rooms are large and well equipped, if without a great deal of personality. It has all the amenities and services that business travelers demand, and a nice round pool for leisure visitors. The El Caballito disco and the happening "Karaoke Solid Gold" casino draw plenty of locals throughout the week.

Av. Federico Villarreal 115, Chiclayo. © 074/234-911. Fax 074/223-961. www.geocities.com/granhch. 129 units. $80 double. Rate includes taxes, breakfast buffet, and airport transfer. AE, DC, MC, V. **Amenities:** Restaurant; bar; disco; casino; outdoor pool; concierge; car-rental desk; business center and conference room; 24-hr. room service; laundry service. *In room:* A/C, TV, minibar, hair dryer, safe.

MODERATE

Costa del Sol   A mini-high-rise building on Chiclayo's most important and busiest street, this midsize hotel offers a good mix of amenities and easygoing charm. The somewhat jarring red-and-white color scheme in the rooms—rather Valentine's Day–like—is a curious choice, but the rooms are ample and comfortable, and bathrooms are also of a good size. Unexpected features are the cute rooftop pool and the Jacuzzi with a dry sauna. All in all, it's a pretty good value, with a dose of quirky personality to set it apart from the Gran Hotel Chiclayo.

Av. José Balta 399, Chiclayo. © 074/227-272. Fax 074/223-961. www.costadelsolperu.com. 40 units. $65 double. Rate includes taxes and continental breakfast buffet. AE, DC, MC, V. **Amenities:** Restaurant; bar; casino; outdoor pool; Jacuzzi; sauna; concierge; small business center; 24-hr. room service; laundry service; safety deposit box. *In room:* A/C, TV, minibar.

Garza Hotel   A pretty standard, rather faceless modern hotel on a busy avenue, the Garza hotel isn't a bad option, but it's not a very exciting one, either. It's in need of an update. Rooms have boring brown carpeting and floral bedspreads. The highlight of the hotel is surely the attractive pool and terrace. Service, though, receives high marks.

Av. Bolognesi 756, Chiclayo. © 074/228-172. Fax 074/228-171. 91 units. $69 double. Rate includes taxes and continental breakfast buffet. MC, V. **Amenities:** Restaurant; karaoke bar; casino; outdoor pool; concierge; small business center; 24-hr. room service; laundry service; safety deposit box. *In room:* A/C, TV, minibar, hair dryer.

Hotel María Alejandra ★ (*Value*) One of the newest hotels in Chiclayo, the pleasant María Alejandra is also one of its best values. Though classified as a 3-star hotel, it's better than the 4-star Garza. It has handsome public rooms and a nice view of the city from a fairly calm residential area. The ample rooms are quite nicely decorated in subdued colors, and all have nice, large bathtubs—a real luxury.

Los Faiques 101 (facing Paseo de las Musas), Urbanización Santa Victoria, Chiclayo. ℂ **074/273-445**. Fax 074/273-450. tours@perutravelnet.com. 60 units. $48 double; $70 suite. Rates include taxes and continental breakfast. AE, DC, MC, V. **Amenities:** Restaurant; bar; karaoke disco; car-rental desk; 24-hr. room service; laundry service. *In room:* A/C, TV, minibar, hair dryer, safe.

INEXPENSIVE

Gran Hotel Santa Rosa A rather nondescript modern hotel on a noisy street, the Santa Rosa has average-size rooms with crummy flowered bedspreads and small bathrooms. Only because Chiclayo doesn't have many decent budget options, it would do in a pinch.

Av. Luis González 927, Chiclayo. ℂ **074/927-935**. Fax 074/236-242. 45 units. S/86 ($25) double. Rate includes continental breakfast buffet and taxes. AE, DC, MC, V. **Amenities:** Restaurant; cafeteria; snack bar; conference center and auditorium; room service; laundry service; safety deposit box. *In room:* A/C, TV, minibar.

Hostal Karla If you're in the area to see the Lord of Sipán exhibit at the Brüning Museum and nothing more, you could stay at the one decent small hotel in Lambayeque, which is right across the street from the museum. In early 2002, the hostal was in the process of building another, nicer small hotel just down the street, which will have 16 rooms on three floors. The rooms at the original location are acceptable, but plain.

Av. Huamachuco 758, Lambayeque. ℂ **074/282-930**. 10 units. S/40 ($11) double. Rate includes taxes and continental breakfast buffet. AE, DC, MC, V. **Amenities:** Cafeteria; laundry service. *In room:* TV.

Hostal Royal This large, rambling old hotel, with a formerly grand, winding central staircase, sits right on the Parque Principal. The place is a bit run-down, though some travelers will find it full of local character. Rooms are large and spartan, with hardwood floors. Beds are a bit soft, though, and bathrooms are tucked behind cheapo partitions, which makes privacy a problem. The best rooms, though surely not the quietest, are those with balconies overlooking the plaza.

San José 787, Chiclayo. ℂ **074/233-421**. Fax 074/228-171. 30 units. S/32 ($9) double. Rate includes taxes. No credit cards. *In room:* No phone.

Hotel America On a busy commercial street not far from the Mercado Modelo, this dimly lit modern hotel with dark furnishings—chic, one supposes for northern Peru—is a slightly better option than the Gran Hotel Santa Rosa next door. It has some very odd, quirky touches, such as leopard-print headboards and large paintings of women in motorcycle helmets, which might give you the idea that it's something other than a standard hotel. Other than the peculiar decorating choices, though, rooms are rather plain.

Av. Luis González 943, Chiclayo. ℂ **074/229-305**. Fax 074/228-171. 52 units. S/86 ($25) double. Rate includes taxes and continental buffet. AE, DC, MC, V. **Amenities:** Restaurant; cafeteria; snack bar; conference center and auditorium; room service; laundry service; safety deposit box. *In room:* A/C, TV, minibar.

WHERE TO DINE

Jhon (*Finds*) SEAFOOD/CEVICHE A tiny neighborhood place with just 10 tables, this informal cevichería, specializes in fish, shellfish, and, of course, several types of ceviche. Among the latter, try the *conchas negras* (black scallops) or *mixto a la Jhon* (with octopus, white fish, shrimp, and conchas). A more

The Ruins of Kuélap

Everyone—at least everyone on his or her way to Peru—has heard of Machu Picchu. Very few have heard of Kuélap  ✪, thought of by some as the true adventurer's alternative to the once lost but today easily accessible Inca city. Tucked in highland cloud forest on top of an Andean mountain ridge at an altitude of 3,000m (9,900 ft.), Kuélap is a stupendous and titanic set of ruins that predates the Incas. More than 800 years old, Kuélap is one of the (least-known) wonders of Peru.

Located northeast of Cajamarca, near the small town of Chachapoyas (itself something of a poor man's Cusco, given the assortment of ruins littered about it), and discovered in the mid–19th century, the site is said to have employed more stone during its 200-year construction than even the Great Pyramids of Egypt. An impossibly scenic but wearying 18- to 24-hour bus ride from Cajamarca, or a less exciting 9- to 10-hour journey from Chiclayo, Kuélap hardly has the name recognition of other ruins in Peru. Ripe for discovery by a wider swath of visitors to Peru, Kuélap is still primarily a destination for independent travelers with a sense of adventure.

A fortress complex of nearly 400 buildings, most of them round, and surrounded by a 30m-high (98 ft.) defensive wall, Kuélap was home to 2,000 people from A.D. 1100 to 1300. Very little, though, is known about its builders and inhabitants. They were most likely the Chachapoyans or Sachupoyans, both groups that were later brought into the Inca fold that unified the highlands. Unlike other ruins in Peru, most of what exists at Kuélap is original, though some reconstruction has been initiated.

The ruins are open daily from 8:30am to 5pm; admission is S/10 ($3). Getting to Kuélap independently remains a laborious endeavor, involving buses to Chachapoyas and/or Tingo plus a long and very difficult 5- to 6-hour hike. Organized visits from Cajamarca may not suit modern-day Hiram Binghams, but they are by far the most convenient way to get to what remains a very remote outpost. Group trips usually cost $200 per person and last 5 days round-trip. If you've got the time and money to spare, and a sense of adventure, check with Cumbe Mayo and Inca Baths Tours (see "Getting Around" in "Cajamarca," below). There's a small Institute of National Culture *albergue* with dorm-style sleeping arrangements available.

substantial entree is one of the *arroces* (rice dishes) with fish or shellfish. There are also several preparations of fish such as *mero* (grouper) and a nice *picante de camarones* (spicy shrimp). Note that Jhon, which is a local favorite, is only open for lunch or a very early dinner.

Colón 276 (at Tacna). ✆ **074/208-593.** Reservations not accepted. Main courses S/7–S/16 ($2–$4.50). No credit cards. Daily 10am–6pm.

La Parra ✪ *Kids* GRILLED MEATS   Enter past a busy, open grill—an indication of the meat-dominated menu you'll find inside. This comfortable, relaxed restaurant is very popular with families. It's nice, if a tad nondescript, with a vaulted wood ceiling, wood paneling, stucco walls, and hardwood floors—and odd incongruous touches such as a framed portrait of Jesus and a deer head. Everyone chows down on grilled meats, served with fries and a salad, not just because it's the house specialty, but also because it's the only thing La Parra serves. *Lomo fino* (sirloin), shish kebab, sausage, or chicken are among the excellent choices from the grill. A great family option is the parrillada for four. Next door is a good chifa by the same owner.

Manuel María Izaga 752. © 074/227-471. Reservations recommended on weekends. Main courses S/7.50–S/21 ($2–$6). AE, DC, MC, V. Daily noon–11pm.

Parrillada Hebrón *Kids* GRILLED MEATS Noisy, brightly lit, and brash, this place lists a wide range of items on the menu, including fish and ceviche, but it really cranks out the grilled meats (baby beef ribs, steaks, and so on) and broiled chicken. It's very popular with families; not only is there a "parrillada for four" on the menu, but there's also a kid's menu and a game area upstairs called "Hebrolandia," where the rambunctious tots who don't want to eat nicely can go to work off their excess energy. The rest of the restaurant has the same chaotic feel, with cooks ringing bells to announce that orders are up; when it's busy, it feels a bit like a war zone, which may explain the name.

Av. José Balta (Sur) 605. © 074/222-709. Reservations not accepted. Main courses S/8–S/17.50 ($2.25–$5); kids' menu, S/7 ($2). MC, V. Daily 8am–midnight.

Pueblo Viejo *Kids* *Value* PERUVIAN Probably Chiclayo's chicest restaurant, this relaxed and attractive two-story place serves traditional Chiclayano cooking and comida criolla, but only for lunch. The menu is interesting and creative, derived from old recipes from the surrounding area. Especially good are the fish and shellfish dishes such as *tiradito de la casa* (sliced fish with lemon, chili pepper, corn, and onions), ceviche, and *tollito a la panca* (dogfish with chicha, cilantro, and corn, served in a clay pot). Other options are fish soup, tender goat, and dried roasted beef. A tasty appetizer is the *humitas de la abuela,* a white-corn tamale stuffed with pork. The nicest area is upstairs under the colored skylights, with lots of plants and wooden walkways, which give it the feel of a well-equipped treehouse. (OK, that may be a stretch, but it's head and shoulders above the norm of plain Peruvian eateries in the north.)

Manuel María Izaga 900 (at Calzoncillo). © 074/228-863. Reservations recommended on weekends. Main courses S/10–S/25 ($3–$7). No credit cards. Daily noon–5pm.

3 Cajamarca

855km (530 miles) NE of Lima; 298km (185 miles) NE of Trujillo; 235km (146 miles) SE of Chiclayo

Delightful and historic Cajamarca, the jewel of Peru's northern highlands, certainly deserves to be better known. The city is frequently called "the Cusco of the north," and comparisons to that tourist-magnet farther south are not illegitimate. This stately and traditional Andean mountain town has some of the same physical attributes as Cusco, but is refreshingly free of many of the hassles associated with a place so beloved by foreign guests. Though it is surrounded by the Andes at an altitude of nearly 2,700m (9,000 ft.) above sea level, Cajamarca is a down-to-earth and unassuming place that doesn't get caught up in its own beauty and grace. Townspeople, nearly all of them decked out in marvelously distinctive *sombreros de paja* (straw hats), merely go about their business.

Cajamarca was the site of a pivotal and horrifically violent moment in Peruvian history, which presaged the downfall of the Inca Empire and the advent of

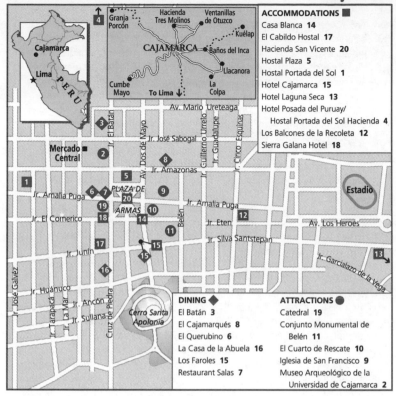

ACCOMMODATIONS ■
Casa Blanca **14**
El Cabildo Hostal **17**
Hacienda San Vicente **20**
Hostal Plaza **5**
Hostal Portada del Sol **1**
Hotel Cajamarca **15**
Hotel Laguna Seca **13**
Hotel Posada del Puruay/
  Hostal Portada del Sol Hacienda **4**
Los Balcones de la Recoleta **12**
Sierra Galana Hotel **18**

DINING ◆
El Batán **3**
El Cajamarqués **8**
El Querubino **6**
La Casa de la Abuela **16**
Los Faroles **15**
Restaurant Salas **7**

ATTRACTIONS ●
Catedral **19**
Conjunto Monumental de
  Belén **11**
El Cuarto de Rescate **10**
Iglesia de San Francisco **9**
Museo Arqueológico de la
  Universidad de Cajamarca **2**

Spanish colonial rule. In 1532, the Inca Atahualpa was attacked and captured by Francisco Pizarro and a small number of Spanish troops. Atahualpa offered the Spaniards a king's ransom for his release, telling his captors he would fill his prison cell to the roof with gold and silver many times over. The outnumbered but heavily armed Spaniards deceived the Incas and assassinated their leader and, within 2 years, had captured the north of Peru and were on their way south toward Cusco.

Cajamarca is the largest town in a fertile agricultural region that is virtually unsurpassed in Peru for its luxurious, verdant countryside. The city is ringed by archaeological sites and handsome hacienda estates, which make getting out to the country a must. Cajamarca's rural roots and agriculture-based economy have been given a jolt with the discovery of one of Latin America's largest gold mines, Yanacocha, which has quickly become the region's largest employer and brought an influx of foreign executives and their families. (The mine is jointly operated by Peruvian and U.S. firms.)

ESSENTIALS
GETTING THERE
BY PLANE   There are daily 2-hour flights from Lima and 1-hour flights from Trujillo aboard **Aero Continente** (© **01/242-4242;** www.aerocontinente.net) and **AeroCondor** (© **01/442-5215;** www.aerocondor.com.pe). Flights from Lima cost around $69.

Caxamarca: A Brief History

The Cajamarca Valley was the epicenter of a pre-Inca culture called Caxamarca, which reached its apex between A.D. 500 and 1000. Cajamarca was part of a small northern highlands kingdom called Cuismango, which was influenced by two great cultures, Chavín and Huari. The Incas, led by Cápac Yupanqui, conquered Cajamarca around 1465, annexing the territory and solidifying the empire's hold on the northern Andes. Cajamarca soon became an important administrative, political, and religious center and a major link in the transcontinental Andes highway; the Incas constructed great palaces and temples in the city.

Francisco Pizarro and a small band of troops, numbering around 160, reached the Cajamarca Valley in November 1532. November 16 shook the very foundations of the Inca Empire and changed Spanish-American and Peruvian history. Pizarro's men ambushed Atahualpa, the last Inca emperor, and held him prisoner. Inca troops, numbering more than 50,000 but already in the midst of civil war, offered no resistance. Atahualpa proposed a huge ransom to win his release, but the Spaniards killed him anyway, 7 months after a staged trial condemning him for attempting to arrange his rescue. The end of the Inca Empire was near, as the Spanish moved south toward Cusco. Cajamarca became a colonial city in 1802. Besides a few stone foundations, only Atahualpa's Cuarto de Rescate (Ransom Room) remains of the grand Inca masonry that once distinguished Cajamarca. But the city's post-Inca colonial roots are very much evident in Spanish-style architecture throughout Cajamarca.

The **Armando Revoredo Aeropuerto de Cajamarca** (© 044/822-523) is just 3km (2 miles) east of the Plaza de Armas. To downtown Cajamarca, a taxi costs S/5 ($1.50).

BY BUS   **Cruz del Sur** (© 01/225-6163) and **Expreso Cia** (© 01/428-5218) make the 12-hour trip from Lima to Cajamarca. **Transportes Línea** (© 044/245-181, or 044/261-482) travels from Lima, Trujillo (6 hr.), and Chiclayo (6 hr.). The bus companies have their own terminals, which are located mostly on Atahualpa, about 3km (1¾ miles) from the center of town.

VISITOR INFORMATION
There's a branch of the **Regional Tourism Office** within the massive Belén complex at Jr. Belén 600 (© 044/822-903). It's open Monday through Friday from 8:30am to 1pm and 2:30 to 6:30pm. The office has a handful of photocopied materials and some brochures for sale, including a self-published tourist information guide. There's another small **Oficina de Información Turística** at Batán 289 (© 044/821-546), which is very helpful and friendly and gives out free city maps. It's open Monday through Friday from 8:30am to 1pm.

FAST FACTS   Two banks are **Interbank,** 2 de Mayo on the Plaza de Armas (© 044/822-4600), and **Banco de Crédito,** Jr. del Comercio 679. Neither of these banks exchange traveler's checks. There are generally money-changers on the Plaza de Armas and Jirón del Batán; there are also several small casas de cambio in the same area.

In an **emergency,** call © **105.** The **police** are located at Amalia Puga 807 (© **044/822-944**). For medical attention, go to **Hospital Regional (Base Cajamarca),** Mario Urteaga 500 (© **044/822-156**); **Clínica San Francisco,** Avenida Grau (© **044/822-050**); or **Clínica Limatambo,** Calle Puno (© **044/824-241**).

For Internet access, try **Efenet,** Jirón Dos de Mayo, or **Atajo,** Jr. del Comercio 716 (© **044/822-245**). Atajo is open until 1am and offers cheap international Internet calls.

Cajamarca's **post office** is located at Amazonas 443, at the corner of Apurímac (© **044/822-245**); it's open Monday through Saturday from 8am to 8pm. There's a **DHL/Western Union** office at Dos de Mayo 323 (© **044/825-674**), within the Cajamarca Tours office. The **Telefónica del Perú** office is at Dos de Mayo 460 on the Plaza de Armas (© **044/821-008**).

GETTING AROUND
The major sights of interest in Cajamarca are all around the Plaza de Armas or within easy walking distance of it. Except for the Inca Baths, you're unlikely to require transportation unless you're staying at one of the country hotels on the outskirts of town, which are serviced by taxi and, to a lesser extent, colectivo.

BY TAXI   Taxis are easy to come by in the center of Cajamarca. They circulate around the Plaza de Armas and the streets leading off it. Most in-town fares are about S/3 (85¢). To call a cab, try **Taxi Seguro** (© **044/825-103**) or **Taxis Unidos** (© **044/828-888**).

BY ORGANIZED TOUR   Reliable tour agencies include **Inca Baths Tours,** Jr. Amalia Puga 653 (© **044/821-828**); **Cumbe Mayo Tours,** Jr. Amalia Puga 635 (© **044/822-938**); **Mega Tours,** Jr. Amalia Puga 643 (© **044/829-642**); and **Cajamarca Tours,** Jr. Dos de Mayo 323 (© **044/825-674**). These companies offer city tours and inexpensive, pooled half- and full-day tours to sights in the countryside around Cajamarca (including Cumbe Mayo, Otuzco, Colpa, and Inca Baths). Most standard tours cost S/12 to S/15 ($3.50–$4.25). Several agencies also offer long-distance tours to Kuélap for around $200. All agencies advertise English-speaking guides, but fluency is a relative term. The best bets are Inca Baths Tours and Cumbe Mayo Tours.

WHAT TO SEE & DO
IN CAJAMARCA
Colonial Cajamarca has several sights of interest, though the town's principal appeal may lie in its relaxed and proudly traditional air, as yet undisturbed by a

---

Tips Carnaval in Cajamarca

Cajamarca is a very traditional Andean highland city, but it lets loose once a year during Carnaval. Its pre-Lenten festivities are said to be the wildest in Peru. Full of music and dance, it also takes on aspects of a high-school locker room. Paint, water, and even bodily fluids (!) are flung around with abandon. Wear a raincoat. If you want to experience (subject yourself to?) Cajamarca's Carnaval, plan ahead. It's very popular with Peruvians, and hotels sell out. Another festive time in Cajamarca, formerly Peru's grandest Inca celebration, is Corpus Christi (in May/June), which includes lots of processions, music, bullfights, and horse shows.

tourist onslaught. Many of Cajamarca's premier tourist attractions are just outside the city in the beautiful pastoral countryside, within easy reach for day trips. Most are best visited by convenient organized tour (see "Getting Around," above).

Plaza de Armas 🏛

The heart of city life, Cajamarca's expansive and utterly graceful Plaza de Armas is one of the loveliest in Peru. In the days of the Incas, it was also the focal point of town, but it was a triangular courtyard rather than a square per se. The plaza was taken in dramatic fashion by Pizarro's small band of invading troops in 1532, and the Inca Emperor Atahualpa was killed there after a mock trial. The fountain at the center of the square dates back more than 300 years, and the plaza is marked by handsome topiaries and low trees. Two grand churches front the square, and it can be difficult to determine which one is the cathedral. On one side is the **Catedral,** built in the 17th and 18th centuries. Its baroque facade is ornately carved from volcanic stone. The gloomy interior features a bold, amazingly carved main altar and a pulpit of carved wood and gold leaf. If the cathedral looks a bit squat and unfinished, it's because its belfry was never completed, a drastic measure to avoid payment of a Spanish tax on finished ecclesiastical buildings. As seen in colonial churches in Cusco, the cathedral is built upon original Inca stonework.

The grander of the two churches, though, is directly across the plaza. The **Iglesia de San Francisco** 🏛, which once formed part of the San Francisco Convent, is entirely wrought from volcanic rock. Built in the first half of the 18th century, the parish church did not add the two bell towers until 1951. Covering every inch of the facade is terrific stone sculpting. Inside is a **Museo de Arte Religioso Colonial,** open Monday through Saturday from 3 to 6pm; admission is S/2 (50¢). The collection of colonial art includes interesting icons and paintings. Beneath the museum are the church's catacombs, good for an eerie visit. Next door to the church is the small and beautiful Santuario de la Virgen de Dolores, or the chapel of **La Dolorosa,** named for the patron saint of Cajamarca. The 18th-century facade is one of the greatest examples of stone carving in the city.

More Attractions

Conjunto Monumental de Belén 🏛   On block 6 of Belén is the city's most important and historic architectural complex, almost entirely constructed of volcanic stone. Dating to the 18th century, it includes a church and colonial women's and men's hospitals, now housing ancient medical and archaeological exhibits. The entire complex is run by the National Institute of Culture. On a small and pretty square, the **Iglesia Belén** may be the most extraordinary work of colonial architecture in Cajamarca. The church, which replaced a primitive adobe-and-wood church on the spot, was begun in 1699 and completed a half century later. Its decorative baroque stone facade is one of the finest in Peru. The interior is replete with delightful and large, carved polychromatic figures of

---

Tips Get Out of Town on Tuesday

Most of Cajamarca's top sights are closed on Tuesday. If you're in town that day, it would be wise to schedule a visit to the Inca Baths or another out-of-town excursion such as Cumbe Mayo or Otuzco.

Cajamarca's Colonial Mansions & Churches

The center of Cajamarca possesses several notable large houses, which feature the carved stone porticoes, slanted roofs, long wooden balconies, and pretty garden courtyards favored by Spanish colonialists. Visitors with an interest in 17th- and 18th-century colonial and republican architecture should check out the following casonas and churches, in addition to those discussed elsewhere in greater detail:

- **Casa Toribio Casanova,** Jr. José Gálvez 938.
- **Casa Santiesteban,** Junín 1123.
- The **house** at Cruz de Piedra 613. Now the property of the municipal government, the house has another excellent carved portico. Also on Cruz de Piedra is a stone cross, which supposedly marks the spot where Simón Bolívar, the Great Libertador, swore to avenge the death of Atahualpa.
- **La Recoleta,** a church about 6 blocks south of the Plaza de Armas, at the end of Amalia Puga.
- **Palacio de los Condes de Uceda** (now the Banco de Crédito), Apurímac 717. A splendid yellowish-orange, well-restored noble house with a carved stone portico.
- **Palacio del Obispo,** next to the Catedral.
- **San Pedro,** a church at the corner of Gálvez and Junín.

angels and warriors. The fantastic, richly decorative cupola was painted by highland natives.

The **Hospital de Hombres** (Men's Hospital) is located on a lovely courtyard marked by a fountain. The hospital, run by Franciscans, began receiving patients in 1630. So that they could focus on prayer, their beds faced the altar and the Virgen de la Piedad. Across the street is the **Hospital de Mujeres** (Women's Hospital); on the facade, note the woman with child above the portal and, on either side of it, female figures with four breasts, symbols of the valley's superpotent fertility. Today, the building houses perhaps the most interesting component of the Belén complex, a **Museo de Arqueología y Etnografía,** well laid out and exhibiting textiles and ceramics dating from as far back as 1500 B.C., replicas of Moche vessels, and local artisanship, dress (including Carnaval costumes), and silver *milagros* (prayer fetishes).

Jr. Belén, s/n (at Junín). ✆ 044/922-601. Admission is by boleto S/4 ($1.25), which also admits visitors to Cuarto de Rescate (see below). Mon, Wed–Fri 9am–1pm and 3–6pm; Sat–Sun 9am–1pm.

El Cuarto de Rescate   Across the street from La Dolorosa Chapel is the most famous building in Cajamarca. When Atahualpa was taken prisoner by Pizarro and his band of men in 1532, the Inca emperor was held in a cell, which he promised to fill with gold and silver many times over if the Spaniards would spare his life. The "Ransom Room" is a small, rectangular stone room, set in the back of a colonial courtyard, once part of Atahualpa's palace. It is made of unadorned Inca masonry—the last intact example of Inca architecture in the city—and is barren except for a red line drawn across one wall, supposedly the very line Atahualpa drew to demonstrate to the Spanish how high his men would fill the cell with treasures. No one knows for sure whether this was

---

Tips **Siesta!**

In many Andean towns and villages, including Cajamarca, the locals take the midafternoon siesta seriously. So plan your day around the knowledge that a lot of places won't be open from 1 to 3pm or so. Have a leisurely lunch, or take a nap.

---

simply Atahualpa's prison cell, or if it was indeed a ransom room. What we do know is that the Inca chief was later executed by Pizarro's men, presumably on a stone right here, even before the Incas had surrendered all of the promised riches. The Cuarto de Rescate represents a crucial moment in Peruvian history, a clash in cultures with ramifications for the entire continent, of course, but it may take some imagination to conjure the drama of the moment. The large painting at the entrance near the ticket booth, of Atahualpa being burned at the stake by the Spanish, is not entirely accurate; after accepting baptism, Atahualpa was merely strangled to death.

Amalia Puga 750 (a half block from Plaza de Armas). © **044/922-601.** Admission by boleto (S/4 or $1.25, adults; S/3 or 75¢, students), which admits visitors to the component parts of the Conjunto Monumental de Belén (see below). Mon, Wed–Fri 9am–1pm and 3–6pm; Sat–Sun 9am–1pm.

Museo Arqueológico de la Universidad Nacional de Cajamarca   This archaeological museum, affiliated with the local university, has a nice collection of ceramics, weavings, and other examples of the pre-Inca Cajamarca culture. The museum, where there is a small tourist information booth, also has photographs of the area's principal archaeological sites. Allow about 45 minutes to see it all.

Jr. Batán 283. © **044/821-546.** Admission S/1 (30¢). Mon–Fri 8:30am–1pm.

ON THE OUTSKIRTS OF CAJAMARCA

Baños del Inca   Just beyond Cajamarca lies the Inca Baths complex of gardens and pools with Cajamarca's famed thermal waters. In use since the time of the Incas (supposedly, Atahualpa had to be roused from his beloved bath when Pizarro and his troops entered the city), the baths are a wonderful respite of clean air and hot waters, ideal for relaxing after days of travel in the highlands. Set in a serene valley, at an elevation of nearly 2,650m (9,000 ft.) with wonderful mountain views, the park's thermal waters are said to be medicinal and effective for treating bronchial and rheumatic conditions. The waters, which reach temperatures of 74°C, or 165°F (but you can control the temperature with spigots in private pools), come from two different sources, Los Perolitos and El Tragadero. The open pools with rising steam make clear the scalding nature of the waters. The modern complex is extremely popular with locals and visitors alike. You can either opt for a private, indoor bath, in which you wait for a room to be vacated and cleaned and the deep pool filled with fresh sulphurous spring waters, or the sauna or outdoor pool. Take a bathing suit and towel with you. Bath products are for sale at the entrance.

6km (4 miles) from Cajamarca. © **044/821-563.** Outdoor pool has assigned entrance times. Admission to the tourist complex (individual bathing cabins), S/4 ($1); to the communal baths S/3 (90¢). Daily 5am–7pm. Colectivos labeled "Baños del Inca" leave from Calle Amazonas and take about 15 min.; virtually everyone gets off at the same stop, across the street from the complex. A taxi costs about S/5–S/8 ($1.50–$2.25).

Cerro Santa Apolonia   A steep but lovely climb up the stairs at the southeast end of the Dos de Mayo leads to Santa Apolonia hill. On the way to the top is a small white chapel, the Virgen de Fátima, built in 1854. Often locked, the interior can still be glimpsed through steel bars of the doorway. Up more paths, through terraced gardens where there are also a handful of caged animals, is a mirador with splendid panoramic views of Cajamarca laid out at your feet. Rocks at the top, carved with petroglyphs, are believed to date to the Chavín civilization (1000–500 B.C.). Nearby, to the right of the white cross (if you're looking down at Cajamarca), sits a stone altar that has earned the popular name "the Inca's Throne." Carved like a chair, the Inca chief reportedly sat here and gazed down on his city and troops. There's also a small tunnel that, according to legend, went all the way from Cajamarca to Cusco.

Reached by stairs at the end of Dos de Mayo. Park admission S/1 (30¢). Daily 8am–6pm.

ATTRACTIONS BEYOND CAJAMARCA

The countryside (*campiña*) around Cajamarca is extraordinary: a verdant expanse of rolling hills, eucalyptus trees, and meadows. If you're not staying at one of the country-style hacienda hotels outside of Cajamarca, a visit to the country is highly recommended to see this gorgeous, fertile region.

Among the standard organized campiña visits are excursions to **La Colpa,** a cattle ranch and manor house in a beautiful setting, where the locally famous "cow calling" prompts cows to enter their stalls when their names are called; **Llacanora,** a small mountain village with ancient cave paintings and hikes to a pretty waterfall; **Tres Molinos,** an agricultural center and gardens, where dairy products are sold; and **Granja Porcón,** a huge cooperative farm and agrotourism experiment supported by the Peruvian government and the European Union. The community runs entirely on hydroelectric power, and hilltop forests have been planted at an altitude of 3,700m (12,136 ft.) to provide paper and wood products without harming the area's natural forests. There is a small *albergue* lodging and a restaurant on the premises (© 044/825-631). In **Lower Porcón,** the Festival of the Crosses (on Palm Sun at the beginning of Easter week) is a famous expression of local folkore. Huge wood and cane crosses, adorned with images of Jesus and saints, flowers, and palm fronds, are carried in devout processions.

The best way to visit one or more of the archaeological sites beyond Cajamarca is to sign on with one of the tour operators in town. Several of the sites are not accessible by public transportation; going with a guide in a small private colectivo is economical and convenient. Most agencies charge S/15 to S/20 ($4.25–$6) for standard day trips. Many combine visits (for example, to the Inca Baths, Colpa, and Llacanora; or to Otuzco and Tres Molinos).

Cumbe Mayo ✮✮   A stunning natural spot of huge and fascinating rock formations set amid rolling green hills at an elevation of 3,400m (11,220 ft.), Cumbe Mayo has been called a stone forest. Equally remarkable, if not more so, is the evidence of human intervention here, first discovered in 1937: caves etched with petroglyphs and a pre-Inca **aqueduct** that is a marvel of hydraulic engineering. The remarkable open canal, carved out of volcanic stone in perfect, polished lines, served to collect and redirect water from various sources on its way to the Pacific Ocean. At points, the canal narrows and introduces right angles to slow the flow of water and lessen the effects of erosion. In all, the aqueduct stretches more than 9km (5 miles). Created, incredibly, around 1000 B.C., it is perhaps the oldest known man-made structure in South America.

Elsewhere in the park, there's a cliff referred to as the **sanctuary,** which looks like a human head with a grotto (and more enigmatic petroglyphs) carved out inside. Stairs carved in stone lead to sacrificial altars (llamas, not humans) and platforms, signs of the ceremonial importance of the zone. As guides lead groups through the "stone forest," they point out figures that can be seen in the stones, such as a group of monks as well as phalluses, breasts, a dog climbing a hill, a tortoise, a pirate's head, and mushrooms. Some are clear, amusing likenesses; others are like trying to identify someone else's images in cloud formations.

20km (12 miles) SW of Cajamarca. Daily 8am–5pm.

Kunturwasi   Three to four hours removed from Cajamarca, in the province of San Pablo, these ceremonial stone ruins date to 1100 B.C. Besides a series of courtyards, plazas, and platforms, many marked with large petroglyphs, burial sites were also discovered here. The gold treasures from the tombs are now exhibited in a small museum in the nearby town of San Pablo.

110km (68 miles) from Cajamarca. Tours to Kunturwasi cost about S/50 ($14) per person and last a full day. Daily 8am–5pm.

Ventanillas de Otuzco   A large necropolis whose gravesites are small square window niches carved out of a hillside, Otuzco was created by the Caxamarca culture, probably around 500 B.C. The niches were funereal tombs for elites. Many held just one body; others housed several corpses. Another 20km (12 miles) beyond Otuzco are the even more impressive (and better preserved) burial niches of **Ventanillas de Comboyo.** More extensive than Otuzco, they are holed out of a sheer volcanic cliff.

7km (4 miles) NW of Cajamarca. Admission S/3 ($1). Daily 8am–5pm. To get there, take an organized tour (S/15, or $4.25), which combines visits with stops at a hacienda. You can also hop on a colectivo along Batán, a few blocks from the Plaza de Armas.

SHOPPING

Relaxed and traditional, untouristy Cajamarca isn't brimming with chic shops and merchants hawking artesanía to visitors. Yet its colorful central market is an enjoyable place to absorb the flavor of an authentic Andean town market and pick up a regional specialty: Cajamarca has excellent handicrafts. The **Mercado Central** on Amazonas, which sprawls among several streets, is a great place to score one of those amazing, finely woven tall straw hats that virtually all natives wear. The sombreros de paja are famous throughout Peru, but some are so finely made that you may be shocked at the prices. I'm told that some campesinos spend up to $400 for their hat, which is their most prideful article of clothing. As you'll see, the hats beg all sorts of individual style; forming and wearing the hat according to one's taste is part of the fashion. I've bought two, though finding them to fit large, non-Andean heads can be trying. Ask the seller to show you how to roll up the hat for easy packing. Other items of interest include saddlebags (*alforjas*), decorative glass-and-silkscreen mirrors, and dairy products.

WHERE TO STAY
EXPENSIVE

Hotel Laguna Seca 🐾 *Kids*   A luxurious country-style hotel renowned for its proximity to the Baños del Inca, this spa resort hotel is where to stay if you're looking for things you don't typically find in Peru: aerobics, massages, and in-room thermal baths. There are also thermal pools (two for adults, one for children), Turkish baths, and a host of outdoors activities for enjoying Cajamarca's clean air. Rooms are large and nicely equipped, but not nearly as luxurious as those at the similarly priced Posada del Puruay (see below).

Av. Manco Cápac, Baños del Inca, Cajamarca. 🕐 044/894-600, or 01/336-7869 for reservations. Fax 044/894-646. hotel@lagunaseca.com.pe. 40 units. $92–$105 double; $120–$139 suite. Rates include taxes and breakfast buffet. AE, DC, MC, V. **Amenities:** Restaurant; cafeteria; bar; disco; 3 thermal water pools; spa; Jacuzzi; concierge; room service; aerobics and massage room; laundry service; travel agency; horseback riding. *In room:* A/C, TV/VCR, minibar, hair dryer.

Hotel Posada del Puruay ★★★ *Kids*   An extraordinary country hotel housed in an impeccably restored, elegant 1830 salmon-colored hacienda, this is one of the most refined and relaxing hotels in Peru. Set amid more than 202,350 hectares (500,000 acres) of land—with eucalyptus forest; lush, beautifully landscaped gardens; and views of the verdant, mountainous countryside—the hotel feels light years removed from any city, yet it's only 7km (4 miles) from downtown Cajamarca. The lovely house, built around a pretty courtyard, has rooms with names such as "La Mansión" and "La Prisión." The first couldn't be truer: Rooms are gigantic and extremely well equipped, with large, luxurious bathrooms. The second room name, though, is very misleading: If this is prison, I want to be thrown in the slammer. The restaurant and public rooms are decorated with well-chosen antiques. Outdoors, horses beckon, as does the trail up the hill to a small structure with stupendous panoramic views. The charming and loquacious owner, Nora, and her husband and daughter live on the premises and couldn't be more gracious. Service is excellent, and the terrific restaurant and vast video-rental library make this a perfect spot to kick back for several days in the northern highlands.

Carretera Porcón-Hualgayoc Km 4.5, Cajamarca. ℂ **044/828-318,** or 01/336-7869 for reservations. Fax 044/827-928. www.puruayhotel.com. 16 units. $93 double; $106–$138 suite. Rates include taxes and breakfast buffet. AE, DC, MC, V. **Amenities:** Restaurant; bar; concierge; room service; laundry service; gift shop; extensive video library; horseback riding. *In room:* A/C, TV/VCR, minibar, hair dryer.

MODERATE

Hacienda San Vicente ★★ *Finds*   Hands-down the funkiest hotel you'll find in Peru, this cool old hacienda is perched on a hill up above Cajamarca. It proclaims itself a "refugio ecológico"; it could just as easily be called a "refugio funkadelico." The seven unique rooms overflow with an oddball, rustic sense of style; some are like caves carved out of the rock. The whole place slides down the hill with cool niches, tight stone stairways, funky spaces, and great views from the gardens. Rooms have wood-beam ceilings and skylights for views of the moon and stars. Room C has a round bed under the skylight. Others have headboards carved right into the stone walls. There is also a group room, where guests stay dorm-style in bunk beds—perfect for trekking groups. For families, there's an apartment. On-site is a Gaudí-esque little chapel.

Jr. Revolución (above Cerro Santa Apolonia), Cajamarca. ℂ and fax **044/822-644.** hacienda-san-vicente@yahoo.com. 7 units. $45 double, $10 per person group room. Rates include taxes, continental breakfast, and airport pickup. Weekend deals available. MC, V. **Amenities:** Restaurant; bar; room service; laundry service; horseback riding; free taxi service to Cajamarca. *In room:* TV, minibar.

Sierra Galana Hotel   A large, modern "turistas" hotel on the Plaza de Armas next door to the cathedral, this large hotel is well positioned, but it feels dated and stale. Rooms are functional and decently decorated (if you're into a plain 1960s aesthetic), but they have very large bathrooms. The location's great, but competing hotels nearby are a better value.

Jr. del Comercio 773, Cajamarca. ℂ and fax **044/822-472,** or 01/446-3652 for reservations. 60 units. $40 double. Rate includes taxes and continental breakfast. AE, DC, MC, V. **Amenities:** Restaurant; bar; laundry service; travel agency. *In room:* TV.

INEXPENSIVE

Casa Blanca   A 100-year-old house located right on the Plaza de Armas, this welcoming small hotel has one key advantage: All the rooms are on the interior, making it more peaceful than one might expect given its location. The lobby has a dirty skylight surrounded by Art Nouveau stained glass. The back courtyard has a small chapel. Rooms are very comfortable, with brightly colored carpets and bedspreads—not fancy, but nice.

Jr. Dos de Mayo 446, Cajamarca. ℂ and fax **044/822-141.** 22 units. S/100 ($29 double). Rate includes taxes and continental breakfast. AE, DC, MC, V. **Amenities:** "Video pub"; game room; laundry service. *In room:* TV, minibar.

El Cabildo Hostal *(Kids*   One block from the Plaza de Armas, this charming small hotel has the swankest colonial courtyard in town: It's sunny, with a central fountain, arches, and balconies on all four sides—a perfect spot to relax. Rooms are a good size with a cozy, comfortable vibe and the beds have carved-wood headboards. Four of the rooms are loft-style, which is perfect for families. Furnishings aren't plush, and the brown-carpet-and-orange-bedspread look could probably do with an update, but given the friendly services and pedigree of the building, it's not a bad deal at all.

Jr. Junín, Cajamarca. ℂ and fax **044/827-025.** cabildoh@latinmail.com. 22 units. S/90–S/95 ($26–$27 double). Rates include taxes and continental breakfast. DC, MC, V. **Amenities:** Restaurant; bar; small gym; spa with massages; room service; laundry service. *In room:* TV, minibar.

Hostal Plaza   This large and rambling old colonial wooden house is loaded with character, even if the rooms are dorm-like and completely unadorned. It's not uncomfortable, though, and it certainly has a great location—right on the Plaza de Armas—for the cheap price. The hotel is spread across two interconnected wings, which are built around a pair of courtyards. Hot water comes and goes. The rickety wooden floors and varied levels have their own kind of charm for travelers looking for a bargain but who need little in the way of creature comforts.

Plaza de Armas, Cajamarca. ℂ **044/822-058.** 22 units. S/25 ($7) per person with bathroom; S/15 ($4) with shared bathroom. Rate includes taxes. No credit cards. *In room:* No phone.

Hostal Portada del Sol *(Value*   A cozy, family inn occupying a beautiful colonial house about 5 minutes from the Plaza de Armas, this is one of the best affordable hotels in town. Rooms have wood-beam ceilings, older-style furnishings, and small bathrooms. Some rooms have upstairs loft areas. The small, covered central courtyard has a marble fountain and is set up with tables beneath the wooden balcony on three sides. El Sol Grill, a charming restaurant with a wood-burning stove, is on the premises, and service is personal and accommodating. The hotel owns the handsome hacienda hotel of the same name in the countryside outside of Cajamarca (see below).

Jr. Pisagua 731, Cajamarca. ℂ and fax **044/823-395,** or 01/225-4306 for reservations. www.terra.com. pe/portadadelsol. 20 units. $27 double. **Amenities:** Restaurant; bar. *In room:* TV.

Hostal Portada del Sol Hacienda *(Kids* *(Value*   A great-value country hacienda, only 6km (3½ miles) from the Plaza de Armas in Cajamarca, this pretty house with beautiful gardens and comfortable, nicely decorated but simple rooms is an excellent option for a relaxed stay. Owned by the same people who run a similarly named inn in town (see above), this cozy Spanish-style hacienda doesn't have the funky character of San Vicente or the classy luxury of Puruay, but it's a great middle-of-the-road choice. Almost unheard of at this price, the hotel has tennis courts, football fields, games for children, horseback riding, and trails for walking.

Camino al Cumbe Mayo Km 6, Cajamarca. ℂ **044/823-395,** or 01/225-4306 for reservations. www.terra.com.pe/portadadelsol. 15 units. $27 double. **Amenities:** Restaurant; bar; tennis courts; children's games; horseback riding. *In room:* TV.

Hostal Cajamarca   This midsize hotel, located in a handsome old house with a pretty patio and fountain, is a clean and straightforward option. It's just a block removed from the Plaza de Armas, on the way up toward Cerro Santa Apolonia. Some rooms have views of Santa Apolonia, but the interior patio rooms are probably quieter and a better choice. The carpeted rooms are simple—unadorned and functional, though they have decent bathrooms. Los Faroles (p. 372) is one of the better hotel restaurants in town.

Jr. Dos de Mayo 311, Cajamarca. © **044/822-532**, or 01/446-3652 for reservations. Fax 044/822-813. 35 units. S/98 ($28 double). Rate includes taxes and continental breakfast. V. **Amenities:** Restaurant; bar; laundry service; travel agency. *In room:* TV.

Los Balcones de la Recoleta *(Value)*   Yet another charming 19th-century house in Cajamarca, this small inn, a 5-minute walk from the Plaza de Armas, is named for its handsome balconies, which drip with vines. The central courtyard is similarly overflowing with plants and flowers. Rooms live up to the colonial character of the place, with hardwood floors and thick ceiling beams; they're nice for the price. The restaurant is recommended for Spanish specialties and the good-value lunch menu.

Jr. Amalia Puga 1050, Cajamarca. © and fax **044/823-003**. 12 units. S/100 ($29 double). Rate includes taxes and continental breakfast. DC, MC, V. **Amenities:** Restaurant; bar. *In room:* TV, minibar.

WHERE TO DINE

El Batán 🍴 PERUVIAN   A sophisticated restaurant—more contemporary than El Cajamarqués (see below), with perhaps the most elevated reputation in town—El Batán uses the tag line "buffet de arte," and in fact, the place is part art gallery upstairs. Elegant but relaxed, inhabiting a handsome 18th-century colonial house entered through the courtyard, it offers a series of relatively expensive fixed-price menús, but there's also a bargain hunter's *menú ejecutivo* for just S/12 ($3.50). You can mix and match appetizers with main courses. You might have a stuffed avocado to start, followed by chicken in mushroom sauce. The menu is, as seems typical in Cajamarca, meat-heavy. Meat-eaters will appreciate dishes such as stuffed tenderloin with peppercorns or filet mignon in whiskey sauce. On weekends, there's peña music. Dine either in the covered courtyard or the relaxed and art-filled interior.

Jr. del Batán 369. © **044/826-025**. Reservations recommended. Main courses S/11.50–S/21 ($3.25–$6); menús del día S/29 ($8) and S/32 ($9); menú ejecutivo S/12 ($3.50). AE, DC, MC, V. Daily noon–midnight.

El Cajamarqués 🍴 *(Value)* PERUVIAN/INTERNATIONAL   A large, elegant restaurant with Cusqueña School paintings (OK, copies) on the walls, a long carved-wood mirror, and a medieval-looking iron chandelier, this is one of Cajamarca's most elegant and traditional restaurants. It has high, wood-beamed ceilings and white walls, much like an old-style Spanish restaurant. It's surprisingly affordable, though, with very economical menús offered midday. The *carta*, which includes standard Peruvian and international dishes including lomo saltado, filet mignon, and beef stroganoff, is heavy on meats. (In fact, there's no fish on it.) The restaurant has a pretty decent wine list. The garden has a small zoo of exotic birds.

Amazonas 770. © **044/822-128**. Reservations recommended. Main courses S/12–S/19 ($3.50–$5.50); menús del día S/6 ($1.75) and S/9 ($2.50). AE, DC, MC, V. Daily noon–midnight.

El Querubino 🍴🍴 PERUVIAN   An elegant new place a half block off the Plaza de Armas, El Querubino has quickly become one of Cajamarca's trendsetters. With mustard-yellow walls, decorative tiles, and a live music duo playing altiplano tunes, it's bright, cheery, friendly, and intimate, and just a few paces from the cathedral. The restaurant qualifies as upscale for low-key Cajamarca, but it's quite popular with locals. House specialties include *mollejas al ajillo* (sweetbreads in garlic) and mustard chicken. Other options among meat dishes are also nice: beef stroganoff, filet mignon, and pork chops. There's a daily list of bargain specials such as lemon chicken written on a board at the entrance. Finally, a Cajamarca restaurant with fish on the menu! (OK, it's only sole, but it's a start.) The wine list is a bit more extensive than at most local restaurants.

Jr. Amalia Puga 589. (✆ **044/830-900.** Reservations recommended. Main courses S/12–S/22 ($3.50–$6). Specials from S/10 ($3). AE, DC, MC, V. Daily 9am–midnight.

La Casa de la Abuela INTERNATIONAL/DESSERT   This cute, country-kitchen-style place has wood beams, a preponderance of baskets with dried flowers, and little tables with blue-and-white-checked tablecloths and blue candles. In short, it's very unusual for Peru—one of the few small restaurants with a conscious and consistent design or look. The first thing to draw your attention will be the wide selection of desserts, including ice cream, cheesecakes, and several other colorful and delectable cakes, in the case at the entrance. But "Grandma's House" also serves a variety of items for breakfast, lunch, and dinner, such as sandwiches and hamburgers, pizzas, pastas, and a gourmet selection of meats. Plenty of people pop in just for dessert and coffee.

Jr. Cruz de Piedra 671. (✆ **044/681-027.** Reservations recommended on weekends. Main courses S/9–S/22 ($2.50–$6). MC. Daily 8am–midnight.

Los Faroles ☏ PERUVIAN   In the Hostal Cajamarca (p. 371), this Spanish colonial-looking restaurant is a perfect fit for the inn. Set at the back of the handsome center courtyard of a historic house, it features a traditional criollo menu, with items such as *palta rellena* (stuffed avocado) and *ají de gallina* (spicy cream chicken), that's well prepared. Service is attentive and friendly. Other menu items include a mixed grill, rabbit in wine sauce, grilled trout and chicken in orange sauce, as well as a selection of pastas. Breakfast features local specialties, such as *chicharrón de puerco* (pork) as well as normal Western fare such as omelets. The midday set menú is a bargain at S/12 ($3.50).

Jr. Dos de Mayo 311. (✆ **044/922-532.** Reservations recommended. Main courses S/8–S/21 ($2.25–$6); menú del día S/12 ($3.50). DC, V. Daily 8am–11pm.

Restaurant Salas (Value PERUVIAN   From the lines at the entrance, you expect this traditional restaurant to be good—it's packed with locals daily (even though some veterans carp that it's not as good as it used to be). Occupying the same spot on the Plaza de Armas since 1947, Salas is a huge eating hall with high ceilings and white-coated waiters scurrying about. Perhaps it's so popular because of the monstrous portions. There's a daily typed list of *platos especiales* (specials), *platos del día* (daily specials) and a set menu with no choices for about $2. *Humitas* (sweet corn tamales) are excellent. Most of the menu focuses on typical Peruvian dishes and things such as churrasco and asado (roasted and barbecued meats).

Amalia Puga 637. (✆ **044/822-867.** Reservations not accepted. Main courses S/6–S/22 ($1.75–$6). V. Daily 9am–10pm.

CAJAMARCA AFTER DARK

Cajamarca is for the most part a pretty quiet town, though it has at least two spots that make an evening out worthwhile.

Peña Usha Usha, at Amalia Puga 142 about 4 blocks from the Plaza de Armas, is a funky little peña bar with kerosene lamps, a smattering of tables and benches, a small altar, and graffiti everywhere. It's very atmospheric and intimate, and Jamie Valera Bazán has been singing songs here, either alone or with a couple friends, for years and years. The bar, which serves simple mixed drinks only, opens at 9pm and doesn't close its doors sometimes until 6am. The cover charge is S/5 ($1.50).

The classiest and most upscale disco in town is **Los Frailones,** Av. Perú 701 (at Cruz de la Piedra, at the base of Santa Apolonia hill). The cover charge is S/15 ($4) for men, S/10 ($3) for women. Other nightclubs worth a look include **Up & Down** at Tarapaca 782 (**044/827-876**), and **El Embrujo** on block 5 of Apurímac.

4 Huaraz & the Cordillera Blanca

Rugged Peru is synonymous with the bold peaks of the Andes, and those mountains, particularly the spectacular Cordillera Blanca range 400km (250 miles) northeast of Lima, are a magnet for several thousand mountaineers and adventure-sports travelers every year. The string of dramatic snowcapped 5,000m (16,500-ft.) peaks east of the Callejón de Huaylas Valley, accessible from the main tourist hub of Huaraz (reached by bus in 7–8 hr. from Lima), is the premier spot in Peru for climbing and trekking and perhaps the best in all of South America. Nearly 3 dozen peaks soar to more than 6,000m (19,800 ft.); Huascarán, topping out at 6,768m (22,199 ft.), is Peru's highest mountain and the highest tropical mountain in the world. Nearly the entire chain is contained within the protected Huascarán National Park, a UNESCO Biosphere Reserve and World Heritage Trust site.

Not surprisingly, the region appeals above all to experienced, veteran mountaineers and adventurers. A burgeoning lineup of other adventure sports, from white-water rafting and mountain biking to hang gliding and rock climbing, have lifted off in popularity in recent years. And for those who would say all play and no culture makes for a dull adventure, visitors can marry their interests in adventure sports and antiquity at the marvelous ruins of Chavín de Huántar, built about 1,500 years ago, about 4 hours from Huaraz.

The extraordinary mountain scenery of the region also appeals to those with limited time and abilities, or only passing interest in testing their physical mettle in Peru. The valley, some 20km (12 miles) wide and 180km (112 miles) long, is also a superb destination for those who are more interested in day walks and village markets.

The best months for climbing are the dry season, between May and September (of those, June–Aug are perhaps best). Mountain biking and trekking can be

---

Fun Fact "La" Huascarán?

The Cordillera Blanca's El Huascarán, the namesake of the mountainous National Park in Peru's central Andes, may seem to be a macho mountain: At 6,768m (22,199 ft.), it's the highest peak in Peru, the fourth highest in the Americas, and the highest tropical-zone mountain in the world. But its north peak was first climbed in 1908 by a woman, the 58-year-old American Annie Smith Peck (who 3 years later climbed Peru's Mt. Coropuna, where she proudly displayed a banner promoting "Votes for Women").

> **_Tips_ Acute Mountain Sickness**
>
> The usual warnings about altitude in the Peruvian Andes especially apply in Huaraz and the Cordillera Blanca. Take at least a couple days to adequately acclimatize to the high elevation of over 3,000m (9,900 ft.), or up to a week if you're planning to attempt a serious ascent. In the early going, don't overextend yourself physically, and drink plenty of mate de coca (coca-leaf tea). If symptoms persist, see a doctor.

practiced other months as well, but the adventurous should be duly prepared for rain.

Extending the length of the valley is the Río Santa. Besides Huaraz, several other small towns and villages at the base of Cordillera mountains serve as starting points for trekking and climbing expeditions, but none is so well equipped as the capital of the Ancash department. Many expeditions to the scenic Llanganuco lakes in the Huascarán National Park begin at Yungay, while Caraz, a pleasant small mountain town known for its agreeable climate and flowers, serves as a quieter alternative to Huaraz and offers similar services required for ascents.

HUARAZ
420km (260 miles) N of Lima

Huaraz is the primary base destination for most visitors who are keen on exploring the Callejón de Huaylas Valley that runs 200km (120 miles) right down the middle of Peru. At an altitude of 3,100m (10,230 ft.), Huaraz enjoys a spectacular setting at the foot of the Cordillera Blanca: The town is dominated by 20 snow-capped peaks, each higher than 6,000m (19,800 ft.), which rise in splendor just beyond reach of the city. Huaraz itself is a far cry from the postcard perfection of a picturesque alpine village, however. It has a major earthquake to blame for its ragged look, which is weighed down by rapid and cheap concrete construction. The massive 1970 earthquake leveled nearly the entire city, eradicating half its population in the process.

Today, though, Huaraz hums with the business of mountain and adventure tourism. A wide range of facilities has sprung up to support outdoor travel; dozens of tour operators and travel agencies, restaurants and bars, and hotels and inns can be found in town, most clustered along the main drag, Avenida Luzuriaga.

ESSENTIALS
Getting There
BY PLANE   Nearly everyone who comes to Huaraz does so by bus. However, there are charter flights from Lima to a small airport in the village of **Anta.** From there, it's only about 15 minutes by taxi to Huaraz. Contact **AeroCondor** (© 01/442-5663; www.aerocondor.com.pe) or a travel agent in Lima to see whether such services are currently being offered.

BY BUS   Traveling by bus from Lima or from other points along the north coast or the northern Andes is the only way to get to Huaraz. Most of the individual bus company terminals are located along Avenida Raymondi or Avenida Fitzcarrald. For the 7- to 8-hour journey from Lima, major companies offering daily service are **CIVA** (© 01/428-5649), **Cruz del Sur** (© 01/225-6163), and

The Cordillera Blanca

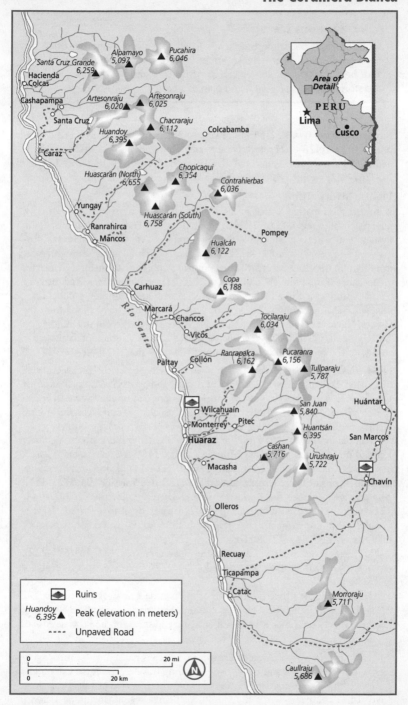

Santa Cruz Grande
6,259
Alpamayo
5,097
Pucahira
6,046
Hacienda
Colcas
Cashapampa
Artesonraju
6,020
Artesonraju
6,025
Santa Cruz
Chacraraju
6,112
Colcabamba
Huandoy
6,395
Caraz
Huascarán (North)
6,655
Chopicaqui
6,354
Contrahierbas
6,036
Yungay
Huascarán (South)
6,758
Ranrahirca
Mancos
Pompey
Hualcán
6,122
Carhuaz
Copa
6,188
Marcará
Chancos
Vicos
Tocilaraju
6,034
Paltay
Collón
Ranrapaka
6,162
Pucaranra
6,156
Tullparaju
5,787
Wilcahuaín
Monterrey
Pitec
San Juan
5,840
Huántar
Huaraz
Huantsán
6,395
San Marcos
Cashan
5,716
Macasha
Urùshraju
5,722
Chavín
Olleros
Recuay
Ticapampa
Catac
Morroraju
5,711
Caullraju
5,686

PERU
Area of Detail
Lima
Cusco

Rio Santa

Legend

Ruins	
Huandoy 6,395 ▲	Peak (elevation in meters)
- - - -	Unpaved Road

0   20 mi
0   20 km

N

> **_Tips_ Safe Bus Travel**
>
> Night bus trips departing Huaraz for Trujillo, Chiclayo, and other cities in northern Peru have earned bad reputations for theft. Be very careful with your belongings on board, even if it means threading your arms through the straps of your carry-on if you plan to sleep.

Móvil Tours (© **044/722-555** in Huaraz). Others include **Empresa de Transportes** (© **01/428-6621**) and **Transportes Rodríguez** (© **01/428-0506**, or 044/721-353). Móvil Tours and **Transportes Línea** (© **044/245-181**, or 044/261-482) are the principal carriers to and from Trujillo (8 hr.).

Visitor Information

A tourist information office is located in the Museo Arqueológico on Av. Luzuriaga s/n (© **044/721-551**). For mountaineering and trekking information, though, you're best off consulting the respected **Casa de Guías de Huaraz,** Parque Ginebra 28 (© **044/721-811**). The office is open Monday through Friday from 9am to 6pm and Saturday from 9am to 1pm. The friendly folks there have up-to-date information on trails, maps, lists of certified guides, and message board postings for those looking to form trekking and climbing groups. Basic information on visiting the Huascarán National Park can be obtained from the **Parque Nacional Huascarán** office, in the Ministerio de Agricultura building on Av. Raymondi (© **044/722-086**). More general tourist information is also available from the **tourist police** office on the Plaza de Armas (© **044/721-341**).

FAST FACTS   Most banks are found around the Plaza de Armas. Among those that exchange traveler's checks and cash and have ATMs are **Banco de Crédito,** Av. Luzuriaga 669 at the corner of Sucre; **Interbanc,** Sucre 913; and **Banco Wiese,** Sucre 766. Money-changers can usually be found hanging around outside banks around the Plaza de Armas.

In an **emergency,** call © **105.** For climbing accidents and assistance, contact **Unidad de Salvamento de Alta Montaña** at © **044/793-333** or 044/793-327, or **Casa de Guías,** Parque Ginebra 28 (© **044/721-811**). If you need the police, the **tourist police** have an office just off the Plaza de Armas (© **044/721-341**); you can also contact the **national police,** Larrea y Loredo 720 (© **044/ 721-461**). For medical attention, go to **Hospital de Apoyo Víctor Ramos Guardia,** Av. Luzuriaga s/n (© **044/721-290**), or **Hospital Regional,** Av. Luzuriaga s/n (© **044/721-861**).

For Internet access, try **Chavín.com**, Gamarra 628 (© **044/691-722**). **Avance,** Av. Luzuriaga 672, 2nd floor (© **044/726-736**), has special deals for repeat visits.

The Huaraz **post office** is located on the Plaza de Armas, Av. Luzuriaga 702 (© **044/721-030**); it's open Monday through Saturday from 8am to 8pm. The **Telefónica del Perú** office is at Bolívar and Sucre, just east of the Plaza de Armas.

Getting Around

The main axis in town is Avenida Luzuriaga, which is packed with tourist agencies, outdoor outfitters, and nearly every strolling traveler who hits Huaraz. The easiest way to get around town is by taking an inexpensive taxi or a colectivo. Myriad bus companies serve the Cordillera Blanca region, including Chavín, Caraz, and Yungay.

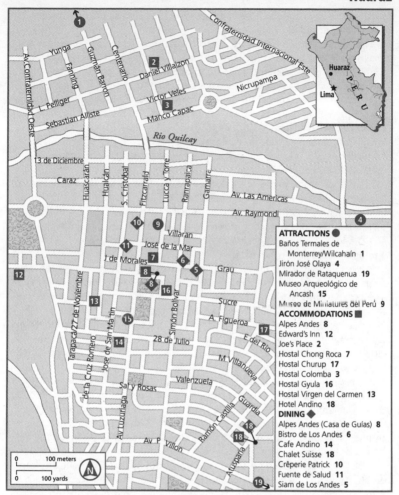

ATTRACTIONS ●
Baños Termales de
  Monterrey/Wilcahaín **1**
Jirón José Olaya **4**
Mirador de Rataquenua **19**
Museo Arqueológico de
  Ancash **15**
Museo de Miniaturas del Perú **9**
ACCOMMODATIONS ■
Alpes Andes **8**
Edward's Inn **12**
Joe's Place **2**
Hostal Chong Roca **7**
Hostal Churup **17**
Hostal Colomba **3**
Hostal Gyula **16**
Hostal Virgen del Carmen **13**
Hotel Andino **18**
DINING ◆
Alpes Andes (Casa de Guías) **8**
Bistro de Los Andes **6**
Cafe Andino **14**
Chalet Suisse **18**
Crêperie Patrick **10**
Fuente de Salud **11**
Siam de Los Andes **5**

BY TAXI Taxis cruise Avenida Luzuriaga in search of travelers day and night. Rides in town cost S/2 (60¢).

BY BUS Combis service towns in the Callejón de Huaylas around Huaraz: Chavín (4 hr.), Caraz (90 min.), and Yungay (90 min.). Most depart from the Quillcay Bridge on Alameda Fitzcarrald; others leave from Calle Caraz, a half block east of Fitzcarrald. Fares are inexpensive, usually S/3 to S/10 ($1–$3).

WHAT TO SEE & DO AROUND HUARAZ

The emphasis on seeing and doing in Huaraz is definitely on the latter—most visitors are in town as long as it takes them to organize an excursion into the mountains and valleys nearby or some sort of adventure-sports activity. The town itself, hastily reconstructed after the devastating 1970 earthquake, would appear to have little to offer beyond one street, **Jirón José Olaya** (to the right of Raymondi), which gives a hint of what Huaraz looked like before it came crumbling down. However, visitors who need a few days to acclimatize can take advantage of their time in town and see what the city has to offer besides its stupendous location.

The **Museo Arqueológico de Ancash** is an interesting and well-organized small museum crammed with exhibits presenting the long history (more than 12,000 years) of the region through mummies, trepanned crania, and a terrific collection of monoliths from the Recuay and Huari cultures. There are textiles, ceramics, and other pieces from the Chavín, Huaraz, Moche, and Chimú cultures, as well as scale models of various ruins sites in the area. The museum, located at Av. Luzuriaga 762 (© 044/721-551), is open Tuesday through Saturday from 8am to 7pm, and Sunday and Monday from 9:30am to 3pm. Admission is S/5 ($1.50); the ticket is also good for same-day entrance to the ruins at Wilcahuaín (see below).

Another diversion might be the **Museo de Miniaturas del Perú** (Miniatures Museum), which houses dolls in traditional Peruvian dress and scale models of the ruins at Chavín de Huántar, pre-earthquake Huaraz, and the city of Yungay. The museum is in the gardens of the Gran Hotel Huascarán, Jr. Lúcar y Torre 46 (© 044/721-466). It's open Monday through Friday from 8am to 1pm and 3 to 6pm. Admission is S/3 ($1).

But because Huaraz is primarily about its stunning location and getting outdoors, more people might be interested in the **Mirador de Rataquenua**⋆, a lookout spot on a 3,650m (12,045-ft.) mountain pass with great panoramic views; it's just under an hour's walk southeast of downtown. The direct trail is pretty steep; there's also a less demanding dirt road with plenty of switchbacks. Go with a group during the day, as the area has experienced a spate of crime in recent years. To get there, head south on Luzuriaga to Villón and follow the road at the end, just beyond the cemetery.

Located about 8km (5 miles) north of Huaraz, the **Monumento Arqueológico de Wilcahuaín** is a set of ruins from the Huari culture, which lived in the region around A.D.1000. Two sites named for their relative size, Grande and Chico, were burial grounds and storage centers. The major temple was built around 1100. The ruins don't have established opening and closing hours, but it's certainly wisest to go during daylight. Admission is S/4 ($1.30) for adults, S/2 (60¢) for students. To get there, take any combi marked "Wilcahuaín" from the Río Quilcay bridge. The trip takes about half an hour and costs S/2 (60¢). After visiting Chico, walk down to Grande and catch a return combi to Huaraz.

A relaxing spot to visit, perhaps after you've indulged in some trekking or other adventure sports, are the thermal baths **Baños Termales de Monterrey.** A series of small wells and two large pools have mineral-rich waters that make the water look dark brown and rather unappealing, but your body may not be as

---

Tips Tour Operators & Travel Agencies

Guides and travel agencies are extremely useful, if not downright indispensable, for most adventure sports. Like Cusco and Iquitos, Huaraz is chock-full of agencies and tour operators. Unfortunately, some of them are less than reliable; others are far worse. See "Trekking & Climbing in the Cordillera Blanca," later in this chapter, for a discussion of guides and agencies. It's best to check with fellow tourists (or, prior to arriving in Huaraz, with the South American Explorers clubs in either Lima or Cusco) to get recent reports about services.

Festival Calendar

Huaraz and the villages in the Callejón de Huaylas celebrate their Andean roots in traditional festivals that are among the country's most spirited. If your visit coincides with a regional festival, you'll see a profusion of folk dances, costumed dances (some with extraordinary masks), and the stirring local music that accompanies them, played on exotic instruments such as *roncadoras, quenas,* and *zampoñas.* Carnaval, the Fiesta de Mayo, the Semana del Andinismo, the Patron Saint Festival, the Fiesta de las Luces, and Virgen de las Mercedes are among the most festive, but be warned that accommodations are at a premium, and prices skyrocket at these times.

The complete list of regional festivals:

- January 18 to 21: La Virgen de Chiquinquirá (Caraz)
- February or March: Carnaval Huaracino (Huaraz)
- March or April: Semana Santa and the steps of the pilgrimage (Huaraz and Callejón de Huaylas)
- May 2 to 10: Fiesta de Mayo, celebrated with traditional dances, ski races, and a lantern procession (Huaraz)
- June: Semana del Andinismo, a celebration of outdoor adventure (Huaraz and Callejón de Huaylas)
- June 22 to 24: San Juan Bautista, Day of the Indian (Pomabamba and the entire Sierra Andina)
- July 6 to 9: La Virgen Santa Isabel (Callejón de Huaylas)
- July 20 to 30: Independence Celebration (Huaraz and Caraz)
- July 28 to 29: Fiestas Patrias
- August 1 to 6: Patron Saint Festival (Coyllur and Huaraz)
- August 13 to 16: Virgen de la Asunción (Huata and Chacas)
- August 29 to 30: Fiesta Patrona (Chiquián and Santa Rosa)
- September 14: Fiesta de las Luces (Huaraz)
- September 14 to 27: Señor de Burgos (Recuay)
- September 23 to 27: Virgen de las Mercedes (Carhuaz)
- October 5 to 7: Virgen del Rosario (Huari)
- October 12: Virgen del Pilar (Ticapampa)
- October 28: Fiesta Cívica (Yungay)

picky as your eyes. The upper pool is the nicer of the two. The baths are open daily from 7am to 6pm, and they're usually very crowded on weekends and holidays. Admission is S/3 ($1). The baths are about 6km (4 miles) north of Huaraz along the road to Caraz; a colectivo from Avenida Luzuriaga drops passengers at the entrance.

SHOPPING

Huaraz is recognized as an artesanía center, and all of the usual Andean handicrafts are available at markets targeting gringos. Some of the best items are custom-made and hand-tooled leather goods, wool sweaters, ponchos, and blankets. There are open-air handicrafts markets, open daily along the covered walkway (Pasaje Cáceres) off Avenida Luzuriaga and along the streets Juan de la Cruz Romero, Avenida Raymondi, and Avenida Tarapaca. A **mercado callejero** (street market) is open Monday and Thursday on Avenida Bolognesi and Confraternidad Oeste.

PeruKraft, on Jirón 28 de Julio, has good-quality alpaca sweaters, while a company called **Andean Expressions** specializes in T-shirts with cool Andean designs; their products are found in several shops in town or their factory site at Jr. J. Arguedas 1246.

But unless you're going on a trekking excursion with all your provisions included, shopping for foodstuffs might be more important. At the **main market** on Cruz Romero, just south of Raymondi, you can find most everything you'll need to sustain yourself for a mountain climb or a trek, including canned foods, nuts, and fresh fruits and vegetables. **Ortiz,** Av. Luzuriaga 401, is a good and well-stocked supermarket. Cheese and *manjar blanco* (a sweet) are good local items to take along on an expedition.

WHERE TO STAY

The high season in Huaraz and the Cordillera Blanca is June through September. During Easter Week and other holidays (such as the Fiestas Patrias at the end of July), hotel prices can double. The Semana del Andinismo, held annually in June, brings mountain climbers from around the world; then and throughout the dry season, climbing groups and student groups (the latter especially in Oct) often take over hostales. Locals with inexpensive accommodations in their homes as well as touts acting (sometimes independently) on behalf of inns often meet incoming buses; take what the hawkers tell you (about location, comfort, and so on) with a grain of salt. Although Huaraz is loaded with budget accommodations aimed at independent trekkers, only a few are nice enough to recommend without reservation.

Expensive

Hotel Andino ⋆   Also known variously as Club Hotel Andino and Hostal Andino, this Swiss-owned upscale alpine lodge is the top place to stay in Huaraz. A modern, raked construction, it's about a 10-minute uphill walk southeast of the Plaza de Armas in the Pedregal district. With a friendly vibe and a very good Swiss restaurant, it's a fine place to prepare for or recover from rugged adventure travel—and it is indeed popular with trekking and climbing groups. In high season, it's wise to book well in advance. The best (but most expensive) rooms are on the second floor and have excellent panoramic views of the Cordillera Blanca and Huascarán peak from private balconies. Accommodations are modern and comfy, with big, thick, striped Andean wool blankets. Some rooms have fireplaces.

Pedro Cochachín 357, Huaraz. © **044/721-662,** or 01/445-9230 for reservations. Fax 044/722-830. www.hotelandino.com. $85–$109 double. Rates include taxes. 41 units. AE, DC, MC, V. **Amenities:** Restaurant; small business center and conference room; laundry service; travel agency; horseback riding; climbing equipment rental. *In room:* TV, hair dryer, safe; fireplaces in some units.

Moderate

Edward's Inn   One of Huaraz's most popular and longest-running inns, Edward's is an easygoing place that packs in the trekkers during high season. Rooms are clean and large and have good mountain views, though some detractors find the inn overpriced, given its fairly basic facilities. (The hot water, fueled by solar power, is best in the late afternoon or early evening.) The inn's also a bit removed from the action in town. Still, it's a fine place to meet and hang out with fellow gringo trekkers and climbers. The eponymous owner, an experienced trekker and mountaineer, rents out gear, speaks good English, and can provide

Tips   **More Budget Accommodations**

Huaraz can fill up with trekking groups and plenty of independent travelers between June and September. Many of the budget inns hawked by people who meet arriving buses are neither clean nor especially comfortable, though. If you arrive without a reservation and are looking for a solid, safe, and inexpensive inn, try one of the following:

Hostal Chong Roca   This hostal has large and pretty decent rooms, which have either a full private bathroom or a toilet and sink. Morales 687 (© 044/721-154). S/30 ($9) per person.

Hostal Gyula   Located opposite the Casa de Guías, this hostal isn't fancy, but it offers hot-water showers and good information on trekking, as well as good views. The inn can get a bit rowdy when taken over by groups. Parque Ginebra 632 (© 044/721-567). $8 per person including breakfast.

Hostal Virgen del Carmen   This comfortable hostal is run by a warm older couple, who have converted their attractive house into an inn with very nice bedrooms. Cruz Romero 622 (© 044/721-729). S/25 ($7) double.

Joe's Place   This is a relaxed and friendly inn with a cool garden terrace, excellent mountain views, and very well-maintained rooms. It's on the north side of the Río Quilcay, a 10- to 15-minute walk from the center of town. The place is pretty popular with a steady stream of backpackers. Jr. Daniel Villaizán 276 (© 044/725-505). $15 double.

Olaza Guest House   This friendly place is run by Julio Olaza, whose agency, Mountain Bike Adventures, is the best for mountain biking in the Cordillera. The hotel has a great rooftop terrace, book exchange, kitchen and laundry facilities, and nice, clean rooms. A great value. Jr. Julio Arguedas 1247, La Soledad, Huaraz (© 044/619-050; www. andeanexplorer.com). $5 per person.

good climbing and trekking information. He can also arrange tours, treks, and climbing trips. The rooftop patio is a good gathering spot.

Av. Bolognesi 121 (near the stadium), Huaraz. © and fax **044/722-692.** edwardsinn@terra.com.pe. 14 units. $30 double with private bathroom, $20 with shared bathroom; $10 per person dormitory. Rates include taxes. DC, V. **Amenities:** Cafe; laundry service; equipment storage and rental; book exchange; safety deposit boxes. *In room:* TV.

Hostal Colomba ☞   A good-value, midrange choice, this family-run hostal occupies the nicely landscaped grounds of an old hacienda and has bungalows in a large and pretty plant-filled garden. Friendly and safe, it's in a tranquil residential area across the river, about 15 to 20 minutes by foot to the main square. The pleasant bungalow rooms are nicely decorated and spacious; all have private bathrooms. It's a good place to unwind after a taxing trip to the mountains.

Jr. Francisco de Zela 278, Huaraz. © **044/721-501.** Fax 044/721-501. www.bed42.com/hotelcolomba. 8 units. $45 double. Rate includes taxes. **Amenities:** Dining room/cafe; room service; laundry service; 24-hr. security; safety deposit boxes. *In room:* TV.

Inexpensive

Alpes Andes *(Value* Huaraz's best official youth hostel is modern, well run and clean—and, best of all, safe. Part of the respected and very informative Casa de Guías, which is a hub for Huaraz/Cordillera visitors, the hostel is a prime meeting place for trekkers and mountaineers looking to form groups. (The bulletin boards are littered with information about trails and expeditions.) The hostel has dorm-room accommodations, plus kitchen and laundry facilities.

Parque Ginebra 28-G (in Casa de Guías), Huaraz. ℂ 044/721-811. Fax 044/722-306. casa_de_guias@ hotmail.com. 2 dorm units (capacity 20 people). $7.50 per person. No credit cards. **Amenities:** Restaurant; kitchen and laundry facilities; luggage storage; trekking and tour information.

Hostal Churup *(★ (Value* One of the friendliest family-run inns in Huaraz, this low-key budget place plays happy host to lots of young gringo trekkers. Located in a quiet residential area just a short 5-block walk from the Plaza de Armas, Hostal Churup has good clean rooms with private bathrooms for two to four people and small dormitory rooms with shared bathrooms. The owners are eager to share not only their knowledge of the area and trekking expeditions but also their home, where a filling and inexpensive breakfast is served with family members each morning. The lovely backyard is a good place to sit, read, and relax. There's also a lounge, and guests can use the kitchen. It's a good idea to reserve in advance from June to September.

Jr. Pedro Campos 735 (near Iglesia Soledad), Huaraz. ℂ **044/722-584.** churup@hotmail.com. 12 units. $10 double with private bathroom; $4 per person with shared bathroom. **Amenities:** Laundry service; kitchen privileges; book exchange; Spanish lessons. *In room:* No phone.

WHERE TO DINE

Huaraz has plenty of good, informal restaurants serving the band of Gore-Tex gringos that come to town. The main drag, Avenida Luzuriaga, is thick with restaurants offering fixed-price menus and other cheap eats. The Andean cuisine of the Cordillera includes hearty items such as Huaracino *picante de cuy* (spicy roasted guinea pig), *jaca-chasqui* (spicy guinea pig soup), *charqui* (dried pork), *huallpa-chasqui* (chicken soup with almonds), and *trucha* (fried river trout). For the less adventurous, there are several chifas and pizzerias in town where you can get a filling, inexpensive meal.

Alpes Andes PIZZA/INTERNATIONAL   The food here may appear to take a back seat to the planning of mountain-climbing expeditions—as many mountain guides as eager tourists come through the doors—but this relaxing and informal cafe next door to the Casa de Guías goes about its business of fortifying trekkers and adventurers for their trips to the Cordillera. Start with a breakfast of granola and yogurt, or chow down on the international trekkers' favorites: pizza and pasta—gotta load up on the carbs, you know.

Morales 753. ℂ **044/721-811.** Reservations not accepted. Main courses S/4–S/15 ($1–$4). No credit cards. Daily 7am–11pm.

Bistro de Los Andes INTERNATIONAL/PERUVIAN   Especially popular for its excellent coffee and crack-of-dawn breakfasts (plenty of tourists straggle in right off the overnight Lima bus), this welcoming cafe also offers an interesting mix of French and Peruvian items for lunch and dinner. The varied menu includes vegetarian dishes, pastas, and nicely done dishes such as *trucha a la almendra* (trout baked with almonds). The tables outside give it that French feel at lunchtime.

Jr. Julio de Morales 823. ℂ **044/726-249.** Reservations not accepted. Main courses S/6–S/18 ($1.50–$5). DC, V. Tues–Sun 6am–11pm; Mon 5–11pm.

Café Andino CAFE This cafe, the most popular hangout in Huaraz, has the best coffee (including cappuccinos and lattes) in town, as well as juices, good breakfasts, and even Mexican food and alcoholic drinks. It's a fun meeting place for gringos looking to hit the trails; it has a library-book exchange with titles in several languages, board games, and good tunes.

Jr. 28 de Julio 562. No phone. Reservations not accepted. Main courses S/4–S/30 ($1–$8.50). No credit cards. Daily 9am–noon and 6pm–midnight.

Chalet Suisse ⍟ SWISS/FONDUE This upscale restaurant, probably the city's finest, is primarily reserved for those staying in the attached Hotel Andino. If you're not a guest, it's best to ring for a reservation. The fondues, while not cheap, are delicious, as are steaks and other dishes. The attractive dining room is the perfect subdued spot to celebrate your big climb (if you're too weary to hit the pubs).

Pedro Cochachín 357. ⓒ **044/721-949.** Reservations recommended. Main courses S/14–S/35 ($4–$10). AE, DC, MC, V. Daily noon–2pm and 7–10pm.

Crêperie Patrick FRENCH/CREPES A taste of sophisticated France in Huaraz, this popular joint does big crepe business, offering a whole range of sweet and savory fillings. There are also good quiches and pastas. Some other items, including steaks and fish dishes, are somewhat less accessible for the budget backpacker, but they're well prepared and worth a celebratory splurge. The rooftop terrace is a great spot for a sunny breakfast.

Av. Luzuriaga 422. ⓒ **044/723-364.** Reservations not accepted. Main courses S/4–S/28 ($1–$8). DC, V. Mon–Sat 8am–noon and 6–11pm.

Fuente de Salud ⍟*Value* VEGETARIAN A simple spot that dares to call itself the "fountain of health," this vegetarian restaurant does its best to serve healthy foods to hikers and travelers who may be feeling a bit done in by the high altitude and the demands of mountain climbing. The menu has a good range of veggie dishes; the lunchtime set-price meals (S/4, or $1) are one of the best values in Huaraz.

José de la Mar 562. No phone. Reservations not accepted. Main courses S/4–S/12 ($1–$3.50). No credit cards. Daily 8am–11pm.

Siam de Los Andes ⍟⍟ THAI It's certainly unusual to alight upon a Thai restaurant in Huaraz, but hungry trekkers looking for a taste of something different are really glad when they do. It's far from the cheapest restaurant in Huaraz, but the food is authentic and very well prepared. The stir-fries and curries are especially delicious. The amiable chef/owner Naresuan likes to greet diners, and, besides cooking, he also knows a thing or two about trekking in the area.

Gamarra 419 (at the corner of Julián de Morales). ⓒ **044/728-006.** Reservations not accepted. Main courses S/12–S/24 ($3.50–$7). DC, V. Daily noon–10pm.

HUARAZ AFTER DARK

It's not hard to find a nightspot in Huaraz. With all the gringos gearing up for or celebrating the completion of trekking expeditions, the place hops in high season.

El Tambo, José de la Mar 776, about 3 blocks from Avenida Luzuriaga (ⓒ **044/723-417**), is the most happening disco in town. There's plenty of drinking, dancing, and smoking until the wee hours, and the music careens between international Top 40 and more home-grown Latin sounds. There's usually a pretty good mix of locals and gringos. The cover charge ranges from S/10 to S/20

($3–$6). **Disco El Sol,** Av. Luzuriaga s/n, is the other top place in town to find late-night revelry. The DJ keeps techno-tinged Latin tunes pumping, and dancers—especially student groups when they flood Huaraz—keep it hopping until dawn. The cover charge is usually about S/5 ($1.50).

Bars worth dropping in on include the bar at El Tambo and **Las Keñas Pub,** Jr. Gabino Uribe 620, both of which have live and recorded (often Andean) music and good pisco sours. **La Cueva del Oso,** Av. Luzuriaga 674, is a lively peña with good music and dancing. A more sedate but still very enjoyable outing is **Café Andino,** Jr. 28 de Julio 562, a cool and intimate coffeehouse hangout with good music, board games, a book exchange, and good drinks and coffee.

SIDE TRIPS FROM HUARAZ

The small towns of the Callejón de Huaylas, the valley that splits the middle between the mountain ranges of the Cordillera Blanca and the Cordillera Negra north of Huaraz, make good bases for hikes and are worthwhile visits in themselves. The entire valley is characterized by spectacular snowcapped scenery, stunning alpine lakes, and tranquil meadows.

Carhuaz
35km (22 miles) N of Huaraz

This quiet, rather plain Andean town stands in stark contrast to the tourism hustle of Huaraz. It's becoming better known as a base in its own right for mountain-adventure travel, but it doesn't have even a fraction of the tourism infrastructure found in Huaraz. Still, it has a couple of nice hostales and restaurants for people looking for a more serene atmosphere. Carhuaz is locally renowned for its Virgen de las Mercedes festival, which takes place for 10 days in mid-September and is perhaps the most raucous festival in the valley.

There aren't many actual sights in town, other than the bustling Sunday market, but there are a few places just outside Carhuaz that are worth a look. Near the small town of Mancos (a half hour from Carhuaz by combi) is the ancient cave Cueva de Guitarreros, which some anthropologists believe to be 12,000 years old. The cave, which contains primitive rock paintings, is a nice 30-minute walk from Mancos south across the river. There are good views of Huascarán. Near Marcará, about 6.5km (4 miles) south of Carhuaz, are the Baños Termales de Chancos (hot springs).

To get to Carhuaz, take a combi from Huaraz; the trip takes about an hour and costs S/4 ($1). If you want to spend the night in Carhuaz, perhaps your best bet is one of the family-run guesthouses, or *casas de alojamiento.* Try **Las Bromelias,** Jr. Brasil 208 (② **044/794-033**), or **Las Torrecitas,** Amazonas 412 (② **044/794-213**). Each costs about S/15 ($4.25) per person.

Yungay
50km (31 miles) N of Huaraz

This small town is permanently marked by tragedy—it was completely buried in a 1970 landslide, precipitated by the massive earthquake that loosened tons of granite from the top of Nevado Huascarán. The hurtling mass killed at least 20,000 people, nearly the town's entire population. Only a few children survived. The rubble, called Campo Santo, is now a macabre tourist attraction. The only reminders of the life that once existed there are four palm trees that graced the Plaza de Armas and rosebushes and monuments honoring the dead. A new settlement was established about a half mile away. Predictably, the rebuilt town isn't too easy on the eyes, save its alpine location; it's mostly a functional transportation hub for those looking to approach the stunning lakes of Llanganuco (see below). In town, there's a small museum, the **Museo de Arqueología e Historia Natural de Yungay,** Avenida Las Palmeras, Ranrahirca (© 044/ 682-322), which exhibits regional flora and fauna, ceramics, textiles, and other historical relics.

Combis leave from the Quillcay Bridge on Alameda Fitzcarrald Huaraz for Yungay. The trip, which takes about 1½ hours, costs S/3 (90¢).

Lagunas de Llanganuco 😿😿
82km (51 miles) N of Huaraz

These two brilliant turquoise alpine lakes, at nearly 4,000m (13,120 ft.) above sea level, compose a dazzling vista at the base of the Cordillera Blanca's highest snowcapped summits. The views of Chopicalqui (6,354m/20,841 ft.), Huandoy (6,395m/20,976 ft.), and hulking Huascarán (6,768m/22,199 ft.) are simply mesmerizing. If possible, wait for a clear morning to go; the sun shining on the lakes makes them shimmer and their colors change. The glacier-fed lakes are a popular day trip from Huaraz, and many tour companies in Huaraz offer Llanganuco as an organized tour for about $25 per person. The lakes are easier to get to from Yungay, which is 26km (16 miles) away; if you're traveling independently, it's simple to catch a combi or truck up to the lakes from the Plaza de Armas in Yungay (about $5 round-trip), but note that the ride can take up to 90 minutes.

Glaciar Pastoruri
The Cordillera is tightly packed with towering peaks that should only be ascended by skilled and properly outfitted climbers. If you're not in that camp, this relatively flat glacier, another popular day trip from Huaraz, might be a draw. Provided that you've already become acclimatized to the altitude of the area, the 45-minute trek up the glacier (5,240m/17,290 ft.) isn't difficult and can be done without special equipment, though horses and mules are frequently available to help those having a hard time trudging through the snow. Though Peruvians often ski and snowboard on the glacier, veteran skiers will be disappointed. Bring sufficient cold-weather gear, though, as it can be very frigid.

As an organized outing, the trip to Pastoruri is usually combined with a visit to the valley of **Pachacoto,** 57km (35 miles) south of Huaraz, an opportunity to see the Callejón de Huaylas's famous **Puya Raimondi** plants. The bizarre, spiky plants, like towering alien cacti, are the largest members of the bromeliad family (a relative of the pineapple). The species is thought to be one of the most ancient in the world, and it is found only in a few isolated, high-altitude parts of the Andes. The plant, which can reach a height of 12m (39 ft.), is like a tragic protagonist: It flowers but once in its life, and though it may live to be 100 years old, it dies immediately after flowering. Flowering is usually in May, when tour groups make pilgrimages to witness the brief, beautiful sight, like a stage set against the snowy mountains.

Caraz
68km (42 miles) N of Huaraz

Caraz is the farthest of the valley towns north of Huaraz that are accessible by public transportation. More attractive than some of the other towns that have suffered great natural disaster, and located at an elevation about 1,000m (3,280 ft.) lower than Huaraz, Caraz makes a good base for trekking and climbing in the Cordillera Blanca. The town has a pleasant Plaza de Armas and a growing amount of infrastructure to serve trekkers and mountaineers, including one of

---

Fun Fact **Top of the Peaks**

Among the best known of Peru's daunting pinnacles are Mount Huascarán 6,768m (22,199 ft.); the Huandoy massif's three summits, all more
than 6,000m (20,000 ft.) high; and Chopicalqui 6,354m (20,841 ft.),
Chacraraju 6,112m (20,047 ft.), Alpamayo 5,957m (19,539 ft.), and Copa
6,118m (20,067 ft.).

---

the area's top outdoor-adventure agencies. Many people end up (and rest up) in
Caraz after trekking the popular Llanganuco–Santa Cruz route, though nearly as
many embark from here onto remote treks into the northern Cordillera Blanca.

Caraz has a couple small museums: a **Museo de Arqueología,** which has
some deformed skulls and artifacts uncovered at the Cueva de Guitarreros, and
the **Museo Amauta de Arte Ancashino,** which contains some ethnographic
exhibits. Nearby are some pre-Chavín ruins, **Tunshucaiko,** about a half mile
from the center of town across the Río Llullán. Though many people make their
way to Caraz to begin some hard-core mountain excursions, there are several
worthwhile and easier excursions that make excellent day trips. Gorgeous
Laguna Parón is a bold, bright blue lake that sits at an elevation of more than
4,000m (13,200 ft.) and is surrounded by a dozen snowcapped peaks, 30km (18
miles) from town. Colectivos run from Santa Rosa in Caraz to Parón (90 min.).
The **Cañón del Pato** is a fantastic, sheer canyon along the Río Santa, dividing
the Cordilleras Blanca and Negra. The road that knifes through the canyon,
from Caraz to Huallanca, is one of the most thrilling in the country; it pene-
trates more than 3 dozen tunnels. By colectivo, it's about 2 hours to Huallanca,
the far end of the canyon, from Caraz.

Caraz is a 2-hour combi ride from Huaraz. If you want to stay overnight
in Caraz, try one of the following nice and inexpensive inns that are popular
with trekkers and backpackers: **Hostal Perla de los Andes,** Plaza de Armas
(© 044/792-007); the youth hostel **Albergue Los Piños,** Parque San Martín
103 (© 044/790-130); or **Caraz Dulzura,** Sáenz Peña 212 (© 044/791-523). In
town is **Pony Expeditions,** one of the best trekking and mountaineering agencies
in the valley, with equipment rental and good guides (see "Recommended Tour
Companies," below). **Café de Rat,** Jr. Sucre 1286, on the Plaza de Armas above
Pony Expeditions, is the place for mountaineers to hang out and fortify themselves
with pizzas, pastas, crepes, and good vegetarian meals. (It also has Internet access,
maps, and guidebooks.)

Chavín de Huántar ⋆
110km (68 miles) E of Huaraz

East of the Cordillera Blanca, some 4 hours from Huaraz, the standout attraction is the nearly 3,000-year-old ruins of Chavín de Huántar, a U-shaped
fortress-temple with excellent stonework constructed by the Chavín culture over
several centuries. The Chavín, who thrived in the region from about 1200 to
300 B.C., are the most ancient of the major cultures known to exist in Peru and
certainly one of its most sophisticated. The Chavín are considered perhaps the
most influential people in the Andes, at least until the arrival of the dynasty-
building Incas (who came along a mere 2,000 years later). Chavín de Huántar,
a UNESCO World Heritage Site, are the best-preserved ruins of the culture,
whose influence was felt from Ecuador all the way to southern Peru.

However, don't expect a stunning set of Machu Picchu–like ruins. The site's archaeological importance isn't nearly as transparently aesthetic. The temple comprises more than a dozen underground galleries or chambers; only a few are open to the public. Some appear as labyrinthine tunnels today because they were interred by a landslide in the 1940s. The main structure on the premises is a large pyramid, called the **Castillo,** built over well-constructed canals where water once flowed. A ways away is a large, sunken central plaza, a ceremonial gathering place. The highlight of the ruins is the **Lanzón,** a remarkable cultist carving in white granite and shaped like a prism or dagger. The monolith is found in an underground passage behind the original temple, which is much smaller than the several-times-enlarged Castillo. The huge 5m (16-ft.) carving depicts three figures worshipped by the Chavín culture: the serpent, the bird, and the feline, the principal deity. The Lanzón remains in its original location, at an underground crossroads, even though other important artifacts, including the famous Tello Obelisk and Raymondi Stela, were removed and are now housed at Museo de la Nación in Lima. A guide and flashlight are good ideas to get the most out of the site.

The **Monumento Arqueológico Chavín de Huántar** (✆ **044/754-042**) is open daily from 8am to 4pm. The most convenient and the fastest way to visit Chavín is by organized tour from Huaraz; most cost about S/30 ($9) per person. Virtually every agency offers the same program, a long day trip leaving Huaraz around 8am and returning around 8pm.

Nearby, the village of Chavín de Huántar is an attractive traditional settlement. Although relatively few tourists stay overnight, there are a couple of decent inns in case you want to (such as the **Hotel La Casona** on the Plaza de Armas), perhaps to make a second day's visit to the ruins. The Lanzón exerts a mystical hold on some visitors.

TREKKING & CLIMBING IN THE CORDILLERA BLANCA

The Cordillera Blanca, the highest tropical mountain chain in the world, is a virtual ocean of glorious and imposing mountain peaks. The range proclaims its beauty and power over a 180km (112-mile) stretch through the heart of Peru. The scenery of snowcapped peaks, glaciers, lakes, and rivers is certainly stunning, but most visitors to the Cordillera Blanca mountain range want to view it from up close and on high. They have one thing in mind: strapping on hi-tech gear and trekking or climbing.

This section of Peru has become one of the world's mountaineering meccas. Fifty summits soar between 4,800m and 6,662m (16,000–22,205 ft.) high, and nearly the entire range forms part of the protected Parque Nacional Huascarán. Though the most challenging peaks are beacons to the some of the most tested mountaineers in the world, there are plenty of trekking and climbing activities for those who haven't quite perfected their ascent techniques. And while some of the peaks are plenty daunting, access to the trailheads is fairly simple, reached by public transportation in just a few hours from Huaraz.

The 340,000-hectare (840,140-acre) Parque Nacional Huascarán was created in 1975 to protect the region's great natural resources. Within the park are the towns Recuay, Huaraz, Carhuaz, Yungay, Huaylas, Bolognesi, Huari, Asunción, Piscobamba, and Pomabamba, several of which serve as bases for explorers. The park counts 32 peaks higher than 6,000m (19,800 ft.) and includes Huascarán, Peru's highest summit, and Alpamayo, whose legendary fourth face is considered by many mountaineers as the most beautiful in the world, as well as 269 lakes and 41 rivers among its spectacular roster of natural blessings.

On Those Camelids

Across the Peruvian highlands, you'll likely have a chance to see three types of South American camelids common to the Andes: the domesticated llama and alpaca, and the considerably rarer wild vicuña. Llamas have been domesticated in the Andes for more than 5,000 years, used for meat, clothing, shelter, and fertilizer. Pre-Columbian civilizations also sacrificed llamas and alpacas as offerings to gods. Vicuñas are the smallest members of the camelid family, as well as the most prized and endangered. These camelids are native to the high plains of the Andes mountains in Bolivia, Chile, and, primarily, Peru.

Alpacas and llamas differ in size and fiber quality. Adult alpacas are usually about a foot shorter than llamas, and the former produces 10 pounds a year or more of high-quality fiber in a single fleece. Alpaca hair is extremely fine, soft, smooth, and lightweight. It is stronger, warmer, and longer lasting than wool. "Baby alpaca" is the first clipping of the shearling, and, extraordinarily soft, it is universally prized and expensive. Llamas, on the other hand, have a less fine dual fiber fleece, and the animals are better equipped to serve as excellent beasts of burden, perfect for mountain-trekking expeditions. Both llamas and alpacas graze at elevations of 3,000m (10,000 ft.) and higher. Llamas and alpacas are intelligent and gentle animals, but they have a reputation for a nasty habit: spitting. They usually spit at each other over food, but female llamas also spit at male llamas to ward off advances.

The vicuña is a national symbol in Peru, which is home to more than half the world's vicuña population. The Incas dressed their nobility in its ultra-soft fibers, considered the finest and warmest in the world, considerably lighter even than cashmere. Vicuña fleece sells for as much as $1,500 a pound; a man's sport coat made of vicuña costs at least $5,000. Poaching nearly rendered the vicuña extinct; it was declared endangered, and trade in vicuña products was banned internationally in 1975. With the vicuña community back up to approximately 200,000 animals throughout the Andean highlands, the animal is now considered threatened rather than endangered, and control over the harvesting of vicuña coats was placed under the ownership and management of Peru's Indian communities in the 1990s. Limited vicuña trade is now allowed; only garments stamped with the "Vicuñandes" trademark or "Vicuña" and the country of origin are deemed legal.

Most of the top climbs in the Cordillera Blanca are best done with the assistance of local guides and experts. Several climbs are not only arduous, but they can also be extremely dangerous. Unless you're a certified member of the hardcore ilk, it's best to contract a guide or organized tour in Huaraz. There, you'll find a whole complement of services, including porters, guides, climbing-gear rentals, and rescue teams.

The fee to enter Huascarán National Park is S/5 ($1.50) for a single-day visit and $20 for visits of 2 days or more. The entrance ticket to Huascarán National Park can be purchased at the Llanganuco and other entrances. You should keep a copy of your passport at the ready for entering and leaving the park.

RECOMMENDED TOUR COMPANIES

In Peru, it's important to pick tour operators carefully to avoid being ripped off. When you're embarking on alpine adventures, especially mountain and ice climbing, it's even more essential: The risks are extreme, so it's paramount to go with an experienced, professional outfit. Accidents happen, and, every year, climbers are injured or killed climbing in the Andes. A good guide from a respected agency knows the routes, the weather, and the risks, and can usually steer you away from the latter. In the event of an emergency, he or she will know how to get injured parties evacuated. Huaraz is littered with freelance guides and somewhat shady agencies offering very cheap fees, but if you're serious about outdoor-adventure sports, you don't want to skimp when it comes to the people to whom you're entrusting your safety and well-being.

The following are all recommended agencies and guides with many years of experience and good reputations in the Huaraz/Cordillera Blanca region. Even so, ask around first. Talk to people who've recently returned from treks and climbing expeditions. Contact the **South American Explorers** either in Lima at Av. Piura 135, Miraflores (© **01/445-3306;** www.samexplo.org), or in Cusco at Choquechaca 188, no. 4 (© **084/245-484;** cuscoclub@saexplorers.org). And of course, speak to the **Casa de Guías de Huaraz,** Parque Ginebra 28 (© **044/ 721-811**), an excellent source of current information. Don't overlook your guide's ability to speak English, which may be critical if your understanding of Spanish is poor. So even if the agency says the guide speaks good English, don't automatically take their word for it.

Virtually every agency in town runs the basic and most popular no- or little-difficulty programs to Lagunas de Llanganuco, Glaciar Pastoruri, and Chavín de Huántar for about $10 to $20 per person.

General Tours

- **Chavín Tours,** Av. Luzuriaga 502, Huaraz (© **044/721-578**). A good company offering standard tours, including trips to Chavín de Huántar, Pastoruri Glacier, and Llanganuco lakes.

Tips A Gear Checklist

Appropriate gear is required for nearly all treks and climbs in the Cordillera Blanca. If you're going with an organized group, you can rent anything you need that's not provided. Independent trekkers and climbers can also rent most anything they need in Huaraz. Some equipment is invariably dated and in less than optimal condition, so experienced mountain climbers pursuing technical climbs will surely want to bring their own equipment. You'll want to bring cold-weather and water-repellent clothing; good backpacking or climbing boots; a tent, a sleeping bag, a camping stove, and cookware; a filter and/or water-purification tablets; a compass; and topographical maps of trails.

- **Pablo Tours,** Av. Luzuriaga 501, Huaraz (© **044/721-145**). A standard tour company, similar to Chavín Tours but offering a few more options. Also organizes good group treks.

Mountain Trekking & Climbing

- **Explorandes** ⚹, Av. Centenario 489, Huaraz (© **044/721-960;** www.explorandes.com). One of the big-name and longest-established adventure-tour operators in Peru, with fixed-departure treks in the Cordillera Blanca. They're expensive, but they're one of the best and most dependable.
- **JM Expeditions,** Av. Luzuriaga 465, office no. 4, Huaraz (© **044/728-017**). Good mountain-climbing equipment and roster of guides.
- **Monttrek** ⚹, Av. Luzuriaga 646, 2nd floor, Huaraz (© **044/721-124;** www.monttrek.com). Offers camping- and climbing-equipment rental, guides, mountain- and ice-climbing classes, as well as horseback riding, mountain biking, river rafting, and hang gliding. A good spot to put together a group of like-minded adventurers.
- **Pony Expeditions** ⚹, Jr. Sucre 1266, Plaza de Armas, Caraz (© **044/791-642;** www.ponyexpeditions.com). Professional outfitter run by a respected guide, Alberto Cafferata, with lots of different treks and climbs available. It offers an extensive program of trekking and climbing itineraries, mountain biking, and rock and ice climbing.
- **Pyramid Adventures,** Luzuriaga 530, Huaraz (© **044/721-864**). One of the better climbing agencies, run by a family of brothers, with good service and knowledge.

Guides & Equipment Rental

- **Galaxia Mountain Shop,** Leoniza y Lescano 603 (© **044/722-792**), and **MountClimb,** Cáceres 421 (© **044/726-060**). Both have a full range of mountain-climbing gear, including boots, sleeping bags, and crampons, for rent ($20–$30 per day for full complement of equipment).
- **Montañero Aventura y Turismo,** Parque Ginebra 30B, Huaraz (© **044/726-386,** or 044/722-603). Climbing equipment, guides, mountain bikes, and standard tours.
- **Mountain Bike Adventures** ⚹, Jr. Lúcar y Torre 530, Huaraz (© **044/724-259;** julio.olaza@terra.com.pe). The top company for single-track riding in the Cordillera, run by Julio Olaza. He has Trek front-suspension bikes for rent and offers several 4- to 7-day itineraries as well as 1-day bike trips. The company also runs a small and enjoyable guesthouse.

TREKKING

The Cordillera Blanca is blessed with some of the greatest trails and most spectacular scenery in South America, and it draws trekkers from the across the world. Across gorgeous valleys and mountain passes nearly 5,000m (16,400 ft.) high, past stunning lakes, waterfalls, and rivers, the region truly earns the cliché so often accorded it: It's a mountaineer's and trekker's paradise. The scenery is enlivened by fantastic indigenous flora and fauna, including 800 varieties of blossoming flowers (the Puya Raimondi and ancient queñual and cacti forests among them), as well as Andean condors, vicuñas, pumas, Andean deer, and 100 species of birds. There are terrific campsites throughout the valley, and excellent guides, porters, and mules to round out your expedition.

There are some 3 dozen well-established treks in the Cordillera Blanca (and many dozens more that draw few tourists). Of the many treks possible from

---

Tips **The Cost of Trekking & Climbing**

All multiday excursions into the Huascarán National Park carry entrance fees of S/65 ($19). If you're going with a tour operator, ask whether this fee is included in your package cost. Single-day entry costs S/5 ($1.50).

Arrieros, local porters with mules who'll lead you on trails, charge $8 to $12 per day, plus food. (Arrieros can be arranged at trailheads or at the Casa de Guías in Huaraz.) Organized treks with one of the firms listed above are generally around $25 to $30 per day, per person. A certified guide to lead technical mountain climbs can cost upwards of $70. Serious climbers should also factor in the cost of insurance (obtained at home), which protects against the prohibitive cost of rescue operations.

Huaraz, the classic **Llanganuco–Santa Cruz** route, one of the most beautiful on the continent, is understandably the most popular. The route across the Santa Cruz gorge begins in the village of Cashapampa and makes its way to the emerald-green lakes at the Llanganuco ravine. The 45km (30-mile) trek usually takes 4 or 5 days. Other popular circuits include **Alpamayo,** a beautiful trek among snowcapped summits that takes about 12 days; **Cedros gorge,** which takes in mountains in the northern sector of the Huascarán Park (4 days); and **Llanganuco** and **Portachuelo,** a less demanding trek through the Quilcayhuanca ravine (1–2 days).

Other well-known routes are:

- **Huaraz to Laguna Llaca,** 35km (22 miles), 2 days
- **Olleros to Chavín** (which ends at Chavín de Huántar), 40km (25 miles), 3 days
- **Cojup Valley** (Huaraz to Laguna Palcacucha), 20km (12 miles), 2 days
- **Lago Churup,** 25km (16 miles), 1 to 2 days
- **Quebrada Quillcayhuanca** (very near Huaraz), 25km (16 miles), 2 to 3 days

The Casa de Guías in Huaraz has detailed information about these and other treks, and South American Explorers produces a good map of various treks in the region. Another good resource is *Peru & Bolivia: Backpacking and Trekking* by Hilary Bradt, et al. (Bradt Publications, 1999), with descriptions of a number of treks in the Cordillera Blanca.

Even the more accessible hikes should be undertaken only by individuals in good physical shape; tackling a mountain pass at nearly 5,000m (16,400 ft.) with gear and food is not easy for those unaccustomed to high altitudes.

Llanganuco–Santa Cruz Trek 🏵🏵

Touted as one of the top five treks in the world by several international outdoor-oriented magazines, the Llanganuco–Santa Cruz trail is one of the most scenic in Peru. It takes in extraordinary mountain scenery of snowcapped peaks, brilliant turquoise lakes, glacier-fed rivers, sparkling waterfalls, and serene meadows. The 45km (28-mile) trail ranges from 2,900m to 4,750m (9,512–15,580 ft.) in altitude but is rated moderate, meaning the hike can be undertaken by anyone in decent physical shape who has allowed him- or herself the time to acclimatize in Huaraz. In peak season, though, the trail's popularity is its enemy. It gets quite crowded, and trash is a problem. There are established campsites and pit toilets along the route.

Packin' Up the Llama

Pack-laden mules on the trail are common, but what could be cooler and more authentic in Peru than trekking with a llama? An organization called Llama 2000, an initiative undertaken by campesino farmers from the Callejón de Huaylas and the Mountain Association of the Olleros-Chavín area, has proposed exactly that. The **Llama-Trek Expedition in Olleros-Chavín** is a roots-based ecotourism initiative, supported by PromPerú and the European Union, which begins in the small alpine town of Olleros (30km/19 miles south of Huaraz). The 4-day trek provides great views of the snowcapped peaks Shaqsha (5,703m/18,706 ft.), Cashan (5,686m/18,650 ft.), and Tuctupunta (5,343m/17,525 ft.), and offers the opportunity to share the customs and traditions of local peasant communities. The route ends at the archaeological site Chavín de Huántar. For more information on llama trekking in the Cordillera, contact **Llama 2000** in Lima at © **01/ 224-3408,** or ask the tourist information office in Huaraz whether treks are currently being organized.

Trekkers can walk the trail in either direction, starting at Cashapampa (2 hr. by bus from Caraz) or Vaquería (2½ hr. by bus from Carhuaz). Many independent travelers prefer to start the trail at Vaquería because the daily bus from Huaraz allows time to make it to the campsite on the first day and get a good jump on the high pass the following day.

All-inclusive treks from Santa Cruz to Llanganuco in a "pooled" service start at about $175 per person.

MOUNTAIN CLIMBING

Climbing in the Cordillera Blanca ranges from highly technical, multipitch ascents to rigorous but nontechnical climbs. The optimal climbing season is May through September. Huaraz serves as the principal hub for contracting qualified guides and tour operators and renting gear, but some similar infrastructure, on a smaller scale, can also be found in Caraz. The Casa de Guías in Huaraz (© **044/721-811**) is your best preclimb resource. It maintains a list of registered guides.

For experienced climbers up to the challenge, the Cordillera Blanca is nirvana. The range includes 50 permanently snowcapped mountain peaks of more than 5,610m (18,700 ft.), amazingly packed into an area just 177km (110 miles) long and 19km (12 miles) wide. Tested mountaineers can hope to bag several 6,000m (20,000-ft.) summits in just a 2- or 3-week trip. Less-experienced climbers can choose among several easier and more popular climbs. For anyone, though, acclimatization is paramount. Allow between 3 days and 1 week before attempting any serious ascent.

The snowy peaks of **Ishinca** (5,534m/18,152 ft.) and **Pisco** (5,752m/18,867 ft.)—essentially 3-day climbs—require appropriate gear, conditioning, and guides, but can be undertaken by inexperienced climbers. Peru's most beautiful mountain, **Alpamayo** (5,957m/19,539 ft.) is an appropriate climb for those with some experience. **Huascarán** (6,768m/22,199 ft.), the highest mountain in the Peruvian Andes and the tallest tropical mountain in the world, takes between

> **Tips   Evacuation Insurance**
>
> Serious mountain climbers would be wise to purchase extra rescue insurance at home, as evacuations can be very costly as well as time-sensitive. See "Insurance, Health & Safety," in chapter 2, for more information about travel insurance.

6 and 9 days and poses a very challenging climb, suitable only for those with technical knowledge and extensive experience.

OTHER ADVENTURE SPORTS

HANG GLIDING   Yungay's hill Pan de Azúcar is the most common spot for hang gliding. For more information, contact **Monttrek** (© 044/721-124; www.monttrek.com).

ICE CLIMBING   The Cordillera Blanca is a great spot to give this serious sport a try. The best mountains for ice climbing are Pisco, Ishinca, Huascarán, Alpamayo, Chopicalqui, and Artesonraju. Contact **Pony Expeditions** (© 044/ 791-642; www.ponyexpeditions.com) or **Monttrek** (© 044/721-124; www.monttrek.com) for more information.

MOUNTAIN BIKING   The Callejón de Huaylas is one of Peru's top destinations for mountain bikers, with hundreds of mountain and valley horse trails cutting across fields, bridges, and creeks, and past traditional Andean villages. Dedicated cyclists can also look forward to the thrill of climbing to 5,000m (16,400-ft.) mountain passes.

In Huaraz, you can rent mountain bikes for an hour, a day, or a week. During the annual Semana del Andinismo in June, there's a mountain-bike competition. Two of Peru's best mountain-bike agencies operate in the area: **Mountain Bike Adventures** in Huaraz (© 044/724-259; julio.olaza@terra.com.pe) and **Pony Expeditions** in Caraz (© 044/791-642; www.ponyexpeditions.com). Both have equipment rental and excellent biking itineraries.

RIVER RAFTING   Near Carhuaz, the Río Santa, which runs the length of the Callejón de Huaylas from Laguna Conococha, is where rafting in the area is practiced. Sections differ in degree of difficulty from easy (classes II and III) to technical (Class V). The section that's most often rafted is between Jangas and Caraz. The season is May through September, when water levels are low. **Monttrek** (© 044/721-124; www.monttrek.com) and a handful of other tour operators in Huaraz offer rafting.

ROCK CLIMBING   Several agencies in Huaraz offer full-day rock-climbing tours in Caraz and Yungay, ranging from easy to moderate. For more information, contact **Monttrek** (© 044/721-124; www.monttrek.com). Monterrey's Rocódromo and Uquia are the most popular spots.

Appendix A:
Peru in Depth

When Francisco Pizarro, the Spanish conquistador, and his fortune-hunting cronies descended on Peru in 1528, they discovered not only vast riches, but also a highly sophisticated culture. The Spaniards soon overpowered the awed and politically weakened Inca Empire, but they didn't find the Incas' greatest secret: the imperial city of Machu Picchu, hidden high in the Andes. Machu Picchu, finally revealed to the world in 1911 by a Yale historian, is acclaimed as the pinnacle achievement of the continent's pre-Columbian societies, yet it is only one of the exhilarating discoveries that await you in Peru.

The Incas left behind numerous examples of their exquisite stone architecture and eye for unparalleled natural settings, but a long line of equally advanced cultures preceded the relatively short-lived Inca Empire. Over several thousand years, civilizations up and down the South Pacific coast and deep in the highlands developed ingenious irrigation systems, created sophisticated pottery and weaving techniques, and built great pyramids, temples, fortresses, and cities of adobe. Early peoples constructed mysterious cylindrical towers and the even more enigmatic Nasca Lines, giant drawings of animals and symbols somehow etched into the desert plains for eternity. Peru's fascinating history is in evidence everywhere: in open graves with bits and pieces of ancient textiles; in mortarless Inca stones that serve as foundations for colonial churches; and in traditional dress, foods, and festivals, as well as Andean customs and beliefs that reveal a country and a people very much rooted in its past.

Peru has a habit of turning virtually every visitor into an amateur archaeologist. Ruins fire the imagination, and outstanding museum collections tell an intricate tale of complex cultures through ceramics, spectacular textiles, and remarkably preserved mummies. You can see the Lord of Sipán in all the glory of the jewels and rituals that accompanied his burial, and the frozen corpse of Juanita the Ice Maiden, an Inca princess sacrificed on a mountain ridge more than 500 years ago. And yet, with so many temples and burial sites still being unearthed, and ruins found in remote jungle regions, Peru still has the rare feeling of a country in the 21st century that hasn't been exhaustively explored or overrun with tourists.

Peru's recent sufferings—2 decades of political mayhem, kidnappings, and assassinations by homegrown Maoist terrorists, cocaine trafficking, and violent street crime—have made international headlines. In the late 1980s and early '90s, Peruvians fled Lima and the countryside, and understandably few foreigners were brave enough to plan vacations in Peru. Many Peruvians are now hopeful that the country has finally turned a corner. It remains desperately poor, but Peru is suddenly safer and more welcoming than it has been in many, many years. In 2001, Peruvians elected a new president, the first with Amerindian roots, who rose from humble beginnings as a shoeshine boy. Too many years of corrupt politicians, lawlessness, and economic disarray clouded but never managed to eclipse the beauty and proud traditions of this vital and alluring Andean nation.

1 A Look at the Past

First inhabited as many as 20,000 years ago, Peru was the cradle of several of the most ancient and sophisticated pre-Columbian civilizations in the Americas. The Chavín, Paracas, Nasca, Huari, Moche, and Incas, among others, form a long line of complicated, occasionally overlapping, and frequently warring, cultures stretching back to 2000 B.C. Before the Incas, two other civilizations, the Chavín and the Huari-Tiahuanaco, achieved pan-Andean empires. Most of what is known about pre-Columbian cultures is based on the unearthing of temples and tombs because none possessed a written language. Further complicating matters is the fact that, as one culture succeeded a previous one, it imposed its values and social structure on the vanquished but also assimilated features useful to it, making distinction among some early cultures exceedingly difficult.

Early societies were located mainly in the coastal areas and highlands. Many fell victim to warfare, cyclical floods, extended drought, and earthquakes. Evidence of pivotal pre-Columbian cultures—including ruined temples; spectacular collections of ceramics, masks, and jewelry; and tombs found with well-preserved mummies—is everywhere in Peru, and some sites are only now being excavated and combed for clues.

The first inhabitants are thought by most historians to have crossed the Bering Strait in Asia during the last ice age, worked their way across the Americas, and settled the region circa 20,000 B.C. (though this migratory pattern has been disputed by some scholars). They were nomadic hunter-gatherers who lived along the central and northern coasts. The Pikimachay cave, which dates to 12,000 B.C., is the oldest site in Peru. The earliest human remains, discovered near Huánaco in

Dateline

* **20,000–10,000 B.C.** The earliest settlers, most likely migrants from Asia, arrive.
* **3000 B.C.** Cotton is first cultivated in Peru.
* **1000 B.C.** Rise of Chavín cult in the central Andes.
* **900 B.C.** Establishment of Chavín de Huántar.
* **700 B.C.** Rise of Paracas culture in the southern desert.
* **300 B.C.–A.D. 700** Rise of Nasca culture; Nasca Lines drawn.
* **100 B.C.** Earliest burials at Paracas Necropolis.
* **A.D. 200** Consolidation of Moche dynasty in northern Peru.
* **ca. 300** Burial of Lord of Sipán.
* **375–500** Rise of the Huari-Tiahuanaco empire.
* **900** Lambayeque and Cajamarca cultures appear in the northern Andes.
* **1000** Appearance of the Chimú culture.
* **1150** Construction of Chan Chan begins.
* **1200** Chimú and Chancay cultures established; Manco Cápac becomes the first Inca (emperor) and founds Inca Empire.
* **1300** Ica-Chincha culture flourishes in south-central Peru.
* **1350** Inca Roca (6th Inca) establishes Cusco dynasty.
* **1375** Chimú takeover of Moche territory.
* **1400** Tschudi Palace at Chan Chan built.
* **1438** Reign of the Inca Pachacútec; Sacsayhuamán & Machu Picchu are built.
* **1460** Inca conquest of southern desert coast.
* **1465** Incas dominate the territory from the northern Andes to Ecuador.
* **1527** Epidemic of smallpox fells the Inca Huayna Cápac. Before his death, the Inca divided the empire in two, giving the northern territory to his son Atahualpa, and the southern half to his other son, Huáscar. Civil war ensues.

continues

highland Peru, are circa 7000 B.C. Early Peruvians were responsible for cave paintings at Toquepala (Tacna, 7000 B.C.) and houses in Chilca (Lima, 5000 B.C.).

PRE-INCA CULTURES

Over the course of nearly 15 centuries, pre-Inca cultures settled principally along the Peruvian coast and highlands. Around 6000 B.C., the Chinchorro people along the southern desert coast mummified their dead, long before the ancient Egyptians had thought of it. By the first century B.C., during what is known as the Formative, or Initial, Period, Andean society had designed sophisticated irrigation canals and produced the first textiles and decorative ceramics. Another important advance was the specialization of labor, aided in large part by the development of a hierarchical society.

The earliest known Peruvian civilization was the **Chavín culture** (1200–400 B.C.), a theocracy that worshipped a feline, jaguar-like god and settled in present-day Huántar, Ancash (central Peru). Over 8 centuries, the Chavín, who never developed into a military or mercantilistic empire, unified groups of peoples across Peru. The most spectacular remnant of this culture, known for its advances in stone carving, pottery, weaving, and metallurgy, is the Chavín de Huántar temple, 40km (25 miles) east of Huaraz. The ceremonial center, a place of pilgrimage, contained wondrous examples of religious carving, such as the Tello Obelisk and the Raimondi Stella. The temple demonstrates evidence of sophisticated engineering and division of labor.

A subsequent society, the **Paracas** culture (700 B.C.–A.D. 200), took hold along the southern coast. It is renowned today for its superior textile weaving, considered perhaps the finest example of pre-Columbian textiles in the Americas. The Paracas peoples were sophisticated enough to dare to practice trepanation, a form of brain

*1530 Francisco Pizarro's third expedition leaves Panama and arrives in Tumbes.

*1532 Atahualpa defeats his brother to gain control of the Inca Empire. Pizarro enters Cajamarca and captures Atahualpa, whom he jails. Atahualpa offers ransom of gold and silver to win his release.

*1533 Spaniards assassinate Atahualpa and name Topa Hualpa his successor (who serves as puppet Inca); Cusco is sacked and burned by Spaniards.

*1535 Francisco Pizarro establishes Lima and makes it the capital of the Viceroyalty of Peru.

*1541 Francisco Pizarro is killed in Lima.

*1572 Tupac Amaru, the last Inca emperor, is captured and executed.

*1780 Tupac Amaru II, an Indian noble who claims to be descended from the final Inca emperor, leads a failed revolt against Spanish.

*1821 General José de San Martín captures Lima and proclaims Peru's independence.

*1824 Peru defeats Spain and becomes the last colony in Latin America to gain its independence.

*1836–39 Peru and Bolivia join together in a short-lived confederation.

*1849–74 Chinese workers numbering up to 100,000 arrive in Peru as menial laborers.

*1866 Peru wins a brief war with Spain.

*1870s The rubber boom in the Peruvian Amazon begins.

*1879–83 Chile defeats Peru and Bolivia in the War of the Pacific; Peru loses southern territory to Chile.

*1884 Treaty of Ancón gives Chile the Peruvian province of Tarapaca.

*1924 Victor Raúl Haya de la Torre sets up the nationalist American Revolutionary Popular Alliance (APRA) in exile in Mexico.

*1941 Peru goes to war with Ecuador over the northern Amazon; the border dispute results in the 1942 treaty of Rio de Janeiro, which gives the land to Peru.

*1945 Civilian government led by center-left APRA assumes power after free elections.

*1948 A coup d'état installs a military government led by General Manuel Odría.

surgery that consisted of drilling holes in the skull to cure various ailments and correct cranial deformation.

The Classical period (A.D. 200–1100) was one of significant social and technological development. Likely descendants of the Paracas, the Moche and Nasca cultures are among the best studied in pre-Columbian Peru. The **Moche** (or **Mochica**) civilization (A.D. 200–700), one of the first true urban societies, dominated the valleys of the north coast near Trujillo and conquered a number of smaller groups in building their widespread empire. The Moche were a highly organized hierarchical civilization that created extraordinary adobe platform complexes, such as the Temples of the Sun and Moon near Trujillo (the former was the largest man-made structure of its day in the Americas), and the burial site of Sipán, near Chiclayo, where the remains and riches of the famous Lord of Sipán, a religious and military authority, were unearthed in remarkably preserved royal tombs. Moche pottery, produced from molds, contains vital clues to their way of life, down to very explicit sexual representations. Its frank depictions of phalluses, labia, and non-traditional bedroom practices may strike some visitors as pre-Columbian pornography.

The **Nasca** culture (A.D. 300–800) established itself along the coastal desert south of Lima. Nasca engineers created outstanding underground aqueducts, which permitted agriculture in one of the most arid regions on earth, and its artisans introduced polychrome techniques in pottery. But the civilization is internationally known for the enigmatic **Nasca Lines,** geometric and animal symbols etched indelibly into the desert, elements of an agricultural and astronomical calendar that are so vast that they can only really be appreciated from the window of an airplane.

* **1963** Peru returns to civilian rule; Fernando Belaúnde Terry becomes the president.
* **1968** The civilian government is ousted in coup led by General Juan Velasco Alvarado.
* **1969** Large-scale land reform and nationalization programs are initiated.
* **1970** A disastrous landslide kills 20,000 in Yungay (Ancash).
* **1975** Velasco is ousted in coup led by General Morales Bermúdez.
* **1980** Peru returns to civilian rule with the re-election of Fernando Belaúnde. Maoist terrorist organization, the Sendero Luminoso (Shining Path), and a smaller group, Tupac Amaru (MRTA), launch armed guerrilla struggle.
* **1981** Peru enters into border war with Ecuador over Cordillera del Cóndor (in Peruvian possession, according to the 1942 protocol).
* **1982** Debt crisis; deaths and "disappearances" escalate following military crackdown on guerrillas and drug traffickers.
* **1985** APRA candidate Alan García Pérez wins the presidency with promises to rid Peru of its military and police "old guard." Belaúnde becomes the first elected president to turn over power to a constitutionally elected successor since 1945.
* **1987** New Libertad movement led by Mario Vargas Llosa, Peru's best-known novelist, blocks plans to nationalize banks.
* **1988** Hyperinflation and bankruptcy rock Peru; the country seeks assistance from International Monetary Fund. Shining Path's guerrilla bombing and assassination campaign intensifies.
* **1990** Human rights groups estimate as many as 10,000 political murders (including thousands of *campesinos*) in Peru. Alberto Fujimori, son of Japanese immigrants, runs on anticorruption platform and defeats the novelist Mario Vargas Llosa for the presidency. Fujimori institutes severe austerity measures and privatization programs.
* **1992** Citing continued terrorism, drug trafficking, and corruption, Fujimori dissolves Congress, suspends the Peruvian constitution, and imposes

continues

The **Huari** (also spelled Wari) culture (A.D. 600–1100), an urban society that was the first in Peru to pursue explicitly expansionist goals through military conquest, settled the south-central sierra near Ayacucho. Along with the **Tiahuanaco** people, with whom they shared a central god figure, they came to dominate the Andes, with an empire spreading all the way to Chile and Bolivia. Both cultures achieved superior agricultural technology, in the form of canal irrigation and terraces.

Separate regional cultures, the best known of which is the **Chimú** culture (A.D. 700), developed and thrived over the next 4 centuries. The Chimú, adroit metallurgists and architects, built the citadel of Chan Chan, a compound of royal palaces and the largest adobe city in the world, near the northern coastal city Trujillo. The Chimú were the dominant culture in Peru prior to the arrival and expansion of the Incas, and they initially represented a great northern and coastal rivalry to the Incas. Other cultures that thrived during the same period were the **Chachapoyas,** who constructed the impressive Kuélap fortress in the northern highlands, the **Ica** (or **Chincha**) south of Lima, and the *altiplano* (high plains) groups that built the finely crafted *chullpa* towers near Puno and Lake Titicaca. The Sicán, or Lambayeque, culture, which built great temple sites and buried its dead with extraordinary riches, fell to the Chimú near the end of the 14th century. The Chimú themselves were in turn conquered by the Incas.

THE INCA EMPIRE

Though Peru is likely to be forever synonymous with the Incas, who built the spectacular city of Machu Picchu high in the Andes and countless other great palaces and temples, the society was merely the last in a long line of pre-Columbian cultures. The Inca Empire (1200–1532) was relatively

censorship. Shining Path leader Abimael Guzmán is arrested and sentenced to life in prison.

*1993 A new constitution is adopted, allowing Fujimori to seek re-election.

*1994 6,000 Shining Path guerrillas surrender to authorities.

*1995 Fujimori is re-elected to a second term. Fighting erupts again along border with Ecuador.

*1996 Tupac Amaru guerrillas seize 490 hostages at the residence of the Japanese ambassador. An American woman, Lori Berenson, is convicted of treason by a secret military court and sentenced to life in prison (reduced to 20 years in 2001) for plotting with the Tupac Amaru Revolutionary Movement.

*1997 Peruvian special forces launch an attack and free hostages held at the Japanese ambassador's residence. El Niño—the worst of the century—causes severe drought in Peru.

*1999 Ecuador and Peru sign treaty ending 6 decades of dispute over a section of the Amazon.

*2000 Fujimori re-elected by landslide to a third 5-year term; opponent, Alejandro Toledo, charges fraud and withdraws from the election. Scandal erupts when Fujimori's chief of intelligence, Vladimiro Montesinos, is caught on videotape attempting to bribe an opposition politician. Fujimori, fending off charges of embezzlement and government drug trafficking, goes into exile in Japan. Peruvian Congress declares Fujimori "morally unfit" to govern; it swears in Valentín Paniagua as interim president.

*2001 A Peruvian judge orders Fujimori to appear in court on charges of dereliction of duty. Alejandro Toledo becomes Peru's first president of native Indian origin. Holds ceremony at Machu Picchu. Massive earthquake rocks Arequipa and southern Peru. In December, a fireworks explosion in downtown Lima ignites a horrific fire that kills 290 people.

*2002 Peruvian authorities issue new international arrest warrant seeking to extradite former president Fujimori from Japan to face charges of corruption and human rights abuses in Peru. A Shining Path car bomb kills 9 people outside of the U.S. embassy in Lima.

short lived, but it remains the best documented of all Peruvian civilizations. Though the height of its power lasted for little more than a century, the Inca Empire extended throughout the Andes, all the way from present-day Colombia down to Chile—a stretch of more than 5,635km (3,500 miles). At its apex, the Inca Empire's reach was longer than even that of the Romans.

The Incas were a naturalistic and ritualistic people who worshipped the sun god Inti and the earth goddess Pachamama, as well as the moon, thunder, lightning, and the rainbow, all regarded as deities. The Inca emperors were believed to be direct descendants of the sun god. The bold Andes mountains were at least as important an element in their system of beliefs: The dwelling places of respected spirits, the 7,000m (22,960-ft.) peaks were the sites of human sacrifices. The Incas founded Cusco, the sacred city and capital of the Inca Empire (which they called Tahuantinsuyo, or Land of Four Quarters). The ruling sovereign was properly called the Inca, but today, the term also refers to the people and the empire.

The Incas' Andean dominance was achieved through formidable organization and a highly developed economic system. The Incas rapidly expanded their empire first through political alliances and absorption, and then by swift military conquest. Though the Incas imposed their social structure and way of life, they also assimilated useful skills and practices, even granting administrative positions to defeated nobles of the Chimú and other cultures. The Incas thus succeeded in achieving political and religious unification across most of their domain.

The Incas recorded an astounding level of achievement. They never developed a system of writing, but they kept extraordinary records with an accounting system of knots on strings, called *quipus*. They laid a vast network of roadways, nearly 32,200km (20,000 miles) total across the difficult territory of the Andes, connecting cities, farming communities, and religious sites. A network of runners, called *chasquis,* operated on the roads, relaying messages and even transporting foodstuffs from the coast to the Andes. *Tambos,* or way stations, dotted the highways, serving as inspection points and shelters for relay runners. The Inca Trail was a sacred highway, connecting the settlements in the Urubamba Valley to the ceremonial center, Machu Picchu.

The Incas' agricultural techniques were exceedingly skilled and efficient, with advanced irrigation systems and soil conservation. The Incas were also extraordinary architects and unparalleled stonemasons. Inca ruins reveal splendid landscaping and graceful construction of perfectly cut stones and terraces on inaccessible sites with extraordinary views of valleys and mountains.

A rigid hierarchy and division of labor ruled Inca society. At the top, just below the Inca sovereign (who was also the chief military and religious figure and considered a descendant of the sun), was the ruling elite: nobles and priests. Tens of thousands of manual laborers provided the massive manpower necessary to construct temples and palaces throughout the empire. The Inca kept chosen maidens, or Virgins of the Sun (*acllas*), who serviced him and Inca nobles.

Extraordinarily tight community organization was replicated across the empire. At the heart of the structure was the Inca's clan, the *panaca,* composed of relatives and descendants. Spanish conquistadors chronicled a dynasty that extended to 12 rulers, from **Manco Cápac,** the empire's founder in 1200 who was said to have risen out of Lake Titicaca, to **Atahualpa,** whose murder in Cajamarca by Spanish conquerors spelled the end of the great power.

The Inca **Pachacútec** ruled from 1438 to 1463, and he is considered the great builder of Inca civilization. Under his rule, Cusco was rebuilt, and some of the

Inca Architecture & Stonemasonry

Much of Peru's greatest architecture, it has to be said, lies in ruins. However, the civilizations that predated the arrival of the Spanish conquistadors were incredibly sophisticated engineers, stonemasons, and architects. The Moche, Sicán, and other cultures built great temples, including some that were the largest man-made structures in the Americas. But it was the Incas, the best-documented pre-Columbian culture in South America and the one that would ultimately succumb to the Spaniards, who left an astounding legacy of innovative building.

Evidence abounds in Peru of superior Inca building techniques. Chief among their architectural prowess is the massive system of roads that crisscrossed the entire empire. Nearly 32,200km (20,000 miles), of which the Inca Trail from the Sacred Valley to Machu Picchu is undoubtedly the most famous stretch, extended from Chile and Bolivia, through the mountainous Andean terrain, and all the way to Quito.

The Incas may not have invented the system of building with huge, mortarless stones or of constructing agricultural terraces on steeply inclined mountainsides, but it is fair to say they perfected it. They also mastered the art of craftily inserting structures—whether citadels, ceremonial temples or palaces—into the nature they so revered. Machu Picchu is perhaps the finest example of this remarkable environmentally sensitive architecture, but it is by no means the only one. Great agricultural terracing can be seen at Ollantaytambo, Moray, and Pisac.

Two of the finest examples of the Incas' ability to construct walls from perfectly integrated, massive stones are the zigzagged defensive walls at Sacsayhuamán and the exquisitely tapered, curved exterior at Qoricancha in Cusco. Visitors who run their hands along the smooth,

most brilliant examples of Inca architecture were erected, including Cusco's Qoricancha (Temple of the Sun), the Ollantaytambo and Sacsayhuamán fortresses, and of course, the famed religious city of Machu Picchu. Pachacútec also initiated the empire's expansion. It was Pachacútec's successor, **Tupac Yupanqui** (1463–93), however, who achieved dominance from Ecuador to Chile. A great conqueror, he defeated his Chimú rivals in northern Peru.

After the death of the Inca **Huayna Cápac** in 1525, civil war ensued, brought on by the empire splitting between his two sons, Atahualpa and Huáscar. The Spaniards, arriving in northern Peru in 1532, found a severely weakened empire—a pivotal reason the Incas so swiftly succumbed to a small band of invading Spaniards. Another key was the Spaniards' superior military technology. Against cannons and cavalry, the Incas' slings, battle-axes, and cotton-padded armor stood little chance. But their defeat remains puzzling to most visitors to Peru, not to mention many scholars.

SPANISH CONQUEST & COLONIALISM

Columbus and his cohorts landed in the Americas in 1492, and by the 1520s, the Spanish conquistadors had reached South America. Francisco Pizarro led an expedition along Peru's coast in 1528. Impressed with the riches of the Inca Empire, he returned to Spain and succeeded in raising money and seamless edges are amazed to discover that such immense and perfectly carved stones, many with beveled edges and some as large as highway tollbooths, simply *fit* together. Some stones were "female" receptors, others "males" with protruding parts: They fit together like a jigsaw puzzle. Inca workers moved these incredible blocks with no machinery, of course, and carved them with only rudimentary tools (none made of iron). As stonemasons, the Incas were peerless. Their architectural achievements, at once formidable and delicate, are mind-boggling.

How did they do it? Well, no one is sure, which is why all kinds of fantastical theories—including the use of magic herbs or the sun to dissolve the stones or even extraterrestrials to raise them—have long circulated to explain the apparently inexplicable. Peter Frost, in his book *Exploring Cusco,* presents interesting theories (complete with sketches) of how the Incas may have lifted and moved such extraordinary stones. He suggests that the Incas' massive and extremely well-organized work force used inclined planes, levers, and wedges to patiently manipulate stone, dragging enormous blocks of granite over long distances and up ramps. Frost delves into technical discussions of horizontal or load-bearing joins, but much of the Incas' technique was ingeniously low-tech. Extensive teams of men used smaller stones to exhaustively pound and smooth the surfaces of the huge building blocks. In addition to Frost's guide, more information is available from **Rutahsa Adventures** (www.rutahsa.com/incaarch.html) and from Susan A. Niles's *The Shape of Inca History: Narrative & Architecture in an Andean Empire* (University of Iowa Press, 1999).

recruiting men for a return expedition. In 1532, Pizarro made his return to Peru overland from Ecuador. After founding the first Spanish city in Peru, San Miguel de Piura, near the Ecuadorian border, he advanced upon the northern highland city of Cajamarca, an Inca stronghold. There, a small number of Spanish troops—about 180 men and 30 horses—cunningly captured the Inca emperor Atahualpa. The emperor promised to pay a king's ransom of gold and silver for his release, offering to fill his cell several times over, but the Spaniards, having received warning of an advancing Inca army, executed the emperor in 1533. It was a catastrophic blow to an already weakened empire.

Pizarro and his men massacred the Inca army, estimated at between 5,000 and 6,000 warriors. The Spaniards installed a puppet Inca, Tupac Huallpa, the brother of Huáscar who had died while Atahualpa was being held. They then marched on Cusco, capturing the capital city on November 15, 1533, and emptying the Sun Temple of its golden treasures. After the death of Tupac Huallpa en route, a new puppet was appointed, Manco Inca.

Pizarro founded the coastal city of Lima 2 years later, which became the capital of the new colony, the Viceroyalty of Peru. The Spanish crown appointed Spanish-born viceroys the rulers of Peru, but Spaniards battled amongst themselves for control of Peru's riches, and the remaining Incas continued to battle the conquistadors. A great siege was laid to Cusco in 1536, with Manco Inca and his brothers directing the rebellion from Sacsayhuamán. Pizarro was assassinated in 1541, and the indigenous insurrection ended with the beheading of Manco Inca, who had escaped to Vilcabamba, deep in the jungle, in 1544. Inca Tupac Amaru led a rebellion in 1572, but also failed and was killed.

Over the next 2 centuries, Lima gained in power and prestige at the expense of the old Inca capital and became the foremost colonial city of the Andean nations. The Peruvian viceroyalty stretched all the way from Panama to Tierra del Fuego. Cusco focused on cultural pursuits and became the epicenter of the Cusco School of painting (Escuela Cusqueña), which incorporated indigenous elements into Spanish styles, in the 16th and 17th centuries.

INDEPENDENT PERU

By the 19th century, grumbling over high taxes and burdensome Spanish controls grew in Peru, as it did in most colonies in the Americas. After liberating Chile and Argentina, José de San Martín set his sights north on Lima in 1821 and declared it an independent nation the same year. Simón Bolívar, the other hero of independence on the continent, came from the other direction. His successful campaigns in Venezuela and Colombia led him south to Ecuador and finally Peru. Peru won its independence from Spain after crucial battles in late 1824. Though Peru mounted its first civilian government, defeat by Chile in the War of the Pacific (1879–83) left Peru in a dire economic position.

Several military regimes ensued, and Peru finally returned to civilian rule in 1895. Land-owning elites dominated this new "Aristocratic Republic." In 1911, the Yale historian Hiram Bingham happened upon the ruins of the imperial city Machu Picchu—a discovery that would begin to unravel the greatness of the Incas and forever associate Peru with the last of its pre-Columbian civilizations.

Peru went to war with Ecuador over a border dispute (just one of several long-running border conflicts) in 1941. Though the 1942 Treaty of Rio de Janeiro granted the area north of the River Marañón to Peru, Ecuador would continue to claim the territory until the end of the 20th century.

2 Modern Peru

Peru's recent political history has been a turbulent mix of military dictatorships, coups d'état, and several disastrous civilian governments, engendering a near-continual cycle of instability.

Peru shook off the mantle of 2 decades of dictatorship in 1945 after a free election (the first in many decades) of José Luis Bustamante y Rivero. Bustamante served for just 3 years. General Manuel A. Odría led a coup and installed a military regime in 1948. In 1963, Peru returned to civilian rule, with Fernando Belaúnde Terry as president. The armed forces overthrew Belaúnde in 1968, but the new military regime (contrary to other right-leaning dictatorships in Latin America) expanded the role of the state, nationalized a number of industries, and instituted agrarian reform. The land-reform initiatives failed miserably. Re-elected in 1980, Belaúnde and his successor, Alan García (1985–90), faced hyperinflation, nationwide strikes, and two guerrilla movements—the Maoist *Sendero Luminoso* (Shining Path) and the Tupac Amaru Revolutionary Movement (MRTA)—that produced violence and terror throughout the late 1980s and early '90s. Meanwhile, Peru's role on the production end of the international cocaine trade grew exponentially.

García, who made a point of refusing to pay Peru's external debt (which prompted both the IMF and World Bank to cut off support), fled into exile after being charged with embezzling millions. With the economy in ruins and the government in chaos, Alberto Fujimori, the son of Japanese immigrants, defeated the Peruvian novelist Mario Vargas Llosa and became president in 1990. Fujimori campaigned on promises to fix the ailing economy and root out terrorist guerrillas, and in 1992, his government succeeded in arresting key members of both the MRTA and the Shining Path (catapulting the president to unprecedented popularity). Fujimori suddenly became authoritarian, however, shutting down Congress in 1992, suspending the constitution, and decreeing an emergency government that he effectively ruled as dictator. His austerity measures got Peru on the right track economically, though, with reforms leading to widespread privatizations, growth of 7%, and a drop in inflation from more than 10,000% annually to about 20%, so many Peruvians were reluctantly accepting of Fujimori's distaste for democracy.

Fujimori pushed to get the constitution amended so that he could run for successive terms, and he was re-elected in 1995, soundly defeating former United Nations Secretary General Javier Pérez de Cuellar. That same year, Peru briefly entered into armed conflict with Ecuador over the decades-old border dispute, though in 1999 Ecuador finally accepted the Rio de Janeiro treaty and the borders as established in 1942.

Most international observers denounced the announced 2000 presidential election results after Fujimori's controversial run-off with Alejandro Toledo, a newcomer from a poor Indian family. Public outcry forced Fujimori to call new elections, but he escaped into exile in Japan and resigned the presidency in late 2000 after a corruption scandal involving his shadowy intelligence chief, Vladimiro Montesinos. Videotape of Montesinos bribing a congressman and subsequent investigations (including a daily barrage of secret videotapes broadcast on national television) revealed a government so thoroughly corrupt that it was itself involved in the narcotics trade it was ostensibly stamping out. Fujimori, who remains in Japan (where he also has citizenship), was discovered to have funneled at least $12 million to private offshore accounts. Montesinos escaped to Venezuela, where he was harbored by the government until he was found and returned to Peru for imprisonment.

Toledo, who most observers believe would have won the 2000 election, ran again in 2001 and, amazingly, entered into a run-off with Alan García, who—though disgraced only a few years earlier—had dared to return from exile to run for the presidency. Toledo, a former shoeshine boy who went on to teach at Harvard and become a World Bank economist, won the election and became Peru's first president of the 21st century in July 2001, formally accepting the post at Machu Picchu. Also in 2001, the U.S. State Department Human Rights Report named Peru among the success stories of the year, praising the country for meeting international standards for free elections and addressing past abuses and corruption under the Fujimori administration.

PERU TODAY

Peru, the third largest country in South America (after Brazil and Argentina), is vastly undervalued as a travel destination. It receives, in its best year, only a million or so visitors. But with spectacular Andes mountains and highland culture, a section of Amazon rain forest second only to Brazil, one of the richest arrays of wildlife in the world, and some of the Americas' greatest ruins of pre-Columbian cultures, Peru deserves to be experienced by so many more people.

Terrorism in Peru

The unprecedented waves of violence that rocked Peru in the late 1980s and early '90s were not a result of cocaine drug trafficking. The violence, which killed as many as 30,000 Peruvians and created a climate of fear across the country, was brought on by small but highly effective, home-grown terrorist groups and the militaristic campaigns by the government to root them out. It made for a highly volatile, perilous situation.

The best-known and largest of Peru's two principal insurgency networks was the **Sendero Luminoso** (or Shining Path). A Maoist terrorist group formed in the late 1960s by a university professor named Abimael Guzmán, the Sendero Luminoso sought nothing less than the destruction of Peruvian institutions. It sought to restructure Peru along the lines of a peasant revolutionary regime. To achieve a peasant, or Amerindian socialist system, the Sendero Luminoso tried to create a rural-based insurgency, appropriating key elements of Indian heritage rather than political ideology to win support.

The government's campaign to identify and destroy the Sendero Luminoso was often just as ruthless as that of the terrorists. As many as half of the terrorism-related deaths are estimated by human rights organizations to have come at the hands of the police and special forces. Yet the government got its man, capturing Guzmán in September 1992 and striking a mortal blow to the Sendero Luminoso. Other leaders were arrested in 1995; defections and an amnesty program further weakened the group. Guzmán himself requested a peace accord from prison in 1995. The group was dormant and considered defunct by many international observers until 2001, when the U.S. State Department warned of a resurgence of activity, supported by the drug trade, in the Upper Huallaga jungle and other rural areas. In late 2001, the Peruvian Interior Ministry announced that it had stopped a planned attack on the U.S. embassy in Lima.

The Sendero Luminoso was a brutal enemy of the state and considered one of the most violent terrorist organizations in the world. It bombed institutions in Peru—from courthouses to diplomatic missions (including the U.S. embassy)—and carried out assassinations. At its height, the Sendero Luminoso was thought to have about 2,000 armed militants and a significant base of support, particularly in rural areas. Its actions resulted in the deaths of more than 10,000 Peruvian nationals since its violent campaign began in 1980. Based in the rural area around Ayacucho, by the late 1980s, the Sendero Luminoso was very active in urban areas in Peru.

In 1990, Alberto Fujimori ran in part on a campaign to eradicate the terrorist network. As president, he won a provision for emergency rule, which resulted in the capture of what the government claimed was 2,500 Sendero Luminoso terrorists. Guzmán (aka Comrade Gonzalo), the brains and spiritual heart of the operation, was sentenced to life in prison along with 100 fellow terrorists.

A smaller terrorist organization operating in Peru was called the **Movimiento Revolucionario Tupac Amaru,** known by its Spanish-language acronym MRTA. Taking the name of an Indian who led a rebellion against Spanish colonizers in the 18th century, the Marxist-Leninist revolutionary movement formed in 1984. It hoped to establish a Marxist regime and rid Peru of imperialist influences. In 1987, it launched a campaign of armed struggle against the government of Alan García. For most of its life, MRTA was much less violent and less organized than the Sendero Luminoso. It orchestrated several atten-tion-getting episodes, such as stealing from supermarkets and distrib-uting free food in poor neighborhoods, prison escapes, and takeovers of foreign press offices, though it was also responsible for a few dozen killings, bombings, and kidnappings.

Before a majority of the organization's militants was imprisoned, MRTA was estimated to have between 300 and 600 members and have operated principally in the northern Amazon region. MRTA became known internationally for two episodes. In December 1996, an MRTA group seized the residence of the Japanese ambassador in Lima during a diplomatic reception, capturing 490 hostages. The group released many, but held 72 hostages—including the brother of President Fuji-mori, Peru's foreign minister, Supreme Court judges, members of Con-gress, and the ambassadors of Japan and Bolivia—until April 1997, when Fujimori ordered a violent raid on the embassy compound by Peruvian special forces. The raid freed the remaining hostages (though one died of heart failure) and killed all 14 MRTA militants, including the group's leader.

The other episode that brought MRTA into the international spot-light was the arrest of a 26-year-old U.S. citizen, Lori Berenson. A free-lance journalist, Berenson was said by the government to be a sympathizer and collaborator of MRTA. She was charged with helping to organize a plan to take over Congress, though Berenson said she was unaware that she was sharing a Lima house with MRTA militants and the bounty of guns and explosives they had hidden there. Convicted of treason in 1996 by a special military court of hooded judges and sen-tenced to life in prison, Berenson's term was later reduced to 20 years. An appeal for her release was denied in 2001. Along with the quiet support of the U.S. embassy in Lima, many organizations in the United States, who see Berenson not as a terrorist but as a human rights activist, continue to try to win her release, citing a wealth of nonstan-dard practices in her arrest and subsequent trials.

Coca Leaves

Coca leaves have been cultivated for thousands of years in Peru—their use by pre-Columbian civilizations dates back 4,000 years. The Incas held the coca plant sacred, restricting its use to nobles and priests. Evidence of coca cultivation and societal uses can be found in the ceramics of the Nasca and instruments of the Moche. Although coca leaves have long had important ritualistic uses in Andean society, they have also been widely masticated to lessen the effects of hunger and high altitude. Amerindian laborers who performed backbreaking tasks in post-Conquest Peru usually did so with coca leaves to spur them on (even though the Spaniards pounced on coca as a pagan element of anti-Christian worship and mysticism).

Campesinos in the Andes widely continue to chew coca leaves, mixed with saliva and lime or *quinua* (a grain) to form a wad called a *llipta* and to produce a dulling sensation in the mouth. Travelers routinely drink *mate de coca,* or coca-leaf tea, to help them deal with the effects of altitude. Coca is as pivotal a component of Andean Peru as tea is in India or Great Britain.

Coca-leaf consumption is not illegal in Peru, though some might expect it to be since coca is the raw material from which cocaine is derived. However, coca leaf contains just 1% of cocaine among its 14 alkaloids. Chemical processing of the leaves turns it into a hard paste (semi-refined cocaine). The refined product cocaine, which *is* illegal in Peru, is a very different animal, producing much different effects in the brain and body.

As the use of cocaine as a narcotic grew in the 1960s and demand in the United States skyrocketed during the '70s and '80s, cultivation of coca grew in Peru, principally on remote slopes of the eastern Andes. For poor farmers, coca was a welcome, revenue-producing crop. Easy to tend and producing as many as a half dozen harvests a year, coca was simply the raw material that others—in those days, Colombian drug lords—refined into cocaine and sold in rapidly growing markets in North America and Europe. Coca as an antidote to widespread rural poverty in rural Peru was not lost on either campesinos or the Peruvian government.

The U.S. Drug Enforcement Agency, in its celebrated but ineffectual war on drugs, focused its attempts to eradicate coca-growing fields in

Most know it only as the land of the Incas, symbolized by the mysteries of Machu Picchu, the famous lost city tucked high in the Andes. Yet Peru is littered with archaeological discoveries of many civilizations, from one end to another, highland to coast. Only a few years ago, a *National Geographic* team discovered Juanita the Ice Maiden, an Inca princess sacrificed on Mount Ampato more than 500 years ago. (Her frozen corpse is now exhibited in Arequipa.) Archaeologists have recently unearthed more than 2,000 extraordinarily well-preserved mummies from one of Peru's largest Inca burial sites, which was found under a shantytown on the outskirts of Lima. Other sites continue to be excavated; many visitors will be shocked to find bits of ancient textiles fluttering around recently opened burial tombs that may be 1,500 years old. Researchers are now calling

Peru (which had become the world's largest provider of cocaine raw materials), usually by strong-arming governments into cooperation. Many Peruvians viewed these efforts to destroy the fields of farmers who were growing a legal crop as a blatantly one-sided approach to the problem, as it did little to solve the problem of demand for cocaine. Such efforts show emphatic disregard for the traditional, religious, and ritualistic role of coca leaves in Peruvian society, which long predates the recent demand for cocaine in Western society. And the campaign is fraught with other problems. The United States believed it had an ally in former Peruvian president Alberto Fujimori—himself no stranger to strong-arm tactics—but it now appears that his government was itself secretly dealing in narco-trafficking, even as it reported its success in eradicating coca-producing fields in the Andes. Fujimori and his cohorts notwithstanding, Peru has never fielded a sophisticated network of drug lords and narco-traffickers, at least not to the extent that Colombia and Mexico have; like Bolivia, it has been much more restricted to a rudimentary role as provider of raw coca leaves. Still, coca was bringing in about $5 billion in annual revenues in Peru in the late 1980s.

Coca continues to serve ritualistic and medicinal purposes in Peru. Every August, villagers make offerings (called *pagos* or *pagapus*) to Pachamama, thanking her for blessing their crops, and the spirits (*Apus*) believed to dwell on mountaintops. Coca remains a sacred plant, one that mediates between the inner, spiritual world and the exterior world inhabited by man. It is a potent symbol of community spirit and respect. Coca leaves are chewed, dispensed from ritualistic pouches during festivals and ceremonies, and spread on blankets to predict the future. Even Pope John Paul II, on a visit to Bolivia, drank coca tea and acknowledged the deeply held respect for it by local peoples. It's one of the best short-term remedies to combat altitude sickness, so drink it liberally, but don't try to take coca leaves back home. Even the leaves are illegal in most North American and European countries, and if you're caught, you'll be treated almost as though you were smuggling cocaine—no matter how much you struggle to explain the difference.

Caral, a site in central Peru north of Lima, the oldest city in the Americas. It is believed to date to 2600 B.C., part of a sophisticated society contemporaneous with the Egyptian pyramids.

Peru is rich in artifacts and culture, but it remains very poor: More than half the population lives at or below the poverty line. The horrendous violence of the late 1980s and early '90s has now almost completely abated, and there are no areas where visitors should not feel welcome. Though the country is beset with economic difficulties, it appears to be entering a more hopeful period. The election of Alejandro Toledo in 2001 follows a disastrous period of sustained political crisis of corruption and scandal; Toledo hopes to attract new foreign investment and triple tourism receipts.

Peru remains a society dominated by elites. Toledo has labeled himself an "Indian rebel with a cause," alluding to his intent to recognize and support the nation's native Andean populations, or *cholos*. To both Peruvians and the international community, Toledo offers an encouraging symbol of hope. A more vivid example of social mobility than a shoeshine boy and son of peasants who goes on to Harvard and Stanford and wrestles the top office from a corrupt leader could not be written.

3 Peruvian People & Culture

SOCIETY
POPULATION

Peruvians are predominantly *mestizo* (of mixed Spanish and indigenous heritage) and Andean Indian, but the population is a true melting pot of ethnic groups. Significant minority groups of Afro-Peruvians (descendants of African slaves, living mainly in the coastal area south of Lima), immigrant Japanese and Chinese populations among the largest in South America, and smaller groups of European immigrants, including Italians and Germans, are among Peru's 28 million people. In the early days of the colony, Peruvian-born offspring of Spaniards were called *criollos*, though that term today refers mainly to coastal residents and Peruvian cuisine.

Peru has, after Bolivia and Guatemala, the largest population by percentage of Amerindians in Latin America. Perhaps half the country lives in the sierra, or highlands, and most of these people, commonly called *campesinos* (peasants), live in either small villages or rural areas. Descendants of Peru's many Andean indigenous groups in remote rural areas continue to speak the native languages Quechua (made an official language in 1975) and Aymara or other Amerindian tongues, and for the most part, they adhere to traditional regional dress. However, massive peasant migration to cities from rural highland villages has contributed to a dramatic weakening of indigenous traditions and culture across Peru. The new government of Alejandro Toledo, himself a proud *cholo*, or person of direct Andean Indian roots, has committed itself to a valorization and preservation of native language and traditions.

Nearly two-thirds of Peru is jungle, and the vast Amazon basin that pertains to Peru holds a phenomenal wealth of flora and fauna, but a dwindling human presence. Indigenous Amazonian tribes have been greatly reduced by centuries of disease, deforestation, and assimilation. There were once some six million people, 2,000 tribes and/or ethnic groups, and innumerable languages in the Amazon basin; today, the indigenous population is less than two million. Still, many traditions and languages have yet to be extinguished, especially deep in the jungle—though most visitors are unlikely to come into contact with groups of unadulterated, non-Spanish-speaking native peoples.

RELIGION

Peruvians are a predominantly Roman Catholic people (more than 90% claim to be Catholic), though Protestant evangelical churches have been winning converts, a fact that is worrisome to the Catholic Church. Animistic religious practices (worship of deities representing nature) inherited from the Incas and others have been incorporated into the daily lives of many Peruvians and can be seen in festivals and small individual rituals such as offerings of food and beverage to Pachamama, or Mother Earth.

ARTS & CULTURE
MUSIC & DANCE

Music and dance are fundamental to the very fabric of Peru, a fact to which the country's innumerable, colorful festivals will attest. Music and dance forms, like dress, vary greatly by region. Amerindian—altiplano and andina (highland)— music, played on wind instruments such as bamboo panpipes, *quena* flutes, bright-sounding and guitar-like *charangos,* and other instruments, is known the world over. It seems that wherever one goes, a Peruvian (or in some cases, Bolivian or Ecuadorian) band is playing panpipes in public places. I've stumbled upon Peruvian musicians from Krakow to Bali. The classic Andean highland tune, *El Cóndor Pasa,* adapted by Simon & Garfunkel in the 1970s, is world-famous. For many visitors, altiplano and highland versions of *música folclórica* are the very rhythm of Peru, but the country also beats to the sounds of *música criolla* (creole music based on a mix of European and African forms), bouncy-sounding *huayno* rhythms played by *orquestas típicas,* and Afro-Peruvian music, adapted from music brought by African slaves.

There is evidence of music in Peru dating back 10,000 years, and each region has its own distinct sounds and dance. Musical historians have identified more than 1,000 genres of music in Peru. Traditional instruments include quenas, *zampoñas, pututos* (trumpets made from seashells), and many other wind instruments crafted from cane, bone, horns, and precious metals, as well as a wide range of percussion instruments. Exposure to Western cultures has introduced new instruments such as the harp, violin, and guitar to Peruvian music. But Peruvian music can still be identified by its distinctive instruments, and there are many besides the basics of highland music.

The *cajón* is a classic percussion instrument, typical in música criolla and *música negra,* as well as *marinera.* A simple wooden box with a sound hole in the back, the cajón is played by a musician who sits on top and pounds the front like a bongo. The cajón has recently been introduced into flamenco music by none other than the legendary flamenco guitarist Paco de Lucía. Another classic Peruvian instrument is the **quena,** an Andean flute that dates to the pre-Columbian era. The best-known wind instrument in Peru, it's usually made out of bamboo, and it usually has five or six holes. Lengths vary to create different pitches. Another popular wind instrument is the **zampoña,** which belongs to the panpipe family and varies greatly in size. The zampoña is never absent at festivals in southern Peru, particularly Puno. String instruments are now fundamental in almost all música folclórica. The **charango,** very popular in the southern Andes, is like a small, high-pitched guitar with five or ten strings. Its resonance box is often crafted from an armadillo or *kirkincho* shell, though increasingly it's made of wood.

Music on the coast is very different from traditional Andean sounds. *Chicha* is a relatively new addition to the list of musical genres. A hybrid of sorts of the *huayno* (see below) and Colombian *cumbia,* chicha is an extremely popular urban dance, especially among the working class. It has spread rapidly across Peru and throughout Latin America. **Música criolla** mixes African and Spanish rhythms, with a taste of everything from the foxtrot to the tango, while **Afro-Peruvian** music, especially popular on the coast around Lima, is contemporary black popular music. It originated with African slaves in Peru but was long dormant before being revived in the 1950s and '60s. The music is soulful and powerful, with intoxicating dance rhythms. Nicomedes Santa Cruz, Susana Baca, and Peru Negro are among the style's greatest exponents. Baca in particular has made a big ripple in the so-called world-music scene in North America and Europe.

Dances associated with Afro-Peruvian music include lively and sensual **festejo** dances, in which participants respond to striking of the cajón, one of the Afro-Peruvian music's essential instruments. The *alcatraz* is an extremely erotic dance. Females enter the dance floor with tissue on their posteriors. The men, meanwhile, dance with lit candles. The not-so-subtle goal on the dance floor is for the man to light the woman's fire (and thus become her partner).

Peruvian tourism authorities produce a guide to festivities, music, and folk art, and it features a diagram of native dances in Peru. Especially up and down the coast, and in the central corridor of the Andes, the map is a bewildering maze of numbers indicating the indigenous dances practiced in given regions. Two dances, though, have become synonymous with Peru, the huayno and marinera.

The **huayno** is the essential dance in the Andes, with pre-Columbian origins fused with Western influences. Couples dancing the huayno perform sharp turns, hops, and tap-like *zapateos* to keep time. Huayno music is played on quena, charango, harp, and violin. The **marinera,** a sleek, sexy, and complex dance of highly coordinated choreography, is derivative of other folkloric dances in Peru, dating back to the 19th century. There are regional variations of the dance, which differs most from the south coast to the northern highlands. Dancers keep time with a handkerchief in one hand. Marinera music in Lima is performed by guitar and cajón, while a marching band is de rigeur in the north. Marinera festivals are held across Peru, but the most celebrated one is in Trujillo in January.

One of the most attention-getting dances in Peru, though, is that performed by **scissors dancers.** Their *danza de las tijeras* is an exercise in athleticism and balance. Dancers perform gymnastic leaps and daring stunts to the sounds of harp and violin. The main instrument played to accompany the dance is the pair of scissors, made up of two independent sheets of metal around 25 centimeters long. The best places to see scissors dancers are Ayacucho, Arequipa, and Lima.

FESTIVALS

Peruvian festivals are some of the most vibrant in the Americas and a highlight of virtually any visit. Though Peruvian festivals have serious foundations—the honoring of patron saints, fertility rituals, prayer, and celebration for harvests—festivals in Peru are colorful escapes for many Peruvians, especially in rural areas where life can be extremely difficult and poverty is widespread. Many festivals are solemn processions, but others are marked by intricate handmade costumes (sometimes involving as many as 16 different skirt layers), elaborate masks, and abundant food and alcoholic drinks (usually *chicha,* beer made from fermented maize), all of which fuel the revelry. A classic feature of many Andean festivals is the appearance of white-stocking-masked jesters called *ukukus* (bears). Symbolic guardians of Apu mountain spirits, ukukus maintain order during religious ceremonies, but they are also playful mischief-makers.

Any of the major festivals would be well worth planning your trip around, but perhaps none so much as **Inti Raymi.** The Festival of the Sun, the single most important feast of the Incas, is still celebrated on the winter solstice (the solar new year, June 24). The festival, once celebrated across the entire Inca Empire, was suppressed by the Catholic Church after the Spanish conquest. Inti Raymi was revived in the mid–20th century as an expression and valuation of native Indian culture in Peru by a group of intellectuals and artists in Cusco. Today, the religious ceremony has taken on colorful, theatrical (and some would say, touristy) proportions at the site of the Inca ruins of Sacsayhuamán. At the end of the ceremony, two llamas are sacrificed to predict the coming year.

See the "Peru Calendar of Events" in chapter 2 for details of some of Peru's most important and exciting festivals.

PERUVIAN TEXTILES

Woven textiles have to be considered among the great traditional arts of Peru. Peru has one of the most ancient and richest weaving traditions in the world; for more than 5,000 years, Peruvian artisans have used fine natural fibers for hand weaving, and the wool produced by alpacas, llamas, and vicuñas is some of the finest in the world, rarer even than cashmere. The most ancient textiles that have been found in Peru come from the Huaca Prieta temple in Chicama and are more than 4,000 years old. In pre-Columbian times, hand-woven textiles, which required extraordinary patience and skill, were prized and extremely valuable; distinctive textiles were indicators of social status and power. They were traded as commodities. Paracas, Huari, and Inca weavings are among the most sophisticated and artful ever produced in Peru. The Paracas designs were stunningly intricate, with detailed animals, human figures, and deities against dark backgrounds. Huari weaving features abstract figures and bold graphics. The Incas favored more minimalist designs, without embroidery. The finest Inca textiles were typically part of ritualistic ceremonies—many were burned as offerings to spirits.

While pre-Columbian civilizations in Peru had no written language, textiles were loaded with symbolic images that serve as indelible clues to the cultures and beliefs of textile artists. Worship of nature and spiritual clues are frequently represented by motifs in textiles. Many of the finest textiles unearthed were sacred and elaborately embroidered blankets that enveloped mummies in burial sites. Found in tombs in the arid coastal desert, one of the world's driest climates, the textiles are in many cases remarkably preserved.

Contemporary Peruvian artisans continue the traditions, sophisticated designs, and techniques of intricate weaving inherited from pre-Columbian civilizations—often employing the very same instruments used hundreds of years ago and still favoring natural dyes. The drop spindle (weaving done with a stick and spinning wooden wheel), for example, is still used in many regions, and it's not uncommon to see women and young girls spinning the wheel as they tend to animals in the fields. Excellent-quality woven items, the best of which are much more than mere souvenirs, include typical Andean *chullo* wool or alpaca hats with earflaps, ponchos, scarves, sweaters, and blankets.

4 Etiquette & Customs

APPROPRIATE ATTIRE   Many travelers to Peru are dressed head-to-toe in adventure or outdoor gear (parkas, fleece wear, hiking boots, and cargo pants). This is perfectly acceptable attire for all but the fanciest restaurants, where "neat casual" would be a better solution. In churches and monasteries, err on the side of discretion (tank tops and very short shorts or skirts are not usually acceptable).

AVOIDING OFFENSE   In Peru, you should be tactful when discussing local politics, though open discussion of the corruption of past presidents Fujimori and García and terrorism in Peru is perfectly acceptable and unlikely to engender heated debate. Discussion of drugs (and coca-plant cultivation) and religion should be handled with great tact. Visitors should understand that chewing coca leaves (or drinking coca tea) is not drug use, and is a longstanding cultural tradition in the Andes.

Tips **Watch Your Language**

The term *cholo* is often used to describe Peruvians of color and obvious Amerindian descent, usually those who have migrated from the highlands to the city. It is frequently employed as a derogatory and racist term by the Limeño population of European descent, but President Alejandro Toledo has claimed the term for himself and all *mestizos* (those of mixed race) of Peru, in an attempt to demonstrate pride in their common culture and to take the sting out of the term. Afro-Peruvians are more commonly called *morenos (-as)* or *negros (-as).* Using any of these terms can potentially be a complicated and charged matter for foreigners, especially those who have little experience in the country or fluency in the language. At any rate, it's best for *gringos* (foreigners; almost always *not* a derogatory term) simply to steer clear of such linguistic territory. It's better to refrain from making distinctions among races and colors than to risk offending someone.

In a country in which nearly half the population is Amerindian, expressing respect for native peoples is important. Try to refer to them not as *indios,* which is a derogatory term, but as *indígenas.* Many Peruvians refer to foreigners as *gringos* (or *gringas*) or the generic "mister," pronounced "*mee*-ster." Neither is intended or should be received as an insult.

On the streets of Cusco and other towns across Peru, shoeshine boys and little girls selling cigarettes or postcards can be very persistent and persuasive. Others just ask directly for money (using the euphemism *propinita,* or little tip). The best way to give money to those who are obviously in need of it is to reward them for their work. I get my scruffy shoes shined on a daily basis in Peru, and I buy postcards I probably don't need. If you don't wish to be hassled, a polite but firm *No, gracias* is usually sufficient, but it's important to treat even these street kids with respect.

Queries about one's marital status and children are considered polite; indeed, women traveling alone or with other women should expect such questions. However, discussion of how much one earns is a generally touchy subject, especially in a poor country such as Peru. Although Peruvians may be curious and ask you directly how much you make, or how much your apartment or house or car or even clothes cost, I'd suggest you deflect the question. At a minimum, explain how much higher the cost of living is in your home country, and how you're not as wealthy as you might seem. Ostentatious display of one's relative wealth is unseemly, even though Peru will be blissfully inexpensive to many budget travelers.

DINING & SHOPPING   Dinner is served later than in some countries, but not as late as in Spain. Nightclubs in large cities often don't get going until after midnight and many stay open until dawn. Many shops in large and small towns close at midday, from 1 to 3 or 2 to 4pm.

If you invite a Peruvian to have a drink or to dine with you, it is expected that you will pay (the Spanish verb *invitar* literally connotes this as an invitation). Do not suggest that a Peruvian acquaintance join you in what will certainly be an expensive restaurant or cafe for him or her and then pony up only half the tab.

Bargaining is considered acceptable in markets and with taxi drivers, and even hotels, but only up to a point—don't overdo it.

GESTURES   Peruvians are more formal in social relations than most North Americans and Europeans. Peruvians shake hands frequently and tirelessly, and while kissing on the cheek is a common greeting for acquaintances, it is not practiced among strangers (as it is in Spain, for example). Amerindian populations are more conservative and even shy; they don't kiss to greet one another, nor do they shake hands as frequently as other Peruvians; if they do, it is a light brush of the hand rather than a firm grip. Many Indians from small villages are reluctant to look a stranger in the eye.

Using your index finger to motion a person to approach you, as practiced in the United States and other places, is considered rude. A more polite way to beckon someone is to place the palm down and gently sweep your fingers toward you.

GREETINGS   When entering a shop or home, always use an appropriate oral greeting (*Buenos días,* or good day; *Buenas tardes,* or good afternoon; *Buenas noches,* or good night). Similarly, upon leaving it is polite to say goodbye, even to shop owners with whom you've had minimal contact (*Adios* or *Hasta luego*). Peruvians often shake hands upon leaving as well as greeting.

PHOTOGRAPHY   With their vibrant dress and expressive faces and festivals, Peruvians across the country make wonderful subjects for photographs. In some heavily touristed areas, such as the Sunday market in Pisac outside of Cusco, locals have learned to offer photo ops for a price at every turn. Some foreigners hand out money and candy indiscriminately, while others grapple with the unseemliness of paying for every photo. Asking for a tip in return for being the subject of a photograph is common in many parts of Peru; in fact, some locals patrol the streets with llamas and kids in tow to pose for photographs as their main source of income. Often, it's more comfortable to photograph people you have made an effort to talk to, rather than responding to those who explicitly beg to be your subject. I usually give a small tip (50 centavos–S/1) if it appears my camera has been an intrusion or nuisance, or especially if I've snapped several shots.

It's not common except in very touristed places (such as the Pisac market), but some young mothers carrying adorable children in knapsacks and with flowers in their hair (and outstretched hands requesting a *propinita,* or tip) aren't actually mothers (or at least, not the mothers of the children they're carrying around); to tug at your tourist heartstrings and pockets, they have essentially "rented" the babies from real moms in remote villages. I don't think it's an especially good idea to reward this practice. If a very young woman has several children in tow, all dolled up for pictures and making the rounds all afternoon, she is very likely one of these rent-a-moms.

Photographing military, police, or airport installations is strictly forbidden. Many churches, convents, and museums also do not allow photography or video.

PUNCTUALITY   Punctuality is not one of the trademarks of Peru or Latin America in general. Peruvians are customarily a half hour late to most personal appointments, and it is not considered very bad form to leave someone hanging in a cafe for up to an hour. It is expected, so if you have a meeting scheduled, unless a strict *hora inglesa* (English hour) is specified, be prepared to wait.

Appendix B:
Useful Terms & Phrases

1 Peruvian Spanish & Quechua

Peruvian Spanish is for the most part straightforward and fairly free of the quirks and national slang that force visitors to page through their dictionaries in desperation. But if you know Spanish, some of the terms you will hear people saying are *chibolo* for *muchacho* (boy); *churro* and *papasito* for *guapo* (good-looking); *jato* instead of *casa* (house); *chapar* (literally to grab or get), slangier than but with the same meaning as *besar* (to kiss); *¡que paja está!* (it's great); *mi pata* to connote a dude or chick from your posse; and *papi* and *mami* (or mamita), affectionate terms for mother and father that are also used as endearments between relatives and lovers (which can get a little confusing to the untrained outsider). The inherited Amerindian respect for nature is evident; words such as *Pachamama* (Mother Earth) tend to make it into conversation remarkably frequently.

Spanish, though, is but one official language of Peru. **Quechua** (the language of the Inca Empire) was recently given official status and is still widely spoken, especially in the highlands, and there's a movement afoot to include **Aymara** as a national language. (Aymara is spoken principally in the southern highlands area around Lake Titicaca.) A couple dozen other native tongues are still spoken. A predominantly oral language (the Incas had no written texts), Quechua is full of glottal and magical, curious sounds. As it is written today, it is mystifyingly vowel-heavy and apostrophe-laden, full of q's, k's, and y's; try to wrap your tongue around *munayniykimanta* (excuse me) or *hayk' atan kubrawanki llamaykikunanmanta* (how much is it to hire a llama?). Very few people seem to agree on spellings of Quechua, as alluded to in chapter 6. Colorful phrases often mix and match Spanish and Amerindian languages: *hacer la tutumeme* is the same as *ir a dormir,* or to go to sleep.

In addition to these primary languages, there are dozens of Indian tongues and dialects in the Amazon region, many of which are in danger of extinction.

2 Basic Spanish Vocabulary

English	Spanish	Pronunciation
Good day	**Buenos días**	*bweh*-nohs *dee*-ahs
Hi/hello	**Hola**	*oh*-lah
Pleasure to meet you	**Mucho gusto/** **Un placer**	*moo*-choh *goos*-toh/oon plah-*sehr*
How are you?	**¿Cómo está?**	*koh*-moh es-*tah*
Very well	**Muy bien**	mwee byehn
Thank you	**Gracias**	*grah*-syahs
How's it going?	**¿Qué tal?**	keh tahl
You're welcome	**De nada**	deh *nah*-dah
Goodbye	**Adiós**	ah-*dyohs*

English	Spanish	Pronunciation
Please	**Por favor**	pohr fah-*bohr*
Yes	**Sí**	see
No	**No**	noh
Excuse me	**Perdóneme/**	pehr-*doh*-neh-meh/
(to get by someone)	**Con permiso**	kohn pehr-*mee*-soh
Excuse me	**Disculpe**	dees-*kool*-peh
(to begin a question)		
Give me	**Déme**	*deh*-meh
What time is it?	**¿Qué hora es?**	keh *ohr*-ah ehs?
Where is . . . ?	**¿Dónde está . . .?**	*dohn*-deh eh-*stah*
the station	**la estación**	lah eh-stah-*syohn*
(bus/train)	**estación de ómnibus/**	eh-stah-*syohn* deh *ohm*-
	tren	nee-boos/trehn
a hotel	**un hotel**	oon oh-*tel*
a gas station	**una estación de**	*oo*-nah eh-stah-*syohn* deh
	servicio	sehr-*bee*-syoh
a restaurant	**un restaurante**	oon res-tow-*rahn*-teh
the toilet	**el baño** (or **servicios**)	el *bah*-nyoh (sehr-*bee*-syohs)
a good doctor	**un buen médico**	oon bwehn *meh*-dee-coh
the road to . . .	**el camino a/hacia . . .**	el cah-*mee*-noh ah/*ah*-syah
To the right	**A la derecha**	ah lah deh-*reh*-chah
To the left	**A la izquierda**	ah lah ee-*skyehr*-dah
Straight ahead	**Derecho**	deh-*reh*-choh
Is it far?	**¿Está lejos?**	eh-*stah* leh-hohs
It is close?	**¿Está cerca?**	eh-*stah* sehr-kah
Open	**Abierto**	ah-*byehr*-toh
Closed	**Cerrado**	seh-*rah*-doh
North	**Norte**	*nohr*-teh
South	**Sur**	soor
East	**Este**	*eh*-steh
West	**Oeste**	oh-*eh*-steh
Expensive	**Caro**	*cah*-roh
Cheap	**Barato**	bah-*rah*-toh
I would like	**Quisiera**	kee-*syeh*-rah
I want	**Quiero**	*kyeh*-roh
to eat	**comer**	koh-*mehr*
a room	**una habitación**	*oo*-nah ah-bee-tah-*syohn*
Do you have . . .?	**¿Tiene usted . . .?**	tyeh-neh oo-*stehd*
a book	**un libro**	oon *lee*-broh
a dictionary	**un diccionario**	oon deek-syoh-*na*-ryoh
change	**cambio**	kahm-byoh
How much is it?	**¿Cuánto cuesta?**	*kwahn*-toh *kwes*-tah
When?	**¿Cuándo?**	*kwahn*-doh
What?	**¿Qué?**	keh
There is	**(¿)Hay (. . . ?)**	eye
(Is/Are there . . .?)		
What is there?	**¿Qué hay?**	keh eye
Yesterday	**Ayer**	ah-*yehr*

English	Spanish	Pronunciation
Today	**Hoy**	oy
Tomorrow	**Mañana**	mah-*nyah*-nah
Good	**Bueno**	*bweh*-noh
Bad	**Malo**	*mah*-loh
Better (best)	**(Lo) Mejor**	(loh) meh-*hohr*
More	**Más**	mahs
Less	**Menos**	*meh*-nohs
No smoking	**Se prohibe fumar**	seh proh-*ee*-beh foo-*mahr*
Postcard	**Tarjeta postal**	tahr-*heh*-tah pohs-*tahl*
Insect repellent	**Rapelente contra insectos**	rah-peh-*lehn*-teh *cohn*-trah een-*sehk*-tohs
Now	**Ahora**	ah-*ohr*-ah
Right now	**Ahora mismo (ahorita)**	ah-*ohr*-ah *mees*-moh (ah-ohr-*ee*-tah)
Later	**Más tarde**	mahs *tahr*-deh
Never	**Nunca**	*noon*-kah
Guide	**Guía**	*ghee*-ah
Heat	**Calor**	kah-*lohr*
It's hot!	**¡Qué calor!**	keh kah-*lohr*
Cold	**Frío**	*free*-oh
Rain	**Lluvia**	*yoo*-byah
It's cold!	**¡Qué frío!**	keh *free*-oh
Wind	**Viento**	*byehn*-toh
It's windy!	**¡Cuánto viento!**	*kwahn*-toh *byehn*-toh
Money-changer	**Cambista**	kahm-*bee*-stah
Bank	**Banco**	*bahn*-koh
Money	**Dinero**	dee-*neh*-roh
Small (correct) change	**Sencillo**	sehn-*see*-yoh
Credit card	**Tarjeta de crédito**	tahr-*heh*-tah deh *creh*-dee-toh
ATM	**Cajero automático**	kah-*heh*-roh ow-toh-*mah*-tee-koh
Tourist information office	**Oficina de información turística**	oh-fee-*see*-nah deh een-for-mah-*syohn* too-*ree*-stee-kah

NUMBERS

1	**uno** (*oo*-noh)	14	**catorce** (kah-*tohr*-seh)
2	**dos** (dohs)	15	**quince** (*keen*-seh)
3	**tres** (trehs)	16	**dieciséis** (*dyeh*-see-sayss)
4	**cuatro** (*kwah*-troh)	17	**diecisiete** (*dyeh*-see-*syeh*-teh)
5	**cinco** (*seen*-koh)	18	**dieciocho** (*dyeh*-see-*oh*-choh)
6	**seis** (sayss)	19	**diecinueve** (*dyeh*-see-*nweh*-beh)
7	**siete** (*syeh*-teh)	20	**veinte** (*bayn*-teh)
8	**ocho** (*oh*-choh)	30	**treinta** (*trayn*-tah)
9	**nueve** (*nweh*-beh)	40	**cuarenta** (kwah-*ren*-tah)
10	**diez** (dyehs)	50	**cincuenta** (seen-*kwen*-tah)
11	**once** (*ohn*-seh)	60	**sesenta** (seh-*sehn*-tah)
12	**doce** (*doh*-seh)	70	**setenta** (seh-*tehn*-tah)
13	**trece** (*treh*-seh)	80	**ochenta** (oh-*chen*-tah)

90	**noventa** (noh-*ben*-tah)	500	**quinientos** (kee-*nyehn*-tohs)
100	**cien** (syehn)	1,000	**mil** (meal)
200	**doscientos** (do-*syehn*-tohs)		

3 More Useful Spanish Phrases

COMMUNICATION

English	Spanish	Pronunciation
Do you speak English?	¿Habla usted inglés?	*ah*-blah oo-*stehd* een-*glehs*
Is there anyone here who speaks English?	¿Hay alguien aquí que hable inglés?	eye *ahl*-gyehn ah-*kee* keh *ah*-bleh een-*glehs*
I speak a little Spanish.	Hablo un poco de español.	*ah*-bloh oon *poh*-koh deh eh-spah-*nyohl*
I don't understand Spanish very well.	No (lo) entiendo muy bien el español.	noh (loh) ehn-*tyehn*-doh mwee byehn ehl eh-spah-*nyohl*
I don't understand you.	No le entiendo/ No comprendo.	noh leh *ehn-tyehn*-doh/ noh kohm-*prehn*-doh
What did you say?	¿Cómo? (colloquial expression for American "Eh?")	*koh*-moh
What does that mean?	¿Qué quiere decir?	keh *kyeh*-reh deh *seer*
How do you say . . . ?	¿Cómo se dice . . .?	*koh*-moh seh-*dee*-seh
May I take a photograph?	¿Puedo sacar una foto?	*pweh*-doh sah-*cahr* oo-nah *foh*-toh

DINING

English	Spanish	Pronunciation
The meal is good.	Me gusta la comida.	meh *goo*-stah lah koh-*mee*-dah
May I see your menu?	¿Puedo ver la carta?	*pweh*-doh behr lah *cahr*-tah
The check, please.	La cuenta, por favor.	lah *kwehn*-tah, pohr fa-*bohr*
What do I owe you?	¿Cuánto le debo?	*kwahn*-toh leh *deh*-boh

ACCOMMODATIONS

English	Spanish	Pronunciation
I would like (to see)	Quisiera (ver)	kee-*syeh*-rah (behr)
a room	un cuarto or una habitación	oon *kwahr*-toh, *oo*-nah ah bee-tah-*syohn*
for two persons	para dos personas	*pah*-rah dohs pehr-*soh*-nahs
with (without) bathroom	con (sin) baño	kohn (seen) *bah*-nyoh
We are staying here only . . .	Nos quedamos aquí solamente . . .	nohs keh-*dah*-mohs ah-*kee* soh-lah-*mehn*-teh
one night	una noche	*oo*-nah *noh*-cheh
one week	una semana	*oo*-nah seh-*mah*-nah
We are leaving . . .	Partimos (Salimos or Nos vamos) . . .	pahr-*tee*-mohs; sah-*lee*-mohs; nohs *bah*-mohs
tomorrow	mañana	mah-*nyah*-nah

English	Spanish	Pronunciation
Do you accept . . . ?	¿Acepta usted (or Se aceptan)?	ah-*sehp*-tah oo-*stehd* (seh ah-*sehp*-tahn)
traveler's checks?	cheques de viajero?	*cheh*-kehs deh byah-*heh*-roh
Is there a laundromat . . .?	¿Hay una lavandería? . . .	eye *oo*-nah lah-*bahn*-deh-*ree*-ah
near here?	cerca de aquí?	*sehr*-kah deh ah-*kee*
Please send these clothes to the	Hágame el favor de mandar esta ropa a la	ah-gah-meh el fah-*bohr* deh mahn-*dahr* eh-stah *roh*-pah
laundry.	lavandería.	ah lah lah-*bahn*-deh-*ree*-

HEALTH & SAFETY

English	Spanish	Pronunciation
I'm sick.	Estoy enfermo(a).	eh-*stoy* ehn-*fehr*-moh
I need a doctor.	Necesito un médico.	neh-seh-*see*-toh oon *meh*-dee-koh
I've been vaccinated.	Estoy vacunado(a).	eh-*stoy* bah-coo-*nah*-doh (dah)
Leave me alone!	¡Déjeme! (or ¡Váyase!)	*deh*-heh-meh/ *bah*-yah-seh
I'm married.	Soy casado(a).	soy kah-*sah*-doh (ah)
Help!	¡Socorro!	soh-*coh*-roh
I've been robbed!	¡Me robaron!	meh roh-*bah*-rohn

POSTAL GLOSSARY

Airmail   **Correo aéreo**
Customs   **Aduana**
General delivery   **Lista de correos**
Insurance (insured mail)   **Seguro (correo asegurado)**
Mailbox   **Buzón**
Money order   **Giro postal**
Parcel   **Paquete**
Post office   **Oficina de correos** (aka **Serpost**)
Post office box (abbreviation)   **Casilla**
Postal service   **Correos**
Registered mail   **Registrado**
Rubber stamp   **Sello**
Special delivery, express   **Entrega inmediata**
Stamp   **Estampilla** or **timbre**

TRANSPORTATION TERMS

English	Spanish	Pronunciation
Airport	Aeropuerto	ah-eh-roh-*pwehr*-toh
Flight	Vuelo	*bweh*-loh
Car-rental agency	Arrendadora (Agencia) de Autos	hh-rehn-dah-*doh*-rah deh *ow*-tohs
Bus	Omnibus	ohm-nee-*boos*
Small local bus/van	Colectivo/micro	koh-lehk-*tee*-boh/ *mee*-kroh
Truck	Camión	kah-*myohn*
Lane	Carril	kah-*reel*
Baggage (claim area)	Equipajes	eh-kee-*pah*-hehs

English	Spanish	Pronunciation
Luggage storage area	**Custodia**	koo-*stoh*-dyah
Arrival gates	**Llegadas**	yeh-*gah*-dahs
Originates at this station	**Local**	loh-*kahl*
Originates elsewhere	**De paso**	deh *pah*-soh
Stops if seats available	**Para si hay lugares**	pah-rah see eye loo-*gah*-rehs
First class	**Primera**	pree-*meh*-rah
Second class	**Segunda**	seh-*goon*-dah
Nonstop	**Sin escala**	seen eh-*skah*-lah
One-way	**Ida**	*ee*-dah
Round-trip	**Ida y vuelta**	*ee*-dah ee *bwehl*-tah
Ticket	**Boleto**	boh-*leh*-toh
Baggage claim area	**Recibo de equipajes**	reh-see-boh deh eh-kee-*pah*-hehs
Waiting room	**Sala de espera**	*Sah*-lah deh eh-*speh*-rah
Toilets	**Baños**	*bah*-nyohs
Ticket window	**Boletería**	boh-leh-teh-*ree*-ah
Street	**Calle/Jirón (Jr.)**	kah-*yeh*/hee-*rohn*
Avenue	**Avenida**	ah-beh-*nee*-dah
Highway	**Autopista**	ow-toh-*pee*-stah
Trail	**Camino**	kah-*mee*-noh

4 Spanish Menu Glossary

GENERAL TERMS

Beef/steak **Lomo**
Bread **Pan**
Chicken **Pollo**
Dessert **Postre**
Eggs **Huevos**
Fish **Pescado**
Fruit **Fruta**
Lamb **Cordero**
Meat **Carne**
Pork **Cerdo/puerco**

Potatoes **Papas**
French fries **Papas fritas**
Rice **Arroz**
Roast **Asado**
Salad **Ensalada**
Seafood **Mariscos**
Shrimp **Camarones**
Soup **Sopa (chupe)**
Sweet potato **Camote**
Vegetables **Verduras**

MEAT

Adobo Meat dish in a spicy chili sauce
Ají de gallina Spicy/creamy chicken
Alpaca Alpaca steak
Anticuchos Shish kebab
Cabrito Goat
Carne de res Beef
Chicharrones Fried pork skins
Conejo Rabbit
Cordero Lamb
Empanada Pastry turnover filled with meat, vegetables, fruit, manjar blanco, or sometimes nothing at all

Estofado Stew
Lomo asado Roast beef
Lomo saltado Strips of beef with fried potatoes, onions, and tomatoes over rice
Parrillada Grilled meats
Pato Duck
Pollo a la brasa Spit-roasted chicken
Venado Venison

420 APPENDIX B · USEFUL TERMS & PHRASES

SEAFOOD

Corvina   Sea bass
Langosta   Lobster
Langostinos   Prawns
Lenguado   Sole

Mero   Mediterranean grouper
Paiche   Large Amazon fish
Tollo   Spotted dogfish

BEVERAGES

Beer   **Cerveza**
Mixed fruit juice   **Refresco**
Juice   **Jugo**
Milk   **Leche**
Soft drink   **Gaseosa**

Water   **Agua**
  with gas   **con gas**
  still   **sin gas**
Wine   **Vino**
Cocktail   **Cóctel**

PREPARATION

Fixed-price menu   **El menú**
Spicy   **Picante**
Hot (temperature)   **Caliente**
Cold (temperature)   **Frío**

Raw   **Crudo**
Cooked   **Cocido**
Fried   **Frito**
Vegetarian   **Vegetariano**

PERUVIAN FAVORITES

Chaufa   Chinese fried rice
Chicha   Fermented maize beer
Chicha morada   Blue-corn non-
  alcoholic refreshment
Chifa   Peruvian-Chinese food
Choclo   Maize (large-kernel corn)
Ceviche   Marinated fish dish
Cuy   Guinea pig
Flan crème   Caramel custard
Manjar blanco   Sweetened con-
  densed milk
Pachamanca   Roast meat and pota-
  toes, prepared underground
Palta   Avocado
Palta rellena (or palta a la Reina)
  Stuffed avocado (with chicken or
  tuna salad)

Panqueque   Crepe
Papa a la huancaína   Boiled potatoes in a creamy and spicy cheese
  sauce
Papa rellena   Stuffed & fried potato
Quinua   Andean grain (quinoa)
Rocoto relleno   Stuffed hot pepper
Sopa a la criolla   Creole soup (noodles or grain, often quinoa, vegetables, and meat)
Tamale   Ground corn cooked and
  stuffed with chicken or pork,
  wrapped in banana leaves or corn
  husks, then steamed

5 Quechua & Quechua-Derived Terms

Quechua ("*kesh*-wa") was the language of the Inca Empire, and it remains widely spoken in Peru and throughout Andean nations 5 centuries after the Spaniards did so much to impose their own culture, language, and religion upon the region. It is the most widely spoken Amerindian language. Called *Runasimi* (literally, language of the people) by Quechua speakers, the language is spoken by more than 10 million people in the highlands of South America. As much as one-third of Peru's 28 million people speak Quechua.

Quechua is an agglutinative language, meaning that words are constructed from a root word and combined with a large number of suffixes and infixes, which are added to words to change meaning and add subtlety. Linguists consider Quechua unusually poetic and expressive. Quechua, though, is not a monolithic language. More than 2 dozen dialects are currently spoken in Peru.

The one of greatest reach, not surprisingly, is the one still spoken in Cusco. Though continually threatened by Spanish, Quechua remains a vital language in the Andes.

In recent decades, however, many Andean migrants to urban areas have tried to distance themselves from their Amerindian roots, fearful that they would be marginalized by the Spanish-speaking majority in cities—many of whom regard Quechua and other native languages as the domain of the poor and uneducated. (Parents often refuse to speak Quechua with their children.) The 2001 presidential election of Alejandro Toledo, himself of Amerindian descent, may lead to a new valuation of Quechua (and Aymara). Toledo has said that he hopes to spur new interest and pride in native culture in schools and among all Peruvians; a telling demonstration of that desire was the Quechua language spoken at his inaugural ceremonies at Machu Picchu. (Even Toledo's Belgian-born wife addressed the crowd in Quechua.)

Quechua has made its influence felt on Spanish, of course. Peruvian Spanish has hundreds of Quechua words, ranging from names of plants and animals (*papa,* or potato; *cuy,* guinea pig) to food (*choclo,* corn on the cob; *pachamanca,* a type of earth oven) and clothing (*chompa,* sweater; *chullu,* knitted cap). Quechua has also made its way into English. Words commonly used in English that are derived from Quechua include coca, condor, guano, gaucho, lima (as in the bean), llama, pampa, and puma.

COMMON TERMS

Altiplano   Plateau/high plains
Apu   Sacred summit/mountain spirit
Campesino   Rural worker/peasant
Chacra   Plot of land
Huayno   Andean musical style
Inca   Inca ruler/emperor
Inti   Sun
Intiwatana   "Hitching post of the sun" (stone pillar at Inca ceremonial sites)
Mestizo   Person of mixed European and Amerindian lineage
Pucara   Fortress
Runasimi   Quechua language
Soroche   Altitude sickness (hypoxia)
Tambo   In-transit checkpoint on Inca highway
Tawantinsuyu   Inca Empire
Tumi   Andean knife
Viracocha   Inca deity (creator god)

TRY A LITTLE QUECHUA

English	Quechua	Pronunciation
Yes	**Riki**	*ree*-kee
No	**Mana**	*mah*-nah
Madam	**Mama**	*mah*-mah
Sir	**Tayta**	*tahy*-tah
Thank you	**Añay**	ah-*nyahy*

Index

Pikillacta, 211
Pisac, 5, 215
Pumamarca, 228
Rumicolca, 211
Sacsayhuamán, 5, 21
Sillustani, 262
Tambo Colorado, 151
Tipon, 210
near Trujillo, 339–342
  Chan Chan, 339–341
  El Brujo, 341–342
  Huacas de Moche, 5, 342
Tunshucaiko, 386
Ventanillas de Otuzco, 368
Archbishop's Palace (Museo de Arte Religioso) (Cusco), 196
Archbishop's Palace (Palacio Episcopal) (Lima), 128
Architecture, 11–13. *See also* Archaeological sites and ruins; Colonial buildings and historical sights
Area codes, 79
Arequipa, 269–288
  accommodations, 278–283
  ATMs and banks, 271
  emergencies and police, 271
  Internet access, 271
  nightlife, 286–287
  post office and courier service, 271
  restaurants, 283–286
  safety, 272
  shopping, 20, 278
  side trips from, 287–288
  sights and attractions, 12, 272–278
  transportation, 272
  traveling to, 270–271
  visitor information, 271
Art Gallery Camu-Camu (Iquitos), 320
Arts and crafts. *See also* Ceramics; Markets; Textiles
  Arequipa, 278
  best places for, 20
  Cusco, 204–205
  customs regulations, 29
  Iquitos, 320
  Lima, 139
  Pisac, 215
  Puno, 258
Atahualpa, Inca emperor, 130, 211, 361, 362, 364–366, 399–401
ATMs (automated-teller machines), 32
Autobuses (buses or *ómnibuses),* 67
Aventours, 219

Ayahuasca ceremonies, 22, 305, 320, 321, 323

B aggage (luggage), lost-luggage insurance, 40–41
Bahuaja-Sonene National Park, 317
Ballestas Islands, 7, 144, 145, 149, 150
  organized tours, 147, 150
  sights and attractions, 150
Ballooning. *See* Hot-air ballooning
Baños de la Ñusta (Ollantaytambo), 225
Baños del Inca (near Cajamarca), 366
Baños Termales de Monterrey, 378–379
Barranco (Lima), 108
  accommodations, 121–122
  restaurants, 126–127
Barrio Chino (Lima), 128
Barrio de Belén (Iquitos), 318–319
Barrio de San Blas (Cusco), 20, 169
  accommodations, 173, 180–184
  arts and crafts, 204–205
  sights and attractions, 195
Batán Grande, 355
Beaches, 137, 142–143
Beer, *chicha,* 16–17
Belén neighborhood (Iquitos), 318–319
BET Tours, 59
Biblioteca Amazónica (Iquitos), 318
Bicycling, Lima, 137
Big Foot Tours, 242
Bingham, Hiram, 77, 227, 232, 234, 240–241, 402
Birding Peru, 313
Bird-watching, 92–93
  Amazon region, 10
  Ballestas Islands, 149, 150
  condors, 4, 7, 77, 136, 150, 270, 287, 289, 291, 292
  Inca Trail, 244, 247, 248
  Mandor Ravine, 247
  Manu Biosphere Reserve, 92, 312
  Pacaya-Samiria National Reserve, 92
  Tambopata-Candamo Reserve Zone, 92, 303–305
  tour operators, 92–93
Biringo, 341
Bisambra aqueduct, 6, 163

Blanquillo Macaw and Parrot Lick, 313
Boat tours and cruises
  Amazon River and its tributaries, 95, 324–326
  Ballestas Islands, 150
  to Iquitos, 313
  Lake Titicaca, 258, 263
  Paracas Bay and Ballestas Islands, 147
Bodega El Catador (near Ica), 155
Bodega Ocucaje (near Ica), 155
Bodegas Vista Alegre (near Ica), 155
Bolívar, Simón, 337, 402
Bolivia, traveling to, 255, 269
Bolivian Consulate
  Puerto Maldonado, 300
  Puno, 255
Bombonaje Adventure Camp, 322
Books, recommended, 77–79
Bucket shops, 54
Bullfighting, Lima, 137–138
Bullfighting Museum (Lima), 128
Business hours, 79
Bus travel, 67–68
  to Peru, 52
Butterflies, 92, 248, 303

C abanaconde, 290–291
Cabezas Largas, 149
Cabo Blanco, 339
Cahuachi, 161
Cajamarca, 9, 360–374
  accommodations, 368–371
  nightlife, 372–373
  restaurants, 371–372
  shopping, 368
  sights and attractions, 363–368
  transportation, 363
  traveling to, 361–362
  visitor information, 362
Cajamarca Valley, 362
Calendar of events, 36–39
Calle del Medio (Ollantaytambo), 225
Callejón de Huaylas, 11, 37, 94, 97, 374, 379, 384, 393
Calle Loreto (Cusco), 194
Camelids, 388
Candelabro, 150
Candlemas (Virgen de la Candelaria) (Puno), 13, 36, 257
Cañón del Cotahuasi, 288, 294

Booked seat 6A, open return.

Rented red 4-wheel drive.

Reserved cabin, no running water.

Discovered space.

With over 700 airlines, 50,000 hotels, 50 rental car companies and 5,000 cruise and vacation packages, you can create the perfect get-away for you. Choose the car, the room, even the ground you walk on.

Travelocity.com
A Sabre Company
Go Virtually Anywhere.

You Need A Vacation.

700 Airlines, 50,000 Hotels, 50 Rental Car Companies, And A Million Ways To Save Money.

Travelocity.com
A Sabre Company
Go Virtually Anywhere.

FROMMER'S® COMPLETE TRAVEL GUIDES

Alaska
Alaska Cruises & Ports of Call
Amsterdam
Argentina & Chile
Arizona
Atlanta
Australia
Austria
Bahamas
Barcelona, Madrid & Seville
Beijing
Belgium, Holland & Luxembourg
Bermuda
Boston
Brazil
British Columbia & the Canadian Rockies
Budapest & the Best of Hungary
California
Canada
Cancún, Cozumel & the Yucatán
Cape Cod, Nantucket & Martha's Vineyard
Caribbean
Caribbean Cruises & Ports of Call
Caribbean Ports of Call
Carolinas & Georgia
Chicago
China
Colorado
Costa Rica
Denmark
Denver, Boulder & Colorado Springs
England
Europe
European Cruises & Ports of Call
Florida

France
Germany
Great Britain
Greece
Greek Islands
Hawaii
Hong Kong
Honolulu, Waikiki & Oahu
Ireland
Israel
Italy
Jamaica
Japan
Las Vegas
London
Los Angeles
Maryland & Delaware
Maui
Mexico
Montana & Wyoming
Montréal & Québec City
Munich & the Bavarian Alps
Nashville & Memphis
Nepal
New England
New Mexico
New Orleans
New York City
New Zealand
Northern Italy
Nova Scotia, New Brunswick & Prince Edward Island
Oregon
Paris
Philadelphia & the Amish Country
Portugal
Prague & the Best of the Czech Republic

Provence & the Riviera
Puerto Rico
Rome
San Antonio & Austin
San Diego
San Francisco
Santa Fe, Taos & Albuquerque
Scandinavia
Scotland
Seattle & Portland
Shanghai
Singapore & Malaysia
South Africa
South America
South Florida
South Pacific
Southeast Asia
Spain
Sweden
Switzerland
Texas
Thailand
Tokyo
Toronto
Tuscany & Umbria
USA
Utah
Vancouver & Victoria
Vermont, New Hampshire & Maine
Vienna & the Danube Valley
Virgin Islands
Virginia
Walt Disney World & Orlando
Washington, D.C.
Washington State

FROMMER'S® DOLLAR-A-DAY GUIDES

Australia from $50 a Day
California from $70 a Day
Caribbean from $70 a Day
England from $75 a Day
Europe from $70 a Day

Florida from $70 a Day
Hawaii from $80 a Day
Ireland from $60 a Day
Italy from $70 a Day
London from $85 a Day

New York from $90 a Day
Paris from $80 a Day
San Francisco from $70 a Day
Washington, D.C. from $80 a Day

FROMMER'S® PORTABLE GUIDES

Acapulco, Ixtapa & Zihuatanejo
Amsterdam
Aruba
Australia's Great Barrier Reef
Bahamas
Baja & Los Cabos
Berlin
Boston
California Wine Country
Cancún
Charleston & Savannah
Chicago
Disneyland
Dublin
Florence

Frankfurt
Hawaii: The Big Island
Hong Kong
Houston
Las Vegas
London
Los Angeles
Maine Coast
Maui
Miami
New Orleans
New York City
Paris
Phoenix & Scottsdale

Portland
Puerto Rico
Puerto Vallarta, Manzanillo & Guadalajara
Rio de Janeiro
San Diego
San Francisco
Seattle
Sydney
Tampa & St. Petersburg
Vancouver
Venice
Virgin Islands
Washington, D.C.

FROMMER'S® NATIONAL PARK GUIDES

Banff & Jasper
Family Vacations in the National Parks
Grand Canyon

National Parks of the American West
Rocky Mountain

Yellowstone & Grand Teton
Yosemite & Sequoia/ Kings Canyon
Zion & Bryce Canyon

FROMMER'S® MEMORABLE WALKS

Chicago	New York	San Francisco
London	Paris	

FROMMER'S® GREAT OUTDOOR GUIDES

Arizona & New Mexico	Northern California	Vermont & New Hampshire
New England	Southern New England	

SUZY GERSHMAN'S BORN TO SHOP GUIDES

Born to Shop: France	Born to Shop: Italy	Born to Shop: New York
Born to Shop: Hong Kong, Shanghai & Beijing	Born to Shop: London	Born to Shop: Paris

FROMMER'S® IRREVERENT GUIDES

Amsterdam	Los Angeles	San Francisco
Boston	Manhattan	Seattle & Portland
Chicago	New Orleans	Vancouver
Las Vegas	Paris	Walt Disney World
London	Rome	Washington, D.C.

FROMMER'S® BEST-LOVED DRIVING TOURS

Britain	Germany	Northern Italy
California	Ireland	Scotland
Florida	Italy	Spain
France	New England	Tuscany & Umbria

HANGING OUT™ GUIDES

Hanging Out in England	Hanging Out in France	Hanging Out in Italy
Hanging Out in Europe	Hanging Out in Ireland	Hanging Out in Spain

THE UNOFFICIAL GUIDES®

Bed & Breakfasts and Country Inns in:	Southwest & South Central Plains	Mid-Atlantic with Kids
California	U.S.A.	Mini Las Vegas
Great Lakes States	Beyond Disney	Mini-Mickey
Mid-Atlantic	Branson, Missouri	New England and New York with Kids
New England	California with Kids	New Orleans
Northwest	Chicago	New York City
Rockies	Cruises	Paris
Southeast	Disneyland	San Francisco
Southwest	Florida with Kids	Skiing in the West
Best RV & Tent Campgrounds in:	Golf Vacations in the Eastern U.S.	Southeast with Kids
California & the West	Great Smoky & Blue Ridge Region	Walt Disney World
Florida & the Southeast	Inside Disney	Walt Disney World for Grown-ups
Great Lakes States	Hawaii	Walt Disney World with Kids
Mid-Atlantic	Las Vegas	Washington, D.C.
Northeast	London	World's Best Diving Vacations
Northwest & Central Plains		

SPECIAL-INTEREST TITLES

Frommer's Adventure Guide to Australia & New Zealand	Frommer's Italy's Best Bed & Breakfasts and Country Inns
Frommer's Adventure Guide to Central America	Frommer's New York City with Kids
Frommer's Adventure Guide to India & Pakistan	Frommer's Ottawa with Kids
Frommer's Adventure Guide to South America	Frommer's Road Atlas Britain
Frommer's Adventure Guide to Southeast Asia	Frommer's Road Atlas Europe
Frommer's Adventure Guide to Southern Africa	Frommer's Road Atlas France
Frommer's Britain's Best Bed & Breakfasts and Country Inns	Frommer's Toronto with Kids
Frommer's Caribbean Hideaways	Frommer's Vancouver with Kids
Frommer's Exploring America by RV	Frommer's Washington, D.C., with Kids
Frommer's Fly Safe, Fly Smart	Israel Past & Present
Frommer's France's Best Bed & Breakfasts and Country Inns	The New York Times' Guide to Unforgettable Weekends
Frommer's Gay & Lesbian Europe	Places Rated Almanac
	Retirement Places Rated